Directory of Residential Facilities for Emotionally Handicapped Children and Youth Second Edition

S0-BSA-724

Edited by Barbara Smiley Sherman

Phoenix • New York

ORYX PRESS

1988

The rare Arabian Oryx is believed to have inspired the myth of the unicorn. This desert antelope became virtually extinct in the early 1960s. At that time several groups of international conservationists arranged to have 9 animals sent to the Phoenix Zoo to be the nucleus of a captive breeding herd. Today the Oryx population is over 400, and herds have been returned to reserves in Israel, Jordan, and Oman.

Copyright © 1988 by The Oryx Press
2214 North Central at Encanto
Phoenix, Arizona 85004-1483

Published simultaneously in Canada

Printed and Bound in the United States of America

ISBN 0-89774-407-1
ISSN 8756-2170

Library of Congress Cataloging-in-Publication Data

Sherman, Barbara Smiley.
    Directory of residential facilities for emotionally
handicapped children and youth / by Barbara Smiley Sherman.
        p. cm.
    Includes indexes.
    ISBN 0-89774-407-1
    1. Child psychotherapy—Residential treatment—United States-
-Directories.   I. Title.
    [DNLM: 1. Affective Symptoms—rehabilitation—United States-
-directories.   2. Child Behavior Disorders—rehabilitation—United
States—directories.   3. Residential Facilities—United States-
-directories.   WS 22 AA1 S5d]
RJ504.5.S54 1987
362.2'3—dc19
DNLM/DLC
for Library of Congress   87-27316
                                                     CIP

Table of Contents

Foreword

I am sure that many of us who participate in diagnostic and planning conferences conducted in schools, psychiatric hospitals, clinics, and community health facilities, have left many of these meetings dissatisfied. Certainly, a comprehensive understanding of a child's special needs may have been reached. But, a critical part of the job was not accomplished well.

Imagine with me one such diagnostic-planning conference that concludes the child in question requires residential treatment. One member of the group, knowledgeable about possible treatment centers in the surrounding area, offers a few details about each. Another member of the group sparks a debate because she is chronically dissatisfied with the brief, and sometimes casual, effort devoted to selecting a placement after much energy and time was put into a careful diagnostic study. She asks if the group isn't being too provincial looking only at the residential treatment programs nearby? What residential treatment facilities are available nationwide?

At this point someone in the group names a facility they have heard of which is located in another state. Now another stream of questions pour out. How did the program get started? What is its physical plant? What particular types of children do they prefer to serve? Will they accept an emotionally disturbed child? An aggressive child? A withdrawn child? A learning disabled child? A child with a low IQ? A child with neurological impairment? What types of social and rehabilitative services do they make available? Do they have formal recreational and milieu programs? Do they have a program for substance abuse? Do they make available individual psychotherapy and family therapy, and exactly who provides these services—are they social workers, nurses, psychiatrists, child care workers? And, what about the educational and vocational programs—how many classrooms, what type of curriculum and what is the daily schedule? How many children are enrolled in the program and what is the student/teacher ratio? Are the teachers certified? Do the students earn degrees? And, what does the program cost? Are insurance funds acceptable? What about state funds?

As the questions continue, professionals and paarents attending this conference are overwhelmed and frustrated, aware that once again there are no answers. But, this time, with an air of authority, the conference chairperson announces she has the answers. A hush of silence surrounds the group as each member turns to the chairperson with a mixture of doubt, anticipation, and relief. The chairperson dramatically reaches for a copy of a *Directory of Residential Facilities for Emotionally Handicapped Children and Youth,* by Barbara Smiley Sherman. This directory, the chairperson declares, contains the answers to their questions and many more.

The reader should note that this directory is more than an alphabetical listing of placements. Its organization and content clearly indicate the author's understanding of the need for strategic placement information. Parents and professionals alike will recognize that this directory has been constructed by someone who has served emotionally disturbed children and who has "lived" the struggle of locating an appropriate residential program for a particular child. The professional course Barbara Smiley Sherman has followed makes clear why the directory she has developed is so informative and relevant for those faced with the task of locating appropriate programs.

After 3 years as a classroom teacher in a college-based day care program for emotionally disturbed and learning disabled children, she served as a clinical educator for 2 years, working collaboratively with clinical child psychologists, child psychiatrists, social workers, and nurses in a psychoeducation program for children under 16 years of age and organized within a children's psychiatric hospital located in the eastern United States. At this point she assimilated issues and needs unique to children handicapped by severe personality disorders, as well as learning disabilities, and cultivated an appreciation for the important roles played by various mental health professionals in providing care.

After this experience, Ms. Sherman held the position of clinical educator in a hospital-based residential school for older children and adolescents. In addition to accumulating further diagnostic and classroom experiences, she was active in recommending and pursuing treatment plans, including securing residential placements when necessary. Ms. Sherman's professional course then moved on to include 2 years as director of education for the same hospital-based program, a position which, in addition to developing quality programs, directly involved her in counseling parents and professionals in their efforts to fit a child's needs with a suitable placement. Most recently, as a professional consultant, she has been active in designing seminars open to the public in special education and mental health issues, assessing community needs, and facilitating the development of services to meet these needs.

Since experiences give rise to an appreciation of relevance, we can now understand why Ms. Sherman's directory is more than a listing of program names and addresses, why the content immediately reveals an understanding of the ingredients of each facility, ingredients which have relevance for finding a good fit between the needs of a particular child and a program, and which make many specifics about the facility which will be working with their child available to parents. With this directory Ms. Sherman has extended to a national level her interest in assessing community needs and locating residential settings for children. Moreover, the indexes of her directory provide many different windows through which the interested reader can begin to look to secure a placement; for example, in terms of characteristics exhibited by a child, type of funding accepted, and type of placement.

Last, with this directory, Ms. Sherman has also made a powerful statement for parents and professionals who believe that education is an effective treatment for emotionally disturbed children.

Sebastiano Santostefano, Ph.D.
Director, Department of Child
Psychology and Psychoeducation,
McLean Hospital and
Associate Professor of Psychology,
Harvard Medical School

Acknowledgments

The author would like to acknowledge those important people who helped make the writing of this book possible.

The memory of my mother, Joyce Skinner Smiley, gave me the desire to help others with special needs, especially children.

The guidance and inspiration given to me by my father, Clenden Karl Smiley, helped create the ambition to write this book.

In particular, I want to give special thanks to my husband, Ian, for his constant support and to my children, Wendy, Wesley and David, for their companionship during the days of writing.

I would also like to express a special thanks to Gene Price, whose dedication and perseverence helped make this directory as comprehensive and informative as it is.

Barbara Smiley Sherman
December 1987

Introduction

This is a nationwide directory of residential treatment facilities for children with emotional handicaps and behavior disorders as their primary diagnosis. It includes a general interpretation of the Education of All Handicapped Act, Public Law 94-142, which describes the rights of handicapped children and the procedures used to obtain special education services. Following the discussion of the federal law is a chapter which describes the procedures for finding and applying to an appropriate residential facility. After this chapter is a comprehensive directory of public and private residential treatment facilities. Each facility is described in terms of its origin, programs, services, and types of population served. The directory is organized alphabetically by state, then alphabetically by facility. There are three indexes in the back of the directory providing specialized access points to facility listings. These indexes are the Characteristics Exhibited by Children Index, the Funding Sources Index, and the Specialized Programs Index.

Residential treatment facilities provide an alternative to youth who need 24-hour out-of-home care in a therapeutic setting. They can provide short- and/or long-term care in a structured environment that is supervised by professionals from the mental health, social service, and education fields. Their campuses can consist of a single-family home or be as large as several dormitory buildings on several acres of land. Their primary purpose is treatment, though residential treatment facilities can offer child care, parent training, family counseling, recreation activities and school programs.

The primary goal of residential treatment facilities is to help children identify and understand their emotional and/or behavioral handicaps and learn more appropriate alternatives. Some of the listed fa-cilities accept children with a secondary diagnosis such as learning disabilities, visual or auditory problems, physical handicaps, and mental retardation. They also provide a variety of programs such as day treatment, transitional group homes, vocational education, and drug rehabilitation. These additional programs are mentioned in this directory, but are not described in length since the focus is on residential services.

The information provided herein was compiled from facilities' responses to a comprehensive questionnaire, along with brochures and fact sheets describing their programs. Any specific piece of information not mentioned in this directory is due to that particular facility not responding to particular questionnaire items. It is also important to note that the programs and fees referred to may alter over time and, therefore, data collected, while current at present, are subject to change.

Some states, such as New York and California, have an abundance of facilities, whereas other states, such as Arkansas and Montana, have very few. Many of the states located in the central part of the country have fewer facilities than the eastern and western states. The entries contained herein should not be considered an endorsement of any particular facility, nor should the omission of an existing facility be construed as anything other than their lack of response or inappropriateness for this type of directory.

It is hoped that lay people and professionals alike who are involved with emotionally handicapped children will utilize this directory to become more familiar with the available residential facilities for children with special needs.

Barbara Smiley Sherman, M.Ed.

The Legal Basis for Educating Special Needs Children

There are more than 8 million handicapped children in the United States, according to a Congressional finding in the Education of All Handicapped Act. The term "handicapped children" includes children who are mentally retarded, hard-of-hearing, deaf, speech impaired, visually handicapped, seriously emotionally disturbed, orthopedically impaired, health impaired, learning disabled, and children who are in need of special education and related services. According to Congress, more than half of these children do not receive the appropriate special education services they require to learn and grow in a standard school setting. Congress found that many handicapped children have undetected handicaps and are attending standard school programs which compromise their ability to have successful educational experiences. The Congressional findings, which culminated in passage of federal legislation, are not difficult to understand, given the fact that the development of special education programs and evaluation procedures by most state and local educational agencies are still in early stages. Although a major factor in the slow development of specialized programs is due to inadequate financial resources, a desire to maintain the status quo and simple lack of knowledge also play a part. The federal government has put into effect the Education of All Handicapped Act, or Public Law 94-142, as an attempt to help state and local educational agencies to meet the increasing educational needs of handicapped children.

Guidelines for Determining Special Education Eligibility

To begin the process of evaluating children who may need special education services, one needs to review the rights of children according to Public Law 94-142. The law now states that all school systems must provide handicapped children between the ages of birth and 21, or until graduation, whichever comes first, an appropriate public education, at no cost to the parents as long as the child resides within the school district.

The Education of All Handicapped Act was amended in 1986 to include infants and toddlers (Chapter 33, Subchapter VIII). The purpose of this subchapter was to provide funding to school systems for the development of programs to detect and reme-diate handicap conditions early to minimize the need for institutionalization. This subchapter defines handicapped infants and toddlers as individuals from birth to age 2 who need early intervention services because of developmental delays in cognitive development, physical development, language and speech development, psychological development, self-help skills, or have been diagnosed as having a physical or mental condition which will probably result in developmental delay. The kinds of services offered are as follows:

1. family training, counseling, and home visits;
2. special instruction;
3. speech pathology and audiology;
4. occupational therapy;
5. physical therapy;
6. psychological services;
7. case management services;
8. medical services for diagnostic and evaluation purposes only;
9. early identification and screening service;
10. health services necessary to enable a child to benefit from early intervention services.

These services must be provided by qualified personnel such as special educators, speech and language pathologists, audiologists, occupational therapists, physical therapists, psychologists, social workers, nurses, and nutritionists. These early intervention services must be public and provided at no cost to families except when specifically stated by state or federal law.

To receive early intervention services an infant or toddler must first be assessed by his/her local school district to determine his/her present functioning levels in the areas of physical development, cognitive development, language and speech development, psycho-social development, and self-help skills. If a child is determined to need early intervention services, then an individualized family service plan is written based on the results of the assessments. The plan will include the following:

1. family's strengths and needs and how they affect the development of the handicapped child;
2. short and long term goals;
3. procedures to be used to evaluate progress and frequency;
4. services to be provided to child and family;

5. procedures for delivering services and frequency;
6. date services will be initiated and estimated time duration;
7. name of case manager responsible for implementing plan;
8. and how the child will be transitioned into receiving future services if necessary.

This subchapter also states that if there is a change in a child's diagnoses, evaluation placement, or services rendered then the parent or guardian must be notified in writing. If the parent or guardian disagrees with the change or with the individualized family service plan, then the subchapter describes the procedure for resolving complaints including the filing of civil action suits. It also discusses the rights of individuals to confidentiality and how parents or guardians can examine records containing assessment reports and individualized family service plans. There is also a procedure for assigning a surrogate parent to a child who doesn't have a parent or guardian to represent the child's best interests at planning conferences.

The federal law provides general guidelines for the states to follow in designing a specific procedure for referring students between the ages of 3 and 21 who may need special education services, determining their eligibility and obtaining the necessary services. PL 94-142 requires that each school district develop a procedure for identifying "exceptional" children. This can be done through annual screening of children from ages 3–5, including hearing and vision screening; speech and language screening when enrolled in school; and annual screening by teachers and other professions for the referral of those children who exhibit problems which may compromise their ability to learn in a standard classroom setting. If a child appears to be in need of special education services, he or she can be referred by school personnel, parents or guardian, community service agencies, professionals having knowledge of the child's problems, state office of education, and by the child. Once the referral is made in writing to the designated school official, then the school has a limited amount of time, usually 30 to 90 days, to determine whether a case study should be performed and to notify the parents and referral source of their decision. To determine whether a child needs a case study evaluation, the school may observe the child, assess methods of instruction, consult with teachers and referral source, and talk with the child. If the school decides that a case study is not appropriate, they must notify the parents and referral source of their decision and the reasons for the decision.

A child cannot be permanently excluded from public school due to the lack of appropriate programs. If a child is waiting for special education services, and exhibits inappropriate behavior that is the result of the exceptional characteristic requiring special services, he or she cannot be expelled from school unless it endangers the child, others, or school property. When it becomes necessary to expel a child waiting for special services due to one or more of the above

criteria, the school system is obligated to provide educational instruction outside of the school itself until the appropriate special education placement is made. To provide education to such a student waiting for services, the school can provide a home tutor or other such alternative.

In the event that the school requests or agrees to a request for a case study or re-evaluation of the child to be performed, parents must give their written consent. If parents refuse to give their written approval, then the school can request an impartial due process hearing. In general, a case study evaluation may include a vision and hearing test, review of child's health status, review of child's academic records and current functioning levels, speech and language evaluation, child and parent conferences, social/emotional and developmental assessment, and a study of the child's learning environment. Special evaluations may also be conducted in addition to those mentioned, depending on the nature of the child's problems. Schools are expected to pay for evaluations which are deemed necessary for the case study. If parents do not agree with the test results, they may seek an independent evaluation outside of the school at public expense if the school agrees. In the case where the school feels that another evaluation is not necessary and, therefore, declines to pay for it, then parents can still have an independent evaluation performed, but at their own expense. In assessing whether tests and procedures are valid, it is important to remember that these evaluation materials cannot be racially or culturally discriminatory, nor can they be inappropriate in relation to the child's sensory, motor, or communication skills.

Multidisciplinary Case Study Conference

When the case study evaluation has been completed, a conference is then held consisting of the director of special education, parents or guardian, child, school personnel (teachers and counselors), and those who may be providing special education services to the child, if deemed necessary. In more complicated case studies where the child may need private or public placement outside the school setting, representatives from the state department of mental health and department of children and family services or their equivalents (depending on the state), should be invited to the conference. The purpose of inviting representatives of agencies and state departments is to allow all possible placement alternatives to be discussed and evaluated in terms of assessing the child's needs, providing services to meet these needs, and to consider what funding sources are available to the child. In terms of funding, sometimes one source pays for the placement and at other times more than one agency or state department will enter into a cooperative agreement. In the case of the latter, the school may fund the tuition of a residential placement and the cooperating agency may fund room and board and/or related services.

The case study conference model was designed and implemented for the purpose of gaining an understanding of the child's learning style, strengths and weaknesses in various skill and social emotional areas; determining whether the standard school program can meet his/her needs; and deciding on whether special education services are needed. If the conference participants agree that the child needs special education services, then it is their responsibility to determine the nature and degree of needed services and to recommend the least restrictive placement that will adequately meet the child's needs and continue to allow him/her to interact with non-handicapped children. Children who exhibit one or more of the following exceptional characteristics are eligible for special education programs and services:

1. visual impairment;
2. hearing impairment;
3. physical and health impairment;
4. speech and/or language impairment;
5. specific learning disability whereupon the child exhibits a disorder in one or more psychological processes necessary to understand or use language, which compromises the ability to listen, think, speak, read, write, spell, or impedes computation skills;
6. educational maladjustment due to social or cultural circumstances;
7. mental impairment, whereupon the child's intellectual development, mental capacity, adaptive behavior, and academic achievement are mildly, severely, or profoundly delayed;
8. behavior disorder, whereupon the child exhibits an affective disorder or maladaptive behavior which compromises learning and/or social functioning;
9. multiple impairment, whereupon the child exhibits 2 or more impairments severe enough to compromise his or her ability to benefit from the standard educational program.

It is necessary, but not sufficient, to have one of the above exceptional characteristics in order to be considered eligible for special education services. The exceptional characteristic must also be shown to compromise his or her social, emotional, and/or educational functioning and, therefore, significantly affect his or her ability to benefit from the standard educational program.

At the conclusion of the multidisciplinary conference, a decision will be made either for or against the child receiving special education services. If a placement recommendation is made and the school personnel and parents agree, then subsequent meetings may be scheduled to write the child's individualized educational plan. An individualized educational plan is a form completed by those who attend the conference, in cooperation with the director of special education. The plan should at least include the child's present levels of academic performance, annual social, emotional, and educational goals, short-term objectives which will lead to the completion of the annual goals, a statement of special education and related services the child needs, a statement of the amount of regular education the child will receive, projected dates for initiating the special program, anticipated duration of placement, and description of the objective criteria and evaluation procedures to be used to assess the child's progress toward objectives and goals. If the parents agree with the individualized educational plan, then they must sign the document before it can be implemented. If the parents disagree with the plan and the school refuses to change it, then the parents can call a due process hearing.

In general, the continuum of special education services available can be described in terms of 7 levels from least restrictive to most restrictive:

Level 1   Standard school program in conjunction with teacher consultations, special education materials, or modified instructional program.

Level 2   Alternative standard program, whereupon the content of the standard curriculum teaching methods are altered to meet the handicapped child's needs.

Level 3   Standard or alternative standard program in conjunction with a resource program which offers more individualized instruction with or without special materials in one or more academic areas.

Level 4   Self-contained special education classroom within the school or in a private school, where a child receives a majority of his or her educational instruction.

Level 5   Self-contained special education classroom in conjunction with a cooperative program set up with work experience programs or programs offered by other agencies.

Level 6   Home or hospital instruction for handicapped children who are unable to attend standard or special education programs due to medical, emotional, or behavioral reasons.

Level 7   Residential treatment placement in private or state facilities.

This last type of placement is viewed as the most restrictive because it is offered to children whose exceptional characteristics are so profound or complex that no special education program offered by the public schools can adequately or appropriately meet the child's special needs. The child must be determined to have exceptional needs and to be in need of placement in either a state or private facility by a multidisciplinary conference at the school.

Public Law 94-142 emphasizes that the lack of available community resources does not relieve the school district of its responsibility to provide a comprehensive special education program. It is important to remember that only those placements approved by the multidisciplinary conference and director of special education are eligible for funding from the school system. The law states that state programs closest to the child's home should be evaluated first, however, the school must refer according primarily to the child's needs, and location secondarily. Children cannot be placed in residential facilities before the funding of such a program has been approved by the school, if the referral source desires school reimbursement. The general criteria used for approving a recommended placement are as follows:

1. Child is presently enrolled in public school.
2. Local education district is in compliance with state law.
3. Facility is appropriate in meeting child's needs.
4. Facility is licensed by state.
5. Facility is registered with the child's home state office of education.
6. Facility is in United States.
7. Facility provides an education program for at least 176 days a year.

When a recommended private placement is approved for a child, then the school district will enter an agreement with the facility which may include the development of an individualized educational plan, procedure for making progress reports, and the establishment of the cost of the program. The school district should also pay for the child's transportation to and from the residential facility at least once each school year.

A residential placement made under PL 94-142 is determined appropriate if 24-hour care is necessary for a student to learn and benefit from an educational environment. Residential placement can be used as a response or alternative to a child's lack of progress in regular school or a less restrictive school setting. The students home school can be responsible for funding an entire residential placement if the school district and those involved in the case conference agree that it is necessary. If the student requires a year round placement to prevent substantial regression over the summer, then the school district will have to pay for room, board and tuition during the summer months. Usually, however, schools do not pay for related services such as psychotherapy because it is a form of medical treatment performed by a psychiatrist and therefore not educational in nature. Likewise, a school district is not required to pay for a students' hospitalization in a psychiatric facility when the placement is for medical or social/emotional problems that are segregable from educational ones. When a free appropriate public education is available to an emotionally disturbed student and the parents choose to place the student in a private school, then the school district is also required to fund the placement.

In choosing the appropriate residential treatment facility, the referral source and/or parent should visit the facility before agreeing to placement. It is important to gather as much information as possible about the facility through phone contacts and requesting printed material about programs and services. Some aspects of a potential placement to be considered include licenses and accreditation, staff credentials, open or closed setting, type of funding sources accepted, referral process, and from what geographical locations applicants are accepted. In terms of educational services, ask if residents can earn credits for their coursework, and whether they are transferable to home schools. It is also important to know whether the school program will continue with the student's present courses or introduce new subjects and books. If the child to be placed needs special education curriculum, ask whether remedial courses and materials are available, along with special education instruction. Above all, make sure that the facility is able to meet the child's needs, socially, emotionally, and academically, as stated in the individualized educational plan.

Due Process Hearing

The child's progress in the special education program should be reviewed annually by all those who wrote the individualized educational plan. If it is recommended at the review conference that the child change his or her special education placement, be re-evaluated, or have his/her special services terminated, then the parents must be notified of the recommendation, along with reasons for the changes. If the parents agree, then the individualized educational plan is revised and signed. If they do not agree and the school persists, then the parents can call a due process hearing. On the other hand, if the parents recommend changes and the school disagrees, then the school can call a due process hearing.

As has been mentioned, if, during or following the multidisciplinary conference, the local school district and parents fail to settle their differences of opinion as to the special services a child should or should not receive, then either party can request a due process hearing. The school district should inform parents and guardians of their rights for requesting a due process hearing and the procedure for doing so. Parents and guardians should also be aware of child advocates and other sources of legal advice which they can obtain to help them cooperatively reach agreements with school districts.

In general, the procedure for requesting a due process hearing by parents and guardians includes the following steps:

1. Parent or guardian sends a certified letter requesting a due process hearing to the designated school official (i.e., superintendent, principal, director of special education). The request should include a summary of the disagreement and reasons for requesting the hearing.

2. Within a week of receiving the request, the school district will send a letter to the state office of education stating the reasons for the hearing and requesting the appointment of an impartial hearing officer.

3. The state office of education will then send a list of hearing officers to the school district, from which the parents and school can jointly choose an officer.

4. The chosen hearing officer, once contacted, will schedule a time and place for the due process hearing to take place.

If the school officials do not acknowledge the parents' request for a hearing and refuse to coooperate, then the parents can appeal to the state office of education directly for assistance. All requests concerning this matter should be made by certified letters so that there is documentation as to when and to whom requests were made.

Before the due process hearing takes place, parents have the right to review the child's school records, request an independent evaluation of the child at their own expense, invite significant people to the hearing who possess important information, and invite those who can represent them, including legal counsel, at their own expense. It is important to remember that the child being discussed has the right to remain in his/her present education setting until the hearing is completed, unless he/she is a danger to self, others, or school property. The child has the right to attend the hearing if the parents feel he/she should. If necessary, an interpreter can be requested to attend the hearing as an aid to the family.

At the due process hearing, the hearing officer will establish the issues to be discussed and designate what evidence, relevant to the issues, can be introduced. Anyone attending the hearing has the right to protest the introduction of evidence which has not been disclosed to him/her prior to the hearing. Within approximately 2 weeks following the hearing, a decision will be made by the hearing officer and sent in written form to the school, parents, and state office of education. This decision will be binding upon the parents and school unless one of the parties appeals. A record of the hearing is kept in the child's temporary school file.

If either party disagrees with the hearing officer's decision, they can send a certified letter requesting an appeal to the state superintendent of education's legal department. This letter should include reasons for the appeal with a copy sent to the other party involved. Upon receipt of a request for a state level review, the state superintendent of education will organize an impartial hearing panel consisting of attorneys and education professionals. The purpose of the review panel is to consider the appeal on the basis of the due process hearing record. Parties may or may not be given an opportunity to give additional information. If they are, then another hearing will be scheduled. The review panel's recommendation will then be submitted to the state superintendent of education for a final decision to be made. This decision, made on appeal, is final and will be binding to all parties concerned. The local school district is then responsible for implementing the decision.

In the event that either party disagrees with the decision made by the superintendent of education, they have the right to bring a civil suit, to state or federal court, seeking a court review adopting their views. Any such action would require the assistance of legal counsel. During the proceedings, the court will review the records of the previous hearings and may allow new evidence to be admitted at the request of the petitioner. The judge is then empowered to make an independent decision, based on all of the evidence. While these proceedings are pending, the child concerned shall remain in his/her current educational setting unless the educational agency and parents otherwise agree.

State Funding for Residential Placement

The Illinois Department of Mental Health and Developmental Disabilities (or its equivalent in other states) has a funding program to assist parents and guardians in paying the cost of residential treatment for mentally ill children. These funds, Individual Care Grants, are usually supplementary in that they are used to pay the remaining cost of residential treatment after all other funding has been applied for. Individual Care Grants, when awarded, continue as long as the child is in need of residential treatment or until his/her 18th birthday. Funds are paid directly to the facility once funding is approved.

The Illinois Department of Mental Health and Development Disabilities offers Individual Care Grants to children who are seriously mentally ill, described as psychotic or borderline psychotic, with significant impairments in reality testing and other areas necessary to function in the community. Those children considered eligible usually have a long history of mental illness, have been unable to benefit from other treatment programs, have had one or more psychiatric hospitalizations, and are in need of 24-hour residential care.

The procedure for applying for an Individual Care Grant in Illinois requires parents or guardians to forward the following family materials: completed family information forms, recent Federal Income Tax Return and W-2s, and, if applicable, a divorce decree. Background information on the child must also be sent, including psychiatric and psychological evaluations, social and developmental history, medical reports, school records, treatment summaries, and treatment recommendations.

A decision regarding a child's eligibility for an Individual Care Grant is usually made by more than one departmental committee review. The department makes its decision on the basis of the child's clinical records, mental illness, and treatment needs. If the necessary services can be provided in the department's own program or community programs, then the funding will not be awarded. It must be noted that the availability of funds can also affect whether an Individual Care Grant will be approved. If awarded, only those programs which have contracts with the department or are on the department's approved list can be used for placement. In-state facilities are considered before out-of-state facilities. There is a formal hearing process available to parents and guardians who wish to appeal the decision of the department in the case that their application for an Individual Care Grant is denied.

The Illinois Department of Children and Family Services (or its equivalent in other states) only becomes involved in case studies when parents either lose or give up the custody of their child. Parents can lose custody of their child, which makes the child a ward of the state, under the following circumstances:

1. Reports of abuse or neglect are proven and the case is referred to juvenile court.

2. Child can no longer be taken care of due to parents' physical or mental illness.

3. Child is ungovernable, truant, a runaway, and determined to be delinquent by the courts. Under these circumstances, the police refer the child to a community agency for approximately 3 weeks. If necessary, the child is then brought before the juvenile court with the parents and custody is taken away.

If parents want to give up custody of their child, the necessary background information must be forwarded to the Department of Children and Family Services (DCFS) before the multidisciplinary conference takes place. The referral packet should at least include a description of presenting problem, a social history, medical records, psychiatric and psychological evaluations, school reports, court reports, and reports from previous placements and/or community counseling services. If DCFS decides that the child needs to be a ward of the state for his/her own welfare, then custody will be taken away from the parents. The child will then be placed in a state residential facility funded by the department. Parents have the right to request that custody be returned to them through the courts, although it is up to the Department of Children and Family Services to determine when the child and parents are ready to be together again as a family.

The interpretation of Public Law 94-142 in this chapter is based on the Education of All Handicapped Act as amended in 1986. Some of the procedures or time lines described were from the point of view of the Illinois Department of Education, Department of Mental Health and Developmental Disabilities, and the Department of Children and Family Services. It is important to contact your local departments and agencies to become familiar with the procedures they utilize to comply with federal mandates. The above described guidelines can be used to evaluate your own state's law for providing special education services to handicapped children.

Procedure for Finding a Residential Placement

A conference with significant family members and professionals should take place before initiating the extensive and complex process of finding an appropriate residential placement. The purpose of this conference is to identify the child's strengths, needs, and goals and to determine the kinds of programs and services that are necessary to provide the child with a therapeutic setting. An individual who requires placement in a residential treatment facility has been determined to need 24-hour care in a controlled environment.

Once the conference participants have agreed that a residential placement would be appropriate for the child, then the source of funding for the placement must be determined. Residential placements can be funded by local and state departments of education, mental health departments, social service agencies, court systems, and insurance agencies. Placements can also be funded by private individuals, but it is often too costly. It is important to identify the funding source before seeking placement because some facilities only accept placements funded by certain sources. Also, funding sources, other than private individuals, often will only fund residential placements in facilities listed on a pre-approved list. In order to seek various funding sources, contact the desired source and ask about eligibility for funding and the application procedure. Once the funding source has been determined, ask the funding source if the residential facility must be on a certain approved list or can the child and parent seek out a placement on their own.

The next step is to decide where the facility should be located according to city, county, state, or region. Most professionals in the education and mental health fields agree that placement should be made near the individual's family and/or friends, especially if either of these groups of people are expected to be involved in the individual's treatment program. Close proximity to the individual's home also allows the facility to help the child make a smooth transition back to the community upon discharge. Some states are very limited in the number of residential facilities they have, so it may be necessary to seek placement out of state.

Once the need for residential placement has been established along with the type of facility, programs required, funding source, and preference of location, then the *Directory of Residential Facilities for Emotionally Handicapped Children and Youth* can be used. First, compile a list of possible facilities by looking them up in the indexes according to specialized programs offered, characteristics of children accepted, funding sources, or by state. It is important to keep in mind the child's strengths, needs, and goals, as determined at the conference. Make sure the facility accepts the individual's funding source, offers the programs and services the individual needs, accepts applicants in the desired age range with the individual's exhibited characteristics and accepts referrals from the individual's referral source.

In terms of social and rehabilitative services offered, be sure that the staff members who implement the services are appropriately trained or licensed to do so. There should be a physician on staff to supervise the administration of medicine if the individual is being medicated. The child may require a psychiatrist or psychologist on staff to provide certain kinds of therapy. A physical therapist should be available if the child has certain handicapping conditions. An individual with a history of alcohol or substance abuse may require a substance abuse program and the appropriate staff to offer guidance and counseling. Check to see if the facility has a follow up program to help children upon discharge.

Children placed in residential treatment facilities should not miss out on their education. They must be able to attend an on-campus or off-campus school program staffed by certified teachers who offer a wide range of curriculum. It is important to contact the home school to arrange for students to acquire the appropriate coursework or credits necessary to pass a grade or graduate. Some facilities use their own coursework and others let students work on their home school coursework through correspondence. If a student needs close supervision and guidance in school then it may be necessary to look for a facility with an on-campus school program. An off-campus program usually sends students to the local school district to attend classes. Small class sizes of 8 or less with a student to teacher ratio of 8 to 1 is preferable. A vocational education program may be a priority for students nearing graduation who are not college bound.

After completing a list of three to five residential facilities, contact their admissions offices to request the necessary application information. Inquire as to what information relating to the child should be forwarded, such as psychologicals, psychiatric reports, family history, school reports, health records, and medical history. Some facilities require a personal interview with the applicant. Inquire as to how long it takes for an admission decision to be made. To minimize the time spent on applying for admission it may be helpful to apply to more than one facility in case a child is not accepted by the first choice.

Once an individual is accepted and placed, be sure to have family members, significant professionals, and home school personnel keep in contact with the residential facility. Progress reports should be sent by the facility at regular intervals, previously agreed upon. The child should be regularly evaluated to determine whether residential treatment should be continued. At this time the education or conference plan should be updated and rewritten to reflect the individual's progress, needs, new goals, and required services for the coming year. If the child is to be mainstreamed, then a discharge planning conference should be held involving family members, school personnel, residential facility staff, involved professionals, and the individual. This meeting should establish a program for the child so that a gradual successful transition can be made back to the home school and community.

ALABAMA

ANNISTON

COOSA VALLEY YOUTH SERVICES, ATTENTION HOME

#1 Sunrise Dr, Anniston, AL 36201 (205) 236-5437 *Contact Person(s):* Charles S Acha, Prog Coord

Setting and Background Information The facility was established in 1978 and is located on 60 wooded acres.

Referral Information Clients are referred to the facility by court order through juvenile probation officers and/or Dept of Human Resource caseworkers.

Type of Facility

Funding Sources County; City.

Average Length of Stay Short and long term.

Types of Admissions Accepted Residential treatment; Wards of the state; Emergency shelter.

Sources of Referral Juvenile courts.

Client Profile

Age Range of Clients Served Residential program: 12-18.

Characteristics Exhibited by Children Emotional handicaps.

IQ Range of Clients 70-120.

Tuition and Fees

Room and Board Short term: $15/diem; Long term: $15/diem.

Placements Primarily Funded By County; Dept of Youth Services; Dept of Human Resources.

Social and Rehabilitative Services

Therapeutic Approach The basic therapeutic approach of the facility is behavior modification.

Therapeutic Services Offered Individual therapy; Group therapy; Family therapy; Independent living skills program; Substance abuse treatment.

Professionals on Staff Social workers; Child care staff.

Educational and Vocational Services

Type(s) of Educational Programs Offered Off campus (Local schools); Summer campus (PACE program).

BIRMINGHAM

GLENWOOD MENTAL HEALTH SERVICES, CHILDREN'S RESIDENTIAL

150 Glenwood Lane, Birmingham, AL 35243 (205) 969-2880 *Contact Person(s):* Betty Milner, Dir-Allan Cott School; Joe Carter, Dir-Children's Residential

Setting and Background Information The facility was established in 1980 with private funding and donations. There are two residential children's homes and a school on the 400-acre Glenwood campus.

Referral Information Contact the facility for referral information.

Type of Facility

Funding Sources Private; State.

Average Length of Stay Long term.

Types of Admissions Accepted Day treatment; Residential treatment.

Sources of Referral State depts of education; State depts of mental health; Private sources; Social service depts.

Client Profile

Age Range of Clients Served Day programs: Birth-18; Residential program: Birth-18.

Characteristics Exhibited by Children Autism; Pervasive developmental disorder.

Tuition and Fees

Room and Board Long term: $27,375/yr.

Tuition $13,000/yr.

Placements Primarily Funded By State depts of education; State depts of mental health; Private sources; Social service depts.

Social and Rehabilitative Services

Therapeutic Approach The facility has a behavioral approach to therapy.

Therapeutic Services Offered Independent living skills program; Recreation activities; Speech therapy.

Professionals on Staff Psychiatrists; Child care staff; Nurses.

Educational and Vocational Services

Type(s) of Educational Programs Offered On campus; Summer campus.

Profile of On Campus School Program Number of teachers 10; *Number of classrooms* 10; *Student to teacher ratio* 4:1; *Credentials of teachers* State Certified; *Grades taught* Un-graded.

Vocational Education Programs/Degrees Offered Pre-vocational training.

JEFFERSON COUNTY FAMILY COURT DETENTION CENTER

120 2nd Ct N, Birmingham, AL 35211 (205) 325-5438 *Contact Person(s):* Willie J Brown, Prog Dir

Setting and Background Information The facility was established in 1927 by a legislative act. There is a residential building, a court house and a detention building. It is a temporary holding facility for delinquents and status offenders awaiting trial or placement.

Referral Information Referrals are made by the courts, families and social workers.

Type of Facility

Funding Sources State; County.

Average Length of Stay Short term.

Types of Admissions Accepted Residential treatment.

Sources of Referral Local depts of education; Social service depts; Courts.

Client Profile

Age Range of Clients Served Residential program: 6-18.

Characteristics Exhibited by Children Delinquency.

Tuition and Fees

Placements Primarily Funded By County commission.

Social and Rehabilitative Services

Therapeutic Approach The facility uses behavior modification.

Therapeutic Services Offered Independent living skills program; Recreation activities.

Professionals on Staff Psychologists; Social workers; Child care staff; Nurses; Physical therapists; Probation services.

Educational and Vocational Services

Type(s) of Educational Programs Offered On campus.

Profile of On Campus School Program Number of teachers 2; *Number of classrooms* 2; Remedial courses offered.

EUFAULA

EUFAULA ADOLESCENT ADJUSTMENT CENTER

PO Box 270, Eufaula, AL 36027 (205) 687-5741 *Contact Person(s):* Carol Driggers

Setting and Background Information Eufaula Adolescent Adjustment Center is a residential treatment which is operated by the Alabama Dept of Mental Health. Its campus is located in a rural

EUFAULA ADOLESCENT ADJUSTMENT CENTER
(continued)

community and consists of 2 large dormitories, recreation hall, school, gymnasium, and swimming pool.

Referral Information Referrals can be made by private and public mental health agencies.

Type of Facility

Funding Sources State.

Average Length of Stay 9-12 mos.

Types of Admissions Accepted Residential treatment.

Sources of Referral State depts of mental health; County.

Client Profile

Age Range of Clients Served Residential program: 12-18.

Characteristics Exhibited by Children Emotional handicaps; Learning disabilities; Mental disabilities.

IQ Range of Clients 89-140.

Tuition and Fees

Placements Primarily Funded By State depts of mental health.

Social and Rehabilitative Services

Therapeutic Approach The program utilizes a wide range of therapeutic approaches, including milieu, behavior, and reality therapies.

Therapeutic Services Offered Individual therapy; Group therapy; Family therapy; Independent living skills program; Recreation activities.

Professionals on Staff Psychiatrists; Psychologists; Social workers; Nurses.

Educational and Vocational Services

Type(s) of Educational Programs Offered On campus (Accredited); Summer campus.

Profile of On Campus School Program Grades taught 6-12; Remedial courses offered.

Degrees Offered GED.

FLORENCE

COLBERT-LAUDERDALE ATTENTION HOME, INC

PO Box 742, 115 ½ E Mobile Plaza, Florence, AL 35631

(205) 767-0972 *Contact Person(s):* Erich H Sigle, Dir

Setting and Background Information The facility was established in 1974 with ALEPA grant monies. There are two residential houses.

Referral Information All referrals to the facility must be made by the court order of a juvenile judge.

Type of Facility

Funding Sources Private; State; Federal; United Way; Churches.

Average Length of Stay Short and long term.

Types of Admissions Accepted Residential treatment; Wards of the state.

Sources of Referral Juvenile court judge.

Client Profile

Age Range of Clients Served Residential program: 10-18.

Characteristics Exhibited by Children Delinquency.

IQ Range of Clients 65+.

Tuition and Fees

Room and Board Short term: $6/diem; Long term: $6/diem.

Placements Primarily Funded By State depts of mental health; Depts of corrections; Social service depts; Dept of Youth Services.

Social and Rehabilitative Services

Therapeutic Approach The facility has a behavioral approach to therapy.

Therapeutic Services Offered Individual therapy; Group therapy.

Professionals on Staff Psychologists; Social workers; Child care staff.

Educational and Vocational Services

Type(s) of Educational Programs Offered Off campus (Public school).

Vocational Education Programs/Degrees Offered State technical schools; High school vocational classes.

GREEN POND

THE BOYD SCHOOL

PO Box 127, Green Pond, AL 35074 (205) 938-7663 *Contact Person(s):* Danny Whitehead, Social Worker

Setting and Background Information The Boyd School is a private residential treatment facility which was established in 1974. The campus is located on 11 acres of land in a rural community and includes a dorm for 12 youth, a group home for 8 youth, and a therapeutic group home for 8 boys. All children are mainstreamed into public schools prior to discharge.

Referral Information Referrals can be made by parents, psychiatrists, psychologists, social workers, school districts, and other social service agencies. Applicants should contact the facility and request a referral packet. A decision as to the appropriateness of the placement will be made within 30 days from the receipt of the background information.

Type of Facility

Funding Sources Private.

Average Length of Stay Long term.

Types of Admissions Accepted Residential treatment; Group home placement; Wards of the state.

Sources of Referral Local depts of education; Private sources; Depts of correction; Social service depts; Courts.

Client Profile

Age Range of Clients Served Residential program: 6-17.

Characteristics Exhibited by Children Emotional handicaps; Learning disabilities; Delinquency.

Tuition and Fees

Room and Board Long term: $75/diem.

Tuition $19/diem (out of state placements).

Placements Primarily Funded By Private sources; Title XX.

Social and Rehabilitative Services

Therapeutic Approach Behavior modification is the primary therapeutic approach used.

Therapeutic Services Offered Individual therapy; Group therapy; Family therapy; Recreation activities; Aftercare program with follow up.

Professionals on Staff Psychiatrists; Psychologists; Social workers; Child care staff; Nurses.

Educational and Vocational Services

Type(s) of Educational Programs Offered On campus; Off campus (Public school).

Profile of On Campus School Program Number of teachers 1 and 2 aides; *Credentials of teachers* MA; *Grades taught* K-8.

GREENPOND

TRI-WIL, INC—PORTA CRAS SCHOOL

PO Box 77, Greenpond, AL 35074 (205) 938-7855 *Contact Person(s):* Soc Wkr

Setting and Background Information The school was established in 1984 with private funding. It provides for the education and treatment of children experiencing serious learning problems or emotional conflicts. It is located on 130 acres and has three family-type dwellings.

Referral Information Referral information should include social and developmental history, an educational report and any clinical material available.

Type of Facility

Funding Sources Private; State; Federal.

Average Length of Stay Long term.

Types of Admissions Accepted Day treatment; Residential treatment.

Sources of Referral State depts of education; Local depts of education; State depts of mental health; Psychiatrists; Private sources; Social service depts; Families.

Client Profile

Age Range of Clients Served Day programs: 6-18; Residential program: 6-18.

Characteristics Exhibited by Children Emotional handicaps; Learning disabilities.

IQ Range of Clients 85+.

Tuition and Fees

Room and Board Long term: $73/diem.

Tuition $19/diem.

Placements Primarily Funded By State depts of education; State depts of mental health; Social service depts.

Social and Rehabilitative Services

Therapeutic Approach The program has a psycho-educational approach to therapy. It is a holistic program.

Therapeutic Services Offered Individual therapy; Group therapy.

Professionals on Staff Psychiatrists; Social workers; Child care staff; Nurses; Medical consultant.

TRI-WIL, INC—PORTA CRAS SCHOOL *(continued)*

Educational and Vocational Services
Type(s) of Educational Programs Offered On campus (Spec Ed); Off campus (Public school).
Profile of On Campus School Program Number of teachers 2; *Number of classrooms* 3; *Credentials of teachers* Certified; *Grades taught* 1-10.

MOBILE

FAIRWAY

1060 Government St, Mobile, AL 36604 (205) 433-3105 *Contact Person(s):* Kathy Veland MEd, Supv Children's Res Srvs
Setting and Background Information The facility was established in 1977 with state funding. The 3-acre campus has a gym, cafeteria, residential and out-patient buildings. It is operated by the Mobile Mental Health Center.
Referral Information Referrals should be made through the program supervisor. Initial referral information should include psychological, social and educational information. Physical exam will be given and a psychological evaluation may be required.
Type of Facility
Funding Sources Private; State.
Average Length of Stay Long term.
Types of Admissions Accepted Residential treatment.
Sources of Referral State depts of mental health; Psychiatrists; Private sources; Social service depts; Local community mental health centers.
Client Profile
Age Range of Clients Served Residential program: 6-12.
Characteristics Exhibited by Children Emotional handicaps; Learning disabilities; Behavior disorders; Family problems.
IQ Range of Clients 70-140.
Tuition and Fees
Room and Board Long term: $100/diem.
Placements Primarily Funded By State depts of mental health; Insurance; Private sources.
Social and Rehabilitative Services
Therapeutic Approach The Fairway program provides treatment for children with significant behavior disorders. The facility uses intensive individual, group and family therapy in a therapeutic milieu.
Therapeutic Services Offered Individual therapy; Group therapy; Family therapy; Adjunctive therapy; Recreation activities; Aftercare program with follow up; Music therapy.
Professionals on Staff Psychiatrists; Psychologists; Social workers; Adjunctive therapists; Child care staff; Nurses; Recreation therapist.
Educational and Vocational Services
Type(s) of Educational Programs Offered Off campus (Public school).

HICKORY HOUSE

1060 Government St, Mobile, AL 36604 (205) 433-9057 *Contact Person(s):* Kathy Veland MEd, Supv Children's Res Srvs
Setting and Background Information This residential program was established in 1981 with funding from the state Dept of Mental Health. The 3-acre campus has a gym, classroom, cafeteria and other residential and out-patient programs. It is operated by the Mobile Mental Health Center.
Referral Information For referral, contact the program supervisor. The child's social history, psychological evaluation, physical evaluation and educational data are required.
Type of Facility
Funding Sources Private; State.
Average Length of Stay Long term.
Types of Admissions Accepted Residential treatment; Wards of the state.
Sources of Referral State depts of mental health; Psychiatrists; Private sources; Social service depts.
Client Profile
Age Range of Clients Served Residential program: 6-12.
Characteristics Exhibited by Children Emotional handicaps; Learning disabilities; Mental disabilities; Psychotic; Severely emotionally disturbed.
IQ Range of Clients 60+.

Tuition and Fees
Placements Primarily Funded By State depts of mental health; Insurance; Private sources.
Social and Rehabilitative Services
Therapeutic Approach The therapeutic approach used is structured behavior modification with individual, group and family therapy. Activity, music and play therapy are also used.
Therapeutic Services Offered Individual therapy; Group therapy; Family therapy; Adjunctive therapy; Recreation activities; Aftercare program with follow up.
Professionals on Staff Psychiatrists; Social workers; Child care staff; Nurses.
Educational and Vocational Services
Type(s) of Educational Programs Offered On campus.
Profile of On Campus School Program Number of teachers 1 and 2 aides; *Number of classrooms* 1; *Student to teacher ratio* 8:1; *Credentials of teachers* MA; *Length of school day* 6 hr; *Grades taught* 1-6.

MOBILE GROUP HOME

563 Stanton St, Mobile, AL 36617 (205) 478-3339, 478-3330
Contact Person(s): Michael G Foley, Dir
Setting and Background Information The facility was established in 1985 by the state. It is a large group home.
Referral Information All referrals are made through the Dept of Youth Services, Diagnostic and Evaluation Center.
Type of Facility
Funding Sources State; Federal.
Average Length of Stay Long term.
Types of Admissions Accepted Group home placement.
Sources of Referral Dept of Youth Svcs only.
Client Profile
Age Range of Clients Served Residential program: 12-18.
Characteristics Exhibited by Children Emotional handicaps; Learning disabilities.
Social and Rehabilitative Services
Therapeutic Approach The basic approach of the facility is reality therapy.
Therapeutic Services Offered Individual therapy; Group therapy; Independent living skills program; Substance abuse treatment.
Professionals on Staff Psychologists; Child care staff.
Educational and Vocational Services
Type(s) of Educational Programs Offered Off campus (Public school).

SOJOURN

1060 Government St, Mobile, AL 36604 (205) 433-4333, 433-4342
Contact Person(s): Billy Golden, Carolyn Collins, Supv
Setting and Background Information This agency was established in 1981 by the Mobile Mental Health Center with a grant from the Runaway and Homeless Youth Act. It has an out-patient counseling center, dorms, a cafeteria and a gym.
Referral Information Referral to the program is available 24 hrs a day, seven days a week. Transportation will be provided if needed.
Type of Facility
Funding Sources Federal; City.
Average Length of Stay Short term.
Types of Admissions Accepted Residential treatment; Emergency shelter.
Sources of Referral Local depts of education; Psychiatrists; Private sources; Social service depts; Self-referred runaways; Homeless youth.
Client Profile
Age Range of Clients Served Residential program: 12-18.
Characteristics Exhibited by Children Emotional handicaps; Learning disabilities; Mental disabilities.
IQ Range of Clients 65+.
Tuition and Fees
Room and Board Short term: $100/diem.
Placements Primarily Funded By Insurance; Private sources; Social service depts; Federal.
Social and Rehabilitative Services
Therapeutic Approach The facility has a family systems approach to therapy, which includes cognitive therapy and behavior management.
Therapeutic Services Offered Individual therapy; Group therapy; Family therapy; Recreation activities; Aftercare program with follow up.

SOJOURN *(continued)*

Professionals on Staff Psychiatrists; Psychologists; Adjunctive therapists; Child care staff; Recreation therapist.
Educational and Vocational Services
Type(s) of Educational Programs Offered Off campus (Public/private schools).

NEW BROCKTON

PATHWAY, INC

Rt 2, Box 352-A, New Brockton, AL 36351 (205) 894-6322 *Contact Person(s):* Skip Hemp, Exec Dir
Setting and Background Information The facility was privately established in 1981. The 60-acre campus has a school, an office, and cabins.
Referral Information Contact the facility and submit a current psychological evaluation, a social history, academic transcripts, court history and current physical report.
Type of Facility
Funding Sources Private; State; Federal.
Average Length of Stay Long term.
Types of Admissions Accepted Residential treatment; Wards of the state.
Sources of Referral State depts of mental health; Psychiatrists; Private sources; Social service depts.
Client Profile
Age Range of Clients Served Residential program: 12-18.
Characteristics Exhibited by Children Emotional handicaps; Learning disabilities; Delinquency.
IQ Range of Clients 60-135.
Tuition and Fees
Room and Board Long term: $1,200/mo (includes school tuition).
Placements Primarily Funded By State depts of education; State depts of mental health; Private sources; Social service depts.
Social and Rehabilitative Services
Therapeutic Approach The facility has a therapeutic milieu.
Therapeutic Services Offered Individual therapy; Group therapy; Adjunctive therapy; Independent living skills program; Recreation activities.
Professionals on Staff Psychologists; Social workers; Adjunctive therapists; Child care staff.
Educational and Vocational Services
Type(s) of Educational Programs Offered On campus; Off campus.
Profile of On Campus School Program Number of classrooms 2; *Student to teacher ratio* 12:1; *Credentials of teachers* MS; *Grades taught* 7-12; Special curriculum electives offered; Remedial courses offered.
Vocational Education Programs/Degrees Offered Construction; Plumbing; Wiring; Roofing; Painting.
Degrees Offered 12th grade diploma.

ONEONTA

THE KING'S RANCH—ONEONTA

PO Box 875, Oneonta, AL 35121 (205) 625-3873 *Contact Person(s):* Bobby Hatter, Soc Wkr
Setting and Background Information This treatment home was established in 1986. It provides services to adolescent boys who need temporary treatment and will eventually be reunited with the family. It is a log cabin home on 4 acres.
Referral Information Referrals can be made by probation officers, judges, social workers, or parents. Contact the social worker. A pre-placement visit will be scheduled.
Type of Facility
Funding Sources Private; State.
Average Length of Stay 6-12 mos.
Types of Admissions Accepted Residential treatment.
Sources of Referral Private sources; Depts of correction; Social service depts.
Client Profile
Age Range of Clients Served Residential program: 12-18.
Characteristics Exhibited by Children Emotional handicaps; Learning disabilities.
Tuition and Fees
Room and Board Long term: $6/diem.
Placements Primarily Funded By Private sources; Depts of corrections; Social service depts.

Social and Rehabilitative Services
Therapeutic Approach The basic approach is reality therapy.
Therapeutic Services Offered Individual therapy; Group therapy; Family therapy; Independent living skills program; Recreation activities.
Professionals on Staff Social workers; Adjunctive therapists; Child care staff.
Educational and Vocational Services
Type(s) of Educational Programs Offered Off campus (Public school).

TALLADEGA

PRESBYTERIAN HOME FOR CHILDREN

PO Drawer 577, Talladega, AL 35160 (205) 362-2114, 362-6601 (for referrals), 245-7099 (emergency shelter) *Contact Person(s):* John Morris, Dir of Soc Srvs; Cathy or David Zabadil, Emergency Shelter Referrals
Setting and Background Information Presbyterian Home for Children is a residential treatment facility which was originally established in 1864 as a home for the children of confederate soldiers. Since then, it has expanded its programs to become a treatment center. The campus is located in east central Alabama, 60 miles from Birmingham, and consists of 7 cottages, activities center, chapel, dining hall, and auxiliary buildings.
Referral Information Anyone can make a referral by contacting the facility, completing application materials, and scheduling a pre-placement visit.
Type of Facility
Funding Sources Private; State.
Average Length of Stay 2 ½ yrs; 30 days (emergency shelter).
Types of Admissions Accepted Residential treatment; Group home placement; Emergency shelter.
Sources of Referral State depts of mental health; Private sources.
Client Profile
Age Range of Clients Served Residential program: 6-18; Emergency shelter: 3-16.
Characteristics Exhibited by Children Emotional handicaps; Learning disabilities.
Tuition and Fees
Placements Primarily Funded By Private sources; Presbyterian church.
Social and Rehabilitative Services
Therapeutic Approach The treatment program utilizes rational therapeutic techniques.
Therapeutic Services Offered Individual therapy; Group therapy; Family therapy; Independent living skills program; Recreation activities; Aftercare program with follow up.
Professionals on Staff Social workers; Adjunctive therapists; Child care staff.
Educational and Vocational Services
Type(s) of Educational Programs Offered Off campus.

UNIVERSITY

BREWER-PORCH CHILDRENS CENTER

PO Box 2232, University, AL 35486 (205) 348-7236 *Contact Person(s):* Susan Powell
Setting and Background Information Brewer-Porch Childrens Center is a state-operated residential treatment facility. The program was established in 1970 by the University of Alabama. Its campus is located on 23 wooded acres and consists of 2 residential cottages and a classroom/administration building.
Referral Information Referrals can be made by mental health centers, school districts, welfare depts, mental health practitioners, and families. To make a referral, contact the admissions coordinator for a referral packet.
Type of Facility
Funding Sources State.
Average Length of Stay Long term.
Types of Admissions Accepted Residential treatment.
Sources of Referral Local depts of education; State depts of mental health; Social service depts.
Client Profile
Age Range of Clients Served Residential program: 8-12.
Characteristics Exhibited by Children Emotional handicaps; Learning disabilities; Mental disabilities.
Tuition and Fees
Placements Primarily Funded By Title XV; Welfare Depts.

BREWER-PORCH CHILDRENS CENTER *(continued)*

Social and Rehabilitative Services

Therapeutic Approach The philosophy of the treatment program is based on behavior modification and psychopharmacological techniques.

Therapeutic Services Offered Individual therapy; Group therapy; Family therapy; Adjunctive therapy; Recreation activities; Aftercare program with follow up.

Professionals on Staff Psychiatrists; Psychologists; Social workers; Child care staff; Nurses.

Educational and Vocational Services

Type(s) of Educational Programs Offered On campus.

Profile of On Campus School Program Number of teachers 2; *Grades taught* 1-12.

ALASKA

ANCHORAGE

ALASKA CHILDREN'S SERVICES, INC
4600 Abbott Rd, Anchorage, AK 99507 (907) 346-2106 *Contact Person(s):* Robert L Griswold, Exec Dir
Setting and Background Information This facility was established in 1970 as a merger of 3 church-related childcare agencies. Currently, it is located on a 13-acre campus.
Referral Information Referral is made through the Division of Family and Youth Services.
Type of Facility
Funding Sources Private; State; United Way.
Average Length of Stay Long term.
Types of Admissions Accepted Residential treatment; Wards of the state.
Sources of Referral Depts of correction; Social service depts.
Client Profile
Age Range of Clients Served Residential program: 6-21+.
Characteristics Exhibited by Children Emotional handicaps; Learning disabilities; Delinquency.
IQ Range of Clients 80-120.
Tuition and Fees
Room and Board Long term: $150/diem.
Placements Primarily Funded By Depts of corrections; Social service depts.
Social and Rehabilitative Services
Therapeutic Services Offered Individual therapy; Group therapy; Family therapy; Adjunctive therapy; Independent living skills program; Recreation activities; Aftercare program with follow up.
Professionals on Staff Psychiatrists; Social workers; Child care staff.
Educational and Vocational Services
Type(s) of Educational Programs Offered On campus (Spec Ed); Off campus (Spec Ed, Mainstream); Summer campus (Spec Ed, Life skills).
Degrees Offered 8th grade diploma; 12th grade diploma; GED.

BETHEL

THE BETHEL GROUP HOME
PO Box 385, Bethel, AK 99559 (907) 543-2846 *Contact Person(s):* Joe Corrigan, Exec Dir
Setting and Background Information The facility was established in 1971 by the Jesuit Volunteer Corp. It is an 8-bed residential treatment program.
Referral Information Referrals are made from the Alaska Division of Family and Youth Services and through the Dept of Corrections.
Type of Facility
Funding Sources Private.
Average Length of Stay Avg 1 yr.
Types of Admissions Accepted Residential treatment; Group home placement; Wards of the state.
Sources of Referral State depts of mental health; Depts of correction; Social service depts.
Client Profile
Age Range of Clients Served Residential program: 12-18.
Characteristics Exhibited by Children Emotional handicaps.
Tuition and Fees
Placements Primarily Funded By Depts of corrections; Social service depts; Fund raising.

Social and Rehabilitative Services
Therapeutic Services Offered Individual therapy; Group therapy; Family therapy; Independent living skills program; Recreation activities; Substance abuse treatment; Aftercare program with follow up.
Professionals on Staff Psychiatrists; Psychologists; Social workers; Adjunctive therapists; Child care staff.

FAIRBANKS

PRESBYTERIAN HOSPITALITY HOUSE
1401 Kellum St, Fairbanks, AK 99701 (907) 456-6445 *Contact Person(s):* Gene Medaris, Exec Dir
Setting and Background Information The facility was established in 1957 in cooperation with the Presbyterian Church. It is located on an acre and has a boys dorm, a girls dorm and three other buildings.
Referral Information Referrals are made by state agencies and are evaluated for admission by a placement committee.
Type of Facility
Funding Sources State.
Average Length of Stay 18 mos.
Types of Admissions Accepted Day treatment; Residential treatment.
Sources of Referral State depts of education; Local depts of education; State depts of mental health; Private sources; Social service depts.
Client Profile
Age Range of Clients Served Day programs: 8-18; Residential program: 12-18.
Characteristics Exhibited by Children Emotional handicaps; Learning disabilities.
IQ Range of Clients 70+.
Tuition and Fees
Room and Board Long term: $129/diem.
Tuition $55/diem.
Placements Primarily Funded By State depts of education; State depts of mental health; Social service depts.
Social and Rehabilitative Services
Therapeutic Services Offered Individual therapy; Group therapy; Art therapy; Substance abuse treatment.
Professionals on Staff Psychiatrists; Psychologists; Social workers; Adjunctive therapists; Child care staff; Art therapists.
Educational and Vocational Services
Type(s) of Educational Programs Offered On campus; Off campus (Activities); Summer campus (Camps).
Profile of On Campus School Program Number of teachers 4; *Number of classrooms* 3; *Student to teacher ratio* 4:1; *Credentials of teachers* Certified; *Grades taught* 6-12.
Degrees Offered 8th grade diploma; 12th grade diploma; GED.

JUNEAU

JUNEAU YOUTH SERVICES, INC
9290 Hurlock, Juneau, AK 99803 (907) 789-7610 *Contact Person(s):* Betty Jo Engelman, Exec Dir
Setting and Background Information The facility was established in 1961. It is a private, non-profit home for children.
Referral Information Contact the facility for referral information.

JUNEAU YOUTH SERVICES, INC *(continued)*

Type of Facility
Funding Sources State.
Average Length of Stay Short and long term.
Types of Admissions Accepted Day treatment; Residential treatment; Wards of the state.
Sources of Referral State depts of education; Social service depts.
Client Profile
Age Range of Clients Served Day programs: 12-18; Residential program: 12-18.
Characteristics Exhibited by Children Emotional handicaps; Learning disabilities.
Tuition and Fees
Placements Primarily Funded By Social service depts.
Social and Rehabilitative Services
Therapeutic Approach The facility offers a positive peer culture.
Therapeutic Services Offered Individual therapy; Group therapy; Family therapy; Independent living skills program; Recreation activities.
Professionals on Staff Psychiatrists; Psychologists; Social workers; Child care staff; Nurses.
Educational and Vocational Services
Type(s) of Educational Programs Offered Off campus (Public school).
Degrees Offered GED.

KODIAK

KODIAK BAPTIST MISSION, INC
1944 Rezanof, Kodiak, AK 99615 (907) 486-4126 *Contact Person(s):* Jeannie Volker, Exec Dir
Setting and Background Information The facility was originally established in 1893 as an orphanage. Currently, the 35-acre campus has three group homes, a gym, an administration building and a barn.
Referral Information For referral, contact the facility for an intake packet. The information will be reviewed by the admission committee in conjunction with local agencies.
Type of Facility
Funding Sources Private; State; Kodiak City; Kodiak Borough.
Average Length of Stay The emergency shelter is short term and the residential program is long term.
Types of Admissions Accepted Residential treatment; Group home placement; Wards of the state; Emergency shelter.
Sources of Referral State depts of education; Local depts of education; State depts of mental health; Psychiatrists; Private sources; Depts of correction; Social service depts.
Client Profile
Age Range of Clients Served Residential program: 6-18.
Characteristics Exhibited by Children Emotional handicaps.
IQ Range of Clients 70-100.
Tuition and Fees
Room and Board Short term: $105/diem; Long term: $105/diem.
Placements Primarily Funded By Social service depts.
Social and Rehabilitative Services
Therapeutic Approach The facility has a behavioral approach to therapy.
Therapeutic Services Offered Individual therapy; Group therapy; Family therapy; Independent living skills program; Substance abuse treatment.
Professionals on Staff Child care staff.
Educational and Vocational Services
Type(s) of Educational Programs Offered Off campus.

NOME

NOME RECEIVING HOME
Box 1653, Nome, AK 99762 (907) 443-2154 *Contact Person(s):* Ruth Nelson, Dir
Setting and Background Information The facility was established in 1971.
Referral Information Referrals to the 6-bed facility are made through the Division of Family and Youth Services.
Type of Facility
Funding Sources State.
Average Length of Stay Short and long term.
Types of Admissions Accepted Residential treatment; Group home placement; Wards of the state.

Sources of Referral Social service depts.
Client Profile
Age Range of Clients Served Residential program: Birth-18.
Characteristics Exhibited by Children Emotional handicaps.
Social and Rehabilitative Services
Professionals on Staff Social workers.

ARIZONA

MESA

PREHAB OF ARIZONA
PO Drawer G, Mesa, AZ 85201 (602) 969-4024 *Contact Person(s):* Mike Hughes, Exec Dir
Setting and Background Information The facility was established in 1971 as an agency designed for treatment of youth experiencing substance abuse problems. Currently, the programs include residential treatment, out-patient counseling, emergency shelter care and a day program.
Referral Information Referrals are accepted throughout the year. Contact the facility for referral information.
Type of Facility
Funding Sources Private.
Average Length of Stay Long term.
Types of Admissions Accepted Day treatment; Residential treatment; Emergency shelter.
Sources of Referral State depts of mental health; Private sources; Courts.
Client Profile
Age Range of Clients Served Day programs: 12-17; Residential program: 12-17.
Characteristics Exhibited by Children Emotional handicaps; Learning disabilities; Delinquency.
Tuition and Fees
Room and Board Long term: $2,295/mo.
Tuition $31.45/diem.
Placements Primarily Funded By Private sources; Depts of corrections; United Way.
Social and Rehabilitative Services
Therapeutic Services Offered Individual therapy; Group therapy; Family therapy; Independent living skills program; Substance abuse treatment; Aftercare program with follow up.
Professionals on Staff Psychologists; Social workers; Adjunctive therapists; Child care staff.
Educational and Vocational Services
Type(s) of Educational Programs Offered On campus.

SUNSHINE ACRES CHILDREN'S HOME
3405 N Higley Rd, Mesa, AZ 85025 (602) 832-2540 *Contact Person(s):* Carol Whitworth, Dir
Referral Information Contact the facility for referral information.
Type of Facility
Types of Admissions Accepted Residential treatment.
Client Profile
Age Range of Clients Served Residential program: 4-18.
Characteristics Exhibited by Children Delinquency.

PEORIA

YOUNG ACRES
6801 W Banff Lane, Peoria, AZ 85345 (602) 979-6740 *Contact Person(s):* Louise M Krieger, Exec Dir
Setting and Background Information The facility was established in 1974 as a group home. Currently it is a child care agency and has 5 residential homes in the Phoenix area.
Referral Information Contact the facility for referral information.

Type of Facility
Funding Sources Private; State.
Average Length of Stay Long term.
Types of Admissions Accepted Residential treatment; Group home placement; Wards of the state.
Sources of Referral Depts of correction; Social service depts.
Client Profile
Age Range of Clients Served Residential program: 6-18.
Characteristics Exhibited by Children Emotional handicaps; Learning disabilities; Speech/Language disorders.
IQ Range of Clients 80-120.
Tuition and Fees
Room and Board Long term: $1,695/mo.
Placements Primarily Funded By Depts of corrections; Social service depts.
Social and Rehabilitative Services
Therapeutic Approach The facility has a behavior modification treatment program.
Therapeutic Services Offered Individual therapy; Group therapy; Family therapy; Independent living skills program; Substance abuse treatment.
Professionals on Staff Psychologists; Social workers; Child care staff; Tutor.
Educational and Vocational Services
Type(s) of Educational Programs Offered On campus (Tutor); Off campus (Local schools).
Degrees Offered GED.

PHOENIX

ABCS LITTLE CANYON SCHOOL
PO Box 27128, 3115 W Missouri Ave, Phoenix, AZ 85061 (602) 973-8131 *Contact Person(s):* Phyllis F McFarland, PhD
Setting and Background Information The school became an agency of the Arizona Baptist Children's Services in 1959 and admitted students in 1961. Its campus is located on 5 acres in a middle-class residential community, and consists of 3 modern residential cottages, educational, and administrative offices.
Referral Information Placements are made through state and local agencies.
Type of Facility
Funding Sources State.
Average Length of Stay Long term.
Types of Admissions Accepted Residential treatment.
Sources of Referral State depts of education; Local depts of education; State depts of mental health; Social service depts.
Client Profile
Age Range of Clients Served Residential program: 13-17.
Characteristics Exhibited by Children Emotional handicaps; Learning disabilities; Speech/Language disorders; Neurological impairments; Mental disabilities.
IQ Range of Clients 70+.
Tuition and Fees
Room and Board Long term: $3,000/mo.
Placements Primarily Funded By State depts of education; Social service depts.
Social and Rehabilitative Services
Therapeutic Approach The treatment program utilizes an eclectic approach with emphasis on milieu therapy, social learning therapy, behavioral contracting, and contingency therapy.

ABCS LITTLE CANYON SCHOOL *(continued)*

Therapeutic Services Offered Individual therapy; Group therapy; Family therapy; Adjunctive therapy; Independent living skills program; Recreation activities; Aftercare program with follow up.
Professionals on Staff Psychologists; Social workers; Adjunctive therapists; Child care staff; Nurses; Educational consultant.
Educational and Vocational Services
Type(s) of Educational Programs Offered On campus; Off campus.
Profile of On Campus School Program Number of teachers 3 and 2 aides; *Student to teacher ratio* 6:1; *Credentials of teachers* Certified; *Grades taught* 1-12; Special curriculum electives offered; Remedial courses offered.
Degrees Offered 8th grade diploma; 12th grade diploma.

ARIZONA STATE HOSPITAL—CHILD AND ADOLESCENT TREATMENT UNIT

2500 E Van Buren St, Phoenix, AZ 85008 (602) 244-1331, ext 466
Setting and Background Information The facility is a state operated psychiatric hospital. The Child and Adolescent Treatment Unit has been a part of the hospital for several years and is located on hospital grounds.
Referral Information Referrals can be made by physicians, social workers, psychologists, clinics, hospitals, and school districts. To make a referral, one of the above mentioned referrants must forward the necessary background information on the child, then a pre-placement interview will be scheduled.
Type of Facility
Funding Sources State.
Average Length of Stay Short and long term.
Types of Admissions Accepted Residential treatment.
Sources of Referral Local depts of education; Psychiatrists; Private sources; Hospitals.
Client Profile
Age Range of Clients Served Residential program: 6-17.
Characteristics Exhibited by Children Emotional handicaps; Learning disabilities; Speech/Language disorders; Mental disabilities.
Social and Rehabilitative Services
Therapeutic Approach The facility has a psychodynamic approach to therapy.
Therapeutic Services Offered Individual therapy; Group therapy; Family therapy; Adjunctive therapy; Independent living skills program; Recreation activities.
Professionals on Staff Psychiatrists; Psychologists; Social workers; Adjunctive therapists; Child care staff; Nurses.
Educational and Vocational Services
Type(s) of Educational Programs Offered On campus.
Profile of On Campus School Program Remedial courses offered.

ARIZONA YOUTH ASSOCIATION, INC

1723 W Mountain View, Phoenix, AZ 85021 (602) 861-0625
Contact Person(s): Dennis Pickering, Exec Dir
Setting and Background Information The facility is a certified residential facility for 9 boys.
Referral Information Contact the facility for referral information.
Type of Facility
Types of Admissions Accepted Residential treatment.
Client Profile
Age Range of Clients Served Residential program: 15-18.
Characteristics Exhibited by Children Emotional handicaps; Mental disabilities; Abused and neglected; Dependent.

CORTEZ HOUSE

3044 W Laurel Lane, Phoenix, AZ 85029 (602) 863-0400 *Contact Person(s):* Vernon Waite, Dir
Setting and Background Information The facility is a certified residential facility for 14 delinquent boys.
Referral Information Contact the facility for referral information.
Type of Facility
Types of Admissions Accepted Residential treatment.
Client Profile
Age Range of Clients Served Residential program: 12-18.
Characteristics Exhibited by Children Delinquency.

FLORENCE CRITTENTON OF ARIZONA, INC

4820 N 7th Ave, Phoenix, AZ 85013 (602) 274-7318 *Contact Person(s):* Donna Leone, Exec Dir
Referral Information Contact the facility for referral information. The facility accepts girls only.
Type of Facility
Types of Admissions Accepted Residential treatment; Emergency shelter.
Client Profile
Age Range of Clients Served Residential program: 12-18.
Characteristics Exhibited by Children Emotional handicaps; Behavior disorders.

JEWISH FAMILY AND CHILDREN'S SERVICES

2033 N 7th St, Phoenix, AZ 85006 (602) 257-1904 *Contact Person(s):* Lois Tuchler, Exec Dir
Referral Information Contact the facility for referral information.
Type of Facility
Types of Admissions Accepted Residential treatment.
Client Profile
Age Range of Clients Served Residential program: Birth-18.
Characteristics Exhibited by Children Emotional handicaps; Behavior disorders; Delinquency.

THE NEW FOUNDATION

PO Box 8500, 6401 S 8th Pl, Phoenix, AZ 85066 (602) 268-3421
Contact Person(s): David S Hedgcock, Exec Dir
Setting and Background Information This facility was established in 1970 to provide drug abuse treatment. There are 6 buildings located on 3 acres.
Referral Information Contact the facility for referral information.
Type of Facility
Funding Sources Private; State; Federal; Contributions.
Average Length of Stay Long term.
Types of Admissions Accepted Residential treatment; Wards of the state.
Sources of Referral State depts of education; Local depts of education; State depts of mental health; Psychiatrists; Private sources; Depts of correction; Social service depts.
Client Profile
Age Range of Clients Served Residential program: 12-18.
Characteristics Exhibited by Children Emotional handicaps; Learning disabilities; Mental disabilities; Delinquency.
IQ Range of Clients 70+.
Tuition and Fees
Room and Board Long term: $100/diem.
Tuition $30.65/diem.
Placements Primarily Funded By State depts of education; Local depts of education; State depts of mental health; Depts of corrections; Social service depts.
Social and Rehabilitative Services
Therapeutic Services Offered Individual therapy; Group therapy; Family therapy; Adjunctive therapy; Art therapy; Independent living skills program; Recreation activities; Substance abuse treatment; Aftercare program with follow up.
Professionals on Staff Psychiatrists; Psychologists; Social workers; Adjunctive therapists; Child care staff; Nurses; Art therapists; Physical therapists.
Educational and Vocational Services
Type(s) of Educational Programs Offered On campus (EH/LD).
Profile of On Campus School Program Number of teachers 2; *Number of classrooms* 2; *Student to teacher ratio* 12:1; *Credentials of teachers* Spec Ed; Remedial courses offered (Individualized).
Degrees Offered Diploma conferred through local school district.

SAN PABLO RESIDENTIAL TREATMENT SCHOOL

4001 N 30th St, Phoenix, AZ 85016 (602) 956-9090 *Contact Person(s):* Hal Elliott, Exec Dir
Setting and Background Information San Pablo Residential Treatment School is a private, non-profit residential treatment facility for boys. The facility, established in 1961, is governed by a Board of Directors consisting of community volunteers and is accredited through the Joint Commission on the Accreditation of Hospitals. There is also a group home which provides a less structured living program.
Referral Information Referrals can be made by parents, guardians, public and social agencies, courts, psychologists, psychiatrists, the clergy, and other professionals. Completed application forms

SAN PABLO RESIDENTIAL TREATMENT SCHOOL
(continued)

provided by San Pablo should be submitted, along with a $100 application fee, social history, psychological and psychiatric assessments, school records, medical history, statement of boy's legal status, and recent photo. The Admissions Committee will review the referral material and arrange for a pre-placement visit with the child, family, and referral source. A placement decision will be made within 24 hours following the visit. Applicants are not accepted with mental retardation, severe delinquency problems, autism, or drug dependency.

Type of Facility
Funding Sources Private.
Average Length of Stay 12-18 mos.
Types of Admissions Accepted Residential treatment; Group home placement.
Sources of Referral State depts of mental health; Private sources; Depts of correction; Champus; Courts.
Client Profile
Age Range of Clients Served Residential program: 12-18.
Characteristics Exhibited by Children Emotional handicaps; Learning disabilities; Behavior disorders; Substance abuse.
Tuition and Fees
Room and Board Long term: $3,000/mo.
Placements Primarily Funded By State depts of mental health; Depts of corrections; Champus.
Social and Rehabilitative Services
Therapeutic Approach The treatment program utilizes 3 treatment modalities: clinical, milieu, and educational. A behavioral approach utilizing a point and level system provides the means for providing students with feedback about their progress and evaluating them for the earning of privileges.
Therapeutic Services Offered Individual therapy; Group therapy; Family therapy; Adjunctive therapy; Independent living skills program; Substance abuse treatment; Aftercare program with follow up.
Professionals on Staff Psychiatrists; Social workers; Child care staff; Nurses.
Educational and Vocational Services
Type(s) of Educational Programs Offered On campus; Off campus.
Profile of On Campus School Program Number of teachers 2; *Student to teacher ratio* 6:1; *Credentials of teachers* Spec Ed; *Grades taught* Individualized; Remedial courses offered.
Vocational Education Programs/Degrees Offered Woodworking; Electrical; Maintenance skills.
Degrees Offered 8th grade diploma; 12th grade diploma; GED.

TOUCHSTONE COMMUNITY, INC—ARIZONA BOYS COMMUNITY
4202 E Union Hills Dr, Phoenix, AZ 85024 (602) 992-2941 *Contact Person(s):* Timothy Dunst
Referral Information Contact the facility for referral information. The facility accepts boys only.
Type of Facility
Types of Admissions Accepted Residential treatment.
Client Profile
Age Range of Clients Served Residential program: 10-18.
Characteristics Exhibited by Children Emotional handicaps; Behavior disorders; Delinquency.

TUMBLEWEED
915 N 5th St, Phoenix, AZ 85004 (602) 271-9849 *Contact Person(s):* Mike Garvey, Dir
Referral Information Contact the facility for referral information.
Type of Facility
Types of Admissions Accepted Residential treatment; Emergency shelter.
Client Profile
Age Range of Clients Served Residential program: 10-18.
Characteristics Exhibited by Children Emotional handicaps; Delinquency.

JANE WAYLAND CENTER
2613 W Campbell, Phoenix, AZ 85017 (602) 242-7491 *Contact Person(s):* Rubin Lara, Dir of Spec Ed; Connie Philips, Dir of Outpt Svcs

Setting and Background Information Jane Wayland Center is a private non-profit mental health agency which was established in 1929. The programs include day and residential treatment. All programs are located on the main campus. There are 5 residential units: 3 for adolescent boys, 1 for adolescent girls and 1 for pre-adolescent boys and girls.
Referral Information To make a referral, contact the facility and forward the necessary background information. If the placement is not recommended by a psychiatrist, psychologist, or social worker, then the child must be evaluated through the facilty's outpatient services before placement will be considered. If the placement seems appropriate, then an interview will be set up with the child, parents, Jane Wayland staff, and referral representative. A placement decision will then be made in less than a week. Referrals are also accepted from out-of-state sources.
Type of Facility
Funding Sources Private.
Average Length of Stay Long term.
Types of Admissions Accepted Day treatment; Residential treatment; Group home placement.
Sources of Referral State depts of mental health; Depts of correction; Courts; BIA.
Client Profile
Age Range of Clients Served Day programs: 4-55+; Residential program: 4-18.
Characteristics Exhibited by Children Emotional handicaps; Learning disabilities; Neurological impairments; Mental disabilities.
Tuition and Fees
Placements Primarily Funded By State depts of mental health; Private sources; United Way.
Social and Rehabilitative Services
Therapeutic Approach The philosophy of the treatment program is psychodynamically oriented and utilizes insight development, relationship building, and behavioral teaching models.
Therapeutic Services Offered Individual therapy; Group therapy; Family therapy; Art therapy; Independent living skills program; Recreation activities; Aftercare program with follow up.
Professionals on Staff Psychologists; Social workers; Adjunctive therapists; Child care staff; Art therapists.
Educational and Vocational Services
Type(s) of Educational Programs Offered On campus (Spec Ed); Off campus (Public school).
Profile of On Campus School Program Number of teachers 5 and 5 aides; *Number of classrooms* 5; *Student to teacher ratio* 6:1.

WESTBRIDGE
702 N 1st St, Phoenix, AZ 85004 (602) 254-0884, 253-2577 *Contact Person(s):* Helene Boinski McConnell, PhD
Setting and Background Information Westbridge is a private residential facility. The business offices are located at the above address. There are 2 campuses—one is for children (age 6-12) at 367 N 21st Ave and the other is for adolescents (age 12-18) at 1830 E Roosevelt.
Referral Information Anyone can make a referral by contacting the Director of Admissions.
Type of Facility
Funding Sources Private.
Average Length of Stay 6 mos.
Types of Admissions Accepted Day treatment; Residential treatment.
Sources of Referral Local depts of education; Psychiatrists; Private sources; Parents.
Client Profile
Age Range of Clients Served Day programs: 12-18; Residential program: 6-18.
Characteristics Exhibited by Children Emotional handicaps; Learning disabilities.
Tuition and Fees
Room and Board Long term: $290/diem.
Placements Primarily Funded By Local depts of education; Private sources.
Social and Rehabilitative Services
Therapeutic Approach The program's philosophy is based on a team approach, using a psychiatric in-patient model.
Therapeutic Services Offered Individual therapy; Group therapy; Family therapy; Art therapy; Occupational therapy, Recreation therapy.

WESTBRIDGE *(continued)*

Professionals on Staff Psychiatrists; Psychologists; Social workers; Adjunctive therapists; Child care staff; Nurses; Art therapists; Occupational therapist; Recreation therapist.

Educational and Vocational Services

Type(s) of Educational Programs Offered On campus (EH certified); Off campus.

Profile of On Campus School Program Number of teachers 3; *Student to teacher ratio* 8:1; *Credentials of teachers* MEd.

Degrees Offered 12th grade diploma; GED.

YOUTH EVALUATION AND TREATMENT CENTERS

801 N 1st Ave, Phoenix, AZ 85003 (602) 258-7282 *Contact Person(s):* Richard E Geasland MSW, Exec Dir

Setting and Background Information The facility was originally established in 1974 as a short-term residential diagnostic center for juvenile court referrals. Currently, the program has many components, including support services, a crisis shelter, and residential treatment centers for adolescents. There are four sites. Two sites consist of residential homes.

Referral Information Contact the facility for referral information.

Type of Facility

Funding Sources Private; State; Local school districs; BIA; Local tribal social services.

Average Length of Stay Long term—9 mo or more.

Types of Admissions Accepted Day treatment; Residential treatment; Wards of the state.

Sources of Referral Local depts of education; Psychiatrists; Private sources; Depts of correction; Social service depts; Local tribal govts; State dept of health; Local county juvenile courts.

Client Profile

Age Range of Clients Served Day programs: 6-18; Residential program: 6-18.

Characteristics Exhibited by Children Emotional handicaps; Learning disabilities; Neurological impairments; Physical handicaps; Mental disabilities.

IQ Range of Clients 70-75+.

Tuition and Fees

Room and Board Long term: $82/diem (residential); $60.66/diem (mimimum treatment and services); $42.54/diem (day support).

Tuition $790/mo.

Placements Primarily Funded By Depts of corrections; Social service depts; County juvenile court.

Social and Rehabilitative Services

Therapeutic Approach The facility has an eclectic approach to therapy and uses reality therapy, behaviorism, developmental psychology, Gestalt and Adlerian therapy.

Therapeutic Services Offered Individual therapy; Group therapy; Family therapy; Adjunctive therapy; Independent living skills program; Recreation activities; Substance abuse treatment; Aftercare program with follow up.

Professionals on Staff Psychiatrists; Psychologists; Social workers; Adjunctive therapists; Child care staff; Recreation specialist.

Educational and Vocational Services

Type(s) of Educational Programs Offered On campus; Off campus; Summer campus.

Profile of On Campus School Program Number of teachers 2; *Number of classrooms* 1 ½ ; *Student to teacher ratio* 15:2; *Credentials of teachers* Certified Spec Ed; *Grades taught* 4-12; Special curriculum electives offered (PE, Music, Variety of arts and spec progs offered thru ASSET); Remedial courses offered.

Degrees Offered 8th grade diploma; 12th grade diploma.

PRESCOTT

MINGUS MOUNTAIN ESTATE—RESIDENTIAL & EDUCATIONAL CENTER FOR GIRLS

Mingus Star Rte, Prescott, AZ 86301 (602) 772-6394 *Contact Person(s):* Dr Pauline Don Carlos, Dir

Setting and Background Information This facility was privately established in 1985. It is a residential treatment and educational center for girls and is located on 120 acres in the Prescott National Forest.

Referral Information Referrals are made by DES, Juvenile Probation Offices, dept of corrections, various tribal govts, and private agencies.

Type of Facility

Funding Sources Private; State.

Average Length of Stay Long term.

Types of Admissions Accepted Residential treatment; Group home placement; Wards of the state.

Sources of Referral State depts of education; Local depts of education; State depts of mental health; Psychiatrists; Private sources; Depts of correction; Social service depts.

Client Profile

Age Range of Clients Served Day programs: 12-18; Residential program: 12-18.

Characteristics Exhibited by Children Emotional handicaps; Learning disabilities.

IQ Range of Clients 85-130.

Tuition and Fees

Room and Board Long term: $1,980/mo (includes school tuition).

Placements Primarily Funded By Depts of corrections; Social service depts; DES & DOC.

Social and Rehabilitative Services

Therapeutic Approach The facility has a holistic approach to therapy.

Therapeutic Services Offered Individual therapy; Group therapy; Family therapy; Adjunctive therapy; Art therapy; Independent living skills program; Recreation activities; Substance abuse treatment.

Professionals on Staff Psychiatrists; Psychologists; Child care staff; Equestrian skills teacher.

Educational and Vocational Services

Type(s) of Educational Programs Offered On campus; Off campus (College; Public school).

Profile of On Campus School Program Number of teachers 1; *Number of classrooms* 1; *Student to teacher ratio* 6:1; *Credentials of teachers* EH, LD; *Length of school day* 7:30-2:30; *Grades taught* All.

Degrees Offered 8th grade diploma; GED.

SCOTTSDALE

THE DEVEREUX CENTER

6436 E Sweetwater, Scottsdale, AZ 85254 (602) 998-2920 *Contact Person(s):* Vicki Bloom, Admis Dir

Setting and Background Information Devereux Center is a private, non-profit residential and day treatment facility which serves the needs of three populations: severely emotionally handicapped children, autistic children and children with head trauma. The Devereux Foundation, a nationwide organization, was founded in 1912 by Helena T Devereux, a Philadelphia teacher. Since then, the organization has built centers in Pennsylvania, Arizona, California, Connecticut, Georgia, Massachusetts, New Jersey, and Texas to provide services to people with mental and emotional handicaps. The Devereux Center campus in Scottsdale was established in 1967 on 10 acres and consists of a school, clinic, residential units, pool, and recreational facilities. The facility also operates a transitional group home for children.

Referral Information Referrals can be made by psychiatrists, psychologists, social workers, counselors, school districts, physicians, and parents. To make a referral, contact the facility and forward the necessary background information. If, upon review of the materials, the child seems appropriate, then he or she will have an interview with each member of the Admission Team. The Team will then make a placement decision.

Type of Facility

Funding Sources Private.

Average Length of Stay Long term.

Types of Admissions Accepted Day treatment; Residential treatment; Group home placement; Wards of the state.

Sources of Referral Local depts of education; Private sources; Hospitals; Courts.

Client Profile

Age Range of Clients Served Day programs 5-18; Residential program: 5-18.

Characteristics Exhibited by Children Emotional handicaps; Learning disabilities; Speech/Language disorders; Mental disabilities; Autism.

Tuition and Fees

Room and Board Long term: $4,280-$4,825/mo.

Placements Primarily Funded By Local depts of education; Insurance; DES; Champus.

THE DEVEREUX CENTER (continued)

Social and Rehabilitative Services

Therapeutic Approach The treatment program is behaviorally oriented, with emphasis on milieu therapy.

Therapeutic Services Offered Individual therapy; Group therapy; Family therapy; Adjunctive therapy; Independent living skills program; Recreation activities; Aftercare program with follow up; Occupational therapy.

Professionals on Staff Psychiatrists; Psychologists; Social workers; Adjunctive therapists; Nurses.

Educational and Vocational Services

Type(s) of Educational Programs Offered On campus.

Profile of On Campus School Program Number of teachers 11 and 11 aides; *Student to teacher ratio* 5:1, 2:1 (autistic), 3:1 (head trauma); *Grades taught* K-12.

GIRL'S RANCH, INC

PO Box 1451, 8204 Monterey Way, Scottsdale, AZ 85252 (602) 941-0150 *Contact Person(s):* Ann Barker, Exec Dir

Referral Information Contact the facility for referral information.

Type of Facility

Types of Admissions Accepted Residential treatment.

Client Profile

Age Range of Clients Served Residential program: 11-18.

Characteristics Exhibited by Children Behavior disorders; Delinquency.

TUCSON

ARIZONA CHILDREN'S HOME ASSOCIATION

2700 S 8th Ave, Tucson, AZ 85713 (602) 622-7611 *Contact Person(s):* Richard A Rikkers, Exec Dir

Setting and Background Information The facility was originally established as an orphanage in 1922. Currently, it is located on 7 acres and has 7 buildings.

Referral Information Contact the facility for referral information.

Type of Facility

Funding Sources Private.

Average Length of Stay Long term.

Types of Admissions Accepted Day treatment; Residential treatment; Group home placement; Wards of the state.

Sources of Referral State depts of education; Local depts of education; State depts of mental health; Psychiatrists; Private sources; Depts of correction; Social service depts.

Client Profile

Age Range of Clients Served Day programs: 6-12; Residential program: 6-15.

Characteristics Exhibited by Children Emotional handicaps.

IQ Range of Clients 70+.

Tuition and Fees

Placements Primarily Funded By State depts of education; Local depts of education; State depts of mental health; Insurance; Private sources; Depts of corrections; Social service depts.

Social and Rehabilitative Services

Therapeutic Services Offered Individual therapy; Group therapy; Family therapy; Independent living skills program; Recreation activities.

Professionals on Staff Psychiatrists; Social workers; Child care staff; Nurses.

Educational and Vocational Services

Type(s) of Educational Programs Offered On campus.

Profile of On Campus School Program Number of teachers 6; *Number of classrooms* 5; *Student to teacher ratio* 7:1; *Credentials of teachers* EH certified; *Grades taught* K-8; Special curriculum electives offered (EH curriculum); Remedial courses offered (Individualized).

CATHOLIC COMMUNITY SERVICES OF SOUTHERN ARIZONA

PO Box 5746, 155 W Helen, Tucson, AZ 85703-0746 (602) 623-0344 *Contact Person(s):* John E Cotter, Chief Exec Off

Setting and Background Information The facility has residential services for adolescent girls and has adoption services.

Referral Information Contact the facility for referral information.

Type of Facility

Types of Admissions Accepted Residential treatment.

Client Profile

Age Range of Clients Served Residential program: Birth-18.

CHARLEE FAMILY CARE, INC

2739 E Speedway, Tucson, AZ 85717 (602) 881-6707 *Contact Person(s):* Shaun McBride, Exec Dir

Setting and Background Information The Menninger Foundation initiated the funding and program design. The facility was established in 1980 and has seven 6-bed group homes.

Referral Information For referrals, contact the facility and forward the application packet. A clinical interview of the potential placement candidate is required.

Type of Facility

Funding Sources State.

Average Length of Stay The shelter program is short term; the group homes have a long term program.

Types of Admissions Accepted Group home placement; Wards of the state; Emergency shelter.

Sources of Referral State depts of mental health; Private sources; Social service depts.

Client Profile

Age Range of Clients Served Residential program: 6-18.

Characteristics Exhibited by Children Emotional handicaps; Learning disabilities; Neurological impairments; Physical handicaps; Mental disabilities; Chronic mental illness; Developmental disabilities.

IQ Range of Clients 55-135.

Tuition and Fees

Room and Board Short term: $1850/mo; Long term: $1809/mo.

Placements Primarily Funded By Social service depts.

Social and Rehabilitative Services

Therapeutic Approach The facility uses milieu therapy in a family-like environment.

Therapeutic Services Offered Individual therapy; Family therapy; Independent living skills program.

Professionals on Staff Psychiatrists; Adjunctive therapists; Child care staff.

Educational and Vocational Services

Type(s) of Educational Programs Offered Off campus.

DESERT HILLS

5245 N Camino De Oeste, Tucson, AZ 85745 (602) 743-7400 *Contact Person(s):* Guy Heidinger, Exec Dir

Setting and Background Information The facility was privately established and is located on 20 acres in desert mountains. There is another campus at 2901 N Silverbell in Tucson.

Referral Information Referrals can be made by mental health professionals, court systems, hospitals, and school districts. All referrals are directed to the intake officer who will schedule a pre-placement interview following the receipt of the necessary background information.

Type of Facility

Funding Sources Private.

Average Length of Stay Short and long term.

Types of Admissions Accepted Day treatment; Residential treatment.

Sources of Referral Local depts of education; Psychiatrists; Court systems.

Client Profile

Age Range of Clients Served Day programs: 11-18; Residential program: 11-18.

Characteristics Exhibited by Children Emotional handicaps.

Tuition and Fees

Placements Primarily Funded By Insurance; Private sources.

Social and Rehabilitative Services

Therapeutic Approach The basic therapeutic approach used is eclectic and reality oriented within an open setting.

Therapeutic Services Offered Individual therapy; Group therapy; Family therapy; Adjunctive therapy; Art therapy; Aftercare program with follow up; Occupational therapy.

Professionals on Staff Psychiatrists; Psychologists; Social workers; Nurses; Art therapists; Occupational therapist.

Educational and Vocational Services

Type(s) of Educational Programs Offered On campus (Spec Ed); Off campus.

Profile of On Campus School Program Grades taught Individualized.

Degrees Offered GED.

VISIONQUEST NATIONAL LTD
PO Box 12906, 600 N Swan Rd, Tucson, AZ 85732 (602) 881-3950
Contact Person(s): Steven Rogers, Exec Dir
Referral Information Contact the facility for referral information.
Type of Facility
Types of Admissions Accepted Day treatment; Residential treatment.
Client Profile
Age Range of Clients Served Day programs: 10-18; Residential program: 10-18.
Characteristics Exhibited by Children Delinquency.

ARKANSAS

LITTLE ROCK

ELIZABETH MITCHELL CHILDREN'S CENTER

6601 W 12th St, Little Rock, AR 72204 (501) 666-8686 *Contact Person(s):* Richard T Hill MSW, Exec Dir

Setting and Background Information The facility was established in 1970. There is a branch facility located at 1006 Burman, Jacksonville, Arkansas 72076.

Referral Information Contact the facility for referral information.

Type of Facility

Funding Sources Private.

Average Length of Stay Short and long term.

Types of Admissions Accepted Day treatment; Residential treatment.

Sources of Referral Psychiatrists; Private sources; Social service depts.

Client Profile

Age Range of Clients Served Residential program: 6-13.

Characteristics Exhibited by Children Emotional handicaps; Learning disabilities.

IQ Range of Clients 80+.

Tuition and Fees

Room and Board Short term: $660/week; Long term: $660/week.

Placements Primarily Funded By Insurance; Private sources; Social service depts.

Social and Rehabilitative Services

Therapeutic Approach A milieu approach is used, involving behavior modification, reality therapy, transactional analysis and attitudinal therapy.

Therapeutic Services Offered Individual therapy; Group therapy; Family therapy; Chemotherapy.

Educational and Vocational Services

Type(s) of Educational Programs Offered On campus.

Profile of On Campus School Program Grades taught individualized.

YOUTH HOME

924 Marshall St, Little Rock, AR 72202 (501) 376-9231 *Contact Person(s):* Bob Tones, Exec Dir

Setting and Background Information The facility was established in 1968.

Referral Information Contact the facility for referral information.

Type of Facility

Funding Sources Private.

Average Length of Stay 8-15 mos.

Types of Admissions Accepted Residential treatment.

Sources of Referral Private sources; Social service depts.

Client Profile

Age Range of Clients Served Residential program: 12-18.

Characteristics Exhibited by Children Emotional handicaps.

Tuition and Fees

Room and Board Long term: $36,000/year.

Placements Primarily Funded By Insurance; Private sources; Social service depts.

Social and Rehabilitative Services

Therapeutic Services Offered Individual therapy; Group therapy; Family therapy; Chemotherapy.

Educational and Vocational Services

Type(s) of Educational Programs Offered On campus.

Profile of On Campus School Program Number of teachers 8; *Grades taught* 6-12.

Vocational Education Programs/Degrees Offered Vocational education program; Manual arts; Shop.

CALIFORNIA

ALTADENA

FIVE ACRES
760 W Mountain View St, Altadena, CA 91001 (818) 798-6793
Contact Person(s): Robert A Ketch, Exec Dir
Setting and Background Information The facility was established in 1888 as an orphanage. Currently, it is located on 5 acres and has 6 buildings.
Referral Information Contact the facility for referral information.
Type of Facility
Funding Sources Private; State; Federal; United Way.
Average Length of Stay Long term.
Types of Admissions Accepted Day treatment; Residential treatment; Group home placement; Wards of the state; Emergency shelter.
Sources of Referral State depts of education; Local depts of education; State depts of mental health; Psychiatrists; Private sources; Depts of correction; Social service depts.
Client Profile
Age Range of Clients Served Day programs: Birth-18; Residential program: Birth-18.
Characteristics Exhibited by Children Emotional handicaps; Learning disabilities.
Tuition and Fees
Room and Board Long term: $3,500/mo.
Placements Primarily Funded By Local depts of education; Social service depts.
Social and Rehabilitative Services
Therapeutic Approach The facility has a psychodynamic approach to therapy and uses behavior modification.
Therapeutic Services Offered Individual therapy; Group therapy; Family therapy; Art therapy; Physical therapy; Recreation activities; Aftercare program with follow up.
Professionals on Staff Psychiatrists; Psychologists; Social workers; Child care staff; Nurses; Art therapists.
Educational and Vocational Services
Profile of On Campus School Program Number of teachers 3; *Number of classrooms* 3; *Credentials of teachers* SED; *Grades taught* K-12.

THE SYCAMORES
2933 El Nido Dr, Altadena, CA 91001 (818) 798-0853 *Contact Person(s):* Michael Schaller, Intake/Training Coord
Setting and Background Information The facility was established in 1902 as an orphanage. The 5-acre campus has residential units, classrooms, group homes, administration and activity buildings.
Referral Information Referrals are made to the facility by the Dept of Child Services and the Dept of Mental Health. A pre-placement interview with the client and the family/liason will be scheduled.
Type of Facility
Funding Sources Private; State; Federal.
Average Length of Stay Long term.
Types of Admissions Accepted Day treatment; Residential treatment; Group home placement; Wards of the state.
Sources of Referral Local depts of education; State depts of mental health; Private sources; Depts of correction; Social service depts.

Client Profile
Age Range of Clients Served Day programs: 6-15; Residential program: 6-18.
Characteristics Exhibited by Children Emotional handicaps; Learning disabilities; Speech/Language disorders; Neurological impairments; Mental disabilities.
IQ Range of Clients 70+.
Tuition and Fees
Room and Board Long term: $2,711/mo.
Tuition $60/diem.
Placements Primarily Funded By State depts of education; State depts of mental health; Depts of corrections.
Social and Rehabilitative Services
Therapeutic Approach The facility has a cognitive behavioral approach to therapy.
Therapeutic Services Offered Individual therapy; Group therapy; Family therapy; Adjunctive therapy; Independent living skills program; Recreation activities.
Professionals on Staff Psychiatrists; Psychologists; Social workers; Child care staff; Nurses.
Educational and Vocational Services
Type(s) of Educational Programs Offered On campus; Off campus.
Profile of On Campus School Program Number of teachers 5; *Number of classrooms* 3; *Student to teacher ratio* 4:1; *Credentials of teachers* Spec Ed; Remedial courses offered.
Degrees Offered 8th grade diploma.

ANGWIN

GRANDVIEW CHILDREN'S RANCH, INC
955 Friesen Dr, Angwin, CA 94508 (707) 965-3495 *Contact Person(s):* Gloria M Burima-Siperko, PhD
Setting and Background Information The facility was established in 1982. There are 4 sites which provide residential group home care.
Referral Information Contact the facility and forward the necessary background information. A pre-placement visit is required if child is over 8 years old.
Type of Facility
Funding Sources Private; State; Federal.
Average Length of Stay Long term.
Types of Admissions Accepted Residential treatment; Group home placement; Wards of the state.
Sources of Referral State depts of education; Local depts of education; State depts of mental health; Psychiatrists; Private sources; Social service depts.
Client Profile
Age Range of Clients Served Residential program: Birth-18.
Characteristics Exhibited by Children Emotional handicaps; Learning disabilities; Speech/Language disorders; Mental disabilities.
IQ Range of Clients 80-120.
Tuition and Fees
Room and Board Long term: $2,431-$2,666/mo.
Placements Primarily Funded By Social service depts.
Social and Rehabilitative Services
Therapeutic Approach The facility uses behavior modification and milieu therapy.
Therapeutic Services Offered Individual therapy; Group therapy; Family therapy; Recreation activities.
Professionals on Staff Psychiatrists; Psychologists; Social workers; Child care staff; Speech therapists.

GRANDVIEW CHILDREN'S RANCH, INC *(continued)*

Educational and Vocational Services
Type(s) of Educational Programs Offered On campus
(Individualized); Off campus (Public school); Summer campus.
Profile of On Campus School Program Number of teachers 1; *Number of classrooms* 1; *Credentials of teachers* Spec Ed; *Grades taught* Individualized; Remedial courses offered.
Degrees Offered Diploma conferred through public school.

ATWATER

THE TREASURE COVE
1160 Oak St, Atwater, CA 95301 (209) 358-9420 *Contact Person(s):*
Peggy Rodenberg, Admin
Setting and Background Information The facility is a large house
which was converted from a foster care home to a group home
for children.
Referral Information Contact the facility for referral information and
forward the necessary information, including a social history, a
psychological evaluation and medical information.
Type of Facility
Funding Sources State.
Average Length of Stay Long term.
Types of Admissions Accepted Residential treatment; Group home
placement; Wards of the state.
Sources of Referral State depts of education; Local depts of education; State depts of mental health; Psychiatrists; Private sources;
Depts of correction; Social service depts.
Client Profile
Age Range of Clients Served Residential program: Birth-12.
Characteristics Exhibited by Children Emotional handicaps; Learning
disabilities; Speech/Language disorders; Neurological impairments; Mental disabilities.
Tuition and Fees
Room and Board Long term: $1,696/mo.
Placements Primarily Funded By Social service depts.
Social and Rehabilitative Services
Therapeutic Approach The basic therapeutic approach used is behavior modification.
Therapeutic Services Offered Individual therapy; Group therapy;
Family therapy; Art therapy; Independent living skills program;
Recreation activities.
Professionals on Staff Psychiatrists; Psychologists; Social workers;
Child care staff.
Educational and Vocational Services
Type(s) of Educational Programs Offered Off campus.

AUBURN

EQUINOX ADOLESCENT TREATMENT CENTER
6540 Grass Valley Hwy, Auburn, CA 95603 (916) 269-1272 *Contact Person(s):* James Dieckman, Exec Dir
Setting and Background Information The center was established in
1981 as a private, non-profit corporation. The 6-acre campus has
a house, office, recreation room, workshop, and a barn.
Referral Information Contact the facility and submit the required
referral information, including a psychological evaluation and
court reports. An interview and pre-placement visit will be
scheduled.
Type of Facility
Funding Sources State; County.
Average Length of Stay Long term.
Types of Admissions Accepted Residential treatment; Wards of the
state.
Sources of Referral Depts of correction; Social service depts.
Client Profile
Age Range of Clients Served Residential program: 12-18.
Characteristics Exhibited by Children Emotional handicaps; Learning
disabilities; Mental disabilities.
IQ Range of Clients 70+.
Tuition and Fees
Room and Board Long term: $3,205/mo.
Placements Primarily Funded By Depts of corrections; Social service
depts.

Social and Rehabilitative Services
Therapeutic Approach The facility uses systems theory in a therapeutic milieu.
Therapeutic Services Offered Individual therapy; Group therapy;
Family therapy.
Professionals on Staff Social workers; Child care staff.
Educational and Vocational Services
Type(s) of Educational Programs Offered Off campus.

GATEWAY RANCH
8010 Mt Vernon Rd, Auburn, CA 95603 (916) 885-4706 *Contact Person(s):* Wes Bjorlin, Dir Soc Work
Setting and Background Information The facility was established in
1975. It is a group home for emotionally disturbed and
educationally handicapped youth.
Referral Information Contact the facility for referral information.
Type of Facility
Funding Sources State; Federal.
Average Length of Stay Long term.
Types of Admissions Accepted Residential treatment; Group home
placement; Wards of the state.
Client Profile
Age Range of Clients Served Residential program: 6-18.
Characteristics Exhibited by Children Emotional handicaps; Learning
disabilities; Neurological impairments; Mental disabilities.
IQ Range of Clients 75-110.
Tuition and Fees
Room and Board Long term: $885/mo.
Placements Primarily Funded By Social service depts.
Social and Rehabilitative Services
Therapeutic Services Offered Individual therapy; Group therapy; Independent living skills program; Recreation activities.
Professionals on Staff Psychologists; Social workers; Child care staff.
Educational and Vocational Services
Type(s) of Educational Programs Offered Off campus.

BEN LOMOND

NEW CHANCE, INC
PO Box 256, 8500 Hihn Rd, Ben Lomond, CA 95005
(408) 336-3279 *Contact Person(s):* Greg Logan, Prog Dir
Setting and Background Information The facility was established in
1983 as a group home in a residential neighborhood. Currently,
there are four group homes on residential sites.
Referral Information For referral, contact the facility and forward
the required information, including a court report, a psychiatric
evaluation, school records and medical information.
Type of Facility
Funding Sources State.
Average Length of Stay Long term.
Types of Admissions Accepted Group home placement; Wards of the
state.
Sources of Referral Private sources; Depts of correction; Social service depts.
Client Profile
Age Range of Clients Served Residential program: 6-18.
Characteristics Exhibited by Children Emotional handicaps; Learning
disabilities.
IQ Range of Clients 60-130.
Tuition and Fees
Room and Board Long term: $1,619/mo.
Placements Primarily Funded By Depts of corrections; Social service
depts.
Social and Rehabilitative Services
Therapeutic Approach The facility uses behavior modification.
Therapeutic Services Offered Individual therapy; Group therapy;
Family therapy; Independent living program; Recreation
activities.
Professionals on Staff Psychologists; Social workers; Child care staff.
Educational and Vocational Services
Type(s) of Educational Programs Offered Off campus.
Vocational Education Programs/Degrees Offered ROP at local community college.

BERKELEY

BERKELEY ACADEMY

3404 King St; 2605 Ashby, Berkeley, CA 94703 (415) 848-4157
Contact Person(s): Dr Ronnie Blakeney, Clin Dir
Setting and Background Information The facility was established in 1979. It is a residential treatment facility for seriously disturbed adolescent girls. There are two self-contained residential schools and an administration building.
Referral Information Contact the facility and forward necessary information. An interview will be scheduled.
Type of Facility
Funding Sources Private; State; Federal.
Average Length of Stay 18 mos.
Types of Admissions Accepted Day treatment; Residential treatment; Wards of the state.
Sources of Referral Local depts of education; State depts of mental health; Psychiatrists; Private sources; Depts of correction; Social service depts.
Client Profile
Age Range of Clients Served Day programs: 11-18; Residential program: 11-18.
Characteristics Exhibited by Children Emotional handicaps; Learning disabilities; Neurological impairments; Mental disabilities; Psychosis; Moral insanity.
IQ Range of Clients 78-156.
Tuition and Fees
Room and Board Long term: $2,500/mo.
Tuition $2,000/mo.
Placements Primarily Funded By Local depts of education; Social service depts.
Social and Rehabilitative Services
Therapeutic Approach The program operates a Piaget-Kohlberg structural development program, including a moral development program.
Therapeutic Services Offered Individual therapy; Group therapy; Family therapy; Art therapy; Independent living skills program; Recreation activities; Aftercare program with follow up; Moral development program; Play group; Drama therapy; Music therapy.
Professionals on Staff Psychologists; Social workers; Child care staff; Nurses; Art therapists.
Educational and Vocational Services
Type(s) of Educational Programs Offered On campus.
Profile of On Campus School Program Number of teachers 7; *Number of classrooms* 4; *Student to teacher ratio* 5:1; *Credentials of teachers* SED; *Grades taught* 6-12; Remedial courses offered (Individualized).
Vocational Education Programs/Degrees Offered Vocational internship program.
Degrees Offered 8th grade diploma; 12th grade diploma; GED.

BOONVILLE

GOOD NEWS SCHOOL, INC

17912 Fitch Lane, Boonville, CA 95415 (707) 895-3512 *Contact Person(s):* Gene Waggoner, Dir
Setting and Background Information The facility was established in 1982 as a non-profit corporation. Located on 7 acres, it is a residential group home.
Referral Information Contact the facility for referral information. A pre-placement visit will be arranged.
Type of Facility
Funding Sources State; Federal.
Average Length of Stay Long term.
Types of Admissions Accepted Residential treatment; Group home placement; Wards of the state.
Sources of Referral Private sources; Depts of correction; Social service depts.
Client Profile
Age Range of Clients Served Residential program: 6-18.
Characteristics Exhibited by Children Emotional handicaps; Learning disabilities.
IQ Range of Clients 68-120.
Tuition and Fees
Room and Board Long term: $1,602/mo.
Placements Primarily Funded By Private sources; Depts of corrections; Social service depts.

Social and Rehabilitative Services
Therapeutic Services Offered Individual therapy; Group therapy; Family therapy; Independent living skills program; Recreation activities.
Professionals on Staff Psychologists; Social workers; Child care staff.
Educational and Vocational Services
Type(s) of Educational Programs Offered Off campus (Public and private schools).
Vocational Education Programs/Degrees Offered Summer youth job training program.

BUELLTON

DAY GROUP HOME, INC

6830 Santa Rosa Rd, Buellton, CA 93427 (805) 688-7851 *Contact Person(s):* Marianna Day, Admin
Setting and Background Information The facility was established in 1981. The residential program is located on 20 acres.
Referral Information Contact the facility for referral information.
Type of Facility
Funding Sources State; Federal; County.
Average Length of Stay Long term.
Types of Admissions Accepted Residential treatment; Group home placement; Wards of the state.
Sources of Referral State depts of mental health; Psychiatrists; Private sources; Depts of correction; Social service depts; Probation dept.
Client Profile
Age Range of Clients Served Residential program: Birth-18.
Characteristics Exhibited by Children Emotional handicaps; Learning disabilities; Mental disabilities; Delinquency.
IQ Range of Clients 70+.
Tuition and Fees
Room and Board Long term: $840/mo.
Placements Primarily Funded By Depts of corrections; Social service depts.
Social and Rehabilitative Services
Therapeutic Services Offered Individual therapy.
Professionals on Staff Psychiatrists; Psychologists; Social workers; Child care staff.
Educational and Vocational Services
Type(s) of Educational Programs Offered Off campus (Regular and Spec Ed programs).

CALABASAS

THE CALABASAS ACADEMY

25000 Mureau Rd, Calabasas, CA 91302 (818) 703-8383 *Contact Person(s):* Dr Richard Kritzer
Setting and Background Information The program was established by Dr Kritzer in 1977. It is certified by the California State Dept of Education to serve children with special needs. The campus is located in a quiet rural area in the hills of Calabasas.
Referral Information Anyone can make a referral by contacting Dr Kritzer and forwarding the necessary background information. A pre-placement interview with the child and family will be held before an admission decision is made.
Type of Facility
Funding Sources Private; State.
Average Length of Stay Long term.
Types of Admissions Accepted Day treatment; Residential treatment; Group home placement.
Sources of Referral Private sources; Social service depts; Probation; Dept of Children Svcs.
Client Profile
Age Range of Clients Served Day programs: 12-18; Residential program: 12-18.
Characteristics Exhibited by Children Emotional handicaps; Learning disabilities; Speech/Language disorders; Mental disabilities.
Tuition and Fees
Room and Board Long term: $2,500/mo.
Placements Primarily Funded By Local depts of education; Private sources; Social service depts; Probation; Dept of Children Services.

THE CALABASAS ACADEMY (continued)

Social and Rehabilitative Services
Therapeutic Approach The treatment program is based on a behavior modification point system.
Therapeutic Services Offered Individual therapy; Group therapy; Family therapy; Independent living skills program; Recreation activities; Substance abuse treatment; Speech/language therapy.
Professionals on Staff Psychiatrists; Psychologists; Social workers; Child care staff.
Educational and Vocational Services
Type(s) of Educational Programs Offered On campus.
Profile of On Campus School Program Number of teachers 2; *Number of classrooms* 2; *Student to teacher ratio* 3:1.
Degrees Offered 12th grade diploma.

CALISTOGA

MCCORMICK FOUNDATION

9000 Franz Valley Rd, Calistoga, CA 94515 (707) 942-9289 *Contact Person(s):* Deborah Lazar PhD, Clinical Dir
Setting and Background Information This private non-profit facility was originally established in 1980 as an adult residential program. An adolescent division was later added.
Referral Information Referrals are made by social workers, psychiatrists, and others. The referral packet should include hospital reports, psychiatric evaluations, and a recent physical exam.
Type of Facility
Funding Sources Private; State.
Average Length of Stay Long term.
Types of Admissions Accepted Residential treatment; Group home placement; Wards of the state.
Sources of Referral State depts of education; Local depts of education; State depts of mental health; Psychiatrists; Private sources; Depts of correction; Social service depts.
Client Profile
Age Range of Clients Served Residential program: 12-21+.
Characteristics Exhibited by Children Emotional handicaps.
IQ Range of Clients 80-130.
Tuition and Fees
Placements Primarily Funded By Private sources; Depts of corrections; Social service depts.
Social and Rehabilitative Services
Therapeutic Approach The facility has a psychoanalytic/psychodynamic approach to therapy.
Therapeutic Services Offered Individual therapy; Group therapy; Family therapy; Art therapy; Independent living skills program; Recreation activities.
Professionals on Staff Psychiatrists; Psychologists; Social workers; Adjunctive therapists; Child care staff; Art therapists.
Educational and Vocational Services
Type(s) of Educational Programs Offered On campus.
Profile of On Campus School Program Number of teachers 1; *Number of classrooms* 1; *Student to teacher ratio* 6:1; *Credentials of teachers* certified; *Grades taught* 6-12.
Degrees Offered 12th grade diploma.

CAMPBELL

EASTFIELD MING QUONG

251 Leewellen Ave, Campbell, CA 95008 (408) 379-3790 *Contact Person(s):* Jerry Doyle, Pres and Chief Exec Off; William Seelig, Clinical Dir
Setting and Background Information Eastfield Ming Quong provides residential treatment, day treatment, outpatient services and has a home-based program. There are 2 campuses; one is in Los Gatos, California, and is located on 73 acres in the foothills of the Santa Cruz Mountains and consists of an administrative building, 7 residential cottages which accomodate 6-8 residents each, a villa (on-grounds apartment to be used by child and family for special events), school building, playground, swimming pool, camping grounds, exercise facility, basketball court, and craft shops. The other campus is at the above address and has residential buildings, a school, and an institute of family training.
Referral Information Referrals can be made by public and private agencies with funding support.

Type of Facility
Funding Sources Private.
Average Length of Stay Avg 18 mos, (90 days-diagnostic assessment).
Types of Admissions Accepted Day treatment; Residential treatment.
Sources of Referral Local depts of education; Psychiatrists; Private sources; Social service depts.
Client Profile
Age Range of Clients Served Day programs: 4-18; Residential program: 4-18.
Characteristics Exhibited by Children Emotional handicaps; Learning disabilities; Speech/Language disorders; Neurological impairments.
Tuition and Fees
Placements Primarily Funded By State depts of mental health; Private sources; Social service depts; Probation.
Social and Rehabilitative Services
Therapeutic Approach The treatment program is family systems oriented, with a variety of therapy approaches used to meet the individual needs of each child.
Therapeutic Services Offered Individual therapy; Group therapy; Family therapy; Adjunctive therapy; Independent living skills program.
Professionals on Staff Psychiatrists; Psychologists; Social workers; Adjunctive therapists; Child care staff; Nurses.
Educational and Vocational Services
Type(s) of Educational Programs Offered On campus; Off campus; Summer campus.
Profile of On Campus School Program Number of teachers 14; *Student to teacher ratio* 4:1; *Grades taught* K-12.
Degrees Offered 8th grade diploma; 12th grade diploma.

CARLSBAD

YMCA OZ NORTH COAST

1212 Oak Ave, Carlsbad, CA 92008 (619) 729-4926 *Contact Person(s):* Geoffrey L Cornish, Prog Dir
Setting and Background Information The agency was established in 1976 with federal funding. It is a coed residential treatment facility.
Referral Information Contact the facility for referral procedures.
Type of Facility
Funding Sources Private; State; Federal; County; City.
Average Length of Stay Short and long term.
Types of Admissions Accepted Residential treatment; Wards of the state.
Sources of Referral Local depts of education; Psychiatrists; Social service depts; Law enforcement.
Client Profile
Age Range of Clients Served Residential program: 12-18.
Characteristics Exhibited by Children Emotional handicaps; Conduct disorders.
Social and Rehabilitative Services
Professionals on Staff Social workers; Adjunctive therapists; Child care staff.

CHINO

BOYS REPUBLIC

State Hwy 71 & Peyton Dr, Chino, CA 91709 (714) 628-1217
Contact Person(s): Bruce Oliver, Intake Dir
Setting and Background Information The facility was privately established in 1907. It is located on 220 acres and has cottages, a school, a recreation facility, a farm, and other buildings.
Referral Information For referrals, contact the facility and forward the applicant's psychosocial history to the intake worker.
Type of Facility
Funding Sources Private; State; Federal; County.
Average Length of Stay Long term.
Types of Admissions Accepted Day treatment; Residential treatment; Group home placement; Wards of the state.
Sources of Referral State depts of education; Local depts of education; State depts of mental health; Psychiatrists; Private sources; Depts of correction; Social service depts.

BOYS REPUBLIC *(continued)*

Client Profile

Age Range of Clients Served Day programs: 15-18; Residential program: 12-18.

Characteristics Exhibited by Children Emotional handicaps; Learning disabilities; Neurological impairments; Mental disabilities; Behavior disorders; Character disorders.

Tuition and Fees

Room and Board Long term: $1,538/mo (includes school tuition).

Placements Primarily Funded By Depts of corrections; Social service depts.

Social and Rehabilitative Services

Therapeutic Services Offered Individual therapy; Group therapy; Family therapy; Independent living skills program; Recreation activities; Substance abuse treatment; Aftercare program with follow up.

Professionals on Staff Psychiatrists; Psychologists; Social workers; Child care staff; Nurses; Family therapists.

Educational and Vocational Services

Type(s) of Educational Programs Offered On campus; Off campus (High school; Vocational programs).

Profile of On Campus School Program Number of teachers 10; *Number of classrooms* 10; *Student to teacher ratio* 10:1; *Credentials of teachers* State licensed; *Grades taught* 8-12; Special curriculum electives offered; Remedial courses offered (LD, Reading, Speech).

Vocational Education Programs/Degrees Offered Printing; Carpentry; Welding; Small engine; Automotive; Farming.

Degrees Offered 12th grade diploma; GED.

HILLVIEW ACRES

3683 Chino Ave, Chino, CA 91710 (714) 628-1272 *Contact Person(s):* Corky Kindsvater, Exec Dir

Setting and Background Information The facility was established in 1929. The 20-acre campus has 5 residences, an office, a dining facility and support buildings.

Referral Information Contact the Director of Professional Services for referral information.

Type of Facility

Funding Sources Private; State.

Average Length of Stay Long term.

Types of Admissions Accepted Residential treatment; Wards of the state.

Sources of Referral State depts of mental health; Social service depts.

Client Profile

Age Range of Clients Served Residential program: 6-18.

Characteristics Exhibited by Children Emotional handicaps.

Tuition and Fees

Room and Board Long term: $2,166/mo.

Placements Primarily Funded By Social service depts.

Social and Rehabilitative Services

Therapeutic Services Offered Individual therapy; Group therapy; Family therapy; Adjunctive therapy; Recreation activities.

Professionals on Staff Psychiatrists; Psychologists; Social workers; Adjunctive therapists; Child care staff; Nurses.

Educational and Vocational Services

Type(s) of Educational Programs Offered On campus; Off campus.

CHULA VISTA

SOUTHWOOD PSYCHIATRIC RESIDENTIAL TREATMENT CENTER, SOUTH BAY

3 N 2nd Ave, Chula Vista, CA 92010 (619) 426-1120 *Contact Person(s):* Howard D Margolis, Asst Admin

Setting and Background Information The facility was established in 1984. It is a part of a continuum of care. There is a full service psychiatric residential treatment center, a school and recreation facilities.

Referral Information Contact the intake coordinator and forward a referral packet.

Type of Facility

Funding Sources Private.

Average Length of Stay Long term.

Types of Admissions Accepted Residential treatment.

Sources of Referral State depts of education; Local depts of education; State depts of mental health; Psychiatrists; Private sources; Depts of correction; Social service depts.

Client Profile

Age Range of Clients Served Residential program: 6-18.

Characteristics Exhibited by Children Emotional handicaps; Learning disabilities.

IQ Range of Clients 70+.

Tuition and Fees

Room and Board Long term: $230/diem.

Placements Primarily Funded By Insurance; Private sources; Champus.

Social and Rehabilitative Services

Therapeutic Approach The center's approach to therapy is psychodynamic. It offers insight oriented milieu therapy.

Therapeutic Services Offered Individual therapy; Group therapy; Family therapy; Adjunctive therapy; Art therapy; Independent living skills program; Recreation activities; Substance abuse treatment; Aftercare program with follow up.

Professionals on Staff Psychiatrists; Psychologists; Social workers; Adjunctive therapists; Child care staff; Nurses; Art therapists.

Educational and Vocational Services

Type(s) of Educational Programs Offered On campus (Spec Ed).

Profile of On Campus School Program Number of teachers 4; *Number of classrooms* 4; *Student to teacher ratio* 12-15:1; *Grades taught* 1-12; Special curriculum electives offered; Remedial courses offered.

Degrees Offered 12th grade diploma; GED.

COMPTON

JOHN/MAR GROUP HOME FOR CHILDREN, INC

1506 S Wilmington, Compton, CA 90220 (213) 637-0180 *Contact Person(s):* Joyce R Krasselt, Admin

Setting and Background Information This facility was established in 1985. It is a group home with a capacity for 4 boys.

Referral Information Contact the facility for referral information.

Type of Facility

Funding Sources State.

Average Length of Stay Short and long term.

Types of Admissions Accepted Group home placement.

Sources of Referral Depts of correction; Social service depts.

Client Profile

Age Range of Clients Served Day programs: 12-18+; Residential program: 12-18+.

Characteristics Exhibited by Children Emotional handicaps; Learning disabilities.

IQ Range of Clients 85-120.

Tuition and Fees

Room and Board Short term: $1351/mo; Long term: $1351/mo. (The cost is determined and paid for by the state).

Placements Primarily Funded By Depts of corrections; Social service depts.

Social and Rehabilitative Services

Therapeutic Services Offered Individual therapy; Group therapy; Family therapy; Independent living skills program; Recreation activities; Substance abuse treatment.

Professionals on Staff Psychologists; Social workers; Child care staff; Nurses.

Educational and Vocational Services

Type(s) of Educational Programs Offered Off campus (Public school).

Vocational Education Programs/Degrees Offered Vocational counseling.

COSTA MESA

SOUTH COAST CHILDREN'S SOCIETY

1065 Santa Cruz Cir, Costa Mesa, CA 92626 (714) 979-1721

Contact Person(s): Bob Ford, Admin

Setting and Background Information The facility was privately established in 1984 and is a 6-bed residential program.

Referral Information Contact the facility for referral information.

Type of Facility

Funding Sources Private; State; County.

Average Length of Stay Long term.

Types of Admissions Accepted Residential treatment; Group home placement.

Sources of Referral State depts of education; Local depts of education; State depts of mental health; Psychiatrists; Private sources; Depts of correction; Social service depts.

SOUTH COAST CHILDREN'S SOCIETY *(continued)*

Client Profile

Age Range of Clients Served Residential program: 6-18.

Characteristics Exhibited by Children Emotional handicaps; Learning disabilities; Hearing impairments/deafness; Vision impairments/blindness; Speech/Language disorders; Neurological impairments; Physical handicaps; Mental disabilities.

IQ Range of Clients 40-70.

Social and Rehabilitative Services

Professionals on Staff Psychologists; Social workers; Child care staff.

Educational and Vocational Services

Type(s) of Educational Programs Offered On campus; Off campus.

EL CAJON

BOYS AND GIRLS AID SOCIETY OF SAN DIEGO— COTTONWOOD CENTER

2815 Steele Canyon Rd, El Cajon, CA 92020 (619) 442-3363

Contact Person(s): Darrell Paulk, Exec Dir

Setting and Background Information The society was originally established as an orphanage in 1903. Currently, there are three facilities. The Cottonwood center has a 27-acre campus with eight buildings. Hawthorn East and Hawthorn West each have one building.

Referral Information Referrals are screened by the intake dept. An MSW, an MD, and a psychiatric RN will review all referrals.

Type of Facility

Funding Sources Private; State; Champus.

Average Length of Stay Long term.

Types of Admissions Accepted Residential treatment; Group home placement; Wards of the state.

Sources of Referral State depts of education; Local depts of education; State depts of mental health; Psychiatrists; Private sources; Social service depts.

Client Profile

Age Range of Clients Served Residential program: 6-18.

Characteristics Exhibited by Children Emotional handicaps; Learning disabilities; Mental disabilities; Substance abuse.

IQ Range of Clients 70-140.

Tuition and Fees

Room and Board Long term: $175/diem (Cottonwood Center); $113/diem (Hawthorn East and West).

Placements Primarily Funded By Insurance; Social service depts; Champus.

Social and Rehabilitative Services

Therapeutic Approach The facility has an eclectic approach to therapy.

Therapeutic Services Offered Individual therapy; Group therapy; Family therapy; Independent living skills program; Recreation activities; Substance abuse treatment; Aftercare program with follow up.

Professionals on Staff Psychiatrists; Psychologists; Social workers; Child care staff; Nurses.

Educational and Vocational Services

Type(s) of Educational Programs Offered On campus (Spec Ed); Off campus (Spec Ed); Summer campus (Spec Ed).

Profile of On Campus School Program Number of teachers 4 and 4 aides; *Number of classrooms* 3; *Student to teacher ratio* 5:1; *Grades taught* 1-12.

Degrees Offered 8th grade diploma; 12th grade diploma.

CALIFORNIA CREST DIAGNOSTIC AND TREATMENT CENTER

15593 Olde Hwy, El Cajon, CA 92021 (619) 561-6909 *Contact Person(s):* Walter Ferris LCSW, Prog Dir

Setting and Background Information The facility was established in 1986. It is an intensive residential program for up to 24 severely emotionally disturbed male and female adolescents. There are 3 group homes and a school.

Referral Information Contact the admissions officer and forward psychological reports, educational records, court reports and hospitalization records.

Type of Facility

Funding Sources State.

Average Length of Stay Long term.

Types of Admissions Accepted Residential treatment; Group home placement; Wards of the state.

Sources of Referral State depts of education; Local depts of education; State depts of mental health; Depts of correction; Social service depts.

Client Profile

Age Range of Clients Served Residential program: 12-18.

Characteristics Exhibited by Children Emotional handicaps; Learning disabilities; Mental disabilities.

IQ Range of Clients 70+.

Tuition and Fees

Room and Board Long term: $3,181/mo.

Placements Primarily Funded By State depts of education; Local depts of education; State depts of mental health; Depts of corrections; Social service depts.

Social and Rehabilitative Services

Therapeutic Approach The facility has a psychoanalytic theoretical approach, integrated with strategic interventions.

Therapeutic Services Offered Individual therapy; Group therapy; Family therapy; Substance abuse treatment.

Professionals on Staff Psychiatrists; Psychologists; Child care staff.

Educational and Vocational Services

Type(s) of Educational Programs Offered On campus (Therapeutic school program).

Profile of On Campus School Program Number of teachers 2; *Number of classrooms* 2; *Student to teacher ratio* 9:1; *Credentials of teachers* SH, LH; *Grades taught* 9-12.

Degrees Offered 12th grade diploma.

EL TORO

FAMILY SOLUTIONS

24432 Muirlands Blvd, Ste 201, El Toro, CA 92630 (714) 770-2362

Contact Person(s): Richard Kaufman, Dir

Setting and Background Information This agency was established in 1975. There are 9 residential group homes.

Referral Information Contact the facility for referral information.

Type of Facility

Funding Sources Private; County.

Average Length of Stay Long term.

Types of Admissions Accepted Residential treatment; Group home placement; Wards of the state.

Sources of Referral State depts of mental health; Psychiatrists; Private sources; Social service depts.

Client Profile

Age Range of Clients Served Residential program: 6-18.

Characteristics Exhibited by Children Emotional handicaps; Learning disabilities; Mental disabilities.

IQ Range of Clients 80+.

Tuition and Fees

Room and Board Long term: $3,000/mo.

Placements Primarily Funded By Insurance; Private sources; Social service depts.

Social and Rehabilitative Services

Therapeutic Approach The facility offers a therapeutic milieu.

Therapeutic Services Offered Individual therapy; Group therapy; Family therapy; Independent living skills program; Aftercare program with follow up.

Professionals on Staff Psychiatrists; Psychologists; Social workers; Child care staff.

Educational and Vocational Services

Type(s) of Educational Programs Offered Off campus.

FRESNO

BELLA VIDA GROUP HOME

3742 Kenmore Dr N, Fresno, CA 93638 (209) 266-4455 *Contact Person(s):* Emma Lozito, Admin

Setting and Background Information This facility was established as a foster home in 1948. In 1973, it became a group home facility. There are 2 residential group homes.

Referral Information Contact the facility for referral information.

Type of Facility

Funding Sources State; Federal.

Average Length of Stay Long term.

Types of Admissions Accepted Residential treatment; Group home placement; Wards of the state.

Sources of Referral State depts of mental health; Psychiatrists; Private sources; Depts of correction; Social service depts.

BELLA VIDA GROUP HOME *(continued)*

Client Profile
Age Range of Clients Served Residential program: 6-18.
Characteristics Exhibited by Children Emotional handicaps; Learning disabilities; Neurological impairments.
Tuition and Fees
Room and Board Long term: $1,184/mo.
Placements Primarily Funded By State depts of mental health; Federal agencies.
Social and Rehabilitative Services
Therapeutic Approach The therapeutic approach of the facility is Gestalt.
Therapeutic Services Offered Individual therapy; Group therapy; Art therapy; Independent living skills program; Recreation activities.
Professionals on Staff Psychiatrists; Psychologists; Social workers; Child care staff.
Educational and Vocational Services
Type(s) of Educational Programs Offered Off campus (Summer school).

FAIRMONT GROUP HOME
651 S 3rd, Fresno, CA 93702 (209) 266-3639 *Contact Person(s):* Debra A Gould, House Dir
Setting and Background Information This facility was established in 1972 by the Junior League. It is a shelter/group home for abused and neglected children.
Referral Information Many referrals are made through the Dept of Social Services and Fresno County Juvenile Probation.
Type of Facility
Funding Sources Private; State; Federal; United Way.
Average Length of Stay Short and long term.
Types of Admissions Accepted Group home placement; Wards of the state.
Sources of Referral Private sources; Depts of correction; Social service depts.
Client Profile
Age Range of Clients Served Residential program: 12-18.
Characteristics Exhibited by Children Emotional handicaps; Learning disabilities.
Tuition and Fees
Room and Board Short term: $1,355/mo; Long term: $1,355/mo.
Placements Primarily Funded By Private sources; Depts of corrections; Social service depts.
Social and Rehabilitative Services
Therapeutic Approach The facility uses behavior modification.
Therapeutic Services Offered Individual therapy; Group therapy; Family therapy; Independent living skills program; Recreation activities; Substance abuse treatment.
Professionals on Staff Social workers; Child care staff.

FRESNO TREATMENT CENTER
205 N Fulton, Fresno, CA 93701 (209) 445-1845 *Contact Person(s):* Nina Hamm, Exec Dir
Setting and Background Information The facility was established in 1974 in response to a community need for residential facilities. The center has 7 group homes.
Referral Information Referrals are considered by a multi-disciplinary team consisting of teachers, counselors and group home staff.
Type of Facility
Funding Sources Private; State; Federal.
Average Length of Stay Long term.
Types of Admissions Accepted Day treatment; Residential treatment; Group home placement; Wards of the state.
Sources of Referral State depts of education; Local depts of education; State depts of mental health; Psychiatrists; Private sources; Social service depts.
Client Profile
Age Range of Clients Served Day programs: 6-18; Residential program: 12-18.
Characteristics Exhibited by Children Emotional handicaps; Learning disabilities; Neurological impairments; Mental disabilities.
Tuition and Fees
Room and Board Short term: $1,762/mo; Long term: $1,762/mo.
Tuition $79/diem.
Placements Primarily Funded By Local depts of education.

Social and Rehabilitative Services
Therapeutic Approach The facility employs both psychological and vocational counseling and brings in AA and NA when needed.
Therapeutic Services Offered Individual therapy; Group therapy; Family therapy; Substance abuse treatment.
Professionals on Staff Psychiatrists; Psychologists; Social workers; Adjunctive therapists; Child care staff.
Educational and Vocational Services
Type(s) of Educational Programs Offered On campus; Summer campus.
Profile of On Campus School Program Number of teachers 4; *Number of classrooms* 4; *Student to teacher ratio* 14:1; *Length of school day* 6 hrs.
Degrees Offered 8th grade diploma; 12th grade diploma; GED.

WASHINGTON STREET HOMES
3320 E Washington St, Fresno, CA 93702 (209) 268-0241 *Contact Person(s):* Carolyn Hoover, Prog Dir
Setting and Background Information The facility was established in 1980 through the EOC of Fresno County. It is a large group home.
Referral Information Youths are referred to the facility by Fresno County Juvenile Justice System through the Juvenile Court or the Juvenile Probation Dept. Youth with a 601 status will be considered for admission—criminal offenders are not accepted.
Type of Facility
Funding Sources State.
Average Length of Stay Long term.
Types of Admissions Accepted Group home placement.
Sources of Referral Depts of correction.
Client Profile
Age Range of Clients Served Residential program: 12-17.
Characteristics Exhibited by Children Behavior disorders; Delinquency.
Tuition and Fees
Placements Primarily Funded By State probationary system.
Social and Rehabilitative Services
Therapeutic Services Offered Group therapy.
Professionals on Staff Social workers; Adjunctive therapists.

GILROY

ODD FELLOW REBEKAH CHILDREN'S HOME
290 IOOF Ave, Gilroy, CA 95020 (408) 842-6451 *Contact Person(s):* Donald Limburg, Dir; Kyle Titus, Asst Dir
Setting and Background Information The facility was established in 1897 as an orphanage by the Odd Fellows and Rebekahs of California. The 10-acre facility has 5 individual living units.
Referral Information Contact the facility for referral information. A pre-placement meeting will be scheduled.
Type of Facility
Funding Sources Private; State; Odd Fellows and Rebekahs of California.
Average Length of Stay Long term.
Types of Admissions Accepted Residential treatment; Wards of the state.
Sources of Referral State depts of education; Local depts of education; State depts of mental health; Private sources; Depts of correction; Social service depts.
Client Profile
Age Range of Clients Served Residential program: 6-18.
Characteristics Exhibited by Children Emotional handicaps; Learning disabilities; Neurological impairments; Mental disabilities.
Tuition and Fees
Room and Board Long term: $2,607/mo.
Placements Primarily Funded By Depts of corrections; Social service depts; Odd Fellows and Rebekahs of California.
Social and Rehabilitative Services
Therapeutic Approach The facility uses behavior modification.
Therapeutic Services Offered Individual therapy; Group therapy; Family therapy; Adjunctive therapy; Recreation activities; Substance abuse treatment.
Professionals on Staff Psychiatrists; Psychologists; Social workers; Adjunctive therapists; Child care staff; Nurses.

ODD FELLOW REBEKAH CHILDREN'S HOME
(continued)

Educational and Vocational Services
Type(s) of Educational Programs Offered On campus; Off campus (Spec Ed classes).
Profile of On Campus School Program Number of teachers 2; *Number of classrooms* 1; *Student to teacher ratio* 5:1; *Grades taught* 7-12.
Degrees Offered 8th grade diploma; 12th grade diploma.

HOLLISTER

CHAMBERLAIN'S CHILDREN'S CENTER, INC
1850 Cienego Rd, Hollister, CA 95023 (408) 637-1677 *Contact Person(s):* Dr Jay Goodman, Res Prog Dir
Setting and Background Information The facility was established in 1965.
Referral Information For referral, contact the facility and forward the necessary material.
Type of Facility
Funding Sources State.
Average Length of Stay Long term.
Types of Admissions Accepted Day treatment; Residential treatment; Group home placement; Wards of the state.
Sources of Referral State depts of education; Local depts of education; State depts of mental health; Private sources; Social service depts.
Client Profile
Age Range of Clients Served Day programs: 6-12; Residential program: 6-15.
Characteristics Exhibited by Children Emotional handicaps; Learning disabilities; Speech/Language disorders; Mental disabilities.
Tuition and Fees
Room and Board Long term: $2,102/mo.
Placements Primarily Funded By Social service depts.
Social and Rehabilitative Services
Therapeutic Services Offered Individual therapy; Group therapy; Aftercare program with follow up.
Professionals on Staff Psychiatrists; Psychologists; Social workers; Child care staff.
Educational and Vocational Services
Type(s) of Educational Programs Offered On campus; Off campus.
Profile of On Campus School Program Number of teachers 1; *Number of classrooms* 1; *Student to teacher ratio* 7:1.

LANCASTER

WALDEN ENVIRONMENT
43545 17th St W, Ste 601, Lancaster, CA 93534 (805) 945-1804
Contact Person(s): Stephen R Lindsey, Asst Exec Dir
Setting and Background Information The facility was established in 1977 as a state licensed group home. There are now several satellite facilities.
Referral Information Referrals are made by social service agencies and parents.
Type of Facility
Funding Sources State AFDC.
Average Length of Stay Long term.
Types of Admissions Accepted Residential treatment; Group home placement; Wards of the state.
Sources of Referral State depts of mental health; Private sources; Depts of correction; Social service depts.
Client Profile
Age Range of Clients Served Residential program: Birth-18.
Characteristics Exhibited by Children Emotional handicaps; Learning disabilities; Mental disabilities.
IQ Range of Clients 70+.
Tuition and Fees
Room and Board Long term: $2,190 (Group homes); $1,214-$1,283 (Foster homes).
Placements Primarily Funded By Social service depts.

Social and Rehabilitative Services
Therapeutic Approach The therapeutic approach is eclectic, primarily using reality therapy and behavior modification.
Therapeutic Services Offered Individual therapy; Group therapy; Family therapy; Art therapy; Recreation activities; Substance abuse treatment.
Professionals on Staff Psychologists; Social workers; Child care staff.
Educational and Vocational Services
Type(s) of Educational Programs Offered Off campus (Public school).

LEMON GROVE

BOSELLI RESIDENTIAL SERVICES, INC
PO Box 1466, Lemon Grove, CA 92045 (619) 589-6300, 589-7878
Contact Person(s): Fran Boselli, Exec Dir
Setting and Background Information The facility was established in 1986 to provide residential care to 6 clients. It now has the capacity for 10 clients. It is in a large house with 7 bedrooms.
Referral Information Contact the facility. A pre-placement interview will be scheduled.
Type of Facility
Funding Sources State.
Average Length of Stay Long term.
Types of Admissions Accepted Residential treatment; Group home placement; Wards of the state.
Sources of Referral Social service depts.
Client Profile
Age Range of Clients Served Residential program: 12-18.
Characteristics Exhibited by Children Emotional handicaps; Learning disabilities; Mental disabilities.
IQ Range of Clients 74+.
Tuition and Fees
Room and Board Long term: $1,949/mo.
Placements Primarily Funded By Social service depts.
Social and Rehabilitative Services
Therapeutic Services Offered Individual therapy; Group therapy; Family therapy; Adjunctive therapy; Art therapy; Independent living skills program; Recreation activities; Substance abuse treatment.
Professionals on Staff Psychiatrists; Psychologists; Social workers; Child care staff.
Educational and Vocational Services
Type(s) of Educational Programs Offered Off campus (Reg school/spec ed).

LOS ANGELES

AVIVA CENTER
7357 Hollywood Blvd, Los Angeles, CA 90046 (213) 876-0550
Contact Person(s): Lois M Tandy, Admin
Setting and Background Information The facility was initially established in 1915 as a residence for working women. Currently, it is a residential treatment program in an urban area.
Referral Information For referral information contact the intake worker of the facility.
Type of Facility
Funding Sources Private.
Average Length of Stay Long term.
Types of Admissions Accepted Residential treatment; Wards of the state.
Sources of Referral State depts of mental health; Psychiatrists; Private sources; Depts of correction; Social service depts.
Client Profile
Age Range of Clients Served Residential program: 15-18.
Characteristics Exhibited by Children Emotional handicaps.
IQ Range of Clients 80-120.
Tuition and Fees
Room and Board Long term: $2,200/mo (includes school tuition).
Placements Primarily Funded By Social service depts.
Social and Rehabilitative Services
Therapeutic Approach The basic therapeutic approach of the facility is clinical in a milieu setting.
Therapeutic Services Offered Individual therapy; Group therapy; Family therapy; Independent living skills program; Substance abuse treatment.
Professionals on Staff Psychiatrists; Social workers; Child care staff.

AVIVA CENTER *(continued)*

Educational and Vocational Services
Type(s) of Educational Programs Offered On campus.
Profile of On Campus School Program Number of teachers 2; *Number of classrooms* 1; *Grades taught* 7-12.
Degrees Offered 12th grade diploma.

GATEWAYS HOSPITAL AND MENTAL HEALTH CENTER

1891 Effie St, Los Angeles, CA 90026 (213) 666-0171 *Contact Person(s):* Norman V Balison MD, Dir Child & Adolescent Srvs; David J Jimenez ED D, Clin Admin, Child & Adolescent Srvs
Setting and Background Information The center was established in 1961 to provide extended services to an incarcerated Jewish population.
Referral Information Referrals are made through depts of correction, social service depts and county mental health depts.
Type of Facility
Funding Sources Private; State; Short/Doyle.
Average Length of Stay Short and long term.
Types of Admissions Accepted Day treatment; Residential treatment; Group home placement; Wards of the state.
Sources of Referral Local depts of education; State depts of mental health; Private sources; Depts of correction; Social service depts.
Client Profile
Age Range of Clients Served Day programs: 13-17; Residential program: 13-17.
Characteristics Exhibited by Children Emotional handicaps.
IQ Range of Clients 80+.
Tuition and Fees
Placements Primarily Funded By Local depts of education; State depts of mental health; Insurance; Private sources; Depts of corrections; Social service depts; Dept of Mental Health; LA County.
Social and Rehabilitative Services
Therapeutic Services Offered Individual therapy; Group therapy; Family therapy; Adjunctive therapy; Recreation activities.
Professionals on Staff Psychiatrists; Psychologists; Social workers; Adjunctive therapists; Child care staff; Nurses.
Educational and Vocational Services
Type(s) of Educational Programs Offered On campus (State certified).
Profile of On Campus School Program Number of teachers 4; *Number of classrooms* 4; *Student to teacher ratio* 11:1.
Degrees Offered 12th grade diploma.

ANNE SIPPI CLINIC

2457 Endicott St, Los Angeles, CA 90032 (213) 221-5177 *Contact Person(s):* Michael D Rosberg, Admin
Setting and Background Information The clinic was founded in 1976 as a non-profit organization to provide a center for the treatment of schizophrenia. It is a residential facility with the capacity to serve the needs of 32 individuals.
Referral Information Referrals can be made by contacting the facility.
Type of Facility
Funding Sources Private.
Average Length of Stay Long term.
Types of Admissions Accepted Day treatment; Residential treatment.
Sources of Referral State depts of mental health; Psychiatrists; Private sources; Social service depts.
Client Profile
Age Range of Clients Served Day programs: 18-21+; Residential program: 18-21+.
Characteristics Exhibited by Children Emotional handicaps; Learning disabilities; Neurological impairments; Mental disabilities; Schizophrenia.
IQ Range of Clients 70+.
Tuition and Fees
Room and Board Long term: $600/mo.
Tuition $2,500/mo.
Placements Primarily Funded By Private sources.

Social and Rehabilitative Services
Therapeutic Approach The basic therapeutic approach of the clinic is an intensive psychological and psycho-social one.
Therapeutic Services Offered Individual therapy; Group therapy; Family therapy; Adjunctive therapy; Art therapy; Physical therapy; Independent living skills program; Recreation activities; Substance abuse treatment; Aftercare program with follow up.
Professionals on Staff Psychiatrists; Psychologists; Social workers; Adjunctive therapists; Art therapists.

TEENS WORLD GROUP HOME, INC

8461 Zamora Ave, Los Angeles, CA 90001 (213) 581-2582 *Contact Person(s):* Eddie Tucker, Exec Dir
Setting and Background Information The facility was privately established in 1983. There is a house and an education/recreation center.
Referral Information Contact the facility for referral procedures.
Type of Facility
Funding Sources State.
Average Length of Stay Long term.
Types of Admissions Accepted Residential treatment; Group home placement; Wards of the state.
Sources of Referral Social service depts; Probation.
Client Profile
Age Range of Clients Served Day programs: 12-18; Residential program: 12-18.
Characteristics Exhibited by Children Emotional handicaps; Learning disabilities.
IQ Range of Clients 70+.
Tuition and Fees
Room and Board Short term: $69.26/diem; Long term: $69.26/diem.
Placements Primarily Funded By Social service depts.
Social and Rehabilitative Services
Therapeutic Approach The facility has a behavioral approach.
Therapeutic Services Offered Individual therapy; Group therapy; Family therapy; Independent living skills program; Recreation activities; Aftercare program with follow up.
Professionals on Staff Psychiatrists; Psychologists; Social workers; Child care staff.

VISTA DEL MAR CHILD CARE SERVICE

3200 Motor Ave, Los Angeles, CA 90034 (213) 836-1223 *Contact Person(s):* Samuel P Berman, Exec Dir
Setting and Background Information The facility was established in 1908 by a local organization who recognized a need for a children's home. Located on 17 acres, there are 22 buildings.
Referral Information For referral, contact the intake worker and forward the necessary information. A pre-placement interview will be scheduled.
Type of Facility
Funding Sources Private; State; Federal; County.
Average Length of Stay Long term.
Types of Admissions Accepted Day treatment; Residential treatment; Group home placement; Wards of the state.
Sources of Referral Local depts of education; State depts of mental health; Psychiatrists; Private sources; Depts of correction; Social service depts.
Client Profile
Age Range of Clients Served Day programs: 6-18; Residential program: 6-18.
Characteristics Exhibited by Children Emotional handicaps; Learning disabilities.
Tuition and Fees
Room and Board Long term: $3,300/mo.
Placements Primarily Funded By Private sources; Social service depts; County.
Social and Rehabilitative Services
Therapeutic Approach The facility uses psychotherapy and behavior modification.
Therapeutic Services Offered Individual therapy; Group therapy; Family therapy; Art therapy; Independent living skills program; Recreation activities; Aftercare program with follow up.
Professionals on Staff Psychiatrists; Psychologists; Social workers; Adjunctive therapists; Child care staff; Nurses; Art therapists.

VISTA DEL MAR CHILD CARE SERVICE *(continued)*

Educational and Vocational Services
Type(s) of Educational Programs Offered On campus.
Profile of On Campus School Program Number of teachers 8; *Number of classrooms* 8; *Student to teacher ratio* 10:1; *Credentials of teachers* MA; *Grades taught* 1-12.
Degrees Offered 8th grade diploma; 12th grade diploma; GED.

LOS OLIVOS

NEW FAMILY VISION
PO Box 503, 2760 Lucca Ave, Los Olivos, CA 93441
(805) 688-1180 *Contact Person(s):* Katrina Yeo, Admin
Setting and Background Information The facility was established in 1983 as a part of the Gorsuch Fleishaur Living Workshop. Currently, the facility consists of a single family residence located on a half acre.
Referral Information Referrals are made by parents, the Dept of Corrections and several service agencies. Candidates for the program must be free from substance abuse and severe mental or emotional disorders.
Type of Facility
Funding Sources Private; State; Federal.
Average Length of Stay 6 mo min.
Types of Admissions Accepted Group home placement.
Sources of Referral Depts of correction; Social service depts.
Client Profile
Age Range of Clients Served Residential program: 12-18.
Characteristics Exhibited by Children Emotional handicaps.
IQ Range of Clients 110+.
Tuition and Fees
Room and Board Long term: $2,000.
Placements Primarily Funded By Depts of corrections; Social service depts.
Social and Rehabilitative Services
Therapeutic Approach The therapeutic approach of the facility is Rogerian.
Therapeutic Services Offered Individual therapy; Family therapy; Independent living skills program; Teen pregnancy program.
Professionals on Staff Psychologists; Social workers; Child care staff; Recreational specialist.
Educational and Vocational Services
Type(s) of Educational Programs Offered Off campus (Public school); Summer campus (Family trips and camp).
Vocational Education Programs/Degrees Offered ROP classes at local high school.
Degrees Offered 8th grade diploma; 12th grade diploma.

MODESTO

KUUBBA EXTENDED FAMILY
531 Truman Ave, Modesto, CA 95351 (209) 523-7120 *Contact Person(s):* Carole Ann Collins, Admin
Setting and Background Information The facility was established in 1984 in response to a local need.
Referral Information For referral information contact the facility.
Type of Facility
Funding Sources State.
Average Length of Stay 6-12 mos.
Types of Admissions Accepted Residential treatment; Group home placement; Wards of the state.
Sources of Referral State depts of education; Local depts of education; State depts of mental health; Psychiatrists; Private sources; Depts of correction; Social service depts.
Client Profile
Age Range of Clients Served Residential program: 6-15.
Characteristics Exhibited by Children Emotional handicaps; Learning disabilities; Mental disabilities.
IQ Range of Clients 65+.
Tuition and Fees
Room and Board Short term: $2,507/mo; Long term: $2,507/mo.
Placements Primarily Funded By State depts of mental health; Depts of corrections; Social service depts.

Social and Rehabilitative Services
Therapeutic Approach The facility uses reality therapy and behavior modification.
Therapeutic Services Offered Individual therapy; Group therapy; Family therapy; Art therapy; Independent living skills program; Recreation activities; Substance abuse treatment; Aftercare program with follow up.
Professionals on Staff Psychiatrists; Psychologists; Social workers; Adjunctive therapists; Child care staff; Nurses; Art therapists.
Educational and Vocational Services
Type(s) of Educational Programs Offered Off campus (Jr college).
Vocational Education Programs/Degrees Offered Vocational education.

NAPA

ALDEA, INC
PO Box 841, Napa, CA 94559 (707) 224-8266 *Contact Person(s):* Allen Ewig, Exec Dir
Setting and Background Information The facility was established in 1971 by a non-profit community group. There are 9 programs in the communities of Napa and Fairfield.
Referral Information For referral, contact the facility and forward evaluative reports. An intake interview and over-night visit will be scheduled.
Type of Facility
Funding Sources State; Federal.
Average Length of Stay Long term.
Types of Admissions Accepted Day treatment; Residential treatment; Group home placement; Wards of the state.
Sources of Referral State depts of mental health; Private sources; Social service depts.
Client Profile
Age Range of Clients Served Day programs: 12-18; Residential program: 12-18.
Characteristics Exhibited by Children Emotional handicaps.
IQ Range of Clients 60-140.
Tuition and Fees
Room and Board Short term: $2,500/mo; Long term: $2,309/mo.
Placements Primarily Funded By Social service depts.
Social and Rehabilitative Services
Therapeutic Approach The facility uses behavior modification in a therapeutic milieu.
Therapeutic Services Offered Individual therapy; Group therapy; Family therapy; Adjunctive therapy; Independent living skills program; Recreation activities.
Professionals on Staff Psychiatrists; Psychologists; Social workers; Adjunctive therapists; Child care staff.
Educational and Vocational Services
Type(s) of Educational Programs Offered Off campus.

OAK RUN

WIDE HORIZONS RANCH, INC
Rt 2 Box 405, Oak Run, CA 96069 (916) 472-3223 *Contact Person(s):* Gene or Merle Anderson, Dir
Setting and Background Information The facility was established in 1974. The 175-acre campus has a house and a mobile home, a barn with an upstairs gym, a craft shop, an equipment shop, and a feed store for vocational education.
Referral Information Referrals are made by outside sources, including parents. Reports from agencies are screened and if appropriate a visit is arranged.
Type of Facility
Funding Sources Private; State.
Average Length of Stay Long term.
Types of Admissions Accepted Residential treatment; Group home placement; Wards of the state.
Sources of Referral State depts of education; Local depts of education; State depts of mental health; Psychiatrists; Private sources; Social service depts.
Client Profile
Age Range of Clients Served Residential program: 10-15.
Characteristics Exhibited by Children Emotional handicaps; Learning disabilities; Speech/Language disorders; Neurological impairments; Mental disabilities.
IQ Range of Clients 70+.

WIDE HORIZONS RANCH, INC *(continued)*

Tuition and Fees
Room and Board Long term: $1,772/mo.
Tuition $40/diem.
Placements Primarily Funded By State depts of education; Local depts of education; State depts of mental health; Insurance; Private sources; Social service depts.
Social and Rehabilitative Services
Therapeutic Approach The basic approach of the facility is reality therapy.
Therapeutic Services Offered Individual therapy; Group therapy; Family therapy.
Professionals on Staff Psychiatrists; Psychologists; Social workers; Child care staff.
Educational and Vocational Services
Type(s) of Educational Programs Offered On campus; Summer campus.
Profile of On Campus School Program Number of teachers 3; *Number of classrooms* 2; *Student to teacher ratio* 3:1; *Credentials of teachers* Spec Ed; *Length of school day* 9-3; *Grades taught* Ungraded; Special curriculum electives offered; Remedial courses offered.
Vocational Education Programs/Degrees Offered Retail experience in feed store.
Degrees Offered 8th grade diploma.

OAKLAND

FRED FINCH YOUTH CENTER
3800 Coolidge Avenue, Oakland, CA 94602 (415) 482-2244 *Contact Person(s):* Barbara B Peterson, Exec Dir
Setting and Background Information The center was originally established in 1891 as an orphanage. The facility is on 7 ½ acres and has an administration building, school buildings, 5 cottages and 2 single family dwellings.
Referral Information All inquiries are made to the Intake Social Worker who reviews material with the Medical Director for appropriateness.
Type of Facility
Funding Sources Private.
Average Length of Stay 14 mos or more.
Types of Admissions Accepted Residential treatment; Wards of the state.
Sources of Referral State depts of education; State depts of mental health; Psychiatrists Champus; Private sources; Depts of correction; Social service depts.
Client Profile
Age Range of Clients Served Residential program: 12-18.
Characteristics Exhibited by Children Emotional handicaps.
IQ Range of Clients 70-120.
Tuition and Fees
Room and Board Long term: $3,567/mo.
Tuition $75/diem.
Placements Primarily Funded By Social service depts.
Social and Rehabilitative Services
Therapeutic Approach The facility has a psychodynamic approach to therapy.
Therapeutic Services Offered Individual therapy; Group therapy; Family therapy; Recreation activities.
Professionals on Staff Psychiatrists; Social workers; Child care staff; Nurses; Recreation therapists.
Educational and Vocational Services
Type(s) of Educational Programs Offered Off campus.
Profile of On Campus School Program Number of teachers 5; *Number of classrooms* 5; *Student to teacher ratio* 8:1; *Credentials of teachers* Spec Ed, EH; *Length of school day* 5 hrs; *Grades taught* 2-12; Remedial courses offered.
Vocational Education Programs/Degrees Offered Limited vocational training (Clerical; Food preparation; Maintenance).
Degrees Offered 12th grade diploma.

GASTON FAMILY HOME
10714 Beverly Ave, Oakland, CA 94603 (415) 568-0930 *Contact Person(s):* Marie Gaston, Admin
Setting and Background Information The facility was established in 1968.
Referral Information Contact the facility for referral information.

Type of Facility
Funding Sources Private; State.
Average Length of Stay Long term.
Types of Admissions Accepted Group home placement.
Sources of Referral Local depts of education; Social service depts.
Client Profile
Age Range of Clients Served Day programs: 15-21+.
Characteristics Exhibited by Children Emotional handicaps; Learning disabilities; Mental disabilities.
Tuition and Fees
Placements Primarily Funded By Local depts of education.
Social and Rehabilitative Services
Therapeutic Services Offered Physical therapy.
Professionals on Staff Child care staff.

SANFORD SOCIETY, INC
1615 Broadway, Ste 510, Oakland, CA 94612 (415) 452-1777
Contact Person(s): Frank A Jones PhD, Exec Dir
Setting and Background Information This facility was established in 1979. There are three buildings.
Referral Information Contact the facility for referral information.
Type of Facility
Funding Sources State.
Average Length of Stay Long term.
Types of Admissions Accepted Residential treatment; Group home placement; Wards of the state.
Sources of Referral State depts of education; State depts of mental health; Private sources; Depts of correction; Social service depts; Probation depts.
Client Profile
Age Range of Clients Served Day programs: 12-18; Residential program: 12-18.
Characteristics Exhibited by Children Emotional handicaps; Learning disabilities; Mental disabilities.
Tuition and Fees
Room and Board Long term: $1,662/mo.
Placements Primarily Funded By Depts of corrections; Social service depts; Probation.
Social and Rehabilitative Services
Therapeutic Approach The facility uses reality therapy.
Therapeutic Services Offered Individual therapy; Group therapy; Family therapy; Adjunctive therapy; Independent living skills program; Substance abuse treatment; Aftercare program with follow up.
Professionals on Staff Psychologists; Social workers; Adjunctive therapists; Child care staff.
Educational and Vocational Services
Type(s) of Educational Programs Offered On campus (Computer literacy); Off campus (Public schools).
Profile of On Campus School Program Number of teachers 1; *Number of classrooms* 3; *Student to teacher ratio* 6:1; Remedial courses offered.
Degrees Offered Certificate.

SENECA CENTER
4500 Redwood Rd, Oakland, CA 94619 (415) 531-1880 *Contact Person(s):* Christine Stoner, Res Coord
Setting and Background Information The center was privately incorporated in 1985 as a non-profit organization. There are two group homes and a school.
Referral Information Contact a social worker at the facility and forward referral material. A pre-placement interview and 2-day visit will be scheduled.
Type of Facility
Funding Sources Private; State; AFDC.
Average Length of Stay Long term.
Types of Admissions Accepted Day treatment; Residential treatment; Group home placement; Wards of the state; Foster care.
Sources of Referral Local depts of education; Social service depts.
Client Profile
Age Range of Clients Served Day programs: 6-15; Residential program: 6-12.
Characteristics Exhibited by Children Emotional handicaps; Learning disabilities; Neurological impairments; Mental disabilities.
IQ Range of Clients 60-140.

SENECA CENTER *(continued)*

Tuition and Fees
Room and Board Long term: $2,807/mo.
Tuition $65/diem.
Placements Primarily Funded By Local depts of education; Social service depts.
Social and Rehabilitative Services
Therapeutic Approach The basic therapeutic approach is behavior modification.
Therapeutic Services Offered Individual therapy; Group therapy; Family therapy; Aftercare program with follow up.
Professionals on Staff Psychiatrists; Psychologists; Social workers; Adjunctive therapists; Child care staff; Speech pathologist.
Educational and Vocational Services
Type(s) of Educational Programs Offered On campus (Spec Ed).
Profile of On Campus School Program Number of teachers 3; *Number of classrooms* 3; *Student to teacher ratio* 5:1; *Credentials of teachers* Spec Ed; *Length of school day* 9-2:30; *Grades taught* K-12; Remedial courses offered (All subjects).

ORANGEVALE

KAPLAN FOUNDATION, INC

7150 Santa Juanita Ave, Orangevale, CA 95662.
Contact Person(s): Karen Fitzgerald, Dir
Setting and Background Information The facility was established in 1979 and is located on 5 acres.
Referral Information Contact the program director for referral information.
Type of Facility
Funding Sources Private; State; Federal; School districts.
Average Length of Stay Long term.
Types of Admissions Accepted Day treatment; Residential treatment.
Sources of Referral State depts of education; Local depts of education; Psychiatrists; Private sources; Social service depts; School districts.
Client Profile
Age Range of Clients Served Day programs: Birth-21+; Residential program: Birth-21+.
Characteristics Exhibited by Children Learning disabilities; Speech/Language disorders; Mental disabilities; Autism.
Tuition and Fees
Tuition $95/diem.
Placements Primarily Funded By State depts of education; Local depts of education; Insurance; Private sources; Social service depts.
Social and Rehabilitative Services
Professionals on Staff Psychologists; Adjunctive therapists.
Educational and Vocational Services
Type(s) of Educational Programs Offered On campus (Full day program).
Profile of On Campus School Program Number of teachers 4; *Number of classrooms* 4; *Student to teacher ratio* 2:1.

PALM DESERT

DIAGNOSTIC AND EDUCATIONAL SERVICES

73-833 El Paseo, Palm Desert, CA 92260 (619) 346-3662 *Contact Person(s):* Carol Proud, Dir
Setting and Background Information The facility was established in 1980 as a day treatment and evaluation program. A residential treatment center was added in 1982.
Referral Information Contact the facility for referral information. Prior to admission, there will be an evaluation and an interview with the director and a social worker. The pre-admission fees are $350.00.
Type of Facility
Funding Sources Private; State.
Average Length of Stay Long term.
Types of Admissions Accepted Day treatment; Residential treatment.
Sources of Referral State depts of education; Local depts of education; State depts of mental health; Psychiatrists; Private sources; Social service depts.

Client Profile
Age Range of Clients Served Day programs: Birth-21+; Residential program: 6-18.
Characteristics Exhibited by Children Emotional handicaps; Learning disabilities; Speech/Language disorders; Neurological impairments; Mental disabilities.
Tuition and Fees
Room and Board Short term: $1,638/mo; Long term: $1,638/mo.
Tuition $1,200/mo (day treatment).
Placements Primarily Funded By Private sources; Social service depts.
Social and Rehabilitative Services
Therapeutic Approach The basic approach of the facility is behavior modification.
Therapeutic Services Offered Individual therapy; Group therapy; Family therapy; Adjunctive therapy; Art therapy; Physical therapy; Independent living skills program; Recreation activities; Substance abuse treatment; Aftercare program with follow up.
Professionals on Staff Psychiatrists; Psychologists; Social workers; Adjunctive therapists; Child care staff; Art therapists.
Educational and Vocational Services
Type(s) of Educational Programs Offered On campus.
Profile of On Campus School Program Number of teachers 5; *Student to teacher ratio* 2:1; *Credentials of teachers* SDL, SH, LD; *Grades taught* K-12; Special curriculum electives offered (Art, Photography, English riding, Ice skating).
Vocational Education Programs/Degrees Offered Retail sales; Banking; Office; Clerical.
Degrees Offered 8th grade diploma; 12th grade diploma; GED.

PALMS

KAM, INC—REALITY RANCH

PO Box 2015, Palms, CA 92277 (714) 367-1336 *Contact Person(s):* Karen A McGinness, Admin
Setting and Background Information Originally established as a foster parent and home facility, in 1974 it became a group home with a capacity to serve 6 male adolescents.
Referral Information Contact the facility and forward referral materials, including psychiatric reports. A pre-placement interview will be scheduled.
Type of Facility
Funding Sources Federal; County.
Average Length of Stay 6 mo - 4 yrs.
Types of Admissions Accepted Group home placement; Wards of the state.
Sources of Referral Social service depts.
Client Profile
Age Range of Clients Served Residential program: 6-18.
Characteristics Exhibited by Children Emotional handicaps; Learning disabilities.
IQ Range of Clients 80+.
Tuition and Fees
Room and Board Short term: $1095/mo; Long term: $1095/mo.
Placements Primarily Funded By Social service depts.
Social and Rehabilitative Services
Therapeutic Approach The facility uses behavior modification.
Therapeutic Services Offered Individual therapy; Group therapy; Family therapy; Recreation activities.
Professionals on Staff Psychiatrists; Psychologists; Social workers; Child care staff.

PALO ALTO

CARAVAN HOUSE

2361 High St, Palo Alto, CA 94301 (415) 321-0690 *Contact Person(s):* Brian Salada MFCC, Dir
Setting and Background Information This facility was established in 1978 for local adolescents. It is a residential house.
Referral Information For referral information, contact the program director.
Type of Facility
Funding Sources Private; Federal.
Average Length of Stay Long term.
Types of Admissions Accepted Residential treatment; Group home placement; Wards of the state.
Sources of Referral State depts of mental health; Depts of correction; Social service depts.

CARAVAN HOUSE *(continued)*

Client Profile
Age Range of Clients Served Residential program: 12-18.
Characteristics Exhibited by Children Emotional handicaps; Learning disabilities; Mental disabilities.
IQ Range of Clients 90+.
Tuition and Fees
Room and Board Long term: $1,935/mo.
Placements Primarily Funded By Private sources; Depts of corrections; Social service depts.
Social and Rehabilitative Services
Therapeutic Approach The basic therapeutic approach of the facility is behavior modification.
Therapeutic Services Offered Individual therapy; Group therapy; Family therapy; Art therapy; Independent living skills program; Substance abuse treatment; Aftercare program with follow up.
Professionals on Staff Social workers; Adjunctive therapists; Art therapists.
Educational and Vocational Services
Type(s) of Educational Programs Offered Off campus (High school).

LA SELVA

652 Forest Ave, Palo Alto, CA 94301 (415) 323-1401 *Contact Person(s):* Paul S Taylor, Prog Dir
Setting and Background Information This is a comprehensive residential treatment program which was established in 1979. It is a program of Miramonte Mental Health Services, Inc. The facility has a capacity for 12 residents.
Referral Information Contact the facility for referral information..
Type of Facility
Funding Sources Private.
Average Length of Stay Approx 1 yr.
Types of Admissions Accepted Residential treatment.
Sources of Referral State depts of education; Local depts of education; State depts of mental health; Psychiatrists; Private sources; Depts of correction; Social service depts; Self; Family.
Client Profile
Age Range of Clients Served Residential program: 15-62.
Characteristics Exhibited by Children Emotional handicaps; Learning disabilities; Mental disabilities.
Tuition and Fees
Room and Board Long term: $115/diem.
Placements Primarily Funded By State depts of mental health; Insurance; Private sources; Depts of corrections; Social service depts; Family; Client.
Social and Rehabilitative Services
Therapeutic Approach The program combines individual counseling with active participation in a small therapeutic community.
Therapeutic Services Offered Individual therapy; Group therapy; Family therapy; Adjunctive therapy; Art therapy; Independent living skills program; Recreation activities; Substance abuse treatment; Aftercare program with follow up.
Professionals on Staff Psychiatrists; Psychologists; Adjunctive therapists; Counselors.
Educational and Vocational Services
Type(s) of Educational Programs Offered Off campus.
Vocational Education Programs/Degrees Offered Full day pre-vocational and vocational program.

SUN PORCH GROUP HOME

610 Cowper, Palo Alto, CA 94301 (415) 323-2103 *Contact Person(s):* Gary Lawson, Dir
Setting and Background Information The facility was established in 1976.
Referral Information Contact the facility for referral information.
Type of Facility
Funding Sources State.
Average Length of Stay Long term.
Types of Admissions Accepted Group home placement; Wards of the state.
Sources of Referral Local depts of education; State depts of mental health; Depts of correction; Social service depts.
Client Profile
Age Range of Clients Served Residential program: 12-18.
Characteristics Exhibited by Children Emotional handicaps; Mental disabilities.

Tuition and Fees
Room and Board Long term: $1,773/mo.
Placements Primarily Funded By Depts of corrections; Social service depts.
Social and Rehabilitative Services
Therapeutic Services Offered Individual therapy; Group therapy; Family therapy; Independent living skills program.
Professionals on Staff Psychologists; Social workers; Adjunctive therapists; Child care staff.
Educational and Vocational Services
Type(s) of Educational Programs Offered Off campus (Public school).

PARADISE

TOYON MESA SCHOOL, INC

5912 Crestview Dr, Paradise, CA 95969 (916) 877-1965 *Contact Person(s):* Kathy Montero, Exec Dir
Setting and Background Information The agency was established in 1973. There are three proprietary group homes for girls.
Referral Information Contact the social worker and submit a referral packet. An intake interview will be held.
Type of Facility
Funding Sources Private; State; Federal.
Average Length of Stay Long term.
Types of Admissions Accepted Group home placement.
Sources of Referral State depts of education; Local depts of education; State depts of mental health; Psychiatrists; Private sources; Depts of correction; Social service depts.
Client Profile
Age Range of Clients Served Residential program: 6-18.
Characteristics Exhibited by Children Emotional handicaps; Learning disabilities; Mental disabilities; Dysfunctional families.
IQ Range of Clients 70+.
Tuition and Fees
Room and Board Long term: $1,359/mo.
Placements Primarily Funded By Depts of corrections; Social service depts.
Social and Rehabilitative Services
Therapeutic Services Offered Individual therapy; Group therapy; Family therapy; Independent living skills program; Recreation activities; Substance abuse treatment.
Professionals on Staff Psychiatrists; Psychologists; Social workers; Child care staff.
Educational and Vocational Services
Type(s) of Educational Programs Offered On campus (Home study); Off campus (Public school); Summer campus.

PETALUMA

FAMILY LIFE CENTER

365 Kuck Lane, Petaluma, CA 94952 (707) 795-6954 *Contact Person(s):* Susan Lemieux, Exec Dir
Setting and Background Information The facility was privately established in 1978. There are two 3-acre country sites with 3 houses, classrooms and out-buildings on each property.
Referral Information Contact the program director and forward psychological evaluations, court reports and other pertinent information.
Type of Facility
Funding Sources State; Federal; Private donations.
Average Length of Stay Long term.
Types of Admissions Accepted Residential treatment; Group home placement; Wards of the state.
Sources of Referral State depts of education; Local depts of education; State depts of mental health; Psychiatrists; Private sources; Depts of correction; Social service depts.
Client Profile
Age Range of Clients Served Residential program: 12-18.
Characteristics Exhibited by Children Emotional handicaps; Learning disabilities; Mental disabilities.
IQ Range of Clients 80-130.
Tuition and Fees
Room and Board Long term: $1,996/mo.
Placements Primarily Funded By Depts of corrections.

FAMILY LIFE CENTER *(continued)*

Social and Rehabilitative Services
Therapeutic Approach The facility has a therapeutic milieu.
Therapeutic Services Offered Individual therapy; Group therapy;
Family therapy; Adjunctive therapy; Art therapy; Independent living skills program; Recreation activities; Substance abuse treatment.
Professionals on Staff Psychologists; Social workers; Adjunctive therapists; Child care staff; Art therapists.
Educational and Vocational Services
Type(s) of Educational Programs Offered On campus.
Profile of On Campus School Program Number of teachers 4; *Number of classrooms* 4; *Student to teacher ratio* 10:1; *Grades taught* 7-12; Special curriculum electives offered; Remedial courses offered.
Vocational Education Programs/Degrees Offered Full vocational training program including job placement.
Degrees Offered 8th grade diploma; 12th grade diploma; GED.

PLEASANT HILL

DRAKE HOUSE GROUP HOME
808 Grayson Rd, Pleasant Hill, CA 94523 (415) 935) 2590 *Contact Person(s):* Wayne Simpson, Exec Dir
Setting and Background Information The facility was privately established in 1971. It is a large 10 bedroom group home.
Referral Information Contact the facility director for referral information.
Type of Facility
Funding Sources Private; State; Federal.
Average Length of Stay Short and long term.
Types of Admissions Accepted Group home placement; Wards of the state.
Sources of Referral State depts of mental health; Psychiatrists; Private sources; Depts of correction; Social service depts.
Client Profile
Age Range of Clients Served Residential program: 12-18.
Characteristics Exhibited by Children Emotional handicaps; Mental disabilities.
Tuition and Fees
Room and Board Short term: $1,950/mo; Long term: $1,950/mo.
Placements Primarily Funded By State depts of mental health; Depts of corrections; Social service depts.
Social and Rehabilitative Services
Therapeutic Approach The facility has an eclectic approach to therapy.
Therapeutic Services Offered Individual therapy; Group therapy;
Family therapy; Adjunctive therapy; Art therapy; Independent living skills program; Recreation activities; Substance abuse treatment.
Professionals on Staff Psychiatrists; Psychologists; Social workers; Adjunctive therapists; Child care staff; Nurses; Art therapists.
Educational and Vocational Services
Type(s) of Educational Programs Offered On campus; Off campus.
Profile of On Campus School Program Number of classrooms 1;
Length of school day 9-2; Special curriculum electives offered; Remedial courses offered.
Vocational Education Programs/Degrees Offered Vocational training and education.

RAMONA

BROAD HORIZONS OF RAMONA, INC
151 Old Julian Hwy, Ramona, CA 92065 (619) 789-7060, 789-4434
Setting and Background Information The facility was established in 1984 by National Psychiatric Centers, Inc. as a private enterprise. The 9 acre campus has 8 cottages, recreation and dining buildings and a pool. There is a second facility which serves adults, located at 1236 'H' St on 3 acres with 4 cottages, recreation and dining buildings and a pool.
Referral Information Referrals are made by hospitals, the Dept of Social Services, and parents.
Type of Facility
Funding Sources Private.
Average Length of Stay Long term.
Types of Admissions Accepted Residential treatment.
Sources of Referral Psychiatrists; Private sources; Social service depts.

Client Profile
Age Range of Clients Served Residential program: 13-55+.
Characteristics Exhibited by Children Emotional handicaps; Mental disabilities.
IQ Range of Clients 80+.
Tuition and Fees
Room and Board Long term: $190/diem (Adolescent program); $125/diem (Adult program).
Placements Primarily Funded By Insurance; Private sources; Social service depts.
Social and Rehabilitative Services
Therapeutic Approach The facility uses psychiatric milieu therapy and has a substance abuse program.
Therapeutic Services Offered Individual therapy; Group therapy;
Family therapy; Adjunctive therapy; Art therapy; Independent living skills program; Recreation activities; Substance abuse treatment; Aftercare program with follow up.
Professionals on Staff Psychiatrists; Psychologists; Social workers; Child care staff; Nurses; Art therapists.
Educational and Vocational Services
Type(s) of Educational Programs Offered On campus; Off campus (Public school).
Profile of On Campus School Program Number of classrooms 2;
Grades taught 8-12; Special curriculum electives offered (Vocational).
Degrees Offered 12th grade diploma; GED.

REDDING

GROUP FOSTER HOMES, INC
1030 Ledell Dr, Redding, CA 96001 (916) 221-1293 *Contact Person(s):* Phil Paulsen LCSW, Admin
Setting and Background Information The facility was established in 1978. There is one building.
Referral Information Contact the administrator for referral. A pre-placement interview will be held.
Type of Facility
Funding Sources Private.
Average Length of Stay Long term.
Types of Admissions Accepted Residential treatment; Group home placement; Wards of the state.
Sources of Referral Depts of correction; Social service depts.
Client Profile
Age Range of Clients Served Residential program: 7-13.
Characteristics Exhibited by Children Emotional handicaps; Learning disabilities; Hearing impairments/deafness; Speech/Language disorders; Neurological impairments; Physical handicaps; Mental disabilities.
IQ Range of Clients 70+.
Tuition and Fees
Room and Board Long term: $1,351/mo.
Placements Primarily Funded By Depts of corrections; Social service depts.
Social and Rehabilitative Services
Therapeutic Services Offered Individual therapy; Group therapy; Recreation activities.
Professionals on Staff Psychiatrists; Psychologists; Social workers; Child care staff.

YMCA YOUTH & FAMILY COUNSELING CENTER
1752 Tehama St, Redding, CA 96001 (916) 244-6226 *Contact Person(s):* Phil Paulsen, Dir
Setting and Background Information The facility was established in 1976 by contracting as a mental health provider. There is a 24-hour intake crisis program and a short term adolescent care facility.
Referral Information The facility accepts walk-in referrals, as well as agency referrals.
Type of Facility
Funding Sources Private.
Average Length of Stay Short term.
Types of Admissions Accepted Emergency shelter.
Sources of Referral County agencies; Law enforcement; Self.
Client Profile
Age Range of Clients Served Residential program: 11-17.
Characteristics Exhibited by Children Emotional handicaps.
IQ Range of Clients 70+.

YMCA YOUTH & FAMILY COUNSELING CENTER
(continued)

Tuition and Fees
Room and Board Short term: $105/diem.
Placements Primarily Funded By State depts of mental health; Social
service depts; County contracts.
Social and Rehabilitative Services
Therapeutic Services Offered Individual therapy; Group therapy;
Family therapy.
Professionals on Staff Psychiatrists; Social workers; Child care staff.

RIVERSIDE

ADVOCATE GROUP HOMES
4317 Jackson, Riverside, CA 92503 (714) 689-5991 *Contact
Person(s):* Bunny Pinchback, Dir
Setting and Background Information The facility was established in
1983 as an outgrowth of a special education program. Each of the
residential facilities is a community based home.
Referral Information Referrals are made by depts of probation,
social service depts (intercounty), and the Dept of Mental Health.
Type of Facility
Funding Sources County.
Average Length of Stay Long term.
Types of Admissions Accepted Residential treatment; Group home
placement.
Sources of Referral State depts of mental health; Depts of correction;
Social service depts.
Client Profile
Age Range of Clients Served Residential program: 12-18.
Characteristics Exhibited by Children Emotional handicaps; Learning
disabilities.
Tuition and Fees
Placements Primarily Funded By Depts of corrections; Social service
depts.
Social and Rehabilitative Services
Therapeutic Services Offered Individual therapy; Group therapy;
Family therapy; Adjunctive therapy; Independent living skills
program; Recreation activities; Substance abuse treatment; After-
care program with follow up.
Professionals on Staff Psychiatrists; Psychologists; Social workers;
Adjunctive therapists; Child care staff.
Educational and Vocational Services
Type(s) of Educational Programs Offered Off campus.

RUNNING SPRINGS

CEDU SCHOOL
Po Box 1176, Running Springs, CA 92382 (714) 867-2722 *Contact
Person(s):* Pat Savage, Dir of Admis
Setting and Background Information The facility was established in
1967 to provide a place for children to develop their intellectual,
social/emotional, and physical skills. Its campus is located in the
National Forest of the San Bernadino Mountains and consists of
a main lodge, dormitories, art studios, performing arts center,
woodshop, and working farm.
Referral Information Anyone can make a referral by contacting the
admissions office.
Type of Facility
Funding Sources Private.
Average Length of Stay 2 ½ yrs.
Types of Admissions Accepted Residential treatment; Group home
placement.
Sources of Referral Private sources.
Client Profile
Age Range of Clients Served Residential program: 13-18.
Characteristics Exhibited by Children Emotional handicaps.
Tuition and Fees
Room and Board Long term: $2,750/mo (includes school tuition).
Placements Primarily Funded By Insurance; Private sources.
Social and Rehabilitative Services
Therapeutic Approach The philosophy of the treatment program is
humanistically oriented, with emphasis on positive peer pressure.
Therapeutic Services Offered Individual therapy; Group therapy;
Family therapy; Independent living skills program; Recreation
activities.

Professionals on Staff Psychologists; Social workers; Adjunctive
therapists; Nurses.
Educational and Vocational Services
Type(s) of Educational Programs Offered On campus.
Profile of On Campus School Program Number of teachers 13;
Student to teacher ratio 4:3; *Credentials of teachers* 4 are LHSH
certified; Special curriculum electives offered (College preparatory
courses, Dance, Drama, Music, Visual and 3-dimensional arts,
Manual arts, Physical education. The Wilderness Program offers
students jogging, hiking, skiing, mountain climbing, and a 2-week
wilderness trek.); Remedial courses offered.
Degrees Offered 12th grade diploma.

SACRAMENTO

GOOD SAMARITAN HOMES
8925 Folsom Blvd, Ste B-2, Sacramento, CA 95826 (916) 366-8444
Contact Person(s): Jeffrey Y Sellwood, Exec Dir
Setting and Background Information The facility was established in
1966 in response to a community need. Currently, the facility
consists of four group homes and an administrative building.
Referral Information Referrals are made by social agencies, parents,
and depts of correction by applying with a letter of request and
background information.
Type of Facility
Funding Sources State; Federal.
Average Length of Stay Long term.
Types of Admissions Accepted Residential treatment; Wards of the
state; Foster care.
Sources of Referral State depts of education; Local depts of educa-
tion; State depts of mental health; Psychiatrists; Private sources;
Depts of correction; Social service depts.
Client Profile
Age Range of Clients Served Residential program: 12-18.
Characteristics Exhibited by Children Emotional handicaps; Learning
disabilities; Delinquency.
IQ Range of Clients 70+.
Tuition and Fees
Room and Board Long term: $1,917/mo.
Placements Primarily Funded By Depts of corrections; Social service
depts.
Social and Rehabilitative Services
Therapeutic Approach The facility uses the mileau approach to
therapy; specifically using peer culture group process.
Therapeutic Services Offered Individual therapy; Group therapy;
Family therapy; Adjunctive therapy; Independent living skills
program; Recreation activities; Substance abuse treatment.
Professionals on Staff Psychiatrists; Psychologists; Social workers;
Adjunctive therapists; Child care staff.
Educational and Vocational Services
Type(s) of Educational Programs Offered Off campus.
Degrees Offered GED.

SALINAS

NATIVIDAD RANCH
700 Old Stage Rd, Salinas, CA 93906 (408) 449-1013 *Contact
Person(s):* Buzz Gray, Prog Dir
Setting and Background Information The ranch was established in
1984. It is located on 100 acres and has a dormitory, a school, a
gym, and offices.
Referral Information For referrals, contact a social worker at the
facility and forward historical information.
Type of Facility
Funding Sources Private.
Average Length of Stay Long term.
Types of Admissions Accepted Group home placement; Wards of the
state.
Sources of Referral Depts of correction; Social service depts.
Client Profile
Age Range of Clients Served Residential program: 12-18.
Characteristics Exhibited by Children Emotional handicaps; Learning
disabilities.
IQ Range of Clients 70+.
Tuition and Fees
Room and Board Long term: $2017/mo (includes school tuition).
Placements Primarily Funded By Depts of corrections; Social service
depts.

NATIVIDAD RANCH (continued)

Social and Rehabilitative Services
Therapeutic Approach The facility uses reality therapy in a milieu setting.
Therapeutic Services Offered Individual therapy; Group therapy; Family therapy; Recreation activities; Substance abuse treatment.
Professionals on Staff Psychologists; Social workers; Adjunctive therapists; Child care staff.
Educational and Vocational Services
Type(s) of Educational Programs Offered On campus; Off campus (Public and vocational schools).
Profile of On Campus School Program Number of teachers 3; *Number of classrooms* 3; *Student to teacher ratio* 8:1; *Length of school day* 4 hrs; Special curriculum electives offered (Wood shop).
Degrees Offered 12th grade diploma; GED.

SAN ANSELMO

SUNNY HILLS CHILDREN'S SERVICES
300 Sunny Hills Dr, San Anselmo, CA 94960-1995 (415) 457-3200 *Contact Person(s):* Robert R McCallie, Exec Dir
Setting and Background Information The facility was established in 1895 as a Presbyterian orphanage. It is located on 11 acres and has an administration building, four cottages, a school, and a therapeutic activities center.
Referral Information For referral information, contact the intake worker. A pre-placement visit will be arranged.
Type of Facility
Funding Sources Private; State; Federal; County.
Average Length of Stay Long term.
Types of Admissions Accepted Residential treatment.
Sources of Referral Psychiatrists; Private sources; Depts of correction; Social service depts.
Client Profile
Age Range of Clients Served Residential program: 12-18.
Characteristics Exhibited by Children Emotional handicaps; Learning disabilities; Mental disabilities.
IQ Range of Clients 70+.
Tuition and Fees
Room and Board Long term: $4,714/mo.
Placements Primarily Funded By Depts of corrections; Social service depts.
Social and Rehabilitative Services
Therapeutic Approach The facility offers a therapeutic milieu.
Therapeutic Services Offered Individual therapy; Group therapy; Family therapy; Art therapy; Recreation activities; Aftercare program with follow up.
Professionals on Staff Psychiatrists; Social workers; Adjunctive therapists; Child care staff; Nurses; Art therapists; MD.
Educational and Vocational Services
Type(s) of Educational Programs Offered On campus; Off campus; Summer campus.
Profile of On Campus School Program Number of teachers 3; *Number of classrooms* 3; *Student to teacher ratio* 6:1; *Credentials of teachers* Spec Ed; *Grades taught* Individualized.
Degrees Offered 8th grade diploma; 12th grade diploma.

SAN BERNARDINO

NEW HOPE TREATMENT CENTERS
2020 N Waterman, Ste F, San Bernardino, CA 92404
(714) 882-7978 *Contact Person(s):* James B Pace PhD, Exec Dir
Setting and Background Information The agency was privately established in 1987. There are 5 residential group homes with the capacity for 6 boys in each one.
Referral Information Referrals are usually made by social workers and probation officers. Contact the facility for referral information.
Type of Facility
Funding Sources County.
Average Length of Stay Long term.
Types of Admissions Accepted Group home placement.
Sources of Referral Private sources; Depts of correction; Social service depts; Private.

Client Profile
Age Range of Clients Served Residential program: 6-18.
Characteristics Exhibited by Children Emotional handicaps; Learning disabilities; Neurological impairments; Mental disabilities.
Tuition and Fees
Room and Board Long term: $1,504/mo.
Placements Primarily Funded By Depts of corrections; Social service depts.
Social and Rehabilitative Services
Therapeutic Approach The facility has an eclectic approach to therapy.
Therapeutic Services Offered Individual therapy; Group therapy; Family therapy; Adjunctive therapy; Independent living skills program; Recreation activities; Substance abuse treatment; Aftercare program with follow up.
Professionals on Staff Psychiatrists; Psychologists; Social workers; Adjunctive therapists; Child care staff.

STEWARTS HOME FOR BOYS
PO Box 7425, San Bernardino, CA 92410 (714) 885-4239 *Contact Person(s):* Clyde A Stewart, Exec Dir
Setting and Background Information The facility was established in 1983. There are 3 residential homes.
Referral Information Contact the facility for referral information.
Type of Facility
Funding Sources State.
Average Length of Stay Long term.
Types of Admissions Accepted Group home placement.
Sources of Referral Depts of correction; Social service depts.
Client Profile
Age Range of Clients Served Residential program: 12-18.
Characteristics Exhibited by Children Substance abuse.
Social and Rehabilitative Services
Therapeutic Approach The primary therapeutic approach is based on social psychological theory.
Therapeutic Services Offered Individual therapy; Group therapy; Substance treatment.
Professionals on Staff Psychiatrists; Social workers; Child care staff.
Educational and Vocational Services
Type(s) of Educational Programs Offered Off campus.
Vocational Education Programs/Degrees Offered Welding and electronics school.
Degrees Offered GED.

SAN DIEGO

THE BRIDGE
3151 Redwood St, San Diego, CA 92104 (619) 280-6150 *Contact Person(s):* Marty Bogan, Prog Dir
Setting and Background Information The facility was established for adolescent runaways in 1970 by the community. The facility consists of a residential house, offices and counseling rooms.
Referral Information Referral is based on the need of the client and on resources in the community. Referrals are made by shelters, community agencies, and state and county agencies.
Type of Facility
Funding Sources Private; State; Federal.
Average Length of Stay Short and long term.
Types of Admissions Accepted Residential treatment; Wards of the state; Emergency shelter.
Sources of Referral Local depts of education; Psychiatrists; Private sources; Depts of correction; Social service depts.
Client Profile
Age Range of Clients Served Residential program: 12-18.
Characteristics Exhibited by Children Emotional handicaps; Learning disabilities.
Tuition and Fees
Room and Board Short term: Sliding scale; Long term: Sliding scale.
Placements Primarily Funded By Private sources; Depts of corrections; Social service depts.
Social and Rehabilitative Services
Therapeutic Approach The facility uses the Adlerian approach to therapy, including individual, group and family counseling in a milieu setting.
Therapeutic Services Offered Individual therapy; Group therapy; Family therapy; Independent living skills program; Recreation activities; Aftercare program with follow up.

THE BRIDGE *(continued)*

Professionals on Staff Psychologists; Child care staff; Recreation therapist.
Educational and Vocational Services
Type(s) of Educational Programs Offered On campus.
Profile of On Campus School Program The on campus school program has two teachers, with 8 children. The teachers come twice a week for 2 hours.
Degrees Offered GED.

HARAMBEE HOUSE
5319 Hilltop Dr, San Diego, CA 92114 (714) 263-2161
Setting and Background Information The facility is licensed by the state Dept of Health for adolescent males.
Referral Information Contact the facility for referral information.
Type of Facility
Funding Sources Private; State; Federal.
Average Length of Stay Long term.
Types of Admissions Accepted Residential treatment.
Sources of Referral Depts of correction.
Client Profile
Age Range of Clients Served Residential program: 13-17.
Characteristics Exhibited by Children Emotional handicaps; Learning disabilities; Youth considered to be incorrigible.
Tuition and Fees
Placements Primarily Funded By Local depts of education; State depts of mental health; Depts of corrections.
Educational and Vocational Services
Type(s) of Educational Programs Offered On campus; Off campus.
Profile of On Campus School Program The education program is coordinated and staffed by the San Diego City Unified School District.
Vocational Education Programs/Degrees Offered Part-time youth employment leading to community job placement.

OZ, SAN DIEGO
3304 Idlewild Way, San Diego, CA 92117 (619) 270-8213 *Contact Person(s):* Stephen J Carmichael, Dir
Setting and Background Information The facility was established in 1970 as a runaway shelter.
Referral Information Contact the facility for referral information.
Type of Facility
Funding Sources Private; Federal; County.
Average Length of Stay Short term.
Types of Admissions Accepted Residential treatment; Group home placement; Wards of the state.
Sources of Referral State depts of education; Local depts of education; State depts of mental health; Psychiatrists; Private sources; Depts of correction; Social service depts; Anyone may make a referral.
Client Profile
Age Range of Clients Served Residential program: 12-18.
Characteristics Exhibited by Children Emotional handicaps.
IQ Range of Clients 70+.
Tuition and Fees
Room and Board Short term: Sliding scale.
Placements Primarily Funded By County general fund.
Social and Rehabilitative Services
Therapeutic Services Offered Individual therapy; Group therapy; Family therapy; Adjunctive therapy; Recreation activities; Substance abuse treatment.
Professionals on Staff Social workers; Adjunctive therapists; Child care staff.
Educational and Vocational Services
Type(s) of Educational Programs Offered On campus.
Profile of On Campus School Program Number of teachers 1; Number of classrooms 1; Student to teacher ratio 8:1; Grades taught 8-12.
Degrees Offered GED.

SAN DIEGO CENTER FOR CHILDREN
3002 Armstrong St, San Diego, CA 92111 (619) 277-9550 *Contact Person(s):* Gerald D Azslaw ACSW, Exec Dir
Setting and Background Information The facility was established in 1887. It is located on 9 acres.
Referral Information Referrals must be made by an MD under a DSM III diagnosis.

Type of Facility
Funding Sources Private; State; Federal.
Average Length of Stay Long term.
Types of Admissions Accepted Day treatment; Residential treatment; Group home placement.
Sources of Referral Local depts of education; State depts of mental health; Psychiatrists; Private sources; Social service depts.
Client Profile
Age Range of Clients Served Day programs: 6-12; Residential program: 6-12.
Characteristics Exhibited by Children Emotional handicaps.
IQ Range of Clients 70+.
Tuition and Fees
Room and Board Long term: $190/diem.
Placements Primarily Funded By State depts of mental health; Insurance; Private sources; Social service depts.
Social and Rehabilitative Services
Therapeutic Approach The facility has an eclectic approach to therapy.
Therapeutic Services Offered Individual therapy; Group therapy; Family therapy; Art therapy; Recreation activities.
Professionals on Staff Psychiatrists; Psychologists; Social workers; Child care staff.
Educational and Vocational Services
Type(s) of Educational Programs Offered On campus (SED).
Profile of On Campus School Program Number of teachers 4; Number of classrooms 4; Student to teacher ratio 8:1; Credentials of teachers SED; Grades taught 1-6.

SAN DIEGO YOUTH INVOLVEMENT PROGRAM
7733 Palm St, San Diego, CA 92045 (619) 463-7800 *Contact Person(s):* Lydia Williams
Setting and Background Information The program was established in 1973 in conjunction with the city. There are three program facilities and 2 administration offices.
Referral Information Referrals are made to the facility by the Dept of Social Services, Juvenile Justice, and the Probation Dept. Walk-ins are also accepted if space allows and client meets entrance criteria.
Type of Facility
Funding Sources Private; State; Federal.
Average Length of Stay Short and long term.
Types of Admissions Accepted Day treatment; Residential treatment.
Sources of Referral State depts of education; Local depts of education; State depts of mental health; Psychiatrists; Private sources; Depts of correction; Social service depts.
Client Profile
Age Range of Clients Served Day programs: 12-17; Residential program: 18-21+.
Characteristics Exhibited by Children Emotional handicaps; Learning disabilities.
Social and Rehabilitative Services
Therapeutic Services Offered Individual therapy; Group therapy; Family therapy; Independent living skills program; Substance abuse treatment; Aftercare program with follow up.
Professionals on Staff Psychiatrists; Psychologists; Social workers.

SAN FRANCISCO

BURT CHILDREN'S CENTER
940 Grove St, San Francisco, CA 94117 (415) 922-7700 *Contact Person(s):* Danielle Crafton, Social Svcs Dir
Setting and Background Information The facility was established in 1969 as a private, non-profit psychiatric treatment center for autistic children.
Referral Information Contact the facility and forward the necessary information. A pre-placement visit will be arranged.
Type of Facility
Funding Sources Private; State; Federal.
Average Length of Stay 2-5 yrs.
Types of Admissions Accepted Day treatment; Residential treatment; Group home placement; Wards of the state.
Sources of Referral Local depts of education; Private sources; Social service depts.
Client Profile
Age Range of Clients Served Day programs: Birth-15; Residential program: Birth-15.
Characteristics Exhibited by Children Emotional handicaps; Autism.

BURT CHILDREN'S CENTER *(continued)*

Tuition and Fees
Room and Board Long term: $3,589/mo.
Tuition $98.72/diem.
Placements Primarily Funded By Local depts of education; Social service depts.
Social and Rehabilitative Services
Therapeutic Approach The facility has a psychodynamic approach to therapy.
Therapeutic Services Offered Individual therapy; Group therapy; Family therapy; Adjunctive therapy; Art therapy; Physical therapy; Independent living skills program; Recreation activities.
Professionals on Staff Psychiatrists; Psychologists; Social workers; Adjunctive therapists; Child care staff; Art therapists.
Educational and Vocational Services
Type(s) of Educational Programs Offered On campus.
Profile of On Campus School Program Number of teachers 4; *Number of classrooms* 4; *Student to teacher ratio* 2:1; *Credentials of teachers* Spec Ed; *Grades taught* Ungraded.
Vocational Education Programs/Degrees Offered Pre-vocational.

EDGEWOOD CHILDREN'S CENTER

1801 Vicente St, San Francisco, CA 94116 (415) 681-3211 *Contact Person(s):* Morris Kilgore, Exec Dir
Setting and Background Information The facility was originally established in 1851 as an orphanage.
Referral Information Contact the Director of Admissions for referral information.
Type of Facility
Funding Sources Private.
Average Length of Stay 18-20 mos.
Types of Admissions Accepted Day treatment; Residential treatment; Wards of the state.
Sources of Referral Local depts of education; Psychiatrists; Private sources; Depts of correction; Social service depts; Local mental health dept.
Client Profile
Age Range of Clients Served Day programs: 6-12; Residential program: 6-12.
Characteristics Exhibited by Children Emotional handicaps; Learning disabilities; Speech/Language disorders; Mental disabilities.
IQ Range of Clients 70+.
Tuition and Fees
Room and Board Long term: $3,602/mo (regular residential); $5,975/mo (intensive residential); $48/diem (day treatment).
Tuition $102/diem (day treatment); $91/diem (residential).
Placements Primarily Funded By Local depts of education; Social service depts; Local mental health.
Social and Rehabilitative Services
Therapeutic Approach The facility has a psychodynamic approach to therapy.
Therapeutic Services Offered Individual therapy; Group therapy; Family therapy; Adjunctive therapy; Art therapy; Recreation activities; Aftercare program with follow up.
Professionals on Staff Psychiatrists; Psychologists; Social workers; Adjunctive therapists; Child care staff; Nurses; Art therapists.
Educational and Vocational Services
Type(s) of Educational Programs Offered On campus; Summer campus.
Profile of On Campus School Program Number of teachers 7; *Number of classrooms* 7; *Student to teacher ratio* 8:1; *Credentials of teachers* Spec Ed; *Grades taught* K-8.

FLORENCE CRITTENTON SERVICES

840 Broderick St, San Francisco, CA 94115 (415) 567-2357 *Contact Person(s):* Sarah N Ngethe Maina, Exec Dir
Setting and Background Information The agency was privately established in 1889 as a shelter for women. Currently, the urban campus has 2 adjacent buildings.
Referral Information Contact intake worker to arrange appointment.
Type of Facility
Funding Sources Private; State; County.
Average Length of Stay Short and long term.
Types of Admissions Accepted Residential treatment; Group home placement; Wards of the state.
Sources of Referral Private sources; Social service depts; Probation depts.

Client Profile
Age Range of Clients Served Day programs: Birth-5; Residential program: 12-21+.
Characteristics Exhibited by Children Emotional handicaps; Learning disabilities; Pregnancy; Single parenting.
IQ Range of Clients 65+.
Tuition and Fees
Room and Board Long term: $1,639/mo (adolescents; adults); $303/mo (infants).
Placements Primarily Funded By Insurance; Social service depts; Probation dept.
Social and Rehabilitative Services
Therapeutic Approach The facility has a psychodynamic approach to therapy.
Therapeutic Services Offered Individual therapy; Group therapy; Family therapy; Independent living skills program; Recreation activities; Parenting classes; Health classes.
Professionals on Staff Psychiatrists; Psychologists; Social workers; Child care staff; Nurses; Recreation worker.
Educational and Vocational Services
Type(s) of Educational Programs Offered On campus; Off campus.
Profile of On Campus School Program Number of teachers 2; *Number of classrooms* 1; Remedial courses offered.
Vocational Education Programs/Degrees Offered Educational/vocational expert helps girls explore vocational options.

HUCKLEBERRY HOUSE II

4127 Kirkham, San Francisco, CA 94122 (415) 731-3670 *Contact Person(s):* Betty Bleicher, Prog Dir
Setting and Background Information The facility was established in 1985 as a foster home. Currently, it is a licensed group home in a large house.
Referral Information Contact the facility for referral information.
Type of Facility
Funding Sources State; United Way.
Average Length of Stay 6 mos.
Types of Admissions Accepted Group home placement; Wards of the state.
Sources of Referral State depts of mental health; Depts of correction; Social service depts.
Client Profile
Age Range of Clients Served Residential program: 12-18.
Characteristics Exhibited by Children Emotional handicaps; Learning disabilities; Behavior disorders.
Tuition and Fees
Room and Board Long term: $2,666/mo.
Placements Primarily Funded By Depts of corrections; Social service depts.
Social and Rehabilitative Services
Therapeutic Approach The facility uses behavior modification.
Therapeutic Services Offered Individual therapy; Group therapy; Family therapy; Recreation activities; Aftercare program with follow up.
Professionals on Staff Psychologists; Social workers; Child care staff.
Educational and Vocational Services
Type(s) of Educational Programs Offered On campus; Summer campus.
Profile of On Campus School Program Number of teachers 1; *Number of classrooms* 1; *Student to teacher ratio* 6:1; *Credentials of teachers* Spec Ed.

SAN JOSE

PALOMARES GROUP HOME

PO Box 8482, San Jose, CA 95155 (408) 265-9092 *Contact Person(s):* Ted L Kitch, Exec Dir
Setting and Background Information The facility was established in 1971 as a non-profit corporation. The homes are located in residential areas of San Jose. Each home is licensed for 6 severely emotionally disturbed girls by the state Dept of Social Services.
Referral Information Referrals are made by forwarding court reports, hospitilization summaries, psychiatric evaluations, prior placement summaries, and school records. If appropriate, an interview and pre-placement visit will be scheduled. A decision will be made within 24 hours.

PALOMARES GROUP HOME *(continued)*

Type of Facility
Funding Sources Private.
Average Length of Stay Long term.
Types of Admissions Accepted Residential treatment; Group home placement; Wards of the state.
Sources of Referral State depts of mental health; Psychiatrists; Social service depts; Probation.
Client Profile
Age Range of Clients Served Residential programs: 12-18.
Characteristics Exhibited by Children Emotional handicaps; Learning disabilities.
IQ Range of Clients 70+.
Tuition and Fees
Room and Board Long term: $100/diem.
Placements Primarily Funded By State depts of mental health; Social service depts; AFDC; Probation.
Social and Rehabilitative Services
Therapeutic Approach The facility has a highly structured program and uses behavior modification.
Therapeutic Services Offered Individual therapy; Group therapy; Family therapy; Independent living skills program; Recreation activities.
Professionals on Staff Psychiatrists; Psychologists; Social workers; Child care staff; Recreation therapist.
Educational and Vocational Services
Type(s) of Educational Programs Offered On campus; Off campus.
Profile of On Campus School Program Student to teacher ratio 5:1.

ST ANDREW'S RESIDENCE FOR BOYS

2845 Moorpark Rd, Ste 103, San Jose, CA 95128 (408) 246-4364
Contact Person(s): Stewart Samuels, Admin Dir
Setting and Background Information The facility was established in 1976 by St. Andrew's Episcopal Church. There are four 6-bed facilities.
Referral Information Contact the facility and submit the necessary referral information, including a family history, immunization records, authorization for medical care, and school records.
Type of Facility
Funding Sources State; Federal; Foundation grants; Solicited donations.
Average Length of Stay Long term.
Types of Admissions Accepted Residential treatment; Group home placement; Wards of the state.
Sources of Referral Local depts of education; Social service depts; Probation depts.
Client Profile
Age Range of Clients Served Residential programs: 12-18.
Tuition and Fees
Room and Board Long term: $1,604/mo.
Social and Rehabilitative Services
Therapeutic Approach The facility has a behavioral approach to therapy.
Therapeutic Services Offered Individual therapy; Group therapy; Family therapy; Independent living skills program; Recreation activities; Substance abuse treatment.
Professionals on Staff Psychiatrists; Social workers; Child care staff.
Educational and Vocational Services
Type(s) of Educational Programs Offered Off campus.

TERRA RESIDENTIAL CENTER

PO Box 53296, San Jose, CA 95153 (408) 866-8090 *Contact Person(s):* Cindy Greer, Prog Dir
Setting and Background Information The facility was established in 1984. It is a community-based residential group home.
Referral Information Contact the facility for referral information. A written background information packet on the child is necessary. An interview will then be arranged.
Type of Facility
Funding Sources Private; State.
Average Length of Stay 9-12 mos.
Types of Admissions Accepted Residential treatment; Group home placement; Wards of the state.
Sources of Referral State depts of mental health; Depts of correction; Social service depts.

Client Profile
Age Range of Clients Served Residential program: 12-18.
Characteristics Exhibited by Children Sexual and/or physical abuse.
Tuition and Fees
Placements Primarily Funded By Social service depts; AFDC.
Social and Rehabilitative Services
Therapeutic Services Offered Individual therapy; Group therapy; Family therapy; Aftercare program with follow up.
Professionals on Staff Psychiatrists; Psychologists; Social workers; Child care staff.
Educational and Vocational Services
Type(s) of Educational Programs Offered Off campus (Local schools).

WE CARE

14926 Union Ave, San Jose, CA 95124 (408) 371-5614 *Contact Person(s):* Jeanne Haight, Admin
Referral Information Contact the facility for referral information.
Type of Facility
Funding Sources Private; State.
Average Length of Stay Short and long term.
Types of Admissions Accepted Residential treatment; Wards of the state.
Sources of Referral State depts of mental health; Social service depts; Regional center.
Client Profile
Age Range of Clients Served Residential program: Birth-18.
Characteristics Exhibited by Children Emotional handicaps; Hearing impairments/deafness; Vision impairments/blindness; Speech/Language disorders; Physical handicaps; Mental disabilities.
Tuition and Fees
Room and Board Short term: $49.19/diem; Long term: $1,033/mo.
Placements Primarily Funded By Social service depts; Regional center.
Social and Rehabilitative Services
Therapeutic Services Offered Physical therapy; Independent living skills program; Recreation activities; Behavior management.
Professionals on Staff Psychologists; Social workers; Child care staff; Nurses.

SAN LORENZO

ULREY HOMES, INC

15919 Hesperian Blvd, San Lorenzo, CA 94580 (415) 276-1881
Contact Person(s): Robert F Jones ACSW, Dir
Setting and Background Information This facility is a group home social services agency which was founded in 1970. There are six group home facilities located in residential communities of Hayward and San Leandro.
Referral Information For referrals, contact the placement supervisor and forward a psychological evaluation, court report and behavior description.
Type of Facility
Funding Sources AFDC-FC/BHI.
Average Length of Stay Short and long term.
Types of Admissions Accepted Group home placement; Wards of the state.
Sources of Referral Depts of correction; Social service depts.
Client Profile
Age Range of Clients Served Residential program: 12-18.
Characteristics Exhibited by Children Emotional handicaps; Mental disabilities; Abused and neglected.
IQ Range of Clients 80+.
Tuition and Fees
Room and Board Short term: $74.86/diem; Long term: $1,643/mo.
Placements Primarily Funded By Depts of corrections; Social service depts.
Social and Rehabilitative Services
Therapeutic Approach The agency has a humanistic approach to therapy and uses behavior modification.
Therapeutic Services Offered Individual therapy; Group therapy; Independent living skills program.
Professionals on Staff Social workers; Child care staff; Counselors.

SAN RAFAEL

BRAUN PROGRAMS INC—BRAUN PLACE

4 Beryl Lane, San Rafael, CA 94901 (415) 453-5451 *Contact Person(s):* Jeff Felix, Exec Dir

Setting and Background Information The facility was established by a task force in 1979. There is a large residential group home and a day treatment facility.

Referral Information All referrals are made through Marin County Community Mental Health. Clients must be residents of Marin County.

Type of Facility

Funding Sources State; Donations; Grants.

Average Length of Stay Long term.

Types of Admissions Accepted Day treatment; Residential treatment; Wards of the state.

Sources of Referral Local depts of education; Psychiatrists; Social service depts; Community mental health.

Client Profile

Age Range of Clients Served Day programs: 12-18; Residential program: 12-18.

Characteristics Exhibited by Children Emotional handicaps; Learning disabilities; Mental disabilities.

Tuition and Fees

Room and Board Long term: $2,002/mo.

Tuition $58/diem.

Placements Primarily Funded By AFDC and Short-Doyle/medical.

Social and Rehabilitative Services

Therapeutic Approach The facility has a psychodynamic approach to therapy and offers a therapeutic milieu.

Therapeutic Services Offered Individual therapy; Group therapy; Family therapy; Adjunctive therapy; Art therapy; Independent living skills program; Recreation activities.

Professionals on Staff Psychiatrists; Psychologists; Social workers; Adjunctive therapists; Child care staff; Nurses; Art therapists; Aikido instruction.

Educational and Vocational Services

Type(s) of Educational Programs Offered On campus; Off campus.

Profile of On Campus School Program Number of teachers 2; *Number of classrooms* 3; *Student to teacher ratio* 7:1; *Credentials of teachers* Spec Ed; *Length of school day* 9-2; *Grades taught* 8-12; Special curriculum electives offered (Spec Ed); Remedial courses offered (Individual curriculum).

Degrees Offered 12th grade diploma; GED.

CHILDREN'S GARDEN

7 Mount Lassen Dr, Ste B256, San Rafael, CA 94903 (415) 472-7620 *Contact Person(s):* Regina Kahn Goodfield, Exec Dir

Setting and Background Information The facility was privately established in 1967 and has group homes, a school and administrative offices on separate sites.

Referral Information For referral, contact the facility and forward the required information.

Type of Facility

Funding Sources Private; State; Federal.

Average Length of Stay Short and long term.

Types of Admissions Accepted Residential treatment; Group home placement; Wards of the state; Evaluation.

Sources of Referral State depts of education; Local depts of education; State depts of mental health; Psychiatrists; Private sources; Social service depts.

Client Profile

Age Range of Clients Served Residential program: Birth-12.

Characteristics Exhibited by Children Emotional handicaps; Learning disabilities.

Tuition and Fees

Placements Primarily Funded By Social service depts.

Social and Rehabilitative Services

Therapeutic Approach The facility has a basic psychodynamic approach to therapy.

Therapeutic Services Offered Individual therapy; Group therapy; Family therapy; Adjunctive therapy; Art therapy; Aftercare program with follow up.

Professionals on Staff Psychiatrists; Psychologists; Social workers; Child care staff; Art therapists.

Educational and Vocational Services

Type(s) of Educational Programs Offered On campus.

Profile of On Campus School Program Number of teachers 6; *Number of classrooms* 3; *Student to teacher ratio* 4:1; *Credentials of teachers* Spec Ed; *Grades taught* K-6; Remedial courses offered.

SANTA ANA

OLIVE CREST TREATMENT CENTERS

1125 E 17th St, Santa Ana, CA 92701 (714) 547-0361 *Contact Person(s):* Dr Don Verluer, Exec Dir

Setting and Background Information Olive Crest Treatment Centers was established in 1973 to provide group home care to abused and displaced children. There are 24 community based homes/centers in Riverside, San Bernardino and Orange County.

Referral Information Referrals to the facility are court designated, having been referred by county social services or by probation for admittance.

Type of Facility

Funding Sources Private; State.

Average Length of Stay Short and long term.

Types of Admissions Accepted Group home placement.

Sources of Referral State depts of mental health; Depts of correction; Social service depts.

Client Profile

Age Range of Clients Served Residential program: 2-18.

Characteristics Exhibited by Children Emotional handicaps; Learning disabilities; Abused and neglected.

IQ Range of Clients 80-110.

Tuition and Fees

Room and Board Short term: $3,155; Long term: $3,158.

Placements Primarily Funded By Depts of corrections; Social service depts.

Social and Rehabilitative Services

Therapeutic Approach The facility has an eclectic approach to therapy.

Therapeutic Services Offered Individual therapy; Group therapy; Family therapy; Art therapy; Independent living skills program; Recreation activities; Substance abuse treatment.

Professionals on Staff Psychiatrists; Psychologists; Social workers; Child care staff; Art therapists.

Educational and Vocational Services

Type(s) of Educational Programs Offered On campus; Off campus.

Profile of On Campus School Program Number of teachers 2; *Number of classrooms* 1; *Student to teacher ratio* 3:1; *Credentials of teachers* State certified; *Length of school day* 5 hrs; *Grades taught* 8-12; Remedial courses offered.

SANTA BARBARA

THE DEVEREUX FOUNDATION

PO Box 1079, Santa Barbara, CA 93102 (805) 968-2525 *Contact Person(s):* David Weisman, Admis Dir

Setting and Background Information The facility was established in 1945 as a private, non-profit residential facility. It is located on 33 acres with 13 cottages, a pool & gym, auditorium and vocational center.

Referral Information Referrals are made by social service agencies, depts of education, psychiatrists and parents. Referrals are evaluated for admission by the Admissions Dept which includes an on-site multi-disciplinary evaluation.

Type of Facility

Funding Sources Private; State; Federal.

Average Length of Stay Long term.

Types of Admissions Accepted Day treatment; Residential treatment; Group home placement; Wards of the state.

Sources of Referral State depts of education; Local depts of education; State depts of mental health; Psychiatrists; Private sources; Social service depts.

Client Profile

Age Range of Clients Served Day programs: 18-55+; Residential program: 12-55+.

Characteristics Exhibited by Children Emotional handicaps; Learning disabilities; Speech/Language disorders; Neurological impairments; Mental disabilities.

IQ Range of Clients 40-100.

THE DEVEREUX FOUNDATION (*continued*)

Tuition and Fees
Placements Primarily Funded By State depts of education; Local depts of education; State depts of mental health; Insurance; Private sources; Social service depts.
Social and Rehabilitative Services
Therapeutic Approach The basic approach used is behavior modification in a therapeutic milieu.
Therapeutic Services Offered Individual therapy; Group therapy; Adjunctive therapy; Art therapy; Independent living skills program; Recreation activities.
Professionals on Staff Psychiatrists; Psychologists; Adjunctive therapists; Child care staff; Nurses; Art therapists.
Educational and Vocational Services
Type(s) of Educational Programs Offered On campus (Certified year-round Spec Ed).
Profile of On Campus School Program Number of teachers 16; *Number of classrooms* 16; *Student to teacher ratio* 8:1; *Grades taught* K-12; Special curriculum electives offered (Human sexuality, Social awareness); Remedial courses offered.
Vocational Education Programs/Degrees Offered CARF approved vocational training; Activity program; Sheltered workshop.
Degrees Offered 12th grade diploma; GED.

KLEIN BOTTLE SOCIAL ADVOCATES FOR YOUTH

301 W Figueroa St, Santa Barbara, CA 93105 (805) 963-8775
Contact Person(s): JoAnn Ferns, Prog Coord
Setting and Background Information The facility was privately established in 1973 with funds from a county drug abuse prevention program. It is a crisis shelter located in a residential building.
Referral Information Contact the facility for referral information.
Type of Facility
Funding Sources Private; State; Federal; County; City; United Way.
Average Length of Stay Short term.
Types of Admissions Accepted Wards of the state; Emergency shelter.
Sources of Referral Local depts of education; Depts of correction; Social service depts.
Client Profile
Age Range of Clients Served Residential program: 12-18.
Characteristics Exhibited by Children Emotional handicaps; Behavior disorders.
IQ Range of Clients 80-120.
Tuition and Fees
Room and Board Short term: $51/diem.
Placements Primarily Funded By Depts of corrections; Social service depts.
Social and Rehabilitative Services
Therapeutic Approach The facility uses behavior modification as a part of crisis intervention.
Therapeutic Services Offered Individual therapy; Group therapy; Family therapy; Substance abuse treatment; Aftercare program with follow up.
Professionals on Staff Adjunctive therapists; Child care staff.
Educational and Vocational Services
Type(s) of Educational Programs Offered Off campus.

SANTA MARIA

KLEIN BOTTLE SOCIAL ADVOCATES FOR YOUTH

900 S Broadway, Santa Maria, CA 93454 (805) 925-1215 *Contact Person(s):* Penny Anderson, Prog Dir
Setting and Background Information The facility was established in 1977 as a runaway shelter in a 2-story home.
Referral Information Referrals to the facility are made through the police, Dept of Child Protective Services, families or individuals.
Type of Facility
Funding Sources Private; State; Federal; Grants; Donations.
Average Length of Stay Short term.
Types of Admissions Accepted Day treatment; Residential treatment; Wards of the state; Emergency shelter.
Sources of Referral State depts of education; Local depts of education; Social service depts; Police; Child Protective Svcs; Parents.
Client Profile
Age Range of Clients Served Day programs: 10-18; Residential program: 10-18.

Social and Rehabilitative Services
Therapeutic Approach The basic therapeutic approach of the facility is family systems combined with behavior modification.
Therapeutic Services Offered Individual therapy; Group therapy; Family therapy; Substance abuse treatment; Aftercare program with follow up.
Professionals on Staff Adjunctive therapists; Child care staff.

SANTA ROSA

CASA DE LUZ

2470 Laguna Rd, Santa Rosa, CA 95401 (707) 546-6809 *Contact Person(s):* Joe Ann Locke, Admin
Setting and Background Information The facility was privately established in 1973. It is a residential group home.
Referral Information Contact the facility for referral information.
Type of Facility
Funding Sources Private; State; Federal; County.
Average Length of Stay Long term.
Types of Admissions Accepted Residential treatment; Group home placement; Wards of the state.
Sources of Referral Psychiatrists; Private sources; Depts of correction; Social service depts.
Client Profile
Age Range of Clients Served Residential program: 12-18.
Characteristics Exhibited by Children Emotional handicaps; Learning disabilities; Mental disabilities.
IQ Range of Clients 70+.
Tuition and Fees
Room and Board Long term: $1,900/mo.
Placements Primarily Funded By Depts of corrections; Social service depts.
Social and Rehabilitative Services
Therapeutic Services Offered Individual therapy; Group therapy; Family therapy; Independent living skills program; Recreation activities; Substance abuse treatment.
Professionals on Staff Psychiatrists; Psychologists; Social workers; Child care staff.
Educational and Vocational Services
Type(s) of Educational Programs Offered Off campus (High school).

VICTOR RESIDENTIAL CENTER—WILLOW CREEK RESIDENTIAL CENTER

2000 Crane Canyon, Santa Rosa, CA 95404 (707) 585-9811 *Contact Person(s):* Dorinda Ennis, Exec Dir
Setting and Background Information This facility was established in 1985 as an alternative to the state mental hospital for SED adolescents. There are three residential group homes.
Referral Information All referrals are processed through the mental health depts of 5 counties. Contact the facility for more information.
Type of Facility
Funding Sources State; Federal; County.
Average Length of Stay Long term.
Types of Admissions Accepted Residential treatment; Group home placement.
Sources of Referral State depts of mental health.
Client Profile
Age Range of Clients Served Residential program: 12-18.
Characteristics Exhibited by Children Emotional handicaps; Learning disabilities.
IQ Range of Clients 70-135.
Tuition and Fees
Room and Board Long term: $3,308/mo.
Placements Primarily Funded By State depts of mental health; Social service depts.
Social and Rehabilitative Services
Therapeutic Services Offered Individual therapy; Group therapy; Family therapy; Art therapy; Recreation activities.
Professionals on Staff Psychiatrists; Psychologists; Social workers; Child care staff.
Educational and Vocational Services
Type(s) of Educational Programs Offered Off campus (Private school); Summer campus.

WILLOW CREEK RESIDENTIAL CENTER

2000 Crane Canyon Rd, Santa Rosa, CA 95404 (707) 585-9811
Contact Person(s): Dorinda Ennis, Dir
Setting and Background Information The facility was established in
1985 by a mental health contract with three counties. There are
three group homes.
Referral Information Contact the facility for referral information.
Type of Facility
Funding Sources State; Federal; County.
Average Length of Stay 12-18 mos.
Types of Admissions Accepted Residential treatment.
Sources of Referral State depts of mental health.
Client Profile
Age Range of Clients Served Residential program: 12-18.

SEBASTOPOL

FULL CIRCLE SONOMA

PO Box 30, Sebastopol, CA 95472 (707) 823-9549 *Contact Person(s):*
Gary D Matlick MS, Dir
Setting and Background Information The facility was established in
1968 as a private school. The 40-acre campus has 2 residences, a
school, gym, and a playing field. There is a group home in the
city.
Referral Information Contact the intake coordinator of the facility
for referral information.
Type of Facility
Funding Sources County.
Average Length of Stay Long term.
Types of Admissions Accepted Day treatment; Residential treatment;
Group home placement; Wards of the state.
Sources of Referral State depts of education; Local depts of educa-
tion; Psychiatrists; Private sources; Social service depts.
Client Profile
Age Range of Clients Served Day programs: 6-15; Residential pro-
gram: 6-18.
Characteristics Exhibited by Children Emotional handicaps; Learning
disabilities; Mental disabilities.
Tuition and Fees
Room and Board Long term: $2,803/mo.
Tuition $65/diem.
Placements Primarily Funded By Local depts of education.
Social and Rehabilitative Services
Therapeutic Services Offered Individual therapy; Group therapy;
Family therapy; Substance abuse treatment; Aftercare program
with follow up.
Professionals on Staff Psychiatrists; Social workers; Adjunctive thera-
pists; Child care staff.
Educational and Vocational Services
Type(s) of Educational Programs Offered On campus; Off campus
(Public schools).
Profile of On Campus School Program Number of teachers 3; *Num-
ber of classrooms* 3; *Student to teacher ratio* 6:1; *Grades taught* 6-
12.

TRUE TO LIFE COUNSELING AND COMPANY

PO Box 207, Sebastopol, CA 95472 (707) 823-7300 *Contact
Person(s):* James Galsterer, Exec Dir
Setting and Background Information The facility was established in
1975 in response to child rehabilitation needs at the state level.
There are 4 coed group homes with 22 children, (12-18 years); a
foster family agency of 12 homes, (3-18 years); and a school.
Referral Information Contact the facility and forward the necessary
information. A pre-placement interview will be scheduled.
Type of Facility
Funding Sources Private; State; Federal.
Average Length of Stay Long term.
Types of Admissions Accepted Residential treatment; Group home
placement; Wards of the state.
Sources of Referral State depts of education; State depts of mental
health; Private sources; Depts of correction; Social service depts.
Client Profile
Age Range of Clients Served Residential program: 3-18.
Characteristics Exhibited by Children Emotional handicaps; Learning
disabilities.
Tuition and Fees
Room and Board Long term: $1,270-$2,078/mo.
Placements Primarily Funded By AFDC-FC.

Social and Rehabilitative Services
Therapeutic Approach The facility uses the family systems approach
to therapy.
Therapeutic Services Offered Individual therapy; Group therapy;
Family therapy; Independent living skills program; Recreation
activities; Substance abuse treatment; Aftercare program with
follow up.
Professionals on Staff Psychiatrists; Psychologists; Social workers;
Child care staff; Art therapists; Foster parents.
Educational and Vocational Services
Type(s) of Educational Programs Offered On campus (Spec Ed); Off
campus (Public school); Summer campus (Spec Ed).
Profile of On Campus School Program Number of teachers 3; *Num-
ber of classrooms* 2; *Student to teacher ratio* 4:1; *Credentials of
teachers* Spec Ed; *Grades taught* 6-12; Special curriculum electives
offered; Remedial courses offered (Reading, Math, Spelling).
Degrees Offered GED.

SOQUEL

MCDOWELL YOUTH HOMES, INC

2901 Park Ave, Soquel, CA 95073 (408) 688-8697 *Contact Person(s):*
Ann McDowell, Prog Dir
Setting and Background Information The facility was privately
established in 1980. There are 25 group homes in different
communities, each serving 6 residents. The facility accepts boys
only.
Referral Information Referral source should contact the facility and
forward the necessary information.
Type of Facility
Funding Sources State; Federal.
Average Length of Stay Short and long term.
Types of Admissions Accepted Residential treatment; Group home
placement; Wards of the state.
Sources of Referral State depts of education; State depts of mental
health; Psychiatrists; Private sources; Depts of correction; Social
service depts.
Client Profile
Age Range of Clients Served Residential program: 12-18.
Characteristics Exhibited by Children Emotional handicaps; Learning
disabilities; Hearing impairments/deafness; Vision impairments/
blindness; Speech/Language disorders; Neurological impairments;
Physical handicaps; Mental disabilities.
Tuition and Fees
Placements Primarily Funded By State depts of mental health; Social
service depts.
Social and Rehabilitative Services
Therapeutic Services Offered Individual therapy; Family therapy;
Independent living skills program; Substance abuse treatment.
Professionals on Staff Psychologists; Social workers.
Educational and Vocational Services
Type(s) of Educational Programs Offered On campus.
Profile of On Campus School Program Number of teachers 4; *Num-
ber of classrooms* 5; *Student to teacher ratio* 5:1; *Grades taught* 8-
12; Remedial courses offered.
Degrees Offered GED.

STOCKTON

CHILDREN'S HOME OF STOCKTON

430 N Pilgrim, Stockton, CA 95205 (209) 466-0853 *Contact
Person(s):* Fred Schmierer, Res Deputy Dir
Setting and Background Information The facility was originally
established in 1888 as an orphanage. Currently, there are 4
community homes, 3 residential units, a school, and an
administration building.
Referral Information Contact the facility for a referral packet. A pre-
placement interview may be arranged.
Type of Facility
Funding Sources State; County of origin.
Average Length of Stay Approx 6-9 mos.
Types of Admissions Accepted Day treatment; Residential treatment;
Group home placement.
Sources of Referral State depts of education; Local depts of educa-
tion; State depts of mental health; Private sources; Depts of
correction; Social service depts.

CHILDREN'S HOME OF STOCKTON *(continued)*

Client Profile
Age Range of Clients Served Day programs: 6-12; Residential program: 10-18.
Characteristics Exhibited by Children Emotional handicaps; Learning disabilities; Speech/Language disorders; Neurological impairments; Mental disabilities; Delinquency.
IQ Range of Clients 75+.
Tuition and Fees
Room and Board Long term: $2,019/mo.
Tuition $75/diem.
Placements Primarily Funded By State depts of education; State depts of mental health; Depts of corrections; Social service depts.
Social and Rehabilitative Services
Therapeutic Services Offered Individual therapy; Group therapy; Family therapy; Independent living skills program; Recreation activities.
Professionals on Staff Psychiatrists; Psychologists; Social workers; Child care staff; Nurses; Activity therapist.
Educational and Vocational Services
Type(s) of Educational Programs Offered On campus (Spec Ed); Off campus.
Profile of On Campus School Program Number of teachers 5; *Number of classrooms* 4; *Student to teacher ratio* 6:1; *Grades taught* 4-12; Special curriculum electives offered; Remedial courses offered.
Degrees Offered 8th grade diploma; 12th grade diploma.

JEFFERSON HOUSE
1117 S Grant St, Stockton, CA 95206 (209) 464-2412 *Contact Person(s):* Ted Freund, Treatment Team Suprv
Setting and Background Information This facility was established in 1979 as a part of the Bear Creek Ranch Program.
Referral Information Contact the facility for referral information.
Type of Facility
Funding Sources State.
Average Length of Stay 9-12 mos.
Types of Admissions Accepted Residential treatment; Group home placement.
Sources of Referral Social service depts; Juvenile probation.
Client Profile
Age Range of Clients Served Residential program: 15-18.
Characteristics Exhibited by Children Emotional handicaps; Learning disabilities.
Tuition and Fees
Room and Board Long term: $1,594/mo.
Placements Primarily Funded By Social service depts; Probation.
Social and Rehabilitative Services
Therapeutic Services Offered Individual therapy; Group therapy; Family therapy; Independent living skills program; Substance abuse treatment.
Professionals on Staff Psychiatrists; Psychologists; Social workers; Child care staff.
Educational and Vocational Services
Type(s) of Educational Programs Offered Off campus.

VICTOR RESIDENTIAL CENTER, INC—DBA
REGIONAL ADOLESCENT TREATMENT PROGRAM
6111 Dill Ct, Stockton, CA 95205 (209) 931-6730 *Contact Person(s):* Roy Alexander, Dir
Setting and Background Information The facility was established in 1982. There are 4 group homes located on a 10-acre site and one group home in another setting.
Referral Information Contact the facility and forward necessary information. Referrals will be assessed by the screening committee.
Type of Facility
Funding Sources State; County.
Average Length of Stay Long term.
Types of Admissions Accepted Residential treatment; Wards of the state.
Sources of Referral State depts of education; Social service depts; County mental health; Probation.
Client Profile
Age Range of Clients Served Residential program: 12-18.
Characteristics Exhibited by Children Emotional handicaps; Learning disabilities; Mental disabilities.
IQ Range of Clients 70+.

Tuition and Fees
Room and Board Long term: $3,308/mo.
Tuition $59/diem.
Placements Primarily Funded By Social service depts; County depts of mental health.
Social and Rehabilitative Services
Therapeutic Services Offered Individual therapy; Group therapy; Family therapy; Independent living skills program; Recreation activities.
Professionals on Staff Psychiatrists; Psychologists; Social workers; Child care staff.
Educational and Vocational Services
Type(s) of Educational Programs Offered On campus; Off campus.
Profile of On Campus School Program Number of teachers 3; *Number of classrooms* 3; *Student to teacher ratio* 10:1; *Grades taught* (Individualized); Remedial courses offered (Reading, Math).
Vocational Education Programs/Degrees Offered Occupational readiness.
Degrees Offered 12th grade diploma; GED.

SUMMIT CITY

SOUTH FORTY RANCH
Coran Rd, Summit City, CA 96089 (916) 275-5630 *Contact Person(s):* Carl W Lubsen, Dir
Setting and Background Information The facility was established in 1977. There are 5 group homes on the 40 acre campus.
Referral Information Contact the facility for referral information.
Type of Facility
Funding Sources State.
Average Length of Stay Long term.
Types of Admissions Accepted Group home placement.
Sources of Referral State depts of education; Local depts of education; State depts of mental health; Psychiatrists; Private sources; Depts of correction; Social service depts.
Client Profile
Age Range of Clients Served Residential program: 12-18.
Characteristics Exhibited by Children Emotional handicaps; Learning disabilities.
IQ Range of Clients 77-114.
Tuition and Fees
Room and Board Long term: $1,307/mo.
Placements Primarily Funded By Social service depts.
Social and Rehabilitative Services
Therapeutic Services Offered Individual therapy; Group therapy; Aftercare program with follow up.
Professionals on Staff Psychiatrists; Psychologists; Child care staff.
Educational and Vocational Services
Type(s) of Educational Programs Offered Off campus.

UKIAH

TRINITY SCHOOL FOR CHILDREN
PO Box 719, 915 Churst St, Ukiah, CA 95482 (707) 462-8721
Contact Person(s): Steven A Katsaris, Dir
Setting and Background Information The facility was established in 1970 for emotionally disturbed children and currently serves 61 children. It consists of residential, educational, recreational and administrative facilities.
Referral Information Most referrals come from placement agencies such as social service depts, probation depts, schools, and hospitals.
Type of Facility
Funding Sources Private; State; Federal.
Average Length of Stay Long term.
Types of Admissions Accepted Residential treatment; Group home placement; Wards of the state.
Sources of Referral Local depts of education; State depts of mental health; Psychiatrists; Private sources; Depts of correction; Social service depts.
Client Profile
Age Range of Clients Served Residential program: 6-18.
Characteristics Exhibited by Children Emotional handicaps; Learning disabilities; Speech/Language disorders; Neurological impairments; Mental disabilities; Delinquency.
IQ Range of Clients 70+.

TRINITY SCHOOL FOR CHILDREN *(continued)*

Tuition and Fees
Room and Board Long term: $3,648/mo (on grounds); $1,917/mo (off-campus).
Placements Primarily Funded By Social service depts.
Social and Rehabilitative Services
Therapeutic Approach The facility uses a structured milieu therapy with group and individual therapy. Children receive nurturing combined with structure, limits, and clear communication.
Therapeutic Services Offered Individual therapy; Group therapy; Family therapy; Adjunctive therapy; Art therapy; Independent living skills program; Recreation activities; Aftercare program with follow up.
Professionals on Staff Psychiatrists; Psychologists; Social workers; Adjunctive therapists; Child care staff; Nurses.
Educational and Vocational Services
Type(s) of Educational Programs Offered On campus; Off campus; Summer campus.
Profile of On Campus School Program Number of teachers 8; *Number of classrooms* 6; *Length of school day* 9 am-2:30 pm; *Grades taught* 1-12; Special curriculum electives offered (Art, Drama, Woodshop, Social studies, Psychology); Remedial courses offered (Reading, Math, Language. Arts).

VAN NUYS

PROJECT SIX
13130 Burbank Blvd, Van Nuys, CA 91401 (818) 782-4655 *Contact Person(s):* Susan Berman PhD, Prog Dir
Setting and Background Information The agency was established in 1976. There are 8 group homes in the community and a school.
Referral Information Referrals can be made to the school program by parents, professionals in the community, school districts. Referrals to the day and residential treatment program can be made by the local Dept of Mental Health and the local Dept of Children's Services.
Type of Facility
Funding Sources Private; State.
Average Length of Stay Long term.
Types of Admissions Accepted Day treatment; Residential treatment; Wards of the state.
Sources of Referral State depts of mental health; Social service depts; County.
Client Profile
Age Range of Clients Served Day programs: 6-18; Residential program: 6-18.
Characteristics Exhibited by Children Emotional handicaps; Learning disabilities; Speech/Language disorders; Neurological impairments; Mental disabilities.
Tuition and Fees
Room and Board Long term: $2,849/mo.
Placements Primarily Funded By State depts of mental health; Social service depts; County.
Social and Rehabilitative Services
Therapeutic Approach The therapeutic approach of the facility is behavioral and psychodynamic.
Therapeutic Services Offered Individual therapy; Group therapy; Family therapy; Adjunctive therapy; Art therapy; Independent living skills program; Recreation activities.
Professionals on Staff Psychiatrists; Psychologists; Social workers; Child care staff.
Educational and Vocational Services
Type(s) of Educational Programs Offered On campus; Off campus; Summer campus.
Profile of On Campus School Program Number of teachers 13; *Number of classrooms* 13; *Student to teacher ratio* 6:1; *Credentials of teachers* LH/SH; *Length of school day* 6 hrs; *Grades taught* K-12; Special curriculum electives offered (Computers, Voc Ed, Horseback riding).
Degrees Offered 12th grade diploma.

WALNUT CREEK

YOUTH HOMES
1537 Sunnyvale Ave, Walnut Creek, CA 94596 (415) 933-2627
Contact Person(s): Richard Pryor, Exec Dir
Setting and Background Information This agency was privately established in 1965 in response to community need. It is a group home agency with seven 6-bed sites, located primarily in Contra Costa county.
Referral Information Contact the facility and submit a referral packet. An intake interview at the group home will be scheduled.
Type of Facility
Funding Sources Private; AFDC-BHI; United Way.
Average Length of Stay Long term.
Types of Admissions Accepted Residential treatment; Group home placement; Wards of the state; Emergency shelter.
Sources of Referral Private sources; Depts of correction; Social service depts; Local mental health agencies.
Client Profile
Age Range of Clients Served Residential program: 12-18.
Characteristics Exhibited by Children Emotional handicaps; Borderline personality disorder.
Tuition and Fees
Room and Board Long term: $2,981/mo (rate is set by the state).
Placements Primarily Funded By Social service depts; AFDC-BHI.
Social and Rehabilitative Services
Therapeutic Approach The treatment team has a family systems approach to therapy and, also, uses reality therapy.
Therapeutic Services Offered Individual therapy; Group therapy; Family therapy; Independent living skills program; Substance abuse treatment.
Professionals on Staff Psychiatrists; Psychologists; Social workers; Child care staff.
Educational and Vocational Services
Type(s) of Educational Programs Offered Off campus.

WHITTIER

CASA VICTORIA I
PO Box 6244, 10621 Victoria Ave, Whittier, CA 90609-6244 (213) 941-1270, 941-1279 *Contact Person(s):* Gloria Moreno-Wycoff, Dir
Setting and Background Information The facility was established in 1985 by a Hispanic Womens organization as a community service. It is a single family 4-bedroom residence.
Referral Information Referrals are made directly from individual probation officers whose wards are in juvenile hall awaiting suitable placements. The agency accepts girls only.
Type of Facility
Funding Sources State; Grants.
Average Length of Stay 9-12 mos.
Types of Admissions Accepted Residential treatment; Group home placement; Wards of the state.
Sources of Referral Probation dept.
Client Profile
Age Range of Clients Served Residential program: 12-18.
Characteristics Exhibited by Children Emotional handicaps; Learning disabilities; Delinquency; Drug and alcohol abuse.
Tuition and Fees
Placements Primarily Funded By Social service depts.
Social and Rehabilitative Services
Therapeutic Services Offered Individual therapy; Group therapy; Family therapy; Adjunctive therapy; Independent living skills program; Recreation activities; Substance abuse treatment; Aftercare program with follow up.
Professionals on Staff Psychiatrists; Psychologists; Adjunctive therapists; Child care staff.
Educational and Vocational Services
Type(s) of Educational Programs Offered Off campus (Continuation and regular high schools); Summer campus.

COLORADO

BROOMFIELD

CLEO WALLACE CENTER
PO Box 345, Broomfield, CO 80020 (303) 466-7391 *Contact Person(s):* Tina Kingery, Admis Coord
Setting and Background Information The center was privately founded in 1943. Currently, it is a residential treatment facility for emotionally disturbed children. It is located on 22 acres and has 7 residential units, a school, a psychiatric hospital unit, pre-vocational buildings and other buildings.
Referral Information Referrals are made by sending psychological, educational, social and medical histories with the application form to the Admissions Committee. A pre-placement evaluation by an in-house psychiatrist is required in most cases to finalize the decision.
Type of Facility
Funding Sources Private.
Average Length of Stay Short term (hospitalization) and Long term (residential).
Types of Admissions Accepted Day treatment; Residential treatment; In-patient psychiatric hospital.
Sources of Referral State depts of education; Local depts of education; State depts of mental health; Psychiatrists; Private sources; Social service depts.
Client Profile
Age Range of Clients Served Day programs: 6-21; Residential program: 6-21.
Characteristics Exhibited by Children Emotional handicaps; Learning disabilities; Hearing impairments/deafness; Speech/Language disorders; Neurological impairments; Mental disabilities.
IQ Range of Clients 60-115.
Tuition and Fees
Room and Board Long term: $150/diem (residential); $340/diem (hospitalization).
Tuition $37.84/diem.
Placements Primarily Funded By State depts of education; Local depts of education; Insurance; Private sources; Social service depts.
Social and Rehabilitative Services
Therapeutic Approach The facility has a behavioral approach to therapy and has a social learning program.
Therapeutic Services Offered Individual therapy; Group therapy; Family therapy; Independent living skills program; Recreation activities; Occupational therapy; Speech/language therapy.
Professionals on Staff Psychiatrists; Psychologists; Social workers; Child care staff; Nurses; Speech therapist; Occupational therapist.
Educational and Vocational Services
Type(s) of Educational Programs Offered On campus.
Profile of On Campus School Program Number of teachers 21; Number of classrooms 21; Student to teacher ratio 6:1 (The ratio on the closed unit is 3:1); Credentials of teachers Certified; Grades taught K-12; Special curriculum electives offered; Remedial courses offered (Individualized educational programs).
Vocational Education Programs/Degrees Offered Pre-vocational training.
Degrees Offered 12th grade diploma; GED.

DENVER

BETHESDA PSYCHEALTH SYSTEM
4400 E Iliff Ave, Denver, CO 80222 (303) 758-1514 *Contact Person(s):* Dr John Aycrigg, Admin Dir
Setting and Background Information Bethesda PsycHealth System is a private residential treatment facility. It was initially established as a tuberculosis hospital in the 1940s and later evolved into a psychiatric hospital. The campus is located on 20 acres of land. It consists of a closed adolescent unit of 20 beds for long term hospitalization, a short term (6 week) evaluation unit, and a partial hospitalization (day treatment) program.
Referral Information Anyone can make a referral but the child must be evaluated by a member of the medical staff to assess whether hospitalization is necessary. Admission also depends on the availability of beds.
Type of Facility
Funding Sources Private.
Average Length of Stay Short and long term.
Types of Admissions Accepted Day treatment; Residential treatment.
Sources of Referral Psychiatrists; Private sources.
Client Profile
Age Range of Clients Served Day programs: 13-18; Residential program: 13-18.
Characteristics Exhibited by Children Emotional handicaps; Learning disabilities.
Tuition and Fees
Room and Board Long term: $391/diem.
Placements Primarily Funded By Insurance; Private sources.
Social and Rehabilitative Services
Therapeutic Approach The treatment program is based on a psychoanalytic, dynamic, therapeutic approach which varies depending on the physician.
Therapeutic Services Offered Individual therapy; Group therapy; Family therapy.
Professionals on Staff Psychiatrists; Psychologists; Social workers; Adjunctive therapists; Child care staff; Nurses.
Educational and Vocational Services
Type(s) of Educational Programs Offered On campus.
Profile of On Campus School Program Number of teachers 5; Student to teacher ratio 6:1; Length of school day 3 hrs.

COLORADO CHRISTIAN HOME
4325 W 29th Ave, Denver, CO 80212 (303) 433-2541 *Contact Person(s):* Bob Cooper, Prog Dir
Setting and Background Information Colorado Christian Home is a private residential and day treatment facility which was initially established as an orphanage in 1904. Owned and operated by the National Benevolent Association of the Christian Church, the facility has evolved into a treatment center for emotionally disturbed children. Its campus is located in a residential area of north Denver. The original buildings were torn down in 1975 and 5 modern cottages were built, including an administration building, school, and gymnasium.
Referral Information Anyone can make a referral by contacting the facility and forwarding the necessary background information. Upon receipt of the referral packet, a staff meeting will take place before a placement decision is made.

COLORADO CHRISTIAN HOME *(continued)*

Type of Facility
Funding Sources Private.
Average Length of Stay 20-24 mos.
Types of Admissions Accepted Day treatment; Residential treatment.
Sources of Referral Psychiatrists; Social service depts.
Client Profile
Age Range of Clients Served Day programs: 5-14; Residential program: 5-12.
Characteristics Exhibited by Children Emotional handicaps; Learning disabilities; Speech/Language disorders; Speech/Language disorders; Neurological impairments; Mental disabilities.
Tuition and Fees
Placements Primarily Funded By Insurance; Private sources; Social service depts.
Social and Rehabilitative Services
Therapeutic Approach The treatment program utilizes behavior modification and play therapy.
Therapeutic Services Offered Individual therapy; Group therapy; Family therapy; Recreation activities; Aftercare program with follow up.
Professionals on Staff Psychiatrists; Psychologists; Social workers; Child care staff.
Educational and Vocational Services
Type(s) of Educational Programs Offered On campus; Off campus.
Profile of On Campus School Program Number of teachers 6 and 6 aides; *Student to teacher ratio* 6:1; *Credentials of teachers* MA, Spec Ed.

THE DENVER CHILDREN'S HOME

1501 Albion St, Denver, CO 80220 (303) 399-4890 *Contact Person(s):* Babe McLagan, Intake Coord
Setting and Background Information The facility was initially established as an orphanage in 1881, but since then has expanded its programs to become a treatment center. The campus has a 3-story building surrounded by grounds used for recreational purposes.
Referral Information Referrals can be made by school districts, mental health professionals, physicians, and state agencies. To make a referral, contact the facility and forward the necessary background information on the child, including a recent psychological evaluation, social history, and educational summary.
Type of Facility
Funding Sources Private.
Average Length of Stay Long term.
Types of Admissions Accepted Day treatment; Residential treatment.
Sources of Referral Private sources; Social service depts.
Client Profile
Age Range of Clients Served Day programs: 10-17; Residential program: 10-17.
Characteristics Exhibited by Children Emotional handicaps; Learning disabilities; Neurological impairments.
Tuition and Fees
Room and Board Long term: $2,012/mo.
Placements Primarily Funded By Insurance; Private sources.
Social and Rehabilitative Services
Therapeutic Services Offered Individual therapy; Group therapy; Family therapy; Adjunctive therapy; Art therapy; Independent living skills program; Recreation activities; Substance abuse treatment; Aftercare program with follow up; Horticulture; Movement therapy; Music therapy.
Professionals on Staff Psychiatrists; Psychologists; Social workers; Adjunctive therapists; Child care staff; Nurses; Art therapists; Music therapist; Movement therapist.
Educational and Vocational Services
Type(s) of Educational Programs Offered On campus; Off campus (Public school); Summer campus.
Profile of On Campus School Program Number of teachers 8; *Student to teacher ratio* 3:1; *Credentials of teachers* Certified Spec Ed; *Grades taught* 4-12; Special curriculum electives offered; Remedial courses offered.
Degrees Offered 8th grade diploma; 12th grade diploma; GED.

MOUNT ST VINCENT'S HOME

4159 Lowell Blvd, Denver, CO 80211 (303) 458-7220 *Contact Person(s):* Charles Dalla, LSW II, Clinical Dir
Setting and Background Information The facility was established in 1883 by the Sisters of Charity of Leavenworth. It is located in northwest Denver on 16 ½ acres of land. The campus consists of residential units, athletic fields, outdoor swimming pool, auditorium, movie theater, and a gymnasium. There is also a large modern lodge in the mountains which is used by children and staff throughout the year.
Referral Information Referrals can be made by parents, private professionals, school disticts, mental health clinics, and state or county agencies. Applicants will be required to submit a social history, recent psychological report, academic information, record of a physical examination, immunization record, and birth certificate. An interview will be scheduled with the child and his/her family, followed by a pre-placement visit. All inquiries should be sent to the Supervisor of Treatment Services.
Type of Facility
Funding Sources Private.
Average Length of Stay 12-36 mos.
Types of Admissions Accepted Day treatment; Residential treatment.
Sources of Referral Local depts of education; Psychiatrists; Private sources; Social service depts.
Client Profile
Age Range of Clients Served Day programs: 5-13; Residential program: 5-13.
Characteristics Exhibited by Children Emotional handicaps; Learning disabilities; Hearing impairments/deafness; Vision impairments/blindness; Speech/Language disorders; Neurological impairments.
Tuition and Fees
Room and Board Long term: $1,675/mo (sliding scale).
Placements Primarily Funded By Social service depts; United Way.
Social and Rehabilitative Services
Therapeutic Approach The facility has a psychodynamic approach to therapy.
Therapeutic Services Offered Individual therapy; Group therapy; Family therapy; Adjunctive therapy; Independent living skills program; Recreation activities; Aftercare program with follow up.
Professionals on Staff Psychiatrists; Social workers; Adjunctive therapists; Child care staff; Nurses.
Educational and Vocational Services
Type(s) of Educational Programs Offered On campus; Summer campus.
Profile of On Campus School Program Number of teachers 4 with 8 aides; *Student to teacher ratio* 3:1; *Credentials of teachers* MA.
Degrees Offered 8th grade diploma.

SAVIO HOUSE

325 King St, Denver, CO 80219 (303) 922-5576 *Contact Person(s):* Beverly Banfield, MSW
Setting and Background Information It is a treatment center for male juvenile delinquents. The campus is located in a residential community and consists of a dormitory, administration building, and school.
Referral Information Referrals can be made by the Colorado State Dept of Social Services and out-of-state agencies. Referrals are made by contacting the facility and forwarding the requested background material. A pre-placement interview with the child, parent, and caseworker will be held and a placement decision will then be made within 24 hours.
Type of Facility
Funding Sources State.
Average Length of Stay Long term.
Types of Admissions Accepted Residential treatment.
Sources of Referral Social service depts; Courts.
Client Profile
Age Range of Clients Served Residential program: 12-17.
Characteristics Exhibited by Children Emotional handicaps.
Tuition and Fees
Placements Primarily Funded By Private sources; Social service depts; County.
Social and Rehabilitative Services
Therapeutic Approach The program's philosophy is based on a positive peer culture approach, in conjunction with reality therapy and behavior modification techniques.

SAVIO HOUSE *(continued)*

Therapeutic Services Offered Individual therapy; Group therapy; Family therapy; Independent living skills program; Recreation activities; Substance abuse treatment; Aftercare program with follow up.
Professionals on Staff Psychiatrists; Psychologists; Social workers; Adjunctive therapists; Child care staff.
Educational and Vocational Services
Type(s) of Educational Programs Offered On campus; Off campus; Summer campus.
Profile of On Campus School Program Number of teachers 1; *Student to teacher ratio* 10:1; *Length of school day* 8-12.
Degrees Offered 12th grade diploma.

EVERGREEN

FOREST HEIGHTS LODGE
PO Box 789, 4761 Forest Hill Rd, Evergreen, CO 80439
(303) 674-6681 *Contact Person(s):* Russell H Colburn, Dir
Setting and Background Information The facility was established in 1954 as a private, non-profit facility. It is located on 10 acres and has a residence, a school, and an administration building. The facility serves moderately to severely emotionally disturbed boys.
Referral Information Referrals are made by contacting the director and may be made by social service agencies, depts of correction, psychiatrists and parents.
Type of Facility
Funding Sources Private; State.
Average Length of Stay Long term.
Types of Admissions Accepted Residential treatment.
Sources of Referral State depts of education; Local depts of education; State depts of mental health; Psychiatrists; Private sources; Social service depts.
Client Profile
Age Range of Clients Served Residential program: 6-18.
Characteristics Exhibited by Children Emotional handicaps; Learning disabilities; Speech/Language disorders; Mental disabilities.
IQ Range of Clients 80+.
Tuition and Fees
Room and Board Long term: $3,536/mo (all inclusive).
Placements Primarily Funded By Insurance.
Social and Rehabilitative Services
Therapeutic Services Offered Individual therapy; Group therapy; Family therapy; Recreation activities; Aftercare program with follow up.
Professionals on Staff Psychiatrists; Psychologists; Social workers; Child care staff.
Educational and Vocational Services
Type(s) of Educational Programs Offered On campus.
Profile of On Campus School Program Number of teachers 3; *Number of classrooms* 3; *Student to teacher ratio* 6:1; *Credentials of teachers* MEd; *Length of school day* 6 hrs; *Grades taught* K-12.

GOLDEN

THE GRIFFITH CENTER
1546 Cole Blvd, Ste 225, Golden, CO 80401 (303) 233-8130 *Contact Person(s):* Kirk Griffith, Res Psychologist & Dir of Treatment Prog
Setting and Background Information The center was privately established in 1927. It is a 100-acre ranch with 4 dormitories and a school.
Referral Information Contact the facility for referral information.
Type of Facility
Funding Sources Private; State; Federal.
Average Length of Stay 9 mos-2 yrs.
Types of Admissions Accepted Residential treatment.
Sources of Referral State depts of education; Local depts of education; Psychiatrists; Private sources; Depts of correction; Social service depts.
Client Profile
Age Range of Clients Served Residential program: 12-18.
Characteristics Exhibited by Children Emotional handicaps; Learning disabilities; Speech/Language disorders.

Tuition and Fees
Tuition $2,950/mo.
Placements Primarily Funded By State depts of education; Local depts of education; State depts of mental health; Insurance; Social service depts.
Social and Rehabilitative Services
Therapeutic Services Offered Individual therapy; Group therapy; Family therapy.
Professionals on Staff Psychologists; Adjunctive therapists; Child care staff; Nurses.
Educational and Vocational Services
Type(s) of Educational Programs Offered On campus; Off campus; Summer campus.
Profile of On Campus School Program Number of teachers 5; *Number of classrooms* 3; *Credentials of teachers* MA; Special curriculum electives offered (Wilderness program); Remedial courses offered.
Vocational Education Programs/Degrees Offered Regular curriculum.

LA JUNTA

COLORADO BOYS RANCH FOUNDATION
PO Box 681, 28071 Hwy 109, La Junta, CO 81050 (303) 384-5981 (La Junta), (303) 320-1646 (Denver) *Contact Person(s):* Bill Butro (La Junta); David Blair (Denver)
Setting and Background Information Colorado Boys Ranch is a private residential treatment facility. There is also an intensive psychiatric care unit for adolescents. The facility was established in 1961 in response to the concern of local citizens regarding youth services. It is located in a semi-rural community on 358 acres of land. The campus consists of 21 buildings and 6 cottages, in addition to 1,900 acres of wilderness area located in the mountains.
Referral Information Referrals are received from anyone and can be made by contacting the Admission Office in either La Junta or Denver (Denver office: 311 Steele St, Suite 10, Denver, CO 80206).
Type of Facility
Funding Sources Private.
Average Length of Stay 8 mos.
Types of Admissions Accepted Residential treatment; Wards of the state.
Sources of Referral State depts of mental health; Private sources; Social service depts.
Client Profile
Age Range of Clients Served Residential program: 12-18.
Characteristics Exhibited by Children Emotional handicaps; Learning disabilities.
Tuition and Fees
Room and Board Long term: $2,012/mo.
Placements Primarily Funded By Insurance; Private sources; Social service depts.
Social and Rehabilitative Services
Therapeutic Approach The philosophy of the program is based on a reality oriented milieu approach with emphasis on family counseling.
Therapeutic Services Offered Individual therapy; Group therapy; Independent living skills program; Substance abuse treatment.
Professionals on Staff Psychiatrists; Psychologists; Social workers; Adjunctive therapists; Child care staff; Nurses.
Educational and Vocational Services
Type(s) of Educational Programs Offered On campus.
Profile of On Campus School Program Student to teacher ratio 5:1; *Credentials of teachers* Spec Ed.
Degrees Offered GED.

LOVELAND

CENTER FOR THERAPEUTIC LEARNING ANNEX
549 E 8th St, Loveland, CO 80537 (303) 669-7550 *Contact Person(s):* Mary Klecan, Dir
Setting and Background Information Center for Therapeutic Learning Annex is a private, non-profit residential treatment facility which was established in 1977 by a group of psychologists in response to a community need for a treatment center. It is located in a brick building with an adjacent school building.

CENTER FOR THERAPEUTIC LEARNING ANNEX
(continued)

Referral Information Anyone can make a referral by requesting an intake packet from the facility. After reviewing the referral information provided on the child, a pre-placement visit will take place before an admission decision is made.

Type of Facility

Funding Sources Private.

Average Length of Stay Long term.

Types of Admissions Accepted Residential treatment.

Client Profile

Age Range of Clients Served Day programs: 5-15; Residential program: 5-15.

Characteristics Exhibited by Children Emotional handicaps; Learning disabilities; Behavior disorders.

Tuition and Fees

Room and Board Long term: $2,102/mo.

Placements Primarily Funded By Local depts of education.

Social and Rehabilitative Services

Therapeutic Approach The treatment program utilizes a token economy system, whereupon residents earn points for appropriate behavior and then purchase activities with the points earned.

Therapeutic Services Offered Individual therapy; Group therapy; Family therapy; Independent living skills program; Aftercare program with follow up; Speech therapy.

Professionals on Staff Psychiatrists; Psychologists; Social workers; Adjunctive therapists; Child care staff.

Educational and Vocational Services

Type(s) of Educational Programs Offered On campus; Off campus; Summer campus.

Profile of On Campus School Program Number of teachers 3; *Student to teacher ratio* 6:1; *Grades taught* K-12.

STERLING

TEEN ACRES, INC

17282 32 County Rd, Box 991, Sterling, CO 80751 (303) 522-5775

Contact Person(s): Dorothy Duncan

Setting and Background Information Teen Acres, Inc is a private, non-profit residential treatment facility for girls. It was established in 1967 and is located on 20 acres of land in a rural setting. The campus consists of 3 homes, one for 16 girls and two for 10 girls each, tennis court, volleyball court, swimming pool, and stables.

Referral Information Referrals can be made by anyone but are primarily made by the Dept of Social Services. It is the responsibility of those making the referral to forward the following information: social history, school report, psychological test reports, current medical exam, immunization records, birth certificate, and social security number. A pre-placement visit will be scheduled when the above information is received.

Type of Facility

Funding Sources Private.

Average Length of Stay 18 mos.

Types of Admissions Accepted Residential treatment; Group home placement.

Sources of Referral Social service depts.

Client Profile

Age Range of Clients Served Residential program: 11-17.

Characteristics Exhibited by Children Emotional handicaps; Learning disabilities.

Tuition and Fees

Room and Board Long term: $1,350/mo.

Placements Primarily Funded By Private sources; Social service depts.

Social and Rehabilitative Services

Therapeutic Approach The primary therapeutic approach used is a level system based on behavior modification, in conjunction with reality therapy and positive peer pressure.

Therapeutic Services Offered Individual therapy; Group therapy; Independent living skills program; Recreation activities.

Professionals on Staff Psychologists; Social workers; Adjunctive therapists; Child care staff; Nurses.

Educational and Vocational Services

Type(s) of Educational Programs Offered On campus; Off campus.

Profile of On Campus School Program Number of teachers 5; *Student to teacher ratio* 5:1; Remedial courses offered.

Degrees Offered 12th grade diploma; GED.

CONNECTICUT

BRIDGEPORT

BRIDGEPORT ACADEMY
516 Laurel Ave, Bridgeport, CT 06605 (203) 366-4793 *Contact Person(s):* Michael Turner
Referral Information Contact the facility for referral information.
Type of Facility
Funding Sources Private.
Sources of Referral Local depts of education; State depts of mental health; Social service depts.
Client Profile
Age Range of Clients Served Residential program: 13-21.
Characteristics Exhibited by Children Emotional handicaps; Learning disabilities.
Tuition and Fees
Room and Board Long term: $9,864/10 mos.
Tuition $9,000/10 mos.

THE UNIVERSITY SCHOOL
Box 6129, 16 Iranistan Ave, Bridgeport, CT 06606.
Contact Person(s): Nicholas G Macol
Referral Information Contact the facility for referral information.
Client Profile
Age Range of Clients Served Residential program: 14-19.
Characteristics Exhibited by Children Emotional handicaps; Learning disabilities.
Tuition and Fees
Tuition $9,000/10 mos.
Educational and Vocational Services
Type(s) of Educational Programs Offered On campus.

DEEP RIVER

MOUNT SAINT JOHN
Kiltland St, Deep River, CT 06417 (203) 526-5391 *Contact Person(s):* James C Mol
Referral Information Contact the facility for referral information.
Client Profile
Age Range of Clients Served Residential program: 10-16.
Characteristics Exhibited by Children Emotional handicaps; Learning disabilities.
Tuition and Fees
Room and Board Long term: $16,173/10 mos.
Tuition $10,638/10 mos, $3,234/summer.
Educational and Vocational Services
Type(s) of Educational Programs Offered On campus.

DURHAM

LAKE GROVE AT DURHAM
PO Box 659, Wallingford Rd, Durham, CT 06422-0659
(203) 349-3467 *Contact Person(s):* Albert Brayson, Dir; Michael Reed, Admin
Referral Information Contact the facility for referral information.
Type of Facility
Types of Admissions Accepted Residential treatment; Crisis intervention.

Client Profile
Age Range of Clients Served Residential program: 11-21.
Characteristics Exhibited by Children Emotional handicaps; Mental disabilities.
Social and Rehabilitative Services
Therapeutic Services Offered Individual therapy; Group therapy; Adjunctive therapy; Art therapy; Physical therapy; Recreation activities.
Professionals on Staff Psychiatrists; Psychologists; Adjunctive therapists; Art therapists; Physical therapists.
Educational and Vocational Services
Type(s) of Educational Programs Offered On campus.
Vocational Education Programs/Degrees Offered Vocational education and assessment.

EAST HAVEN

BENHAVEN
Maple St, East Haven, CT 06512 (203) 469-9819
Referral Information Contact the facility for referral information.
Client Profile
Age Range of Clients Served Residential program: 5-21.
Characteristics Exhibited by Children Emotional handicaps; Learning disabilities; Hearing impairments/deafness; Vision impairments/blindness; Neurological impairments; Mental disabilities; Autism.
Tuition and Fees
Room and Board Long term: $37,605/10 mos.
Tuition $25,245/10 mos.

HARTFORD

SHELTER FOR WOMEN, INC—GRAY LODGE
105 Spring St, Hartford, CT 06105 (203) 522-9363 *Contact Person(s):* Rose Alma Senatore, Exec Dir
Setting and Background Information The facility was established in 1901 by the community. There are two facilities- one is in Hartford and the other is in Manchester. Both are large residential homes.
Referral Information Contact the facility and forward an intake packet, including a social summary, and psychological, educational, and medical records. A pre-placement interview will be held.
Type of Facility
Funding Sources Private; State; Federal.
Average Length of Stay Min 1 yr.
Types of Admissions Accepted Residential treatment; Independent living program.
Sources of Referral State depts of education; Local depts of education; Dept of Children and Youth Svcs.
Client Profile
Age Range of Clients Served Residential program: 12-18.
Characteristics Exhibited by Children Emotional handicaps; Learning disabilities; Delinquency.
Tuition and Fees
Room and Board Long term: $42/diem.
Tuition $11,500 yr.
Placements Primarily Funded By Local depts of education; DCYS.

SHELTER FOR WOMEN, INC—GRAY LODGE
(continued)

Social and Rehabilitative Services
Therapeutic Approach The basic approach of the facility is reality therapy.
Therapeutic Services Offered Individual therapy; Group therapy; Family therapy; Independent living skills program; Recreation activities; Aftercare program with follow up.
Professionals on Staff Psychiatrists; Social workers; Child care staff.
Educational and Vocational Services
Type(s) of Educational Programs Offered On campus; Summer campus.
Profile of On Campus School Program Number of teachers 4; *Number of classrooms* 4; *Student to teacher ratio* 4:1; *Credentials of teachers* Spec Ed & Business Degrees; *Grades taught* 7-12; Special curriculum electives offered (Computers, Accounting, Consumer Ed); Remedial courses offered (Reading, Math, English).
Vocational Education Programs/Degrees Offered Typing; Word processing; Cooking; Home Ec.
Degrees Offered 8th grade diploma; 12th grade diploma.

WOODSTOCK SCHOOL
500 Blue Hills Ave, Hartford, CT 06112 (203) 242-4431 *Contact Person(s):* Anthony Rigazio-Digilio
Referral Information Contact the facility for referral information.
Client Profile
Age Range of Clients Served Residential program: 13-19.
Characteristics Exhibited by Children Emotional handicaps.
Tuition and Fees
Room and Board Long term: $60-75/diem.
Social and Rehabilitative Services
Therapeutic Services Offered Individual therapy; Group therapy; Family therapy.

LITCHFIELD

CONNECTICUT JUNIOR REPUBLIC
Goshen Rd, Litchfield, CT 06759 (203) 567-9423 *Contact Person(s):* Bernard Flannery, MSW
Setting and Background Information The facility was established in 1906 by staff from the George Junior Republic in New York, but is now no longer connected with the New York facility. It is located on 209 acres in a rural setting and consists of 7 residential units, school, shops, indoor pool, gymnasium, and playing fields.
Referral Information Applicants should apply for admission through a referring agency. A referral packet must be completed before a pre-placement visit can take place and an admission decision is made.
Type of Facility
Funding Sources Private; State; Federal.
Average Length of Stay Long term.
Types of Admissions Accepted Day treatment; Residential treatment; Group home placement; Wards of the state.
Sources of Referral State depts of education; Local depts of education; Depts of correction; Social service depts.
Client Profile
Age Range of Clients Served Day programs: 12-16 ½; Residential program: 12-16 ½.
Characteristics Exhibited by Children Emotional handicaps; Learning disabilities; Speech/Language disorders.
IQ Range of Clients 80+.
Tuition and Fees
Placements Primarily Funded By State depts of education; Local depts of education; Social service depts.
Social and Rehabilitative Services
Therapeutic Services Offered Individual therapy; Group therapy; Family therapy; Adjunctive therapy; Art therapy; Physical therapy; Independent living skills program; Recreation activities; Aftercare program with follow up.
Professionals on Staff Psychiatrists; Psychologists; Social workers; Child care staff; Nurses.
Educational and Vocational Services
Type(s) of Educational Programs Offered On campus; Summer campus.
Profile of On Campus School Program Number of teachers 13; *Student to teacher ratio* 8:1; *Length of school day* 3 hrs; Special curriculum electives offered; Remedial courses offered.
Degrees Offered 8th grade diploma.

MADISON

GROVE SCHOOL, INC
PO Box 646, 175 Copse Rd, Madison, CT 06443 (203) 245-2778
Contact Person(s): Ethel Chorney
Setting and Background Information The facility was established in 1934 on 90 acres of land. Its campus consists of 11 cottages, a gymnasium, ballfield, and lake.
Referral Information Referrals can be made by any interested agency or individual. Applicants are requested to forward psychiatric, psychological, and academic material to the central office. A pre-placement interview will be scheduled with the child and his parents before an admission decision is made. The facility accepts boys only.
Type of Facility
Funding Sources Private.
Average Length of Stay Long term.
Types of Admissions Accepted Residential treatment.
Sources of Referral State depts of education; Local depts of education; State depts of mental health; Psychiatrists; Private sources; Depts of correction; Social service depts.
Client Profile
Age Range of Clients Served Residential program: 11-19.
Characteristics Exhibited by Children Emotional handicaps; Learning disabilities; Speech/Language disorders.
Tuition and Fees
Placements Primarily Funded By Insurance; Private sources.
Social and Rehabilitative Services
Therapeutic Approach The program's philosophy is psychoanalytically oriented with emphasis on milieu, individual, and group therapy.
Therapeutic Services Offered Individual therapy; Group therapy; Family therapy; Adjunctive therapy; Art therapy; Physical therapy; Independent living skills program; Recreation activities.
Professionals on Staff Psychiatrists; Psychologists; Social workers; Child care staff; Art therapists.
Educational and Vocational Services
Type(s) of Educational Programs Offered On campus.
Profile of On Campus School Program Number of teachers 20; *Number of classrooms* 20; *Student to teacher ratio* 4:1; *Grades taught* 5-12; Special curriculum electives offered; Remedial courses offered.
Degrees Offered 12th grade diploma.

MANCHESTER

SUMMIT SCHOOL
48 Hartford Rd, Manchester, CT 06040 (203) 643-2701 *Contact Person(s):* Trisha Donahue
Setting and Background Information The facility was established in 1972 to provide a substance abuse program for girls. The program is housed in a mansion with spacious grounds.
Referral Information Anyone can make a referral by forwarding the necessary background information on the child. If the referral seems appropriate, a pre-placement visit will be scheduled before an admission decision is made. The facility accepts girls only.
Type of Facility
Funding Sources Private; State.
Average Length of Stay Long term.
Types of Admissions Accepted Residential treatment; Group home placement.
Sources of Referral State depts of education; Local depts of education; State depts of mental health; Psychiatrists; Private sources; Depts of correction; Social service depts.
Client Profile
Age Range of Clients Served Residential program: 12-18.
Characteristics Exhibited by Children Emotional handicaps; Learning disabilities.
Tuition and Fees
Placements Primarily Funded By Local depts of education; Insurance; Private sources; Social service depts.
Social and Rehabilitative Services
Therapeutic Approach The facility has a holistic approach to therapy.
Therapeutic Services Offered Individual therapy; Group therapy; Family therapy; Recreation activities; Substance abuse treatment; Aftercare program with follow up.

SUMMIT SCHOOL *(continued)*

Professionals on Staff Psychiatrists; Social workers.
Educational and Vocational Services
Type(s) of Educational Programs Offered On campus; Summer campus.
Profile of On Campus School Program Number of teachers 3; *Number of classrooms* 3; *Student to teacher ratio* 5:1; *Length of school day* 6 hrs; *Grades taught* 7-12; Special curriculum electives offered; Remedial courses offered.
Degrees Offered 12th grade diploma.

MERIDEN

CURTIS SCHOOL

380 Crown St, Meriden, CT 06450 (203) 237-9526
Referral Information Contact the facility for referral information.
Client Profile
Age Range of Clients Served Residential program: 6-14.
Characteristics Exhibited by Children Emotional handicaps; Learning disabilities.
Tuition and Fees
Room and Board Long term: $17,145/10 mos; $3,429/summer.
Tuition $9,950/10 mos, $1,105/summer.
Social and Rehabilitative Services
Professionals on Staff Psychologists; Social workers; Educational advocate.
Educational and Vocational Services
Type(s) of Educational Programs Offered On campus.

MILFORD

BOY'S VILLAGE YOUTH AND FAMILY SERVICES, INC

528 Wheelers Farm Rd, Milford, CT 06460 (203) 877-0300 *Contact Person(s):* Donald A Gaskill, Exec Dir
Setting and Background Information The facility was established in 1942 as a summer camp for youth offenders. Currently, the 11-acre campus has three buildings and provides both residential and day treatment.
Referral Information Referrals are made by the Dept of Children and Youth Services, the courts, school systems, clinics, and hospitals by submitting referral materials, including a recent psychological evaluation, a school history, and clinical data.
Type of Facility
Funding Sources Private; State.
Average Length of Stay Long term.
Types of Admissions Accepted Day treatment; Residential treatment; Day school.
Sources of Referral State depts of education; Local depts of education; Social service depts; Psychiatric hospitals; Mental health clinics.
Client Profile
Age Range of Clients Served Day programs: 6-15; Residential program: 6-15.
Characteristics Exhibited by Children Emotional handicaps; Learning disabilities.
IQ Range of Clients 70-130.
Tuition and Fees
Room and Board Long term: $26,794/yr.
Tuition $11,900.
Placements Primarily Funded By State depts of education; Local depts of education; Dept of Children and Youth Services.
Social and Rehabilitative Services
Therapeutic Approach The facility offers a therapeutic milieu.
Therapeutic Services Offered Individual therapy; Group therapy; Family therapy; Adjunctive therapy; Independent living skills program; Recreation activities; Aftercare program with follow up.
Professionals on Staff Psychiatrists; Social workers; Child care staff.
Educational and Vocational Services
Type(s) of Educational Programs Offered On campus (Spec Ed); Off campus (CETA); Summer campus (Spec Ed tutoring).
Profile of On Campus School Program Number of teachers 9; *Number of classrooms* 7; *Student to teacher ratio* 6:1; *Credentials of teachers* Certified; *Grades taught* K-8; Remedial courses offered (Tutoring).
Vocational Education Programs/Degrees Offered Job training.

Degrees Offered 8th grade diploma.

NEW BRITAIN

KLINGBERG FAMILY CENTERS

370 Linwood St, New Britain, CT 06052 (203) 224-9113 *Contact Person(s):* Lynne Vasear Roe, Intake Coord
Setting and Background Information The agency was founded in 1903 by John Eric Klingberg, a Swedish Baptist minister, as a child care center for homeless children. Over the years, the programs have expanded and new buildings have been acquired. It has evolved into a residential treatment center with extensive in-patient and out-patient services. The Center is licensed as a child care facility and child placing agency by the Connecticut Dept of Children and Youth Services. The school program is certified by the State Dept of Education. The campus is located on a hill surrounded by 40 acres of land, overlooking New Britain. There are several buildings which house offices, residential units, school, library, medical unit, and conference rooms. Recreational facilities include an outdoor swimming pool, playgrounds, and athletic fields.
Referral Information Referrals can be made by school districts, juvenile courts, Dept of Children and Youth Services, and private individuals. Applicants are requested to forward an intake packet consisting of psychological evaluations, educational reports, and a family history. If the referral seems appropriate, then an overnight visit will be arranged so that the child can be further evaluated by unit staff, teacher, and family counselor. Following the overnight assessment, a placement decision will be made.
Type of Facility
Funding Sources State.
Average Length of Stay Long term.
Types of Admissions Accepted Day treatment; Residential treatment; Wards of the state.
Sources of Referral State depts of education; Local depts of education; State depts of mental health; Psychiatrists; Private sources; Depts of correction; Social service depts.
Client Profile
Age Range of Clients Served Day programs: 8-14 ½ ; Residential program: 8-14 ½ .
Characteristics Exhibited by Children Emotional handicaps; Learning disabilities.
Tuition and Fees
Placements Primarily Funded By Local depts of education; Insurance; Private sources; Social service depts.
Social and Rehabilitative Services
Therapeutic Approach The primary therapeutic approaches used are cognitive behavior modification, reality therapy, and family therapy.
Therapeutic Services Offered Individual therapy; Group therapy; Family therapy; Adjunctive therapy; Independent living skills program; Recreation activities.
Professionals on Staff Psychiatrists; Psychologists; Social workers; Child care staff; Nurses.
Educational and Vocational Services
Type(s) of Educational Programs Offered On campus.
Profile of On Campus School Program Number of teachers 6; *Number of classrooms* 6; *Student to teacher ratio* 4:1; *Length of school day* 5 hrs; *Grades taught* K-12; Remedial courses offered.

NEW HAVEN

HIGHLAND HEIGHTS

651 Prospect St, New Haven, CT 06505 (203) 777-5513 *Contact Person(s):* Gerald Leventhal, Dir of Residential Group Care
Setting and Background Information The facility was initially established as an orphanage in 1852. It expanded its programs to become a residential treatment center in 1962. The campus consists of 5 buildings, including an on-grounds school, playgrounds, and beach property nearby on Long Island Sound.
Referral Information Referrals can be made by school systems, Dept of Children and Family Services, psychiatric hospitals, and community hospital psychiatric units. Applicants should apply in writing and include family history, developmental history, testing data, school records, medical records, and other pertinent information. Once the referral packet is received, a pre-placement visit will be set up with the intake coordinator. A placement decision will be made following the interview.

HIGHLAND HEIGHTS *(continued)*

Type of Facility
Funding Sources Private; State; Federal.
Average Length of Stay Long term.
Types of Admissions Accepted Day treatment; Residential treatment.
Sources of Referral State depts of education; Local depts of education; State depts of mental health.
Client Profile
Age Range of Clients Served Day program: 7-10; Residential program: 5-19.
Characteristics Exhibited by Children Emotional handicaps; Learning disabilities.
Tuition and Fees
Placements Primarily Funded By State depts of education; Local depts of education; Social service depts.
Social and Rehabilitative Services
Therapeutic Services Offered Individual therapy; Group therapy; Family therapy; Independent living skills program; Recreation activities; Aftercare program with follow up.
Professionals on Staff Psychiatrists; Psychologists; Social workers; Adjunctive therapists; Child care staff; Nurses.
Educational and Vocational Services
Type(s) of Educational Programs Offered On campus; Summer campus.
Profile of On Campus School Program Number of teachers 12; *Number of classrooms* 8; *Student to teacher ratio* 5:1; *Length of school day* 5 hrs; *Grades taught* K-8; Remedial courses offered.

NEWTOWN

CENTER OF PROGRESSIVE EDUCATION

Greenwich House, Newtown, CT 06470 (203) 787-7188 *Contact Person(s):* Peter Williams, MSW
Referral Information Contact the facility for referral information.
Client Profile
Age Range of Clients Served Residential program: 14-21.
Characteristics Exhibited by Children Emotional handicaps; Learning disabilities.
Tuition and Fees
Room and Board Long term: $102/diem; based on sliding scale.
Tuition $10,500/yr.

NORWALK

VITAM CENTER, INC

PO Box 730, 57 W Rock Rd, Norwalk, CT 06852 (203) 846-2091
Contact Person(s): Peter Gonda, Dir of Intake
Setting and Background Information The facility was established in 1969 as a treatment center for drug abusers. Its campus is located on 13 acres consisting of a male dorm, main building, administration building, student activities center, off-site leased school, short term/re-entry house and an off-site girls dorm.
Referral Information Referrals can be made by social workers, physicians, probation officers, police, courts, drug programs, and parents. To make a referral, call the facility to determine the appropriateness of the referral.
Type of Facility
Funding Sources Private; State.
Average Length of Stay Long term.
Types of Admissions Accepted Residential treatment.
Sources of Referral State depts of education; Local depts of education; Psychiatrists; Private sources; Depts of correction; Social service depts.
Client Profile
Age Range of Clients Served Residential program: 12-18.
Characteristics Exhibited by Children Emotional handicaps; Learning disabilities.
IQ Range of Clients 80+.
Tuition and Fees
Placements Primarily Funded By State depts of education; Local depts of education; Insurance; Private sources; Social service depts.
Social and Rehabilitative Services
Therapeutic Approach The treatment program utilizes positive peer pressure, in conjunction with behavior modification and reality therapy.

Therapeutic Services Offered Individual therapy; Group therapy; Family therapy; Art therapy; Physical therapy; Independent living skills program; Recreation activities; Substance abuse treatment; Aftercare program with follow up.
Professionals on Staff Psychiatrists; Psychologists; Social workers; Child care staff; Nurses; Art therapists; Physical therapists; MD.
Educational and Vocational Services
Type(s) of Educational Programs Offered Off campus; Summer campus.
Profile of On Campus School Program Number of teachers 15; *Number of classrooms* 8; *Student to teacher ratio* 6:1; *Grades taught* 1-12; Remedial courses offered.
Degrees Offered 12th grade diploma; GED.

PLAINVILLE

WHEELER CLINIC

91 Worthwest Dr, Plainville, CT 06062 (203) 793-0249 *Contact Person(s):* Dennis Keenan
Referral Information Contact the facility for referral information.
Client Profile
Age Range of Clients Served Residential program: 2-16.
Characteristics Exhibited by Children Emotional handicaps; Learning disabilities; Autism.
Tuition and Fees
Room and Board Long term: $17,261/10 mos.

PORTLAND

ELMCREST SCHOOL

25 Marlborough St, Portland, CT 06480.
Contact Person(s): Lane Ameen, MD
Referral Information Contact the facility for referral information.
Client Profile
Age Range of Clients Served Residential program: 8-18.
Social and Rehabilitative Services
Therapeutic Services Offered Individual therapy; Group therapy; Family therapy.

QUAKER HILL

WATERFORD COUNTY SCHOOL, INC

78 Hunts Brook Rd, Quaker Hill, CT 06375 (203) 442-9454 *Contact Person(s):* Pat Marten, Intake Coord; T J Butcher, Clin Dir
Setting and Background Information The facility was initially set up as a summer camp for handicapped children. It has gradually expanded its programs to become a residential/educational program. The campus consists of 3 dormitories (2 for boys and 1 for girls), transitional group home, independent living unit, school, and a full working farm.
Referral Information Referrals are mostly made by the Dept of Children and Youth Services, juvenile court, school board, psychiatric hospitals, and parents. Applicants are requested to forward psychological reports, school records, family history, medical records, and court information. If, upon reviewing the background information, a child is considered appropriate for the program, then a pre-placement meeting will take place and a placement decision made.
Type of Facility
Funding Sources Private.
Average Length of Stay Long term.
Types of Admissions Accepted Day treatment; Residential treatment; Group home placement.
Sources of Referral State depts of mental health; Psychiatrists; Depts of correction.
Client Profile
Age Range of Clients Served Day programs: 9-17; Residential program: 9-17.
Characteristics Exhibited by Children Emotional handicaps; Learning disabilities; Speech/Language disorders; Mental disabilities.
Tuition and Fees
Room and Board Long term: $19,886/yr.
Tuition $14,000/yr (usually funded by the Board of Education).
Placements Primarily Funded By State depts of mental health; Private sources.

WATERFORD COUNTY SCHOOL, INC *(continued)*

Social and Rehabilitative Services
Therapeutic Approach The primary therapeutic approach used is that of behavior modification, with emphasis on individual and family counseling.
Therapeutic Services Offered Individual therapy; Group therapy; Family therapy; Independent living skills program; Recreation activities.
Professionals on Staff Psychiatrists; Psychologists; Social workers; Adjunctive therapists; Child care staff; Nurses.
Educational and Vocational Services
Type(s) of Educational Programs Offered On campus; Off campus.
Profile of On Campus School Program Number of teachers 12; *Student to teacher ratio* 6:1; *Credentials of teachers* Spec Ed, Voc Ed; *Grades taught* 1-12.
Degrees Offered GED; Diploma conferred through public schools.

WASHINGTON

THE DEVEREUX FOUNDATION—GLENHOLM
2 Sabbaday Lane, Washington, CT 06793 (203) 868-7377
Referral Information Contact the facility for referral information.
Client Profile
Age Range of Clients Served Residential program: 5-21.
Characteristics Exhibited by Children Emotional handicaps; Learning disabilities.
Tuition and Fees
Room and Board Long term: $12,043/yr.
Tuition $12,389/yr.

WEST HARTFORD

AMERICAN SCHOOL FOR THE DEAF, PACES PROGRAM
139 N Main St, West Hartford, CT 06107 (203) 727-1420 (Voice), 727-1423 (TDD) *Contact Person(s):* Martha J Rosen, Dir
Setting and Background Information This program is located on the American School for the Deaf campus, which has 54 acres and 10 buildings for educational, residential, vocational and medical services. The PACES program was established in 1982 by ASD.
Referral Information For referral, contact the facility and forward educational, psychological, audiological, familial and other relevant background information on the student. Only students with stable home placements in the Southern New England area are eligible for this facility. A day-long evaluation visit will be arranged. If the candidate is appropriate, a 6-8 week diagnostic placement will be made.
Type of Facility
Funding Sources State; Local educational agencies.
Average Length of Stay Long term.
Types of Admissions Accepted Day treatment; Residential treatment.
Sources of Referral Local depts of education; Social service depts.
Client Profile
Age Range of Clients Served Day programs: 12-22; Residential program: 12-22.
Characteristics Exhibited by Children Emotional handicaps; Hearing impairments/deafness; Behavior disorders.
IQ Range of Clients 75-130.
Tuition and Fees
Placements Primarily Funded By State depts of education; Local depts of education; State depts of mental health; Social service depts.
Social and Rehabilitative Services
Therapeutic Approach The basic approach of the facility is behavioral, within a therapeutic milieu.
Therapeutic Services Offered Individual therapy; Group therapy; Art therapy; Independent living skills program.
Professionals on Staff Psychiatrists; Psychologists; Adjunctive therapists; Child care staff; Art therapists.
Educational and Vocational Services
Type(s) of Educational Programs Offered On campus (Spec Ed); Off campus.
Profile of On Campus School Program Number of teachers 7; *Number of classrooms* 5; *Student to teacher ratio* 2:1; *Credentials of teachers* BA, MA in Spec Ed; *Grades taught* 6-12.

Vocational Education Programs/Degrees Offered High school vocational curriculum.
Degrees Offered 12th grade diploma.

WESTPORT

HALL-BROOKE FOUNDATION
47 Long Lots Rd, Westport, CT 06881 (203) 227-1251 *Contact Person(s):* Admissions Officer
Setting and Background Information The facility was originally established in 1898 as a psychiatric hospital. Its 25-acre campus has residential facilities, a school and a partial hospital building.
Referral Information Contact the facility for referral information.
Type of Facility
Funding Sources Private.
Average Length of Stay The adult program is short term; the adolescent program is long term.
Types of Admissions Accepted Day treatment; Residential treatment.
Sources of Referral State depts of education; Local depts of education; State depts of mental health; Psychiatrists; Private sources; Depts of correction; Social service depts.
Client Profile
Age Range of Clients Served Day programs: 12-55+; Residential program: 12-55+.
Characteristics Exhibited by Children Emotional handicaps; Learning disabilities.
Tuition and Fees
Room and Board Long term: $2,200/wk (hospital treatment).
Tuition $300/wk.
Placements Primarily Funded By Local depts of education; Insurance; Private sources; Social service depts.
Social and Rehabilitative Services
Therapeutic Approach The facility offers individual, group and family therapy within the context of a medical model.
Therapeutic Services Offered Individual therapy; Group therapy; Family therapy; Adjunctive therapy; Art therapy; Recreation activities; Substance abuse treatment.
Professionals on Staff Psychiatrists; Psychologists; Social workers; Adjunctive therapists; Nurses; Art therapists.
Educational and Vocational Services
Type(s) of Educational Programs Offered On campus.
Profile of On Campus School Program Number of teachers 12; *Number of classrooms* 7-12; *Student to teacher ratio* 5:1; *Credentials of teachers* State licensed, BA, BS; *Grades taught* K-12 (primarily Jr and Sr High School).
Degrees Offered 12th grade diploma.

DELAWARE

BEAR

AU CLAIR SCHOOL

4185 Kirkwood-St Goerge Rd, Bear, DE 19701 (302) 834-7018
Contact Person(s): Diane Wolff, Admis Dir
Referral Information Contact the facility for referral information.
Type of Facility
Average Length of Stay Long term.
Types of Admissions Accepted Residential treatment.
Client Profile
Age Range of Clients Served Residential program: 5-21.
Characteristics Exhibited by Children Autism.
Social and Rehabilitative Services
Therapeutic Services Offered Individual therapy; Group therapy;
   Family therapy.
Professionals on Staff Psychiatrists; Psychologists; Adjunctive thera-
   pists; Physical therapists; Speech therapist; Recreational thera-
   pists.
Educational and Vocational Services
Type(s) of Educational Programs Offered On campus.
Vocational Education Programs/Degrees Offered Vocational assess-
   ment and education.

MIDDLETOWN

HILLHAVEN CENTER

Bayview Road, RD 2 Box 78, Middletown, DE 19709
(302) 834-4811 *Contact Person(s):* Carol Smith, Dir
Referral Information For referral information contact the facility.
Type of Facility
Types of Admissions Accepted Residential treatment.
Client Profile
Age Range of Clients Served Residential program: 6-21.
Characteristics Exhibited by Children Emotional handicaps; Learning
   disabilities; Mental disabilities.
Social and Rehabilitative Services
Therapeutic Approach The basic therapeutic approach used at the
   facility is behavior modification.
Therapeutic Services Offered Individual therapy; Adjunctive therapy;
   Physical therapy; Recreation activities.

NEW CASTLE

TERRY CHILDREN'S PSYCHIATRIC CENTER

10 Central Ave, New Castle, DE 19720 (302) 421-6661 *Contact
Person(s):* Anita L Amurao MD, Hosp Dir
Setting and Background Information The facility was established in
   1969 with federal funds. Currently, the state is responsible for the
   program. The facility consists of one building with adjunct pool
   and gym on 3 ½ acres.
Referral Information Referrals are accepted from all child-related
   agencies, schools, physicians, and parents. Referrals by telephone
   or letter preferred. Walk-ins can be accommodated at times.
Type of Facility
Funding Sources State.
Average Length of Stay Short and long term.
Types of Admissions Accepted Day treatment; Residential treatment;
   Out-patient.

Sources of Referral State depts of education; Local depts of educa-
   tion; State depts of mental health; Psychiatrists; Private sources;
   Depts of correction; Social service depts; Family.
Client Profile
Age Range of Clients Served Day programs: Birth-12; Residential
   program Birth-12.
Characteristics Exhibited by Children Emotional handicaps; Learning
   disabilities; Speech/Language disorders; Neurological impair-
   ments; Mental disabilities.
Tuition and Fees
Room and Board Short term: $119.79/diem; Long term: $119.79/
   diem.
Tuition $86.81/diem.
Placements Primarily Funded By State of Delaware.
Social and Rehabilitative Services
Therapeutic Services Offered Individual therapy; Group therapy;
   Family therapy; Adjunctive therapy; Art therapy; Recreation ac-
   tivities; Aftercare program with follow up; Music therapy; Drama
   therapy; Occupational therapy.
Professionals on Staff Psychiatrists; Psychologists; Social workers;
   Adjunctive therapists; Child care staff; Nurses; Art therapists;
   Pediatrician; Child Dev counselor.
Educational and Vocational Services
Type(s) of Educational Programs Offered On campus; Summer cam-
   pus.
Profile of On Campus School Program Number of teachers 9; Num-
   ber of classrooms 7; Student to teacher ratio 7:1; Credentials of
   teachers SEM; Length of school day 5 hrs; Grades taught K-6.

DISTRICT OF COLUMBIA

WASHINGTON

EPISCOPAL CENTER FOR CHILDREN

5901 Utah Ave NW, Washington, DC 20015 (202) 363-1333
Contact Person(s): Sean C Kurz, Dir
Referral Information Contact the facility for referral information.
Type of Facility
Funding Sources .
Average Length of Stay Long term.
Types of Admissions Accepted Day treatment; Residential treatment.
Client Profile
Age Range of Clients Served Day programs: 5-12; Residential program: 5-12.
Characteristics Exhibited by Children Emotional handicaps.
Tuition and Fees
Room and Board Long term: $24,500/year.
Social and Rehabilitative Services
Therapeutic Services Offered Individual therapy; Group therapy; Family therapy; Substance abuse treatment; Occupational therapy.
Professionals on Staff Adjunctive therapists; Occupational therapist.
Educational and Vocational Services
Type(s) of Educational Programs Offered On campus; Off campus.

ST ELIZABETH'S HOSPITAL—DIVISON OF CHILDREN AND ADOLESCENT SERVICES

Martin Luther King Jr Ave SE, Washington, DC 20032
(202) 562-4000 *Contact Person(s):* S P Hershad Md, Dir
Setting and Background Information The facility was established in 1978.
Referral Information For referral information, contact the facility.
Type of Facility
Types of Admissions Accepted Residential treatment.
Client Profile
Age Range of Clients Served Residential program: 6-18.
Characteristics Exhibited by Children Emotional handicaps.
Social and Rehabilitative Services
Therapeutic Services Offered Individual therapy.
Educational and Vocational Services
Type(s) of Educational Programs Offered On campus.
Profile of On Campus School Program Special curriculum electives offered; Remedial courses offered.
Vocational Education Programs/Degrees Offered Manual arts; Shop.

ST JOHN'S CHILD DEVELOPMENT CENTER

5005 MacArthur Blvd NW, Washington, DC 20016 (202) 363-7032
Contact Person(s): Thomas F Welds MA, Dir
Setting and Background Information The facility was established in 1882 and is a non-profit organization. The facility accepts boys only.
Referral Information Contact the facility for referral information.
Type of Facility
Average Length of Stay Short and long term.
Types of Admissions Accepted Residential treatment.
Client Profile
Age Range of Clients Served Day programs: 11-18; Residential program: 11-18.
Characteristics Exhibited by Children Mental disabilities; Autism.
Tuition and Fees
Room and Board Long term: $52,208/yr.

Social and Rehabilitative Services
Therapeutic Services Offered Individual therapy; Family therapy; Physical therapy.
Educational and Vocational Services
Type(s) of Educational Programs Offered On campus; Summer campus.

FLORIDA

BRADENTON

MANATEE PALMS, RESIDENTIAL TREATMENT CENTER

1324 37th Ave E, Bradenton, FL 33508 (813) 746-1388 *Contact Person(s):* Colleen Bekiempts, Marketing Dir

Setting and Background Information The center was privately established in 1987 in response to a community need for residential treatment. Located on 15 acres, there are three major buildings.

Referral Information For referral, contact the facility. An admissions committee will review all applications.

Type of Facility
Funding Sources Private; State; Federal.
Average Length of Stay Long term.
Types of Admissions Accepted Residential treatment.

Client Profile
Age Range of Clients Served Residential program: Birth-18.
Characteristics Exhibited by Children Emotional handicaps; Learning disabilities; Speech/Language disorders; Neurological impairments; Physical handicaps; Mental disabilities; Substance abuse; Eating disorders; Addictive disorders.

Tuition and Fees
Room and Board Long term: $235/diem.
Placements Primarily Funded By State depts of mental health; Insurance.

Social and Rehabilitative Services
Therapeutic Approach The facility has a multi-disciplinary approach to therapy.
Therapeutic Services Offered Individual therapy; Group therapy; Family therapy; Adjunctive therapy; Art therapy; Physical therapy; Independent living skills program; Recreation activities; Substance abuse treatment; Aftercare program with follow up.
Professionals on Staff Psychiatrists; Psychologists; Social workers; Adjunctive therapists; Child care staff; Nurses; Art therapists; Physical therapists.

Educational and Vocational Services
Type(s) of Educational Programs Offered On campus; Off campus; Summer campus.
Profile of On Campus School Program Number of classrooms 2; *Student to teacher ratio* 6:1; *Credentials of teachers* MA, Certified; *Grades taught* K-12; Special curriculum electives offered; Remedial courses offered.
Degrees Offered 8th grade diploma; 12th grade diploma; GED.

CLEARWATER

ECKERD WILDERNESS EDUCATIONAL SYSTEM CAMPING PROGAMS

PO Box 7450, 100 N Starcrest Dr, Clearwater, FL 33518-7450, 33575 (813) 461-2990, (800) 544-4357 *Contact Person(s):* Dwight Lord, Dir of Agency Relations

Setting and Background Information The program was established in 1968 as an alternative to institutionalization. Each facility has approximately 250 acres that contain a office/dining building, a classroom building and residential buildings.

Referral Information Contact the admissions office for referral information.

Type of Facility
Funding Sources Private; State; Federal.
Average Length of Stay Long term.
Types of Admissions Accepted Residential treatment; Wards of the state.
Sources of Referral State depts of education; Local depts of education; State depts of mental health; Psychiatrists; Private sources; Social service depts.

Client Profile
Age Range of Clients Served Residential program: 6-18.
Characteristics Exhibited by Children Emotional handicaps.
IQ Range of Clients 70+.

Tuition and Fees
Room and Board Long term: $49/diem.
Placements Primarily Funded By Local depts of education; State depts of mental health; Private sources; Social service depts.

Social and Rehabilitative Services
Therapeutic Approach The facility uses an eclectic blend of proven therapies, including reality therapy, guided group interaction, Rogerian, and Maslow.
Therapeutic Services Offered Individual therapy; Group therapy; Family therapy; Recreation activities; Aftercare program with follow up.
Professionals on Staff Social workers; Child care staff.

Educational and Vocational Services
Type(s) of Educational Programs Offered On campus (Remedial & grade level instruction).
Profile of On Campus School Program Number of teachers 2; *Number of classrooms* 1; *Student to teacher ratio* 5:1; *Credentials of teachers* certified; *Grades taught* 4-12.

FT LAUDERDALE

OUTREACH BROWARD—SOLOMON CENTER FOR BOYS

1036 NE 3rd Ave, Ft Lauderdale, FL 33304 (305) 523-3148 *Contact Person(s):* Amy Gilson, Prog Therapist

Setting and Background Information The facility was established in 1981 as a private, non-profit organization. It is a residential group home.

Referral Information Referrals are made through the state Dept of HRS. Staff of the facility will assist with the process.

Type of Facility
Funding Sources Private; State.
Average Length of Stay Long term; Avg 1 yr.
Types of Admissions Accepted Residential treatment; Wards of the state.
Sources of Referral Local depts of education; State depts of mental health; Psychiatrists; Social service depts.

Client Profile
Age Range of Clients Served Residential program: 12-18.
Characteristics Exhibited by Children Emotional handicaps; Mental disabilities.
IQ Range of Clients 85-120.

Tuition and Fees
Room and Board Long term: $70/diem.
Placements Primarily Funded By State depts of mental health.

OUTREACH BROWARD—SOLOMON CENTER FOR BOYS (continued)

Social and Rehabilitative Services
Therapeutic Approach The facility uses a systems approach to family therapy.
Therapeutic Services Offered Individual therapy; Group therapy; Family therapy; Independent living skills program; Aftercare program with follow up.
Professionals on Staff Psychologists; Social workers.
Educational and Vocational Services
Type(s) of Educational Programs Offered Off campus (Special ed center and local school).

OUTREACH BROWARD—SOLOMON CENTER FOR GIRLS

1048 NE 3rd Ave, Ft Lauderdale, FL 33304 (305) 760-9149 *Contact Person(s):* Betty Blair, Prog Therapist
Setting and Background Information The facility was established in 1986 as a private, non-profit organization. It is a residential group home.
Referral Information Referrals are made through the state Dept of HRS. The staff of the facility will assist with the process.
Type of Facility
Funding Sources Private; State.
Average Length of Stay Long term; Avg 1 yr.
Types of Admissions Accepted Residential treatment; Wards of the state.
Sources of Referral Local depts of education; State depts of mental health; Psychiatrists; Social service depts.
Client Profile
Age Range of Clients Served Residential program 12-18.
Characteristics Exhibited by Children Emotional handicaps; Mental disabilities.
IQ Range of Clients 85-120.
Tuition and Fees
Room and Board Long term: $70/diem.
Placements Primarily Funded By State depts of mental health.
Social and Rehabilitative Services
Therapeutic Approach The facility uses the systems approach to family therapy.
Therapeutic Services Offered Individual therapy; Group therapy; Family therapy; Independent living skills program; Aftercare program with follow up.
Professionals on Staff Psychologists; Social workers.
Educational and Vocational Services
Type(s) of Educational Programs Offered Off campus (Special Ed center & local school).

SHERIDAN HOUSE

4200 SW 54 Ct, Ft Lauderdale, FL 33021 (305) 583-1552
Setting and Background Information The facility was established by a church in 1968.
Referral Information Contact the facility for referral information. Children must be residents of Broward County.
Type of Facility
Funding Sources Private.
Average Length of Stay Long term.
Types of Admissions Accepted Residential treatment.
Sources of Referral State depts of education; Local depts of education; State depts of mental health; Psychiatrists; Social service depts.
Client Profile
Age Range of Clients Served Day programs: 12-15.
Characteristics Exhibited by Children Emotional handicaps; Learning disabilities.
Tuition and Fees
Room and Board Long term: $20/wk.
Placements Primarily Funded By Private sources.
Social and Rehabilitative Services
Therapeutic Services Offered Individual therapy; Group therapy; Family therapy.
Professionals on Staff Psychologists; Social workers.
Educational and Vocational Services
Type(s) of Educational Programs Offered Off campus.

ANN STORCK CENTER, INC.

1790 SW 43rd Way, Ft Lauderdale, FL 33317 (305) 584-8000
Contact Person(s): James J. McGuire, Exec Dir
Setting and Background Information The center was incorporated in 1981 as a non-profit comprehensive facility for mentally retarded children and young adults, and has a preschool, a developmental training program and a residential program. In addition, the facility operates two cluster programs, one in Pembroke Pines and the other in Lantana, which have three group homes in each.
Referral Information Contact the facility for referral information.
Type of Facility
Funding Sources Private; State.
Average Length of Stay Long term.
Types of Admissions Accepted Day treatment; Residential treatment; Group home placement.
Sources of Referral Social service depts.
Client Profile
Age Range of Clients Served Day programs: Birth-5; Residential programs: 10-55+.
Characteristics Exhibited by Children Emotional handicaps; Learning disabilities; Hearing impairments/deafness; Vision impairments/blindness; Speech/Language disorders; Neurological impairments; Physical handicaps; Mental disabilities.
Tuition and Fees
Placements Primarily Funded By Social service depts; Donations.
Social and Rehabilitative Services
Therapeutic Services Offered Physical therapy; Independent living skills program; Recreation activities; Speech therapy; Occupational therapy;.
Professionals on Staff Social workers; Child care staff; Nurses; Physical therapists; Speech therapist; Recreational therapist; Occupational therapist.
Educational and Vocational Services
Type(s) of Educational Programs Offered On campus (Pre-school; Independent living skills); Off campus.

JACKSONVILLE

DANIEL MEMORIAL, INC

3725 Belfort Rd, Jacksonville, FL 32316 (904) 737-1677 *Contact Person(s):* Sylvia Hammond
Setting and Background Information Daniel Memorial is a private residential treatment facility. There is also a group home for girls, a foster care program, and an independent living program for older children who are transitioning back into the community. This facility was originally established in 1883 and expanded its programs to become a treatment facility in 1973. The campus is located on a 10 acre wooded area, 15 miles from the Atlantic Ocean. There are 4 cottages, a school complex, infirmary, shop, swimming pool, and athletic field.
Referral Information Referrals can be made by any concerned individual. Applicants are requested to forward psychiatric, psychological, educational, and medical reports before a placement decision can be made.
Type of Facility
Funding Sources Private.
Average Length of Stay Long term.
Types of Admissions Accepted Residential treatment.
Sources of Referral State depts of mental health; Psychiatrists; Private sources; Depts of correction; Social service depts.
Client Profile
Age Range of Clients Served Residential program: 5-17.
Characteristics Exhibited by Children Emotional handicaps; Learning disabilities.
Tuition and Fees
Room and Board Long term: $216/diem.
Placements Primarily Funded By State depts of mental health; Insurance; Private sources; Champus.
Social and Rehabilitative Services
Therapeutic Approach The philosophy of the treatment program is based on the Educator Model.
Therapeutic Services Offered Individual therapy; Group therapy; Family therapy.
Educational and Vocational Services
Type(s) of Educational Programs Offered On campus (Through Duval county); Off campus.
Profile of On Campus School Program Student to teacher ratio 6:1; Credentials of teachers Certified Spec Ed; Grades taught K-12.

MIAMI

DADE COUNTY DEPT OF YOUTH AND FAMILY DEVELOPMENT—GROUP HOME PROGRAM

1701 NW 30 Ave, Miami, FL 33125 (305) 633-6481 *Contact Person(s):* Pamela Waters, Soc Srvs Supr

Setting and Background Information This program was established in 1974 as an alternative to institutional care. There are 5 group homes.

Referral Information Referral is initiated by phone to the social services supervisor. A brief history and identifying data are taken at that time. An intake interview with the social worker and houseparents will be scheduled.

Type of Facility

Funding Sources Dade county.

Average Length of Stay 6-9 mo.

Types of Admissions Accepted Group home placement.

Sources of Referral State depts of education; Local depts of education; State depts of mental health; Psychiatrists; Private sources; Depts of correction; Social service depts; Self.

Client Profile

Age Range of Clients Served Residential program: 10-18.

Characteristics Exhibited by Children Emotional handicaps; Learning disabilities; Mental disabilities.

IQ Range of Clients 80+.

Tuition and Fees

Room and Board Long term: Sliding scale.

Placements Primarily Funded By Dade county.

Social and Rehabilitative Services

Therapeutic Approach The facility has a structured, individualized program in a family type, community-based setting.

Therapeutic Services Offered Individual therapy; Group therapy; Family therapy; Independent living skills program; Aftercare program with follow up.

Professionals on Staff Social workers; Child care staff.

Educational and Vocational Services

Type(s) of Educational Programs Offered Off campus (Public school programs).

HCA GRANT CENTER HOSPITAL

20601 SW 157 Ave, Miami, FL 33187 (305) 251-0710 *Contact Person(s):* Janet Fenner, Adm Dir

Setting and Background Information The facility was established in 1970 with a grant from the School of Miami. It is a private, non-profit school for developmentally delayed children. Its 20-acre campus has dormitories, recreation areas, and greenhouses.

Referral Information Anyone can make a referral by calling the facility.

Type of Facility

Funding Sources Private; State.

Average Length of Stay Long term.

Types of Admissions Accepted Day treatment; Residential treatment.

Sources of Referral State depts of education; Local depts of education; State depts of mental health; Psychiatrists; Private sources; Depts of correction; Social service depts.

Client Profile

Age Range of Clients Served Day programs: 6-21; Residential program: 3-21.

Characteristics Exhibited by Children Emotional handicaps; Learning disabilities; Neurological impairments; Mental disabilities; Psychiatric diagnosis.

IQ Range of Clients 80-140.

Tuition and Fees

Placements Primarily Funded By Local depts of education; Insurance; Private sources; Social service depts.

Social and Rehabilitative Services

Therapeutic Approach The facility's approach to therapy is psychodynamic, with a strong family component.

Therapeutic Services Offered Individual therapy; Group therapy; Family therapy; Art therapy; Physical therapy; Recreation activities; Substance abuse treatment; Aftercare program with follow up; Horticulture.

Professionals on Staff Psychiatrists; Psychologists; Social workers; Adjunctive therapists; Child care staff; Nurses; Art therapists; Physical therapists.

Educational and Vocational Services

Type(s) of Educational Programs Offered On campus (Fully accredited K-12).

Degrees Offered 12th grade diploma.

MIAMI CHILDREN'S HOSPITAL—DIVISION OF PSYCHIATRY

6125 SW 31 St, Miami, FL 33155 (305) 666-6511, ext 2465 *Contact Person(s):* Lori White, Proj Coord

Setting and Background Information Miami Children's Hospital was established in 1951. The Division of Psychiatry was established in 1964 as a 12-bed unit for children 5-12 years. Currently, the unit has 20 beds in a 188 bed pediatric hospital.

Referral Information Referrals are made by parents, school counselors, pediatricians. If not appropriate for the program or out-patient clinic, referrals are made by the facility to agencies in the community.

Type of Facility

Funding Sources Private.

Average Length of Stay Short and long term.

Types of Admissions Accepted Day treatment; Residential treatment; Wards of the state.

Sources of Referral State depts of education; Local depts of education; State depts of mental health; Psychiatrists; Private sources; Depts of correction; Social service depts.

Client Profile

Age Range of Clients Served Day programs: 12-18; Residential program: 11-18.

Characteristics Exhibited by Children Emotional handicaps; Learning disabilities; Neurological impairments; Physical handicaps; Mental disabilities.

Tuition and Fees

Room and Board Long term: $390/diem.

Placements Primarily Funded By Insurance; Private sources; Medicaid.

Social and Rehabilitative Services

Therapeutic Approach The basic therapeutic approach used is pychotherapy and systemic/structural family therapy.

Therapeutic Services Offered Individual therapy; Group therapy; Family therapy; Adjunctive therapy; Art therapy; Physical therapy; Independent living skills program; Recreation activities; Substance abuse treatment; Aftercare program with follow up.

Professionals on Staff Psychiatrists; Psychologists; Social workers; Adjunctive therapists; Child care staff; Nurses; Art therapists; Physical therapists; Music therapist; Movement therapist; Occupational therapists.

Educational and Vocational Services

Type(s) of Educational Programs Offered On campus (Individualized academic).

Profile of On Campus School Program Number of teachers 1; *Number of classrooms* 1; *Length of school day* 3 hrs; *Grades taught* All; Special curriculum electives offered (Life mgmt, Computer, PE); Remedial courses offered (Reading, Math, Grammar).

Degrees Offered 12th grade diploma.

PINELLAS PARK

PINELLAS EMERGENCY MENTAL HEALTH SERVICES

11254 58th St, Pinellas Park, FL 34666 (813) 545-5636 *Contact Person(s):* Children's Residential Intake Worker

Setting and Background Information The facility was originally established as a treatment center called Pinellas Youth People's Treatment Home. There were 4 programs or homes located in Pinellas County, each serving 4-11 children. In 1986, the center merged with Pinellas Emergency Mental Health Services and currently provides a full range of services, from crisis intervention to residential treatment.

Referral Information Anyone can make a referral by contacting the facility.

Type of Facility

Funding Sources Private.

Average Length of Stay Short and long term.

Types of Admissions Accepted Day treatment; Residential treatment; Group home placement; Wards of the state; Emergency shelter.

Sources of Referral State depts of mental health; Private sources; County.

PINELLAS EMERGENCY MENTAL HEALTH SERVICES *(continued)*

Client Profile
Age Range of Clients Served Day programs: 4-17; Residential program: 4-17.
Characteristics Exhibited by Children Emotional handicaps; Learning disabilities; Neurological impairments.
Tuition and Fees
Placements Primarily Funded By State depts of mental health; Private sources; County.
Social and Rehabilitative Services
Therapeutic Approach The philosophy of the treatment program is based on behavior modification and milieu therapy.
Therapeutic Services Offered Individual therapy; Group therapy; Family therapy; Independent living skills program; Recreation activities.
Professionals on Staff Psychiatrists; Psychologists; Social workers; Adjunctive therapists; Child care staff; Nurses.
Educational and Vocational Services
Type(s) of Educational Programs Offered On campus.
Profile of On Campus School Program Number of teachers 3; *Student to teacher ratio* 8:1; *Grades taught* Individualized.

POMPANO BEACH

OUTREACH BROWARD—THE CHORD

113 NE 7th St, Pompano Beach, FL 33060 (305) 785-7588 *Contact Person(s):* Lynn Dorfman, Prog Therapist
Setting and Background Information The facility was established in 1975 as a private, non-profit organization. It is a residential group home.
Referral Information For referral, contact the facility. An interview will be held with the parents, the child and the referring agency. A psychological evaluation is required.
Type of Facility
Funding Sources Private; State; United Way.
Average Length of Stay Long term; Avg 7 mos.
Types of Admissions Accepted Residential treatment; Group home placement.
Sources of Referral Local depts of education; State depts of mental health; Psychiatrists; Private sources; Social service depts; Families.
Client Profile
Age Range of Clients Served Residential program: 12-18.
Characteristics Exhibited by Children Emotional handicaps.
IQ Range of Clients 85-135.
Tuition and Fees
Room and Board Long term: Sliding scale.
Placements Primarily Funded By Private sources; Parents.
Social and Rehabilitative Services
Therapeutic Approach The facility has a systems approach to family therapy.
Therapeutic Services Offered Individual therapy; Group therapy; Family therapy; Aftercare program with follow up.
Professionals on Staff Psychologists; Social workers.
Educational and Vocational Services
Type(s) of Educational Programs Offered Off campus (Local school).

TALLAHASSEE

WATEROAK SPECIALTY HOSPITAL TREATMENT PROGRAM

2634-G Capital Cir NE, Tallahassee, FL 32308 (904) 487-2930, ext 33 *Contact Person(s):* Catherine E McNabb, Dir
Setting and Background Information The program was established in 1977 to provide group residential treatment for youth as an alternative to psychiatric hospitalization.
Referral Information Contact the facility for referral information. A psychological/psychiatric evaluation is needed to enter the residential treatment program.
Type of Facility
Funding Sources Private; State.
Average Length of Stay Long term.
Types of Admissions Accepted Residential treatment.
Sources of Referral Local depts of education; State depts of mental health; Psychiatrists; Social service depts.

Client Profile
Age Range of Clients Served Residential program: 12-18.
Characteristics Exhibited by Children Emotional handicaps.
IQ Range of Clients 70-120.
Tuition and Fees
Room and Board Long term: $92/diem.
Placements Primarily Funded By Insurance; Social service depts.
Social and Rehabilitative Services
Therapeutic Approach The facility uses cognitive and behavioral therapies.
Therapeutic Services Offered Individual therapy; Group therapy; Family therapy; Adjunctive therapy; Independent living skills program; Aftercare program with follow up.
Professionals on Staff Psychiatrists; Psychologists; Social workers; Adjunctive therapists; Child care staff; Nurses.
Educational and Vocational Services
Type(s) of Educational Programs Offered Off campus (Public school).

TAMPA

NORTHSIDE COMMUNITY MENTAL HEALTH CENTER, INC

1330 N 30th St, Tampa, FL 33612 (813) 977-8700 *Contact Person(s):* Susan Perez
Setting and Background Information Northside Community Mental Health Center has an adolescent in-patient unit and a group home. The facility was established in 1980 with cooperation from the University of South Florida, Psychiatry Dept. It is located on the University of South Florida campus in a one-story building.
Referral Information Anyone can make a referral, however, most referrals come from community agencies. The following referral information on the child will be requested: psycho-educational assessments, social and developmental history, and arrangements for funding.
Type of Facility
Funding Sources Private.
Average Length of Stay Short and long term.
Types of Admissions Accepted Residential treatment; Group home placement.
Sources of Referral Depts of correction; Crisis centers; Short term facilities.
Client Profile
Age Range of Clients Served Residential program: 13-18.
Characteristics Exhibited by Children Emotional handicaps; Learning disabilities; Neurological impairments.
Tuition and Fees
Placements Primarily Funded By State depts of mental health; Insurance.
Social and Rehabilitative Services
Therapeutic Approach The philosophy of the residential treatment program is insight oriented with the use of a behavioral level system.
Therapeutic Services Offered Individual therapy; Group therapy; Family therapy; Independent living skills program; Community meetings.
Professionals on Staff Psychiatrists; Psychologists; Social workers; Adjunctive therapists; Child care staff; Nurses.
Educational and Vocational Services
Type(s) of Educational Programs Offered On campus (Through public school system).
Profile of On Campus School Program Number of teachers 3; *Number of classrooms* 1; *Student to teacher ratio* 4:1; *Credentials of teachers* EH.
Degrees Offered 12th grade diploma; GED.

GEORGIA

ATLANTA

HILLSIDE, INC

690 Courtenay Dr NE, Atlanta, GA 30306 (404) 875-4551 *Contact Person(s):* Lori Hogeman, Social Wkr
Setting and Background Information The facility was originally established in 1888 as an orphanage. The 8-acre campus has 4 living units, an office, and a school.
Referral Information Contact the facility for referral information. A pre-placement interview will be scheduled.
Type of Facility
Funding Sources Private; State; Federal.
Average Length of Stay Long term.
Types of Admissions Accepted Residential treatment; Wards of the state.
Sources of Referral State depts of education; Local depts of education; State depts of mental health; Psychiatrists; Private sources; Depts of correction; Social service depts.
Client Profile
Age Range of Clients Served Residential program: 10-18.
Characteristics Exhibited by Children Emotional handicaps; Learning disabilities; Mental disabilities.
IQ Range of Clients 70+.
Tuition and Fees
Room and Board Long term: $80/diem.
Tuition $80/diem.
Placements Primarily Funded By State depts of education; Local depts of education; State depts of mental health; Insurance; Private sources; Depts of corrections; Social service depts.
Social and Rehabilitative Services
Therapeutic Approach The basic approach of the facility is reality therapy.
Therapeutic Services Offered Individual therapy; Group therapy; Family therapy; Adjunctive therapy; Independent living skills program; Recreation activities.
Professionals on Staff Psychiatrists; Psychologists; Social workers; Adjunctive therapists; Child care staff; Nurses.
Educational and Vocational Services
Type(s) of Educational Programs Offered On campus; Off campus; Summer campus.
Profile of On Campus School Program Number of teachers 2; *Number of classrooms* 2; *Student to teacher ratio* 10:1; *Credentials of teachers* MA; *Grades taught* 3-12.
Degrees Offered 8th grade diploma; 12th grade diploma.

VILLAGE OF ST JOSEPH

2969 Butner Rd SW, Atlanta, GA 30331-0120 (404) 349-2400
Contact Person(s): Sr Mary Frances Bruns, Admin
Setting and Background Information The facility was established in 1967 by the Archdiocese of Atlanta. The 45-acre campus has 4 cottages, an administration/activity building, and a chapel.
Referral Information Contact the intake worker for referral information. A pre-placement conference will be scheduled.
Type of Facility
Funding Sources Private; Archdiocesan subsidy.
Average Length of Stay 2 ½ - 3 yrs.
Types of Admissions Accepted Day treatment; Residential treatment.
Sources of Referral State depts of education; Local depts of education; State depts of mental health; Psychiatrists; Private sources; Social service depts; Psychiatric hospitals.

Client Profile
Age Range of Clients Served Day programs: 6-18; Residential program: 6-18.
Characteristics Exhibited by Children Emotional handicaps; Learning disabilities.
IQ Range of Clients 90-130.
Tuition and Fees
Room and Board Long term: $1,200/mo.
Tuition $400/mo.
Placements Primarily Funded By Private sources; Archdiocese of Atlanta.
Social and Rehabilitative Services
Therapeutic Approach The facility has an eclectic approach to therapy.
Therapeutic Services Offered Individual therapy; Group therapy; Family therapy.
Professionals on Staff Psychiatrists; Psychologists; Social workers; Child care staff.
Educational and Vocational Services
Type(s) of Educational Programs Offered On campus; Summer campus.
Profile of On Campus School Program Number of teachers 6; *Number of classrooms* 6; *Student to teacher ratio* 8:1; *Credentials of teachers* MA; *Length of school day* 9-2:30; *Grades taught* 1-10; Remedial courses offered.

CARTERSVILLE

CHILDREN'S EMERGENCY SHELTER

127 W Church St, Cartersville, GA 30120 (404) 382-6180 *Contact Person(s):* Ava Norton-Gehman, Exec Dir
Setting and Background Information The facility was established in 1985 in response to a community need. It is an emergency shelter located in a residential home.
Referral Information All referrals are made through the Dept of Family and Children Services.
Type of Facility
Funding Sources Private.
Average Length of Stay Short term.
Types of Admissions Accepted Wards of the state; Emergency shelter.
Sources of Referral Social service depts.
Client Profile
Age Range of Clients Served Residential program: Birth-18.
Characteristics Exhibited by Children Emotional handicaps; Learning disabilities.
Tuition and Fees
Placements Primarily Funded By Private sources; Social service depts.
Social and Rehabilitative Services
Professionals on Staff Psychologists; Social workers; Child care staff.
Educational and Vocational Services
Type(s) of Educational Programs Offered Off campus.

CEDARTOWN

MURPHY-HARPST UNITED METHODIST CHILDREN AND FAMILY SERVICES

740 Fleltcher St, Cedartown, GA 30125 (404) 748-1500 *Contact Person(s):* John R Steiner, Exec Dir

MURPHY-HARPST UNITED METHODIST CHILDREN AND FAMILY SERVICES *(continued)*

Setting and Background Information The facility was established in 1926 as an orphanage. There are 5 residential cottages.
Referral Information Referrals are made through state DFCS, DHR and Dept of Ed. Private referrals are also accepted.
Type of Facility
Funding Sources Private; State.
Average Length of Stay Short and long term.
Types of Admissions Accepted Residential treatment.
Sources of Referral State depts of education; Private sources; Social service depts.
Client Profile
Age Range of Clients Served Residential program: 6-18.
Characteristics Exhibited by Children Emotional handicaps; Learning disabilities.
IQ Range of Clients 54-100.
Tuition and Fees
Room and Board Long term: $60/diem (Intermediate care); $20/diem (Basic care).
Placements Primarily Funded By State depts of education; Insurance; Private sources; Social service depts.
Social and Rehabilitative Services
Therapeutic Approach The facility has a multi-disciplinary therapeutic milieu.
Therapeutic Services Offered Individual therapy; Group therapy; Family therapy; Independent living skills program.
Professionals on Staff Psychiatrists; Psychologists; Social workers; Child care staff; Nurses.
Educational and Vocational Services
Type(s) of Educational Programs Offered On campus; Off campus.
Profile of On Campus School Program Number of teachers 2; *Number of classrooms* 2; *Student to teacher ratio* 6:1; *Credentials of teachers* BS, MA; *Grades taught* Ungraded; Remedial courses offered.

COLUMBUS

ANNE ELIZABETH SHEPHERD HOME
751 Double Churches Rd, Columbus, GA 31904 (404) 322-8984
Contact Person(s): Calvin Bunn, Dir
Setting and Background Information The facility was established in 1845 by a state charter. Currently, it is located on 7 acres with an administration building and two cottages with the capacity for 14 adolescents each.
Referral Information Contact the facility for an application form. Submit this form with psychological and social histories, school and health records.
Type of Facility
Funding Sources Private; State.
Average Length of Stay Long term.
Types of Admissions Accepted Residential treatment; Group home placement; Wards of the state.
Sources of Referral State depts of education; Local depts of education; State depts of mental health; Psychiatrists; Private sources; Depts of correction; Social service depts.
Client Profile
Age Range of Clients Served Residential program: 12-18.
Characteristics Exhibited by Children Emotional handicaps.
IQ Range of Clients 70+.
Tuition and Fees
Room and Board Long term: $500/mo.
Placements Primarily Funded By Social service depts.
Social and Rehabilitative Services
Therapeutic Approach The facility uses reality therapy with behavior modification.
Therapeutic Services Offered Individual therapy; Group therapy; Family therapy; Independent living skills program; Recreation activities.
Professionals on Staff Psychiatrists; Psychologists; Social workers; Child care staff.
Educational and Vocational Services
Type(s) of Educational Programs Offered On campus (Public school).

JULIETTE

APPLETON FAMILY MINISTRIES
PO Box 210, Juliette, GA 31046 (912) 986-4620
Setting and Background Information This facility was originally established in 1865 as an orphanage. Currently, its 400-acre campus has a lodge, a bathhouse, an office and a school.
Referral Information Contact the facility for referral information.
Type of Facility
Funding Sources Private.
Average Length of Stay Long term; 12-18 mos.
Types of Admissions Accepted Residential treatment.
Sources of Referral Psychiatrists; Private sources; Social service depts.
Client Profile
Age Range of Clients Served Residential program: 12-16.
Characteristics Exhibited by Children Emotional handicaps; Behavior disorders.
IQ Range of Clients 85+.
Tuition and Fees
Room and Board Long term: $80/diem.
Placements Primarily Funded By Private sources; Social service depts.
Social and Rehabilitative Services
Therapeutic Approach This facility has an outdoor therapeutic program and uses positive peer culture as a therapeutic intervention.
Therapeutic Services Offered Individual therapy; Group therapy; Family therapy; Recreation activities.
Professionals on Staff Psychiatrists; Social workers; Child care staff; Nurses.
Educational and Vocational Services
Type(s) of Educational Programs Offered On campus (Individualized instruction).
Profile of On Campus School Program Number of teachers 2; *Number of classrooms* 3; *Student to teacher ratio* 10:1; *Grades taught* 7-12.

KENNESAW

THE DEVEREUX CENTER IN GEORGIA
1980 Stanley Rd, Kennesaw, GA 30144 (404) 427-0147 *Contact Person(s):* Lyn H Crowe, Admis Dir
Setting and Background Information The facility was established in 1973 by the National Devereux Foundation. Located on 47 acres, there is an acute care hospital, residential buildings, educational buildings and others.
Referral Information Contact the facility and forward psychiatric and social histories, and educational information. If appropriate, the admissions dept will schedule an evaluation.
Type of Facility
Funding Sources Private; State; Champus.
Average Length of Stay Long term.
Types of Admissions Accepted Residential treatment; Wards of the state; Psychiatric hospital.
Sources of Referral State depts of education; Local depts of education; State depts of mental health; Psychiatrists; Private sources; Depts of correction; Social service depts.
Client Profile
Age Range of Clients Served Residential program: 12-18.
Characteristics Exhibited by Children Emotional handicaps; Learning disabilities; Speech/Language disorders; Mental disabilities.
IQ Range of Clients 75+.
Tuition and Fees
Room and Board Long term: $5,039-$8,432/mo (includes school tuition).
Placements Primarily Funded By State depts of education; Local depts of education; State depts of mental health; Insurance; Private sources; Depts of corrections; Social service depts.
Social and Rehabilitative Services
Therapeutic Approach The facility has a behavioral approach to therapy.
Therapeutic Services Offered Individual therapy; Group therapy; Family therapy; Adjunctive therapy; Art therapy; Independent living skills program; Recreation activities; Substance abuse treatment; Aftercare program with follow up.
Professionals on Staff Psychiatrists; Psychologists; Social workers; Adjunctive therapists; Child care staff; Nurses; Art therapists.

THE DEVEREUX CENTER IN GEORGIA *(continued)*

Educational and Vocational Services
Type(s) of Educational Programs Offered On campus; Summer campus.
Profile of On Campus School Program Number of teachers 13; *Number of classrooms* 9; *Student to teacher ratio* 8:1; *Credentials of teachers* BS, MS; *Grades taught* 3-12; Remedial courses offered.
Vocational Education Programs/Degrees Offered Nurses Aide; Childcare.
Degrees Offered GED.

LAGRANGE

WEST GA YOUTH COUNCIL, INC
PO Box 2522, LaGrange, GA 30240 (404) 884-1717 *Contact Person(s):* Leslie Chastain, Social Svcs Coord
Setting and Background Information The facility was established in 1978. There are 3 homes licensed to serve 8 adolescents each and a day treatment facility.
Referral Information For referral, contact the intake worker and forward an application packet. A pre-placement visit will be scheduled.
Type of Facility
Funding Sources State.
Average Length of Stay Short term (emergency shelter); Long term (group homes).
Types of Admissions Accepted Day treatment; Group home placement; Wards of the state; Emergency shelter.
Sources of Referral Local depts of education; Depts of correction; Social service depts.
Client Profile
Age Range of Clients Served Day programs: 6-18; Residential program: 12-18.
Characteristics Exhibited by Children Emotional handicaps; Learning disabilities.
IQ Range of Clients 70+.
Social and Rehabilitative Services
Therapeutic Services Offered Individual therapy; Group therapy; Family therapy; Independent living skills program.
Professionals on Staff Psychologists; Social workers; Child care staff.
Educational and Vocational Services
Type(s) of Educational Programs Offered Off campus.

MARIETTA

THE OPEN GATE
330 Victory Dr, Marietta, GA 30060 (404) 426-1919 *Contact Person(s):* Carolyn Campbell, Dir
Setting and Background Information The facility was established in 1984. It is a private, non-profit residential shelter.
Referral Information All referrals are made through Cobb County Family and Children Services as a result of abuse or neglect.
Type of Facility
Funding Sources Private; State.
Average Length of Stay Short term.
Types of Admissions Accepted Emergency shelter.
Sources of Referral State depts of mental health; Cobb County.
Client Profile
Age Range of Clients Served Residential program: Birth-17.
Characteristics Exhibited by Children Abused and neglected.
Tuition and Fees
Placements Primarily Funded By .
Social and Rehabilitative Services
Therapeutic Services Offered Individual therapy; Group therapy.
Professionals on Staff Social workers; Child care staff.
Educational and Vocational Services
Type(s) of Educational Programs Offered Off campus.

PALMETTO

GEORGIA BAPTIST CHILDREN'S HOMES AND FAMILY MINISTRIES, INC
9250 Hutcheson Ferry Rd, Palmetto, GA 30268 (404) 463-3344
Contact Person(s): Jimmy McAdams, North Area Admin

Setting and Background Information The facility was established in 1973. There are 22 buildings on the 400 acre campus, which include cotttages, offices and a gym.
Referral Information Contact the facility for referral information.
Type of Facility
Funding Sources Private; Foundations.
Average Length of Stay Short and long term.
Types of Admissions Accepted Residential treatment; Group home placement; Wards of the state.
Sources of Referral Private sources; Depts of correction; Social service depts; Private.
Client Profile
Age Range of Clients Served Residential program: Birth-55+.
Characteristics Exhibited by Children Emotional handicaps.
IQ Range of Clients 68-110.
Tuition and Fees
Placements Primarily Funded By Churches.
Social and Rehabilitative Services
Therapeutic Services Offered Individual therapy; Group therapy; Family therapy; Recreation activities; Aftercare program with follow up.
Professionals on Staff Psychologists; Social workers; Child care staff.
Educational and Vocational Services
Type(s) of Educational Programs Offered On campus; Off campus.
Profile of On Campus School Program Number of teachers 1; *Credentials of teachers* MA; Remedial courses offered.

SMYRNA

RIDGEVIEW INSTITUTE
3995 S Cobb Dr, Smyrna, GA 30080 (404) 434-4567 *Contact Person(s):* Robert J Alpern MD, Dir Child and Adolescent Srvs
Setting and Background Information The facility was established in 1976 as a private, non-profit psychiatric hospital. The facility has an 80-acre campus with professional office buildings, a conference center, an administration building, and 5 residential treatment cottages.
Referral Information Contact the facility for referral information. A psychiatrist is on call 24-hours.
Type of Facility
Funding Sources Private.
Average Length of Stay Short term (Adults); Long term (Children, Adolescents).
Types of Admissions Accepted Day treatment; Residential treatment.
Sources of Referral State depts of education; Local depts of education; State depts of mental health; Psychiatrists; Private sources; Depts of correction; Social service depts.
Client Profile
Age Range of Clients Served Day programs: 12-55+; Residential program: 6-55+.
Characteristics Exhibited by Children Emotional handicaps; Learning disabilities; Mental disabilities; Chemical abuse.
Tuition and Fees
Placements Primarily Funded By Insurance; Private sources.
Social and Rehabilitative Services
Therapeutic Approach The facility has a psychodynamic approach to therapy.
Therapeutic Services Offered Individual therapy; Group therapy; Family therapy; Adjunctive therapy; Art therapy; Physical therapy; Recreation activities; Substance abuse treatment; Aftercare program with follow up.
Professionals on Staff Psychiatrists; Psychologists; Social workers; Adjunctive therapists; Nurses; Art therapists.
Educational and Vocational Services
Type(s) of Educational Programs Offered On campus; Off campus; Summer campus.
Profile of On Campus School Program Number of teachers 18; *Number of classrooms* 17; *Student to teacher ratio* 6:1; *Credentials of teachers* Certified; *Grades taught* 4-12; Special curriculum electives offered (PE, Computers, Languages, Drug education, Music, Home ec, Art, Photography); Remedial courses offered.
Vocational Education Programs/Degrees Offered Clerical; Computers; Drafting; Accounting; Interior design.
Degrees Offered Degrees earned through home school.

THOMASVILLE

SOUTHWESTERN STATE HOSPITAL—CHILD AND ADOLESCENT UNIT

Pinetree Blvd, Thomasville, GA 31792 (912) 228-2234 *Contact Person(s):* Donna Steffen, MSW

Setting and Background Information The program was established in 1975 with the help of a federal grant, but is now state funded. The 25-bed Child and Adolescent Unit is located on the grounds of Southwestern State Hospital, which is a comprehensive regional psychiatric hospital.

Referral Information Referrals are made through county mental health agencies.

Type of Facility

Funding Sources State.

Average Length of Stay Short and long term.

Types of Admissions Accepted Day treatment; Residential treatment.

Sources of Referral State depts of mental health; Private sources.

Client Profile

Age Range of Clients Served Day programs: Birth-17; Residential program: Birth-17.

Characteristics Exhibited by Children Emotional handicaps; Learning disabilities.

Tuition and Fees

Room and Board Long term: $225/diem.

Placements Primarily Funded By State depts of mental health; Insurance; Private sources.

Social and Rehabilitative Services

Therapeutic Approach The treatment program is based on a interdisciplinary team approach.

Therapeutic Services Offered Individual therapy; Group therapy; Family therapy; Adjunctive therapy; Independent living skills program; Substance abuse treatment; Aftercare program with follow up.

Professionals on Staff Psychiatrists; Psychologists; Social workers; Adjunctive therapists; Child care staff; Nurses.

Educational and Vocational Services

Type(s) of Educational Programs Offered On campus.

Profile of On Campus School Program Number of teachers 2; *Student to teacher ratio* 6:1; *Credentials of teachers* Certified Spec Ed.

VIDALIA

PAUL ANDERSON YOUTH HOME, INC

PO Box 525, Vidalia, GA (912) 537-7237 (912) 537-7237 *Contact Person(s):* Mrs Paul Anderson, Asst Dir

Setting and Background Information This Christian youth home was privately established in 1961 to provide an alternative to juvenile penal institutions. It has a 52 acre campus.

Referral Information Contact the facility for referral information.

Type of Facility

Funding Sources Private.

Average Length of Stay Long term.

Types of Admissions Accepted Residential treatment.

Sources of Referral State depts of education; Local depts of education; State depts of mental health; Psychiatrists; Private sources; Depts of correction; Social service depts.

Client Profile

Age Range of Clients Served Residential program: 15-18.

Characteristics Exhibited by Children Emotional handicaps; Learning disabilities.

Tuition and Fees

Room and Board Long term: Sliding scale.

Tuition Sliding scale.

Placements Primarily Funded By .

Social and Rehabilitative Services

Therapeutic Services Offered Individual therapy; Group therapy; Family therapy; Independent living skills program; Recreation activities; Substance abuse treatment; Aftercare program with follow up.

Professionals on Staff Social workers; Child care staff; Counselors.

Educational and Vocational Services

Type(s) of Educational Programs Offered On campus.

Profile of On Campus School Program Number of teachers 8; *Number of classrooms* 6; *Student to teacher ratio* 5:1; *Length of school day* 8-4; *Grades taught* 8-12; Special curriculum electives offered; Remedial courses offered.

Degrees Offered 12th grade diploma; GED.

WARM SPRINGS

FD ROOSEVELT WILDERNESS CAMP—OUTDOOR THERAPEUTIC PROGRAM

PO Drawer 427, Hwy 190, Warm Springs, GA 31830 (404) 655-3303 *Contact Person(s):* Michael Angstadt, Dir

Setting and Background Information The facility was established in 1983 by the Dept of Human Resources. The 600-acre campus has residential buildings, an administration building, a dining hall, a school and support buildings.

Referral Information All divisions of the Dept of Human Resources can refer. Applications are screened monthly by the screening committee. A family interview will be arranged. Client must be a Georgia resident.

Type of Facility

Funding Sources State; Federal.

Average Length of Stay Long term.

Types of Admissions Accepted Residential treatment.

Sources of Referral Local depts of education; State depts of mental health.

Client Profile

Age Range of Clients Served Residential program: 6-15.

Characteristics Exhibited by Children Emotional handicaps; Learning disabilities; Neurological impairments; Mental disabilities.

IQ Range of Clients 60+.

Tuition and Fees

Placements Primarily Funded By State depts of mental health.

Social and Rehabilitative Services

Therapeutic Services Offered Individual therapy; Group therapy; Family therapy; Adjunctive therapy; Art therapy; Physical therapy; Independent living skills program; Recreation activities; Substance abuse treatment; Aftercare program with follow up.

Professionals on Staff Psychiatrists; Social workers; Adjunctive therapists; Child care staff; Nurses.

Educational and Vocational Services

Type(s) of Educational Programs Offered On campus (Academic; Vocational).

Profile of On Campus School Program Number of teachers 2; *Number of classrooms* 2; *Student to teacher ratio* 16:1; *Credentials of teachers* MA; *Length of school day* 10-3; *Grades taught* 1-11; Special curriculum electives offered; Remedial courses offered.

HAWAII

HONOLULU

PO'AILANI, INC

1111 Hola Dr, Honolulu, HI 96817 (808) 841-0421 *Contact Person(s):* Sherry Chong, Exec Dir
Setting and Background Information This agency was established in 1979. There are 4 programs at facilities located throughout Oahu: a Transitional Living Unit, Crisis Housing, a Cooperative Living Program, and a Dual Diagnosis program.
Referral Information Contact the facility for referral information.
Type of Facility
Funding Sources Private; State; Federal.
Average Length of Stay Short and long term.
Types of Admissions Accepted Residential treatment; Emergency shelter.
Sources of Referral State depts of mental health; Psychiatrists; Private sources; Depts of correction; Social service depts.
Client Profile
Age Range of Clients Served Residential program: 18-55+.
Characteristics Exhibited by Children Emotional handicaps; Mental disabilities.
Tuition and Fees
Placements Primarily Funded By State depts of mental health; Social service depts.
Social and Rehabilitative Services
Therapeutic Services Offered Individual therapy; Group therapy; Family therapy; Adjunctive therapy; Independent living skills program; Recreation activities; Substance abuse treatment; Aftercare program with follow up.
Professionals on Staff Social workers; Adjunctive therapists.
Educational and Vocational Services
Type(s) of Educational Programs Offered On campus; Off campus.

THE SALVATION ARMY RESIDENTIAL TREATMENT FACILITIES FOR CHILDREN AND YOUTH

845 22nd Ave, Honolulu, HI 96816 (808) 732-2802 *Contact Person(s):* Edmund Leong MSW ACSW, Soc Srvs Super
Setting and Background Information The facility was established in 1906 as a home for dependent children. Located on 10 acres, there are 3 living units, a school, and other buildings.
Referral Information For referral, contact the social services supervisor and forward necessary information. A treament team will review the application packet.
Type of Facility
Funding Sources Private; State; Federal; United Way.
Average Length of Stay Long term.
Types of Admissions Accepted Residential treatment.
Sources of Referral State depts of mental health; Psychiatrists; Social service depts; Family courts; Social agencies.
Client Profile
Age Range of Clients Served Residential program: 6-18.
Characteristics Exhibited by Children Emotional handicaps; Learning disabilities; Behavioral problems related to psychiatric/emotional disturbances.
IQ Range of Clients 80+.
Tuition and Fees
Room and Board Long term: $105.94/diem.
Placements Primarily Funded By State depts of education; Social service depts; Family courts.

Social and Rehabilitative Services
Therapeutic Services Offered Individual therapy; Group therapy; Family therapy; Adjunctive therapy; Recreation activities.
Professionals on Staff Psychiatrists; Psychologists; Social workers; Adjunctive therapists; Child care staff; Nurses.
Educational and Vocational Services
Type(s) of Educational Programs Offered On campus (Spec Ed); Off campus (Spec Ed, Mainstream).
Profile of On Campus School Program *Number of teachers* 6; *Number of classrooms* 6; *Student to teacher ratio* 6:1; *Credentials of teachers* BA, BEd, MEd; *Length of school day* 8:30am-5pm; *Grades taught* K-12; Special curriculum electives offered; Remedial courses offered.

KEALAKEKUA

KONA ASSOCIATION FOR RETARDED CITIZENS DBA KONA KRAFTS

PO Box 127, Kealakekua, HI 96750 (808) 323-2626 *Contact Person(s):* Yash Y Deguchi, Exec Dir
Setting and Background Information The association was established in 1986 as a pilot program funded by a federal grant.
Referral Information Contact the facility for referral procedures.
Type of Facility
Funding Sources State; Federal.
Average Length of Stay Short and long term.
Types of Admissions Accepted Residential treatment.
Sources of Referral State depts of mental health.
Client Profile
Age Range of Clients Served Residential program: 18-21+.
Characteristics Exhibited by Children Emotional handicaps; Learning disabilities; Mental disabilities.
Tuition and Fees
Room and Board Short term: $30/diem; Long term: $225/mo.
Placements Primarily Funded By State depts of mental health.
Social and Rehabilitative Services
Therapeutic Services Offered Individual therapy; Group therapy; Family therapy; Independent living skills program; Substance abuse treatment; Aftercare program with follow up.
Professionals on Staff Psychiatrists; Psychologists; Social workers; Nurses.

MAKAWAO

MAUI YOUTH & FAMILY SERVICES BOYS' GROUP HOME

200 Ike Dr, Makawao, HI 96779 (808) 579-8441 *Contact Person(s):* Colleen O'Shea Wallace, Social Worker
Setting and Background Information The facility was established in 1986.
Referral Information Contact the facility for referral information.
Type of Facility
Funding Sources Private; State.
Average Length of Stay Long term.
Types of Admissions Accepted Residential treatment; Group home placement; Wards of the state.
Sources of Referral State depts of education; Local depts of education; State depts of mental health; Psychiatrists; Private sources; Depts of correction; Social service depts.

MAUI YOUTH & FAMILY SERVICES BOYS' GROUP HOME *(continued)*

Client Profile

Age Range of Clients Served Residential program: 12-18.

Characteristics Exhibited by Children Emotional handicaps; Learning disabilities.

Tuition and Fees

Room and Board Long term: $1,200/mo.

Placements Primarily Funded By Depts of corrections; Social service depts.

Social and Rehabilitative Services

Therapeutic Approach The basic approach of the facility is rational behavior therapy.

Therapeutic Services Offered Individual therapy; Group therapy; Family therapy; Independent living skills program; Recreation activities; Substance abuse treatment; Aftercare program with follow up.

Professionals on Staff Psychologists; Social workers; Child care staff.

IDAHO

BOISE

THE BOISE GIRLS HOME

2300 W Boise Ave, Boise, ID 83706 (208) 343-8741 *Contact Person(s):* Mary Lou Pierce, Social Worker
Setting and Background Information The home is a duplex which has been remodeled into a single home and is located in a residential neighborhood near Boise State University.
Referral Information Contact the facility for referral information. The home does not accept habitual runaways, girls with drug related problems or with serious emotional disturbances. It is operated by the Idaho Youth Ranch.
Type of Facility
Types of Admissions Accepted Residential treatment; Group home placement.
Client Profile
Age Range of Clients Served Residential program: 13-18.
Characteristics Exhibited by Children Emotional handicaps.
Tuition and Fees
Room and Board Long term: $32/diem.
Social and Rehabilitative Services
Therapeutic Services Offered Individual therapy; Group therapy.
Professionals on Staff Psychiatrists; Psychologists; Social workers.
Educational and Vocational Services
Type(s) of Educational Programs Offered Off campus.

HAYS HOUSE

924 W Franklin St, Boise, ID 83702 (208) 345-5591 *Contact Person(s):* Tracy Everson, Prog Mgr
Setting and Background Information Hays House is a well-established facility which has provided temporary, short-term care for girls in the Boise area for a number of years. The facility has recently expanded and is able to take children from any area of the state.
Referral Information Contact the facility for referral information.
Type of Facility
Average Length of Stay Short term.
Types of Admissions Accepted Group home placement; Emergency shelter.
Client Profile
Age Range of Clients Served Residential program: 12-18.
Characteristics Exhibited by Children Abused and neglected.
Tuition and Fees
Room and Board Short term: $26/diem.

BUHL

MCCAULEY GIRL'S HOME

Box 413, 1629 Poplar, Buhl, ID 83316 (208) 543-5542 *Contact Person(s):* Marilyn Ault, Dir
Setting and Background Information The home is a modern, 2-story building, located in the small town of Buhl.
Referral Information Contact the facility for referral information.
Type of Facility
Types of Admissions Accepted Residential treatment; Group home placement.
Client Profile
Age Range of Clients Served Residential program: 13-18.
Characteristics Exhibited by Children Emotional handicaps; Behavior disorders; Runaways.

Tuition and Fees
Room and Board Long term: $39.60/diem.
Social and Rehabilitative Services
Therapeutic Approach The treatment program is based upon the Adlerian approach of a carefully balanced program of encouragement and natural consequences.
Therapeutic Services Offered Individual therapy; Group therapy.
Professionals on Staff Counselors; Resident advisors.

EAGLE

CHALLENGE GROUP HOME

2150 Elliot, Eagle, ID 83616 (208) 939-8555 *Contact Person(s):* Dan Henderson, Dir
Setting and Background Information The home is licensed for eight children and is located on an acre just east of Eagle, Idaho.
Referral Information Contact the facility for referral information.
Type of Facility
Types of Admissions Accepted Residential treatment; Group home placement.
Client Profile
Age Range of Clients Served Residential program: 4-18.
Characteristics Exhibited by Children Emotional handicaps; Mental disabilities; Behavior disorders.
Tuition and Fees
Room and Board Long term: $41.02/diem.
Social and Rehabilitative Services
Therapeutic Approach The home's program includes an inter-disciplinary treatment team and a highly structured home life with skilled live-in houseparents.
Therapeutic Services Offered Individual therapy.

LEWISTON

CEDAR HOUSE

PO Box 319, Lewiston, ID 83501 (208) 743-9404 *Contact Person(s):* Dan Mahler, Dir Res Svcs
Setting and Background Information The home is licensed for eight adolescent boys as a satellite program of the North Idaho Children's Home and is located in a residential area about four miles from the main campus.
Referral Information Referrals to the facility are made through the North Idaho Children's Home. For referrals contact Dan Mahler at (208) 743-9404.
Type of Facility
Average Length of Stay Short and long term.
Client Profile
Age Range of Clients Served Residential program: 12-18.
Characteristics Exhibited by Children Emotional handicaps; Behavior disorders.
Tuition and Fees
Room and Board Long term: $39/diem.

NORTH IDAHO CHILDREN'S HOME

Box 319, Lewiston, ID 83501 (208) 743-9404 *Contact Person(s):* Dan Mahler, Dir Res Svcs
Referral Information Contact the facility for referral information.

NORTH IDAHO CHILDREN'S HOME *(continued)*

Type of Facility
Types of Admissions Accepted Residential treatment; Group home placement.
Sources of Referral Social service depts.
Client Profile
Age Range of Clients Served Residential program: 10-16.
Characteristics Exhibited by Children Emotional handicaps; Behavior disorders.
Tuition and Fees
Room and Board Long term: $64/diem.
Placements Primarily Funded By Social service depts.
Social and Rehabilitative Services
Therapeutic Approach The treatment program is highly structured and conducted in an open setting in conjunction with behavior management.
Therapeutic Services Offered Individual therapy; Group therapy; Art therapy; Recreation activities; Medical evaluation.
Professionals on Staff Psychiatrists; Psychologists; Social workers; Art therapists; Physical therapists.
Educational and Vocational Services
Type(s) of Educational Programs Offered On campus (Spec Ed); Off campus.
Profile of On Campus School Program Special curriculum electives offered; Remedial courses offered.

NAMPA

NAMPA BOYS GROUP HOME
Rte 3 Box 3832, Nampa, ID 83651 (208) 467-1750 *Contact Person(s):* Tom Steeves, CSW
Referral Information Contact the facility for referral information.
Type of Facility
Types of Admissions Accepted Residential treatment; Group home placement.
Client Profile
Age Range of Clients Served Residential program: 12-18.
Characteristics Exhibited by Children Behavior disorders.
Tuition and Fees
Room and Board Long term: $32/diem.
Social and Rehabilitative Services
Therapeutic Services Offered Group therapy.
Educational and Vocational Services
Type(s) of Educational Programs Offered Off campus.

PLANTATION (I BELIEVE) ATTENTION HOME
Box 5959, Rte 5, Karcher Rd, Nampa, ID 83651 (208) 466-7919
Contact Person(s): Marion Clarkson
Setting and Background Information The Plantation Attention Home is a privately operated shelter home designed to provide care to 12 youths.
Referral Information Contact the facility for referral information.
Type of Facility
Funding Sources Private.
Types of Admissions Accepted Residential treatment; Emergency shelter.
Sources of Referral Social service depts.
Client Profile
Age Range of Clients Served Residential program: 9-18.
Characteristics Exhibited by Children Emotional handicaps.
Tuition and Fees
Room and Board Short term: $18/diem.
Social and Rehabilitative Services
Therapeutic Services Offered Individual therapy; Family therapy.

POCATELLO

SOUTH IDAHO GIRLS HOME
PO Box 4669, 1552 S 4th, Pocatello, ID 83201 (208) 232-0537
Contact Person(s): Carol Dillon
Setting and Background Information The home is tri-level and modern, located in a residential area five blocks from the Idaho State University Campus, and in close proximity to both indoor and outdoor recreational facilities. It is operated by Idaho Youth Ranch.
Referral Information Contact the facility for referral information.

Type of Facility
Types of Admissions Accepted Day treatment; Residential treatment.
Client Profile
Age Range of Clients Served Day programs: 12-18; Residential program: 12-18.
Tuition and Fees
Room and Board Long term: $32/diem.
Social and Rehabilitative Services
Therapeutic Services Offered Individual therapy.
Professionals on Staff Psychiatrists; Psychologists; Social workers.
Educational and Vocational Services
Type(s) of Educational Programs Offered Off campus (Public school; College).

RUPERT

IDAHO YOUTH RANCH
Box 534, Rupert, ID 83350 (208) 532-4117, 436-9365 *Contact Person(s):* Charles Yeaton
Setting and Background Information The ranch consists of 3 lodges, each with up to 15 boys.
Referral Information Contact the facility for referral information.
Type of Facility
Average Length of Stay Long term.
Client Profile
Age Range of Clients Served Residential program: 9-18.
Tuition and Fees
Room and Board Long term: $36/diem.
Social and Rehabilitative Services
Professionals on Staff Counselors; Houseparents.
Educational and Vocational Services
Type(s) of Educational Programs Offered On campus; Off campus; Summer campus.

ILLINOIS

ADDISON

LUTHERBROOK CHILDREN'S CENTER

343 W Lake St, Addison, IL 60101 (312) 543-6900 *Contact Person(s):* Wayne Nafzger
Referral Information Contact the facility for referral information.
Type of Facility
Funding Sources State.
Client Profile
Age Range of Clients Served Residential program: 4-12.
Characteristics Exhibited by Children Emotional handicaps; Learning disabilities; Neurological impairments; Physical handicaps.
IQ Range of Clients 40-139.
Social and Rehabilitative Services
Therapeutic Services Offered Individual therapy; Group therapy; Family therapy; Aftercare program with follow up.
Educational and Vocational Services
Type(s) of Educational Programs Offered On campus; Off campus.

ALTON

CATHOLIC CHILDREN'S HOME

1400 State St, Alton, IL 62002 (618) 465-3594 *Contact Person(s):* Marcia Lilley, Admin
Setting and Background Information The facility was originally established in 1879 as an orphanage. The 7-acre campus has a group home, a school and a large residential building.
Referral Information Contact the facility for referral information.
Type of Facility
Funding Sources Private; State; Federal.
Average Length of Stay Short and long term.
Types of Admissions Accepted Group home placement; Wards of the state.
Sources of Referral State depts of education; Local depts of education; State depts of mental health; Private sources; Depts of correction; Social service depts.
Client Profile
Age Range of Clients Served Day programs: 6-18; Residential program: 6-18.
Characteristics Exhibited by Children Emotional handicaps; Learning disabilities; Hearing impairments/deafness; Speech/Language disorders; Neurological impairments; Mental disabilities.
IQ Range of Clients 54-135.
Tuition and Fees
Room and Board Short term: $75.39/diem; Long term: $57.41/diem.
Tuition $40.71/diem.
Placements Primarily Funded By State depts of education; Local depts of education; Social service depts.
Social and Rehabilitative Services
Therapeutic Approach The facility uses the teaching family model, adapted from Boystown.
Therapeutic Services Offered Individual therapy; Group therapy; Family therapy; Art therapy; Recreation activities; Occupational therapy.
Professionals on Staff Psychologists; Social workers; Adjunctive therapists; Child care staff; Art therapists; Occupational therapist.

Educational and Vocational Services
Type(s) of Educational Programs Offered On campus; Off campus; Summer campus.
Profile of On Campus School Program Number of teachers 12; *Number of classrooms* 95; *Student to teacher ratio* 3:1; *Credentials of teachers* Spec Ed; *Grades taught* K-12; Remedial courses offered.
Degrees Offered 8th grade diploma; 12th grade diploma.

BLOOMINGTON

KALEIDOSCOPE

530 N Center, Bloomington, IL 61701 (312) 827-0407 *Contact Person(s):* Mel Breed, Pres
Setting and Background Information The agency was established in 1973 to deinstitutionalize the state facility for dependent children. There are 6 group homes, 50 foster family homes, 50 independent living units and 60 family outreach units.
Referral Information Most referrals come from the state Dept of Children and Family Service.
Type of Facility
Funding Sources State.
Average Length of Stay Long term.
Types of Admissions Accepted Residential treatment; Group home placement; Wards of the state.
Sources of Referral State depts of education; Local depts of education; State depts of mental health; Private sources; Depts of correction; Social service depts.
Client Profile
Age Range of Clients Served Residential program: 12-21+.
Characteristics Exhibited by Children Emotional handicaps; Learning disabilities; Hearing impairments/deafness; Vision impairments/blindness; Speech/Language disorders; Neurological impairments; Physical handicaps; Mental disabilities.
IQ Range of Clients 30-120+.
Tuition and Fees
Room and Board Long term: $45-110/diem.
Placements Primarily Funded By State depts of mental health; Social service depts.
Social and Rehabilitative Services
Therapeutic Services Offered Individual therapy; Group therapy; Family therapy; Adjunctive therapy; Art therapy; Physical therapy; Independent living skills program; Recreation activities; Substance abuse treatment; Aftercare program with follow up.
Professionals on Staff Psychiatrists; Psychologists; Social workers; Adjunctive therapists; Child care staff; Nurses.
Educational and Vocational Services
Type(s) of Educational Programs Offered Off campus.

SCOTT CENTER

403 S State St, Bloomington, IL 61701 (309) 827-0374 *Contact Person(s):* Darrell Torrence, Exec Dir
Setting and Background Information The facility was established in 1889 as a non-profit charitable organization. The 4-acre campus has an administration/education building and a therapeutic group home.
Referral Information Contact the facility and forward the required materials.

SCOTT CENTER *(continued)*

Type of Facility
Funding Sources Private; State; United Way.
Average Length of Stay Long term.
Types of Admissions Accepted Day treatment; Residential treatment; Group home placement; Wards of the state.
Sources of Referral State depts of education; Local depts of education; State depts of mental health; Psychiatrists; Private sources; Social service depts; Families.
Client Profile
Age Range of Clients Served Day programs: 12-18; Residential program: 12-18.
Characteristics Exhibited by Children Emotional handicaps; Learning disabilities.
Tuition and Fees
Room and Board Long term: $85/diem.
Tuition $57/diem.
Placements Primarily Funded By State depts of education; Local depts of education; State depts of mental health; Social service depts.
Social and Rehabilitative Services
Therapeutic Approach The facility has a cognitive, behavioral approach to therapy.
Therapeutic Services Offered Individual therapy; Group therapy; Family therapy; Adjunctive therapy; Aftercare program with follow up; Music therapy.
Professionals on Staff Psychiatrists; Psychologists; Social workers; Adjunctive therapists; Child care staff; Music therapist.
Educational and Vocational Services
Type(s) of Educational Programs Offered On campus; Off campus; Summer campus.
Profile of On Campus School Program Number of teachers 4; *Number of classrooms* 3; *Student to teacher ratio* 8:1; *Credentials of teachers* BD/LD; *Grades taught* 6-12.
Degrees Offered 12th grade diploma.

CARBONDALE

BREHM PREPARATORY SCHOOL

1245 E Grand, Carbondale, IL 62901 (618) 457-0371 *Contact Person(s):* Janet Hanson, Dir
Setting and Background Information The facility was endowed in 1982 by Carol Brehm of Mt. Vernon, IL. The 8-acre campus has 4 dormitories and 2 classroom buildings.
Referral Information For referral, contact the facility for an application form, which should be submitted with a non-refundable application fee of $50.00.
Type of Facility
Funding Sources Private.
Average Length of Stay Long term.
Types of Admissions Accepted Day treatment; Residential treatment.
Sources of Referral State depts of education; Local depts of education; State depts of mental health; Psychiatrists; Private sources; Social service depts.
Client Profile
Age Range of Clients Served Day programs: 12-21; Residential program: 12-21.
Characteristics Exhibited by Children Emotional handicaps; Learning disabilities; Hearing impairments/deafness; Vision impairments/blindness; Speech/Language disorders; Neurological impairments; Physical handicaps; Mental disabilities.
IQ Range of Clients 80-140.
Tuition and Fees
Room and Board Long term: $17,500/yr (includes school tuition).
Tuition $12,500/yr (day students).
Placements Primarily Funded By Private sources.
Social and Rehabilitative Services
Therapeutic Services Offered Individual therapy; Group therapy; Art therapy; Independent living skills program.
Professionals on Staff Psychiatrists; Psychologists; Nurses; Speech/language therapist.
Educational and Vocational Services
Type(s) of Educational Programs Offered On campus.
Profile of On Campus School Program Number of teachers 13; *Number of classrooms* 13; *Student to teacher ratio* 4:1; *Credentials of teachers* Certified; Special curriculum electives offered (ACT/ SAT review, Art, Photography); Remedial courses offered (LD, Reading, Speech, Adaptive PE).
Degrees Offered 8th grade diploma; 12th grade diploma.

CARMI

BAPTIST CHILDREN'S HOME, INC

PO Box 379, Carmi, IL 62821 (618) 382-4164
Referral Information Contact the facility for referral information.
Type of Facility
Sources of Referral Private sources; Public.
Client Profile
Age Range of Clients Served Residential program: 4-18.
Characteristics Exhibited by Children Emotional handicaps; Learning disabilities; Physical handicaps; Mental disabilities.
Social and Rehabilitative Services
Therapeutic Approach The basic therapeutic approaches of the facility are behavior modification and reality therapy.
Therapeutic Services Offered Individual therapy; Group therapy; Family therapy; Physical therapy; Independent living skills program; Aftercare program with follow up; Speech therapy; Occupational therapy; Maternity care; Foster care.
Educational and Vocational Services
Type(s) of Educational Programs Offered Off campus.

CENTRALIA

HUDELSON BAPTIST CHILDREN'S HOME

PO Box 548, 1400 E 2nd, Centralia, IL 62801 (618) 532-4311
Contact Person(s): Michael Goodwin
Referral Information For referral information contact the facility.
Type of Facility
Sources of Referral Private sources; Public.
Client Profile
Age Range of Clients Served Residential program: 13-18.
Characteristics Exhibited by Children Emotional handicaps.
Social and Rehabilitative Services
Therapeutic Approach The basic therapeutic approaches used at the facility are behavior modification and reality therapy.
Therapeutic Services Offered Individual therapy; Family therapy.
Educational and Vocational Services
Type(s) of Educational Programs Offered On campus; Off campus.

WARREN G MURRAY DEVELOPMENTAL CENTER

1717 W Broadway, Centralia, IL 62801 (618) 532-1811 *Contact Person(s):* Galen Goode, Dir
Setting and Background Information The facility was established in 1964 by the state Dept of Mental Health and Developmental Disabilities. Located on 120 acres, there are 7 residential units, office buildings, and others.
Referral Information Contact the county case coordination unit and forward current evaluations. A pre-admission staffing will determine appropriateness of admission.
Type of Facility
Funding Sources State.
Average Length of Stay Long term.
Types of Admissions Accepted Residential treatment.
Sources of Referral State depts of education; Local depts of education; State depts of mental health; Psychiatrists; Private sources; Depts of correction.
Client Profile
Age Range of Clients Served Residential program: Birth-55+.
Characteristics Exhibited by Children Emotional handicaps; Mental disabilities.
IQ Range of Clients 01-60.
Tuition and Fees
Placements Primarily Funded By State depts of mental health.
Social and Rehabilitative Services
Therapeutic Services Offered Adjunctive therapy; Physical therapy; Independent living skills program; Recreation activities.
Professionals on Staff Psychologists; Social workers; Adjunctive therapists; Child care staff; Nurses; Physical therapists.

WARREN G MURRAY DEVELOPMENTAL CENTER (*continued*)

Educational and Vocational Services
Type(s) of Educational Programs Offered On campus (Sponsored by local school district); Off campus; Summer campus.
Profile of On Campus School Program Number of teachers 13 and 27 aides; *Number of classrooms* 13; *Student to teacher ratio* 7:1; *Credentials of teachers* State certified; *Grades taught* Pre K-12; Special curriculum electives offered (Speech pathology).
Vocational Education Programs/Degrees Offered Pre-vocational.

CHICAGO

CHICAGO-READ MENTAL HEALTH CENTER
4200 N Oak Park Ave, Chicago, IL 60634 (312) 794-4000 *Contact Person(s):* Dr Kris Lall, Facility Dir
Setting and Background Information The facility was established in 1960 and is a state psychiatric hospital.
Referral Information Contact the facility. Admission decisions are made by the intake psychiatrist.
Type of Facility
Funding Sources State.
Average Length of Stay Short term.
Types of Admissions Accepted Acute psychiatric care.
Sources of Referral State depts of education; Local depts of education; State depts of mental health; Psychiatrists; Private sources; Depts of correction; Social service depts.
Client Profile
Age Range of Clients Served Residential program: 6-55+.
Characteristics Exhibited by Children Emotional handicaps.
IQ Range of Clients 70+.
Social and Rehabilitative Services
Therapeutic Approach The facility offers short term psychiatric hospital treatment.
Therapeutic Services Offered Individual therapy; Group therapy; Family therapy; Adjunctive therapy; Art therapy; Independent living skills program; Recreation activities.
Professionals on Staff Psychiatrists; Psychologists; Social workers; Adjunctive therapists; Nurses; Activity therapist.

LAWRENCE HALL SCHOOL FOR BOYS
4833 N Francisco, Chicago, IL 60625 (312) 769-3500 *Contact Person(s):* Carole Cotter, Admis Coord
Setting and Background Information The facility was initially established following the Civil War as the Chicago Newsboys and Bootblacks Assoc. Currently, it is a residential treament facility for boys. Its 5-acre campus has six cottages, an administration/education building and other buildings.
Referral Information Contact the facility for referral procedures.
Type of Facility
Funding Sources State; Federal.
Average Length of Stay Long term; 12-18 mos.
Types of Admissions Accepted Day treatment; Residential treatment; Group home placement; Wards of the state.
Sources of Referral State depts of education; Local depts of education; Social service depts; State Dept of Children/Family Svcs; County Dept of Public Welfare.
Client Profile
Age Range of Clients Served Day programs: 6-18; Residential program: 6-18.
Characteristics Exhibited by Children Emotional handicaps; Learning disabilities; Mental disabilities.
IQ Range of Clients 70-120+.
Tuition and Fees
Room and Board Long term: $71.86/diem (campus); $67.75/diem (group home).
Tuition $70.95/diem.
Placements Primarily Funded By State depts of education; Local depts of education; Social service depts; Illinois Dept of Children and Family Services.
Social and Rehabilitative Services
Therapeutic Approach The facility uses milieu therapy and behavior modification.
Therapeutic Services Offered Individual therapy; Group therapy; Family therapy; Adjunctive therapy; Art therapy; Independent living skills program; Recreation activities; Substance abuse treatment; Aftercare program with follow up.

Professionals on Staff Psychiatrists; Psychologists; Social workers; Nurses; Art therapists.
Educational and Vocational Services
Type(s) of Educational Programs Offered On campus; Off campus; Summer campus.
Profile of On Campus School Program Number of teachers 19 and 2 aides; *Student to teacher ratio* 6:1; *Credentials of teachers* Spec Ed; *Length of school day* 8:45-2:30; *Grades taught* 1-12; Special curriculum electives offered (Computer programming, Industrial arts, Home economics); Remedial courses offered (Reading, Math).
Vocational Education Programs/Degrees Offered Vocational assessment; Vocational experience; Job placement.
Degrees Offered 8th grade diploma; 12th grade diploma.

MCCORMICK HOUSE
5414 S Greenwood, Chicago, IL 60615 (312) 752-6790 *Contact Person(s):* Susan Carlton, Prog Dir
Setting and Background Information The facility was established in 1962. It is a group home.
Referral Information All residents are wards of the Dept of Children and Family Services. All referrals are made through that department.
Type of Facility
Funding Sources Private; State.
Average Length of Stay Long term.
Types of Admissions Accepted Group home placement.
Sources of Referral Dept of Children and Family Services.
Client Profile
Age Range of Clients Served Residential program: 12-19.
Characteristics Exhibited by Children Emotional handicaps; Learning disabilities; Physical handicaps; Mental disabilities.
IQ Range of Clients 70+.
Tuition and Fees
Placements Primarily Funded By Department of Children and Family Services.
Social and Rehabilitative Services
Therapeutic Approach The facility has a psychodynamic approach in a therapeutic milieu.
Therapeutic Services Offered Individual therapy; Group therapy; Family therapy; Independent living skills program; Aftercare program with follow up.
Professionals on Staff Psychiatrists; Social workers; Child care staff; Nurses.
Educational and Vocational Services
Type(s) of Educational Programs Offered Off campus (Public school).

MERCY BOYS HOME
1140 W Jackson Blvd, Chicago, IL 60607 (312) 738-7590 *Contact Person(s):* Dan King
Setting and Background Information The facility has a capacity for 40 youth and accepts boys only.
Referral Information Contact the facility for referral information.
Type of Facility
Funding Sources Private.
Client Profile
Age Range of Clients Served Residential program: 15-18.
Characteristics Exhibited by Children Emotional handicaps; Learning disabilities.
IQ Range of Clients 80+.
Social and Rehabilitative Services
Therapeutic Approach The facility has an eclectic approach to therapy, which includes a psychoanalytic approach and a humanistic family systems approach.
Therapeutic Services Offered Individual therapy; Group therapy; Family therapy; Independent living skills program; Substance abuse treatment; Aftercare program with follow up; Career counseling.
Educational and Vocational Services
Type(s) of Educational Programs Offered Off campus.

METHODIST YOUTH SERVICES
4350 N Beacon St, Chicago, IL 60640 (312) 728-1818 *Contact Person(s):* James E Powl
Setting and Background Information The facility has a capacity for 50 youth and accepts males only.
Referral Information Contact the facility for referral information.
Type of Facility
Funding Sources Private; State.

METHODIST YOUTH SERVICES *(continued)*

Client Profile
Age Range of Clients Served Residential program: 16-21.
Characteristics Exhibited by Children Emotional handicaps.
Social and Rehabilitative Services
Therapeutic Approach The facility has an eclectic approach to therapy.
Therapeutic Services Offered Individual therapy; Group therapy; Independent living skills program; Aftercare program with follow up.
Educational and Vocational Services
Type(s) of Educational Programs Offered Off campus.

ST JOSEPH'S CARDENDELET CHILD CENTER
739 E 35 St, Chicago, IL 60616 (312) 624-7443 *Contact Person(s):* Intake Worker
Setting and Background Information The facility has a capacity for 28 youth and accepts males only.
Referral Information Contact the facility for referral information.
Type of Facility
Funding Sources Public.
Client Profile
Age Range of Clients Served Residential program: 4-14.
Characteristics Exhibited by Children Emotional handicaps; Learning disabilities; Speech/Language disorders; Neurological impairments.
IQ Range of Clients 70-139.
Social and Rehabilitative Services
Therapeutic Approach The facility has an eclectic approach to therapy.
Therapeutic Services Offered Individual therapy; Group therapy; Family therapy; Speech therapy.
Educational and Vocational Services
Type(s) of Educational Programs Offered On campus.

SONIA SHANKMAN ORTHOGENIC SCHOOL
1365 E 60th St, Chicago, IL 60637 (312) 962-1203 *Contact Person(s):* Dr Frank Lani, Acting Dir
Setting and Background Information The facility was established as a laboratory of Rush Medical School in 1915 and became part of the University of Chicago in the 1920s. In 1944, the school modified its focus to the treatment of emotionally disturbed youth. The school is located on the University of Chicago campus and has dormitories, offices, classrooms, a library, activity rooms and therapy rooms.
Referral Information Referrals can be made by parents, school districts and mental health professionals by contacting the facility.
Type of Facility
Types of Admissions Accepted Residential treatment.
Client Profile
Age Range of Clients Served Residential program: 6-21.
Characteristics Exhibited by Children Emotional handicaps.
Social and Rehabilitative Services
Therapeutic Approach The philosophy of the treatment program is based on progressive education and child psychoanalysis through the use of intensive milieu therapy.
Therapeutic Services Offered Individual therapy; Group therapy; Family therapy; Adjunctive therapy; Art therapy; Physical therapy; Recreation activities.
Professionals on Staff Psychiatrists; Psychologists; Adjunctive therapists; Art therapists; Physical therapists.
Educational and Vocational Services
Type(s) of Educational Programs Offered On campus.
Vocational Education Programs/Degrees Offered Vocational assessment and education.

THRESHOLDS
2700 N Lakeview, Chicago, IL 60614 (312) 281-3800, 880-2468, 880-2470 *Contact Person(s):* Diane Farrell, Supv Young Adult Prog
Setting and Background Information This agency was established in 1959 by the National Council of Jewish Women. There are two group homes with a capacity for 10 each and a day treatment program.
Referral Information Contact the facility and forward the required materials.

Type of Facility
Funding Sources Private; State; Federal.
Average Length of Stay 1 ½ -3 yrs.
Types of Admissions Accepted Day treatment; Group home placement.
Sources of Referral Local depts of education; State depts of mental health; Psychiatrists; Private sources; Social service depts; Dept of Vocational Rehabilitation.
Client Profile
Age Range of Clients Served Day programs: 16-21+; Residential program: 16-21+.
Characteristics Exhibited by Children Emotional handicaps; Learning disabilities; Mental disabilities.
Tuition and Fees
Room and Board Long term: $59.66/diem.
Tuition $45.10/diem.
Placements Primarily Funded By Local depts of education; Private sources; DORS.
Social and Rehabilitative Services
Therapeutic Approach The facility offers psychosocial rehabilitation.
Therapeutic Services Offered Individual therapy; Group therapy; Family therapy; Independent living skills program; Recreation activities; Substance abuse treatment.
Professionals on Staff Psychiatrists; Social workers; Child care staff.
Educational and Vocational Services
Type(s) of Educational Programs Offered On campus.
Profile of On Campus School Program Number of teachers 5; *Number of classrooms* 4; *Student to teacher ratio* 5:1; *Credentials of teachers* Spec Ed; Special curriculum electives offered; Remedial courses offered.
Vocational Education Programs/Degrees Offered Pre-vocational training; Job placement.
Degrees Offered 12th grade diploma; GED.

TRANSITIONAL LIVING
3179 N Broadway, Chicago, IL 60657.
Contact Person(s): Patricia G Berg MSW CSW, Exec Dir
Setting and Background Information The facility was established in 1977 by a contractual agreement with the Illinois Dept of Children and Family Services.
Referral Information Referrals to the facility are made through police, social service agencies, and the Dept of Children and Family Services.
Type of Facility
Funding Sources Private; State; Federal.
Average Length of Stay Short and long term.
Types of Admissions Accepted Wards of the state; Emergency shelter; Independent living.
Sources of Referral Private sources; Social service depts; Individuals; Hospitals.
Client Profile
Age Range of Clients Served Residential program: 16-20.
Characteristics Exhibited by Children Learning disabilities; Abused and neglected; Runaways.
Tuition and Fees
Placements Primarily Funded By State depts of education; Local depts of education; State depts of mental health; Social service depts.
Social and Rehabilitative Services
Therapeutic Approach The basic therapeutic approach used at the facility is reality therapy.
Therapeutic Services Offered Individual therapy; Family therapy; Independent living skills program; Aftercare program with follow up; Crisis intervention.

UNITED CITIZEN COMMUNITY ORGANIZATION
5927 W Washington, Chicago, IL 60644 (312) 921-5037 *Contact Person(s):* Joseph Sanders, Group Home Admin
Setting and Background Information The facility was established in 1978 to provide shelter and foster home care for children. There is a large residential home.
Referral Information Contact the facility.
Type of Facility
Funding Sources State.
Average Length of Stay Short and long term.
Types of Admissions Accepted Group home placement; Wards of the state.
Sources of Referral Depts of correction; Social service depts.

UNITED CITIZEN COMMUNITY ORGANIZATION
(continued)

Client Profile
Age Range of Clients Served Residential program: 6-18.
Tuition and Fees
Room and Board Long term: $60/diem.
Placements Primarily Funded By Depts of corrections; Social service depts.
Social and Rehabilitative Services
Therapeutic Approach The facility has an eclectic approach to therapy which is geared toward individual needs.
Therapeutic Services Offered Individual therapy; Group therapy; Family therapy; Independent living skills program.
Professionals on Staff Psychologists; Child care staff.
Educational and Vocational Services
Type(s) of Educational Programs Offered Off campus.

COAL VALLEY

ARROWHEAD RANCH
12200 104th St, Coal Valley, IL 61240 (309) 799-7044 *Contact Person(s):* Robert Eastlund
Setting and Background Information The facility has the capacity for 72 youth and accepts males only.
Referral Information For referral information contact the facility.
Type of Facility
Funding Sources Public.
Client Profile
Age Range of Clients Served Residential program: 13-17.
Characteristics Exhibited by Children Emotional handicaps; Learning disabilities; Substance abuse.
Social and Rehabilitative Services
Therapeutic Approach The facility offers positive peer group therapy.
Therapeutic Services Offered Group therapy; Family therapy; Independent living skills program; Aftercare program with follow up.
Educational and Vocational Services
Type(s) of Educational Programs Offered On campus.

DECATUR

WEBSTER-CANTRELL HALL
1942 E Cantrell St, Decatur, IL 62521 (217) 423-6961 *Contact Person(s):* Merlin Outcalt
Referral Information Contact the facility for referral information.
Type of Facility
Funding Sources Public.
Client Profile
Age Range of Clients Served Residential program: 12-17.
Characteristics Exhibited by Children Emotional handicaps; Learning disabilities; Neurological impairments; Physical handicaps.
Social and Rehabilitative Services
Therapeutic Approach The facility has an eclectic approach to therapy.
Therapeutic Services Offered Individual therapy; Group therapy; Family therapy.
Educational and Vocational Services
Type(s) of Educational Programs Offered On campus; Off campus.

EDWARDSVILLE

EDUCATIONAL THERAPY CENTER
100 W 5th St, Edwardsville, IL 62025 (618) 692-6200, ext 4487 *Contact Person(s):* David Blue, Dir
Setting and Background Information The facility was established in 1982 with a grant from the state board of education. It is one building with a recreational area.
Referral Information Referrals are made by local school districts.
Type of Facility
Funding Sources State.
Average Length of Stay Long term.
Types of Admissions Accepted Group home placement.
Sources of Referral Local depts of education; State depts of mental health.

Client Profile
Age Range of Clients Served Day programs: 6-21+; Residential program: 12-18.
Characteristics Exhibited by Children Emotional handicaps; Mental disabilities.
Tuition and Fees
Room and Board Long term: $63/diem.
Tuition $5,000/yr.
Placements Primarily Funded By Local depts of education; State depts of mental health; Social service depts.
Social and Rehabilitative Services
Therapeutic Approach The facility has a behavioral orientation.
Therapeutic Services Offered Individual therapy; Group therapy; Family therapy; Adjunctive therapy; Recreation activities.
Professionals on Staff Psychologists; Adjunctive therapists; Child care staff.
Educational and Vocational Services
Type(s) of Educational Programs Offered Off campus.

ELGIN

LARKIN HOME FOR CHILDREN
1212 Larkin Ave, Elgin, IL 60123 (312) 695-5656 *Contact Person(s):* Michael R Horwitz, Exec Dir
Setting and Background Information The facility was established in 1896 as a shelter for orphans. Currently, there are five group homes, two school sites, and an administration building.
Referral Information Referrals are made to either the residential coordinator or the day treatment coordinator.
Type of Facility
Funding Sources Private; State; Investment income.
Average Length of Stay Long term.
Types of Admissions Accepted Day treatment; Residential treatment; Group home placement; Wards of the state.
Sources of Referral State depts of education; Local depts of education; State depts of mental health; Private sources; Depts of correction.
Client Profile
Age Range of Clients Served Day programs: Birth-18; Residential program: 6-18.
Characteristics Exhibited by Children Emotional handicaps; Learning disabilities; Neurological impairments; Mental disabilities.
IQ Range of Clients 60+.
Tuition and Fees
Room and Board Long term: $85/diem.
Tuition $65/diem.
Placements Primarily Funded By Local depts of education.
Social and Rehabilitative Services
Therapeutic Approach The facility has a multi-disciplinary, electic approach to therapy.
Therapeutic Services Offered Individual therapy; Group therapy; Family therapy; Adjunctive therapy; Art therapy; Independent living skills program; Recreation activities; Substance abuse treatment; Aftercare program with follow up.
Professionals on Staff Psychiatrists; Psychologists; Social workers; Adjunctive therapists; Child care staff; Nurses; Art therapists; Recreation/activities staff.
Educational and Vocational Services
Type(s) of Educational Programs Offered On campus (Spec Ed); Off campus (Public school); Summer campus (Environmental camp).
Profile of On Campus School Program Number of teachers 15; *Number of classrooms* 15; *Student to teacher ratio* 3 ½ :1; *Credentials of teachers* Spec Ed; *Grades taught* K-12; *Remedial courses offered* (Independent living skills).
Vocational Education Programs/Degrees Offered Career counseling.
Degrees Offered 12th grade diploma.

EVANSTON

EVANSTON CHILDREN'S CENTER
826 Ridge Ave, Evanston, IL 60202 (312) 866-3800 *Contact Person(s):* William P Martone, Dir
Setting and Background Information The center was originally established in 1904 as an orphanage. Currently, it is a residential treatment facility for latency age children with social and emotional difficulties and provides services to 30 girls and boys.
Referral Information For referral information, contact the intake coordinator.

EVANSTON CHILDREN'S CENTER *(continued)*

Type of Facility
Funding Sources Private; State.
Average Length of Stay Long term.
Types of Admissions Accepted Residential treatment.
Sources of Referral State depts of education; Local depts of education; State depts of mental health; Social service depts.
Client Profile
Age Range of Clients Served Residential program: 5-14.
Characteristics Exhibited by Children Emotional handicaps.
IQ Range of Clients 70+.
Tuition and Fees
Room and Board Long term: $105/diem.
Placements Primarily Funded By State depts of education; Local depts of education; State depts of mental health; Social service depts.
Social and Rehabilitative Services
Therapeutic Approach The program offers individual and milieu therapy including family treatment.
Therapeutic Services Offered Individual therapy; Group therapy; Family therapy; Independent living skills program; Recreation activities.
Professionals on Staff Psychiatrists; Social workers; Child care staff; Nurses.
Educational and Vocational Services
Type(s) of Educational Programs Offered On campus (Provided by local school district); Off campus (Public school).
Profile of On Campus School Program Number of teachers 3 and 3 aides; *Number of classrooms* 3; *Student to teacher ratio* 5:2; *Credentials of teachers* Certified Spec Ed; *Grades taught* 1-8.
Degrees Offered 8th grade diploma.

FLANAGAN

SALEM CHILDREN'S HOME

RR 1, Flanagan, IL 61740 (815) 796-4561 *Contact Person(s):* Stephen M Yahnig, Exec Dir
Setting and Background Information The facility was established as an orphanage by a religious organization in 1896. The 100-acre campus has 3 cottages, an administration building, and other buildings.
Referral Information Contact the facility and forward the necessary information. A pre-placerment interview will be scheduled.
Type of Facility
Funding Sources Private; State; Donations.
Average Length of Stay Short and long term.
Types of Admissions Accepted Residential treatment; Group home placement; Wards of the state.
Sources of Referral State depts of education; State depts of mental health; Private sources; Depts of correction; Social service depts; Juvenile court.
Client Profile
Age Range of Clients Served Residential program: 12-18.
Characteristics Exhibited by Children Emotional handicaps; Learning disabilities; Mental disabilities.
IQ Range of Clients Below 80.
Tuition and Fees
Room and Board Short term: $25/diem; Long term: $37.50-$55/diem.
Placements Primarily Funded By State depts of mental health; Social service depts; Contributions.
Social and Rehabilitative Services
Therapeutic Approach The facility uses behavior modification.
Therapeutic Services Offered Individual therapy; Group therapy; Adjunctive therapy; Independent living skills program; Recreation activities.
Professionals on Staff Psychologists; Social workers; Adjunctive therapists; Child care staff.
Educational and Vocational Services
Type(s) of Educational Programs Offered Off campus; Summer campus.
Vocational Education Programs/Degrees Offered Horse husbandry; Horticulture; Food management; Maintenance.

FREEPORT

NORMAN C SLEEZER JUVENILE HOMES, INC

PO Box 895, 1250 S Adams, Freeport, IL 61032 (815) 232-8336
Contact Person(s): Raymond H Hughes, Exec Dir
Setting and Background Information The facility was established in 1975. There are 2 residences, an office building and a classroom building.
Referral Information Contact the intake coordinator and forward the social history and psychological, educational, and medical records.
Type of Facility
Funding Sources Private.
Average Length of Stay Long term; 7-16 mos.
Types of Admissions Accepted Residential treatment.
Sources of Referral State depts of education; Local depts of education; Depts of correction; Social service depts; Probation depts.
Client Profile
Age Range of Clients Served Residential program: 12-18.
Characteristics Exhibited by Children Behavior disorders.
IQ Range of Clients 80+.
Tuition and Fees
Room and Board Long term: $47.79-$56.71/diem.
Placements Primarily Funded By State depts of education; Local depts of education; Depts of corrections; Social service depts; Probation depts.
Social and Rehabilitative Services
Therapeutic Services Offered Group therapy; Independent living skills program; Recreation activities.
Professionals on Staff Psychologists; Social workers; Child care staff.
Educational and Vocational Services
Type(s) of Educational Programs Offered On campus; Off campus (Local school).
Profile of On Campus School Program Number of teachers 2; *Number of classrooms* 2; *Student to teacher ratio* 9:1; *Credentials of teachers* Spec Ed Certified; *Length of school day* 8-3; *Grades taught* Individualized.
Degrees Offered Certificate of completion.

HIGHLAND PARK

ARDEN SHORE

1875 Stratford Rd, Highland Park, IL 60035 (312) 234-1730 *Contact Person(s):* Thomas Pfeiffer
Setting and Background Information The facility has the capacity for 10 female adolescents.
Referral Information Contact the facility for referral information.
Type of Facility
Funding Sources Public.
Client Profile
Age Range of Clients Served Residential program: 13-17.
Characteristics Exhibited by Children Emotional handicaps; Learning disabilities.
Social and Rehabilitative Services
Therapeutic Approach The facility offers a positive peer culture.
Therapeutic Services Offered Group therapy; Family therapy.
Educational and Vocational Services
Type(s) of Educational Programs Offered Off campus.

HINES

JOHN J MADDEN MENTAL HEALTH CENTER

1200 S 1st Ave, Hines, IL 60141 (312) 345-9870 ext 247 *Contact Person(s):* Dan Williams, Volunteer Svcs Coord
Setting and Background Information The facility was established in 1967 and is state operated. The 33-acre campus has 11 residential pavilions and an administration building.
Referral Information Contact the facility for referral information.
Type of Facility
Funding Sources State; Federal.
Average Length of Stay Short term.
Types of Admissions Accepted Residential treatment; Wards of the state.
Sources of Referral State depts of mental health.
Client Profile
Age Range of Clients Served Residential program: 6-55+.
Characteristics Exhibited by Children Emotional handicaps.

JOHN J MADDEN MENTAL HEALTH CENTER
(continued)

Tuition and Fees
Placements Primarily Funded By State depts of mental health.
Social and Rehabilitative Services
Therapeutic Approach The facility offers a therapeutic milieu.
Therapeutic Services Offered Individual therapy; Group therapy; Family therapy; Recreation activities; Aftercare program with follow up.
Professionals on Staff Psychiatrists; Psychologists; Social workers; Child care staff; Nurses.
Educational and Vocational Services
Type(s) of Educational Programs Offered On campus.
Profile of On Campus School Program Number of teachers 7.5; *Number of classrooms* 8.

JOLIET

GUARDIAN ANGEL HOME OF JOLIET
1550 Plainfield Rd, Joliet, IL 60435 (815) 729-0930 *Contact Person(s):* Mary Beth Meyers ACSW, Dir of Residential Svcs
Setting and Background Information The facility was initially established as an orphanage in 1897 by the Sisters of St Francis of Mary Immaculate. In 1971, it reorganized and expanded its programs and services to become a treatment center for emotionally disturbed children. The campus is located on 9.3 acres and consists of an administration building, residential units, school, child and family guidance center, gymnasium, and outdoor pool.
Referral Information Referrals can be made by any legal guardian or school district with available funding for placement. To make a referral, contact the facility and forward the necessary background information to the Dir of Residential Services. A pre-placement visit and interview will take place before an admission decision is made.
Type of Facility
Funding Sources Private.
Average Length of Stay 18-24 mos.
Types of Admissions Accepted Residential treatment.
Sources of Referral State depts of education; Local depts of education; State depts of mental health; Psychiatrists; Private sources; Depts of correction.
Client Profile
Age Range of Clients Served Residential program: 7-14.
Characteristics Exhibited by Children Emotional handicaps.
IQ Range of Clients 70+.
Tuition and Fees
Room and Board Long term: $85/diem.
Tuition $55/diem.
Placements Primarily Funded By State depts of education; Local depts of education; State depts of mental health; Depts of corrections; Social service depts.
Social and Rehabilitative Services
Therapeutic Services Offered Individual therapy; Group therapy; Family therapy; Adjunctive therapy; Recreation activities; Aftercare program with follow up.
Professionals on Staff Psychiatrists; Social workers; Child care staff.
Educational and Vocational Services
Type(s) of Educational Programs Offered On campus; Off campus.
Profile of On Campus School Program Number of teachers 6; *Student to teacher ratio* 6:1; *Grades taught* 1-12; Special curriculum electives offered; Remedial courses offered.

LAKE VILLA

ALLENDALE
PO Box 277, Lake Villa, IL 60046 (312) 356-2351 *Contact Person(s):* Robert Mount, Intake Supv
Setting and Background Information The facility was founded in 1897 by Edward L Bradley for the purpose of helping children and adolescents with emotional problems. It is located on the west shore of Cedar Lake, 50 miles northwest of Chicago. The campus covers 120 acres and includes a gymnasium, chapel, library, school, kitchen, main office building, and 7 large resident homes.

Referral Information Referrals can be made by school districts, state agencies, professionals in private practice, and parents at any time during the year. Referral materials are reviewed by the intake committee. Potential candidates visit Allendale for a diagnostic pre-placement visit.
Type of Facility
Funding Sources Private.
Average Length of Stay 18-24 mos.
Types of Admissions Accepted Day treatment; Residential treatment.
Sources of Referral State depts of education; Local depts of education; State depts of mental health; Psychiatrists; Private sources; Depts of correction.
Client Profile
Age Range of Clients Served Day programs: 8-16; Residential program: 8-16.
Characteristics Exhibited by Children Emotional handicaps; Learning disabilities; Mental disabilities.
Tuition and Fees
Placements Primarily Funded By State depts of education; Local depts of education; State depts of mental health; Insurance; Private sources; Depts of corrections; Social service depts; Champus.
Social and Rehabilitative Services
Therapeutic Services Offered Individual therapy; Group therapy; Family therapy; Independent living skills program; Recreation activities; Aftercare program with follow up.
Professionals on Staff Psychiatrists; Psychologists; Social workers; Child care staff; Nurses.
Educational and Vocational Services
Type(s) of Educational Programs Offered On campus; Off campus.
Profile of On Campus School Program Number of teachers 12; *Student to teacher ratio* 4:1; *Grades taught* 1-12.

MATTESON

INTERVENTIONS, SMA RESIDENTIAL SCHOOL
PO Box 77, 4200 Maple Ave, Matteson, IL 60443 (312) 663-0817
Contact Person(s): Myra Nichols, Asst to Clinical Dir
Setting and Background Information The school was established in 1984 in coordination with SMA - a special education cooperative. It is a residential facility on 3 acres.
Referral Information Referrals are made by DCFS, DMHDD, and local school districts.
Type of Facility
Funding Sources Public Law 94-142.
Average Length of Stay Long term.
Types of Admissions Accepted Residential treatment; Wards of the state.
Sources of Referral State depts of education; Local depts of education; State depts of mental health; Psychiatrists; Private sources; Dept of Children and Family Svcs.
Client Profile
Age Range of Clients Served Residential program: 12-21.
Characteristics Exhibited by Children Emotional handicaps; Learning disabilities; Neurological impairments.
IQ Range of Clients 80-120.
Tuition and Fees
Room and Board Long term: $76.15/diem.
Tuition $30/diem.
Placements Primarily Funded By State depts of education.
Social and Rehabilitative Services
Therapeutic Approach The school provides a therapeutic community for its residents.
Therapeutic Services Offered Individual therapy; Group therapy; Family therapy; Adjunctive therapy; Art therapy; Independent living skills program; Recreation activities.
Professionals on Staff Psychiatrists; Social workers; Child care staff; Nurses.
Educational and Vocational Services
Type(s) of Educational Programs Offered On campus; Off campus; Summer campus.
Profile of On Campus School Program Number of teachers 1; *Number of classrooms* 1; *Student to teacher ratio* 5:1; *Credentials of teachers* MEd; *Grades taught* K-12; Remedial courses offered.
Degrees Offered 8th grade diploma; 12th grade diploma.

MOLINE

BETHANY HOME, INC

PO Box 638, 220 11th Ave, Moline, IL 61265 (309) 797-7700
Contact Person(s): Larry Chasey, Vice-Pres
Setting and Background Information This facility was initially
established as an orphanage in 1899. Currently, it offers both
residential and day treatment programs. The main campus is
located on 6 acres and has residential and administration
buildings. There are three additional counseling sites.
Referral Information The referral procedure is to submit the current
social, educational, medical and psychological information. An
extended pre-placement visit will be arranged.

Type of Facility
Funding Sources Private; State; Federal; United Way.
Average Length of Stay Long term.
Types of Admissions Accepted Day treatment; Residential treatment;
Wards of the state.
Sources of Referral State depts of education; Local depts of educa-
tion; State depts of mental health; Depts of correction; Social
service depts.

Client Profile
Age Range of Clients Served Day programs: 12-18; Residential pro-
gram: 6-15.
Characteristics Exhibited by Children Emotional handicaps; Learning
disabilities; Mental disabilities.
IQ Range of Clients 70+.

Tuition and Fees
Room and Board Long term: $71.99/diem.
Placements Primarily Funded By Social service depts.

Social and Rehabilitative Services
Therapeutic Approach The facility uses a family process model as its
therapeutic approach.
Therapeutic Services Offered Individual therapy; Group therapy;
Family therapy; Adjunctive therapy; Independent living skills
program; Recreation activities.
Professionals on Staff Psychiatrists; Psychologists; Social workers;
Adjunctive therapists; Child care staff; Nurses; Recreational thera-
pist.

Educational and Vocational Services
Type(s) of Educational Programs Offered Off campus (Public school).

NACHUSA

LUTHERAN SOCIAL SERVICES OF ILLINOIS, NACHUSA LUTHERAN HOME

PO Box 100, 1261 Illinois Rt #38, Nachusa, IL 61057
(815) 284-7796 *Contact Person(s):* James Czerwionka MS MEd, Dir
Setting and Background Information The facility was originally
established in 1903 as an orphanage.
Referral Information Contact the facility for referral information. A
two-day pre-placement visit is required.

Type of Facility
Funding Sources Private; State.
Average Length of Stay Short and long term.
Types of Admissions Accepted Day treatment; Residential treatment;
Wards of the state.
Sources of Referral State depts of education; Local depts of educa-
tion; State depts of mental health; Psychiatrists; Private sources;
Social service depts.

Client Profile
Age Range of Clients Served Day programs: 12-18; Residential pro-
gram: 12-18.
Characteristics Exhibited by Children Emotional handicaps; Learning
disabilities; Neurological impairments; Mental disabilities.
IQ Range of Clients 55-125.

Tuition and Fees
Room and Board Short term: $77.20/diem; Long term: $77.20/diem.
Tuition $58.23/diem.
Placements Primarily Funded By State depts of education; Local
depts of education; State depts of mental health; Social service
depts.

Social and Rehabilitative Services
Therapeutic Approach The facility utilizes both the
psychoeducational and the behavioral therapeutic approaches.
Therapeutic Services Offered Individual therapy; Group therapy;
Family therapy; Adjunctive therapy; Art therapy; Independent
living skills program; Recreation activities; Aftercare program
with follow up; Music therapy.
Professionals on Staff Psychiatrists; Psychologists; Social workers;
Adjunctive therapists; Child care staff; Nurses; Art therapists;
Music therapist.

Educational and Vocational Services
Type(s) of Educational Programs Offered On campus; Off campus;
Summer campus.
Profile of On Campus School Program Number of teachers 10;
Number of classrooms 4; *Student to teacher ratio* 4:1; *Credentials
of teachers* Certified; *Grades taught* Ungraded; Remedial courses
offered.
Vocational Education Programs/Degrees Offered Work training
through JTPA Grant.
Degrees Offered 8th grade diploma; 12th grade diploma.

NORMAL

BABY FOLD RESIDENTIAL TREATMENT CENTER

108 E Willow St, Normal, IL 61761 (309) 452-1170 *Contact
Person(s):* Benjamine Moore, Dir of Clinical Svcs
Setting and Background Information This facility was originally
established as a place for homeless children in 1902. It later
expanded its program to become a treatment facility. The campus
is located in central Illinois, 125 miles south of Chicago and
includes a school, gymnasium, media center, administrative
offices, large play yard, and 2 playgrounds.
Referral Information Referrrals can be made by school districts,
special education cooperatives, Dept of Children and Family
Services, and other state agencies. Background information on the
child, such as psychological reports, medical history, educational
reports, and social data, should be forwarded to the facility. After
the referral is reviewed, a pre-placement visit and conference will
take place before a placement decision is made.

Type of Facility
Funding Sources Private.
Average Length of Stay 18-24 mos.
Types of Admissions Accepted Residential treatment.
Sources of Referral State depts of education; Local depts of educa-
tion; Social service depts.

Client Profile
Age Range of Clients Served Residential program: 3-11.
Characteristics Exhibited by Children Emotional handicaps; Learning
disabilities; Mental disabilities; Behavior disorders.
IQ Range of Clients 60+.

Tuition and Fees
Room and Board Long term: $71/diem.
Tuition $47/diem.
Placements Primarily Funded By State depts of education; Social
service depts.

Social and Rehabilitative Services
Therapeutic Approach The primary therapeutic approaches used by
the treatment program are based on behavioral and social learning theories.
Therapeutic Services Offered Individual therapy; Group therapy;
Family therapy; Recreation activities; Aftercare program with
follow up.
Professionals on Staff Psychologists; Adjunctive therapists; Child care
staff; Nurses.

Educational and Vocational Services
Type(s) of Educational Programs Offered On campus; Off campus.
Profile of On Campus School Program Number of teachers 20;
Student to teacher ratio 4:1; *Grades taught* K-5; Special curricu-
lum electives offered (Pre-school).

PALATINE

CAMELOT CARE CENTER, INC
1502 NW Highway, Palatine, IL 60067 (312) 359-5600 *Contact Person(s):* Peggy Williams
Setting and Background Information Camelot Care Center operates a group of private residential treatment facilities. The initial facility was established in 1972. Since then, the agency has built 4 facilities in Illinois, one in Tennessee, and another in Florida.
Referral Information Referrals can be made by parents, insurance companies, and state agencies.
Type of Facility
Funding Sources Private.
Average Length of Stay Short and long term.
Types of Admissions Accepted Residential treatment.
Sources of Referral Psychiatrists; Private sources; Depts of correction; Hospitals.
Client Profile
Age Range of Clients Served Residential program: 3-18.
Characteristics Exhibited by Children Emotional handicaps.
IQ Range of Clients 75+.
Tuition and Fees
Room and Board Long term: $287/diem.
Tuition $287/diem.
Placements Primarily Funded By State depts of mental health; Insurance; Private sources; County.
Social and Rehabilitative Services
Therapeutic Approach The treatment program utilizes a developmental behavioral model.
Therapeutic Services Offered Individual therapy; Group therapy; Family therapy; Adjunctive therapy; Independent living skills program; Recreation activities; Substance abuse treatment; Aftercare program with follow up.
Professionals on Staff Psychiatrists; Psychologists; Social workers; Adjunctive therapists; Child care staff; Nurses.
Educational and Vocational Services
Type(s) of Educational Programs Offered On campus.
Profile of On Campus School Program Number of teachers 3; Grades taught K-12; Remedial courses offered.

PARK RIDGE

EDISON PARK HOME
1800 Canfield Rd, Park Ridge, IL 60068 (312) 825-7176 *Contact Person(s):* Elizabeth Andrade
Setting and Background Information The facility was initially established as an orphange in 1892. It later expanded its programs to become a residential facility with a group home component. The campus is located in suburban Chicago on 13 acres of land. There are residential units designed as boys, girls, and co-ed. A group home is located in nearby Aurora.
Referral Information Referrals can be made by the Dept of Children and Family Services or local school districts. Applicants should contact the Admissions Office to set up an intitial interview. If the placement is deemed possible, then a 24-hour visit will be arranged, along with a second interview before a placement decision is made.
Type of Facility
Funding Sources Private.
Average Length of Stay 18 mos.
Types of Admissions Accepted Residential treatment; Group home placement.
Sources of Referral State depts of education; Local depts of education; Depts of correction; Social service depts.
Client Profile
Age Range of Clients Served Residential program: 13-18.
Characteristics Exhibited by Children Emotional handicaps; Learning disabilities.
Tuition and Fees
Room and Board Long term: $89/diem.
Placements Primarily Funded By State depts of education; Local depts of education; Private sources; Depts of corrections; Courts.
Social and Rehabilitative Services
Therapeutic Services Offered Individual therapy; Group therapy; Family therapy; Adjunctive therapy; Independent living skills program; Recreation activities; Aftercare program with follow up.
Professionals on Staff Psychiatrists; Social workers; Child care staff; Nurses.

Educational and Vocational Services
Type(s) of Educational Programs Offered Off campus.

PARK RIDGE YOUTH CAMPUS
733 N Prospect Ave, Park Ridge, IL 60068 (312) 823-5161 *Contact Person(s):* Maurs West, Dir of Treatment Srvs
Setting and Background Information The facility was established in 1876 as an orphanage for girls. The 13-acre campus has 13 buildings, which include 6 group homes, a school, and office buildings.
Referral Information Contact the facility for referral information.
Type of Facility
Funding Sources Private; State.
Average Length of Stay Long term.
Types of Admissions Accepted Residential treatment; Group home placement.
Sources of Referral State depts of education; Local depts of education; Cook and DuPage Juvenile Court.
Client Profile
Age Range of Clients Served Residential program: 12-18.
Characteristics Exhibited by Children Emotional handicaps; Learning disabilities.
Tuition and Fees
Room and Board Long term: $57.88/diem.
Tuition $32/diem.
Placements Primarily Funded By Local depts of education; Juvenile Court.
Social and Rehabilitative Services
Therapeutic Approach The facility has a family systems approach.
Therapeutic Services Offered Individual therapy; Family therapy; Substance abuse treatment; Aftercare program with follow up.
Professionals on Staff Psychiatrists; Psychologists; Social workers; Child care staff.
Educational and Vocational Services
Type(s) of Educational Programs Offered On campus; Off campus (Mainstream); Summer campus.
Profile of On Campus School Program Number of teachers 6; Number of classrooms 6; Student to teacher ratio 6:1; Credentials of teachers Certified Spec Ed; Length of school day 4 ½ hrs; Grades taught 7-12; Remedial courses offered (Math, Reading, Speech).
Degrees Offered 8th grade diploma; 12th grade diploma.

JEANINE SCHULTZ MEMORIAL SCHOOL
2101 W Oakton St, Park Ridge, IL 60068 (312) 696-3315
Setting and Background Information The school was established in 1965 to provide a day treatment program for severely emotionally disturbed children and their families. The day school is located in Park Ridge, 15 minutes northwest of Chicago. A residential component has evolved over the past few years in nearby Des Plaines.
Referral Information Referrals can be made by public and private schools, psychiatrists, mental health facilities, and state agencies. Applicants should contact the school's office for placement information. A series of diagnostic interviews will be scheduled to determine the appropriateness of the placement and to assess whether the child's parent or guardian can meet program expectations.
Type of Facility
Funding Sources Private.
Average Length of Stay 4 years.
Types of Admissions Accepted Day treatment; Residential treatment.
Sources of Referral State depts of education; Local depts of education.
Client Profile
Age Range of Clients Served Day programs: 5-18; Residential program: 5-18.
Characteristics Exhibited by Children Emotional handicaps; Learning disabilities; Mental disabilities.
Tuition and Fees
Placements Primarily Funded By State depts of education; Local depts of education.
Social and Rehabilitative Services
Therapeutic Approach The highly structured treatment program uses a dynamic approach in a child centered therapeutic milieu.
Therapeutic Services Offered Individual therapy; Group therapy; Independent living skills program.
Professionals on Staff Psychiatrists; Social workers; Child care staff.

JEANINE SCHULTZ MEMORIAL SCHOOL
(continued)

Educational and Vocational Services
Type(s) of Educational Programs Offered On campus.
Profile of On Campus School Program Number of teachers 9; *Grades taught* K-12; Remedial courses offered.

PEORIA

EDWARD HALL OF GUARDIAN ANGEL HOME
2900 W Heading Ave, Peoria, IL 61604 (309) 671-5760 *Contact Person(s):* Patricia A O'Connell
Setting and Background Information The facility was established in 1983 and is licensed by the Dept of Children and Family Services. It is also approved by the Illinois State Board of Education. Located in a residential area of west Peoria, the facility is housed in one building with a living room, dining room, recreation room, kitchen, laundry facilities, bedrooms, and classroom.
Referral Information Referrals can be made by school districts and special education associations or cooperatives. To make a referral, a letter stating the need for residential services, short and long-term goals, and estimated length of stay should be sent to the facility. The necessary background information on the child should be forwarded, including a social, emotional, and developmental study.
Type of Facility
Funding Sources Private.
Average Length of Stay Short and long term.
Types of Admissions Accepted Day treatment; Residential treatment.
Sources of Referral State depts of education; Local depts of education; Social service depts.
Client Profile
Age Range of Clients Served Day programs: 13-21; Residential program: 13-21.
Characteristics Exhibited by Children Emotional handicaps; Learning disabilities; Neurological impairments; Mental disabilities.
Tuition and Fees
Room and Board Long term: $87/diem.
Placements Primarily Funded By State depts of education; Local depts of education; Social service depts.
Social and Rehabilitative Services
Therapeutic Approach The treatment program has an eclectic therapeutic approach in conjunction with a behavior management system used to earn privileges.
Therapeutic Services Offered Individual therapy; Group therapy; Family therapy; Independent living skills program; Recreation activities.
Professionals on Staff Psychologists; Social workers; Child care staff.
Educational and Vocational Services
Type(s) of Educational Programs Offered On campus.
Profile of On Campus School Program Number of teachers 6; *Grades taught* 7-12; Remedial courses offered.

PRINCETON

CONVENANT CHILDREN'S HOME
502 Elm Pl, Princeton, IL 61356 (815) 875-1129 *Contact Person(s):* Donna Linder
Setting and Background Information The facility was originally established as an orphanage in 1921 and later evolved into a residential center. It is located 120 miles west of Chicago, on Route I-80. The campus includes a new building with 4 living units, a co-educational independent living unit in a separate house, school building, recreational building, and a gymnasium.
Referral Information Referrals are accepted from anyone by contacting the facility and forwarding the child's social and medical histories, school records, and recent psychological reports. A pre-placement interview will take place before a placement decision is made.
Type of Facility
Funding Sources Private.
Average Length of Stay 12-18 mos.
Types of Admissions Accepted Residential treatment.

Sources of Referral State depts of education; Local depts of education; State depts of mental health; Psychiatrists; Private sources; Depts of correction.
Client Profile
Age Range of Clients Served Residential program: 12-18.
Characteristics Exhibited by Children Emotional handicaps; Learning disabilities; Physical handicaps.
IQ Range of Clients 65+.
Tuition and Fees
Room and Board Long term: $95/diem.
Placements Primarily Funded By State depts of education; Local depts of education; State depts of mental health; Insurance; Private sources; Depts of corrections; Social service depts.
Social and Rehabilitative Services
Therapeutic Services Offered Individual therapy; Group therapy; Family therapy; Adjunctive therapy; Independent living skills program.
Professionals on Staff Psychiatrists; Psychologists; Social workers; Adjunctive therapists; Child care staff; Nurses.
Educational and Vocational Services
Type(s) of Educational Programs Offered On campus; Summer campus.
Profile of On Campus School Program Number of teachers 5 and 2 aides; *Grades taught* 6-12.
Degrees Offered 8th grade diploma; 12th grade diploma.

QUINCY

CHADDOCK
205 S 24th St, Quincy, IL 62301 (217) 222-0034 *Contact Person(s):* Kevin Blickhan, Assoc Dir of Res Svcs
Setting and Background Information Chaddock has evolved from an English and German College (1853) to a boys' military school, an orphanage, a home for dependent boys, and currently, a treatment center for boys. It is licensed by the Illinois Dept of Children and Family Services. The campus is located on 35 acres of land and includes an administration building, school, activity building, and 5 cottage living units.
Referral Information Referrals can be made by school districts, Dept of Children and Family Services, courts, religious organizations, and private individuals. Those interested in making a referral should contact the facility.
Type of Facility
Funding Sources Private.
Average Length of Stay 9-12 mos.
Types of Admissions Accepted Day treatment; Residential treatment.
Sources of Referral State depts of education; Local depts of education; State depts of mental health; Social service depts; Courts.
Client Profile
Age Range of Clients Served Day programs: 9-17; Residential program: 9-17.
Characteristics Exhibited by Children Emotional handicaps; Learning disabilities.
IQ Range of Clients 75+.
Tuition and Fees
Placements Primarily Funded By State depts of education; Local depts of education; State depts of mental health; Social service depts; Courts.
Social and Rehabilitative Services
Therapeutic Services Offered Individual therapy; Group therapy; Family therapy; Recreation activities; Aftercare program with follow up.
Professionals on Staff Psychologists; Adjunctive therapists; Child care staff; Nurses.
Educational and Vocational Services
Type(s) of Educational Programs Offered On campus; Off campus.
Profile of On Campus School Program Number of teachers 10; *Student to teacher ratio* 5:1; *Grades taught* Individualized; Special curriculum electives offered; Remedial courses offered.

ROCKTON

FLOBERG CENTER FOR CHILDREN
58 W Rockton Rd, Rockton, IL 61072 (815) 624-8431 *Contact Person(s):* Dan J Pennell MSW, Exec Dir
Setting and Background Information This facility was originally established as an orphanage in 1922. In 1975, it began to serve a DD population. Located on 40 acres, there are three buildings.

FLOBERG CENTER FOR CHILDREN *(continued)*

Referral Information State funded placements are referred through Illinois DMH/DD. Privately funded placements may be made by directly contacting the facility.

Type of Facility
Funding Sources State.
Average Length of Stay Long term.
Types of Admissions Accepted Residential treatment; Wards of the state.
Sources of Referral State depts of education; State depts of mental health; Private sources.

Client Profile
Age Range of Clients Served Residential programs: 6-18.
Characteristics Exhibited by Children Emotional handicaps; Vision impairments/blindness; Neurological impairments; Physical handicaps; Must have primary diagnosis of DD.
IQ Range of Clients Moderate to profound MR.

Tuition and Fees
Room and Board Short term: $49.67/diem; Long term: $49.67/diem.
Placements Primarily Funded By State depts of mental health.

Social and Rehabilitative Services
Therapeutic Approach The basic therapeutic approach is behavior modification.
Therapeutic Services Offered Physical therapy; Independent living skills program; Recreation activities; Occupational therapy; Speech therapy.
Professionals on Staff Psychiatrists; Psychologists; Social workers; Adjunctive therapists; Child care staff; Nurses; Physical therapists; Occupational therapist; Recreational therapist.

Educational and Vocational Services
Type(s) of Educational Programs Offered On campus (Spec Ed); Off campus (Spec Ed).
Profile of On Campus School Program Number of teachers 6 and 14 aides; *Number of classrooms* 3; *Student to teacher ratio* 3:1; *Credentials of teachers* BS, MEd; *Grades taught* Individualized instruction.

URBANA

CUNNINGHAM CHILDREN'S HOME

1301 N Cunningham Ave, Urbana, IL 61801 (217) 367-3728, 367-4064 *Contact Person(s):* John Duchene, Dir of Admis

Setting and Background Information The facility was originally established as an orphanage in 1895 by the Methodist Women's Organization. It has since evolved into a treatment center, which has been in operation for the past 50 years. The 11-building campus is located on 16 acres of land and consists of 5 cottages, administration building, social services building, recreation complex with a pool and school, and maintenance buildings.
Referral Information Referrals can be made by the Illinois Dept of Public Welfare, Dept of Children and Family Services, Dept of Mental Health, probation officers, Governors Youth Service, school districts, and private individuals. To make a referral, contact the facility and forward the following background information: social history, psychological and psychiatric evaluations, school records, court reports, and prior placement reports. Upon receipt of the information, a pre-placement interview will take place before a placement decision is made.

Type of Facility
Funding Sources Private.
Average Length of Stay 18 mos.
Types of Admissions Accepted Residential treatment; Group home placement.
Sources of Referral State depts of education; Local depts of education; State depts of mental health; Psychiatrists; Private sources; Depts of correction; Social service depts.

Client Profile
Age Range of Clients Served Residential program: 11-18.
Characteristics Exhibited by Children Emotional handicaps; Learning disabilities; Mental disabilities; Behavior disorders.

Tuition and Fees
Placements Primarily Funded By State depts of education; Local depts of education; State depts of mental health; Insurance; Private sources; Depts of corrections; Social service depts.

Social and Rehabilitative Services
Therapeutic Services Offered Individual therapy; Group therapy; Family therapy; Adjunctive therapy; Independent living skills program; Recreation activities; Substance abuse treatment; Aftercare program with follow up.
Professionals on Staff Psychologists; Social workers; Adjunctive therapists; Child care staff; Nurses.

Educational and Vocational Services
Type(s) of Educational Programs Offered On campus; Off campus; Summer campus.
Profile of On Campus School Program Student to teacher ratio 4:1; Special curriculum electives offered; Remedial courses offered.

WHEATON

SUNNY RIDGE FAMILY CENTER

2 S 426 Orchard Rd, Wheaton, IL 60187 (312) 668-5117 *Contact Person(s):* Robert G McNeill

Setting and Background Information Initially, this facility was established as a children's home in 1926. It has expanded its programs to become a residential treatment center which also offers outpatient services to families and individuals. The campus consists of an old country estate on 18 acres of land south of Wheaton.
Referral Information Referrals can be made by the Dept of Children and Family Services, juvenile courts, and private individuals. Applicants are requested to forward a referral packet, including social history, psychological report, school records, health records, and court reports. A pre-placement visit will be scheduled and then an admission decision will be made.

Type of Facility
Funding Sources Private.
Average Length of Stay 1 year.
Types of Admissions Accepted Residential treatment.
Sources of Referral Private sources; Depts of correction; Social service depts.

Client Profile
Age Range of Clients Served Residential program: 13-17.
Characteristics Exhibited by Children Emotional handicaps; Learning disabilities; Behavior disorders.

Tuition and Fees
Placements Primarily Funded By Private sources; Depts of corrections; Social service depts.

Social and Rehabilitative Services
Therapeutic Approach The primary therapeutic approach used is based on the peer group treatment model.
Therapeutic Services Offered Individual therapy; Group therapy; Family therapy; Recreation activities.
Professionals on Staff Social workers; Adjunctive therapists; Child care staff.

Educational and Vocational Services
Type(s) of Educational Programs Offered On campus; Off campus.
Profile of On Campus School Program Number of teachers 2; *Grades taught* 9-12; Remedial courses offered.

INDIANA

ANDERSON

MADISON COUNTY BOYS RESIDENTIAL UNIT

3420 Mounds Rd, Anderson, IN 46013 (317) 646-9264 *Contact Person(s):* Harold A Coles, Dir

Setting and Background Information The facility was established in 1982 in order to meet the needs of adolescent males who had been charged with committing a status offense, misdemeanor, felony, or who were in need of temporary shelter care. The program is directly operated by Madison County Probation Services.

Referral Information All referrals are made through Madison County Juvenile Probation Dept. The final decision regarding placement rests with the Superior Court Division II Judge.

Type of Facility

Funding Sources County.

Average Length of Stay Short and long term.

Types of Admissions Accepted Residential treatment; Group home placement; Emergency shelter.

Sources of Referral Juvenile probation dept.

Client Profile

Age Range of Clients Served Residential program: 12-17.

Characteristics Exhibited by Children Emotional handicaps; Learning disabilities; Delinquency; Conduct disorders.

IQ Range of Clients 70+.

Tuition and Fees

Placements Primarily Funded By County.

Social and Rehabilitative Services

Therapeutic Approach The program offers a structured environment through behavior management. The emotional, psychological and additional needs of the resident are dealt with through community agencies.

Therapeutic Services Offered Individual therapy; Group therapy; Family therapy; Independent living skills program; Recreation activities.

Professionals on Staff Psychologists; Social workers.

Educational and Vocational Services

Type(s) of Educational Programs Offered Off campus (Public school).

ARCADIA

HAMILTON CENTERS YSB, ARCADIA HOME

510 E Hamilton St, Arcadia, IN 46030 (317) 773-6342 *Contact Person(s):* Ron Duke Carpenter, Exec Dir

Setting and Background Information The facility was established in 1974 as an alternative to housing status offenders in jail. It is a community-based group home for boys.

Referral Information Contact the facility and forward an information package, including a social history, diagnostic evaluations, a health history, and education reports. A pre-placement visit will be scheduled.

Type of Facility

Funding Sources Private; State.

Average Length of Stay Short and long term.

Types of Admissions Accepted Group home placement; Wards of the state.

Sources of Referral State depts of mental health; Private sources; Depts of correction; Social service depts.

Client Profile

Age Range of Clients Served Residential program: 6-18.

Characteristics Exhibited by Children Emotional handicaps; Learning disabilities; Physical handicaps; Mental disabilities; Delinquency.

IQ Range of Clients 65+.

Tuition and Fees

Room and Board Short term: $35/diem; Long term: $35/diem.

Placements Primarily Funded By State depts of mental health; Social service depts; Courts; Probation.

Social and Rehabilitative Services

Therapeutic Approach The basic approach of the facility is reality therapy.

Therapeutic Services Offered Individual therapy; Group therapy; Family therapy; Recreation activities; Aftercare program with follow up.

Professionals on Staff Psychiatrists; Social workers; Adjunctive therapists; Child care staff.

Educational and Vocational Services

Type(s) of Educational Programs Offered Off campus (Public schools).

BLOOMINGTON

DELTA TREATMENT CENTERS OF INDIANA, INC

PO Box 2024, Bloomington, IN 47402 (812) 825-7400 *Contact Person(s):* Sandra S Berndt, Dir of Admin

Setting and Background Information The facility was established in 1981. There are 4 residential group homes.

Referral Information Contact the facility for referral information. Court-ordered placement is required before admission.

Type of Facility

Funding Sources State; Title XX.

Average Length of Stay Avg 18 mos.

Types of Admissions Accepted Residential treatment; Wards of the state.

Sources of Referral State depts of mental health.

Client Profile

Age Range of Clients Served Residential program: 6-18.

Characteristics Exhibited by Children Emotional handicaps; Learning disabilities; Hearing impairments/deafness; Speech/Language disorders; Mental disabilities; Epileptic.

IQ Range of Clients 50+.

Tuition and Fees

Room and Board Long term: $84/diem.

Placements Primarily Funded By Insurance; Title XX.

Social and Rehabilitative Services

Therapeutic Approach The facility has a therapeutic milieu.

Therapeutic Services Offered Individual therapy; Group therapy; Family therapy; Recreation activities; Substance abuse treatment; Aftercare program with follow up.

Professionals on Staff Psychiatrists; Psychologists; Social workers; Adjunctive therapists; Child care staff.

Educational and Vocational Services

Type(s) of Educational Programs Offered Off campus (Public school).

Profile of On Campus School Program Remedial courses offered Tutoring.

THE VILLAGES OF INDIANA, INC

1641 Kinser Pike, Bloomington, IN 47401 (812) 332-1245 *Contact Person(s):* Gina Alexander, Prog Dir

Setting and Background Information This program was established in 1980 and is a part of The Villages, Inc, which was founded in 1964 by Dr Karl Menninger. It is a non-profit corporation established for the purpose of operating quality homes for children in need of care. There a 6 group homes in communities in Indiana.

Referral Information Referrals are accepted from depts of public welfare and juvenile courts. Available space, the Village family, and the child's educational and emotional needs are all factors which enter into the placement decision.

Type of Facility

Funding Sources State.

Average Length of Stay Long term; 12-48 mo.

Types of Admissions Accepted Group home placement; Wards of the state; Foster care and special needs adoption.

Sources of Referral Depts of correction; Social service depts.

Client Profile

Age Range of Clients Served Residential program: 6-18.

Characteristics Exhibited by Children Emotional handicaps; Learning disabilities; Mental disabilities.

IQ Range of Clients 65+.

Tuition and Fees

Room and Board Long term: $56/diem.

Placements Primarily Funded By Depts of corrections; Social service depts.

Social and Rehabilitative Services

Therapeutic Approach The program offers individual psychotherapy in the context of a supportive homelike environment. Behavior modification is also used.

Therapeutic Services Offered Individual therapy; Group therapy; Independent living skills program; Aftercare program with follow up.

Professionals on Staff Psychiatrists; Psychologists; Social workers; Child care staff.

Educational and Vocational Services

Type(s) of Educational Programs Offered Off campus (Public schools).

CORYDON

WYANDOTTE HOUSE

270 Wyandotte Ave, Corydon, IN 47112 (812) 738-3273 *Contact Person(s):* Pat Ray, Dir

Setting and Background Information This residential facility was established in 1981. It is a 3 bedroom house with an attached garage, that will be converted to 3 additional bedrooms.

Referral Information The facility accepts status offenders. Children with a history of violence, sexual abuse or serious mental illness are not accepted. Contact the facility for referral information.

Type of Facility

Funding Sources Private.

Average Length of Stay Short and long term.

Types of Admissions Accepted Group home placement; Wards of the state.

Sources of Referral Depts of correction; Social service depts.

Client Profile

Age Range of Clients Served Residential program: 2-17.

Characteristics Exhibited by Children Emotional handicaps; Family dysfunction.

IQ Range of Clients 70+.

Tuition and Fees

Room and Board Short term: $35/diem; Long term: $35/diem.

Placements Primarily Funded By Social service depts.

Social and Rehabilitative Services

Professionals on Staff Child care staff.

Educational and Vocational Services

Type(s) of Educational Programs Offered Off campus (Public school).

EVANSVILLE

UNITED METHODIST YOUTH HOME

2521 N Burkhardt Rd, Evansville, IN 47715 (812) 479-7535 *Contact Person(s):* Doris A Murphy, Admin

Setting and Background Information The facility was established in 1978. It is a large building on a 3-acre campus.

Referral Information Referring agency should submit social history, psychological evaluation, medical examination, school records and reason for referral. A pre-placement interview is required.

Type of Facility

Funding Sources Private.

Average Length of Stay Long term.

Types of Admissions Accepted Residential treatment; Group home placement; Wards of the state.

Sources of Referral Depts of correction; Social service depts.

Client Profile

Age Range of Clients Served Residential program: 12-21+.

Characteristics Exhibited by Children Emotional handicaps; Learning disabilities; Hearing impairments/deafness; Vision impairments/ blindness; Speech/Language disorders; Mental disabilities.

IQ Range of Clients 49-130.

Tuition and Fees

Room and Board Long term: $56.51/diem.

Placements Primarily Funded By Social service depts.

Social and Rehabilitative Services

Therapeutic Approach The facility offers individual and group therapy, and uses a behavior modification system.

Therapeutic Services Offered Individual therapy; Group therapy; Family therapy; Independent living skills program; Recreation activities; Substance abuse treatment; Aftercare program with follow up.

Professionals on Staff Psychiatrists; Psychologists; Social workers; Child care staff.

Educational and Vocational Services

Type(s) of Educational Programs Offered Off campus (Public school).

YOUTH CARE CENTER

300 SE 7th St, Evansville, IN 47711 (812) 867-6576 *Contact Person(s):* Roger C Mason, Admin

Setting and Background Information The center was established in 1982 as a pilot project to determine the need for emergency shelter for juveniles (abused, neglected, delinquent).

Referral Information Referrals to the facility are made by contacting the office for an intitial placement interview.

Type of Facility

Funding Sources Private; County.

Average Length of Stay Short term.

Types of Admissions Accepted Residential treatment; Wards of the state; Emergency shelter.

Sources of Referral Social service depts; Probation dept.

Client Profile

Age Range of Clients Served Residential program: 12-18.

Characteristics Exhibited by Children Emotional handicaps; Learning disabilities; Mental disabilities; Delinquency.

IQ Range of Clients 75+.

Tuition and Fees

Room and Board Short term: $29/diem.

Placements Primarily Funded By Social service depts.

Social and Rehabilitative Services

Therapeutic Approach The basic therapeutic approaches used by the facility include behavior modification, reality, and client centered therapy.

Therapeutic Services Offered Individual therapy; Family therapy; Independent living skills program; Recreation activities.

Professionals on Staff Adjunctive therapists; Child care staff.

Educational and Vocational Services

Type(s) of Educational Programs Offered Summer campus (Tutoring).

FORT WAYNE

CROSSROAD

PO Box 5038, 2525 Lake Ave, Fort Wayne, IN 46895 (219) 484-4153 *Contact Person(s):* John M Gantt, Exec Dir

Setting and Background Information The facility was established in 1883 by the German Reformed Church. The 60-acre campus has 3 dorms, an administration building, and other buildings.

CROSSROAD *(continued)*

Referral Information For referral, contact the facility and submit social and psychological histories.
Type of Facility
Funding Sources Private; County.
Average Length of Stay Short and long term.
Types of Admissions Accepted Residential treatment; Wards of the state; Diagnostic evaluations.
Sources of Referral Private sources; Social service depts; Courts.
Client Profile
Age Range of Clients Served Residential program: 12-18.
Characteristics Exhibited by Children Emotional handicaps; Learning disabilities.
IQ Range of Clients 80+.
Tuition and Fees
Room and Board Short term: $82/diem; Long term: $82/diem.
Tuition $1,500/yr.
Placements Primarily Funded By Depts of corrections; Social service depts; County.
Social and Rehabilitative Services
Therapeutic Approach The facility uses insight-oriented psychotherapy as a therapeutic intervention.
Therapeutic Services Offered Individual therapy; Group therapy; Family therapy; Independent living skills program; Recreation activities; Aftercare program with follow up.
Professionals on Staff Psychiatrists; Psychologists; Social workers; Child care staff; Nurses; Recreation therapist.
Educational and Vocational Services
Type(s) of Educational Programs Offered On campus (Spec Ed); Off campus (Public school).
Profile of On Campus School Program Number of teachers 4; Number of classrooms 6; Student to teacher ratio 8:1; Credentials of teachers MA; Grades taught 6-12; Special curriculum electives offered.

FRANKLIN

JOHNSON COUNTY YOUTH SERVICE BUREAU, INC

PO Box 115, 101 N Hurricane, Franklin, IN 46131 (317) 738-3273
Contact Person(s): Karen Bullington, Exec Dir
Setting and Background Information The agency was established to provide an alternative to incarceration of abused, neglected and status offender youth. It is a residential group home.
Referral Information Contact the facility for a referral packet. An interview with the client will be arranged prior to admission.
Type of Facility
Funding Sources Private; State; County.
Average Length of Stay Short and long term.
Types of Admissions Accepted Residential treatment; Group home placement; Wards of the state.
Sources of Referral Depts of correction; Social service depts.
Client Profile
Age Range of Clients Served Residential program: 12-18.
Characteristics Exhibited by Children Emotional handicaps; Learning disabilities; Abused and neglected.
Tuition and Fees
Room and Board Short term: $47.37/diem; Long term: $47.37/diem.
Social and Rehabilitative Services
Therapeutic Approach The facility uses behavior modification.
Therapeutic Services Offered Individual therapy; Group therapy; Family therapy; Independent living skills program; Recreation activities.
Professionals on Staff Adjunctive therapists; Child care staff.
Educational and Vocational Services
Type(s) of Educational Programs Offered Off campus (Local schools).

GOSHEN

BASHOR HOME OF THE UNITED METHODIST CHURCH, INC

PO Box 843, 62226 County Rd #15, Goshen, IN 46526
(219) 875-5117
Setting and Background Information The facility was established by a gift made by John and Emmaline Bashor to the United Methodist Church. The campus is located in a rural community on 160 acres of land, including a 5 acre lake. There are 4 residential units and a central dining and administration building.
Referral Information Referrals can be made by state agencies, mental health professionals, pastors, or family throughout the year. Applicants should contact the main office to submit the necessary application materials and arrange a pre-placement interview.
Type of Facility
Funding Sources Private.
Average Length of Stay 9-12 mos.
Types of Admissions Accepted Residential treatment.
Sources of Referral State depts of mental health; Depts of correction.
Client Profile
Age Range of Clients Served Residential program: 9-18.
Characteristics Exhibited by Children Emotional handicaps; Learning disabilities.
Tuition and Fees
Placements Primarily Funded By State depts of mental health; Depts of corrections; Social service depts.
Social and Rehabilitative Services
Therapeutic Services Offered Individual therapy; Group therapy; Family therapy; Adjunctive therapy; Independent living skills program; Recreation activities.
Professionals on Staff Psychiatrists; Psychologists; Social workers; Child care staff.
Educational and Vocational Services
Type(s) of Educational Programs Offered On campus; Off campus; Summer campus.
Profile of On Campus School Program Number of teachers 2.

HAMMOND

CARMELITE HOME FOR BOYS

4007 Sheffield Ave, Hammond, IN 46327 (219) 931-6451 *Contact Person(s):* Sr M Francis Robillard, Admin
Setting and Background Information The facility was established in 1915 as a home for boys. The facility consists of 2 buildings, a gym and a chapel.
Referral Information Referrals are made by parents and local agencies.
Type of Facility
Funding Sources State; Federal; Contributions; Title XX.
Average Length of Stay Long term.
Types of Admissions Accepted Residential treatment; Group home placement; Wards of the state.
Sources of Referral State depts of education; Local depts of education; State depts of mental health; Psychiatrists; Depts of correction; Social service depts; Courts.
Client Profile
Age Range of Clients Served Residential program: 6-18.
Characteristics Exhibited by Children Emotional handicaps; Learning disabilities; Speech/Language disorders; Neurological impairments; Mental disabilities.
IQ Range of Clients 70+.
Tuition and Fees
Room and Board Long term: $62.10/diem.
Placements Primarily Funded By Social service depts; Donations.
Social and Rehabilitative Services
Therapeutic Approach Therapy is provided by Tri-City Mental Health Association.
Therapeutic Services Offered Individual therapy; Group therapy; Family therapy; Adjunctive therapy; Art therapy; Physical therapy; Recreation activities; Substance abuse treatment; Aftercare program with follow up.
Professionals on Staff Psychiatrists; Psychologists; Social workers; Adjunctive therapists; Child care staff; Therapists; Neurologist; MDs.
Educational and Vocational Services
Type(s) of Educational Programs Offered Off campus.
Profile of On Campus School Program Remedial courses offered (Reading, Speech).

INDIANAPOLIS

LUTHERWOOD RESIDENTIAL TREATMENT CENTER

1525 N Ritter Ave, Indianapolis, IN 46219 (317) 353-8211 *Contact Person(s):* Glenn R Johnson, Dir

LUTHERWOOD RESIDENTIAL TREATMENT CENTER *(continued)*

Setting and Background Information This facility was originally established as an orphanage in 1883. Currently, its 16-acre campus has 2 boys units, a girls unit and an administration building. It is a residential treatment center for emotionally disturbed children.

Referral Information Contact the director and send social history, education evaluations and psychological reports.

Type of Facility

Funding Sources Private; County; Title XX.

Average Length of Stay Long term.

Types of Admissions Accepted Residential treatment.

Sources of Referral State depts of education; State depts of mental health; Psychiatrists; Private sources; Social service depts; Court welfare depts; Juvenile courts.

Client Profile

Age Range of Clients Served Residential program: 6-18.

Characteristics Exhibited by Children Emotional handicaps; Learning disabilities; Neurological impairments; Mental disabilities.

IQ Range of Clients 70+.

Tuition and Fees

Room and Board Long term: $70.50/diem.

Placements Primarily Funded By State depts of education; Insurance; Private sources; County child welfare fund; Title XX.

Social and Rehabilitative Services

Therapeutic Approach The basic approach of the facility is reality therapy.

Therapeutic Services Offered Individual therapy; Group therapy; Family therapy; Independent living skills program.

Professionals on Staff Psychiatrists; Social workers; Child care staff.

Educational and Vocational Services

Type(s) of Educational Programs Offered On campus; Off campus (Public school).

Profile of On Campus School Program Number of teachers 2; *Number of classrooms* 2; *Student to teacher ratio* 5:1; *Credentials of teachers* MA; *Grades taught* 6-12; Remedial courses offered (Math, Reading).

LADOGA

INDIANA CHILDREN'S CHRISTIAN HOME

PO Box 276, W Main St, Ladoga, IN 47954 (317) 942-2245 *Contact Person(s):* Jeffery L Sparks, Exec Dir

Setting and Background Information This facility was established in 1961 for dependent and neglected youth. Its 18-acre campus has residential units, offices and a school.

Referral Information Referrals are made through the courts and welfare depts.

Type of Facility

Funding Sources Private.

Average Length of Stay Long term.

Types of Admissions Accepted Residential treatment.

Sources of Referral Local depts of education; Depts of correction; Social service depts.

Client Profile

Age Range of Clients Served Residential program: 6-18.

Characteristics Exhibited by Children Emotional handicaps; Learning disabilities.

Tuition and Fees

Room and Board Long term: $69.50/diem.

Placements Primarily Funded By Local welfare and probation depts.

Social and Rehabilitative Services

Therapeutic Approach The facility uses an integrated, behavior modification model.

Therapeutic Services Offered Individual therapy; Group therapy; Family therapy; Independent living skills program; Recreation activities; Substance abuse treatment; Aftercare program with follow up.

Professionals on Staff Psychologists; Social workers; Child care staff; Nurses.

Educational and Vocational Services

Type(s) of Educational Programs Offered On campus (Non-graded).

Profile of On Campus School Program Number of teachers 7; *Number of classrooms* 8; *Student to teacher ratio* 10:1; *Credentials of teachers* LD/EH; *Grades taught* K-12; Special curriculum electives offered (Art, Music, Shop, Home Ec); Remedial courses offered.

Degrees Offered 12th grade diploma.

LAFAYETTE

CARY HOME FOR CHILDREN

1530 S 18th St, Lafayette, IN 47905 (317) 423-9367 *Contact Person(s):* Cecil R Geary, Exec Dir

Setting and Background Information The facility was established in 1930 by the county.

Referral Information Contact the facility and forward a brief social history, medical and school records. Immediate acceptance is possible, depending on space availability.

Type of Facility

Funding Sources County.

Average Length of Stay Short and long term.

Types of Admissions Accepted Residential treatment; Wards of the state; Emergency shelter.

Sources of Referral Social service depts; Courts; Probation dept.

Client Profile

Age Range of Clients Served Residential program: 12-18.

Characteristics Exhibited by Children Emotional handicaps; Delinquency.

Tuition and Fees

Room and Board Short term: $30/diem (emergency shelter); Long term: $48/diem (residential treatment).

Placements Primarily Funded By Social service depts; County.

Social and Rehabilitative Services

Therapeutic Services Offered Individual therapy; Group therapy; Family therapy; Independent living skills program; Substance abuse treatment; Aftercare program with follow up.

Professionals on Staff Psychiatrists; Psychologists; Social workers; Child care staff.

Educational and Vocational Services

Type(s) of Educational Programs Offered Off campus.

LEBANON

INDIANA UNITED METHODIST CHILDREN'S HOME, INC.

515 W Camp St, Lebanon, IN 46052 (317) 482-5900 *Contact Person(s):* Michael J Waggoner ACSW

Setting and Background Information The facility was originally established in 1915 as an orphanage. It became a residential treatment center in 1959. Its 14-acre campus has 11 buildings. There are 2 group homes off campus.

Referral Information Contact the facility for referral procedures. A pre-placement visit is required.

Type of Facility

Funding Sources Private.

Average Length of Stay Long term.

Types of Admissions Accepted Residential treatment; Group home placement; Wards of the state.

Sources of Referral State depts of education; Local depts of education; State depts of mental health; Psychiatrists; Private sources; Depts of correction; Social service depts.

Client Profile

Age Range of Clients Served Residential program: 6-18.

Characteristics Exhibited by Children Emotional handicaps; Learning disabilities; Hearing impairments/deafness; Vision impairments/blindness; Speech/Language disorders; Neurological impairments; Physical handicaps; Mental disabilities.

Tuition and Fees

Room and Board Long term: $51/diem (in state); $85/diem (out of state).

Tuition $900.

Placements Primarily Funded By Depts of corrections; Social service depts; Church.

Social and Rehabilitative Services

Therapeutic Approach The facility teaches independent living skills and offers counseling in a therapetic milieu.

Therapeutic Services Offered Individual therapy; Group therapy; Family therapy; Independent living skills program; Recreation activities; Substance abuse treatment; Aftercare program with follow up.

Professionals on Staff Psychiatrists; Psychologists; Social workers; Child care staff; Nurses; Activities staff.

INDIANA UNITED METHODIST CHILDREN'S HOME, INC. *(continued)*

Educational and Vocational Services
Type(s) of Educational Programs Offered On campus; Off campus (Public schools); Summer campus.
Profile of On Campus School Program Number of teachers 5; *Number of classrooms* 5; *Student to teacher ratio* 10:1; *Credentials of teachers* Certified Spec Ed; *Grades taught* Individualized instruction.
Degrees Offered 8th grade diploma; 12th grade diploma; GED.

LEO

APOSTOLIC CHRISTIAN CHILDRENS HOME
PO Box 151, 11947 Klopfenstein Rd, Leo, IN 46765 (219) 627-2159
Contact Person(s): Timothy D Sander, Admin
Setting and Background Information This facility was established in 1976 by the Apostolic Christian Church. Its 63 acre campus has 2 residential buildings, an administration building, a barn and a machine shop.
Referral Information Referring party should contact by phone, mail referral materials, and schedule a pre-placement interview.
Type of Facility
Funding Sources Private.
Average Length of Stay Long term.
Types of Admissions Accepted Residential treatment; Group home placement; Wards of the state.
Sources of Referral State depts of mental health; Psychiatrists; Private sources; Social service depts.
Client Profile
Age Range of Clients Served Residential program: 6-21+.
Characteristics Exhibited by Children Emotional handicaps; Learning disabilities; Mental disabilities.
IQ Range of Clients 70+.
Tuition and Fees
Room and Board Long term: $24/diem.
Tuition $800/semester.
Placements Primarily Funded By Private sources; Social service depts; Contributions.
Social and Rehabilitative Services
Therapeutic Services Offered Individual therapy; Group therapy; Family therapy; Independent living skills program; Recreation activities.
Professionals on Staff Social workers; Child care staff; Nurses.
Educational and Vocational Services
Type(s) of Educational Programs Offered On campus (Tutorial/remedial); Off campus (Special ed/independent living); Summer campus (Psych testing/computer workshop).
Profile of On Campus School Program Number of teachers 1 and 2 aides; *Number of classrooms* 1; Special curriculum electives offered (This is a tutorial and remedial program only).
Vocational Education Programs/Degrees Offered Woodwork; Animal husbandry.

MARION

GRANT COUNTY RESIDENTIAL TREATMENT CENTER
532 E 5th St, Marion, IN 46953 (317) 662-9864 *Contact Person(s):* Joyce N Inskeep, Dir
Setting and Background Information The facility was established in 1982 through a grant. Its campus consists of one building on 4 acres of land.
Referral Information Contact the facility and forward the necessary information. A pre-placement interview will be held and then a decision will be made on the appropriateness of placement.
Type of Facility
Funding Sources County.
Average Length of Stay Long term.
Types of Admissions Accepted Residential treatment.
Sources of Referral Depts of correction; Social service depts.
Client Profile
Age Range of Clients Served Residential program: 12-15.
Characteristics Exhibited by Children Emotional handicaps; Learning disabilities.
IQ Range of Clients 75-130.

Tuition and Fees
Room and Board Long term: $60/diem.
Placements Primarily Funded By Welfare dept.
Social and Rehabilitative Services
Therapeutic Approach The facility uses reality therapy, including behavior modification.
Therapeutic Services Offered Individual therapy; Group therapy; Family therapy; Recreation activities; Substance abuse treatment; Aftercare program with follow up.
Professionals on Staff Psychiatrists; Psychologists; Social workers; Adjunctive therapists; Child care staff.
Educational and Vocational Services
Type(s) of Educational Programs Offered Off campus (Tucker Area Vocational Center & Marion community schools).
Profile of On Campus School Program Number of teachers 2; *Number of classrooms* 2; *Credentials of teachers* Certified; *Grades taught* 5-11.

NEW HORIZONS MINISTRIES
1000 S 350 E, Marion, IN 46953 (317) 668-4009 *Contact Person(s):* Tim Blossom, Admis
Setting and Background Information The facility was established in 1972 and is located on 100 acres, with four buildings.
Referral Information Referrals are made by social service agencies and parents.
Type of Facility
Funding Sources Private.
Average Length of Stay Long term.
Types of Admissions Accepted Residential treatment.
Sources of Referral Private sources; Social service depts.
Client Profile
Age Range of Clients Served Residential program: 12-18.
Characteristics Exhibited by Children Emotional handicaps.
Tuition and Fees
Room and Board Long term: $1,620/mo (includes school tuition).
Placements Primarily Funded By Private sources; Social service depts.
Social and Rehabilitative Services
Therapeutic Approach Behavior modification is the therapeutic approach of the facility.
Therapeutic Services Offered Individual therapy; Group therapy; Family therapy; Aftercare program with follow up.
Professionals on Staff Psychologists; Social workers; Child care staff; Clergy.
Educational and Vocational Services
Type(s) of Educational Programs Offered On campus; Off campus; Summer campus.
Profile of On Campus School Program Number of teachers 8; *Number of classrooms* 5; *Student to teacher ratio* 4:1; *Grades taught* 7-12; Special curriculum electives offered; Remedial courses offered.
Degrees Offered 8th grade diploma; 12th grade diploma.

MISHAWAKA

THE CHILDREN'S CAMPUS
1411 Lincoln Way W, Mishawaka, IN 46544 (219) 259-5666
Contact Person(s): Michael Puthoff, Exec Dir
Setting and Background Information The facility was established in 1882 by the Women's Christian Temperance Union. Currently, its 15-acre campus has 4 cottages, a gym, 2 school buildings and an administration building.
Referral Information Contact intake coordinator for referral information.
Type of Facility
Funding Sources Private; State; Federal.
Average Length of Stay Long term; 12 mos.
Types of Admissions Accepted Residential treatment; Group home placement; Wards of the state.
Sources of Referral State depts of mental health; Private sources; Depts of correction; Social service depts.
Client Profile
Age Range of Clients Served Residential program: 6-18.
Characteristics Exhibited by Children Emotional handicaps; Learning disabilities; Hearing impairments/deafness; Vision impairments/blindness; Speech/Language disorders; Neurological impairments; Physical handicaps; Mental disabilities.
IQ Range of Clients 85+.

THE CHILDREN'S CAMPUS *(continued)*

Tuition and Fees
Room and Board Long term: $73.98/diem.
Social and Rehabilitative Services
Therapeutic Approach The basic approach is reality therapy and behavior management.
Therapeutic Services Offered Individual therapy; Group therapy; Family therapy; Independent living skills program; Recreation activities; Substance abuse treatment; Aftercare program with follow up.
Professionals on Staff Psychiatrists; Psychologists; Social workers; Adjunctive therapists; Child care staff.
Educational and Vocational Services
Type(s) of Educational Programs Offered On campus; Off campus (Public school); Summer campus.
Profile of On Campus School Program Number of teachers 6; *Number of classrooms* 10; *Student to teacher ratio* 10:1; *Credentials of teachers* State certified; *Length of school day* 8-3; *Grades taught* 3-11; *Remedial courses offered.*
Degrees Offered 8th grade diploma; GED.

MUNCIE

CAMBRIDGE HOUSE, INC
608 E Washington St, Muncie, IN 47305 (317) 289-2802 *Contact Person(s):* Imogene Nusbaum Snyder, Dir
Setting and Background Information The facility was established in 1971 by a group of local citizens as an alternative to large institutions. There is a 3-story house and an office building.
Referral Information Contact the facility and forward social, psychological, and educational histories. A pre-placement visit can be arranged.
Type of Facility
Funding Sources Private; County.
Average Length of Stay Long term.
Types of Admissions Accepted Residential treatment; Group home placement; Wards of the state.
Sources of Referral Private sources; Depts of correction; State Dept of Public Welfare; City and state depts; Individuals.
Client Profile
Age Range of Clients Served Residential program: 12-21.
Characteristics Exhibited by Children Emotional handicaps; Learning disabilities; Mental disabilities.
IQ Range of Clients 70+.
Tuition and Fees
Room and Board Long term: $51/diem.
Tuition Funded by public school.
Social and Rehabilitative Services
Therapeutic Approach The facility has an eclectic approach to therapy and uses behavior management.
Therapeutic Services Offered Individual therapy; Group therapy; Family therapy; Adjunctive therapy; Independent living skills program; Recreation activities.
Professionals on Staff Psychologists; Adjunctive therapists; Child care staff.
Educational and Vocational Services
Type(s) of Educational Programs Offered Off campus (Public school system).

YOUTH SERVICE BUREAU
722 E Main St, Muncie, IN 47305 (317) 289-8940 *Contact Person(s):* Debra Gray, Exec Dir
Setting and Background Information The facility is a large group home which provides residential and out-patient services.
Referral Information Referrals to the out-patient program may be made by anyone. Referrals to the residential program are court-ordered through the juvenile court.
Type of Facility
Funding Sources Private; State; County.
Average Length of Stay Short and long term.
Types of Admissions Accepted Residential treatment; Group home placement.
Sources of Referral Depts of correction; Social service depts.

Client Profile
Age Range of Clients Served Day programs: Birth-18; Residential program: 10-18.
Characteristics Exhibited by Children Emotional handicaps; Learning disabilities; Mental disabilities; Behavior disorders; Delinquency.
Tuition and Fees
Room and Board Short term: $30/diem; Long term: $48/diem.
Placements Primarily Funded By Depts of corrections; Social service depts.
Social and Rehabilitative Services
Therapeutic Approach The basic approach of the facility is behavior modification.
Therapeutic Services Offered Individual therapy; Group therapy; Family therapy; Substance abuse treatment; Aftercare program with follow up.
Professionals on Staff Psychologists; Social workers; Child care staff.
Educational and Vocational Services
Type(s) of Educational Programs Offered Off campus (Public schools).

NOBLESVILLE

HAMILTON CENTERS YSB—CHERRY ST HOME
PO Box 401, 1035 Cherry St, Noblesville, IN 46060 (317) 773-6342
Contact Person(s): Ron Duke Carpenter, Exec Dir
Setting and Background Information The facility was established in 1974 as an alternative to housing status offenders in jail. It is a community-based group home for boys.
Referral Information Contact the facility and submit an information package, including a social history, diagnostic evaluations, a health history and education reports. A pre-placement visit will be arranged.
Type of Facility
Funding Sources Private; State.
Average Length of Stay Long term.
Types of Admissions Accepted Group home placement; Wards of the state.
Sources of Referral State depts of mental health; Private sources; Depts of correction; Social service depts.
Client Profile
Age Range of Clients Served Residential program: 6-18.
Characteristics Exhibited by Children Emotional handicaps; Learning disabilities; Physical handicaps; Mental disabilities.
IQ Range of Clients 75+.
Tuition and Fees
Room and Board Short term: $35/diem; Long term: $35/diem.
Placements Primarily Funded By State depts of mental health; Social service depts; Courts; Probation.
Social and Rehabilitative Services
Therapeutic Approach The basic approach of the facility is reality therapy.
Therapeutic Services Offered Individual therapy; Group therapy; Family therapy; Recreation activities; Aftercare program with follow up.
Professionals on Staff Psychiatrists; Social workers; Adjunctive therapists; Child care staff.
Educational and Vocational Services
Type(s) of Educational Programs Offered Off campus (Public schools).

HAMILTON CENTERS YSB—REGIONAL SHELTER HOME
PO Box 401, 294 S 9th St, Noblesville, IN 46060 (317) 773-6342
Contact Person(s): Ron Duke Carpenter, Exec Dir
Setting and Background Information The facility was established in 1974 as an alternative to jail for status offenders. It is a co-ed group home.
Referral Information Contact the facility and submit an information packet. In emergency situations, the packet can be forwarded after placement has been made.
Type of Facility
Funding Sources Private; State.
Average Length of Stay Short term.
Types of Admissions Accepted Group home placement; Wards of the state; Foster care.
Sources of Referral State depts of mental health; Private sources; Depts of correction; Social service depts.

HAMILTON CENTERS YSB—REGIONAL SHELTER HOME *(continued)*

Client Profile
Age Range of Clients Served Residential program: 6-18.
Characteristics Exhibited by Children Emotional handicaps; Learning disabilities; Mental disabilities.
IQ Range of Clients 75+.
Tuition and Fees
Room and Board Short term: $35/diem.
Placements Primarily Funded By State depts of mental health; Social service depts; Courts; Probation.
Social and Rehabilitative Services
Therapeutic Approach The basic approach of the facility is reality therapy.
Therapeutic Services Offered Individual therapy; Group therapy; Family therapy; Recreation activities; Aftercare program with follow up.
Professionals on Staff Psychiatrists; Social workers; Adjunctive therapists; Child care staff.
Educational and Vocational Services
Type(s) of Educational Programs Offered Off campus (Public schools).

SCHERERVILLE

HOOSIER BOYS TOWN, INC
7403 Cline Ave, Schererville, IN 46375 (219) 838-7723 *Contact Person(s):* Gary Adzia
Setting and Background Information Hoosier Boys Town is a private residential treatment facility. Monsignor Michael A Compagna founded Hoosier Boys Town in 1947.
Referral Information Referrals can be made by welfare depts, courts, and private individuals. Applicants should forward a social history report.
Type of Facility
Funding Sources Private.
Average Length of Stay 12 mos.
Types of Admissions Accepted Residential treatment.
Sources of Referral Depts of correction; Social service depts.
Client Profile
Age Range of Clients Served Residential program: 8-18.
Characteristics Exhibited by Children Emotional handicaps; Learning disabilities.
Tuition and Fees
Placements Primarily Funded By Depts of corrections; Social service depts.
Social and Rehabilitative Services
Therapeutic Services Offered Individual therapy; Group therapy; Family therapy; Recreation activities; Substance abuse treatment.
Professionals on Staff Psychologists; Social workers; Adjunctive therapists.
Educational and Vocational Services
Type(s) of Educational Programs Offered On campus; Off campus.
Profile of On Campus School Program Number of teachers 2.

TERRE HAUTE

GIBAULT SCHOOL FOR BOYS
PO Box 2316, 5901 Dixie Bee Rd, Terre Haute, IN 47802
(812) 299-1156 *Contact Person(s):* Marlene Redman, Admis Coord
Setting and Background Information The school was established in 1921 by the Indiana Knights of Columbus. It is a residential treatment facility for troubled and delinquent boys. It is located on 360 acres and has 4 residential buildings, two school buildings, two gyms and a swimming pool.
Referral Information Referrals are made by submitting a complete social and medical history. In many cases, a pre-placement visit will be required. The admissions committee reviews the material and makes a decision.
Type of Facility
Funding Sources Private.
Average Length of Stay 12 mos.
Types of Admissions Accepted Residential treatment.
Sources of Referral State depts of education; Depts of correction; Social service depts.

Client Profile
Age Range of Clients Served Residential program: 12-18.
Characteristics Exhibited by Children Emotional handicaps; Learning disabilities.
IQ Range of Clients 72-130.
Tuition and Fees
Room and Board Long term: $75/diem (includes school tuition).
Placements Primarily Funded By Depts of corrections.
Social and Rehabilitative Services
Therapeutic Approach The facility uses reality therapy as its basic therapeutic approach.
Therapeutic Services Offered Individual therapy; Group therapy; Family therapy; Art therapy; Recreation activities; Substance abuse treatment; Aftercare program with follow up.
Professionals on Staff Psychiatrists; Psychologists; Social workers; Adjunctive therapists; Child care staff; Nurses; Art therapists.
Educational and Vocational Services
Type(s) of Educational Programs Offered On campus; Off campus; Summer campus.
Profile of On Campus School Program Number of teachers 13; *Number of classrooms* 13; *Student to teacher ratio* 5:1; *Credentials of teachers* BA, MA certified; *Grades taught* 5-10; Special curriculum electives offered (Music, Crafts, Woodshop).
Degrees Offered 8th grade diploma; GED.

VALPARAISO

BAPTIST CHILDREN'S HOME AND FAMILY MINISTRIES
354 West St, Valparaiso, IN 46383 (219) 462-4111 *Contact Person(s):* Lindel R Brothers, Supr of Soc Serv
Setting and Background Information The facility was established in 1952 by local churches. There is a 52 acre campus with three buildings and group homes in Valparaiso and Indianapolis.
Referral Information For referral, contact the facility for an intake application. An in-house interview will be scheduled.
Type of Facility
Funding Sources Private; Churches.
Average Length of Stay Long term.
Types of Admissions Accepted Group home placement.
Sources of Referral Psychiatrists; Private sources; Social service depts; Pastors.
Client Profile
Age Range of Clients Served Residential program: 6-18.
Characteristics Exhibited by Children Emotional handicaps; Learning disabilities.
IQ Range of Clients 70+.
Tuition and Fees
Room and Board Long term: $30/diem.
Placements Primarily Funded By Private sources.
Social and Rehabilitative Services
Therapeutic Approach The facility offers milieu christian counseling.
Therapeutic Services Offered Individual therapy; Family therapy.
Professionals on Staff Social workers; Child care staff.
Educational and Vocational Services
Type(s) of Educational Programs Offered Off campus.

WABASH

WHITE'S
RR 5 Box 78, Wabash, IN 46992 (219) 563-1158 *Contact Person(s):* Richard E Davis, Supt
Setting and Background Information The facility was established in 1850. There are 800 acres of wooded land with about 40 buildings.
Referral Information Contact the facility for referral information.
Type of Facility
Funding Sources Federal; County; Title XX.
Average Length of Stay 12-18 mos.
Types of Admissions Accepted Residential treatment.
Sources of Referral State depts of mental health; Social service depts; Juvenile courts.
Client Profile
Age Range of Clients Served Residential program: 12-18.
Characteristics Exhibited by Children Emotional handicaps; Character disorders.
IQ Range of Clients 65-120.

WHITE'S *(continued)*

Tuition and Fees
Room and Board Long term: $45/diem.
Placements Primarily Funded By Social service depts; Juvenile
courts.
Social and Rehabilitative Services
Therapeutic Approach The facility uses reality therapy in a milieu
setting.
Therapeutic Services Offered Individual therapy; Group therapy;
Family therapy; Adjunctive therapy; Recreation activities; Substance abuse treatment.
Professionals on Staff Psychologists; Social workers; Child care staff;
Nurses.
Educational and Vocational Services
Type(s) of Educational Programs Offered On campus.
Profile of On Campus School Program Number of teachers 19;
Number of classrooms 19; *Student to teacher ratio* 10:1; *Credentials of teachers* MS; *Length of school day* 8:30-3; *Grades taught* 7-12; *Remedial courses offered* (Reading, Math).
Vocational Education Programs/Degrees Offered Construction; Horticulture; Small engine repair; Food service; Secretarial.
Degrees Offered 8th grade diploma; 12th grade diploma; GED.

WHEATFIELD

CHRISTIAN HAVEN HOMES, INC

R 1, Box 17, Wheatfield, IN 46392 (219) 956-3125 *Contact*
Person(s): Carl Lange, Exec Dir; Joseph Tierney, Intake Counselor
Setting and Background Information The facility was established in
1958 by donations, bequests and church involvement. There are
two locations- a 40-acre campus with 3 cottages, a school and an
office; and a 105-acre campus with 7 cottages, a gym, a school
and an administrative office. There is also a group home in
Valpariso, Indiana.
Referral Information Contact the facility and forward the necessary
material.
Type of Facility
Funding Sources Private; State; Title XX.
Average Length of Stay Long term.
Types of Admissions Accepted Residential treatment.
Sources of Referral Depts of correction; Social service depts.
Client Profile
Age Range of Clients Served Residential program: 9-18.
Characteristics Exhibited by Children Emotional handicaps; Learning
disabilities.
IQ Range of Clients 50-110.
Tuition and Fees
Room and Board Long term: $57.95/diem.
Placements Primarily Funded By Depts of corrections; Social service
depts.
Social and Rehabilitative Services
Therapeutic Approach The basic approach of the facility is reality
therapy.
Therapeutic Services Offered Individual therapy; Group therapy;
Family therapy; Independent living skills program; Recreation
activities; Substance abuse treatment; Aftercare program with
follow up.
Professionals on Staff Psychiatrists; Psychologists; Social workers;
Child care staff.
Educational and Vocational Services
Type(s) of Educational Programs Offered On campus (Remedial); Off
campus (Public school).
Profile of On Campus School Program Number of teachers 5; *Number of classrooms* 5; *Student to teacher ratio* 2:1; *Credentials of
teachers* BA; Special curriculum electives offered; Remedial
courses offered.
Vocational Education Programs/Degrees Offered Landscaping; Woodworking; Food Services; Custodial; Auto shop.
Degrees Offered GED.

WHITING

PHOENIX HOUSE

2118 Indianapolis Blvd, Whiting, IN 46394 (219) 398-7050
Setting and Background Information The facility was established
jointly by Tri-City Mental Health and Lake County Juvenile
Court in 1980. Phoenix House is a 3-story brick building located
in a small industrial city of approximately 12,000 people.
Referral Information Referrals can be made by juvenile court, Dept
of Public Welfare, school districts, and parents. All referrals
should make an initial phone contact to schedule a pre-placement
interview.
Type of Facility
Funding Sources Private.
Average Length of Stay 12 mos.
Types of Admissions Accepted Residential treatment.
Sources of Referral State depts of education; Local depts of education; Depts of correction; Social service depts.
Client Profile
Age Range of Clients Served Residential program: 13-17.
Characteristics Exhibited by Children Emotional handicaps; Learning
disabilities.
IQ Range of Clients 75+.
Tuition and Fees
Room and Board Long term: $81.63/diem.
Placements Primarily Funded By Depts of corrections; Social service
depts; Title XX.
Social and Rehabilitative Services
Therapeutic Approach The basic therapeutic approach used is client
centered therapy, in conjunction with family, milieu and
problem-solving therapy.
Therapeutic Services Offered Individual therapy; Group therapy; Independent living skills program; Recreation activities; Substance
abuse treatment; Aftercare program with follow up.
Professionals on Staff Psychiatrists; Psychologists; Social workers;
Adjunctive therapists; Child care staff.
Educational and Vocational Services
Type(s) of Educational Programs Offered Off campus.

IOWA

AMES

MARY GREELEY MEDICAL CENTER
117 11th St, Ames, IA 50010 (515) 239-2011 *Contact Person(s):*
John D Worley Jr, Pres
Referral Information Contact the facility for referral information.
Type of Facility
Types of Admissions Accepted Residential treatment.
Client Profile
Age Range of Clients Served Residential program: Birth-55+.
Characteristics Exhibited by Children Emotional handicaps; Hearing
   impairments/deafness; Vision impairments/blindness; Physical
   handicaps; Mental disabilities; Behavior disorders; Multiple
   handicapped.
Social and Rehabilitative Services
Therapeutic Services Offered Individual therapy; Group therapy;
   Family therapy; Independent living skills program; Diagnosis and
   evaluation.
Educational and Vocational Services
Type(s) of Educational Programs Offered On campus.
Vocational Education Programs/Degrees Offered Vocational training.

MAINSTREAM LIVING, INC
PO Box 1621, 1200 McCormick Ave, Ames, IA 50010
(515) 232-8405 *Contact Person(s):* Reinhold V Berg, Dir
Referral Information Contact the facility for referral information.
Type of Facility
Types of Admissions Accepted Residential treatment; Group home
   placement.
Client Profile
Age Range of Clients Served Residental program: 3-59.
Characteristics Exhibited by Children Emotional handicaps; Hearing
   impairments/deafness; Physical handicaps; Mental disabilities; Be-
   havior disorders; Multiple handicaps.
Social and Rehabilitative Services
Therapeutic Services Offered Individual therapy; Independent living
   skills program; Diagnosis and evaluation; Case management.
Professionals on Staff Social workers; Child care staff.

CEDAR RAPIDS

CHILDREN'S HOME OF CEDAR RAPIDS
2309 C St SW, Cedar Rapids, IA 52404 (319) 365-9164 *Contact
Person(s):* George Estle, Exec Dir
Referral Information Contact the facility for referral information.
Type of Facility
Types of Admissions Accepted Residential treatment.
Client Profile
Age Range of Clients Served Residential program: 3-18.
Characteristics Exhibited by Children Emotional handicaps; Hearing
   impairments/deafness; Vision impairments/blindness; Physical
   handicaps; Mental disabilities; Behavior disorders.
Social and Rehabilitative Services
Therapeutic Services Offered Individual therapy; Independent living
   skills program; Diagnosis and evaluation.
Educational and Vocational Services
Type(s) of Educational Programs Offered On campus.
Vocational Education Programs/Degrees Offered Vocational training;
   Supported work program.

CLINTON

JANE LAMB HEALTH CENTER
638 S Bluff Blvd, Clinton, IA 52732 (319) 243-1131 *Contact
Person(s):* Jackie Kramer, Admin
Referral Information Contact the facility for referral information.
Type of Facility
Types of Admissions Accepted Residential treatment.
Client Profile
Age Range of Clients Served Residential program: 12-55+.
Characteristics Exhibited by Children Emotional handicaps; Hearing
   impairments/deafness; Vision impairments/blindness; Physical
   handicaps; Mental disabilities; Behavior disorders.
Social and Rehabilitative Services
Therapeutic Services Offered Individual therapy; Group therapy;
   Family therapy; Independent living skills program; Diagnosis and
   evaluation.
Educational and Vocational Services
Vocational Education Programs/Degrees Offered Vocational training.

COUNCIL BLUFFS

JENNIE EDMUNDSON MEMORIAL HOSPITAL
933 E Pierce St, Council Bluffs, IA 51501 (712) 328-6222 *Contact
Person(s):* Edward R Lynn, Admin
Referral Information Contact the facility for referral information.
Type of Facility
Types of Admissions Accepted Residential treatment.
Client Profile
Age Range of Clients Served Residential program: Birth-55+.
Characteristics Exhibited by Children Emotional handicaps; Hearing
   impairments/deafness; Vision impairments/blindness; Physical
   handicaps; Mental disabilities; Behavior disorders; Multiple
   handicapped.
Social and Rehabilitative Services
Therapeutic Services Offered Individual therapy; Group therapy;
   Family therapy; Independent living skills program; Diagnosis and
   evaluation.
Educational and Vocational Services
Type(s) of Educational Programs Offered On campus.
Vocational Education Programs/Degrees Offered Vocational training.

DES MOINES

IOWA CHILDREN'S AND FAMILY SERVICES
1101 Walnut, Des Moines, IA 50309 (515) 288-1981 *Contact
Person(s):* Lawrence Scales, Jr, Admin
Referral Information Contact the facility for referral information.
Type of Facility
Types of Admissions Accepted Day treatment; Residential treatment;
   Group home placement; Foster care.
Client Profile
Age Range of Clients Served Day programs: Birth-55+; Residential
   program: Birth-55+.
Characteristics Exhibited by Children Emotional handicaps; Vision
   impairments/blindness; Physical handicaps; Mental disabilities;
   Behavior disorders; Multiple handicapped.
Social and Rehabilitative Services
Therapeutic Services Offered Individual therapy; Independent living
   skills program; Diagnosis and evaluation.

IOWA CHILDREN'S AND FAMILY SERVICES
(continued)

Educational and Vocational Services
Vocational Education Programs/Degrees Offered Vocational training.

IOWA LUTHERAN HOSPITAL, CHILDREN'S SERVICES

University at Penn Ave, Des Moines, IA 50316 (515) 263-5187, 5584, 5322 *Contact Person(s):* Dr Dewdney, Physician-in-Charge
Setting and Background Information The hospital was privately established in 1978. There is a 14 bed adolescent unit, a 12 bed pre-adolescent unit, and an 8 bed childrens unit.
Referral Information Referrals to the hospital are made by psychiatrists only.
Type of Facility
Funding Sources Private; Title 19.
Average Length of Stay Short and long term.
Types of Admissions Accepted Residential treatment.
Sources of Referral Psychiatrists.
Client Profile
Age Range of Clients Served Residential program: 4-18.
Characteristics Exhibited by Children Emotional handicaps.
IQ Range of Clients 76+.
Tuition and Fees
Room and Board Long term: $280-320/diem.
Placements Primarily Funded By Insurance.
Social and Rehabilitative Services
Therapeutic Approach The facility offers a therapeutic milieu.
Therapeutic Services Offered Individual therapy; Group therapy; Family therapy; Adjunctive therapy; Art therapy; Physical therapy; Independent living skills program; Recreation activities.
Professionals on Staff Psychiatrists; Psychologists; Social workers; Adjunctive therapists; Child care staff; Nurses; Art therapists; Physical therapists.
Educational and Vocational Services
Type(s) of Educational Programs Offered On campus; Off campus.
Profile of On Campus School Program Number of teachers 3 and 3 aides; *Number of classrooms* 3; Remedial courses offered.

ORCHARD PLACE, DES MOINES CHILDREN'S HOME

925 SW Porter, Des Moines, IA 50315 (515) 285-6781 *Contact Person(s):* Carolyn Hejtmanek, ACSW
Setting and Background Information The Des Moines Children's Home has been providing services to children since 1886. The agency opened Orchard Place in 1962 on a 5-acres wooded campus. There are 3 residential treatment units (Orchard Place, Kenyon House, Porter House), each having its own distinct program and population.
Referral Information Referrals can be made by parents, Dept of Human Services, physicians, courts, and public or private agencies. To make a referral, contact the facility and forward the necessary background information, including social history, psychiatric and psychological reports, school records, and recent medical report. Upon review of these materials, a pre-placement visit will take place before an admission decision is made.
Type of Facility
Funding Sources Private.
Average Length of Stay 18-24 mos.
Types of Admissions Accepted Day treatment; Residential treatment.
Sources of Referral Depts of correction; Social service depts.
Client Profile
Age Range of Clients Served Day programs: 5-18; Residential program: 5-18.
Characteristics Exhibited by Children Emotional handicaps; Learning disabilities; Neurological impairments; Physical handicaps; Mental disabilities.
Tuition and Fees
Room and Board Long term: $68/diem; $30/diem (day treatment).
Placements Primarily Funded By Local depts of education; Private sources; Depts of corrections; Social service depts.
Social and Rehabilitative Services
Therapeutic Approach The programs' philosophy is based on psychoanalytic concepts, however, a variety of therapeutic approaches are used, including reality therapy, behavior modification, and play therapy.

Therapeutic Services Offered Individual therapy; Group therapy; Family therapy; Recreation activities; Aftercare program with follow up.
Professionals on Staff Psychiatrists; Psychologists; Social workers; Adjunctive therapists; Child care staff; Nurses.
Educational and Vocational Services
Type(s) of Educational Programs Offered On campus; Off campus.
Profile of On Campus School Program Number of teachers 25; *Student to teacher ratio* 5:1; *Grades taught* K-12; Special curriculum electives offered; Remedial courses offered.

DUBUQUE

HILLCREST FAMILY SERVICES

PO Box 1160, 2005 Asbury Rd, Dubuque, IA 52001 (319) 583-3756
Setting and Background Information The agency was founded by Dr Nancy Hill in 1896 for the purpose of providing services to unwed mothers. Supervision of the home was transferred to St Lukes Methodist Church in 1914. Since then, it has expanded its programs and services to include residential treatment and outpatient services. The agency operates 5 residential treatment facilities, 2 of which are located on the main campus. The other 3 are separate facilities in residential neighborhoods.
Referral Information Referrals can be made by mental health centers, juvenile courts, ministers, and families, and through the Dept of Human Services. No private placements are accepted. Most residents are admitted upon court order after being adjudicated as delinquents. A pre-placement visit is necessary before an admission decision is made.
Type of Facility
Funding Sources State.
Average Length of Stay 1-2 years.
Types of Admissions Accepted Residential treatment.
Sources of Referral State depts of mental health; Social service depts.
Client Profile
Age Range of Clients Served Residential program: 10-17.
Characteristics Exhibited by Children Emotional handicaps; Learning disabilities; Mental disabilities; Delinquency.
IQ Range of Clients 60+.
Tuition and Fees
Room and Board Long term: $66/diem.
Placements Primarily Funded By Social service depts.
Social and Rehabilitative Services
Therapeutic Approach The treatment programs utilize milieu therapy in conjunction with a behavior modification level system designed for the earning of privileges.
Therapeutic Services Offered Individual therapy; Group therapy; Family therapy; Independent living skills program; Recreation activities.
Professionals on Staff Psychiatrists; Psychologists; Social workers; Child care staff.
Educational and Vocational Services
Type(s) of Educational Programs Offered On campus; Off campus.

MERCY HEALTH CENTER

Mercy Drive, Dubuque, IA 52001 (319) 589-9000 *Contact Person(s):* Sr Mary Corita Heid, Chief Oper Off
Referral Information Contact the facility for referral information.
Type of Facility
Types of Admissions Accepted Day treatment; Residential treatment.
Client Profile
Age Range of Clients Served Day programs: Birth-55+; Residential program: Birth-55+.
Characteristics Exhibited by Children Emotional handicaps; Physical handicaps; Behavior disorders.
Social and Rehabilitative Services
Therapeutic Services Offered Individual therapy; Group therapy; Family therapy; Independent living skills program; Diagnosis and evaluation.

FORT DODGE

JERRY RABINER MEMORIAL BOYS RANCH, INC
Rte 3, Box E, Fort Dodge, IA 50501 (515) 576-7388 *Contact Person(s):* David D Kilian, Exec Dir
Setting and Background Information The facility was established by the Iowa State Policemen's Association in 1964. Its campus is located 5 miles from Fort Dodge and consists of 4 cottages, gymnasium, swimming pool, and tennis courts.
Referral Information Referrals can be made by the Dept of Human Services, courts, mental health facilities, schools, law enforcement officials, county attorney, and private individuals. To make a referral, forward the necessary background information, including a social history, psychological evaluation, and school records. An intake assessment is required before a placement decision is made.
Type of Facility
Funding Sources Private.
Average Length of Stay 9 mos.
Types of Admissions Accepted Residential treatment.
Sources of Referral Depts of correction; Social service depts.
Client Profile
Age Range of Clients Served Residential program: 13-17.
Characteristics Exhibited by Children Emotional handicaps; Delinquency.
Social and Rehabilitative Services
Therapeutic Approach The program uses an eclectic therapeutic approach involving reality therapy and behavior modification.
Therapeutic Services Offered Individual therapy; Group therapy; Family therapy; Recreation activities.
Professionals on Staff Psychiatrists; Social workers; Child care staff.
Educational and Vocational Services
Type(s) of Educational Programs Offered Off campus.

TRINITY REGIONAL HOSPITAL
Psychiatric Unit, S Kenyon Rd, Fort Dodge, IA 50501
(515) 573-3101 *Contact Person(s):* Dr S O Lee, Dir
Referral Information Contact the facility for referral information.
Type of Facility
Types of Admissions Accepted Residential treatment.
Client Profile
Age Range of Clients Served Residential program: 3-55+.
Characteristics Exhibited by Children Emotional handicaps; Hearing impairments/deafness; Vision impairments/blindness; Physical handicaps; Mental disabilities; Behavior disorders; Psychological problem as primary diagnosis.
Social and Rehabilitative Services
Therapeutic Services Offered Individual therapy; Group therapy; Family therapy; Independent living skills program; Diagnosis and evaluation.

MARION

LINNHAVEN, INC
601 7th Ave, Marion, IA 52302 (319) 377-9788 *Contact Person(s):* C Richard Beavers, Admin
Referral Information Contact the facility for referral information.
Type of Facility
Types of Admissions Accepted Residential treatment; Group home placement; Foster care.
Client Profile
Age Range of Clients Served Residential program: Birth-55+.
Characteristics Exhibited by Children Emotional handicaps; Hearing impairments/deafness; Vision impairments/blindness; Neurological impairments; Physical handicaps; Mental disabilities; Behavior disorders.
Social and Rehabilitative Services
Therapeutic Services Offered Individual therapy; Independent living skills program; Diagnosis; Evaluation.
Educational and Vocational Services
Type(s) of Educational Programs Offered Off campus (Public school).
Vocational Education Programs/Degrees Offered Vocational training; Supported work program.

MASON CITY

GERARD OF IOWA
PO Box 1353, Mason City, IA 50401 (515) 423-3222 *Contact Person(s):* Admissions Dir
Setting and Background Information Gerard was established in 1969. It operates 2 facilities, one in Mason City, Iowa, and another in Austin, Minnesota. The Iowa program is located on 10 acres of land, in a 35-room English country home. The facility houses bedrooms, recreational and community rooms, and library. A swimming pool, tennis court, and recreational facilities are also located on the grounds. Gerard of Iowa is accredited by the Joint Commission of Accreditation of Hospitals.
Referral Information Referrals can be made by psychiatrists, physicians, psychologists, and social agencies (only with psychiatric consultation). To make a referral, contact the facility and forward the following information: psychiatric evaluations, psychological reports, school records, family history, and developmental history reports.
Type of Facility
Funding Sources Private.
Average Length of Stay 17 mos.
Types of Admissions Accepted Residential treatment.
Sources of Referral State depts of education; Local depts of education; State depts of mental health; Psychiatrists; Private sources; Depts of correction; Social service depts.
Client Profile
Characteristics Exhibited by Children Emotional handicaps; Learning disabilities; Neurological impairments; Physical handicaps; Mental disabilities.
Tuition and Fees
Placements Primarily Funded By Insurance; Private sources.
Social and Rehabilitative Services
Therapeutic Approach The philosophy of the treatment program is based on developmental theory and is implemented through a highly structured individual milieu therapy program.
Therapeutic Services Offered Individual therapy; Group therapy; Family therapy; Recreation activities.
Professionals on Staff Psychiatrists; Psychologists; Social workers; Child care staff; Nurses.
Educational and Vocational Services
Type(s) of Educational Programs Offered On campus; Off campus.
Profile of On Campus School Program Special curriculum electives offered; Remedial courses offered.

FRANCIS LAUER YOUTH SERVICES
Rte 1, Mason City, IA 50401 (515) 423-2582 *Contact Person(s):* Nora Giefe, Social Worker
Setting and Background Information The facility evolved from a group home serving the juvenile courts to become a treatment facility in 1983. It is licensed by the Iowa Dept of Social Services and owned by Cerro Gordo County. The large ranch-style home is located in rural Mason City and contains 7 bedrooms, recreation room, mult-purpose room, dining room, kitchen, living room, laundry facilities, and office space. There is also a youth shelter for short term placements.
Referral Information Referrals can be made by probation officers and the court system. Background information on the child should be forwarded, including a social history, school reports, psychological evaluation, and reports from previous placements. Upon receipt of the referral information, a pre-placement visit with the child, family, and referral agency worker will take place before a placement decision is made. Adolescents who are chemically dependent, persistant runaways, physically abusive, or diagnosed as severely mentally ill are not accepted.
Type of Facility
Funding Sources State; County.
Average Length of Stay Short and long term.
Types of Admissions Accepted Residential treatment.
Sources of Referral Depts of correction; Social service depts.
Client Profile
Age Range of Clients Served Residential program: 11-17.
Characteristics Exhibited by Children Emotional handicaps.
Tuition and Fees
Room and Board Long term: $65/diem.
Placements Primarily Funded By Depts of corrections; Social service depts.

FRANCIS LAUER YOUTH SERVICES (continued)

Social and Rehabilitative Services
Therapeutic Approach The philosophy of the treatment program is based on behavior modification theory, using a 5-step level system.
Therapeutic Services Offered Individual therapy; Group therapy; Family therapy; Independent living skills program; Recreation activities.
Professionals on Staff Social workers; Adjunctive therapists; Child care staff.
Educational and Vocational Services
Type(s) of Educational Programs Offered On campus; Off campus.
Profile of On Campus School Program Remedial courses offered.

ST JOSEPH MERCY HOSPITAL

84 Beaumont Dr, Mason City, IA 50401 (515) 424-7211 *Contact Person(s):* Dave Vellinga
Referral Information Contact the facility for referral information.
Type of Facility
Types of Admissions Accepted Day treatment; Residential treatment.
Client Profile
Age Range of Clients Served Day programs: 3-55+; Residential program: 3-55+.
Characteristics Exhibited by Children Emotional handicaps; Hearing impairments/deafness; Vision impairments/blindness; Physical handicaps; Mental disabilities; Behavior disorders; Multiple handicapped.

NEW PROVIDENCE

QUAKERDALE HOME

New Providence, IA 50206 (515) 497-5294 *Contact Person(s):* Lawrence Bailey
Setting and Background Information The first facility was founded in 1851 by Josiah White, a Quaker philanthropist. There are 4 facilities that now exist, governed by a board of directors appointed by the Iowa Yearly Meeting of Friends. The main campus is located in a rural area near New Providence and includes 4 residential cottages housing 10 children each, administrative building, gymnasium/shops complex, executive director's home, farm, and maintenance garages.
Referral Information Referrals must be made by the Dept of Human Services or juvenile probation officers. Out of state placements are accepted, but private placements are no longer accepted.
Type of Facility
Funding Sources Private.
Average Length of Stay 10-13 mos.
Types of Admissions Accepted Residential treatment.
Sources of Referral Depts of correction.
Client Profile
Age Range of Clients Served Residential program: 11-18.
Characteristics Exhibited by Children Emotional handicaps; Learning disabilities.
Tuition and Fees
Room and Board Long term: $55.71/diem.
Placements Primarily Funded By Depts of corrections.
Social and Rehabilitative Services
Therapeutic Approach The primary therapeutic approach used is that of reality therapy.
Therapeutic Services Offered Individual therapy; Group therapy; Family therapy; Art therapy; Recreation activities; Spiritual life program.
Professionals on Staff Psychologists; Social workers; Child care staff; Nurses; Art therapists.
Educational and Vocational Services
Type(s) of Educational Programs Offered Off campus.

OTTUMWA

OTTUMWA REGIONAL HEALTH CENTER

1001 E Pennsylvania, Ottumwa, IA 52501 (515) 682-7511 *Contact Person(s):* Clarence Corry, Admin
Referral Information Contact the center for referral information.
Type of Facility
Types of Admissions Accepted Residential treatment.

Client Profile
Age Range of Clients Served Residential program: Birth-55+.
Characteristics Exhibited by Children Emotional handicaps; Vision impairments/blindness; Physical handicaps; Mental disabilities; Behavior disorders; Multiple handicapped.
Social and Rehabilitative Services
Therapeutic Services Offered Individual therapy; Group therapy; Family therapy; Independent living skills program; Diagnosis and evaluation.
Educational and Vocational Services
Vocational Education Programs/Degrees Offered Vocational training; Supported work programs.

PETERSON

MIDWEST CHRISTIAN CHILDREN'S HOME

Rte 1 Box 154, Peterson, IA 51047 (712) 295-7601 *Contact Person(s):* Karl Peterson
Referral Information Contact the facility for referral information.
Type of Facility
Types of Admissions Accepted Residential treatment.
Client Profile
Age Range of Clients Served Residential program: 3-18.
Characteristics Exhibited by Children Emotional handicaps; Behavior disorders.
Social and Rehabilitative Services
Therapeutic Services Offered Individual therapy; Independent living skills program; Diagnosis and evaluation.
Educational and Vocational Services
Type(s) of Educational Programs Offered On campus.
Vocational Education Programs/Degrees Offered Vocational training; Supported work programs.

ROCK VALLEY

HOPE HAVEN, INC

1800 19th St, Rock Valley, IA 51247 (712) 476-2737 *Contact Person(s):* David VanNingen, Exec Dir
Referral Information Contact the facility for referral information.
Type of Facility
Types of Admissions Accepted Residential treatment; Group home placement.
Client Profile
Age Range of Clients Served Residential program: 3-55+.
Characteristics Exhibited by Children Emotional handicaps; Hearing impairments/deafness; Vision impairments/blindness; Physical handicaps; Mental disabilities; Multiple handicapped.
Social and Rehabilitative Services
Therapeutic Services Offered Individual therapy; Independent living skills program; Diagnosis and evaluation.
Educational and Vocational Services
Vocational Education Programs/Degrees Offered Vocational training.

SIOUX CITY

FLORENCE CRITTENTON HOME

1105 28th St, Sioux City, IA 51104 (712) 255-4321
Referral Information Contact the facility for referral information.
Type of Facility
Types of Admissions Accepted Day treatment; Group home placement; Foster care.
Client Profile
Age Range of Clients Served Day programs: 2-59; Residential program: 0-59.
Characteristics Exhibited by Children Emotional handicaps; Hearing impairments/deafness; Vision impairments/blindness; Physical handicaps; Mental disabilities.
Social and Rehabilitative Services
Therapeutic Services Offered Individual therapy; Independent living skills program; Diagnosis and evaluation.
Educational and Vocational Services
Type(s) of Educational Programs Offered Off campus.

WALLINGFORD

FOREST RIDGE COMMUNITY YOUTH CENTER
RR 1, Wallingford, IA 51365 (712) 867-4724 *Contact Person(s):*
Patricia Mitchell ACSW, Exec Dir
Referral Information Contact the facility for referral information.
Type of Facility
Types of Admissions Accepted Residential treatment.
Client Profile
Age Range of Clients Served Residential program: 13-18.
Characteristics Exhibited by Children Emotional handicaps; Mental
   disabilities; Behavior disorders.
Social and Rehabilitative Services
Therapeutic Services Offered Individual therapy; Independent living
   skills program; Diagnosis and evaluation.
Educational and Vocational Services
Type(s) of Educational Programs Offered On campus.
Vocational Education Programs/Degrees Offered Vocational training;
   Supported work program.

WATERLOO

ST FRANCIS HOSPITAL
3421 W 9th St, Psyc Living Ctr, Waterloo, IA 50702 (319) 236-4513
Contact Person(s): Kathleen Wernimont, RN Coord
Referral Information Contact the facility for referral information.
Type of Facility
Types of Admissions Accepted Residential treatment.
Client Profile
Age Range of Clients Served Residential program: 3-55+.
Characteristics Exhibited by Children Emotional handicaps; Hearing
   impairments/deafness; Vision impairments/blindness; Physical
   handicaps; Mental disabilities; Behavior disorders; Multiple
   handicapped.
Social and Rehabilitative Services
Therapeutic Services Offered Individual therapy; Group therapy;
   Family therapy; Independent living skills program; Diagnosis and
   evaluation.
Educational and Vocational Services
Type(s) of Educational Programs Offered On campus.
Vocational Education Programs/Degrees Offered Vocational training;
   Supported work programs.

WAVERLY

BREMWOOD LUTHERAN CHILDREN'S HOME SOCIETY
Box 848, 106 16th St SW, Waverly, IA 50677 (319) 352-2630
Contact Person(s): Ardell M Banker ACSW, Dir
Referral Information Contact the facility for referral information.
Type of Facility
Types of Admissions Accepted Residential treatment; Group home
   placement.
Client Profile
Age Range of Clients Served Residential program: 3-18.
Characteristics Exhibited by Children Emotional handicaps; Mental
   disabilities; Behavior disorders.
Social and Rehabilitative Services
Therapeutic Services Offered Individual therapy; Independent living
   skills program.

KANSAS

KANSAS CITY

RAINBOW MENTAL HEALTH FACILITY

2205 W 36th St, Kansas City, KS 66103 (913) 384-1880

Setting and Background Information Rainbow Mental Health Facility is a state operated psychiatric hospital. The facility was established in 1974 as a short-term acute care psychiatric hospital. It is a 59-bed hospital with an accredited special education school.

Referral Information Referrals can be made by mental health centers, medical centers, and the Dept of Social and Rehabilitative Services. Screening for admission is conducted by one of the referral agencies listed above.

Type of Facility

Funding Sources State.

Average Length of Stay Short term (Adults); Long term (Children, Adolescents).

Types of Admissions Accepted Day treatment; Residential treatment.

Sources of Referral State depts of mental health.

Client Profile

Age Range of Clients Served Day programs: 4-55+; Residential program: 4-55+.

Characteristics Exhibited by Children Emotional handicaps; Learning disabilities; Mental disabilities; Psychotic.

Tuition and Fees

Placements Primarily Funded By State depts of mental health.

Social and Rehabilitative Services

Therapeutic Approach A multi-disciplinary approach is used in conjunction with behavior management therapy and chemotherapy.

Therapeutic Services Offered Individual therapy; Group therapy; Family therapy; Adjunctive therapy; Independent living skills program; Recreation activities.

Professionals on Staff Psychiatrists; Psychologists; Social workers; Adjunctive therapists; Child care staff; Nurses.

Educational and Vocational Services

Type(s) of Educational Programs Offered On campus.

Profile of On Campus School Program Number of teachers 16; *Student to teacher ratio* 7:1; *Grades taught* K-12; Remedial courses offered (Reading, Math).

Degrees Offered Conferred through local school district.

LARNED

LARNED STATE HOSPITAL

RR #3 Box 89, Larned, KS 67550 (316) 285-2131 *Contact Person(s):* G W Getz, Supt & Clin Dir

Setting and Background Information The facility was established in 1914 by state statute. The 78-acre grounds have 52 major buildings, including residential buildings for patients and for staff, and office buildings.

Referral Information Contact the facility for referral information.

Type of Facility

Funding Sources State.

Average Length of Stay Short and long term.

Types of Admissions Accepted Residential treatment.

Sources of Referral Depts of correction; Courts.

Client Profile

Age Range of Clients Served Residential program: 6-55+.

Characteristics Exhibited by Children Emotional handicaps; Neurological impairments; Mental disabilities.

Tuition and Fees

Placements Primarily Funded By State depts of mental health.

Social and Rehabilitative Services

Therapeutic Approach The hospital has a psycho-social approach to therapy.

Therapeutic Services Offered Individual therapy; Group therapy; Adjunctive therapy; Art therapy; Independent living skills program; Recreation activities; Substance abuse treatment.

Professionals on Staff Psychiatrists; Psychologists; Social workers; Adjunctive therapists; Child care staff; Nurses; Art therapists.

Educational and Vocational Services

Type(s) of Educational Programs Offered On campus (Elementary and secondary).

Profile of On Campus School Program Number of teachers 20; *Number of classrooms* 15; *Student to teacher ratio* 8:1; *Credentials of teachers* Certified; *Grades taught* 1-12; Special curriculum electives offered; Remedial courses offered.

Vocational Education Programs/Degrees Offered Pre-vocational training.

Degrees Offered 12th grade diploma; GED.

PITTSBURG

RESIDENTIAL CENTER FOR YOUTH, INC

30th & Michigan, Pittsburg, KS 66762 (316) 232-1500 *Contact Person(s):* John Bozich, Exec Dir

Setting and Background Information The facility initially opened as a regional detention center in 1973. It expanded its programs to become a treatment facility by 1979. The campus is located on 9 acres of land in a rural community of 20,000 residents. There are 3 living units; one is for 12 girls, and two are for 14 boys.

Referral Information Referrals can be made by the Dept of Social and Rehabilitative Services.

Type of Facility

Funding Sources Private.

Average Length of Stay 5-7 mos.

Types of Admissions Accepted Day treatment; Residential treatment.

Sources of Referral State depts of mental health.

Client Profile

Age Range of Clients Served Day programs: 13-17; Residential program: 13-17.

Characteristics Exhibited by Children Emotional handicaps; Learning disabilities; Conduct disorders.

IQ Range of Clients 75+.

Tuition and Fees

Room and Board Long term: $56.72/diem.

Placements Primarily Funded By State depts of mental health.

Social and Rehabilitative Services

Therapeutic Approach The program utilizes an eclectic therapeutic approach involving the use of reality therapy, with emphasis on remedial development counseling within a highly structured environment.

Therapeutic Services Offered Individual therapy; Group therapy; Family therapy; Adjunctive therapy; Independent living skills program; Substance abuse treatment.

Professionals on Staff Psychologists.

Educational and Vocational Services

Type(s) of Educational Programs Offered On campus (Through local school district).

Profile of On Campus School Program Number of teachers 3 and 4 aides; *Student to teacher ratio* 6:1; *Grades taught* 6-12.

RESIDENTIAL CENTER FOR YOUTH, INC
(continued)

Degrees Offered 8th grade diploma; 12th grade diploma; GED.

SALINA

THE ST FRANCIS BOYS' HOMES
PO Box 1348, Salina, KS 67402 (913) 825-0541 *Contact Person(s):*
Richard W Burnett ACSW, Clinical Coord

Setting and Background Information St Francis Boys' Homes has 3
private residential treatment facilities. The initial facility was
established by the Rt Rev Robert H Mize, Jr, as a non-profit
treatment center for delinquent boys. There are 3 homes, one
each in Ellsworth and Salina, Kansas, and one in Lake Placid,
New York. Each home has a living unit and activities center,
including a gymnasium and chapel. There is also a program called
Passport for Adventure for girls (grades 4-5) and boys (grades 5-6)
which is a 72-day wilderness program that includes a family
therapy week.

Referral Information Referrals can be made by parents, mental
health professionals, school counselors, courts, and clergy by
forwarding the necessary application materials. A placement
decision will be made within 10 days of receipt of the application
materials.

Type of Facility
Funding Sources Private.
Average Length of Stay 13 ½ mos.
Types of Admissions Accepted Residential treatment.
Sources of Referral Private sources; Courts.

Client Profile
Age Range of Clients Served Residential program: 12-18.
Characteristics Exhibited by Children Emotional handicaps; Learning
disabilities; Conduct disorders.

Tuition and Fees
Room and Board Long term: $162-$183/diem (residential); $140/
diem (Passport for Adventure).
Placements Primarily Funded By State depts of mental health; Insurance; Private sources; Donations; Endowments.

Social and Rehabilitative Services
Therapeutic Approach The basic approach of the facilities is thera-
peutic community living.
Therapeutic Services Offered Individual therapy; Group therapy;
Family therapy; Adjunctive therapy; Independent living skills
program.
Professionals on Staff Psychiatrists; Psychologists; Social workers;
Adjunctive therapists; Child care staff; Nurses.

Educational and Vocational Services
Type(s) of Educational Programs Offered On campus (Lake Placid,
NY); Off campus (Ellsworth and Salina); Summer campus.
Profile of On Campus School Program Number of teachers 3; *Student
to teacher ratio* 8:1; *Grades taught* 7-12; Special curriculum elec-
tives offered; Remedial courses offered.
Degrees Offered 12th grade diploma; GED.

TOPEKA

THE MENNINGER FOUNDATION—CHILDRENS DIVISION
Children's Division, PO Box 829, Topeka, KS 66601
(913) 273-7500, Ext 800 *Contact Person(s):* Les Letulle ACSW, Dir
of Hospital Admis

Setting and Background Information The Menninger Foundation has
been in operation for over 60 years. Children's Division evolved
out of the Southard School, established in 1926. The campus is
located on a secluded 35 acres of land and consists of 4 main
buildings which house administrative and out-patient offices,
Southard School, 7 residential units, outdoor swimming pool,
tennis courts, and fishing and camping areas. The Southard
School has a gymnasium, library, student computer lab, and
classrooms. Children's Hospital is licensed by the Kansas State
Dept of Social and Rehabilitative Services and is accredited by
the Joint Commission on Accreditation of Hospitals.

Referral Information Anyone can make a referral by contacting the
Director of Hospital Admissions.

Type of Facility
Funding Sources Private.
Average Length of Stay 9-24 mos.
Types of Admissions Accepted Day treatment; Residential treatment.
Sources of Referral Psychiatrists; Private sources.

Client Profile
Age Range of Clients Served Day programs: 5-17; Residential
progrm: 5-17.
Characteristics Exhibited by Children Emotional handicaps; Learning
disabilities; Primary diagnosis of psychiatric illness.

Tuition and Fees
Room and Board Long term: $550/diem; $390/diem (diagnostic
unit).
Placements Primarily Funded By Insurance; Private sources.

Social and Rehabilitative Services
Therapeutic Approach The treatment program utilizes a multi-
disciplinary team approach.
Therapeutic Services Offered Individual therapy; Group therapy;
Family therapy; Adjunctive therapy; Art therapy; Independent
living skills program; Recreation activities; Aftercare program
with follow up.
Professionals on Staff Psychiatrists; Psychologists; Social workers;
Adjunctive therapists; Child care staff; Nurses; Art therapists.

Educational and Vocational Services
Type(s) of Educational Programs Offered On campus; Off campus
(Public school); Summer campus.
Profile of On Campus School Program Number of teachers 15;
Number of classrooms 11; *Student to teacher ratio* 4.6:1; *Grades
taught* 1-12; Remedial courses offered.
Degrees Offered 12th grade diploma.

TOPEKA STATE HOSPITAL—CAPITAL CITY SCHOOLS
2700 W 6th St, Topeka, KS 66606 (913) 296-4343 *Contact
Person(s):* Abigail B Calkin, Principal

Setting and Background Information The facility was established in
1955 by a contract between Topeka State Hospital and the local
school district to provide educational services. The school
occupies 3 buildings on the 400 acre hospital grounds.

Referral Information Referrals are made by the Topeka State
Hospital, by the Dept of Social and Rehabilitative Services, and
by local school districts.

Type of Facility
Funding Sources State; Local school districts.
Average Length of Stay Short and long term.
Types of Admissions Accepted Day treatment; Residential treatment.
Sources of Referral Local depts of education; State depts of mental
health; Psychiatrists; Social service depts.

Client Profile
Age Range of Clients Served Day programs: 12-21+; Residential
program: Birth-21+.
Characteristics Exhibited by Children Emotional handicaps; Mental
disabilities.
IQ Range of Clients 80-140.

Tuition and Fees
Placements Primarily Funded By State depts of education; Local
depts of education; State depts of mental health; Social service
depts.

Social and Rehabilitative Services
Therapeutic Approach The facility has a psychodynamic approach to
therapy and uses behavior modification.
Therapeutic Services Offered Individual therapy; Group therapy;
Family therapy; Recreation activities.
Professionals on Staff Psychiatrists; Psychologists; Social workers;
Child care staff; Nurses.

Educational and Vocational Services
Type(s) of Educational Programs Offered On campus; Off campus;
Summer campus.
Profile of On Campus School Program Number of teachers 53;
Number of classrooms 42; *Student to teacher ratio* 5:1; *Credentials
of teachers* MA; *Grades taught* K-12; Special curriculum electives
offered; Remedial courses offered.
Vocational Education Programs/Degrees Offered Basic vocational
courses.
Degrees Offered 8th grade diploma; 12th grade diploma; GED.

WICHITA

MAUDE CARPENTER'S CHILDRENS HOME

1501 N Meridian, Wichita, KS 67203 (316) 942-3221 *Contact Person(s):* Jim Laney, Dir of Children's Svcs

Setting and Background Information Maude Carpenter's Childrens Home is a private treatment facilty. It also offers foster care and adoption services. The agency was founded in 1948 by several Church of Christ churches in the Wichita area. The teaching family program (residential program) was started in 1973 and is located on 22 acres in a suburban setting with 4 cottages (6-8 residents each), gymnasium, tennis courts, and softball fields.

Referral Information Referrals can be made by contacting the facility. Adolescents who are psychotic, dangerous, or who will not consent to attend the program are not accepted.

Type of Facility

Funding Sources Private.

Average Length of Stay Long term.

Types of Admissions Accepted Residential treatment; Foster care.

Client Profile

Age Range of Clients Served Residential program: 13-17.

Characteristics Exhibited by Children Emotional handicaps; Behavior disorders.

Social and Rehabilitative Services

Therapeutic Approach The philosophy of the treatment program is oriented towards the teaching family approach to child care.

Therapeutic Services Offered Individual therapy; Family therapy; Independent living skills program; Aftercare program with follow up.

Educational and Vocational Services

Type(s) of Educational Programs Offered Off campus (Public school).

WICHITA CHILDREN'S HOME, INC

810 N Holyoke, Wichita, KS 67208 (316) 684-6581

Setting and Background Information Wichita Children's Home is a private residential treatment facility for short-term placements, 90 days or less. The facility was established in 1888 by Mrs M L Garver, a Wichita resident. It is located in northeast Wichita on 6 acres of land.

Referral Information Referrals are mostly made by law enforcement agencies and social workers. Private referrals are accepted on children between birth and 12 years of age. The referral process is initiated by contacting the facility by phone.

Type of Facility

Funding Sources Private.

Average Length of Stay 48 hrs-90 days.

Types of Admissions Accepted Residential treatment; Emergency shelter.

Sources of Referral State depts of mental health; Private sources; Police (runaways).

Client Profile

Age Range of Clients Served Residential program: Birth-17.

Characteristics Exhibited by Children Emotional handicaps; Learning disabilities.

Tuition and Fees

Room and Board Short term: $59/diem (based on sliding scale).

Placements Primarily Funded By State depts of mental health; United Way.

Social and Rehabilitative Services

Therapeutic Approach The program's philosophy is based on the Teaching Family Model as developed at Kansas University.

Therapeutic Services Offered Individual therapy; Group therapy; Independent living skills program; Recreation activities.

Professionals on Staff Psychiatrists; Psychologists; Social workers; Child care staff; Tutors.

Educational and Vocational Services

Type(s) of Educational Programs Offered Off campus (Public school).

KENTUCKY

CRITTENDEN

NORTHERN KENTUCKY TREATMENT CENTER

PO Box 100, Crittenden, KY 41030 (606) 356-3172 *Contact Person(s):* Melody Adams, Admis

Setting and Background Information The facility was originally established as a treatment center for delinquent children by the Dept of Social Services in 1972. In 1981, it was transferred to the Dept of Health Services, became a licensed hospital, and expanded its programs to include moderately emotionally disturbed children between the ages of 11 and 17. In 1987, it became a facility for emotionally disturbed adolescents. The campus is located in rural northern Kentucky, and consists of dormitories, school, cafeteria, office building, fenced-in recreational areas, and indoor recreational areas.

Referral Information For admission to the program, contact the placement and assessment branch of Children's Residential Services at (502) 564-7220.

Type of Facility
Funding Sources State.
Average Length of Stay 10-112 mos.
Types of Admissions Accepted Residential treatment.
Sources of Referral Court committed.

Client Profile
Age Range of Clients Served Residential program: 12-17.
Characteristics Exhibited by Children Emotional handicaps; Delinquency.

Tuition and Fees
Placements Primarily Funded By State depts of mental health.

Social and Rehabilitative Services
Therapeutic Approach The basic therapeutic approach used is behavior modification in the form of a contingency phase system.
Therapeutic Services Offered Individual therapy; Group therapy; Family therapy; Art therapy.
Professionals on Staff Psychiatrists; Psychologists; Social workers; Adjunctive therapists; Child care staff; Nurses; Art therapists.

Educational and Vocational Services
Type(s) of Educational Programs Offered On campus; Summer campus.
Profile of On Campus School Program Number of teachers 6; *Student to teacher ratio* 6:1; *Grades taught* Ungraded; Special curriculum electives offered; Remedial courses offered.
Degrees Offered GED.

LEXINGTON

CENTRAL KENTUCKY RE-ED CENTER

690 Newtown Pike, Lexington, KY 40508 (606) 253-2436 *Contact Person(s):* Gail Gillespie

Setting and Background Information Central Kentucky Re-Ed Center is a 5-day a week residential treatment facility which was established in 1971 by the Bluegrass Regional Mental Health-Mental Retardation board. The campus is located on the grounds of Eastern State Mental Hospital, though separate from it. There are 4 'living space' cottages, a 3-story classroom building, and an office building. Children must live close enough to the facility to be able to return home on weekends.

Referral Information Referrals can be made by parents or guardians, schools, and state agencies. Applicants should contact the facility to receive information regarding what records need to be

forwarded and to schedule an interview with the Re-Ed Admissions Committee. If the child is accepted, then he/she will be placed on a waiting list, depending on the census at the time.

Type of Facility
Funding Sources Private; State.
Average Length of Stay 7 mos.
Types of Admissions Accepted Residential treatment.
Sources of Referral State depts of mental health; Private sources.

Client Profile
Age Range of Clients Served Residential program: 6-12.
Characteristics Exhibited by Children Emotional handicaps; Learning disabilities; Neurological impairments; Mental disabilities.
IQ Range of Clients 75+.

Tuition and Fees
Room and Board Long term: $8.75/diem (sliding scale).
Placements Primarily Funded By State depts of mental health; Private sources.

Social and Rehabilitative Services
Therapeutic Approach Behavior modification is the primary therapeutic approach used in the educational program. The facility puts a strong emphasis on family therapy.
Therapeutic Services Offered Individual therapy; Group therapy; Family therapy; Independent living skills program; Aftercare program with follow up.
Professionals on Staff Psychologists; Social workers; Adjunctive therapists; Child care staff; Nurses.

LOUISVILLE

CARDINAL TREATMENT CENTER

2915 Freys Hill Rd, Louisville, KY 40222 (502) 425-2172 *Contact Person(s):* Tom Andis, Prog Dir

Setting and Background Information The facility was established in 1982 by the Children's Division for Residential Services, Dept of Social Services, and Kentucky Dept for Human Resources. The campus consists of 3 cottages and recreation areas for softball, basketball, and volleyball. It is located near a state park which offers swimming, tennis, and gym.

Referral Information The assessment and placement branch of the Dept of Social Services should be contacted for admission information at (502) 588-3161.

Type of Facility
Funding Sources State.
Average Length of Stay 3-6 mos.
Types of Admissions Accepted Residential treatment; Wards of the state.
Sources of Referral State depts of mental health.

Client Profile
Age Range of Clients Served Residential program: 13-17.
Characteristics Exhibited by Children Emotional handicaps.
IQ Range of Clients 70+.

Tuition and Fees
Placements Primarily Funded By State depts of mental health.

Social and Rehabilitative Services
Therapeutic Approach The program philosophy is based on behavior modification and reality therapy.
Therapeutic Services Offered Individual therapy; Group therapy; Recreation activities.
Professionals on Staff Psychiatrists; Psychologists; Social workers; Adjunctive therapists; Child care staff; Nurses.

CARDINAL TREATMENT CENTER (continued)

Educational and Vocational Services
Type(s) of Educational Programs Offered On campus (Through Jefferson County); Off campus; Summer campus.
Profile of On Campus School Program Number of teachers 10;
Student to teacher ratio 3:1; *Credentials of teachers* Certified;
Grades taught Individualized; Special curriculum electives offered;
Remedial courses offered.
Degrees Offered GED.

CHILDREN'S TREATMENT SERVICE

10510 LaGrange Rd, Louisville, KY 40223 (502) 245-4121 ext 477
Contact Person(s): Thomas D Schell, Prog Dir
Setting and Background Information The facility was established in
1956 as a children's unit of a psychiatric hospital. There are 7
buildings on extensive grounds.
Referral Information For referral, contact the facility and send
results of psychiatric, psychological and social assessments to
Director of Admissions.
Type of Facility
Funding Sources State.
Average Length of Stay Long term.
Types of Admissions Accepted Residential treatment.
Sources of Referral Local depts of education; State depts of mental
health; Psychiatrists; Private sources; Social service depts.
Client Profile
Age Range of Clients Served Residential program: 6-18.
Characteristics Exhibited by Children Emotional handicaps; Mental
disabilities.
Tuition and Fees
Room and Board Long term: $250/diem.
Placements Primarily Funded By Medicaid.
Social and Rehabilitative Services
Therapeutic Approach The facility offers psychiatric treatment.
Therapeutic Services Offered Individual therapy; Group therapy;
Family therapy; Art therapy; Recreation activities.
Professionals on Staff Psychiatrists; Psychologists; Adjunctive therapists; Child care staff; Nurses; Art therapists.
Educational and Vocational Services
Type(s) of Educational Programs Offered On campus.
Profile of On Campus School Program Number of teachers 8; *Number of classrooms* 8.

RE-ED TREATMENT PROGRAM

1804 Bluegrass Ave, Louisville, KY 40214 (502) 368-2591 *Contact
Person(s):* JoAnn Tivnan, Denise Tischendorf
Setting and Background Information Re-Ed Treatment Program is a
residential state operated treatment facility. Children return home
or to foster care on weekends.
Referral Information Families, schools, private physicians, and
community agencies can make referrals by contacting the facility.
Admission criteria requires that the child be a resident of
Kentucky, be able to return home on weekends and holidays, and
have a complete physical exam.
Type of Facility
Funding Sources State.
Average Length of Stay 6-12 mos.
Types of Admissions Accepted Residential treatment; Wards of the
state.
Sources of Referral Local depts of education; Social service depts.
Client Profile
Age Range of Clients Served Residential program: 5-12.
Characteristics Exhibited by Children Emotional handicaps; Learning
disabilities.
Tuition and Fees
Room and Board Long term: $5.75/diem (sliding scale).
Placements Primarily Funded By State depts of mental health.
Social and Rehabilitative Services
Therapeutic Approach The treatment program is based on an educational and behavioral model which focuses on the child's interactions with significant others.
Therapeutic Services Offered Individual therapy; Group therapy;
Family therapy; Independent living skills program; Recreation
activities; Aftercare program with follow up.
Professionals on Staff Psychologists; Social workers; Adjunctive
therapists; Child care staff.

Educational and Vocational Services
Type(s) of Educational Programs Offered On campus.
Profile of On Campus School Program Number of teachers 4 and 4
aides; *Student to teacher ratio* 4:1; *Grades taught* K-8.

VERSAILLES

THE METHODIST HOME OF KENTUCKY, INC

PO Drawer B, Versailles, KY 40383 (606) 873-4481 *Contact
Person(s):* Dr Donald W Durham, Exec Dir
Setting and Background Information The facility was opened in 1871
as a home for widows and orphans by the Kentucky and
Louisville Conferences of the Methodist Church. There are three
facilities in the state. In Lexington, there is a group home in a
residential setting; in Owensboro, there are 2 buildings on 4 acres;
and there is a 251-acre campus in Versailles which has 7 cottages,
an administration building, a gym, a chapel, a school, a day care
center, a pre-school and a dining hall.
Referral Information Contact the facility for referral information.
Type of Facility
Funding Sources Private; State.
Average Length of Stay Short and long term.
Types of Admissions Accepted Residential treatment; Group home
placement; Wards of the state; Foster-care; Adoptions.
Sources of Referral Social service depts; Families.
Client Profile
Age Range of Clients Served Residential program: Birth-18.
Characteristics Exhibited by Children Emotional handicaps; Learning
disabilities; Hearing impairments/deafness; Vision impairments/
blindness; Speech/Language disorders; Neurological impairments;
Physical handicaps; Mental disabilities; Behavior disorders.
IQ Range of Clients 70+.
Tuition and Fees
Room and Board Short term: Sliding scale; Long term: Sliding scale.
Placements Primarily Funded By Private sources; Social service
depts; Private donations.
Social and Rehabilitative Services
Therapeutic Approach The therapeutic approaches used by the facility are behavior modification and milieu therapy.
Therapeutic Services Offered Individual therapy; Group therapy; Recreation activities.
Professionals on Staff Psychiatrists; Psychologists; Social workers;
Child care staff; Nurses.
Educational and Vocational Services
Type(s) of Educational Programs Offered On campus (ED/BD); Off
campus (Public school).
Profile of On Campus School Program Number of teachers 3; *Number of classrooms* 4; *Student to teacher ratio* 8:1; *Credentials of
teachers* State Certified; *Grades taught* Individualized.

LOUISIANA

GREENWOOD

JOY HOME FOR BOYS II

PO Box 550, Greenwood, LA 71033 (318) 938-5365 *Contact Person(s):* Rev Robert Scudder, Exec Dir

Setting and Background Information This facility was established in 1981 in response to a community need as manifested through a suicide hotline. It is located on 32 acres and has 3 dormitories, offices and dining facilities.

Referral Information For referral, contact the facility and forward pertinent reports, including a social summary.

Type of Facility

Funding Sources Private; State.

Average Length of Stay Long term.

Types of Admissions Accepted Residential treatment; Group home placement; Wards of the state.

Sources of Referral Social service depts.

Client Profile

Age Range of Clients Served Residential program: 6-21+.

Characteristics Exhibited by Children Emotional handicaps; Learning disabilities.

Tuition and Fees

Room and Board Long term: $49.11/diem.

Placements Primarily Funded By Social service depts.

Social and Rehabilitative Services

Therapeutic Services Offered Individual therapy; Group therapy; Family therapy; Independent living skills program.

Professionals on Staff Psychiatrists; Psychologists; Social workers; Child care staff.

Educational and Vocational Services

Type(s) of Educational Programs Offered Off campus (Public school).

HOUMA

MACDONELL UNITED METHODIST CHILDREN'S SERVICES, INC

1210 E Main St, Houma, LA 70363 (504) 868-8362 *Contact Person(s):* Michael Guidroz, Dir, Social Svcs

Setting and Background Information MacDonell United Methodist Children's Services is a private agency which operates a residential treatment facility and an emergency shelter care program. The campus is located on 17 acres of land in an older section of Houma.

Referral Information Anyone can make a referral by contacting the facility to arrange for a pre-placement interview and the forwarding of the necessary background information. Most referrals come from social service agencies. An intake committee will review the referral information and then make a placement decision.

Type of Facility

Funding Sources State.

Average Length of Stay 60-90 days (emergency shelter), 12-24 mos (residential treatment).

Types of Admissions Accepted Residential treatment; Wards of the state; Emergency shelter.

Sources of Referral State depts of mental health; Social service depts.

Client Profile

Age Range of Clients Served Residential program: 5-16.

Characteristics Exhibited by Children Emotional handicaps; Learning disabilities; Behavior disorders; Abused and neglected.

Tuition and Fees

Room and Board Long term: $65/diem.

Placements Primarily Funded By State depts of mental health.

Social and Rehabilitative Services

Therapeutic Approach The treatment program utilizes developmental task completion as its primary therapeutic model.

Therapeutic Services Offered Individual therapy; Group therapy; Family therapy; Independent living skills program; Recreation activities; Aftercare program with follow up.

Professionals on Staff Psychiatrists; Social workers; Child care staff; Nurses.

Educational and Vocational Services

Type(s) of Educational Programs Offered Off campus (Spec Ed; Regular public school).

LACOMBE

K-BAR-B YOUTH RANCH

PO Box 1517, Lacombe, LA 70445 (504) 523-5063 *Contact Person(s):* Herbert W Smith, Exec Dir

Setting and Background Information K-Bar-B Youth Ranch is a private, non-profit residential treatment facility. The ranch was established in 1971 on 75 acres of wooded land.

Referral Information Referrals can be made by anyone through the local Regional Review Committee and then to Herbert W Smith, Executive Director. The necessary background information on the child should be forwarded, including a social summary, psychiatric and psychological evaluation, multi-disciplanary team evaluation, individualized educational plan, medical records, current physical, social security number, school reports, Medicaid number, and birth certificate.

Type of Facility

Funding Sources Private.

Average Length of Stay 8 mos.

Types of Admissions Accepted Residential treatment.

Sources of Referral State depts of mental health.

Client Profile

Age Range of Clients Served Residential program: 8-18.

Characteristics Exhibited by Children Emotional handicaps; Learning disabilities; Speech/Language disorders; Mental disabilities; Behavior disorders.

IQ Range of Clients 70+.

Tuition and Fees

Tuition Provided by St Tammany Parish School System.

Placements Primarily Funded By State depts of mental health.

Social and Rehabilitative Services

Therapeutic Approach The philosophy of the treatment program is based on reality and cognitive therapy. A behavioral management program involving the use of a level system is used to encourage residents to meet behavioral and attitudinal expectations.

Therapeutic Services Offered Individual therapy; Group therapy; Family therapy; Adjunctive therapy; Independent living skills program; Recreation activities; Substance abuse treatment; Aftercare program with follow up.

Professionals on Staff Social workers; Child care staff.

K-BAR-B YOUTH RANCH *(continued)*

Educational and Vocational Services
Type(s) of Educational Programs Offered On campus; Off campus
(Public school; Vocational education); Summer campus.
Profile of On Campus School Program Number of teachers 4 and 4
aides; *Student to teacher ratio* 7:1; *Credentials of teachers* Certified Spec Ed; *Grades taught* Individualized; Special curriculum
electives offered.
Degrees Offered 12th grade diploma; GED.

LOGANSPORT

COOL SPRINGS OF LOGANSPORT
PO Box 610, Logansport, LA 71049 (318) 697-4365 *Contact
Person(s):* Joe Williams, Admin
Setting and Background Information The facility was privately
established in 1976. Located on 85 acres, there are offices, a
dorm and a school.
Referral Information Referrals are made through the Dept of
Corrections and are reviewed by an interdisciplinary team.
Type of Facility
Funding Sources State.
Average Length of Stay Long term.
Types of Admissions Accepted Residential treatment.
Sources of Referral Depts of correction.
Client Profile
Age Range of Clients Served Residential program: 12-18.
Characteristics Exhibited by Children Emotional handicaps; Learning
disabilities.
IQ Range of Clients 55+.
Tuition and Fees
Room and Board Long term: $56/diem.
Placements Primarily Funded By Depts of corrections.
Social and Rehabilitative Services
Therapeutic Approach The facility uses behavior modification.
Therapeutic Services Offered Individual therapy; Group therapy;
Family therapy; Independent living skills program; Recreation
activities.
Professionals on Staff Psychologists; Social workers; Child care staff.
Educational and Vocational Services
Type(s) of Educational Programs Offered On campus (Spec Ed).
Profile of On Campus School Program Number of teachers 3; *Number of classrooms* 3; *Student to teacher ratio* 9:1; *Credentials of
teachers* Certified Spec Ed; *Length of school day* 9-3; *Grades
taught* 1-12; Remedial courses offered (Every subject).
Degrees Offered 12th grade diploma.

MANDEVILLE

SOUTHEAST LOUISIANA HOSPITAL
PO Box 3850, Mandeville, LA 70448 (504) 626-8161 *Contact
Person(s):* Diana Marse, Social Service Adm Counselor
Setting and Background Information The facility was established in
1950 and is located 28 miles from New Orleans.
Referral Information Applicants are requested to forward psychiatric
reports, psychological reports, social history, immunization
records, birth certificate, and school reports. Psychiatric
recommendations are required.
Type of Facility
Funding Sources Private; State.
Average Length of Stay Long term.
Types of Admissions Accepted Residential treatment.
Sources of Referral State depts of mental health; Psychiatrists.
Client Profile
Age Range of Clients Served Residential program: 6-18.
Characteristics Exhibited by Children Emotional handicaps.
Tuition and Fees
Room and Board Long term: Sliding scale.
Placements Primarily Funded By State depts of mental health; Private sources.
Social and Rehabilitative Services
Therapeutic Approach Behavior modification is the basic therapeutic
approach used, in conjunction with milieu therapy and
psychotropic medications.

Therapeutic Services Offered Individual therapy; Group therapy;
Family therapy; Adjunctive therapy; Independent living skills
program; Recreation activities; Aftercare program with follow up;
Music therapy; Occupational therapy.
Professionals on Staff Psychiatrists; Psychologists; Social workers;
Adjunctive therapists; Child care staff; Nurses; Occupational
therapist, Music therapist.
Educational and Vocational Services
Type(s) of Educational Programs Offered On campus; Summer campus.
Profile of On Campus School Program Number of teachers 28;
Number of classrooms 24; *Student to teacher ratio* 7:1.
Degrees Offered 8th grade diploma; 12th grade diploma; GED.

MARRERO

HOPE HAVEN-MADONNA MANOR RESIDENTIAL TREATMENT CENTER
1101 Barataua Blvd, Marrero, LA 70072 (504) 347-5581 *Contact
Person(s):* Intake Worker
Setting and Background Information Hope Haven-Madonna Manor
is a private residential treatment facility for boys. Hope Haven
was established as an agricultural and vocational home for boys
by Msgr Peter Wynhoven. Madonna Manor was founded as an
orphanage in 1932. Catholic Charities of New Orleans combined
the 2 institutions in 1975 to establish a treatment center for
emotionally disturbed boys. The facility is located on 54 acres in
suburban New Orleans and consists of multi-bed, highly
structured dormitories and independent living cottages.
Referral Information Referrals are accepted from the Louisiana Dept
of Health and Human Resources—Office of Human
Development, through the Division of Evaluation Services or
Division of Youth Services, and through psychiatrists. Applicants
who are actively psychotic, severely mentally retarded, actively
addicted to drugs or alcohol, or cannot cooperate with the
program are not accepted.
Type of Facility
Funding Sources Private.
Average Length of Stay Long term.
Types of Admissions Accepted Residential treatment.
Sources of Referral State depts of mental health; Private sources;
Courts.
Client Profile
Age Range of Clients Served Residential program: 6-18.
Characteristics Exhibited by Children Emotional handicaps; Learning
disabilities; Mental disabilities.
Tuition and Fees
Placements Primarily Funded By State depts of mental health.
Social and Rehabilitative Services
Therapeutic Approach The treatment program utilizes individual and
group behavior modification programs to help residents modify
inappropriate behaviors and develop self-care and social skills.
Therapeutic Services Offered Individual therapy; Group therapy;
Family therapy; Independent living skills program; Recreation
activities; Aftercare program with follow up.
Professionals on Staff Psychiatrists; Psychologists; Social workers;
Child care staff; Nurses.
Educational and Vocational Services
Type(s) of Educational Programs Offered On campus (Spec Ed); Off
campus (Public school).
Profile of On Campus School Program Number of teachers 12;
Student to teacher ratio 5:1; Special curriculum electives offered;
Remedial courses offered (Reading, Math).

MERAUX

ST BERNARD GROUP HOMES
PO Box 1866, Meraux, LA 70075-1866 (504) 278-1511 *Contact
Person(s):* Paul F Bussell, Exec Dir
Setting and Background Information The facility was established in
1977 with LEAA grant monies and state funding. There are two
group homes—one is for boys and the other is for girls.
Referral Information Referrals are made by the local courts, mental
health clinics, the Dept of Health and Human Resources, and the
Dept of Corrections. A social history, a psychological evaluation,
a psychiatric evaluation, and educational records are required.

ST BERNARD GROUP HOMES (continued)

Type of Facility
Funding Sources State; Local government.
Average Length of Stay Long term.
Types of Admissions Accepted Group home placement; Wards of the state.
Sources of Referral Local depts of education; State depts of mental health; Depts of correction; Social service depts.
Client Profile
Age Range of Clients Served Residential program: 12-18.
Characteristics Exhibited by Children Emotional handicaps.
IQ Range of Clients 70+.
Tuition and Fees
Room and Board Long term: $75/diem.
Placements Primarily Funded By Depts of corrections; Social service depts.
Social and Rehabilitative Services
Therapeutic Services Offered Individual therapy; Group therapy; Family therapy; Independent living skills program; Aftercare program with follow up.
Professionals on Staff Psychiatrists; Psychologists; Social workers; Adjunctive therapists; Child care staff.
Educational and Vocational Services
Type(s) of Educational Programs Offered Off campus (Public school, Vocational school).
Degrees Offered Degrees conferred through public school.

METAIRIE

MAISON MARIE GROUP HOME
3020 Independence St, Metairie, LA 70006 (504) 888-9555 *Contact Person(s):* Gordon R Wadge, Prog Dir
Setting and Background Information The facility was established in 1973.
Referral Information Contact the facility for referral information.
Type of Facility
Funding Sources State.
Average Length of Stay Short and long term.
Types of Admissions Accepted Group home placement.
Sources of Referral State depts of mental health; Psychiatrists; Depts of correction; Social service depts.
Client Profile
Age Range of Clients Served Residential program: 15-18.
Characteristics Exhibited by Children Emotional handicaps; Learning disabilities.
Tuition and Fees
Placements Primarily Funded By Dept of Health and Human Resources.
Social and Rehabilitative Services
Therapeutic Services Offered Individual therapy; Group therapy; Family therapy; Independent living skills program.
Professionals on Staff Psychiatrists; Psychologists; Social workers; Child care staff; Nurses.
Educational and Vocational Services
Type(s) of Educational Programs Offered Off campus (Public; Private; Vocational).

NEW ORLEANS

BETHLEHEM CHILDREN'S CENTER
4430 Bundy Rd, New Orleans, LA 70127 (504) 241-1337 *Contact Person(s):* Marsha Whittenburg, Dir
Setting and Background Information Bethlehem Children's Center is a private residential treatment facility which was originally established as an orphanage in the late 1890s. It evolved into a residential facility in the 1960s. The residential programs are housed in 3 homes which are set in suburban communities.
Referral Information Referrals can be made by state agencies, private parties, and parents. Applicants will be requested to forward referral material, whereupon it will be reviewed by an Admission Committee. An interview with the child will be scheduled before a placement decision is made.
Type of Facility
Funding Sources Private.
Average Length of Stay Long term.
Types of Admissions Accepted Residential treatment; Group home placement.

Sources of Referral State depts of mental health.
Client Profile
Age Range of Clients Served Residential program: 5-17.
Characteristics Exhibited by Children Emotional handicaps; Learning disabilities; Speech/Language disorders.
Tuition and Fees
Placements Primarily Funded By State depts of mental health; Private sources.
Social and Rehabilitative Services
Therapeutic Approach The therapeutic approaches used include developmental therapy, reality therapy, and behavior modification.
Therapeutic Services Offered Individual therapy; Group therapy; Family therapy; Adjunctive therapy; Recreation activities.
Professionals on Staff Psychiatrists; Psychologists; Social workers; Adjunctive therapists; Child care staff; Nurses.
Educational and Vocational Services
Type(s) of Educational Programs Offered On campus; Off campus.
Profile of On Campus School Program Number of teachers 2; *Student to teacher ratio* 6:1; *Credentials of teachers* MA; *Grades taught* Individualized.

DE PAUL HOSPITAL
1040 Calhoun St, New Orleans, LA 70118 (504) 899-8282 *Contact Person(s):* Shirley B Lancaster, Admis
Setting and Background Information De Paul Hospital is a private psychiatric hospital. The facility was established in 1861 by the Daughters of Charity, but is presently owned by Hospital Corporation of America. The campus consists of 4 in-patient buildings on 12 acres of land.
Referral Information Referrals can be made by courts, clergy, agencies, civilian and military medical facilites, psychiatrists, psychologists, employees, and parents. All referrals are directed to the Admission Office.
Type of Facility
Funding Sources Private.
Average Length of Stay Long term.
Types of Admissions Accepted Day treatment; Residential treatment.
Sources of Referral Psychiatrists.
Client Profile
Age Range of Clients Served Day programs: 6-18; Residential program: 6-18.
Characteristics Exhibited by Children Emotional handicaps.
Tuition and Fees
Placements Primarily Funded By Insurance; Private sources; Medicare.
Social and Rehabilitative Services
Therapeutic Approach The basic therapeutic approach used at the hospital is psychoanalytic.
Therapeutic Services Offered Individual therapy; Group therapy; Family therapy; Adjunctive therapy; Independent living skills program; Recreation activities; Substance abuse treatment; Aftercare program with follow up.
Professionals on Staff Psychiatrists; Psychologists; Social workers; Adjunctive therapists; Child care staff; Nurses.
Educational and Vocational Services
Type(s) of Educational Programs Offered On campus.
Degrees Offered GED.

THE METHODIST HOME OF NEW ORLEANS
815 Washington Ave, New Orleans, LA 70130 (504) 895-7709 *Contact Person(s):* James C Akins, Dir of Child Care
Setting and Background Information The facility was originally established in 1886 as a home and hospital for unwed mothers.
Referral Information All referrals are made through the State of Louisiana.
Type of Facility
Funding Sources Private; State; Church.
Average Length of Stay Short and long term.
Types of Admissions Accepted Residential treatment; Wards of the state.
Sources of Referral Social service depts.
Client Profile
Age Range of Clients Served Residential program: Birth-15.
Characteristics Exhibited by Children Emotional handicaps; Learning disabilities; Hearing impairments/deafness; Speech/Language disorders; Mental disabilities; Abused and neglected.
IQ Range of Clients 29-160.

THE METHODIST HOME OF NEW ORLEANS
(continued)

Tuition and Fees
Room and Board Short term: $48/diem; Long term: $48/diem.
Placements Primarily Funded By Social service depts.
Social and Rehabilitative Services
Therapeutic Approach The facility offers a therapeutic milieu.
Therapeutic Services Offered Group therapy; Family therapy; Independent living skills program; Recreation activities; Music therapy.
Professionals on Staff Social workers; Adjunctive therapists; Child care staff; Music therapist.
Educational and Vocational Services
Type(s) of Educational Programs Offered On campus; Off campus (Public schools).
Profile of On Campus School Program Number of teachers 1; *Number of classrooms* 1; *Student to teacher ratio* 10:1; *Credentials of teachers* Certified; *Grades taught* 1-8.

NEW ORLEANS ADOLESCENT HOSPITAL
210 State St, New Orleans, LA 70118 (504) 897-3400 *Contact Person(s):* Catherine Kidd, Admis Coord
Setting and Background Information New Orleans Adolescent Hospital is a state funded psychiatric hospital which was founded in December 1981 by an act of the Louisiana State Legislature. The campus consists of a 5 story building, a school and administrative annex located on 17 acres in uptown New Orleans.
Referral Information Referrals can be made by private individuals, community mental health centers, courts and state agencies. The facility and the Review Committee have an agreement with the state Office of Mental Health and Substance Abuse for the admission of emergency cases.
Type of Facility
Funding Sources State.
Average Length of Stay 6 mos.
Types of Admissions Accepted Residential treatment.
Sources of Referral State depts of mental health; Psychiatrists; Social service depts; Courts.
Client Profile
Age Range of Clients Served Residential program: 3-17.
Characteristics Exhibited by Children Emotional handicaps; Learning disabilities.
Tuition and Fees
Room and Board Long term: $235/diem.
Placements Primarily Funded By State depts of mental health.
Social and Rehabilitative Services
Therapeutic Approach The basic therapeutic approach of the facility is psychodynamic.
Therapeutic Services Offered Individual therapy; Group therapy; Family therapy; Adjunctive therapy; Independent living skills program; Recreation activities; Substance abuse treatment; Aftercare program with follow up.
Professionals on Staff Psychiatrists; Psychologists; Social workers; Adjunctive therapists; Child care staff; Nurses.
Educational and Vocational Services
Type(s) of Educational Programs Offered On campus; Off campus (Public school).
Profile of On Campus School Program Number of teachers 9; *Student to teacher ratio* 8:1; *Grades taught* K-12; Special curriculum electives offered (Nursery school program); Remedial courses offered.
Degrees Offered 8th grade diploma; 12th grade diploma; GED.

PINEVILLE

CENTRAL LOUISIANA STATE HOSPITAL, ADOLESCENT SERVICE
PO Box 5031, Pineville, LA 71360 (318) 485-6524 *Contact Person(s):* John C Simoneaux PhD, Dir
Setting and Background Information This facility was established in 1968. The adolescent unit consists of 4 wards of the state hospital and a school.
Referral Information Once a referral call is received, a pre-admission interview is scheduled. This interview is a multi-disciplinary effort to determine eligibility and appropriateness for admission.

Type of Facility
Funding Sources State.
Average Length of Stay Short and long term.
Types of Admissions Accepted Residential treatment; Wards of the state.
Sources of Referral State depts of education; Local depts of education; State depts of mental health; Psychiatrists; Private sources; Depts of correction; Social service depts.
Client Profile
Age Range of Clients Served Residential program: 12-18.
Characteristics Exhibited by Children Emotional handicaps; Learning disabilities; Hearing impairments/deafness; Neurological impairments; Mental disabilities.
IQ Range of Clients 70-120+.
Tuition and Fees
Placements Primarily Funded By State depts of mental health; Insurance.
Social and Rehabilitative Services
Therapeutic Services Offered Individual therapy; Group therapy; Family therapy; Adjunctive therapy; Art therapy; Recreation activities.
Professionals on Staff Psychiatrists; Psychologists; Social workers; Adjunctive therapists; Nurses; Art therapists.
Educational and Vocational Services
Type(s) of Educational Programs Offered On campus (Special school district).
Profile of On Campus School Program Credentials of teachers MA+; *Grades taught* K-12.
Degrees Offered 12th grade diploma.

SLIDELL

TOWERING PINES CENTER
PO Box 925, Howze Beach Rd, Slidell, LA 70459 (504) 643-3665 or New Orleans (504) 524-1155 *Contact Person(s):* Soledad P Martinez, BCSW, Dir
Setting and Background Information Towering Pines Center is a private residential treatment facility for boys. The facility was previously known as Lee Hall and in 1976 came under new ownership to be renamed Towering Pines Center. Its campus is located 30 miles east of New Orleans on 5 acres of land. On-grounds facilities include 4 dormitories, administration building, school, kitchen/dining hall, and a service building containing a recreation room, nurse's station, group therapy room, and office space. There is also an on-grounds basketball court, and a large recreation field. The facility is licensed by the Dept of Health and Human Resources as a child care institution which can receive state funds in caring for the handicapped.
Referral Information Referrals can be made by state agencies, school districts, private agencies, and parents or guardians. To make a referral, contact the facility and forward the following information: psychiatric evaluation, psychological report, social history, medical records, school evaluations, birth certificate, and current photograph. The referral package will be reviewed by the Treatment Team, and if appropriate, a pre-placement interview will take place before an admission decision is made.
Type of Facility
Funding Sources Private.
Average Length of Stay Long term.
Types of Admissions Accepted Residential treatment.
Sources of Referral Local depts of education; State depts of mental health; Private sources; Social service depts.
Client Profile
Age Range of Clients Served Residential program: 7-17.
Characteristics Exhibited by Children Emotional handicaps; Learning disabilities; Mental disabilities.
IQ Range of Clients 40-139.
Tuition and Fees
Room and Board Long term: $2,000/mo.
Placements Primarily Funded By State depts of mental health; Private sources.
Social and Rehabilitative Services
Therapeutic Approach The treatment program utilizes an eclectic therapeutic approach which includes psychoanalysis, reality therapy, Gestalt therapy, behavior modification, and object relations theory.
Therapeutic Services Offered Individual therapy; Group therapy; Family therapy; Adjunctive therapy; Recreation activities.

TOWERING PINES CENTER *(continued)*

Professionals on Staff Psychiatrists; Psychologists; Social workers; Adjunctive therapists; Child care staff; Nurses; Recreational therapist.

Educational and Vocational Services

Type(s) of Educational Programs Offered On campus; Off campus (Public school); Summer campus.

Profile of On Campus School Program Number of teachers 3 and 3 aides; *Student to teacher ratio* 7:1; *Grades taught* Individualized; Remedial courses offered.

Vocational Education Programs/Degrees Offered Pre-vocational.

WEST MONROE

YOUTH HOUSE OF OUACHITA, INC

101 Ludwig Ave, West Monroe, LA 71291 (318) 323-6644 *Contact Person(s):* Bernardine S Fontana, Exec Dir

Setting and Background Information The facility was established in 1975 with funding from JJDP and LEAA. The 8-acre campus has 4 buildings.

Referral Information Referrals to facility are made by state agencies.

Type of Facility

Funding Sources Private; State; Federal.

Average Length of Stay Long term.

Types of Admissions Accepted Residential treatment; Group home placement; Wards of the state.

Sources of Referral State depts of mental health; Depts of correction; Social service depts.

Client Profile

Age Range of Clients Served Residential program: 6-18.

Characteristics Exhibited by Children Emotional handicaps; Neurological impairments; Mental disabilities; Maladaptive behavior.

Tuition and Fees

Placements Primarily Funded By State depts of mental health; Depts of corrections; Social service depts.

Social and Rehabilitative Services

Therapeutic Approach The facility uses reality therapy, including behavior modification.

Therapeutic Services Offered Individual therapy; Group therapy; Family therapy; Recreation activities; Substance abuse treatment.

Professionals on Staff Psychologists; Social workers; Child care staff; Nurses.

Educational and Vocational Services

Type(s) of Educational Programs Offered On campus; Off campus; Summer campus.

Profile of On Campus School Program Number of teachers 2; *Number of classrooms* 2; *Student to teacher ratio* 10:1; *Credentials of teachers* MS.

MAINE

AUGUSTA

AUGUSTA MENTAL HEALTH INSTITUTE

Box 724, Hospital St, Augusta, ME 04330 (207) 622-3751 *Contact Person(s):* Jim Burton, Unit Dir

Setting and Background Information The facility was established in 1978 with federal grant monies.

Referral Information All referrals to the facility are made through Community Mental Health Systems of Maine.

Type of Facility

Funding Sources State.

Average Length of Stay Short and long term.

Types of Admissions Accepted Residential treatment; Emergency shelter.

Sources of Referral State depts of mental health; Social service depts.

Client Profile

Age Range of Clients Served Residential program: 12-18.

Characteristics Exhibited by Children Emotional handicaps; Mental disabilities.

Tuition and Fees

Placements Primarily Funded By State depts of mental health.

Social and Rehabilitative Services

Therapeutic Approach The facility offers a therapeutic milieu.

Therapeutic Services Offered Individual therapy; Group therapy; Family therapy; Physical therapy; Recreation activities; Substance abuse treatment; Aftercare program with follow up.

Professionals on Staff Psychiatrists; Psychologists; Social workers; Child care staff; Nurses.

Educational and Vocational Services

Type(s) of Educational Programs Offered On campus; Off campus.

CARIBOU

DIOCESAN HUMAN RELATIONS SERVICE, CHRISTOPHER HOME OF AROOSTOOK

PO Box 748, Caribou, ME 04736 (207) 498-2575 *Contact Person(s):* Dianne Raymond, Dir of Svcs

Setting and Background Information This facility was established in 1979 by a local citizen's action group.

Referral Information For referral, contact the director of services. The screening process consists of a series of interviews.

Type of Facility

Funding Sources State.

Average Length of Stay Long term.

Types of Admissions Accepted Residential treatment.

Sources of Referral Private sources; Depts of correction; Social service depts; Low-income families.

Client Profile

Age Range of Clients Served Residential program: 12-18.

Characteristics Exhibited by Children Emotional handicaps; Behavior disorders.

Social and Rehabilitative Services

Therapeutic Approach The facility has an eclectic approach to therapy.

Therapeutic Services Offered Individual therapy; Group therapy; Family therapy; Recreation activities; Substance abuse treatment education.

Professionals on Staff Social workers; Child care staff.

ELLSWORTH

HOMESTEAD RESIDENTIAL CENTER

Box 663, Ellsworth, ME 04605 (207) 667-2021 *Contact Person(s):* Dr Douglas W Houck, Exec Dir

Setting and Background Information The center was established in 1977. The 155-acre campus has a lodge, a wilderness building, and classroom buildings. It is a residential treatment center for behaviorally handicapped adolescents.

Referral Information Forward a referral packet to the administrative assistant.

Type of Facility

Funding Sources State.

Average Length of Stay Long term.

Types of Admissions Accepted Residential treatment.

Sources of Referral State depts of education; Local depts of education; State depts of mental health; Psychiatrists; Social service depts.

Client Profile

Age Range of Clients Served Residential program: 12-18.

Characteristics Exhibited by Children Emotional handicaps.

IQ Range of Clients 85-130.

Tuition and Fees

Room and Board Long term: $28/diem.

Tuition $50.69/diem.

Placements Primarily Funded By State depts of education; Local depts of education; State depts of mental health; Social service depts.

Social and Rehabilitative Services

Therapeutic Approach The facility offers individual and group therapy.

Therapeutic Services Offered Individual therapy; Group therapy; Family therapy; Recreation activities; Substance abuse treatment; Aftercare program with follow up.

Professionals on Staff Psychiatrists; Psychologists; Social workers; Adjunctive therapists; Child care staff; Nurses; Art therapists.

Educational and Vocational Services

Type(s) of Educational Programs Offered On campus.

Profile of On Campus School Program Number of teachers 7; Number of classrooms 6; Student to teacher ratio 8:1; Credentials of teachers Certified Spec Ed; Grades taught 7-12; Special curriculum electives offered; Remedial courses offered.

LEWISTON

ST ANDRE GROUP HOME

188 Sabattus St, Lewiston, ME 04240 (207) 783-8003 *Contact Person(s):* Intake Worker

Setting and Background Information This group home for girls was established in 1974.

Referral Information For referral to the facility, contact the social worker. A pre-placement visit with the girl and her parents (or with her social worker) will be scheduled.

Type of Facility

Funding Sources Private; State; Federal.

Average Length of Stay Long term.

Types of Admissions Accepted Group home placement; Wards of the state.

ST ANDRE GROUP HOME (continued)

Sources of Referral State depts of education; Local depts of education; State depts of mental health; Psychiatrists; Private sources; Depts of correction; Social service depts.

Client Profile

Age Range of Clients Served Residential program: 15-18.

Characteristics Exhibited by Children Emotional handicaps.

IQ Range of Clients 75+.

Tuition and Fees

Room and Board Long term: $59.85/diem.

Placements Primarily Funded By Social service depts.

Social and Rehabilitative Services

Therapeutic Approach The facility uses a form of reality therapy in combination with other eclectic approaches.

Therapeutic Services Offered Individual therapy; Group therapy; Family therapy; Independent living skills program; Aftercare program with follow up.

Professionals on Staff Social workers; Child care staff.

Educational and Vocational Services

Type(s) of Educational Programs Offered Off campus (Public school).

POLAND SPRING

ELAN SCHOOL

RR1 Box 370, Poland Spring, ME 04274-9711 (207) 998-4666

Contact Person(s): Dir of Admis

Setting and Background Information The facility was privately established in 1971. It is a 170-bed co-educational residential school for adolescents. It has four self-contained units and is located on 70 acres.

Referral Information For referral, contact the director of admissions and request an admissions package.

Type of Facility

Funding Sources Private.

Average Length of Stay 18-22 mos.

Types of Admissions Accepted Residential treatment; Wards of the state.

Sources of Referral State depts of education; Local depts of education; State depts of mental health; Psychiatrists; Private sources; Depts of correction; Social service depts.

Client Profile

Age Range of Clients Served Residential program: 12-21+.

Characteristics Exhibited by Children Emotional handicaps; Conduct disorder.

Tuition and Fees

Placements Primarily Funded By State depts of education; Local depts of education; State depts of mental health; Insurance; Private sources; Depts of corrections; Social service depts.

Social and Rehabilitative Services

Therapeutic Services Offered Individual therapy; Group therapy; Independent living skills program; Aftercare program with follow up.

Professionals on Staff Psychiatrists; Psychologists; Social workers; Adjunctive therapists; Child care staff; Nurses; Speech pathologist.

Educational and Vocational Services

Type(s) of Educational Programs Offered On campus; Summer campus.

Profile of On Campus School Program Number of teachers 24; *Student to teacher ratio* 8:1; *Credentials of teachers* MA, Certified; *Grades taught* 7-12; Special curriculum electives offered (Computer, Spec Ed, Gym, Language); Remedial courses offered (Special tutorial programs).

Degrees Offered 12th grade diploma; GED.

PORTLAND

THE SPURWINK SCHOOL

899 Riverside St, Portland, ME 04103 (207) 871-1200 *Contact Person(s):* John Rosser

Setting and Background Information The facility was established as a treatment center for boys in 1960. It is licensed as a child caring agency by the Maine Dept of Human Services, and as a mental health facility by the Maine Dept of Mental Health and Corrections. There are 3 residential programs offered as follows: Riverside serves 16 boys between the ages of 5 and 13; Edgefield, located in Casco, Maine, has 9 boys aged 13 to 18 years of age; and 10 therapeutic foster homes for boys from 5 to 18 years.

These residences consist of self-sufficient homes having their own kitchen, living room, and bedrooms. Spurwink also operates the Cumberland County Day Treatment Program.

Referral Information Referrals can be made by mental health professionals and school districts. All referrals are directed to John Rosser to assess the child's problems and determine the appropriate program.

Type of Facility

Funding Sources Private.

Average Length of Stay Long term.

Types of Admissions Accepted Day treatment; Residential treatment; Group home placement.

Client Profile

Age Range of Clients Served Day programs: 5-18; Residential program: 5-18.

Characteristics Exhibited by Children Emotional handicaps; Learning disabilities; Neurological impairments; Mental disabilities.

Tuition and Fees

Placements Primarily Funded By Local depts of education; State depts of mental health; Social service depts.

Social and Rehabilitative Services

Therapeutic Approach The programs use an eclectic treatment approach involving psychoanalytic, psychodynamic, developmental, and conceptual theory.

Therapeutic Services Offered Individual therapy; Group therapy; Family therapy; Adjunctive therapy; Independent living skills program; Recreation activities; Play therapy.

Professionals on Staff Psychiatrists; Psychologists; Social workers; Adjunctive therapists; Child care staff.

Educational and Vocational Services

Type(s) of Educational Programs Offered On campus.

RUMFORD

RUMFORD GROUP HOME, INC

346 Pine St, Rumford, ME 04276 (207) 364-3551 *Contact Person(s):* Kevin LaBree, Dir

Setting and Background Information The facility was established in 1975 with a LEAA grant.

Referral Information Contact the facility for referral information.

Type of Facility

Funding Sources Private; State; Federal.

Average Length of Stay Long term.

Types of Admissions Accepted Group home placement; Wards of the state.

Sources of Referral Social service depts.

Client Profile

Age Range of Clients Served Residential program: 12-18.

Characteristics Exhibited by Children Emotional handicaps; Learning disabilities.

IQ Range of Clients 88-110.

Tuition and Fees

Room and Board Long term: $1,475/mo.

Placements Primarily Funded By Social service depts.

Social and Rehabilitative Services

Therapeutic Approach The basic approach of the facility is reality therapy.

Therapeutic Services Offered Individual therapy; Group therapy; Art therapy; Independent living skills program; Recreation activities; Substance abuse treatment.

Professionals on Staff Psychiatrists; Psychologists; Social workers; Child care staff; Art therapists.

Educational and Vocational Services

Type(s) of Educational Programs Offered Off campus (Public schools; Outward bound); Summer campus (Agassiz Village).

SACO

SWEETSER CHILDRENS HOME

50 Moody St, Saco, ME 04072 (207) 284-5981 *Contact Person(s):* Barbara Fowler

Setting and Background Information The facility is a result of combining 4 Maine orphanages in 1949; Children's Home of Portland, Maine Home for Boys, Children's Aid Society, and the Sweetser Home for Boys. The purpose of this amalgamation was to provide services to children exhibiting emotional disturbances and learning disabilities. The main campus is located in southern Maine on a 400-acre farm and consists of 4 co-educational

SWEETSER CHILDRENS HOME *(continued)*

cottages (13-14 residents each), farm buildings, recreational building, administration building, residential school, and day school. There are also 2 group homes, one in Sanford and another in Lewiston. Both are co-educational and can house up to 6 residents. Sweetser also serves New Hampshire residents.

Referral Information Contact the facility for referral information. An on-campus intake evaluation will be conducted by staff before a final placement decision is made.

Type of Facility

Funding Sources State; Local school districts.

Average Length of Stay 18 mos.

Types of Admissions Accepted Day treatment; Residential treatment; Group home placement; Wards of the state.

Sources of Referral State depts of education; Local depts of education.

Client Profile

Age Range of Clients Served Day programs: 6-18; Residential program: 6-18.

Characteristics Exhibited by Children Emotional handicaps; Learning disabilities; Speech/Language disorders; Neurological impairments; Physical handicaps; Mental disabilities.

Tuition and Fees

Placements Primarily Funded By Local depts of education; Dept of Human Services.

Social and Rehabilitative Services

Therapeutic Approach The treatment program uses a multi-model approach in conjunction with eclectic services.

Therapeutic Services Offered Individual therapy; Group therapy; Family therapy; Adjunctive therapy; Art therapy; Independent living skills program; Recreation activities; Substance abuse treatment; Aftercare program with follow up.

Professionals on Staff Psychiatrists; Psychologists; Social workers; Child care staff; Nurses; Art therapists; Speech and language therapists.

Educational and Vocational Services

Type(s) of Educational Programs Offered On campus; Off campus; Summer campus.

Profile of On Campus School Program Number of teachers 15; *Student to teacher ratio* 6:1; *Grades taught* K-12; Special curriculum electives offered; Remedial courses offered.

MARYLAND

BALTIMORE

WALTER P CARTER COMMUNITY MENTAL HEALTH CENTER

630 W Fayette St, Baltimore, MD 21201 (301) 328-2139 *Contact Person(s):* P Flowers Whitmore PhD, Supt
Setting and Background Information The facility was established in 1976 as part of the Dept of Mental Health and Hygiene. The campus has an in-patient unit and an administration building. There are four out-patient clinics in the community.
Referral Information Contact the facility for referral information.
Type of Facility
Funding Sources State.
Average Length of Stay Short and long term.
Types of Admissions Accepted Day treatment; Residential treatment.
Sources of Referral Psychiatrists; Court ordered.
Client Profile
Age Range of Clients Served Day programs: 12-55+; Residential program: 12-55+.
Characteristics Exhibited by Children Emotional handicaps; Mental disabilities.
Tuition and Fees
Placements Primarily Funded By State depts of mental health.
Social and Rehabilitative Services
Therapeutic Services Offered Individual therapy; Group therapy; Family therapy.
Professionals on Staff Psychiatrists; Psychologists; Social workers; Occupational therapist.
Educational and Vocational Services
Type(s) of Educational Programs Offered On campus (Level V school).
Profile of On Campus School Program Number of teachers 5; *Number of classrooms* 8; *Student to teacher ratio* 6:1; *Credentials of teachers* Certified; *Length of school day* 8-2:30.

GUNDRY HOSPITAL

2 N Wickham Rd, Baltimore, MD 21229 (311) 644-9917 *Contact Person(s):* Nathan Muler, Admin
Setting and Background Information The facility was established in 1900 as a private psychiatric hospital. Located on 21 acres, there are 5 buildings.
Referral Information Contact the admissions office to make a referral.
Type of Facility
Funding Sources Private.
Average Length of Stay Long term.
Types of Admissions Accepted Residential treatment.
Sources of Referral State depts of education; Local depts of education; State depts of mental health; Psychiatrists; Private sources; Social service depts.
Client Profile
Age Range of Clients Served Residential program: 12-18.
Characteristics Exhibited by Children Emotional handicaps.
Tuition and Fees
Room and Board Short term: $250/diem (includes school tuition); Long term: $250/diem (includes school tuition).
Placements Primarily Funded By Private sources; Depts of corrections; Social service depts.

Social and Rehabilitative Services
Therapeutic Services Offered Individual therapy; Group therapy; Family therapy; Adjunctive therapy; Art therapy; Independent living skills program; Recreation activities.
Professionals on Staff Psychiatrists; Psychologists; Social workers; Adjunctive therapists; Nurses; Art therapists.
Educational and Vocational Services
Type(s) of Educational Programs Offered On campus.

BETHESDA

BAPTIST HOME FOR CHILDREN

6301 Greentree Rd, Bethesda, MD 20817 (301) 365-4480 *Contact Person(s):* Delores D'Elia
Setting and Background Information Baptist Home for Children is a private residential treatment facility which was established by the Washington, DC Baptist Convention of Churches in 1914. Its campus is located in a suburban setting on 16 acres of land outside of Washington, DC.
Referral Information Referrals can be made by parents, guardians, or custodians of the child.
Type of Facility
Funding Sources State.
Average Length of Stay Long term.
Types of Admissions Accepted Residential treatment.
Sources of Referral Social service depts.
Client Profile
Age Range of Clients Served Residential program: 13-19.
Characteristics Exhibited by Children Emotional handicaps; Learning disabilities; Speech/Language disorders; Neurological impairments; Mental disabilities.
Tuition and Fees
Placements Primarily Funded By Social service depts.
Social and Rehabilitative Services
Therapeutic Approach The program uses a reality oriented therapeutic approach.
Therapeutic Services Offered Individual therapy; Group therapy; Family therapy; Adjunctive therapy; Independent living skills program; Recreation activities; Aftercare program with follow up.
Professionals on Staff Psychiatrists; Social workers; Adjunctive therapists; Child care staff; Nurses.
Educational and Vocational Services
Type(s) of Educational Programs Offered Off campus.

CHELTENHAM

REGIONAL INSTITUTE FOR CHILDREN AND ADOLESCENTS—CHELTENHAM

PO Box 100, Cheltenham, MD 20623 (301) 372-6121 *Contact Person(s):* Deborah Hoppe, Acting Admin
Setting and Background Information The facility was established in 1976 with a state grant through the local health dept. Located on the campus of another state facility, there are 2 residential buildings, a school and an administration building.
Referral Information Referrals are made through local county boards of education and the courts.
Type of Facility
Funding Sources State.
Average Length of Stay Short and long term.
Types of Admissions Accepted Day treatment; Residential treatment.

REGIONAL INSTITUTE FOR CHILDREN AND ADOLESCENTS—CHELTENHAM *(continued)*

Sources of Referral Local depts of education; State depts of mental health; Psychiatrists; Social service depts; Court ordered.
Client Profile
Age Range of Clients Served Day programs: 12-18; Residential program: 12-18.
Characteristics Exhibited by Children Emotional handicaps; Learning disabilities; Neurological impairments; Mental disabilities.
IQ Range of Clients 75-135.
Tuition and Fees
Placements Primarily Funded By State depts of mental health.
Social and Rehabilitative Services
Therapeutic Approach The facility offers milieu therapy.
Therapeutic Services Offered Individual therapy; Group therapy; Family therapy.
Professionals on Staff Psychiatrists; Psychologists; Social workers; Child care staff; Nurses; Occupational therapist.
Educational and Vocational Services
Type(s) of Educational Programs Offered On campus (Academic/vocational); Off campus (Academic/vocational); Summer campus (Vocational).
Profile of On Campus School Program Number of teachers 15; *Number of classrooms* 16; *Student to teacher ratio* 9:1; *Credentials of teachers* BA; *Grades taught* 7-12; Special curriculum electives offered (Art, Music, PE, Business); Remedial courses offered (Reading, Math).
Vocational Education Programs/Degrees Offered Automotive.
Degrees Offered 12th grade diploma.

OLDTOWN

NEW DOMINION, INC

PO Box 8, Oldtown, MD 21555 (301) 395-5252 *Contact Person(s):* Tim Snyder
Setting and Background Information New Dominion is a private year round residential camping program for boys. The program was started in 1980 by staff from the original school located in Dellwyn, Virginia. The camp is located on 150 acres and consists of 5 campsites (10 boys each), main dining area, administration buildings, and a school.
Referral Information Referrals can be made by school districts, mental health clinics, Dept of Juvenile Services, Dept of Social Services, and parents or guardians. To make a referral forward the necessary background information including academic, social, and professional records. If the placement seems appropriate, a pre-placement interview will take place before a final decision is made.
Type of Facility
Funding Sources Private.
Average Length of Stay Long term.
Types of Admissions Accepted Residential treatment.
Sources of Referral State depts of mental health; Psychiatrists; Private sources; Social service depts.
Client Profile
Age Range of Clients Served Residential program: 13-18.
Characteristics Exhibited by Children Emotional handicaps.
IQ Range of Clients 80+.
Tuition and Fees
Room and Board Long term: $1,620.75/mo.
Placements Primarily Funded By Private sources; Social service depts.
Social and Rehabilitative Services
Therapeutic Approach The program is based on a group process problem solving model.
Therapeutic Services Offered Individual therapy; Group therapy; Family therapy; Recreation activities; Substance abuse treatment; Aftercare program with follow up.
Professionals on Staff Psychologists; Social workers; Child care staff; Nurses.
Educational and Vocational Services
Type(s) of Educational Programs Offered On campus; Summer campus.
Profile of On Campus School Program Number of teachers 3; *Number of classrooms* 5.

ROCKVILLE

CHESTNUT LODGE HOSPITAL

Adolescent and Child Division, 500 W Montgomery Ave, Rockville, MD 20850 (301) 424-8300 *Contact Person(s):* Patricia Holland, Admis Coord
Setting and Background Information Chestnut Lodge is a private residential facility. The Adolescent and Child Division was established in 1974. The facility is located one-half hour from Washington, DC, on 80 acres of land. The campus consists of 4 small residential units organized around a family model with 7 residents in each, a school, gymnasium, pool, clinical center, and recreational facilities.
Referral Information Referrals can be made by parents, schools, physicians, social workers, and mental health agencies. The pre-admission procedure requires the forwarding of psychiatric evaluations, educational reports, and medical reports. A pre-placement visit and interviews with the child and family will then be arranged before a placement decision is made.
Type of Facility
Funding Sources Private; State.
Average Length of Stay Long term.
Types of Admissions Accepted Residential treatment.
Sources of Referral State depts of education; Local depts of education; State depts of mental health; Psychiatrists; Private sources; Social service depts.
Client Profile
Age Range of Clients Served Residential program: 12-18.
Characteristics Exhibited by Children Emotional handicaps; Learning disabilities.
IQ Range of Clients 90+.
Tuition and Fees
Room and Board Long term: $300/diem plus physicians fees.
Tuition $15,000/yr.
Placements Primarily Funded By Insurance; Private sources.
Social and Rehabilitative Services
Therapeutic Approach The facility uses psychotherapy and milieu therapy.
Therapeutic Services Offered Individual therapy; Group therapy; Family therapy; Adjunctive therapy; Art therapy; Independent living skills program; Recreation activities; Substance abuse treatment; Aftercare program with follow up; Dance therapy; Music therapy; Occupational therapy.
Professionals on Staff Psychiatrists; Psychologists; Social workers; Adjunctive therapists; Child care staff; Nurses; Art therapists.
Educational and Vocational Services
Type(s) of Educational Programs Offered On campus.
Profile of On Campus School Program Number of teachers 8; *Number of classrooms* 9; *Student to teacher ratio* 6:1.
Degrees Offered 8th grade diploma; 12th grade diploma.

REGIONAL INSTITUTE FOR CHILDREN & ADOLESCENTS—ROCKVILLE

15000 Broschart Rd, Rockville, MD 20850 (301) 251-6844 *Contact Person(s):* Julie McLeod, Coord of Public Relations & Vol Srvcs
Setting and Background Information This facility was established jointly in 1980 by the state Dept of Mental Health and Mental Hygiene and the Montgomery County Public Schools. The 14.7-acre campus has an administration building, three residential buildings, a school, and an activities building.
Referral Information The majority of students are referred by the school system or the court system. Contact the facility for referral procedures.
Type of Facility
Funding Sources State; County school.
Average Length of Stay Long term.
Types of Admissions Accepted Day treatment; Residential treatment.
Sources of Referral State depts of education; Local depts of education; State depts of mental health; Psychiatrists; Private sources; Depts of correction; Social service depts.
Client Profile
Age Range of Clients Served Day programs: 6-18; Residential program: 12-18.
Characteristics Exhibited by Children Emotional handicaps; Learning disabilities.
IQ Range of Clients 80-145.

REGIONAL INSTITUTE FOR CHILDREN & ADO-LESCENTS—ROCKVILLE *(continued)*

Tuition and Fees
Room and Board Long term: $46,000/yr (includes school tuition).
Placements Primarily Funded By State depts of mental health.
Social and Rehabilitative Services
Therapeutic Approach The facility has an interdisciplinary approach to therapy.
Therapeutic Services Offered Individual therapy; Group therapy; Family therapy; Art therapy; Independent living skills program; Recreation activities; Aftercare program with follow up; Music therapy; Dance therapy.
Professionals on Staff Psychiatrists; Psychologists; Social workers; Child care staff; Nurses; Art therapists; Dance therapist; Music therapist; Occupational therapist.
Educational and Vocational Services
Type(s) of Educational Programs Offered On campus; Off campus; Summer campus.
Profile of On Campus School Program Number of teachers 70; *Number of classrooms* 25; *Student to teacher ratio* 12:1; *Credentials of teachers* Certified; *Length of school day* 9:30-3:30; *Grades taught* 1-12; Special curriculum electives offered (Print shop, Cooking, Woodwork).

TIMONIUM

ST VINCENT'S CENTER—CHILD AND FAMILY CARE
2600 Pot Spring Rd, Timonium, MD 21093 (301) 252-4000 *Contact Person(s):* Mary Giovanni, Supv
Setting and Background Information St Vincent's Center is a private residential treatment facility. The facility was initially established as a home for orphans and single mothers by the Daughters of Charity of St Vincent de Paul in 1856. In 1949, it was consolidated with the Associate Catholic Charities, Inc of Baltimore, Maryland. By 1974, St Vincent's Center had expanded its program to become a treatment center for youth with emotional and/or physical problems. Its campus is located 25 miles from Baltimore and consists of 6 cottages; 2 for multiply handicapped and 4 for abuse, neglect, and behavior problem cases.
Referral Information Referrals can be made by the Dept of Social Services. To make a referral, contact the facility, forward the necessary background information, and arrange for a pre-placement visit.
Type of Facility
Funding Sources State.
Average Length of Stay Long term.
Types of Admissions Accepted Residential treatment.
Sources of Referral Social service depts.
Client Profile
Age Range of Clients Served Residential program: 3-10.
Characteristics Exhibited by Children Emotional handicaps; Learning disabilities; Speech/Language disorders; Neurological impairments; Mental disabilities.
IQ Range of Clients 70+.
Tuition and Fees
Room and Board Long term: $30,000/yr.
Placements Primarily Funded By Social service depts.
Social and Rehabilitative Services
Therapeutic Services Offered Individual therapy; Group therapy; Family therapy; Art therapy; Aftercare program with follow up.
Professionals on Staff Social workers.
Educational and Vocational Services
Type(s) of Educational Programs Offered On campus; Off campus.
Profile of On Campus School Program Number of teachers 2; *Number of classrooms* 2; *Student to teacher ratio* 10:1.

WILLIAMSPORT

CEDAR RIDGE CHILDREN'S HOME AND SCHOOL
Rte 2, Box 325, Williamsport, MD 21795 (301) 582-0282 *Contact Person(s):* Stephen T Griffith, Res Clinical Dir
Setting and Background Information Cedar Ridge is a private residential treatment facility which was established in response to a request by Maryland judges and the Dept of Social Services. Its campus is located on 158 acres, 6 miles west of Hagerstown, in western Maryland. On-ground facilities include an administration building, 3 residential cottages, group home, school, gymnasium, playground, basketball and softball area, tennis court, and a swimming pool.
Referral Information Referrals can be made by the Dept of Social Services, Dept of Juvenile Services, professionals, and families. To make a referral, contact the facility and forward the following background information to the Clinical Director: school records, hospital reports, psychological evaluations, psychiatric reports, and social history. An intake interview and a 4 to 5 day pre-placement visit will take place before an admission decision is made.
Type of Facility
Funding Sources Private; State.
Average Length of Stay Long term.
Types of Admissions Accepted Residential treatment.
Sources of Referral Private sources; Social service depts.
Client Profile
Age Range of Clients Served Residential program: 6-18.
Characteristics Exhibited by Children Emotional handicaps; Learning disabilities.
Tuition and Fees
Placements Primarily Funded By Private sources; Social service depts.
Social and Rehabilitative Services
Therapeutic Approach The basic therapeutic approach used at the facility is behavior modification.
Therapeutic Services Offered Individual therapy; Group therapy; Family therapy; Art therapy; Independent living skills program; Recreation activities.
Professionals on Staff Psychiatrists; Psychologists; Social workers; Child care staff; Nurses.
Educational and Vocational Services
Type(s) of Educational Programs Offered On campus.
Profile of On Campus School Program Number of teachers 4; *Number of classrooms* 5.

MASSACHUSETTS

ARLINGTON

THE GERMAINE LAWRENCE SCHOOL

18 Clarement Ave, Arlington, MA 02174 (617) 648-6200 *Contact Person(s):* Deirdre Maltais, Adm Asst

Setting and Background Information The Germaine Lawrence School is a private facility, which was initially established in 1928 as St Anne's School. It was later developed into a residential facility in 1980. The campus is located on 10 acres of land in Arlington, a suburb of Boston.

Referral Information Referrals can be made by social service depts, school districts, psychiatric hospitals, and mental health clinics. Applicants will be screened and a pre-placement interview scheduled. If the facility's staff feel the placement may be appropriate, then diagnostic visits of either 1, 2 or 30 days will be arranged. The facility accepts girls only.

Type of Facility
Funding Sources State.
Average Length of Stay Long term.
Types of Admissions Accepted Residential treatment.
Sources of Referral State depts of education; Local depts of education; State depts of mental health; Social service depts; Dept of Youth Svcs.

Client Profile
Age Range of Clients Served Residential program: 12-19.
Characteristics Exhibited by Children Emotional handicaps; Learning disabilities.
IQ Range of Clients 80+.

Tuition and Fees
Room and Board Long term: $118.18/diem.
Placements Primarily Funded By State depts of education; Local depts of education.

Social and Rehabilitative Services
Therapeutic Approach The core of the treatment program is based on a point and level system in a highly structured milieu setting.
Therapeutic Services Offered Individual therapy; Group therapy; Family therapy; Independent living skills program; Recreation activities; Substance abuse treatment.
Professionals on Staff Social workers; Child care staff; Nurses.

Educational and Vocational Services
Type(s) of Educational Programs Offered On campus.
Profile of On Campus School Program Number of teachers 9; *Number of classrooms* 8; *Student to teacher ratio* 6:1; *Remedial courses offered.*
Degrees Offered 12th grade diploma.

ATTLEBORO

ATTLEBORO YOUTH SHELTER

11 Peck St, Attleboro, MA 02703 (617) 226-6031 *Contact Person(s):* Ernest Campagnone, Prog Dir

Setting and Background Information The facility was established in 1982 with a contract from the Massachusetts Dept of Mental Health. The facility consists of a large 3-story building, self-contained, for 12 clients.

Referral Information The facility has a 24-hour, 7-day a week admission schedule. Contact the intake worker of the facility for referral information.

Type of Facility
Funding Sources Private; State.
Average Length of Stay Short and long term.
Types of Admissions Accepted Wards of the state; Emergency shelter.
Sources of Referral State depts of education; Local depts of education; State depts of mental health; Psychiatrists; Private sources; Social service depts.

Client Profile
Age Range of Clients Served Emergency placements: 12-18.
Characteristics Exhibited by Children Emotional handicaps; Learning disabilities.

Tuition and Fees
Room and Board Short term: $118/diem (includes tuition).
Placements Primarily Funded By Social service depts.

Social and Rehabilitative Services
Therapeutic Approach The facility uses structured reality therapy.
Therapeutic Services Offered Individual therapy; Group therapy; Recreation activities.
Professionals on Staff Psychiatrists; Psychologists; Social workers; Child care staff.

Educational and Vocational Services
Type(s) of Educational Programs Offered On campus.
Profile of On Campus School Program Number of teachers 1; *Number of classrooms* 1; *Student to teacher ratio* 4:1; *Credentials of teachers* MA; Remedial courses offered.

BEDFORD

NORTHEASTERN FAMILY INSTITUTE—NORTH CROSSING ADOLESCENT AND FAMILY TREATMENT PROGRAM

460 North Rd, Bedford, MA 01730 (617) 275-9494 *Contact Person(s):* Paul L Dann, Prog Dir

Setting and Background Information This residential treatment center was established in 1984.

Referral Information Referrals are made through the Dept of Mental Health. A pre-placement visit will be scheduled.

Type of Facility
Funding Sources State; Local school systems.
Average Length of Stay Long term.
Types of Admissions Accepted Residential treatment.
Sources of Referral State depts of mental health.

Client Profile
Age Range of Clients Served Residential program: 12-21.
Characteristics Exhibited by Children Emotional handicaps; Learning disabilities; Mental disabilities.
IQ Range of Clients 70-135.

Tuition and Fees
Room and Board Long term: $38,500/yr.
Tuition $12,500/yr.
Placements Primarily Funded By State depts of mental health.

Social and Rehabilitative Services
Therapeutic Approach The facility uses a systems approach, and includes cognitive and behavioral therapies.
Therapeutic Services Offered Individual therapy; Group therapy; Family therapy; Independent living skills program; Recreation activities.
Professionals on Staff Psychiatrists; Psychologists; Social workers; Child care staff.

NORTHEASTERN FAMILY INSTITUTE—NORTH CROSSING ADOLESCENT AND FAMILY TREATMENT PROGRAM *(continued)*

Educational and Vocational Services
Type(s) of Educational Programs Offered On campus; Summer campus.
Profile of On Campus School Program Number of teachers 2; *Number of classrooms* 2; *Student to teacher ratio* 4:1; *Credentials of teachers* MA; *Grades taught* 7-12; Special curriculum electives offered; Remedial courses offered.
Vocational Education Programs/Degrees Offered Pre-voc program.
Degrees Offered 12th grade diploma.

BELMONT

MCLEAN HOSPITAL—COMMUNITY RESIDENTIAL AND TREATMENT SERVICES
115 Mill St, Belmont, MA 02178 (617) 855-3100 *Contact Person(s):* Jody Dzuris Daniels, Admin; Richard D Budson, MD
Setting and Background Information The hospital is a 328-bed private non-profit psychiatric hospital affiliated with the Massachusetts General Hospital and the Harvard Medical School. There are five residential buildings on the grounds of the hospital and three residential programs off grounds in Belmont and Boston.
Referral Information Referrals are usually made by mental health professionals or family members. Contact the facility for further information.
Type of Facility
Funding Sources Private; State; Federal.
Average Length of Stay Long term.
Types of Admissions Accepted Day treatment; Residential treatment.
Sources of Referral State depts of education; Local depts of education; State depts of mental health; Psychiatrists; Private sources; Social service depts.
Client Profile
Age Range of Clients Served Day programs: 18-21+; Residential program: 12-55+.
Characteristics Exhibited by Children Emotional handicaps; Neurological impairments; Mental disabilities.
IQ Range of Clients 70+.
Tuition and Fees
Placements Primarily Funded By Private sources; Social service depts.
Social and Rehabilitative Services
Therapeutic Approach The approach of the facility is to foster and develop the highest adaptive capability of the residents by using a variety of therapeutic interventions.
Therapeutic Services Offered Individual therapy; Group therapy; Family therapy; Adjunctive therapy; Independent living skills program; Recreation activities; Substance abuse treatment; Aftercare program with follow up.
Professionals on Staff Psychiatrists; Psychologists; Social workers; Adjunctive therapists; Child care staff; Nurses.
Educational and Vocational Services
Type(s) of Educational Programs Offered On campus; Off campus.

BRAINTREE

YOUTH RESOURCES, INC—PILGRIM CENTER
140 Adams St, Braintree, MA 02184 (617) 848-5510 *Contact Person(s):* Rev Phillip Early, Exec Dir
Setting and Background Information The center was established in 1970 as a residential treatment center for court involved youth. There are two residences and a school on the 7 acre campus.
Referral Information Referrals are made by the Dept of Youth Services and the Dept of Social Services.
Type of Facility
Funding Sources State.
Average Length of Stay Long term.
Types of Admissions Accepted Residential treatment; Group home placement.
Sources of Referral State depts of education; Local depts of education; Depts of correction; Social service depts.

Client Profile
Age Range of Clients Served Residential program: 15-18.
Characteristics Exhibited by Children Emotional handicaps; Learning disabilities; Speech/Language disorders; Mental disabilities.
IQ Range of Clients 70-110.
Tuition and Fees
Room and Board Long term: $73.24/diem.
Placements Primarily Funded By Local depts of education; Depts of corrections; Social service depts.
Social and Rehabilitative Services
Therapeutic Approach The facility offers a therapeutic milieu.
Therapeutic Services Offered Individual therapy; Group therapy; Family therapy; Recreation activities; Substance abuse treatment; Aftercare program with follow up.
Professionals on Staff Psychologists; Social workers; Adjunctive therapists; Child care staff; Nurses.
Educational and Vocational Services
Type(s) of Educational Programs Offered On campus (Academic; Vocational).
Profile of On Campus School Program Number of teachers 6; *Number of classrooms* 6; *Student to teacher ratio* 7:1; *Grades taught* All.
Vocational Education Programs/Degrees Offered Automotive; Carpentry; Computers.
Degrees Offered 8th grade diploma; 12th grade diploma; GED.

BREWSTER

THE LATHAM SCHOOL
1646 Main St, Brewster, MA 02631 (617) 896-5755, 896-5776
Contact Person(s): Karl F Hoyt, Prog Dir
Setting and Background Information The facility was established in 1970 as a non-profit school for emotionally disturbed children. There is a main dormitory housing 21 girls and a transitional cottage housing 7 girls on 4 acres.
Referral Information Referral materials, including psychological evaluations, a social history and educational information are sent to the intake worker. An intake team will review the information and interview the child. The facility accepts girls only.
Type of Facility
Funding Sources State; Local educational funding.
Average Length of Stay Long term.
Types of Admissions Accepted Residential treatment.
Sources of Referral State depts of education; Local depts of education; State depts of mental health; Psychiatrists; Social service depts.
Client Profile
Age Range of Clients Served Residential program: 6-22.
Characteristics Exhibited by Children Emotional handicaps; Learning disabilities; Speech/Language disorders; Neurological impairments; Mental disabilities.
IQ Range of Clients 45-80+.
Tuition and Fees
Room and Board Long term: $110.80/diem.
Tuition $55.40/diem.
Placements Primarily Funded By State depts of education; Local depts of education; State depts of mental health; Social service depts.
Social and Rehabilitative Services
Therapeutic Approach The therapeutic approach of the school is reality therapy, including behavior modification.
Therapeutic Services Offered Individual therapy; Group therapy; Physical therapy; Independent living skills program; Recreation activities.
Professionals on Staff Psychiatrists; Psychologists; Social workers; Child care staff; Nurses; Recreational therapist.
Educational and Vocational Services
Type(s) of Educational Programs Offered On campus.
Profile of On Campus School Program Number of teachers 4; *Number of classrooms* 4; *Student to teacher ratio* 4:1; *Credentials of teachers* BA; Special curriculum electives offered; Remedial courses offered.

BROCKTON

GREENTREE GIRLS PROGRAM

659 Summer St, Brockton, MA 02402 (617) 588-2978 *Contact Person(s):* Nancy Parnell, Dir

Setting and Background Information The facility was established in 1978. It is a large residential home.

Referral Information For referral, contact the facility and forward the necessary information. A pre-placement interview and overnight visit will be scheduled.

Type of Facility

Funding Sources Private.

Average Length of Stay Long term.

Types of Admissions Accepted Group home placement.

Sources of Referral State depts of mental health; Social service depts.

Client Profile

Age Range of Clients Served Residential program: 12-18.

Characteristics Exhibited by Children Emotional handicaps; Mental disabilities.

IQ Range of Clients 65-110.

Tuition and Fees

Placements Primarily Funded By Social service depts.

Social and Rehabilitative Services

Therapeutic Approach The basic approach of the facility is behavior management.

Therapeutic Services Offered Individual therapy; Group therapy; Family therapy; Independent living skills program.

Professionals on Staff Psychiatrists; Psychologists; Social workers; Child care staff.

Educational and Vocational Services

Type(s) of Educational Programs Offered Off campus.

CAMBRIDGE

CASTLE SCHOOL, INC

298 Harvard St, Cambridge, MA 02139 (617) 354-5410 *Contact Person(s):* Linda Corwin, Dir

Setting and Background Information The facility was established in 1978 through a local mental health area board. It is a large house in an urban neighborhood.

Referral Information Contact the facility and forward a psycho-social history, and psychological, educational and family assessments. A pre-placement interview will be held with the child and family.

Type of Facility

Funding Sources Private; State; Local school districts.

Average Length of Stay Long term.

Types of Admissions Accepted Residential treatment; Group home placement; Wards of the state.

Sources of Referral State depts of education; Local depts of education; State depts of mental health; Depts of correction; Social service depts.

Client Profile

Age Range of Clients Served Residential program: 12-18.

Characteristics Exhibited by Children Emotional handicaps; Learning disabilities.

IQ Range of Clients 75-120.

Tuition and Fees

Placements Primarily Funded By Local depts of education; Social service depts.

Social and Rehabilitative Services

Therapeutic Approach The facility has a milieu therapy approach in a well-structured setting.

Therapeutic Services Offered Individual therapy; Group therapy; Family therapy; Art therapy; Recreation activities; Substance abuse treatment.

Professionals on Staff Social workers; Child care staff; Art therapists.

Educational and Vocational Services

Type(s) of Educational Programs Offered On campus (Spec Ed); Off campus.

Profile of On Campus School Program Number of teachers 3; *Student to teacher ratio* 4:1; *Credentials of teachers* Spec Ed; *Grades taught* 5-12; Remedial courses offered.

Vocational Education Programs/Degrees Offered Computers; Wood working.

Degrees Offered 12th grade diploma.

CHATHAM

MAY INSTITUTE

Box 703, 100 Seaview St, Chatham, MA 02633 (617) 945-1147 *Contact Person(s):* Dr Walter Christian, Dir; Dr Stephen Luce, Dir Clin Svcs

Setting and Background Information The facility accepts boys only.

Referral Information For referral information contact the facility.

Type of Facility

Types of Admissions Accepted Residential treatment; Crisis intervention.

Client Profile

Age Range of Clients Served Residential program: 3-16.

Characteristics Exhibited by Children Autism.

Social and Rehabilitative Services

Therapeutic Services Offered Individual therapy; Group therapy; Family therapy; Adjunctive therapy; Physical therapy; Recreation activities.

Professionals on Staff Psychiatrists; Psychologists; Adjunctive therapists; Physical therapists; Speech therapist.

Educational and Vocational Services

Type(s) of Educational Programs Offered On campus.

Vocational Education Programs/Degrees Offered Vocational assessment and education.

COLRAIN

AQUARIUS HOUSE

182 A Greenfield Rd, Colrain, MA 01340 (413) 624-3954 *Contact Person(s):* Ella T Cosimini, Dir

Setting and Background Information The facility was established in 1978 by the Dept of Youth Services to meet the needs of younger delinquent boys.

Referral Information All referrals are made through Dept of Youth Services.

Type of Facility

Funding Sources State.

Average Length of Stay Long term.

Types of Admissions Accepted Residential treatment.

Sources of Referral Dept of Youth Services.

Client Profile

Age Range of Clients Served Residential program: 12-15.

Characteristics Exhibited by Children Emotional handicaps; Delinquency.

IQ Range of Clients 80+.

Tuition and Fees

Room and Board Long term: $94.90/diem.

Placements Primarily Funded By Dept of Youth Services.

Social and Rehabilitative Services

Therapeutic Approach The facility uses reality therapy in a milieu setting.

Therapeutic Services Offered Individual therapy; Group therapy; Family therapy.

Professionals on Staff Child care staff.

Educational and Vocational Services

Type(s) of Educational Programs Offered On campus (Certified school).

Profile of On Campus School Program Number of teachers 1; *Number of classrooms* 1; *Student to teacher ratio* 6:1; *Credentials of teachers* certified.

Vocational Education Programs/Degrees Offered Wood shop.

Degrees Offered Credits towards public education.

CONCORD

CONCORD ASSABET ADOLESCENT SERVICES

PO Box 114, Concord, MA 01742 (617) 263-1750 *Contact Person(s):* Stephen A Joffe, Exec Dir

Setting and Background Information The facility was established in 1978 by community members.

Referral Information Referrals are made through the local dept of education.

Type of Facility

Funding Sources State; Local school authorities.

Average Length of Stay The shelter program is short-term; the school offers a long-term program.

CONCORD ASSABET ADOLESCENT SERVICES
(continued)

Types of Admissions Accepted Residential treatment; Emergency shelter.

Sources of Referral State depts of education; Local depts of education; State depts of mental health; Psychiatrists; Private sources; Depts of correction; Social service depts.

Client Profile

Age Range of Clients Served Residential program: 12-21.

Characteristics Exhibited by Children Emotional handicaps.

Tuition and Fees

Room and Board Short term: $113.95/diem (shelter); Long term: $49,685/yr (includes school tuition).

Placements Primarily Funded By Local depts of education; State depts of mental health; Social service depts.

Social and Rehabilitative Services

Therapeutic Services Offered Group therapy; Family therapy.

Professionals on Staff Social workers; Child care staff.

Educational and Vocational Services

Type(s) of Educational Programs Offered On campus (High school).

Profile of On Campus School Program Number of teachers 5; *Number of classrooms* 3; *Student to teacher ratio* 4:1; *Credentials of teachers* Certified; *Grades taught* 9-12; Special curriculum electives offered (Woodworking, Photography, Theatre, Computers); Remedial courses offered (Reading, Math, Science).

Degrees Offered 12th grade diploma.

DANVERS

INSTITUTE FOR FAMILY AND LIFE LEARNING

78 Liberty St, Danvers, MA 01923 (617) 777-4480 *Contact Person(s):* Shelby Liner, William Layfield, Brian LaCroix

Setting and Background Information The facility was established in 1971 on 5 acres of land, 20 miles north of Boston.

Referral Information Referrals can be made by contacting the facility and forwarding the following background information: psychological evaluations, educational evaluations, and placement objectives and goals.

Type of Facility

Funding Sources State.

Average Length of Stay Long term.

Types of Admissions Accepted Residential treatment.

Sources of Referral State depts of education; Local depts of education; Social service depts.

Client Profile

Age Range of Clients Served Residential program: 14-18.

Characteristics Exhibited by Children Emotional handicaps; Learning disabilities.

Tuition and Fees

Room and Board Long term: $119.60/diem.

Placements Primarily Funded By State depts of education; Local depts of education; Social service depts.

Social and Rehabilitative Services

Therapeutic Approach The treatment program utilizes reality therapy, confrontation, and peer group processes to help residents change their inappropriate attitudes and behaviors.

Therapeutic Services Offered Individual therapy; Group therapy; Family therapy; Adjunctive therapy; Independent living skills program; Recreation activities; Substance abuse treatment.

Professionals on Staff Psychiatrists; Psychologists; Social workers; Adjunctive therapists; Child care staff; Nurses.

Educational and Vocational Services

Type(s) of Educational Programs Offered On campus; Summer campus.

Profile of On Campus School Program Number of teachers 7; *Number of classrooms* 7; *Student to teacher ratio* 5:1; Remedial courses offered.

Degrees Offered 12th grade diploma.

DORCHESTER

THE CHARLES HAYDEN GOODWILL SCHOOL

21 Queen St, Dorchester, MA 02122 (617) 288-1500 *Contact Person(s):* Maria Fowler, Prog Coord

Setting and Background Information The facility was established in 1932 as a division of Morgan Memorial Goodwill Industries. It is licensed by the Massachusetts Office for Children and accredited by the Massachusetts Dept of Education, Division of Special Education. The main campus is located in Dorchester and overlooks Dorchester Bay. There is also a separate residential program for co-educational placements. A group home program is located nearby in Jamaica Plain for residents making a transition from the residential program to independent living.

Referral Information Referrals can be made by the Massachusetts Dept of Social Services, Dept of Youth Services, Dept of Mental Health, and school districts through Chapter 766 Special Education Law. The referring agency must purchase a service agreement in order to set up funding of the child's treatment services. All referrals are directed to Marcia Fowler. The facility accepts boys only.

Type of Facility

Funding Sources State.

Average Length of Stay Long term.

Types of Admissions Accepted Residential treatment; Group home placement.

Sources of Referral State depts of education; Local depts of education; Social service depts.

Client Profile

Age Range of Clients Served Residential program: 12-18.

Characteristics Exhibited by Children Emotional handicaps; Learning disabilities; Hearing impairments/deafness.

Tuition and Fees

Room and Board Long term: $183.24/diem.

Placements Primarily Funded By State depts of education; Local depts of education; Social service depts.

Social and Rehabilitative Services

Therapeutic Approach The treatment programs use behavior management and psychodrama in conjunction with bioenergetics.

Therapeutic Services Offered Individual therapy; Group therapy; Family therapy; Art therapy; Independent living skills program; Recreation activities; Substance abuse treatment; Movement therapy; Dance/music therapy.

Professionals on Staff Psychiatrists; Psychologists; Social workers; Child care staff; Nurses; Art therapists.

Educational and Vocational Services

Type(s) of Educational Programs Offered On campus.

Profile of On Campus School Program Special curriculum electives offered; Remedial courses offered.

Vocational Education Programs/Degrees Offered Woodworking; Plumbing; Electrical.

Degrees Offered 12th grade diploma.

EAST FREETOWN

CRANWOOD

Palmer Court Extension, East Freetown, MA 02717 (617) 763-4217 *Contact Person(s):* Lynda M Rounsevell, Exec Dir

Setting and Background Information The facility was established in 1973 as an extension of a larger institution. There is one building on 3 ½ acres of land.

Referral Information For referral, contact the facility and forward the necessary background information. An initial interview with the Director and direct care workers will take place followed by a 3 day/2 overnight pre-placement visit.

Type of Facility

Funding Sources State.

Average Length of Stay Long term.

Types of Admissions Accepted Residential treatment; Group home placement.

Sources of Referral Social service depts.

Client Profile

Age Range of Clients Served Residential program: 6-12.

Characteristics Exhibited by Children Emotional handicaps; Learning disabilities.

IQ Range of Clients 75-100.

CRANWOOD *(continued)*

Tuition and Fees
Room and Board Long term: $67.17/diem.
Placements Primarily Funded By Social service depts.
Social and Rehabilitative Services
Therapeutic Services Offered Individual therapy; Group therapy;
Family therapy; Recreation activities.
Professionals on Staff Psychiatrists; Psychologists; Social workers;
Child care staff.
Educational and Vocational Services
Type(s) of Educational Programs Offered Off campus (Public school).

FALL RIVER

ST VINCENT'S HOME

2425 Highland Ave, Fall River, MA 02720 (617) 679-8511 *Contact
Person(s):* Thomas W Dunse, Intake Dir
Setting and Background Information The facility was initially
established as an orphanage in 1885 but has since expanded its
programs to become a treatment center. In 1971, St Vincent's
relocated to a modern building which houses a school, social
services, and administrative offices. There are 8 residential
cottages.
Referral Information Referrals can be made by school systems and
state agencies. The process of making a referral involves
completing a referral packet, and scheduling a pre-placement
interview.
Type of Facility
Funding Sources State.
Average Length of Stay Long term.
Types of Admissions Accepted Residential treatment.
Sources of Referral Social service depts; Dept of Youth Svcs; Out-of-
State Agencies.
Client Profile
Age Range of Clients Served Residential program: 6-18.
Characteristics Exhibited by Children Emotional handicaps; Learning
disabilities; Speech/Language disorders.
IQ Range of Clients 65+.
Tuition and Fees
Room and Board Long term: $112.22/diem.
Placements Primarily Funded By Social service depts.
Social and Rehabilitative Services
Therapeutic Services Offered Individual therapy; Group therapy;
Family therapy; Adjunctive therapy; Independent living skills
program.
Professionals on Staff Psychiatrists; Psychologists; Social workers;
Child care staff.
Educational and Vocational Services
Type(s) of Educational Programs Offered On campus.
Profile of On Campus School Program Number of teachers 9 and 9
aides; *Student to teacher ratio* 4:1.
Vocational Education Programs/Degrees Offered Woodwork; Car-
pentry; Culinary arts; Hotel and restaurant management; Graphic
arts and video; Computer lab; Job placement; Career counseling.
Degrees Offered 8th grade diploma; 12th grade diploma; GED.

FRAMINGHAM

REED ACADEMY

1 Winch St, Framingham, MA 01701 (617) 877-1222 *Contact
Person(s):* Barbara Nichols, Clin Dir
Setting and Background Information The facility was established in
1975 on 3 acres of land surrounded by 500 acres of state forest.
The program is located in a 28-room house, which includes
classrooms, therapy rooms, recreational area, and library. There is
also a physical education building and outdoor recreation space.
Referral Information Referrals can be made by parents, school
districts, and state agencies. Facility staff will arrange a pre-
placement interview with the child and family.
Type of Facility
Funding Sources State.
Average Length of Stay Long term.
Types of Admissions Accepted Residential treatment.
Sources of Referral State depts of education; Local depts of educa-
tion; State depts of mental health; Social service depts.

Client Profile
Age Range of Clients Served Residential program: 7-18.
Characteristics Exhibited by Children Emotional handicaps; Learning
disabilities; Speech/Language disorders; Neurological impair-
ments.
Tuition and Fees
Room and Board Long term: $37,500/year.
Placements Primarily Funded By State depts of education; Local
depts of education; State depts of mental health; Social service
depts.
Social and Rehabilitative Services
Therapeutic Approach The philosophy of the treatment program is
based on a behavioral therapeutic approach, with emphasis on
socialization and basic living skills in a family-like setting.
Therapeutic Services Offered Individual therapy; Group therapy;
Family therapy; Adjunctive therapy; Independent living skills
program; Recreation activities; Aftercare program with follow up;
Speech therapy.
Professionals on Staff Psychiatrists; Psychologists; Social workers;
Adjunctive therapists; Child care staff; Nurses.
Educational and Vocational Services
Type(s) of Educational Programs Offered On campus.
Profile of On Campus School Program Number of teachers 8; *Num-
ber of classrooms* 4; *Student to teacher ratio* 4:1.

GREAT BARRINGTON

EAGLETON SCHOOL

Star Rt 62 Box 10, Great Barrington, MA 01230 (413) 528-4385
Contact Person(s): Bruce Bona, Dir
Setting and Background Information The facility accepts males only.
Referral Information For referral information contact the facility.
Type of Facility
Types of Admissions Accepted Residential treatment; Crisis interven-
tion.
Client Profile
Age Range of Clients Served Residential program: 9-21.
Characteristics Exhibited by Children Emotional handicaps; Learning
disabilities; Mental disabilities.
Social and Rehabilitative Services
Therapeutic Services Offered Individual therapy; Group therapy; Art
therapy; Physical therapy.
Professionals on Staff Psychiatrists; Psychologists; Adjunctive thera-
pists; Art therapists; Physical therapists; Speech therapist.
Educational and Vocational Services
Type(s) of Educational Programs Offered On campus.
Vocational Education Programs/Degrees Offered Vocational assess-
ment and education.

GREENFIELD

OUR HOUSE, INC

139 Shelburne Rd, Greenfield, MA 01301 (413) 772-6422 *Contact
Person(s):* Donald G Harris, Exec Dir
Setting and Background Information This facility was established in
1971. There are two residential facilities.
Referral Information Contact the facility for referral information.
Type of Facility
Funding Sources State.
Average Length of Stay Long term.
Types of Admissions Accepted Residential treatment.
Sources of Referral Private sources; Depts of correction; Social ser-
vice depts.
Client Profile
Age Range of Clients Served Residential program: 12-18.
Characteristics Exhibited by Children Delinquency.
Tuition and Fees
Room and Board Long term: $80/diem.
Placements Primarily Funded By Private sources; Social service
depts.
Social and Rehabilitative Services
Therapeutic Approach The basic therapeutic approach of the facility
is behavior modification.
Therapeutic Services Offered Individual therapy; Group therapy;
Family therapy; Independent living skills program; Recreation
activities; Substance abuse treatment.
Professionals on Staff Psychologists; Child care staff.

OUR HOUSE, INC *(continued)*

Educational and Vocational Services
Type(s) of Educational Programs Offered On campus.
Profile of On Campus School Program Number of teachers 4; *Number of classrooms* 3; *Student to teacher ratio* 4:1; *Credentials of teachers* State Certified; *Grades taught* All.

LAKEVILLE

BISHOP RUOCCO HOUSE
22 Highland Rd, Lakeville, MA 02346 (617) 947-2823 *Contact Person(s):* Robert M Turillo, Dir
Setting and Background Information The facility was established in 1981 through the Archdiocese of Boston. Located on 14 acres, there is one main building.
Referral Information Contact the facility for referral information.
Type of Facility
Funding Sources Private.
Average Length of Stay Long term; 9-12 mos.
Types of Admissions Accepted Residential treatment.
Sources of Referral State depts of education; Local depts of education; Social service depts.
Client Profile
Age Range of Clients Served Residential program: 15-18.

LANCASTER

ROBERT F KENNEDY ACTION CORPS
PO Box 319, Wellington Hall, Old Common Rd, Lancaster, MA 01523 (617) 365-7358 *Contact Person(s):* Leslie F Goodwill, Adm Dir
Setting and Background Information The facility was established in 1968 in memory of Robert F Kennedy. Its campus is located in a rural setting 50 miles west of Boston and consists of residential living units for 27 children and on-grounds school.
Referral Information Referrals can be made by the Dept of Social Services, private agencies, community mental health centers, physicians, mental health professionals, school systems, and parents. To make a referral, contact the facility and forward the necessary background information. A pre-placement visit and interview will take place before an admission decision is made.
Type of Facility
Funding Sources State.
Average Length of Stay Short and long term.
Types of Admissions Accepted Residential treatment.
Sources of Referral Local depts of education; State depts of mental health; Social service depts.
Client Profile
Age Range of Clients Served Residential program: 6-13.
Characteristics Exhibited by Children Emotional handicaps; Learning disabilities; Speech/Language disorders; Neurological impairments; Mental disabilities.
IQ Range of Clients 65+.
Tuition and Fees
Room and Board Short term: $120/diem; Long term: $120/diem.
Placements Primarily Funded By Social service depts.
Social and Rehabilitative Services
Therapeutic Approach The basic therapeutic approach used at the facility is behavior modification.
Therapeutic Services Offered Individual therapy; Group therapy; Family therapy; Art therapy; Recreation activities; Speech/language therapy.
Professionals on Staff Psychiatrists; Psychologists; Social workers; Adjunctive therapists; Child care staff; Nurses; Art therapists.
Educational and Vocational Services
Type(s) of Educational Programs Offered On campus.
Profile of On Campus School Program Number of teachers 12; *Number of classrooms* 8; *Student to teacher ratio* 7:1.

ROBERT F KENNEDY ACTION CORPS ADOLESCENT TREATMENT UNIT
PO Box 319, Wellington Hall, Old Common Rd, Lancaster, MA 01523 (617) 365-6412 *Contact Person(s):* Joe Healy
Setting and Background Information The facility accepts males only.

Referral Information Referrals can be made by the Dept of Social Services, private agencies, community mental health centers, physicians, mental health professionals, school systems, and parents. To make a referral, contact the facility and forward the necessary background information. A pre-placement visit and interview will take place before an admission decision is made.
Type of Facility
Funding Sources State.
Average Length of Stay Long term.
Types of Admissions Accepted Residential treatment.
Sources of Referral State depts of education; Local depts of education; Social service depts; Courts; Dept of Youth Svcs.
Client Profile
Age Range of Clients Served Residential program: 12-15.
Characteristics Exhibited by Children Emotional handicaps; Learning disabilities.
Tuition and Fees
Room and Board Long term: $166.64/diem.
Placements Primarily Funded By State depts of education; Local depts of education; Social service depts.
Social and Rehabilitative Services
Therapeutic Services Offered Individual therapy; Group therapy; Family therapy; Substance abuse treatment; Movement therapy.
Professionals on Staff Psychiatrists; Psychologists; Social workers; Child care staff; Nurses.
Educational and Vocational Services
Type(s) of Educational Programs Offered On campus; Summer campus.
Profile of On Campus School Program Number of teachers 12; *Number of classrooms* 8; *Student to teacher ratio* 7:1.

ROBERT F KENNEDY ACTION CORPS CHILDREN'S CENTER
PO Box 319, Wellington Hall, Old Common Rd, Lancaster, MA 01523 (617) 365-7359 *Contact Person(s):* Marjorie Johnson, Prog Dir
Setting and Background Information This center accepts males only.
Referral Information Referrals can be made by the Dept of Social Services, private agencies, community mental health centers, physicians, mental health professionals, school systems, and parents. To make a referral, contact the facility and forward the necessary information. A pre-placement visit and interview will take place before an admission decision is made.
Type of Facility
Funding Sources State.
Average Length of Stay Long term.
Types of Admissions Accepted Residential treatment.
Sources of Referral Local depts of education; State depts of mental health; Social service depts.
Client Profile
Age Range of Clients Served Residential program: 6-13.
Characteristics Exhibited by Children Emotional handicaps; Learning disabilities.
IQ Range of Clients 70+.
Tuition and Fees
Room and Board Long term: $119.23/diem.
Placements Primarily Funded By Local depts of education; Social service depts.
Social and Rehabilitative Services
Therapeutic Services Offered Individual therapy; Group therapy; Family therapy; Art therapy; Recreation activities; Aftercare program with follow up.
Professionals on Staff Psychiatrists; Psychologists; Social workers; Child care staff; Nurses; Art therapists.
Educational and Vocational Services
Type(s) of Educational Programs Offered On campus; Off campus.
Profile of On Campus School Program Number of teachers 12; *Number of classrooms* 8; *Student to teacher ratio* 7:1.

LEICESTER

ARCHWAY, INC
77 Mulberry St, Leicester, MA 01524 (617) 892-4707 *Contact Person(s):* Ellen Price, Exec Dir
Setting and Background Information The facility was privately established in 1975.
Referral Information Contact the facility and submit historical information. A pre-placement visit will be scheduled.

ARCHWAY, INC *(continued)*

Type of Facility
Funding Sources State.
Average Length of Stay Long term.
Types of Admissions Accepted Residential treatment.
Sources of Referral State depts of education; Local depts of education; State depts of mental health; Social service depts.
Client Profile
Age Range of Clients Served Residential program: 12-21+.
Characteristics Exhibited by Children Speech/Language disorders; Neurological impairments; Mental disabilities; Autism.
Tuition and Fees
Tuition $61,529/yr.
Placements Primarily Funded By State depts of education; Local depts of education; State depts of mental health; Social service depts.
Social and Rehabilitative Services
Therapeutic Approach The facility has a behavioral approach to therapy.
Therapeutic Services Offered Independent living skills program.
Professionals on Staff Social workers; Child care staff; Nurses; Physical therapists.
Educational and Vocational Services
Type(s) of Educational Programs Offered On campus.
Profile of On Campus School Program Number of teachers 2; *Number of classrooms* 4; *Student to teacher ratio* 3:1; *Credentials of teachers* Certified; *Grades taught* Ungraded.
Vocational Education Programs/Degrees Offered Pre-vocational.

LENOX

HILLCREST EDUCATIONAL CENTERS, INC

PO Box 794, 224 Housatonic St, Lenox, MA 01240 (413) 637-1821
Contact Person(s): Mary Beth Yarmey, Dir of Plan & Prog Dev
Setting and Background Information The center was established in 1985. There are 4 locations throughout Berkshire County.
Referral Information Referrals are received from depts of education, local educational authorities, depts of mental health and are processed by the intake coordinator.
Type of Facility
Funding Sources State.
Average Length of Stay Long term.
Types of Admissions Accepted Residential treatment.
Sources of Referral State depts of education.
Client Profile
Age Range of Clients Served Residential program: 6-21+.
Characteristics Exhibited by Children Emotional handicaps; Learning disabilities; Hearing impairments/deafness; Vision impairments/blindness; Speech/Language disorders; Neurological impairments; Mental disabilities.
Tuition and Fees
Placements Primarily Funded By State depts of education; Local depts of education; State depts of mental health.
Social and Rehabilitative Services
Therapeutic Approach The facility has a behavioral approach to therapy.
Therapeutic Services Offered Individual therapy; Group therapy; Art therapy; Physical therapy; Independent living skills program; Recreation activities.
Professionals on Staff Psychiatrists; Psychologists; Social workers; Child care staff; Nurses; Art therapists; Physical therapists; Speech therapist; Music therapists.
Educational and Vocational Services
Type(s) of Educational Programs Offered On campus; Off campus.
Profile of On Campus School Program Number of teachers 28; *Number of classrooms* 28; *Length of school day* 5 ½ hrs; *Grades taught* Ungraded; Special curriculum electives offered; Remedial courses offered.
Vocational Education Programs/Degrees Offered Vocational programs.
Degrees Offered 8th grade diploma; 12th grade diploma; GED.

VALLEYHEAD

PO Box 714, Lenox, MA 01240 (413) 637-3635 *Contact Person(s):* Judith Fun, Admis Coord
Setting and Background Information The facility accepts girls only.
Referral Information For referral information contact the facility.

Type of Facility
Types of Admissions Accepted Residential treatment; Crisis intervention.
Client Profile
Age Range of Clients Served Residential program: 10-21.
Characteristics Exhibited by Children Emotional handicaps; Learning disabilities; Mental disabilities.
Social and Rehabilitative Services
Therapeutic Services Offered Individual therapy; Group therapy; Family therapy; Adjunctive therapy; Art therapy; Physical therapy; Recreation activities.
Professionals on Staff Psychiatrists; Psychologists; Adjunctive therapists; Art therapists; Physical therapists.
Educational and Vocational Services
Type(s) of Educational Programs Offered On campus.
Vocational Education Programs/Degrees Offered Vocational assessment and education.

LEXINGTON

MYSTIC VALLEY ADOLESCENT RESIDENCE

10 Sunnyknoll Terr, Lexington, MA 02173 (617) 862-1846 *Contact Person(s):* Joan Murray, Prog Dir
Setting and Background Information This residential group home was established in 1974 by the Mystic Valley Mental Health Clinic.
Referral Information Referrals to the facility are made through the Dept of Social Services.
Type of Facility
Funding Sources State.
Average Length of Stay Long term.
Types of Admissions Accepted Group home placement.
Sources of Referral Social service depts.
Client Profile
Age Range of Clients Served Residential program: 15-18.
Characteristics Exhibited by Children Emotional handicaps.
IQ Range of Clients 70+.
Tuition and Fees
Placements Primarily Funded By Social service depts.
Social and Rehabilitative Services
Therapeutic Services Offered Individual therapy; Group therapy; Family therapy; Independent living skills program; Aftercare program with follow up.
Professionals on Staff Psychiatrists; Psychologists; Social workers; Adjunctive therapists; Child care staff; Nurses.
Educational and Vocational Services
Type(s) of Educational Programs Offered Off campus (Public schools).

LITTLETON

ALPHA OMEGA

544 Newtown Rd, Littleton, MA 01460 (617) 486-8919 *Contact Person(s):* Lori Prehl, Intake Coord; Joseph P O'Malley Jr, Dir
Setting and Background Information The Adolescent Program was established in 1969 to offer services to drug users, but has since evolved into a treatment center for emotionally disturbed boys. The program is licensed by the Office for Children and Dept of Education (Chapter 766). The campus is located 30 miles northwest of Boston, in a rural setting.
Referral Information Referrals can be made by courts, school districts, professionals, and families. The referral process requires the forwarding of background information, including a recent psychological and/or psychiatric evaluation, family history, medical evaluation (when appropriate). Upon receiving the referral information, appropriate applicants will be asked to return with their family and referral source for a pre-placement interview, before a final decision is made.
Type of Facility
Funding Sources State.
Average Length of Stay Long term.
Types of Admissions Accepted Residential treatment; Group home placement.
Sources of Referral State depts of education; Local depts of education; Private sources; Social service depts; Dept of Youth Svcs.

ALPHA OMEGA (continued)

Client Profile
Age Range of Clients Served Residential program: 13-17.
Characteristics Exhibited by Children Emotional handicaps; Learning disabilities.
Tuition and Fees
Placements Primarily Funded By State depts of education; Local depts of education; Private sources; Social service depts; Dept of Youth Services.
Social and Rehabilitative Services
Therapeutic Services Offered Individual therapy; Group therapy; Family therapy; Independent living skills program; Recreation activities; Substance abuse treatment; Aftercare program with follow up.
Educational and Vocational Services
Type(s) of Educational Programs Offered On campus; Summer campus.
Profile of On Campus School Program Remedial courses offered.
Degrees Offered GED.

LITTLETON GIRLS HOUSE, SECURE TREATMENT FACILITY

PO Box 2335, 22 King St, Littleton, MA 01460 (617) 486-9227
Contact Person(s): Donna Grisi, Dir
Setting and Background Information The facility was established in 1979 by the Dept of Youth Service. This is a secure girls residential program.
Referral Information Clients are committed to DYS by juvenile judges. DYS then refers the girls to the facility.
Type of Facility
Funding Sources State.
Average Length of Stay 10-12 mos.
Types of Admissions Accepted Residential treatment.
Sources of Referral Dept of Youth Services only.
Client Profile
Age Range of Clients Served Residential program: 14-17.
Characteristics Exhibited by Children Emotional handicaps; Learning disabilities; Delinquency.
IQ Range of Clients 70-115.
Tuition and Fees
Room and Board Long term: $134/diem.
Placements Primarily Funded By Dept of Youth Services.
Social and Rehabilitative Services
Therapeutic Approach The facility uses reality therapy.
Therapeutic Services Offered Individual therapy; Group therapy; Family therapy; Independent living skills program; Recreation activities; Substance abuse treatment; Aftercare program with follow up.
Professionals on Staff Psychologists; Social workers; Child care staff; Nurses.
Educational and Vocational Services
Type(s) of Educational Programs Offered On campus.
Vocational Education Programs/Degrees Offered Pre-vocational.
Degrees Offered GED.

METHUEN

ST ANN'S HOME, INC

100A Haverhill St, Methuen, MA 01844 (617) 682-5276 *Contact Person(s):* Patrick T Villani PhD, Exec Dir
Setting and Background Information The facility was originally established in 1925 as an orphanage. It was incorporated as a residential treatment facility in 1966. The main campus of 7 acres has a school building and a dormitory. There are 2 group homes nearby.
Referral Information Contact the facility for referral information. Pre-admission interviews will be scheduled.
Type of Facility
Funding Sources Private; State; Federal; School systems.
Average Length of Stay Long term.
Types of Admissions Accepted Day treatment; Residential treatment; Group home placement; Wards of the state.
Sources of Referral State depts of education; Local depts of education; State depts of mental health; Private sources; Social service depts.

Client Profile
Age Range of Clients Served Day programs: 6-18; Residential program: 6-18.
Characteristics Exhibited by Children Emotional handicaps; Learning disabilities; Speech/Language disorders.
IQ Range of Clients 80-130.
Tuition and Fees
Room and Board Long term: $27,055/yr.
Tuition $13,686/yr.
Placements Primarily Funded By Social service depts.
Social and Rehabilitative Services
Therapeutic Approach The basic therapeutic approach of the facility is ego-psychological.
Therapeutic Services Offered Individual therapy; Group therapy; Family therapy.
Professionals on Staff Psychiatrists; Psychologists; Social workers; Child care staff; Nurses.
Educational and Vocational Services
Type(s) of Educational Programs Offered On campus; Off campus (Public schools).
Profile of On Campus School Program Number of teachers 15; Number of classrooms 12; Student to teacher ratio 5:1; Credentials of teachers Certified in Sp Needs; Grades taught Ungraded.

MIDDLETON

WREATH HOUSE

89 E St, Middleton, MA 01949 (617) 774-3294 *Contact Person(s):* Carole Small, Dir of Res Srvs
Setting and Background Information The facility was established in 1981. The two buildings on the campus contain a school/day program and a residential program.
Referral Information Contact the facility for referral information.
Type of Facility
Funding Sources State; Dept of mental health.
Average Length of Stay 1 yr or more.
Types of Admissions Accepted Residential treatment.
Sources of Referral State depts of education; Local depts of education; State depts of mental health; Psychiatrists; Private sources; Depts of correction; Social service depts.
Client Profile
Age Range of Clients Served Day programs: 12-18; Residential program: 12-18.
Characteristics Exhibited by Children Emotional handicaps; Learning disabilities.
Tuition and Fees
Placements Primarily Funded By Local depts of education; Social service depts.
Social and Rehabilitative Services
Therapeutic Approach The facility uses reality therapy, including behavior modification.
Therapeutic Services Offered Individual therapy; Group therapy; Family therapy; Independent living skills program.

NATICK

BRANDON SCHOOL

27 Winter St, Natick, MA 01760 (617) 655-6400 *Contact Person(s):* Timothy M Callahan, Exec Dir
Setting and Background Information The facility, founded in 1966, is located on 37 wooded acres of land. Its one-story brick building was specially designed to house programs for emotionally disturbed children. There are 8 classrooms, a gymnasium, woodworking shop, several therapy rooms, and administrative offices. There are 2 group homes in the community. The facility accepts boys only.
Referral Information Referrals can be made by school districts, Dept of Social Services, and Dept of Mental Health.
Type of Facility
Funding Sources State.
Average Length of Stay Long term.
Types of Admissions Accepted Day treatment; Residential treatment; Group home placement.
Sources of Referral State depts of education; Local depts of education; Social service depts.

BRANDON SCHOOL *(continued)*

Client Profile
Age Range of Clients Served Day programs: 10-16; Residential program: 10-16.
Characteristics Exhibited by Children Emotional handicaps; Learning disabilities.
IQ Range of Clients 70+.
Tuition and Fees
Room and Board Long term: $40,000/yr.
Placements Primarily Funded By State depts of education; Local depts of education; Social service depts.
Social and Rehabilitative Services
Therapeutic Approach Therapeutic approaches used include a psychoanalytic view of child development, expressive therapy, reality therapy, and cognitive behavioral techniques.
Therapeutic Services Offered Individual therapy; Group therapy; Family therapy; Adjunctive therapy; Art therapy; Independent living skills program; Recreation activities.
Professionals on Staff Psychiatrists; Psychologists; Social workers; Adjunctive therapists; Child care staff; Nurses; Art therapists.
Educational and Vocational Services
Type(s) of Educational Programs Offered On campus; Summer campus.
Profile of On Campus School Program Number of teachers 9; *Number of classrooms* 8; *Student to teacher ratio* 6:1.

NEEDHAM

THE WALKER HOME AND SCHOOL

1968 Central Ave, Needham, MA 02192 (617) 449-4500 *Contact Person(s):* Dr Richard Small, Exec Dir
Setting and Background Information The facility is located on 7 acres and includes school/administration buildings, an activity/clinical building, industrial arts building, 2 residential facilities, and recreation fields. There are also 2 off-campus group foster homes in Needham, Massachusetts.
Referral Information Referrals are made by the Dept of Social Services, local school systems and through the courts.
Type of Facility
Funding Sources State.
Average Length of Stay Long term.
Types of Admissions Accepted Day treatment; Residential treatment.
Sources of Referral State depts of education; Local depts of education; State depts of mental health; Social service depts; Courts.
Client Profile
Age Range of Clients Served Day programs: 6-13; Residential program: 6-13.
Characteristics Exhibited by Children Emotional handicaps; Learning disabilities.
Tuition and Fees
Placements Primarily Funded By State depts of education; Local depts of education; Social service depts.
Social and Rehabilitative Services
Therapeutic Services Offered Individual therapy; Group therapy; Family therapy; Art therapy; Recreation activities; Aftercare program with follow up.
Professionals on Staff Psychiatrists; Psychologists; Social workers; Child care staff; Nurses; Art therapists; Pediatrician.
Educational and Vocational Services
Type(s) of Educational Programs Offered On campus; Summer campus.
Profile of On Campus School Program Number of classrooms 6.

NEW MARLBOROUGH

THE KOLBURNE SCHOOL, INC

Southfield Rd, New Marlborough, MA 01230 (413) 229-8787
Contact Person(s): John C Zola, Admin Dir
Setting and Background Information The facility was established by the Kolburne family in 1947. The 1,500-acre campus has 2 residential buildings, 2 school buildings, 2 gyms, an indoor pool, 7 group homes, a vocational building, and a greenhouse.
Referral Information Contact the facility and forward a referral packet. A pre-admission interview will be arranged.

Type of Facility
Funding Sources Private; State.
Average Length of Stay Avg 36 mos.
Types of Admissions Accepted Residential treatment; Group home placement.
Sources of Referral State depts of education; Local depts of education; State depts of mental health; Psychiatrists; Private sources; Social service depts.
Client Profile
Age Range of Clients Served Residential program: 6-21+.
Characteristics Exhibited by Children Emotional handicaps; Learning disabilities; Speech/Language disorders; Neurological impairments; Mental disabilities; Head injury.
IQ Range of Clients 70-150.
Tuition and Fees
Room and Board Long term: $42,282-59,282/yr (includes tuition).
Placements Primarily Funded By State depts of education; Local depts of education; State depts of mental health; Private sources; Social service depts.
Social and Rehabilitative Services
Therapeutic Approach The facility has a psychodynamic approach to therapy and uses behavior modification.
Therapeutic Services Offered Individual therapy; Group therapy; Family therapy; Art therapy; Independent living skills program.
Professionals on Staff Psychiatrists; Psychologists; Social workers; Adjunctive therapists; Child care staff; Nurses; Art therapists.
Educational and Vocational Services
Type(s) of Educational Programs Offered On campus.
Profile of On Campus School Program Number of teachers 22; *Number of classrooms* 18; *Student to teacher ratio* 8:1; *Credentials of teachers* Certified Spec Ed; *Grades taught* Individualized; Special curriculum electives offered (Computers, Art, Reading, Speech).
Vocational Education Programs/Degrees Offered Small engine repair; EKG technician.
Degrees Offered 12th grade diploma.

NEWBURYPORT

THE HARBOR SCHOOLS, INC

11 Market Sq, Newburyport, MA 01950 (617) 462-3151 *Contact Person(s):* Arthur C DiMauro, Exec Dir
Setting and Background Information This residential school was established in 1972. There are 4 facilities. One is in Amesbury, one is in Haverhill and two are in Newburyport.
Referral Information Contact the facility and forward a referral packet which should include psychological, medical and educational evaluations and a family development history. The funding source also should be identified.
Type of Facility
Funding Sources State.
Average Length of Stay Long term.
Types of Admissions Accepted Residential treatment.
Sources of Referral State depts of education; Local depts of education; State depts of mental health; Private sources; Depts of correction; Social service depts.
Client Profile
Age Range of Clients Served Residential program: 12-18.
Characteristics Exhibited by Children Emotional handicaps; Learning disabilities.
IQ Range of Clients 65+.
Tuition and Fees
Room and Board Long term: $38,228/yr (includes school tuition).
Placements Primarily Funded By State depts of education; Local depts of education; State depts of mental health; Private sources; Depts of corrections; Social service depts.
Social and Rehabilitative Services
Therapeutic Approach The primary therapeutic medium of the facility is the milieu.
Therapeutic Services Offered Individual therapy; Group therapy; Family therapy; Independent living skills program; Aftercare program with follow up.
Professionals on Staff Psychiatrists; Psychologists; Social workers; Child care staff; Nurses.

THE HARBOR SCHOOLS, INC *(continued)*

Educational and Vocational Services
Type(s) of Educational Programs Offered On campus (Academic, Vocational).
Profile of On Campus School Program Number of teachers 12; *Number of classrooms* 16; *Student to teacher ratio* 4:1; *Credentials of teachers* Certified special needs; Remedial courses offered (Reading).
Vocational Education Programs/Degrees Offered Pre-vocational classes.

NEWTON

KEYSTONE ADOLESCENT PROGRAM, NORTHEASTERN FAMILY INSTITUTE

47 Park St, Newton, MA 02158 (617) 527-6098 *Contact Person(s):* Christine Cahill, Dir
Setting and Background Information The facility was established in 1983 and was originally located on the grounds of the state hospital. Currently, the facility is in a single family residence.
Referral Information Referrals are made through the Newton Area Office, Dept of Mental Health, and by social service agencies.
Type of Facility
Funding Sources State.
Average Length of Stay Long term.
Types of Admissions Accepted Residential treatment.
Sources of Referral State depts of mental health; Social service depts.
Client Profile
Age Range of Clients Served Residential program: 12-21+.
Characteristics Exhibited by Children Emotional handicaps; Learning disabilities; Mental disabilities.
IQ Range of Clients 70+.
Tuition and Fees
Room and Board Long term: $132.97/diem.
Tuition $12,000/yr.
Placements Primarily Funded By Local depts of education; State depts of mental health.
Social and Rehabilitative Services
Therapeutic Services Offered Individual therapy; Group therapy; Family therapy; Independent living skills program; Recreation activities; Substance abuse treatment; Aftercare program with follow up.
Professionals on Staff Psychiatrists; Psychologists; Social workers; Adjunctive therapists; Child care staff.
Educational and Vocational Services
Type(s) of Educational Programs Offered On campus; Summer campus.
Profile of On Campus School Program Number of teachers 3; *Number of classrooms* 1; *Student to teacher ratio* 3:1; *Length of school day* 8-4; *Grades taught* 8-12; Special curriculum electives offered; Remedial courses offered.
Degrees Offered 12th grade diploma; GED.

NORTH BROOKFIELD

VALLEY VIEW SCHOOL

PO Box 338, North Brookfield, MA 01535 (617) 867-6505 *Contact Person(s):* Philip G Spiva PhD, Dir
Setting and Background Information Valley View School is a private residential treatment facility for boys which was established by its director, Philip G Spiva, PhD, in 1970 to provide a therapeutic environment for emotionally disturbed boys. Its campus is located on a 215-acre farm site and consists of a remodeled farm building which has dormitory rooms, dining room, lounges, and recreational areas. There is also an on-campus school, gymnasium, educational resource/computer center, woodworking shop, athletic field, art center and library.
Referral Information Referrals can be made by psychiatrists, psychologists, social workers, school districts, educational consultants, and parents. To make a referral, contact the director.
Type of Facility
Funding Sources Private.
Average Length of Stay Long term.
Types of Admissions Accepted Residential treatment.
Sources of Referral State depts of education; Local depts of education; Psychiatrists; Private sources.

Client Profile
Age Range of Clients Served Residential program: 12-16.
Characteristics Exhibited by Children Emotional handicaps; Learning disabilities.
Tuition and Fees
Room and Board Long term: $27,500/yr.
Placements Primarily Funded By Private sources.
Social and Rehabilitative Services
Therapeutic Approach The treatment program provides a structured therapeutic milieu.
Therapeutic Services Offered Individual therapy; Group therapy; Recreation activities.
Professionals on Staff Psychologists; Social workers; Child care staff; Nurses.
Educational and Vocational Services
Type(s) of Educational Programs Offered On campus; Off campus.
Profile of On Campus School Program Number of teachers 9; *Number of classrooms* 8; *Student to teacher ratio* 3:1.
Degrees Offered 12th grade diploma.

PEABODY

LAKESIDE SCHOOL

629 Lowell St, Peabody, MA 01960 (617) 535-0250 *Contact Person(s):* Debra Ankeles
Setting and Background Information Lakeside School is a psychoeducational, residential, and day treatment facility which was established in 1972 in the semi-rural community of West Peabody on 8 acres of wooded land. The campus has a restored 19th century farmhouse which provides facilities for the residential program, a modern building housing the school program, library, administrative offices, and a building housing the pre-vocational program. There is also a completely fenced-in playground which has a large assortment of activity equipment and an in-ground pool.
Referral Information Referrals can be made by the public schools, social service agencies, hospitals, and physicians. Applicants must submit a completed referral packet with an evaluation summary to the Admission Office. An interview with the child, parents, and facility staff will take place at the center. The clinical team will review the referral packet and may arrange a one day visit for the child before a placement decision is made.
Type of Facility
Funding Sources State.
Average Length of Stay Long term.
Types of Admissions Accepted Day treatment; Residential treatment.
Sources of Referral State depts of education; Local depts of education; Social service depts.
Client Profile
Age Range of Clients Served Day program: 9-17; Residential program: 9-17.
Characteristics Exhibited by Children Emotional handicaps; Learning disabilities; Speech/Language disorders.
IQ Range of Clients 60+.
Tuition and Fees
Room and Board Long term: $34,274/yr; $12,417/yr (Day treatment).
Placements Primarily Funded By State depts of education; Local depts of education; Social service depts.
Social and Rehabilitative Services
Therapeutic Approach The treatment program is based on a humanistic-educational philosophy.
Therapeutic Services Offered Individual therapy; Group therapy; Family therapy; Adjunctive therapy; Independent living skills program; Recreation activities; Occupational therapy.
Professionals on Staff Psychiatrists; Psychologists; Social workers; Adjunctive therapists; Child care staff; Nurses; Occupational therapist.
Educational and Vocational Services
Type(s) of Educational Programs Offered On campus.
Profile of On Campus School Program Number of teachers 7; *Number of classrooms* 6; *Student to teacher ratio* 10:1.

PITTSFIELD

BERKSHIRE LEARNING CENTER

PO Box 1224, Pittsfield, MA 01202 (413) 442-5531 *Contact Person(s):* Christine Whalen, Adm Dir; Dr Marianne E Rud
Setting and Background Information The facility was established in 1971 and presently operates 2 residential programs, one for adolescents and one for young adults. Its main campus has 3 dormitories, an administration building, and school building. The young adult residence, named The Country Place, is a larger house with spacious grounds on the outskirts of Pittsfield.
Referral Information Referrals can be made by school districts, social service agencies, mental health centers or depts, private individuals, and families.
Type of Facility
Funding Sources Private; State.
Types of Admissions Accepted Residential treatment.
Sources of Referral State depts of education; Local depts of education; State depts of mental health; Private sources; Social service depts.
Client Profile
Age Range of Clients Served Residential program: 13-33.
Characteristics Exhibited by Children Emotional handicaps; Learning disabilities; Neurological impairments.
Tuition and Fees
Room and Board Long term: $36,088/yr.
Placements Primarily Funded By State depts of education; Local depts of education; State depts of mental health; Private sources; Social service depts.
Social and Rehabilitative Services
Therapeutic Approach The philosophy of the treatment program is psychoanalytically oriented.
Therapeutic Services Offered Individual therapy; Group therapy; Family therapy; Independent living skills program; Recreation activities; Aftercare program with follow up.
Professionals on Staff Psychiatrists; Psychologists; Social workers; Child care staff; Nurses.
Educational and Vocational Services
Type(s) of Educational Programs Offered On campus; Off campus; Summer campus.
Profile of On Campus School Program Number of teachers 9; *Number of classrooms* 7; *Student to teacher ratio* 6:1; Remedial courses offered.
Degrees Offered 12th grade diploma; GED.

PLYMOUTH

THE BAIRD CENTER

Great Outlook Way, Plymouth, MA 02360 (617) 224-8041 *Contact Person(s):* Stephen Yerdon, Dir
Setting and Background Information This residential program was established in 1974 as an extension of summer camping for disturbed youth. There are 15 buildings on 47 acres.
Referral Information Referrals are made through DYS, DSS, DMH and local depts of education.
Type of Facility
Funding Sources Private; State.
Average Length of Stay Long term.
Types of Admissions Accepted Residential treatment; School day treatment.
Sources of Referral State depts of education; Local depts of education; State depts of mental health; Psychiatrists; Private sources; Social service depts.
Client Profile
Age Range of Clients Served Day programs: 12-15; Residential program: 12-15.
Characteristics Exhibited by Children Emotional handicaps; Learning disabilities; Mental disabilities.
Tuition and Fees
Room and Board Long term: $115/diem.
Tuition $55/diem.
Placements Primarily Funded By State depts of education; Local depts of education; State depts of mental health; Social service depts.

Social and Rehabilitative Services
Therapeutic Approach The facility has a reality based approach to therapy.
Therapeutic Services Offered Individual therapy; Group therapy; Family therapy; Recreation activities; Substance abuse treatment; Aftercare program with follow up.
Professionals on Staff Social workers; Child care staff; Nurses.
Educational and Vocational Services
Type(s) of Educational Programs Offered On campus.
Profile of On Campus School Program Number of teachers 8; *Number of classrooms* 11; *Student to teacher ratio* 4:1; *Credentials of teachers* Special needs Certified; *Length of school day* 9am-3pm; *Grades taught* 3-12; Remedial courses offered.

ROWLEY

SOLSTICE ADOLESCENT PROGRAM

PO Box 522, Rowley, MA 01969 (617) 948-2346 *Contact Person(s):* Bob Johnston, Dir of Res Svcs
Setting and Background Information The Dept of Mental Health established this facility in 1979. There are 2 buildings on the 4-acre campus.
Referral Information The Dept of Mental Health pre-screens all referrals to the facility.
Type of Facility
Funding Sources State.
Average Length of Stay Long term.
Types of Admissions Accepted Residential treatment.
Sources of Referral State depts of mental health.
Client Profile
Age Range of Clients Served Residential program: 12-18.
Characteristics Exhibited by Children Emotional handicaps.
Tuition and Fees
Room and Board Long term: $44,000/yr.
Tuition $16,000/yr.
Placements Primarily Funded By State depts of education; State depts of mental health.
Social and Rehabilitative Services
Therapeutic Services Offered Individual therapy; Group therapy; Family therapy; Independent living skills program; Recreation activities.
Professionals on Staff Psychiatrists; Social workers; Adjunctive therapists; Child care staff; Nurses.
Educational and Vocational Services
Type(s) of Educational Programs Offered On campus (Spec Ed); Off campus (Public school).
Profile of On Campus School Program Number of teachers 5; *Number of classrooms* 6; *Student to teacher ratio* 3:1; *Credentials of teachers* Certified; *Grades taught* 7-12; Special curriculum electives offered; Remedial courses offered (Math, English).
Degrees Offered Diploma conferred through public school.

ROXBURY

PERRIN HOUSE

46 Perrin St, Roxbury, MA 02119 (617) 427-5571 *Contact Person(s):* George Brice, Exec Dir
Setting and Background Information The facility was established in 1978. It is a group home for adolescent boys.
Referral Information For referral, contact the facility and forward the necessary materials. An interview will be scheduled.
Type of Facility
Funding Sources State.
Average Length of Stay 12-18 mos.
Types of Admissions Accepted Residential treatment; Group home placement; Wards of the state.
Sources of Referral Depts of correction; Social service depts.
Client Profile
Age Range of Clients Served Residential program: 12-18.
Characteristics Exhibited by Children Emotional handicaps; Learning disabilities.
IQ Range of Clients 70+.
Tuition and Fees
Room and Board Long term: $85.49/diem.
Placements Primarily Funded By Depts of corrections; Social service depts.

PERRIN HOUSE *(continued)*

Social and Rehabilitative Services
Therapeutic Services Offered Individual therapy; Group therapy; Family therapy; Independent living skills program; Recreation activities.
Professionals on Staff Social workers; Child care staff.
Educational and Vocational Services
Type(s) of Educational Programs Offered Off campus (Public; Private schools).

RUTLAND

THE DEVEREAUX FOUNDATION

2 Miles Rd, Rutland, MA 01543 (617) 886-4746 *Contact Person(s):* Kenneth Ayers, Admis Dir
Setting and Background Information The foundation was originally established in 1964 by a teacher. It is a division of a national organization, which was founded in 1912. Its 220-acre campus has educational buildings, dormitories and cottages. It has a residential treatment center and an autistic treatment center.
Referral Information For referral, contact the facility and forward necessary material. If appropriate, an 8-hr pre-placement evaluation will be held.
Type of Facility
Funding Sources Private; State; School depts.
Average Length of Stay Long term.
Types of Admissions Accepted Day treatment; Residential treatment.
Sources of Referral State depts of education; Local depts of education; State depts of mental health; Psychiatrists; Private sources; Depts of correction; Social service depts.
Client Profile
Age Range of Clients Served Residential program: 6-18.
Characteristics Exhibited by Children Emotional handicaps; Learning disabilities; Speech/Language disorders; Neurological impairments; Mental disabilities.
Tuition and Fees
Placements Primarily Funded By State depts of education; Local depts of education; State depts of mental health; Private sources; Depts of corrections; Social service depts.
Social and Rehabilitative Services
Therapeutic Approach The facility has a cognitive-developmental approach, combined with milieu treatment.
Therapeutic Services Offered Individual therapy; Group therapy; Family therapy; Independent living skills program; Recreation activities.
Professionals on Staff Psychiatrists; Psychologists; Social workers; Child care staff; Nurses.
Educational and Vocational Services
Type(s) of Educational Programs Offered On campus.
Profile of On Campus School Program Student to teacher ratio 8:1; *Credentials of teachers* Certified Special Needs; *Grades taught* Ungraded.
Vocational Education Programs/Degrees Offered Pre-vocational.

SPRINGFIELD

CHILDREN'S STUDY HOME

44 Sherman St, Springfield, MA 01109 (413) 739-5626 *Contact Person(s):* Teresa A Harris, Asst Dir
Setting and Background Information The facility was originally established in 1865 as a home for friendless women and children. There are 2 campus locations.
Referral Information Contact the facility and forward an application packet.
Type of Facility
Funding Sources Private; State.
Average Length of Stay Long term.
Types of Admissions Accepted Day treatment; Residential treatment.
Sources of Referral Local depts of education; Private sources; Social service depts.
Client Profile
Age Range of Clients Served Day programs: 6-18; Residential program: 6-18.
Characteristics Exhibited by Children Emotional handicaps; Learning disabilities.

Tuition and Fees
Placements Primarily Funded By Local depts of education; Social service depts.
Social and Rehabilitative Services
Therapeutic Services Offered Individual therapy; Group therapy; Family therapy; Recreation activities; Aftercare program with follow up.
Professionals on Staff Psychiatrists; Psychologists; Social workers; Child care staff; Nurses.
Educational and Vocational Services
Type(s) of Educational Programs Offered On campus; Off campus.
Degrees Offered 12th grade diploma; Certificate.

WAREHAM

WAREHAM KEY, FAMILY REUNIFICATION PROGRAM

102 Charge Pond Rd, Wareham, MA 02571 (617) 291-0058 *Contact Person(s):* Bart King, Prog Supv
Setting and Background Information The facility was established in 1986 by the Dept of Social Services.
Referral Information Referrals come only from Dept of Social Services.
Type of Facility
Funding Sources State.
Average Length of Stay 90 days, followed by 90 days of aftercare.
Types of Admissions Accepted Residential treatment.
Sources of Referral Social service depts; DSS.
Client Profile
Age Range of Clients Served Residential program: 12-16.
Characteristics Exhibited by Children Emotional handicaps.
Tuition and Fees
Placements Primarily Funded By Social service depts; DSS.
Social and Rehabilitative Services
Therapeutic Services Offered Family therapy; Recreation activities; Aftercare program with follow up.
Professionals on Staff Child care staff.
Educational and Vocational Services
Type(s) of Educational Programs Offered On campus.
Profile of On Campus School Program Number of teachers 1; *Number of classrooms* 1; *Student to teacher ratio* 5:1; *Length of school day* 9-2pm.

WATERTOWN

ORCHARD HOME

917 Belmont St, Watertown, MA 02172 (617) 489-1760 *Contact Person(s):* Brenda English, Dir
Setting and Background Information The facility was established in 1954 for younger adolescent girls. There is a large Victorian house and a school.
Referral Information Contact the facility and forward the necessary materials, including the presenting problem, psychological reports, and social history. If appropriate, an intake will be scheduled.
Type of Facility
Funding Sources Private.
Average Length of Stay Long term.
Types of Admissions Accepted Residential treatment; Group home placement.
Sources of Referral State depts of education; Local depts of education; State depts of mental health; Social service depts.
Client Profile
Age Range of Clients Served Residential program: 12-15.
Characteristics Exhibited by Children Emotional handicaps; Learning disabilities.
IQ Range of Clients 70-120.
Tuition and Fees
Room and Board Long term: $112.34/diem.
Tuition $41,000/year.
Placements Primarily Funded By Local depts of education; Social service depts.
Social and Rehabilitative Services
Therapeutic Approach The facility has a therapeutic milieu.
Therapeutic Services Offered Individual therapy; Group therapy; Family therapy; Recreation activities.
Professionals on Staff Psychiatrists; Psychologists; Social workers; Adjunctive therapists; Child care staff; Nurses.

ORCHARD HOME *(continued)*

Educational and Vocational Services
Type(s) of Educational Programs Offered On campus; Summer campus.
Profile of On Campus School Program Number of teachers 2; *Number of classrooms* 3; *Student to teacher ratio* 7:1; *Credentials of teachers* Certified Spec Ed; Remedial courses offered.

WENDELL

MAPLE VALLEY SCHOOL

PO Box 248, Wendell, MA 01379 (617) 544-6913 *Contact Person(s):* Trish White
Setting and Background Information Maple Valley School is a private residential and day treatment facility for boys which was established in 1973 as an approved special education facility by the Division of Special Education and as a group care facility by the Dept of Social Services. It is also licensed as a group care facility by the Massachusetts Office for Children. The campus is located in western Massachusetts in a rural community and consists of a large renovated farmhouse, office building, and dorm building.
Referral Information Referrals can be made by public agencies. The referral process includes forwarding the necessary background information and scheduling an interview. After the pre-placement visit, an admission decision will be made.
Type of Facility
Funding Sources State.
Average Length of Stay Long term.
Types of Admissions Accepted Day treatment; Residential treatment.
Sources of Referral State depts of education; Local depts of education; Social service depts.
Client Profile
Age Range of Clients Served Day programs: 13-18; Residential program: 13-18.
Characteristics Exhibited by Children Emotional handicaps; Learning disabilities.
Tuition and Fees
Room and Board Long term: $148.03/diem.
Placements Primarily Funded By Social service depts.
Social and Rehabilitative Services
Therapeutic Approach The philosophy of the treatment program is based on a wide range of treatment modalities with emphasis on milieu, behavior modification, and reality therapy.
Therapeutic Services Offered Individual therapy; Group therapy; Family therapy; Adjunctive therapy; Independent living skills program; Recreation activities; Substance abuse treatment.
Professionals on Staff Psychiatrists; Social workers; Adjunctive therapists; Child care staff; Nurses.
Educational and Vocational Services
Type(s) of Educational Programs Offered On campus.
Profile of On Campus School Program Number of teachers 5; *Number of classrooms* 6; *Student to teacher ratio* 5:1.
Degrees Offered 12th grade diploma; GED.

WEST SPRINGFIELD

OUR LADY OF PROVIDENCE CHILDREN'S CENTER

2112 Riverdale St, West Springfield, MA 01089 (413) 788-7366
Contact Person(s): C David Scanlin, Dir of Res & Day Treatment Srvs
Setting and Background Information The facility was originally established in 1881 as an orphanage. Its 23-acre campus has 5 cottages and an administration building.
Referral Information For referral, contact the facility.
Type of Facility
Funding Sources State; Federal; Donations.
Average Length of Stay Long term.
Types of Admissions Accepted Day treatment; Residential treatment; Group home placement.
Sources of Referral State depts of education; Local depts of education; State depts of mental health; Depts of correction; Social service depts.

Client Profile
Age Range of Clients Served Day programs: 6-15; Residential program: 6-15.
Characteristics Exhibited by Children Emotional handicaps; Learning disabilities; Speech/Language disorders.
Tuition and Fees
Placements Primarily Funded By State depts of education; Local depts of education; Social service depts.
Social and Rehabilitative Services
Therapeutic Approach The center has a psychodynamic approach to therapy and uses behavior management.
Therapeutic Services Offered Individual therapy; Group therapy; Family therapy.
Professionals on Staff Psychiatrists; Psychologists; Social workers; Child care staff; Nurses.
Educational and Vocational Services
Type(s) of Educational Programs Offered On campus; Off campus.
Profile of On Campus School Program Number of teachers 10; *Number of classrooms* 7; *Student to teacher ratio* 8:1; *Credentials of teachers* Spec Ed; *Grades taught* 1-8; Special curriculum electives offered (Woodworking, Cooking, Sewing, Swimming, Outdoor education).
Degrees Offered GED.

PACE CENTER

470 Westfield St, West Springfield, MA 01089 (413) 737-2679
Contact Person(s): Kally Walsh, Res Coord
Setting and Background Information This program was established in 1982. There is a school/office building, with three residences in the community.
Referral Information Contact the facility for a group care referral packet. If appropriate, a pre-placement interview and overnight visit will be scheduled.
Type of Facility
Funding Sources State.
Average Length of Stay Long term.
Types of Admissions Accepted Day treatment school; Residential treatment.
Sources of Referral State depts of education; Local depts of education; State depts of mental health; Social service depts.
Client Profile
Age Range of Clients Served Day programs: 12-21+; Residential program: 12-21+.
Characteristics Exhibited by Children Emotional handicaps.
IQ Range of Clients 80-125.
Tuition and Fees
Room and Board Long term: $89.03/diem.
Tuition $74.38/diem.
Placements Primarily Funded By Local depts of education; Social service depts.
Social and Rehabilitative Services
Therapeutic Services Offered Individual therapy; Group therapy; Family therapy; Independent living skills program.
Professionals on Staff Psychiatrists; Social workers; Child care staff; Nurses.
Educational and Vocational Services
Type(s) of Educational Programs Offered On campus.
Profile of On Campus School Program Number of teachers 2; *Number of classrooms* 1; *Student to teacher ratio* 4:1; *Grades taught* 7-12; Special curriculum electives offered (Art).

WESTBORO

JUSTICE RESOURCE INSTITUTE, THE BUTLER CENTER

PO Box 432, Lyman St, Westboro, MA 01591 (617) 366-8870
Contact Person(s): Edward St John ACSW, Dir
Setting and Background Information The institute was established in 1984 with funding from a DYS contract. It is a secure residential treatment facility.
Referral Information Adjudicated youth are referred to the facility through the Dept of Youth Services based on a history of violent and sexually deviant behaviors.
Type of Facility
Funding Sources State.
Average Length of Stay Approx 18 mos.
Types of Admissions Accepted Residential treatment.
Sources of Referral Dept of Youth Svcs.

JUSTICE RESOURCE INSTITUTE, THE BUTLER CENTER (continued)

Client Profile
Age Range of Clients Served Residential program: 15-18.
Characteristics Exhibited by Children Emotional handicaps; Learning disabilities.
Tuition and Fees
Room and Board Long term: $60,000/yr.
Tuition $20,000/yr.
Placements Primarily Funded By State depts of education; Dept of Youth Svcs.
Social and Rehabilitative Services
Therapeutic Approach The basic therapeutic approach of the facility is ego developmental.
Therapeutic Services Offered Individual therapy; Group therapy; Family therapy; Art therapy; Recreation activities.
Professionals on Staff Psychiatrists; Psychologists; Social workers; Adjunctive therapists; Child care staff; Nurses; Art therapists.
Educational and Vocational Services
Type(s) of Educational Programs Offered On campus.
Profile of On Campus School Program Number of teachers 4; *Number of classrooms* 4; *Student to teacher ratio* 4:1; *Credentials of teachers* Licensed; *Grades taught* Individualized; Remedial courses offered.

WESTBORO SECURE TREATMENT

Box 432, Westboro, MA 01581 (617) 727-7845 *Contact Person(s):* John A DeBenedetto, Jr, Dir
Setting and Background Information The facility was established in 1979 by establishing a treatment unit within the Dept of Youth Services. It is located on the grounds of the Westboro State Hospital.
Referral Information Referrals are made through the Dept of Youth Services.
Type of Facility
Funding Sources State.
Average Length of Stay Long term.
Types of Admissions Accepted Residential treatment; Locked facility.
Sources of Referral Dept of Youth Svcs.
Client Profile
Age Range of Clients Served Residential program: 15-18.
IQ Range of Clients 80+.
Tuition and Fees
Room and Board Long term: $55,000/yr.
Placements Primarily Funded By Dept of Youth Services.
Social and Rehabilitative Services
Therapeutic Approach The basic approach of the facility is reality therapy.
Therapeutic Services Offered Individual therapy; Group therapy; Family therapy; Independent living skills program; Recreation activities; Substance abuse treatment; Aftercare program with follow up.
Professionals on Staff Psychologists; Social workers; Adjunctive therapists; Child care staff; Nurses.
Educational and Vocational Services
Type(s) of Educational Programs Offered On campus.
Profile of On Campus School Program Number of teachers 4; *Number of classrooms* 4; *Student to teacher ratio* 4:1; *Credentials of teachers* Certified; Special curriculum electives offered (Computers, GED, Photography, Carpentry).
Degrees Offered GED; Certificates.

WESTLAKE ACADEMY

PO Box 288, Westboro, MA 01851 (617) 366-9887 *Contact Person(s):* Donald Mosher, Dir
Setting and Background Information The facility was established in 1985 with monies from the Dept of Mental Health in order to establish programs for adolescents. It is a unit in a psychiatric hospital.
Referral Information Contact the facility for referral information.
Type of Facility
Funding Sources State.
Average Length of Stay 1 ½ yrs.
Types of Admissions Accepted Residential treatment.
Sources of Referral State depts of mental health; Depts of correction; Social service depts.

Client Profile
Age Range of Clients Served Residential program: 15-21.
Characteristics Exhibited by Children Emotional handicaps; Learning disabilities; Neurological impairments; Mental disabilities.
Tuition and Fees
Room and Board Long term: $57,000/yr.
Social and Rehabilitative Services
Therapeutic Approach The facility offers milieu therapy.
Therapeutic Services Offered Individual therapy; Group therapy; Family therapy; Adjunctive therapy; Independent living skills program; Recreation activities; Substance abuse treatment.
Professionals on Staff Psychiatrists; Social workers; Adjunctive therapists; Child care staff; Nurses; Clinical director.
Educational and Vocational Services
Type(s) of Educational Programs Offered On campus.
Profile of On Campus School Program Number of teachers 4; *Number of classrooms* 4; *Student to teacher ratio* 3:1; *Credentials of teachers* BA, MA; Remedial courses offered.
Degrees Offered 12th grade diploma; GED.

WOODS HOLE

PENIKESE ISLAND SCHOOL

PO Box 161, 3 Little Harbor Rd, Woods Hole, MA 02543
(617) 548-7276 *Contact Person(s):* David Masch, Dir
Setting and Background Information The school was established in 1973. The 75-acre campus has a large house, a barn and boat building shop, a school, a large workshop, and out buildings.
Referral Information Contact the facility for referral information. There is a two-week trial period.
Type of Facility
Funding Sources Private.
Average Length of Stay Long term.
Types of Admissions Accepted Residential treatment.
Sources of Referral State depts of education; Local depts of education; State depts of mental health; Private sources; Depts of correction; Social service depts.
Client Profile
Age Range of Clients Served Residential program: 12-18.
Characteristics Exhibited by Children Learning disabilities; Behavior disorders; Delinquency.
IQ Range of Clients 70+.
Tuition and Fees
Room and Board Long term: $93.39/diem.
Placements Primarily Funded By Local depts of education; Social service depts; Dept of Youth Svcs.
Social and Rehabilitative Services
Therapeutic Approach The basic approach of the facility is reality therapy.
Professionals on Staff Psychiatrists; Psychologists; Social workers; Child care staff.
Educational and Vocational Services
Type(s) of Educational Programs Offered On campus; Summer campus.
Profile of On Campus School Program Student to teacher ratio 3:1.
Vocational Education Programs/Degrees Offered Pre-vocational.
Degrees Offered GED.

WORCESTER

COMMUNITY TREATMENT COMPLEX

340 Main St, Worcester, MA 01608 (617) 755-3698 *Contact Person(s):* Barry Walsh, Exec Dir
Setting and Background Information The facility was established in 1976 with DMH funding for disturbed adolescents. There are three community residential sites.
Referral Information Contact the facility for referral information.
Type of Facility
Funding Sources Private; State; Local schools.
Average Length of Stay Long term.
Types of Admissions Accepted Day treatment; Residential treatment; Group home placement; Wards of the state.
Sources of Referral Local depts of education; State depts of mental health; Private sources; Social service depts.
Client Profile
Age Range of Clients Served Day programs: 12-21+; Residential program: 12-21+.
Characteristics Exhibited by Children Emotional handicaps.

COMMUNITY TREATMENT COMPLEX *(continued)*

IQ Range of Clients 80-130.

Tuition and Fees

Room and Board Long term: $21,000-38,000/yr.

Tuition $15,603/yr.

Placements Primarily Funded By Local depts of education; State depts of mental health; Social service depts.

Social and Rehabilitative Services

Therapeutic Services Offered Individual therapy; Group therapy; Family therapy; Psychopharmacology.

Professionals on Staff Psychiatrists; Psychologists; Social workers; Child care staff; Nurses.

Educational and Vocational Services

Type(s) of Educational Programs Offered On campus; Off campus (Academic; Vocational training).

Profile of On Campus School Program Number of teachers 6; *Number of classrooms* 7; *Student to teacher ratio* 6:1; *Credentials of teachers* BA, MEd; *Grades taught* 6-12; Special curriculum electives offered; Remedial courses offered.

Vocational Education Programs/Degrees Offered Vocational training; Supported work placement.

Degrees Offered 12th grade diploma.

MICHIGAN

ADRIAN

MAURICE SPEAR CAMPUS

2910 Airport Rd, Adrian, MI 49221 (517) 265-5171 *Contact Person(s):* Dorman Borders

Setting and Background Information Maurice Spear Campus is a county operated facility for court ordered placements. The facility was established in 1962 as a treatment center for delinquent youth by Lenawee County Commissioners and Judge Maurice Spear. The campus is located on 35 acres of farmland, across from the Lenawee County Airport, and consists of a secure detention unit (20 adolescents), residential treatment center (40 adolescents), special education school, gymnasium, and chapel.

Referral Information Referrals can be made by Michigan Probate Courts and Dept of Social Services. The facility accepts only adjudicated delinquents.

Type of Facility
Funding Sources Private; State; County.
Average Length of Stay Long term.
Types of Admissions Accepted Residential treatment; Wards of the state.
Sources of Referral Depts of correction.

Client Profile
Age Range of Clients Served Residential program: 13-16.
Characteristics Exhibited by Children Emotional handicaps; Learning disabilities; Speech/Language disorders; Delinquency.
IQ Range of Clients 85+.

Tuition and Fees
Room and Board Long term: $75/diem.
Placements Primarily Funded By Depts of corrections; Social service depts.

Social and Rehabilitative Services
Therapeutic Approach The treatment program utilizes reality therapy, behavior modification, and milieu therapy approaches.
Therapeutic Services Offered Individual therapy; Group therapy; Family therapy; Adjunctive therapy; Art therapy; Physical therapy; Independent living skills program; Recreation activities; Substance abuse treatment; Aftercare program with follow up.
Professionals on Staff Social workers; Child care staff.

Educational and Vocational Services
Type(s) of Educational Programs Offered On campus; Off campus; Summer campus.
Profile of On Campus School Program Number of teachers 6; *Number of classrooms* 7; *Student to teacher ratio* 10:1; *Credentials of teachers* Spec Ed; *Grades taught* K-12; Special curriculum electives offered.

ANN ARBOR

ARBOR HEIGHTS CENTER

1447 Washington Heights, Ann Arbor, MI 48104 (313) 994-1661
Contact Person(s): Jan Fisher

Setting and Background Information The facility was established by the Michigan Dept of Services for Children who were wards of the state. It is located on the University of Michigan campus.

Referral Information To make a referral, a community worker from the Social Services Dept must forward the necessary background information. After reviewing the material, the facility will arrange an interview with the child and family before a placement decision is made.

Type of Facility
Funding Sources State; Federal.
Average Length of Stay Long term.
Types of Admissions Accepted Residential treatment; Wards of the state.
Sources of Referral Social service depts.

Client Profile
Age Range of Clients Served Residential program: 13-19.
Characteristics Exhibited by Children Emotional handicaps; Learning disabilities; Speech/Language disorders.

Tuition and Fees
Placements Primarily Funded By Social service depts; Federal.

Social and Rehabilitative Services
Therapeutic Approach The philosophy of the treatment program is based on a systems approach involving transactional analysis and positive peer culture.
Therapeutic Services Offered Individual therapy; Group therapy; Family therapy; Recreation activities.
Professionals on Staff Psychiatrists; Psychologists; Social workers; Child care staff.

Educational and Vocational Services
Type(s) of Educational Programs Offered On campus.
Profile of On Campus School Program Student to teacher ratio 5:1.
Degrees Offered 8th grade diploma; 12th grade diploma; GED.

DEARBORN HEIGHTS

VISTA MARIA

20651 W Waren, Dearborn Heights, MI 48127 (313) 271-3050
Contact Person(s): Beth Jeross

Setting and Background Information The original facility, House of the Good Shepherd, was founded in 1883 by the Sisters of the Good Shepherd to provide services to girls with problems. In 1942, the program moved to its present location and was renamed Vista Maria. The campus is located in a suburb of Detroit on 37 acres and consists of 5 residence buildings, school and training center, gymnasium, exercise rooms, administration building, 2 convents, chapel, swimming pool, tennis court, ball field and power house.

Referral Information Referrals can be made by state or county social workers and juvenile court. A pre-placement visit will be scheduled.

Type of Facility
Funding Sources Private.
Average Length of Stay Short and long term.
Types of Admissions Accepted Residential treatment; Group home placement; Wards of the state; Emergency shelter.
Sources of Referral Depts of correction; Social service depts.

Client Profile
Age Range of Clients Served Day programs: 13-17; Residential program: 13-17.
Characteristics Exhibited by Children Emotional handicaps; Learning disabilities.

Tuition and Fees
Placements Primarily Funded By Depts of corrections; Social service depts.

Social and Rehabilitative Services
Therapeutic Services Offered Individual therapy; Group therapy; Family therapy; Independent living skills program; Recreation activities; Aftercare program with follow up.

VISTA MARIA *(continued)*

Educational and Vocational Services
Type(s) of Educational Programs Offered On campus; Off campus;
Summer campus.
Profile of On Campus School Program Number of teachers 18;
Number of classrooms 18; *Student to teacher ratio* 6:1; *Grades
taught* 7-12; Remedial courses offered.
Degrees Offered 12th grade diploma; GED.

EATON RAPIDS

VETERANS OF FOREIGN WARS NATIONAL HOME

Eaton Rapids, MI 48827 (517) 663-1521 *Contact Person(s):* Dr
Theodore H Wilson III
Setting and Background Information The home was established in
1925 to care for widows and children of members of the Veterans
of Foreign Wars. Its campus is located 20 miles south of Lansing,
on 640 acres, and consists of 35 group homes (4-6 children per
cottage), gymnasium, library, chapel, and recreation field.
Referral Information Referrals can be made by members of the
Veterans of Foreign Wars and its Ladies Auxiliary. To make a
referral, contact the facility and complete application materials. A
pre-placement visit is necessary before an admission decision is
made.
Type of Facility
Funding Sources Private.
Average Length of Stay Long term.
Types of Admissions Accepted Residential treatment; Group home
placement; Wards of the state.
Sources of Referral Private sources.
Client Profile
Age Range of Clients Served Residential program: Birth-18.
Characteristics Exhibited by Children Emotional handicaps; Learning
disabilities.
Tuition and Fees
Placements Primarily Funded By Private sources; VFW.
Social and Rehabilitative Services
Therapeutic Approach The treatment program utilizes insight coun-
seling, in conjunction with milieu therapy.
Therapeutic Services Offered Individual therapy; Group therapy;
Family therapy; Independent living skills program; Recreation
activities; Aftercare program with follow up.
Professionals on Staff Psychologists; Social workers; Adjunctive
therapists; Child care staff; Nurses.
Educational and Vocational Services
Type(s) of Educational Programs Offered Off campus.

EVART

PINEVIEW HOMES, INC

4490 E Oak Rd, Evart, MI 49631 (616) 734-2045 *Contact Person(s):*
Jerry Hendrick, Caseworker
Setting and Background Information The facility was established as a
group home approximately 19 years ago by Rev Lowell Dersheid.
It has gradually changed and expanded its programs to
encompass a larger population. The campus is located 2 miles
north of Evart, Michigan and consists of an office building, 3
residential units, director's home, school, chapel, gymnasium, and
an indoor swimming pool. The facility accepts boys only.
Referral Information Most referrals come from the Dept of Social
Services and the courts. Referrals can be made by contacting the
facility's director, or the casework supervisor.
Type of Facility
Funding Sources Private; State; Federal.
Average Length of Stay Long term.
Types of Admissions Accepted Residential treatment.
Sources of Referral State depts of education; Local depts of educa-
tion; State depts of mental health; Psychiatrists; Private sources;
Depts of correction; Social service depts.
Client Profile
Age Range of Clients Served Residential program: 7-17.
Characteristics Exhibited by Children Emotional handicaps; Learning
disabilities; Speech/Language disorders; Neurological impair-
ments; Physical handicaps; Mental disabilities.
Tuition and Fees
Room and Board Long term: $47.88/diem.
Placements Primarily Funded By Social service depts.

Social and Rehabilitative Services
Therapeutic Approach Staff are trained to implement transactional
analysis, reality therapy, and the psychoanalytic model in helping
students process their emotional and psychological problems.
Therapeutic Services Offered Individual therapy; Group therapy;
Physical therapy; Independent living skills program; Recreation
activities.
Professionals on Staff Psychiatrists; Psychologists; Social workers;
Adjunctive therapists; Child care staff.
Educational and Vocational Services
Type(s) of Educational Programs Offered On campus; Summer cam-
pus.
Profile of On Campus School Program Number of teachers 4; *Num-
ber of classrooms* 3; *Student to teacher ratio* 7:1; *Grades taught* 1-
12.

FARMINGTON HILLS

ST VINCENT—SARAH FISHER CENTER

27400 W 12 Mile Rd, Farmington Hills, MI 48018 (313) 626-7527
Contact Person(s): Catherine Lamb
Setting and Background Information The facility was initially
established as an orphanage and home for neglected children in
1851 and has since expanded its program to become a treatment
center. The campus is located on 50 acres of land and consists of
5 treatment cottages and an administration building with
recreational facilities.
Referral Information Referrals can be made by the courts, Dept of
Mental Health, and Dept of Social Services. Applicants are
requested to contact the facility through one of the agencies above
and forward the necessary background infomation. A pre-
placement visit will take place before an admission decision is
made.
Type of Facility
Funding Sources State.
Average Length of Stay Long term.
Types of Admissions Accepted Residential treatment; Wards of the
state.
Sources of Referral State depts of education; Local depts of educa-
tion; State depts of mental health; Psychiatrists; Social service
depts.
Client Profile
Age Range of Clients Served Residential program: 5-14.
Characteristics Exhibited by Children Emotional handicaps; Learning
disabilities; Speech/Language disorders; Neurological impair-
ments; Physical handicaps; Mental disabilities.
Tuition and Fees
Room and Board Long term: $175/diem.
Placements Primarily Funded By State depts of mental health; Social
service depts.
Social and Rehabilitative Services
Therapeutic Services Offered Individual therapy; Group therapy;
Family therapy; Recreation activities; Aftercare program with
follow up.
Professionals on Staff Psychiatrists; Psychologists; Social workers;
Child care staff; Nurses.
Educational and Vocational Services
Type(s) of Educational Programs Offered On campus; Off campus;
Summer campus.
Profile of On Campus School Program Number of teachers 5.

JONESVILLE

MANOR FOUNDATION

115 E St, Jonesville, MI 49250 (517) 849-2152 *Contact Person(s):*
Fred Prasser
Setting and Background Information The Manor Foundation was
started by a special education teacher for the Toledo School
System as a profit-making organization. It was converted to a
non-profit corporation in the 1940s and is governed by a board of
7 directors. The campus is located in the village of Jonesville, 90
miles west of Detroit, on 35 acres of land. It consists of an
educational facility, gymnasium, and recreational building.
Referral Information Anyone can make a referral by contacting Fred
Prasser. Applicants must forward psychological testing reports,
psychiatric reports, social history, and academic reports as part of
the admission procedure.

MANOR FOUNDATION *(continued)*

Type of Facility
Funding Sources Private; State.
Average Length of Stay Long term.
Types of Admissions Accepted Residential treatment; Wards of the state.
Sources of Referral State depts of education; Local depts of education; State depts of mental health; Psychiatrists; Private sources; Depts of correction.
Client Profile
Characteristics Exhibited by Children Emotional handicaps; Learning disabilities; Hearing impairments/deafness; Speech/Language disorders; Mental disabilities.
Tuition and Fees
Room and Board Long term: $77/diem (boys); $105/diem (girls).
Placements Primarily Funded By State depts of mental health; Private sources; Depts of corrections; Social service depts.
Social and Rehabilitative Services
Therapeutic Approach The primary therapeutic approach used is behavior modification in combination with dynamic and milieu therapy.
Therapeutic Services Offered Individual therapy; Group therapy; Independent living skills program; Recreation activities.
Professionals on Staff Social workers; Child care staff.
Educational and Vocational Services
Type(s) of Educational Programs Offered On campus; Off campus; Summer campus.
Profile of On Campus School Program Number of teachers 7; Number of classrooms 5; Student to teacher ratio 6:1; Grades taught K-12.
Vocational Education Programs/Degrees Offered Sheltered workshop program.
Degrees Offered 8th grade diploma; 12th grade diploma.

LOWELL

RIVERVIEW RESIDENTIAL TREATMENT FACILITIES

791 Flat River Dr, Lowell, MI 49331 (616) 897-5806 *Contact Person(s):* Jeffrey T Conklin
Setting and Background Information The facility consists of 4 group residential facilities located in the rural town of Lowell. There are also licensed intensive treatment foster homes located in and near the Kent County area. These homes are directly related to the residential facility and provide a thorough follow-up program.
Referral Information Referrals are made by probation officers, case workers, and social workers throughout the year.
Type of Facility
Funding Sources State.
Average Length of Stay Long term.
Types of Admissions Accepted Residential treatment; Wards of the state.
Sources of Referral State depts of mental health; Psychiatrists; Social service depts.
Client Profile
Age Range of Clients Served Residential program: 8-18.
Characteristics Exhibited by Children Emotional handicaps; Learning disabilities; Neurological impairments; Mental disabilities; Abused and neglected.
IQ Range of Clients 65+.
Tuition and Fees
Room and Board Long term: $115.14/diem.
Placements Primarily Funded By State depts of mental health; Social service depts.
Social and Rehabilitative Services
Therapeutic Approach A behavioral system makes up the core of the programs in conjunction with an eclectic reality based therapeutic approach.
Therapeutic Services Offered Individual therapy; Group therapy; Family therapy; Adjunctive therapy; Art therapy; Independent living skills program; Recreation activities; Aftercare program with follow up.
Professionals on Staff Psychiatrists; Psychologists; Social workers; Adjunctive therapists; Child care staff; Art therapists.

PRUDENVILLE

YOUTH REHABILITATION CAMPS—NOKOMIS

6300 S Reserve Rd, #G, Prudenville, MI 48651 (517) 366-5368
Contact Person(s): John J Castle
Setting and Background Information Youth Rehabilitation Camps is a state residential treatment program for the treatment of delinquent youth. The Nokomis Camp is located 4 ½ miles south of Houghton Lake.
Referral Information Referrals are accepted from the Michigan Dept of Social Services for adjudicated delinquent youth.
Type of Facility
Funding Sources State.
Average Length of Stay Long term.
Types of Admissions Accepted Residential treatment.
Sources of Referral Social service depts.
Client Profile
Age Range of Clients Served Residential program: 15-17.
Characteristics Exhibited by Children Emotional handicaps; Learning disabilities; Neurological impairments; Mental disabilities; Delinquency.
Tuition and Fees
Room and Board Long term: $97/diem.
Placements Primarily Funded By Social service depts.
Social and Rehabilitative Services
Therapeutic Services Offered Individual therapy; Group therapy; Family therapy; Independent living skills program; Recreation activities; Substance abuse treatment; Aftercare program with follow up.
Professionals on Staff Psychiatrists; Psychologists; Child care staff.
Educational and Vocational Services
Type(s) of Educational Programs Offered On campus.
Profile of On Campus School Program Number of teachers 3; Student to teacher ratio 10:1; Special curriculum electives offered.

WHITMORE LAKE

MAXEY TRAINING SCHOOL

PO Box 349, Whitmore Lake, MI 48189 (313) 449-4422
Setting and Background Information The facility was established in 1952 as a state training school for juvenile delinquents. Its campus is located in a rural area and consists of 5 residential centers; 3 medium security units and 2 maximum security units.
Referral Information Referrals can only be made by the Dept of Social Services.
Type of Facility
Funding Sources State.
Average Length of Stay Short and long term.
Types of Admissions Accepted Residential treatment.
Sources of Referral Social service depts.
Client Profile
Age Range of Clients Served Residential program: 12-19.
Characteristics Exhibited by Children Emotional handicaps; Learning disabilities; Hearing impairments/deafness; Vision impairments/blindness; Speech/Language disorders; Neurological impairments; Physical handicaps; Mental disabilities.
Tuition and Fees
Placements Primarily Funded By Social service depts.
Social and Rehabilitative Services
Therapeutic Approach The treatment programs utilize a group centered therapeutic approach based on Positive Peer Culture.
Therapeutic Services Offered Individual therapy; Group therapy; Adjunctive therapy; Recreation activities.
Professionals on Staff Psychiatrists; Psychologists; Social workers; Adjunctive therapists; Child care staff; Nurses.
Educational and Vocational Services
Type(s) of Educational Programs Offered On campus; Summer campus.
Profile of On Campus School Program Number of teachers 55; Number of classrooms 50; Student to teacher ratio 10:1; Special curriculum electives offered; Remedial courses offered.
Vocational Education Programs/Degrees Offered Vocational education program.
Degrees Offered GED.

MINNESOTA

ANOKA

BAR-NONE RESIDENTIAL TREATMENT SERVICES

22426 St Francis Blvd, Anoka, MN 55303 (612) 753-2500 *Contact Person(s):* Verlyn R Wenndt, Dir; Cathy Eareckson, Dir of Clin Srvs
Setting and Background Information The facility was established in 1955 with support from the Volunteers of America. The 700-acre campus has residential buildings, a school, offices and a lake. There is a residential center for youth with psychiatric problems and an intensive center for children with autism or neurological problems.
Referral Information Contact the facility. Written referral material is reviewed and evaluated. A pre-placement visit is arranged.
Type of Facility
Funding Sources Volunteers of America.
Average Length of Stay Long term.
Types of Admissions Accepted Residential treatment.
Sources of Referral State depts of education; Local depts of education; State depts of mental health; Psychiatrists; Private sources; Depts of correction; Social service depts.
Client Profile
Age Range of Clients Served Residential program: 6-21+.
Characteristics Exhibited by Children Emotional handicaps; Learning disabilities; Speech/Language disorders; Neurological impairments; Mental disabilities; Autism.
IQ Range of Clients 40-120.
Tuition and Fees
Room and Board Long term: $93.84/diem (residental center); $128/diem (intensive center).
Placements Primarily Funded By State depts of education; State depts of mental health; Insurance; Social service depts.
Social and Rehabilitative Services
Therapeutic Approach The residential center offers individual and milieu therapy. The intensive center uses behavior modification.
Therapeutic Services Offered Individual therapy; Group therapy; Family therapy; Adjunctive therapy; Independent living skills program; Recreation activities; Substance abuse treatment; Speech therapy.
Professionals on Staff Psychiatrists; Psychologists; Social workers; Adjunctive therapists; Child care staff; Nurses; Behavior analyst; Neurologist.
Educational and Vocational Services
Type(s) of Educational Programs Offered On campus (EBD; Vocational; DD); Off campus (Mainstream); Summer campus (EBD; Vocational; DD).
Profile of On Campus School Program Number of teachers 40; *Number of classrooms* 14; *Credentials of teachers* State licensed; *Grades taught* 1-12; Special curriculum electives offered (Woodshop, Art, Computer); Remedial courses offered (Math, Language, Arts, Speech).
Vocational Education Programs/Degrees Offered Pre-vocational program; Vocation program for neurologically impaired.
Degrees Offered 8th grade diploma; 12th grade diploma.

AUSTIN

GERARD OF MINNESOTA

PO Box 715, Austin, MN 55912 (507) 433-1843 *Contact Person(s):* Donna Gerlach, Dir of Admis
Setting and Background Information Gerard was established in 1969. It operates 2 facilities; one in Austin, Minnesota and another in Mason City, Iowa. The Minnesota facility is located northeast of Austin on a 12-acre estate. A 97-room mansion and 2 cottages house residential units, school, and a large arboretum, along with recreational areas. Gerard of Minnesota is accredited by the Joint Commission of Accreditation of Health Care Facilites.
Referral Information Referrals can be made by psychiatrists, physicians, psychologists, and social agencies (only with psychiatric consultation). To make a referral, contact the facility and forward the following information: psychiatric evaluations, psychological reports, school records, family history, neurological and physical reports, and developmental history reports.
Type of Facility
Funding Sources Private; State; Federal; Champus.
Average Length of Stay Long term.
Types of Admissions Accepted Residential treatment; Wards of the state.
Sources of Referral State depts of education; Local depts of education; State depts of mental health; Psychiatrists; Private sources; Depts of correction; Social service depts.
Client Profile
Age Range of Clients Served Residential program: 12-17.
Characteristics Exhibited by Children Emotional handicaps; Learning disabilities; Hearing impairments/deafness; Vision impairments/blindness; Speech/Language disorders; Neurological impairments; Physical handicaps; Mental disabilities.
IQ Range of Clients 80+.
Tuition and Fees
Placements Primarily Funded By State depts of education; Local depts of education; State depts of mental health; Insurance; Private sources; Depts of corrections; Social service depts.
Social and Rehabilitative Services
Therapeutic Approach The philosophy of the treatment program is based on developmental theory and is implemented through a highly structured individualized milieu therapy program.
Therapeutic Services Offered Individual therapy; Group therapy; Family therapy; Recreation activities.
Professionals on Staff Psychiatrists; Psychologists; Child care staff; Nurses; Physical therapists.
Educational and Vocational Services
Type(s) of Educational Programs Offered On campus; Off campus; Summer campus.
Profile of On Campus School Program Number of teachers 7; *Number of classrooms* 7; *Grades taught* 7-12; Remedial courses offered.
Degrees Offered 12th grade diploma; GED.

SHERIFFS YOUTH PROGRAMS

PO Box 249, Austin, MN 55912 (507) 433-0100 *Contact Person(s):* Sandy Jarvis
Setting and Background Information The organization was founded by the Minnesota State Sheriffs Association and has a variety of treatment programs. The Austin Ranch facility has 4 residential cottages, a school, shop/arts and crafts building, barn, and other farm buildings. The Isanti Ranch has 4 residential cottages, school, gymnasium, greenhouse, dining hall, and offices. There is

SHERIFFS YOUTH PROGRAMS *(continued)*

also a 10-bed group home in Mankato, a 12-bed co-educational group home in Hayward, and 14 community-based foster homes.

Referral Information Referrals can be made by social workers and probation officers from any county in Minnesota. To make a referral contact the intake worker to provide her with the necessary preliminary information. A pre-placement visit with the Program Director will take place before a placement decision is made.

Type of Facility
Funding Sources Private; State.
Average Length of Stay Long term.
Types of Admissions Accepted Residential treatment; Group home placement; Wards of the state.
Sources of Referral Depts of correction; Social service depts.
Client Profile
Age Range of Clients Served Residential program: 11-18.
Characteristics Exhibited by Children Emotional handicaps; Learning disabilities; Mental disabilities.
IQ Range of Clients 65+.
Tuition and Fees
Room and Board Long term: $92/diem.
Placements Primarily Funded By Private sources; Depts of corrections; Social service depts.
Social and Rehabilitative Services
Therapeutic Approach The philosophy of the treatment program is based on humanistic psychology and developmental theory.
Therapeutic Services Offered Individual therapy; Group therapy; Family therapy; Adjunctive therapy; Independent living skills program; Recreation activities; Aftercare program with follow up.
Professionals on Staff Psychologists; Social workers; Adjunctive therapists; Child care staff; Nurses; Family therapist.
Educational and Vocational Services
Type(s) of Educational Programs Offered On campus; Off campus; Summer campus.
Profile of On Campus School Program Number of teachers 16; *Number of classrooms* 9; *Student to teacher ratio* 5:1; Remedial courses offered.
Degrees Offered 8th grade diploma; 12th grade diploma; GED.

BEMIDJI

NORTHWESTERN MINNESOTA JUVENILE TRAINING CENTER

B-Wing, Birch Hall, Bemidji State University, Bemidji, MN 56601-2651 (218) 751-3196 *Contact Person(s):* Joseph Vene, Supt

Setting and Background Information The facility was established in 1972 and is licensed by the state Dept of Corrections. It has a site on the Bemidji State University and 4 extension satellite homes in outlying communities.
Referral Information Referrals are made through the courts.
Type of Facility
Funding Sources State; County.
Average Length of Stay Short and long term.
Types of Admissions Accepted Residential treatment.
Sources of Referral Depts of correction; Social service depts.
Client Profile
Age Range of Clients Served Residential program: 12-18.
Characteristics Exhibited by Children Emotional handicaps; Learning disabilities; Character disorders.
IQ Range of Clients 60-150.
Tuition and Fees
Room and Board Short term: $48/diem; Long term: $52/diem.
Tuition $19/diem.
Placements Primarily Funded By Depts of corrections; Social service depts.
Social and Rehabilitative Services
Therapeutic Approach The basic approach of the facility is reality therapy.
Therapeutic Services Offered Individual therapy; Group therapy; Family therapy; Adjunctive therapy; Independent living skills program; Substance abuse treatment.
Professionals on Staff Psychiatrists; Psychologists; Social workers; Adjunctive therapists; Child care staff; Nurses.

Educational and Vocational Services
Type(s) of Educational Programs Offered On campus; Off campus; Summer campus.
Profile of On Campus School Program Number of teachers 4; *Number of classrooms* 3; *Student to teacher ratio* 6:1; *Credentials of teachers* LD/EBD; *Grades taught* 6-12; Special curriculum electives offered; Remedial courses offered (Basic skills).
Degrees Offered GED.

BRAINERD

MINNESOTA LEARNING CENTER

1777 Highway 18 E, Brainerd, MN 56401 (218) 828-2317 *Contact Person(s):* Sue Roelandt, Intake Sco Wkr

Setting and Background Information The facility was established in 1972 by legislative action. It is located on the campus of Brainerd Regional Human Services Center and offers a range of services.
Referral Information Referrals are made through the county social service agency.
Type of Facility
Funding Sources Private; State; Federal.
Average Length of Stay Long term.
Types of Admissions Accepted Day treatment; Residential treatment.
Sources of Referral Social service depts.
Client Profile
Age Range of Clients Served Day programs: 6-18; Residential program: 6-18.
Characteristics Exhibited by Children Emotional handicaps; Learning disabilities; Mental disabilities.
IQ Range of Clients 76-115.
Tuition and Fees
Room and Board Long term: Sliding scale.
Placements Primarily Funded By Social service depts.
Social and Rehabilitative Services
Therapeutic Approach The facility uses the behavioral and cognitive therapies.
Therapeutic Services Offered Individual therapy; Group therapy; Family therapy; Recreation activities; Aftercare program with follow up.
Professionals on Staff Psychiatrists; Psychologists; Social workers; Adjunctive therapists; Child care staff; Nurses.
Educational and Vocational Services
Type(s) of Educational Programs Offered On campus (EBD program); Off campus (Public school); Summer campus.
Profile of On Campus School Program Number of teachers 3; *Number of classrooms* 3; *Student to teacher ratio* 9:1; *Credentials of teachers* EBD; *Grades taught* Ungraded; Special curriculum electives offered (Art, Home Ec, Wood working); Remedial courses offered (Reading, Math, Language).
Vocational Education Programs/Degrees Offered Vocational class, Supervised work experience.

PORT OF CROW WING COUNTY, INC

110 NW 2nd St, Brainerd, MN 56401 (218) 829-0263 *Contact Person(s):* John Fellerer, Exec Dir

Setting and Background Information The facility was established in 1972 when a group of citizens formed a corporation. Located on the Mississippi River, there are two large houses on three acres.
Referral Information Referrals are made through court services or social services.
Type of Facility
Funding Sources County.
Average Length of Stay Long term.
Types of Admissions Accepted Group home placement.
Sources of Referral Depts of correction; Social service depts.
Client Profile
Age Range of Clients Served Residential program: 12-18.
Characteristics Exhibited by Children Emotional handicaps; Mental disabilities.
IQ Range of Clients 75-100.
Tuition and Fees
Room and Board Long term: $48.50/diem (includes school tuition).
Placements Primarily Funded By Depts of corrections; Social service depts.

PORT OF CROW WING COUNTY, INC *(continued)*

Social and Rehabilitative Services
Therapeutic Approach The facility uses directive counseling.
Therapeutic Services Offered Individual therapy; Group therapy;
Family therapy; Independent living skills program; Substance
abuse treatment.
Professionals on Staff Psychologists; Social workers; Adjunctive
therapists; Child care staff.

BRECKENRIDGE

VALLEY-LAKE BOYS HOME, INC
Box 411, Breckenridge, MN 56520 (218) 643-4036 *Contact
Person(s):* Mark Engebretson, Dir
Setting and Background Information The facility was established in
1975 with monies from federal and state grants. The 9.5-acre
campus is located in a rural setting with an office, a main
building, and various outbuildings.
Referral Information Referrals are made by court services and social
service agencies.
Type of Facility
Funding Sources County.
Average Length of Stay Long term.
Types of Admissions Accepted Residential treatment; Group home
placement.
Sources of Referral Depts of correction; Social service depts.
Client Profile
Age Range of Clients Served Residential program: 12-18.
Characteristics Exhibited by Children Emotional handicaps.
IQ Range of Clients 80+.
Tuition and Fees
Room and Board Long term: $22.55/diem.
Tuition $32.45/diem.
Placements Primarily Funded By Social service depts.
Social and Rehabilitative Services
Therapeutic Approach The facility uses reality therapy and behavior
modification.
Therapeutic Services Offered Individual therapy; Group therapy;
Family therapy; Independent living skills program; Aftercare pro-
gram with follow up.
Professionals on Staff Child care staff.
Educational and Vocational Services
Type(s) of Educational Programs Offered Off campus (Public school).

CLOQUET

SHELTER SERVICES OF CARLTON COUNTY, INC
531 Slate St, Cloquet, MN 55720 (218) 879-1527, 879-1528 *Contact
Person(s):* Barbara Petersen, Exec Dir
Setting and Background Information The facility was established in
1978 by a community task force.
Referral Information Children are referred to the facility by courts,
law enforcement agencies, and local social service agencies. Self
referrals are also accepted.
Type of Facility
Funding Sources Private.
Average Length of Stay Short term.
Types of Admissions Accepted Emergency shelter.
Sources of Referral Depts of correction; Social service depts; Law
enforcement.
Client Profile
Age Range of Clients Served Residential program: Birth-18.
Characteristics Exhibited by Children Emotional handicaps; Learning
disabilities; Hearing impairments/deafness; Vision impairments/
blindness; Speech/Language disorders; Neurological impairments;
Physical handicaps; Mental disabilities; Abused and neglected.
IQ Range of Clients 80-140.
Tuition and Fees
Room and Board Short term: $68/diem.
Placements Primarily Funded By Social service depts.
Social and Rehabilitative Services
Therapeutic Approach The facility has an eclectic approach to ther-
apy.
Therapeutic Services Offered Individual therapy; Group therapy;
Family therapy; Family assessment.
Professionals on Staff Adjunctive therapists; Child care staff.

Educational and Vocational Services
Type(s) of Educational Programs Offered Off campus (Public school).

DULUTH

NORTHWOOD CHILDREN'S HOME
714 College St, Duluth, MN 55811 (218) 724-8815 *Contact
Person(s):* James Yeager, Exec Dir
Setting and Background Information The facility was originally
established in 1883 as a home for unmarried women and their
babies. Currently, the 4-acre campus has 3 large buildings. There
are also 3 satellite homes.
Referral Information Contact the facility and complete the referral
packet. A visit will be arranged.
Type of Facility
Funding Sources Private; State; Federal.
Average Length of Stay Long term.
Types of Admissions Accepted Day treatment; Residential treatment;
Group home placement; Wards of the state.
Sources of Referral State depts of education; Local depts of educa-
tion; State depts of mental health; Psychiatrists; Private sources;
Depts of correction; Social service depts; Parents.
Client Profile
Age Range of Clients Served Day programs: 6-15; Residential pro-
gram: 6-18.
Characteristics Exhibited by Children Emotional handicaps; Learning
disabilities; Speech/Language disorders; Neurological impair-
ments; Mental disabilities.
IQ Range of Clients 60-130.
Tuition and Fees
Room and Board Long term: $92/diem.
Placements Primarily Funded By Social service depts.
Social and Rehabilitative Services
Therapeutic Approach The facility uses a psycho-educational model.
Therapeutic Services Offered Individual therapy; Group therapy;
Family therapy; Art therapy; Independent living skills program;
Recreation activities; Aftercare program with follow up; Occupa-
tional therapy.
Professionals on Staff Psychiatrists; Psychologists; Social workers;
Child care staff; Nurses; Art therapists; Occupational therapists.
Educational and Vocational Services
Type(s) of Educational Programs Offered On campus.
Profile of On Campus School Program Number of teachers 8; *Num-
ber of classrooms* 8; *Student to teacher ratio* 8:1; *Credentials of
teachers* ED; *Length of school day* 6 hrs; *Grades taught* K-12;
Special curriculum electives offered (Music); Remedial courses
offered.
Vocational Education Programs/Degrees Offered Work experience
program; Welding; Upholstery; Bicycle repair; Small engine re-
pair.
Degrees Offered 8th grade diploma; 12th grade diploma.

WOODLAND HILLS
4321 Allendale Ave, Duluth, MN 55803 (218) 724-8528 *Contact
Person(s):* Ken Stafford
Setting and Background Information The facility was established in
1910 as a service agency for Catholic Charities, but became
incorporated as a separate agency in 1971. The campus is located
in Duluth on 150 acres of land and consists of residential units,
athletic facilities, and educational buildings.
Referral Information Referral can be made by parents, probation
officers, social service depts, and school districts. The referral
process is initiated by contacting an intake worker, then
completing the referral packet, whereupon a pre-placement visit is
arranged.
Type of Facility
Funding Sources Private; State; Federal.
Average Length of Stay Short and long term.
Types of Admissions Accepted Residential treatment; Wards of the
state.
Sources of Referral State depts of education; Local depts of educa-
tion; State depts of mental health; Psychiatrists; Private sources;
Depts of correction; Social service depts.
Client Profile
Age Range of Clients Served Residential program: 13-17.
Characteristics Exhibited by Children Emotional handicaps; Learning
disabilities.
IQ Range of Clients 80+.

WOODLAND HILLS *(continued)*

Tuition and Fees
Room and Board Long term: $87.95/diem.
Tuition $20.83/diem.
Placements Primarily Funded By Insurance; Private sources; Social service depts.
Social and Rehabilitative Services
Therapeutic Services Offered Individual therapy; Group therapy; Family therapy; Adjunctive therapy; Independent living skills program; Substance abuse treatment; Aftercare program with follow up.
Professionals on Staff Psychologists; Social workers; Adjunctive therapists; Child care staff; Nurses.
Educational and Vocational Services
Type(s) of Educational Programs Offered On campus.
Profile of On Campus School Program Number of teachers 6; *Number of classrooms* 4; *Student to teacher ratio* 2:1; *Grades taught* K-12; Special curriculum electives offered; Remedial courses offered.
Degrees Offered 12th grade diploma; GED.

EXCELSIOR

GATEWAY GROUP HOME
2600 Arboretum Blvd, Excelsior, MN 55331 (612) 474-4786 *Contact Person(s):* Charles T Gabrielson, Admin
Setting and Background Information The facility was established in 1976.
Referral Information For referral information contact the facility. A pre-placement inerview and visit will be scheduled. There is a 30-day probationary period.
Type of Facility
Funding Sources State.
Average Length of Stay Long term.
Types of Admissions Accepted Group home placement; Wards of the state.
Sources of Referral Depts of correction; Social service depts.
Client Profile
Age Range of Clients Served Residential program: 12-18.
Characteristics Exhibited by Children Emotional handicaps; Learning disabilities; Delinquency.
IQ Range of Clients 80+.
Tuition and Fees
Room and Board Long term: $64.50/diem.
Placements Primarily Funded By Depts of corrections; Social service depts.
Social and Rehabilitative Services
Therapeutic Approach The basic approach of the facility is reality therapy.
Therapeutic Services Offered Individual therapy; Group therapy; Family therapy; Independent living skills program; Recreation activities; Aftercare program with follow up; Pet therapy.
Educational and Vocational Services
Type(s) of Educational Programs Offered Off campus.

FARIBAULT

THE CONSTANCE BULTMAN WILSON CENTER
Box 917, Faribault, MN 55021 (507) 334-5561, 1-800-328-4873 (referrals only) *Contact Person(s):* Dee Monson, Dir of Admis; Bernie Orhn, Asst Dir of Admis
Setting and Background Information The Wilson Center is a private, psychiatric hospital for adolescents, which was founded by M Robert Wilson, MD, in 1971. Dr Wilson came from the Mayo Clinic to establish a psychiatric unit for adolescents which included treatment, medical care, and accredited school program. The facility is located 50 miles south of Minneapolis on 35 acres of wooded bluffs. Its modern facilities include 5 separate units, each having 10 patient rooms, lounge, laundry facilities, staff office, snack kitchen, and nurses' station. The campus also has a swimming pool, tennis courts, football field, and gymnasium.
Referral Information Referrals can be made by psychiatrists, psychologists, social workers, consultants, probation officers, or parents. To make a referral, contact the admissions dept and forward the necessary background information on the applicant, including approval of funding source. The facility will arrange for a 3 day 'Collaborative Evaluation' at the Center. This evaluation includes individual psychiatric and medical interviews with parents and adolescent, along with psychological and academic testing. Evaluation results are then presented to the Medical Director who will make the decision regarding admission.
Type of Facility
Funding Sources Private.
Average Length of Stay Long term.
Types of Admissions Accepted Residential treatment; Group home placement; Wards of the state.
Sources of Referral State depts of education; Local depts of education; State depts of mental health; Psychiatrists; Private sources; Depts of correction; Social service depts.
Client Profile
Age Range of Clients Served Residential program: 13-22.
Characteristics Exhibited by Children Emotional handicaps; Learning disabilities; Hearing impairments/deafness; Vision impairments/blindness; Speech/Language disorders; Neurological impairments; Physical handicaps; Mental disabilities; Behavior disorders.
IQ Range of Clients 70+.
Tuition and Fees
Placements Primarily Funded By State depts of education; Local depts of education; Insurance; Private sources.
Social and Rehabilitative Services
Therapeutic Approach The philosophy of the treatment program is psychoanalytically oriented.
Therapeutic Services Offered Individual therapy; Group therapy; Adjunctive therapy; Art therapy; Art therapy; Physical therapy; Independent living skills program; Recreation activities; Substance abuse treatment; Aftercare program with follow up.
Professionals on Staff Psychiatrists; Psychologists; Social workers; Adjunctive therapists; Child care staff; Nurses; Art therapists; Occupational therapist.
Educational and Vocational Services
Type(s) of Educational Programs Offered On campus; Summer campus.
Profile of On Campus School Program Number of teachers 17; *Number of classrooms* 17; *Student to teacher ratio* 4:1; Special curriculum electives offered (Tutoring); Remedial courses offered (College preparatory).
Degrees Offered 12th grade diploma; GED.

LACRESCENT

HOUSTON COUNTY GROUP HOME, LACRESCENT
1700 Lancer Blvd, LaCrescent, MN 55947 (507) 895-8111 *Contact Person(s):* Dennis Theede, Exec Dir
Setting and Background Information The facility was established in 1982 and has a capacity for 15 clients.
Referral Information Referrals to the facility are made through the Houston County Social Services.
Type of Facility
Funding Sources State; Federal.
Average Length of Stay Long term.
Types of Admissions Accepted Group home placement.
Sources of Referral Local depts of education; State depts of mental health; Social service depts.
Client Profile
Age Range of Clients Served Residential program: 6-55+.
Characteristics Exhibited by Children Emotional handicaps; Learning disabilities; Hearing impairments/deafness; Vision impairments/blindness; Speech/Language disorders; Neurological impairments; Physical handicaps; Mental disabilities.
IQ Range of Clients 0-70.
Tuition and Fees
Room and Board Long term: $100.72/diem.
Placements Primarily Funded By State depts of mental health; Social service depts.
Social and Rehabilitative Services
Therapeutic Approach The facility uses behavior management.
Therapeutic Services Offered Physical therapy; Independent living skills program; Recreation activities.
Professionals on Staff Psychologists; Social workers; Adjunctive therapists; Child care staff; Nurses; Physical therapists.
Educational and Vocational Services
Type(s) of Educational Programs Offered Off campus.

MARSHALL

TRY HOUSE CENTER

409 S 4th St, Marshall, MN 56258 (507) 532-9609 *Contact Person(s):* Karl Pfeiffer, Prog Dir

Setting and Background Information The facility was established in 1981. It is a community-based residential treatment center.

Referral Information Contact the facility for a referral application. An interview and/or visit will be arranged.

Type of Facility

Funding Sources Private.

Average Length of Stay Short and long term.

Types of Admissions Accepted Residential treatment; Wards of the state; Emergency shelter.

Sources of Referral Depts of correction; Social service depts; Juvenile court.

Client Profile

Age Range of Clients Served Residential program: 12-18.

Characteristics Exhibited by Children Emotional handicaps; Learning disabilities.

Tuition and Fees

Room and Board Short term: $68/diem; Long term: $68/diem.

Placements Primarily Funded By Depts of corrections; Social service depts.

Social and Rehabilitative Services

Therapeutic Services Offered Individual therapy; Group therapy; Family therapy; Adjunctive therapy; Independent living skills program; Recreation activities; Aftercare program with follow up.

Professionals on Staff Psychologists; Social workers; Adjunctive therapists; Child care staff.

Educational and Vocational Services

Type(s) of Educational Programs Offered Off campus (Local schools).

MINNEAPOLIS

THE CITY, INC—GROUP HOME

3222 16th Ave S, Minneapolis, MN 55407 (612) 729-0556 *Contact Person(s):* Deborah S Riba, Dir

Setting and Background Information The facility was established in 1975 in response to a community need.

Referral Information Contact the facility for referral information.

Type of Facility

Funding Sources Federal; County.

Average Length of Stay Long term.

Types of Admissions Accepted Group home placement.

Sources of Referral Social service depts.

Client Profile

Age Range of Clients Served Residential program: 12-18.

Characteristics Exhibited by Children Emotional handicaps.

Tuition and Fees

Room and Board Long term: $67.73/diem.

Placements Primarily Funded By Social service depts.

Social and Rehabilitative Services

Therapeutic Approach The facility uses cognitive therapy and behavior modification

Therapeutic Services Offered Individual therapy; Group therapy; Family therapy; Adjunctive therapy.

Professionals on Staff Psychologists; Child care staff.

FREEPORT WEST TREATMENT GROUP HOME

1-27th Ave SE, Minneapolis, MN 55414 (612) 338-7440 *Contact Person(s):* Janet E Berry, Exec Dir

Setting and Background Information The facility was established in 1976 with LEAA funds. It is a residential treatment group home with the capacity for 11 male residents.

Referral Information For referral, contact the facility and forward the most recent psychological, medical and dental records, and discharge summaries from other facilities. An intake interview will be scheduled.

Type of Facility

Funding Sources Private; County.

Average Length of Stay Long term.

Types of Admissions Accepted Group home placement; Wards of the state.

Sources of Referral Depts of correction; Social service depts.

Client Profile

Age Range of Clients Served Residential program: 12-18.

Characteristics Exhibited by Children Emotional handicaps; Learning disabilities.

Tuition and Fees

Room and Board Long term: $81.46/diem.

Placements Primarily Funded By Depts of corrections; Social service depts.

Social and Rehabilitative Services

Therapeutic Approach The program offers primarily an individual, relationship-based approach. It uses reality therapy and a concept of normalization.

Therapeutic Services Offered Individual therapy; Group therapy; Family therapy; Independent living skills program; Aftercare program with follow up.

Professionals on Staff Social workers; Child care staff.

Educational and Vocational Services

Type(s) of Educational Programs Offered Off campus (Community resources).

FRIENDSHIP HOUSE

2427 Park Ave S, Minneapolis, MN 55404 (612) 874-1231 *Contact Person(s):* Mary Sperl

Setting and Background Information The facility was established in South Minneapolis in 1974. It is housed in a large mansion containing a living room, dining room, kitchen, 3 recreation rooms, 9 bedrooms, 10 bathrooms, office space, storage areas, and a spacious yard. The facility accepts girls only.

Referral Information Referrals can be made by county social service agencies. The referring agency should contact the facility and forward the necessary background information.

Type of Facility

Funding Sources Private.

Average Length of Stay Long term.

Types of Admissions Accepted Residential treatment; Group home placement; Wards of the state.

Sources of Referral State depts of education; Local depts of education; Social service depts.

Client Profile

Age Range of Clients Served Residential program: 11-17.

Characteristics Exhibited by Children Emotional handicaps; Learning disabilities.

Tuition and Fees

Room and Board Long term: $103/diem.

Placements Primarily Funded By Insurance; Private sources; Social service depts.

Social and Rehabilitative Services

Therapeutic Services Offered Individual therapy; Group therapy; Family therapy; Adjunctive therapy; Independent living skills program; Recreation activities.

Professionals on Staff Psychiatrists; Psychologists; Social workers; Child care staff.

Educational and Vocational Services

Type(s) of Educational Programs Offered On campus; Off campus; Summer campus.

Profile of On Campus School Program Number of teachers 2; *Number of classrooms* 3; *Student to teacher ratio* 5:1; *Length of school day* 3 hrs; Remedial courses offered.

HOME AWAY CENTERS, INC.

2119 Pleasant Ave S, Minneapolis, MN 55404 (612) 871-7599 *Contact Person(s):* Corky Johnson, Dir

Setting and Background Information The facility was privately established in 1970. There are 2 residential homes in an urban community.

Referral Information Referral is made through depts of correction or social service depts.

Type of Facility

Funding Sources Private.

Average Length of Stay Long term.

Types of Admissions Accepted Residential treatment; Group home placement; Wards of the state.

Sources of Referral Depts of correction; Social service depts.

Client Profile

Age Range of Clients Served Residential program: 12-18.

Characteristics Exhibited by Children Emotional handicaps; Learning disabilities.

HOME AWAY CENTERS, INC. *(continued)*

Tuition and Fees
Room and Board Long term: $75.74/diem.
Placements Primarily Funded By Depts of corrections; Social service depts.
Social and Rehabilitative Services
Therapeutic Services Offered Group therapy; Family therapy; Adjunctive therapy; Aftercare program with follow up; Sexuality group.
Professionals on Staff Social workers; Adjunctive therapists; Child care staff.
Educational and Vocational Services
Type(s) of Educational Programs Offered Off campus (Public school).

NORTH STAR
3217 Nicolet Ave S, Minneapolis, MN 55417 (612) 871-3613
Contact Person(s): Nancy Hite, Dir
Setting and Background Information The facility was established in 1982 by a multi-disciplinary task force and funded by the local government. There is one small building with 8 beds.
Referral Information Referrals are made directly to the facility which accepts only females (aged 12-18) who are involved in prostitution.
Type of Facility
Funding Sources County.
Average Length of Stay Short and long term.
Sources of Referral Depts of correction; Social service depts; Self.
Client Profile
Age Range of Clients Served Residential program: 12-18.
Characteristics Exhibited by Children Emotional handicaps; Learning disabilities.
Tuition and Fees
Room and Board Long term: $100/diem.
Placements Primarily Funded By Social service depts.
Social and Rehabilitative Services
Therapeutic Approach The basic therapeutic approach of the facility is eclectic.
Therapeutic Services Offered Individual therapy; Group therapy; Family therapy; Art therapy; Independent living skills program; Aftercare program with follow up.
Professionals on Staff Psychologists; Social workers; Child care staff; Art therapists.
Educational and Vocational Services
Type(s) of Educational Programs Offered Off campus (Public school; Alternative schools).

PINE CITY

THERAPEUTIC SERVICES AGENCY
Rt 1 Box 9, Pine City, MN 55063 (612) 629-6748 *Contact Person(s):* Cheryl Snetana McHugh, Prog Dir
Setting and Background Information The agency was established in 1978. There are two buildings.
Referral Information Contact the facility for referral information.
Type of Facility
Funding Sources State; Federal; County.
Average Length of Stay Long term.
Types of Admissions Accepted Residential treatment.
Sources of Referral Depts of correction; Social service depts.
Client Profile
Age Range of Clients Served Residential program: 6-18.
Characteristics Exhibited by Children Emotional handicaps; Learning disabilities.
Tuition and Fees
Room and Board Long term: $75/diem.
Placements Primarily Funded By Social service depts.
Social and Rehabilitative Services
Therapeutic Services Offered Individual therapy; Group therapy; Family therapy; Recreation activities; Substance abuse treatment; Aftercare program with follow up.
Professionals on Staff Social workers; Adjunctive therapists; Child care staff.
Educational and Vocational Services
Type(s) of Educational Programs Offered Off campus.

ST CLOUD

ST CLOUD CHILDREN'S HOME
1726 7th Ave S, St Cloud, MN 53601 (612) 251-8811 *Contact Person(s):* John Doman
Setting and Background Information The facility was initially established as an orphanage in 1924. Its programs and services were expanded to become a treatment center in 1961 by Catholic Charities of the Diocese of St Cloud. The campus is located on 42 acres in a residential area, on the west bank of the Mississippi River. There are 6 cottage units, connected by hallways to a central area housing school facilities, gymnasium, and chapel. They are also connected to administrative and support service buildings.
Referral Information Referrals can be made by parents, social service agencies, psychiatrists, and other interested individuals. To make a referral, contact the Intake Coordinator and forward the necessary background information, including a psychological evaluation, social history, school records, medical and immunization records, and reports from previous placements.
Type of Facility
Funding Sources Private; State.
Average Length of Stay Long term.
Types of Admissions Accepted Day treatment; Residential treatment.
Sources of Referral State depts of education; Local depts of education; State depts of mental health; Psychiatrists; Private sources; Depts of correction; Social service depts.
Client Profile
Age Range of Clients Served Day programs: 8-18; Residential program: 8-18.
Characteristics Exhibited by Children Emotional handicaps; Learning disabilities.
Tuition and Fees
Room and Board Long term: $94.27/diem (includes school tuition).
Placements Primarily Funded By Insurance; Private sources; Depts of corrections; Social service depts.
Social and Rehabilitative Services
Therapeutic Approach The treatment program is primarily based on reality therapy, but at times, utilizes other approaches including behavior modification and Adlerian methods.
Therapeutic Services Offered Individual therapy; Group therapy; Family therapy; Adjunctive therapy; Independent living skills program; Recreation activities; Substance abuse treatment; Aftercare program with follow up.
Professionals on Staff Psychologists; Social workers; Adjunctive therapists; Child care staff; Nurses.
Educational and Vocational Services
Type(s) of Educational Programs Offered On campus; Off campus; Summer campus.
Profile of On Campus School Program Number of teachers 17; *Number of classrooms* 14; *Student to teacher ratio* 6:1; Remedial courses offered.
Degrees Offered 12th grade diploma.

ST PAUL

ALTERNATIVE HOMES, INC
1210 Albermarle, St Paul, MN 55117 (612) 488-7951 *Contact Person(s):* Howard Rod, Dir
Setting and Background Information The facility was established in 1977. It is a non-profit corporation and is funded by foundations. It is located in a residential area.
Referral Information Contact the facility for referral information.
Type of Facility
Funding Sources Private; State; Federal.
Average Length of Stay Long term.
Types of Admissions Accepted Residential treatment.
Client Profile
Age Range of Clients Served Day programs: 6-15; Residential program: 6-15.
Characteristics Exhibited by Children Emotional handicaps; Learning disabilities; Neurological impairments; Mental disabilities.
IQ Range of Clients 65-140.
Tuition and Fees
Placements Primarily Funded By Insurance; Private sources; Depts of corrections.

ALTERNATIVE HOMES, INC (continued)

Social and Rehabilitative Services
Therapeutic Approach The facility has an individualized approach to therapy.
Therapeutic Services Offered Individual therapy; Family therapy; Adjunctive therapy; Physical therapy; Independent living skills program; Recreation activities; Substance abuse treatment.
Professionals on Staff Psychiatrists; Psychologists; Social workers; Adjunctive therapists; Child care staff; Nurses; Physical therapists.
Educational and Vocational Services
Profile of On Campus School Program Remedial courses offered.
Vocational Education Programs/Degrees Offered Pre-vocational.

MARIA GROUP HOME

193 Maria Ave, St Paul, MN 55106 (612) 772-1344 *Contact Person(s):* Linda Kolander, Dir
Setting and Background Information This group home was established in 1972. It is a large home in a residential neighborhood.
Referral Information Contact the facility for referral information.
Type of Facility
Funding Sources Federal.
Average Length of Stay Long term.
Types of Admissions Accepted Group home placement.
Sources of Referral Social service depts.
Client Profile
Age Range of Clients Served Residential program: 12-18.
Characteristics Exhibited by Children Emotional handicaps; Learning disabilities.
IQ Range of Clients 70+.
Tuition and Fees
Room and Board Long term: $62.51.
Placements Primarily Funded By Depts of corrections; Social service depts.
Social and Rehabilitative Services
Therapeutic Approach The basic approach of the facility is reality therapy.
Therapeutic Services Offered Individual therapy; Group therapy; Family therapy; Independent living skills program; Substance abuse treatment.
Professionals on Staff Social workers; Child care staff.
Educational and Vocational Services
Type(s) of Educational Programs Offered On campus; Off campus.

NEW CONNECTION PROGRAMS, INC.

73 Leech St, St Paul, MN 55102 (612) 224-4384 *Contact Person(s):* Charles Mulvaney, Dir of Comm Relations
Setting and Background Information The program was established in 1970 with grant monies.
Referral Information Contact the admissions office for referral procedures.
Type of Facility
Funding Sources Private.
Average Length of Stay Short and long term.
Types of Admissions Accepted Day treatment; Residential treatment.
Sources of Referral State depts of education; Local depts of education; State depts of mental health; Psychiatrists; Private sources; Depts of correction; Social service depts.
Client Profile
Age Range of Clients Served Day programs: 12-18; Residential program: 12-18.
Characteristics Exhibited by Children Chemical abuse.
Tuition and Fees
Room and Board Short term: $215/diem; Long term: $125/diem.
Placements Primarily Funded By Insurance; Private sources; Depts of corrections; Social service depts.
Social and Rehabilitative Services
Therapeutic Approach The facility has a family systems approach to therapy, which includes reality therapy.
Therapeutic Services Offered Individual therapy; Group therapy; Family therapy; Adjunctive therapy; Art therapy; Recreation activities; Substance abuse treatment; Aftercare program with follow up.
Professionals on Staff Psychiatrists; Psychologists; Adjunctive therapists; Child care staff; Nurses; Art therapists.

Educational and Vocational Services
Type(s) of Educational Programs Offered On campus; Off campus.
Profile of On Campus School Program Number of teachers 3; *Number of classrooms* 3; *Student to teacher ratio* 5:1; Remedial courses offered.

THE SALVATION ARMY BOOTH BROWN HOUSE SERVICES

1471 Como Ave W, St Paul, MN 55108 (612) 646-2601 *Contact Person(s):* Capt Carole Bacon
Setting and Background Information The program was initially established as a service to unwed mothers in 1890. In 1971, it expanded its services to become a treatment center and, in 1976, a shelter care program was added. The campus is located in a residential area and consists of a 3-story building built around 1913, with 2 3-story wings added in the 1960s.
Referral Information Referrals can be made to the residential program by Ramsey County Human Services Dept or Corrections Dept, and by the Minnesota County Social Services Dept or Corrections Dept. To make a referral, contact the Program Director to arrange the forwarding of background information to schedule a pre-placement interview. The shelter care program has a contract solely with Ramsey County, and, therefore, accepts referrals from that county's human services and correction workers only.
Type of Facility
Funding Sources State.
Average Length of Stay Short and long term.
Types of Admissions Accepted Residential treatment; Group home placement; Wards of the state; Emergency shelter.
Sources of Referral Private sources; Depts of correction; Social service depts.
Client Profile
Age Range of Clients Served Residential program: 12-17.
Characteristics Exhibited by Children Emotional handicaps; Learning disabilities; Speech/Language disorders; Physical handicaps.
Tuition and Fees
Room and Board Short term: $93.80/diem; Long term: $80.61/diem.
Placements Primarily Funded By Insurance; Private sources; Depts of corrections; Social service depts.
Social and Rehabilitative Services
Therapeutic Approach The residential treatment program utilizes Adlerian therapy with a family systems approach, in conjunction with a point system for behavior management. The shelter care program utilizes a level system without a formal therapeutic approach.
Therapeutic Services Offered Individual therapy; Group therapy; Family therapy; Independent living skills program; Recreation activities.
Professionals on Staff Psychiatrists; Social workers; Child care staff; Nurses.
Educational and Vocational Services
Type(s) of Educational Programs Offered On campus; Off campus; Summer campus.
Profile of On Campus School Program Number of teachers 3; *Number of classrooms* 4; *Student to teacher ratio* 7:1; *Length of school day* 6 hrs; Remedial courses offered.
Degrees Offered 12th grade diploma; GED.

ST PETER

LEO A HOFFMANN CENTER

100 Freeman Dr, St Peter, MN 56082 (507) 931-6020 *Contact Person(s):* David Compton, Dir
Setting and Background Information The center was established in 1979 with monies from county grants. It is located on the grounds of St Peter State Hospital.
Referral Information Contact the facility for referral information.
Type of Facility
Funding Sources County.
Average Length of Stay Long term.
Types of Admissions Accepted Residential treatment.
Sources of Referral Depts of correction; Social service depts.
Client Profile
Age Range of Clients Served Residential program: 12-18.
Characteristics Exhibited by Children Sex offenders.
IQ Range of Clients 70+.

LEO A HOFFMANN CENTER (continued)

Tuition and Fees
Room and Board Long term: $93.28/diem.
Placements Primarily Funded By Depts of corrections; Social service depts.
Social and Rehabilitative Services
Therapeutic Approach The basic therapeutic approach of the facility is reality therapy.
Therapeutic Services Offered Individual therapy; Group therapy; Family therapy; Recreation activities; Aftercare program with follow up.
Professionals on Staff Psychologists; Social workers; Child care staff; Recreational therapist.
Educational and Vocational Services
Type(s) of Educational Programs Offered On campus; Off campus; Summer campus.
Profile of On Campus School Program Number of teachers 2; *Number of classrooms* 2; *Grades taught* 7-12.
Vocational Education Programs/Degrees Offered Through public school.

STILLWATER

HARBOR SHELTER & COUNSELING CENTER, INC
310 W Myrtle St, Stillwater, MN 55082.
Contact Person(s): David Genter, Proj Dir
Setting and Background Information The facility was established in 1986.
Referral Information Referrals to the facility come directly from social service agencies.
Type of Facility
Funding Sources State; Federal.
Average Length of Stay Short term.
Types of Admissions Accepted Wards of the state; Emergency shelter.
Sources of Referral Depts of correction; Social service depts.
Client Profile
Age Range of Clients Served Residential program: 12-18.
Characteristics Exhibited by Children Emotional handicaps; Learning disabilities.
Tuition and Fees
Room and Board Short term: $64.44/diem.
Placements Primarily Funded By Local depts of education; Social service depts.
Social and Rehabilitative Services
Therapeutic Services Offered Individual therapy; Group therapy.
Professionals on Staff Social workers; Adjunctive therapists; Child care staff.
Educational and Vocational Services
Type(s) of Educational Programs Offered On campus.

JAMESTOWN
11550 Jasmine Trail N, Stillwater, MN 55082 (612) 429-5307
Contact Person(s): Judith Hill
Setting and Background Information Jamestown is a private, non-profit residential treatment facility for adolescents who abuse drugs and/or are chemically dependent. The facility was established in 1971 on 10 acres of land in a rural setting.
Referral Information Anyone can make a referral by contacting the facility and arranging a pre-placement visit.
Type of Facility
Funding Sources Private.
Average Length of Stay Long term.
Types of Admissions Accepted Residential treatment; Group home placement; Wards of the state.
Sources of Referral State depts of education; Local depts of education; State depts of mental health; Psychiatrists; Private sources; Depts of correction; Social service depts.
Client Profile
Age Range of Clients Served Residential program: 13-18.
Characteristics Exhibited by Children Emotional handicaps; Learning disabilities; Hearing impairments/deafness; Speech/Language disorders; Neurological impairments; Mental disabilities.

Tuition and Fees
Room and Board Long term: $143/diem (county and private) $209/diem (insurance).
Placements Primarily Funded By State depts of education; Local depts of education; State depts of mental health; Insurance; Private sources; Depts of corrections; Social service depts.
Social and Rehabilitative Services
Therapeutic Approach The treatment program is based on the philosophy that drug use and abuse are symptoms of developmental crisis in adolescence.
Therapeutic Services Offered Individual therapy; Group therapy; Family therapy; Adjunctive therapy; Art therapy; Recreation activities; Substance abuse treatment; Aftercare program with follow up.
Professionals on Staff Psychiatrists; Psychologists; Adjunctive therapists; Child care staff; Nurses.
Educational and Vocational Services
Type(s) of Educational Programs Offered On campus; Off campus.
Profile of On Campus School Program Number of teachers 2; *Number of classrooms* 5; *Student to teacher ratio* 5:1; *Length of school day* 3; *Grades taught* 8-12; Remedial courses offered.
Degrees Offered 8th grade diploma; 12th grade diploma; GED.

WAHKON

GALLOWAY BOYS RANCH
Rte 1 Box 69, Wahkon, MN 56386 (612) 495-3344 *Contact Person(s):* Max Allen
Setting and Background Information The ranch was established by the Volunteers of America and is licensed by the Minnesota Dept of Public Welfare. Its campus is located two miles of Wahkon, Minnesota, on 515 acres of woodland. The ranch consists of 6 modern homes (6-8 boys per home), school, gymnasium, and athletic field.
Referral Information Referrals can be made by county welfare workers, probation officers, and school personnel. To make a referral, contact the facility and forward the necessary background information, including family history, testing reports, and description of present problems. Upon receipt of the information, a pre-placement visit will take place before a placement decision is made. Placement may be made the same day.
Type of Facility
Funding Sources Private; State.
Average Length of Stay Long term.
Types of Admissions Accepted Residential treatment.
Sources of Referral State depts of education; Local depts of education; State depts of mental health; Psychiatrists; Private sources; Depts of correction; Social service depts.
Client Profile
Age Range of Clients Served Residential program: 10-17.
Characteristics Exhibited by Children Emotional handicaps; Learning disabilities; Neurological impairments; Mental disabilities.
Tuition and Fees
Room and Board Long term: $97.88/diem.
Tuition $22/diem.
Placements Primarily Funded By Local depts of education; Insurance; Depts of corrections; Social service depts.
Social and Rehabilitative Services
Therapeutic Approach The treatment program utilizes Adlerian principles and reality therapy.
Therapeutic Services Offered Individual therapy; Group therapy; Family therapy; Adjunctive therapy; Independent living skills program; Recreation activities; Substance abuse treatment.
Professionals on Staff Social workers; Child care staff.
Educational and Vocational Services
Type(s) of Educational Programs Offered On campus; Off campus; Summer campus.
Profile of On Campus School Program Number of teachers 1; *Number of classrooms* 6; *Student to teacher ratio* 4:1; *Length of school day* 6 hrs; *Grades taught* Ungraded; Remedial courses offered.
Degrees Offered 12th grade diploma; GED.

WAVERLY

WRIGHT DIRECTION HOME

Rt 1 Box 453, Waverly, MN 55390 (612) 658-4881 *Contact Person(s):* James Reese, Admin
Setting and Background Information The facility was established in 1979. There is one building.
Referral Information Contact the facility.
Type of Facility
Funding Sources State; County.
Average Length of Stay Long term.
Types of Admissions Accepted Residential treatment; Group home placement.
Sources of Referral State depts of mental health; Psychiatrists; Depts of correction; Social service depts.
Client Profile
Age Range of Clients Served Residential programs: 12-18.
Characteristics Exhibited by Children Emotional handicaps; Learning disabilities; Mental disabilities.
Tuition and Fees
Placements Primarily Funded By Social service depts.
Social and Rehabilitative Services
Therapeutic Services Offered Individual therapy; Group therapy; Family therapy; Independent living skills program; Recreation activities; Substance abuse treatment; Aftercare program with follow up.
Professionals on Staff Psychiatrists; Psychologists; Social workers; Adjunctive therapists; Child care staff; Art therapists; Physical therapists.
Educational and Vocational Services
Type(s) of Educational Programs Offered Off campus.

WILLMAR

TEMPORARY RESIDENCE, CRISIS

PO Box 787, SE 6th St & Willmar Ave, Willmar, MN 56201 (612) 235-4613 *Contact Person(s):* Barry Evans, Unit Dir
Setting and Background Information This facility was established in 1987 with a grant from the state Dept of Human Services as a program of a community mental health center. It is housed in a portion of a two-building complex and has the capacity for 9 clients.
Referral Information Contact the facility for referral information.
Type of Facility
Funding Sources Private; State; County.
Average Length of Stay Short term.
Types of Admissions Accepted Emergency shelter.
Sources of Referral Local depts of education; Psychiatrists; Private sources; Depts of correction; Social service depts; Families.
Client Profile
Age Range of Clients Served Residential program: 6-55+.

WILLMAR REGIONAL TREATMENT CENTER

Box 128, Willmar, MN 56201 (612) 231-5100 *Contact Person(s):* Ted Olsen, Unit Dir
Setting and Background Information The facility was established in 1912 by the state legislature. It is located on 100 acres and has more than 20 buildings.
Referral Information All referrals are made through county social service agencies, but many are originated by families or the courts.
Type of Facility
Funding Sources State.
Average Length of Stay Long term.
Types of Admissions Accepted Residential treatment.
Sources of Referral Social service depts.
Client Profile
Age Range of Clients Served Residential program: 12-55+.
Characteristics Exhibited by Children Emotional handicaps; Learning disabilities; Mental disabilities; Chemical dependency.
Tuition and Fees
Room and Board Long term: $120/diem (includes school tuition).
Placements Primarily Funded By Social service depts.

Social and Rehabilitative Services
Therapeutic Approach The center has an eclectic approach to therapy, including behavior modification.
Therapeutic Services Offered Individual therapy; Group therapy; Family therapy; Adjunctive therapy; Physical therapy; Independent living skills program; Recreation activities; Substance abuse treatment.
Professionals on Staff Psychiatrists; Psychologists; Social workers; Adjunctive therapists; Child care staff; Nurses; Physical therapists.
Educational and Vocational Services
Type(s) of Educational Programs Offered On campus; Off campus (Sheltered work; Public school).
Profile of On Campus School Program Number of teachers 3; *Number of classrooms* 2; *Student to teacher ratio* 1:3; *Credentials of teachers* Certified; *Grades taught* 9-12; Remedial courses offered.
Degrees Offered GED.

MISSISSIPPI

CORINTH

NORTHEAST MISSISSIPPI EMERGENCY SHELTER FOR CHILDREN

1322 Jackson St, Corinth, MS 38834 (601) 287-8243 *Contact Person(s):* Judy Miller, Dir
Setting and Background Information The facility was established in 1980 with a Title XX grant.
Referral Information All referrals to the facility are children in custody of the Dept of Public Welfare.
Type of Facility
Funding Sources Private; State; Federal.
Average Length of Stay Short term.
Types of Admissions Accepted Residential treatment; Wards of the state; Emergency shelter.
Sources of Referral Social service depts.
Client Profile
Age Range of Clients Served Residential program: Birth-18.
Characteristics Exhibited by Children Emotional handicaps.
Tuition and Fees
Placements Primarily Funded By Social service depts.
Social and Rehabilitative Services
Therapeutic Services Offered Individual therapy.
Professionals on Staff Social workers.
Educational and Vocational Services
Type(s) of Educational Programs Offered Off campus (Local schools).

JACKSON

THE ARK

942 North St, Jackson, MS 39202 (601) 355-0077, 352-7784 *Contact Person(s):* Angela Robertson, Prog Supv
Setting and Background Information The facility is a program of the Mississippi Children's Home Society and Family Service Association. It was established in 1985 with funds from the Dept of Mental Health. It is a residential treatment center for chemically dependent youth.
Referral Information For referrals, contact the facility and provide basic background information. If placement is appropriate, a screening interview will be scheduled and a decision rendered following the interview.
Type of Facility
Funding Sources Private; State; Federal.
Average Length of Stay Long term.
Types of Admissions Accepted Residential treatment; Group home placement; Wards of the state.
Sources of Referral State depts of mental health; Depts of correction; Social service depts; Parents.
Client Profile
Age Range of Clients Served Residential program: 14-17.
Characteristics Exhibited by Children Emotional handicaps; Learning disabilities; Mental disabilities; Chemical dependency.
IQ Range of Clients 70+.
Tuition and Fees
Room and Board Long term: Sliding scale.
Placements Primarily Funded By State depts of mental health.

Social and Rehabilitative Services
Therapeutic Approach The facility uses a combination of behavior modification and the 12 step program of AA/NA.
Therapeutic Services Offered Individual therapy; Group therapy; Family therapy; Independent living skills program; Recreation activities; Substance abuse treatment; Aftercare program with follow up.
Professionals on Staff Psychiatrists; Psychologists; Social workers.
Educational and Vocational Services
Type(s) of Educational Programs Offered On campus (GED preparation and high school credits).
Profile of On Campus School Program Number of teachers 1; *Number of classrooms* 1; *Student to teacher ratio* 5:1; *Credentials of teachers* Fully certified; *Grades taught* 7-12; *Remedial courses offered* (Extensive tutoring).

MISSISSIPPI CHILDREN'S HOME SOCIETY AND FAMILY SERVICE ASSOCIATION

PO Box 1078, 1801 N West St, Jackson, MS 39205 (601) 352-7784 *Contact Person(s):* Christopher M Cherney, Exec Dir
Setting and Background Information This agency is a statewide, private, non-profit child and family service agency and was established in 1912. The facility offers a variety of services, including a licensed adoption agency, a program for runaway youth, residential services and public awareness programs.
Referral Information Referral procedures are to contact the facility.
Type of Facility
Funding Sources Private; State; Federal; United Way; Foundations; Individual contributions.
Average Length of Stay Long term.
Types of Admissions Accepted Residential treatment; Group home placement; Wards of the state; Out-patient.
Sources of Referral State depts of education; Local depts of education; State depts of mental health; Psychiatrists; Private sources; Depts of correction; Social service depts; Self; Parents.
Client Profile
Age Range of Clients Served Day programs: Birth-55+; Residential program: 12-18.
Characteristics Exhibited by Children Emotional handicaps; Learning disabilities; Chemical dependency; Runaways; Dysfunctioning individuals and families.
Tuition and Fees
Room and Board Long term: Sliding scale.
Placements Primarily Funded By State depts of mental health; Insurance; Private sources.
Social and Rehabilitative Services
Therapeutic Services Offered Individual therapy; Group therapy; Family therapy; Adjunctive therapy; Independent living skills program; Recreation activities; Substance abuse treatment; Aftercare program with follow up.
Professionals on Staff Psychiatrists; Psychologists; Social workers; Adjunctive therapists.

POWERS THERAPEUTIC GROUP HOME FOR ADOLESCENT GIRLS

PO Box 1078, 1801 N West St, Jackson, MS 39205 (601) 353-3101, 352-7784 *Contact Person(s):* Kay Fortenberry, Prog Supv

POWERS THERAPEUTIC GROUP HOME FOR ADOLESCENT GIRLS *(continued)*

Setting and Background Information The facility is a program of the Mississippi Children's Home Society and Family Service Association. It was established in 1983 with funds from the state Dept of Mental Health.

Referral Information Referrals are made by contacting the facility. Appropriate applicants and parents are interviewed. The treatment team determines placement based on a number of factors.

Type of Facility

Funding Sources Private; State; Federal.

Average Length of Stay Long term.

Types of Admissions Accepted Residential treatment; Group home placement; Wards of the state.

Sources of Referral State depts of education; Local depts of education; State depts of mental health; Psychiatrists; Private sources; Depts of correction; Social service depts; Dept of Public Welfare.

Client Profile

Age Range of Clients Served Residential program: 12-18.

Characteristics Exhibited by Children Emotional handicaps; Learning disabilities.

IQ Range of Clients 75+.

Tuition and Fees

Room and Board Long term: Sliding scale.

Placements Primarily Funded By State depts of mental health.

Social and Rehabilitative Services

Therapeutic Approach The basic therapeutic approach of the facility is the behavioral treatment model.

Therapeutic Services Offered Individual therapy; Group therapy; Family therapy; Independent living skills program; Recreation activities; Substance abuse treatment; Aftercare program with follow up.

Professionals on Staff Psychiatrists; Psychologists; Social workers; Adjunctive therapists.

Educational and Vocational Services

Type(s) of Educational Programs Offered Off campus (Public schools).

PASCAGOULA

RHONDA CRANE MEMORIAL YOUTH SHELTER

4903 Telephone Rd, Pascagoula, MS 39567 (601) 762-7370 *Contact Person(s):* Cynthia Wilson, Dir

Setting and Background Information The shelter was built in 1977 with funds from Title XX and the county.

Referral Information Referrals must be residents of Jackson, George, Greene or Perry counties. Contact the facility for referral information.

Type of Facility

Funding Sources County; Title XX.

Average Length of Stay Short term.

Types of Admissions Accepted Emergency shelter.

Sources of Referral Any source can make referrals.

Client Profile

Age Range of Clients Served Residential program: Birth-17.

Characteristics Exhibited by Children Abused and neglected.

Tuition and Fees

Placements Primarily Funded By County; Title XX.

Social and Rehabilitative Services

Therapeutic Services Offered These services are offered outside of the program.

Professionals on Staff Psychologists; Social workers.

Educational and Vocational Services

Type(s) of Educational Programs Offered Off campus (Public schools).

MISSOURI

BRIGHTON

GOOD SAMARITAN BOYS RANCH

PO Box 617, Brighton, MO 65617 (417) 756-2238 *Contact Person(s):*
Wayne Richards, Exec Dir
Setting and Background Information The facility was established in
1954 for homeless boys by the Baptist Church. It is located on
110 acres and has 2 dormitories, a school, an administration
building, and a gym.
Referral Information Contact the facility for a referral packet. A two-
week pre-placement visit will be scheduled.
Type of Facility
Funding Sources Private; State; Federal.
Average Length of Stay Short and long term.
Types of Admissions Accepted Residential treatment; Wards of the
state.
Sources of Referral State depts of education; Local depts of educa-
tion; State depts of mental health; Private sources; Depts of
correction; Social service depts.
Client Profile
Age Range of Clients Served Residential program: 12-18.
Characteristics Exhibited by Children Emotional handicaps; Learning
disabilities; Mental disabilities.
Tuition and Fees
Room and Board Short term: $30/diem; Long term: $55/diem.
Placements Primarily Funded By State depts of mental health; Social
service depts.
Social and Rehabilitative Services
Therapeutic Services Offered Individual therapy; Group therapy;
Family therapy; Independent living skills program; Recreation
activities; Substance abuse treatment; Aftercare program with
follow up.
Professionals on Staff Social workers; Adjunctive therapists; Child
care staff.
Educational and Vocational Services
Type(s) of Educational Programs Offered On campus (Self-contained
Spec Ed); Off campus.
Profile of On Campus School Program Number of teachers 3; *Num-
ber of classrooms* 4; *Student to teacher ratio* 2:1; *Credentials of
teachers* Certified; *Grades taught* Ungraded; Special curriculum
electives offered; Remedial courses offered.
Vocational Education Programs/Degrees Offered Local vocational
school.
Degrees Offered 8th grade diploma; 12th grade diploma; GED.

FARMINGTON

PRESBYTERIAN HOME FOR CHILDREN

412 W Liberty, Farmington, MO 63640 (314) 756-6744 *Contact
Person(s):* Jerry Sullivan, Dir
Setting and Background Information The facility was established in
1914 as an orphanage. Currently, there is a 200 acre farm and 2
campuses with 8 residences on each.
Referral Information Contact the facility for referral information.
Type of Facility
Funding Sources Private; State.
Average Length of Stay Short and long term.
Types of Admissions Accepted Residential treatment; Group home
placement; Wards of the state.

Sources of Referral State depts of mental health; Private sources;
Depts of correction; Social service depts.
Client Profile
Age Range of Clients Served Residential program: 12-18.
Characteristics Exhibited by Children Emotional handicaps; Learning
disabilities.
IQ Range of Clients 75+.
Tuition and Fees
Room and Board Short term: $30/diem; Long term: $38-63/diem.
Placements Primarily Funded By Social service depts.
Social and Rehabilitative Services
Therapeutic Services Offered Individual therapy; Group therapy;
Family therapy; Independent living skills program; Recreation
activities; Substance abuse treatment; Aftercare program with
follow up.
Professionals on Staff Social workers; Child care staff; Recreation
therapist.
Educational and Vocational Services
Type(s) of Educational Programs Offered On campus; Off campus.
Profile of On Campus School Program Number of teachers 2; *Num-
ber of classrooms* 2; *Student to teacher ratio* 8:1; *Credentials of
teachers* Spec Ed; *Length of school day* 8-3.
Degrees Offered GED.

FLORISSANT

MARYGROVE

2705 Mullanphy Ln, Florissant, MO 63031 (314) 837-1702 *Contact
Person(s):* Sr Helen Negri, Admin
Setting and Background Information This facility was established in
1869 for delinquent girls. Currently, it is a residential program,
located on 50 acres with 7 buildings.
Referral Information All referrals to the facility are made through the
Child Center of Our Lady, 7900 Natural Bridge Road, St. Louis,
Missouri, 63121.
Type of Facility
Funding Sources Private.
Average Length of Stay Avg 18-24 mos.
Types of Admissions Accepted Day treatment; Residential treatment.
Sources of Referral State depts of education; Local depts of educa-
tion; State depts of mental health; Psychiatrists; Private sources;
Depts of correction; Social service depts.
Client Profile
Age Range of Clients Served Residential program: 6-18.
Characteristics Exhibited by Children Emotional handicaps.
IQ Range of Clients 70-120.
Tuition and Fees
Room and Board Long term: $72/diem.
Tuition $45/diem.
Placements Primarily Funded By Local depts of education; State
depts of mental health; Social service depts.
Social and Rehabilitative Services
Therapeutic Services Offered Individual therapy; Group therapy;
Family therapy; Physical therapy; Independent living skills pro-
gram; Recreation activities.
Professionals on Staff Psychiatrists; Psychologists; Social workers;
Child care staff; Nurses; Art therapists.

MARYGROVE *(continued)*

Educational and Vocational Services
Type(s) of Educational Programs Offered On campus; Off campus; Summer campus.
Profile of On Campus School Program Number of teachers 12; *Number of classrooms* 5; *Student to teacher ratio* 7:1; *Grades taught* Ungraded.

JOPLIN

OZARK CENTER YOUTH RESIDENTIAL SERVICES
PO Box 2526, Joplin, MO 64803 (417) 781-0821 *Contact Person(s):* David Nethery, Coord of Res Srvs
Setting and Background Information The agency was established in 1981 by the Ozark Center in order to supplement out-patient services for children. Its 40-acre campus has 3 residential buildings, an administration building and a gym.
Referral Information The referring agency or therapist should forward the social history, recent psychological evaluations, educational reports and any other pertinent information. The referral packet will be reviewed by the screening team.
Type of Facility
Funding Sources Private; State.
Average Length of Stay Long term.
Types of Admissions Accepted Residential treatment.
Sources of Referral State depts of mental health; Psychiatrists; Private sources; Social service depts.
Client Profile
Age Range of Clients Served Residential program: 6-18.
Characteristics Exhibited by Children Emotional handicaps; Learning disabilities; Mental disabilities.
IQ Range of Clients 80+.
Tuition and Fees
Room and Board Long term: $85/diem.
Placements Primarily Funded By State depts of mental health; Insurance; Social service depts.
Social and Rehabilitative Services
Therapeutic Approach The facility has a behavioral approach to therapy.
Therapeutic Services Offered Individual therapy; Group therapy; Family therapy; Recreation activities.
Professionals on Staff Psychiatrists; Psychologists; Social workers; Child care staff; Recreation therapists.
Educational and Vocational Services
Type(s) of Educational Programs Offered Off campus (Public school).

KANSAS CITY

CRITTENTON CENTER
10918 Elm Ave, Kansas City, MO 64134-4199 (816) 765-6600
Contact Person(s): Pat Coleman, Asst to the President
Setting and Background Information The center was established in 1896 to provide services to unwed mothers. The 150-acre campus has a main center, a group home, and a greenhouse. There are two other group homes located off campus.
Referral Information Contact the facility for referral information.
Type of Facility
Funding Sources Private.
Average Length of Stay 4 mos (children's psychiatric hospital), 14 mos (residential treatment).
Types of Admissions Accepted Day treatment; Residential treatment; Group home placement; Wards of the state; Psychiatric hospital.
Sources of Referral State depts of education; Local depts of education; State depts of mental health; Psychiatrists; Private sources; Depts of correction; Social service depts.
Client Profile
Age Range of Clients Served Day programs: 6-18; Residential program: 12-18.
Characteristics Exhibited by Children Emotional handicaps; Learning disabilities; Mental disabilities.
IQ Range of Clients 70+.
Tuition and Fees
Room and Board Long term: $220/diem (hospital); $110/diem (residential).
Placements Primarily Funded By State depts of mental health; Insurance; Private sources; Social service depts.

Social and Rehabilitative Services
Therapeutic Services Offered Individual therapy; Group therapy; Family therapy; Adjunctive therapy; Art therapy; Physical therapy; Independent living skills program; Recreation activities; Substance abuse treatment; Aftercare program with follow up.
Professionals on Staff Psychiatrists; Psychologists; Social workers; Child care staff; Nurses; Art therapists; Physical therapists.
Educational and Vocational Services
Type(s) of Educational Programs Offered On campus (Spec Ed); Off campus; Summer campus (Spec Ed).
Profile of On Campus School Program Number of teachers 13; *Number of classrooms* 13; *Student to teacher ratio* 8:1; *Length of school day* 8:15-2:30; *Grades taught* K-8; Special curriculum electives offered (Small business, Cooking, Math, Marriage & family, PE, Speech).
Degrees Offered 8th grade diploma; 12th grade diploma; GED.

EVANGELICAL CHILDREN'S HOME
5100 Noland Rd, Kansas City, MO 64133 816) 356-0187 *Contact Person(s):* Sharron Bowen, Prog Dir
Setting and Background Information The facility was established in 1978 as a branch of the Evangelical Children's Home in St. Louis. The 17-acre campus has an office, a children's residence, a shed and barn.
Referral Information Contact the facility and forward the required information, including family background, educational information, psychological or psychiatric evaluations, and medical information.
Type of Facility
Funding Sources Private; State.
Average Length of Stay Avg 18 mos.
Types of Admissions Accepted Residential treatment.
Sources of Referral State depts of mental health; Private sources; Social service depts.
Client Profile
Age Range of Clients Served Residential program: 12-18.
Characteristics Exhibited by Children Emotional handicaps; Learning disabilities; Mental disabilities.
Tuition and Fees
Room and Board Long term: $57/diem.
Placements Primarily Funded By State depts of mental health; Social service depts.
Social and Rehabilitative Services
Therapeutic Approach The facility uses individual treatment plans with a therapeutic milieu approach.
Therapeutic Services Offered Individual therapy; Group therapy; Family therapy; Adjunctive therapy; Art therapy; Independent living skills program; Recreation activities; Aftercare program with follow up; Music therapy; Therapeutic riding program.
Professionals on Staff Psychiatrists; Psychologists; Social workers; Adjunctive therapists; Child care staff; Art therapists.
Educational and Vocational Services
Type(s) of Educational Programs Offered On campus.
Profile of On Campus School Program Number of teachers 1; *Number of classrooms* 1; *Student to teacher ratio* 5:1; *Grades taught* 6-12.

MARILLAC CENTER FOR CHILDREN
310 W 106th St, Kansas City, MO 64114 (816) 941-9700 *Contact Person(s):* Jim Veverka
Setting and Background Information The facility was initially established as an orphanage in the 1890s. Its programs have gradually expanded to become a psychiatric residential and day treatment facility. The campus is located in the south part of Kansas City on 14 acres of land. There is one large building which houses residence halls, classrooms, gymnasium, swimming pool, kitchen, and offices.
Referral Information Contact the facility for referral information.
Type of Facility
Funding Sources Private; State; United Way.
Average Length of Stay Long term.
Types of Admissions Accepted Day treatment; Residential treatment; Wards of the state.
Sources of Referral State depts of education; Local depts of education; State depts of mental health; Psychiatrists; Private sources; Social service depts.

MARILLAC CENTER FOR CHILDREN *(continued)*

Client Profile
Age Range of Clients Served Day programs: 5-13; Residential program: 5-13.
Characteristics Exhibited by Children Emotional handicaps; Learning disabilities; Speech/Language disorders; Neurological impairments.
Tuition and Fees
Room and Board Long term: Sliding scale.
Placements Primarily Funded By State depts of education; Local depts of education; State depts of mental health; Insurance; Private sources; Social service depts.
Social and Rehabilitative Services
Therapeutic Services Offered Individual therapy; Group therapy; Family therapy; Adjunctive therapy; Independent living skills program; Aftercare program with follow up.
Professionals on Staff Psychiatrists; Psychologists; Social workers; Adjunctive therapists; Child care staff; Nurses.
Educational and Vocational Services
Type(s) of Educational Programs Offered On campus; Off campus; Summer campus.
Profile of On Campus School Program Number of classrooms 5; *Student to teacher ratio* 7:1; *Length of school day* 6 hrs; *Grades taught* K-8; Remedial courses offered.
Degrees Offered 8th grade diploma.

NILES HOME FOR CHILDREN

1911 E 23rd St, Kansas City, MO 64127 (816) 241-3448 *Contact Person(s):* Tonya Sydnor,
Setting and Background Information The facility was originally established as an orphanage for destitute children in 1883. It has since evolved into a treatment center consisting of a modern 3-building complex surrounding a courtyard on one-half acre of land in the heart of the inner city.
Referral Information Referrals can be made by anyone by contacting the facilty.
Type of Facility
Funding Sources State.
Average Length of Stay Long term.
Types of Admissions Accepted Residential treatment; Wards of the state.
Sources of Referral State depts of education; Local depts of education; State depts of mental health; Psychiatrists; Private sources; Depts of correction; Social service depts.
Client Profile
Age Range of Clients Served Residential program: 6-14.
Characteristics Exhibited by Children Emotional handicaps; Learning disabilities; Mental disabilities.
Tuition and Fees
Room and Board Long term: $91/diem.
Placements Primarily Funded By State depts of mental health; Social service depts.
Social and Rehabilitative Services
Therapeutic Approach The therapeutic approaches used are eclectic and designed to meet the individual needs of the children.
Therapeutic Services Offered Individual therapy; Group therapy; Family therapy; Art therapy; Independent living skills program; Recreation activities; Aftercare program with follow up.
Professionals on Staff Psychiatrists; Psychologists; Social workers; Child care staff; Nurses.
Educational and Vocational Services
Type(s) of Educational Programs Offered On campus.
Profile of On Campus School Program Number of teachers 2; *Number of classrooms* 14; *Student to teacher ratio* 7:1; *Length of school day* 6.5 hrs; Remedial courses offered.
Degrees Offered GED.

OZANAM HOME FOR BOYS, INC

421 E 137th St, Kansas City, MO 64145 (816) 942-5600 *Contact Person(s):* Arlene Finney
Setting and Background Information The facility was initially established as an orphanage by a local social worker in 1948. Since then, it has expanded its programs to become a residential treatment center for emotionally disturbed adolescent boys, including a spiritual life center and a family center. The main campus is located south of Kansas City on 40 acres and consists of 2 dormitories, school, and a gymnasium. A group home program is located in Kansas City.
Referral Information Referrals can be made by juvenile courts, social workers, and parents. The referral process requires the forwarding of the necessary background information on the child, including a psychiatric exam, testing, and social history. Upon receipt of the referral materials, a pre-placement interview will be scheduled with the boy, his parents, intake coordinator, and clinical director. An admission decision will be made following the pre-placement evaluation and interview.
Type of Facility
Funding Sources Private; State.
Average Length of Stay Long term.
Types of Admissions Accepted Day treatment; Residential treatment; Group home placement; Wards of the state.
Sources of Referral State depts of education; Local depts of education; State depts of mental health; Psychiatrists; Private sources; Social service depts.
Client Profile
Age Range of Clients Served Day programs: 12-18; Residential program: 12-18.
Characteristics Exhibited by Children Emotional handicaps; Learning disabilities; Speech/Language disorders; Neurological impairments; Mental disabilities.
Tuition and Fees
Room and Board Long term: $95/diem.
Placements Primarily Funded By State depts of mental health; Insurance; Private sources; Social service depts.
Social and Rehabilitative Services
Therapeutic Approach The facility has a multi-faceted approach to therapy.
Therapeutic Services Offered Individual therapy; Group therapy; Family therapy; Adjunctive therapy; Art therapy; Independent living skills program; Recreation activities; Substance abuse treatment; Aftercare program with follow up.
Professionals on Staff Psychiatrists; Social workers; Adjunctive therapists; Art therapists.
Educational and Vocational Services
Type(s) of Educational Programs Offered On campus; Off campus; Summer campus.
Profile of On Campus School Program Number of teachers 14; *Student to teacher ratio* 5:1; *Grades taught* K-12; Special curriculum electives offered; Remedial courses offered.
Degrees Offered 12th grade diploma; GED.

THE SPOFFORD HOME

PO Box 9888, 9700 Grandview Rd, Kansas City, MO 64134 (816) 765-4060 *Contact Person(s):* Mark Cedarburg, ACSW
Setting and Background Information The facility was initially established in 1917 for the care of homeless children, but has since evolved into a treatment center. Its campus is located in South Kansas City, on 33 acres, in a suburban community and consist of residential units, school, gymnasium, and outdoor swimming pool.
Referral Information Referrals can be made by the Division of Family Services, Social and Rehabilitation Services, Dept of Mental Health, mental health centers, and private individuals.
Type of Facility
Funding Sources Private; State.
Average Length of Stay Long term.
Types of Admissions Accepted Residential treatment; Wards of the state.
Sources of Referral State depts of education; Local depts of education; State depts of mental health; Psychiatrists; Private sources; Social service depts.
Client Profile
Age Range of Clients Served Residential program: 4-11.
Characteristics Exhibited by Children Emotional handicaps; Learning disabilities; Speech/Language disorders; Mental disabilities.
Tuition and Fees
Placements Primarily Funded By State depts of mental health; Insurance; Private sources; Social service depts.
Social and Rehabilitative Services
Therapeutic Services Offered Individual therapy; Group therapy; Family therapy; Adjunctive therapy; Art therapy; Recreation activities.
Professionals on Staff Psychiatrists; Social workers; Adjunctive therapists; Child care staff; Nurses.

THE SPOFFORD HOME (continued)

Educational and Vocational Services
Type(s) of Educational Programs Offered On campus; Summer campus.
Profile of On Campus School Program Number of teachers 6; *Number of classrooms* 6; *Student to teacher ratio* 10:1; *Credentials of teachers* Spec Ed; *Credentials of teachers* 6 hrs; Special curriculum electives offered; Remedial courses offered.

NEVADA

HSA HEARTLAND HOSPITAL

1500 W Ashland, Nevada, MO 64772 (417) 667-2666 *Contact Person(s):* Debbie Schicke
Setting and Background Information The facility was established in 1983 as a private, for profit hospital. It is located on 20 acres and has dormitories, horse stables, and various other buildings.
Referral Information Contact the facility and forward referral information, including psychological, educational and social histories, and a psychiatric evaluation prior to admission.
Type of Facility
Funding Sources Private.
Average Length of Stay Long term.
Types of Admissions Accepted Residential treatment.
Sources of Referral State depts of education; Local depts of education; Psychiatrists; Private sources; Champus.
Client Profile
Age Range of Clients Served Residential program: 12-18.
Characteristics Exhibited by Children Emotional handicaps.
IQ Range of Clients 80+.
Tuition and Fees
Room and Board Long term: $330/diem.
Placements Primarily Funded By Insurance.
Social and Rehabilitative Services
Therapeutic Approach The facility offers psychotherapy in a milieu setting.
Therapeutic Services Offered Individual therapy; Group therapy; Family therapy; Adjunctive therapy; Physical therapy; Independent living skills program; Recreation activities; Substance abuse treatment; Aftercare program with follow up.
Professionals on Staff Psychiatrists; Psychologists; Social workers; Adjunctive therapists; Child care staff; Nurses.
Educational and Vocational Services
Type(s) of Educational Programs Offered On campus (Jr & Sr High).
Profile of On Campus School Program Number of teachers 9; *Number of classrooms* 9; *Student to teacher ratio* 10:1; *Grades taught* K-12; Special curriculum electives offered; Remedial courses offered.
Degrees Offered 12th grade diploma; GED.

ST CHARLES

CORNERSTONE

316 Jefferson, St Charles, MO 63301 (314) 946-2814, 946-3771 *Contact Person(s):* Steven Tenebaum, Prog Coord
Setting and Background Information The facility was established in 1984 with grant monies. It is a large home.
Referral Information Contact the facility.
Type of Facility
Funding Sources Private.
Average Length of Stay Long term.
Types of Admissions Accepted Residential treatment; Group home placement.
Sources of Referral State depts of mental health; Social service depts.
Client Profile
Age Range of Clients Served Residential program: 12-18.
Characteristics Exhibited by Children Emotional handicaps; Learning disabilities.
IQ Range of Clients 90+.
Tuition and Fees
Room and Board Long term: $55/diem.
Placements Primarily Funded By State depts of mental health; Social service depts.
Social and Rehabilitative Services
Therapeutic Services Offered Individual therapy; Group therapy; Family therapy.
Professionals on Staff Psychologists; Child care staff.

YOUTH IN NEED

529 Jeferson, St Charles, MO 63301 (314) 946-3771 *Contact Person(s):* Liza Andrew-Miller, Exec Dir
Setting and Background Information The agency was established in 1974 through a cooperative effort by community leaders. There are three separate buildings within a 6 block radius of each other.
Referral Information Referrals by parents, youth, psychiatrists, schools, are accepted by phone or as walk-ins. A 24-hour hotline is maintained.
Type of Facility
Funding Sources Private; State; Federal.
Average Length of Stay Short and long term.
Types of Admissions Accepted Day treatment; Group home placement; Emergency shelter.
Sources of Referral Local depts of education; State depts of mental health; Psychiatrists; Private sources; Depts of correction; Social service depts.
Client Profile
Age Range of Clients Served Day programs: 12-18; Residential program: 12-18.
Characteristics Exhibited by Children Emotional handicaps; Learning disabilities.
IQ Range of Clients 70+.
Tuition and Fees
Room and Board Short term: Sliding scale; Long term: $55/diem.
Tuition Negotiated with individual school districts.
Placements Primarily Funded By Local depts of education; Private sources and Dept of Family Services (group home); Private sources (emergency shelter); Depts of corrections (emergency shelter); Social service depts (emergency shelter).
Social and Rehabilitative Services
Therapeutic Approach The facility has a broad eclectic approach relying heavily on providing a therapeutic milieu and some behavior modification techniques.
Therapeutic Services Offered Individual therapy; Group therapy; Family therapy.
Professionals on Staff Psychologists; Social workers; Child care staff.
Educational and Vocational Services
Type(s) of Educational Programs Offered On campus.
Profile of On Campus School Program Number of teachers 3; *Number of classrooms* 3; *Student to teacher ratio* 6:1; *Credentials of teachers* LD, BD Certified; *Grades taught* Individualized instruction.
Degrees Offered Degrees are conferred by originating school district..

ST JOSEPH

TRANSITIONAL LIVING COMMUNITY FOR GIRLS

312 N 20th, St Joseph, MO 64507 (816) 232-3478 *Contact Person(s):* Joan Collins, Prog Dir
Setting and Background Information The facility was established in 1974 by the Jr League of St Joseph. It is a residential home with a capacity for 8 youth.
Referral Information Contact the facility and forward a referral packet including social, psychological, and school information.
Type of Facility
Funding Sources Private; State.
Average Length of Stay Long term.
Types of Admissions Accepted Residential treatment; Group home placement; Wards of the state.
Sources of Referral State depts of mental health; Social service depts.
Client Profile
Age Range of Clients Served Residential program: 12-18.
Characteristics Exhibited by Children Emotional handicaps; Learning disabilities; Mental disabilities.
IQ Range of Clients 90+.
Tuition and Fees
Placements Primarily Funded By State depts of mental health; Social service depts.
Social and Rehabilitative Services
Therapeutic Approach The basic approach of the facility is milieu therapy.
Therapeutic Services Offered Individual therapy; Group therapy; Family therapy; Adjunctive therapy; Independent living skills program; Recreation activities.
Professionals on Staff Social workers; Adjunctive therapists; Child care staff.

ST LOUIS

BOYS HOPE

4970 Oakland Ave, St Louis, MO 63110 (314) 652-9405 *Contact Person(s):* Joseph M Stortz, Prog Dir

Setting and Background Information The facility was established in 1976. There are 3 group homes in residential neighborhoods.

Referral Information Contact the facility and forward the necessary information. A pre-placement visit will be arranged.

Type of Facility

Funding Sources Private; Foundations; Corporations.

Average Length of Stay Long term.

Types of Admissions Accepted Group home placement; Wards of the state.

Sources of Referral State depts of education; Local depts of education; State depts of mental health; Psychiatrists; Private sources; Social service depts; Juvenile courts; Private agencies; Individuals.

Client Profile

Age Range of Clients Served Residential program: 12-18.

Characteristics Exhibited by Children Emotional handicaps; Neglected and dependent youth.

Tuition and Fees

Room and Board Long term: Sliding scale.

Placements Primarily Funded By Private sources; Fund raising.

Social and Rehabilitative Services

Therapeutic Approach The facility uses reality therapy, behavior modification and has a therapeutic milieu.

Therapeutic Services Offered Individual therapy; Group therapy; Family therapy; Independent living skills program; Aftercare program with follow up.

Professionals on Staff Psychologists; Social workers; Adjunctive therapists; Child care staff.

Educational and Vocational Services

Type(s) of Educational Programs Offered Off campus (Private schools).

CHILD CENTER OF OUR LADY

7900 Natural Bridge Rd, St Louis, MO 63121 (314) 383-0200

Contact Person(s): Sr Helen Negri, Admin

Setting and Background Information The facility was established in 1959 by Catholic Charities of St Louis as a child guidance center. Located on 7 acres, there are 4 buildings.

Referral Information Contact the facility for referral information..

Type of Facility

Funding Sources Private; State.

Average Length of Stay Long term.

Types of Admissions Accepted Day treatment; Residential treatment.

Sources of Referral State depts of education; Local depts of education; State depts of mental health; Psychiatrists; Private sources; Social service depts.

Client Profile

Age Range of Clients Served Day programs: 6-12; Residential program: 6-12.

Characteristics Exhibited by Children Emotional handicaps.

Tuition and Fees

Placements Primarily Funded By State depts of education; State depts of mental health; Social service depts.

Social and Rehabilitative Services

Therapeutic Approach The facility has a family systems approach to therapy.

Therapeutic Services Offered Individual therapy; Group therapy; Family therapy; Adjunctive therapy; Art therapy; Recreation activities.

Professionals on Staff Psychiatrists; Psychologists; Social workers; Adjunctive therapists; Child care staff; Nurses.

Educational and Vocational Services

Type(s) of Educational Programs Offered On campus.

Profile of On Campus School Program Number of teachers 12; *Number of classrooms* 5; *Student to teacher ratio* 2:1; *Credentials of teachers* Spec Ed; *Length of school day* 6 hrs; *Grades taught* Ungraded.

EDGEWOOD CHILDREN'S CENTER

330 N Gore Ave, St Louis, MO 63119 (314) 968-2060 *Contact Person(s):* Ralph S Lehman, Exec Dir

Setting and Background Information The facility was initially established in 1834 as an orphanage and is now a residential treatment facility. The 23-acre campus has 3 residential buildings, a school, administration and support services buildings.

Referral Information For referrals, contact the facility and forward information about the child's medical, social, and educational history.

Type of Facility

Funding Sources Private; State; Federal; United Way.

Average Length of Stay Long term.

Types of Admissions Accepted Day treatment; Residential treatment; Wards of the state; Respite care.

Sources of Referral State depts of education; Local depts of education; State depts of mental health; Psychiatrists; Private sources; Depts of correction; Social service depts.

Client Profile

Age Range of Clients Served Day programs: 6-15; Residential program: 6-18.

Characteristics Exhibited by Children Emotional handicaps; Learning disabilities; Speech/Language disorders; Neurological impairments; Mental disabilities.

IQ Range of Clients 70+.

Tuition and Fees

Room and Board Long term: $83/diem.

Tuition $43/diem.

Placements Primarily Funded By State depts of education; Local depts of education; State depts of mental health; Private sources; Social service depts.

Social and Rehabilitative Services

Therapeutic Approach The center has an eclectic approach to therapy, which includes psychotherapy.

Therapeutic Services Offered Individual therapy; Group therapy; Family therapy; Adjunctive therapy; Art therapy; Physical therapy; Independent living skills program; Recreation activities; Substance abuse treatment; Aftercare program with follow up.

Professionals on Staff Psychiatrists; Psychologists; Social workers; Adjunctive therapists; Child care staff; Nurses; Art therapists; Physical therapists.

Educational and Vocational Services

Type(s) of Educational Programs Offered On campus; Summer campus.

Profile of On Campus School Program Number of teachers 7; *Number of classrooms* 7; *Student to teacher ratio* 9:1; *Student to teacher ratio* MA, certified Spec Ed; *Grades taught* K-9; Remedial courses offered (Reading, Math, English).

EVANGELICAL CHILDREN'S HOME

8240 St Charles Rock Rd, St Louis, MO 63114 (314) 427-3755

Contact Person(s): Robert A Baur, Exec Dir

Setting and Background Information The facility was established in 1858 by a church organization. There are 3 campuses and 4 community group homes.

Referral Information Contact the facility and forward required materials. A pre-placement visit will be arranged.

Type of Facility

Funding Sources Private; State; Federal.

Average Length of Stay Long term.

Types of Admissions Accepted Day treatment; Residential treatment; Group home placement; Wards of the state.

Sources of Referral State depts of education; Local depts of education; State depts of mental health; Psychiatrists; Private sources; Social service depts; Juvenile courts.

Client Profile

Age Range of Clients Served Day programs: Birth-18; Residential program: 6-21+.

Characteristics Exhibited by Children Emotional handicaps; Learning disabilities.

IQ Range of Clients 69+.

Tuition and Fees

Room and Board Long term: $72.24/diem.

Tuition $32.

Placements Primarily Funded By State depts of education; Local depts of education; State depts of mental health; Private sources; Social service depts; Juvenile courts.

EVANGELICAL CHILDREN'S HOME *(continued)*

Social and Rehabilitative Services
Therapeutic Approach The facility has an eclectic approach to therapy.
Therapeutic Services Offered Individual therapy; Group therapy; Family therapy; Adjunctive therapy; Art therapy; Independent living skills program; Recreation activities; Aftercare program with follow up.
Professionals on Staff Psychiatrists; Psychologists; Social workers; Adjunctive therapists; Child care staff; Art therapists.
Educational and Vocational Services
Type(s) of Educational Programs Offered On campus; Off campus; Summer campus.
Profile of On Campus School Program Number of teachers 4; *Number of classrooms* 8; *Student to teacher ratio* 6:1; *Credentials of teachers* BD & LD; *Grades taught* K-12.
Degrees Offered 8th grade diploma; 12th grade diploma.

FATHER DUNNE'S NEWSBOYS HOME

4253 Clarence, St Louis, MO 63115 (314) *Contact Person(s):* Samuel Owusu Agyemang, Serra Bording-Jones
Setting and Background Information Father Dunne's Newsboys Home is a private residential treatment facility for boys.
Referral Information Contact the facility for referral information.

GENERAL PROTESTANT CHILDREN'S HOME

12685 Olive St Rd, St Louis, MO 63141 (314) 434-5858 *Contact Person(s):* E A Lenz
Setting and Background Information The facility was originally established as an orphanage 106 years ago. Since then it has expanded its programs to become a treatment center consisting of 4 cottages.
Referral Information Referrals can be made by the Dept of Family Services, school districts, courts, and parents. Applicants are requested to forward a social history, school records, medical history, and psychological evaluation. A pre-placement interview will take place before an admission decision is made.
Type of Facility
Funding Sources Private; State.
Average Length of Stay Long term.
Types of Admissions Accepted Residential treatment; Group home placement; Wards of the state.
Sources of Referral State depts of education; Local depts of education; Private sources; Social service depts.
Client Profile
Age Range of Clients Served Residential program: 6-19.
Characteristics Exhibited by Children Emotional handicaps; Learning disabilities.
Tuition and Fees
Room and Board Long term: Sliding scale.
Placements Primarily Funded By Private sources; Social service depts.
Social and Rehabilitative Services
Therapeutic Services Offered Individual therapy; Group therapy; Family therapy; Adjunctive therapy; Recreation activities.
Educational and Vocational Services
Type(s) of Educational Programs Offered Off campus.

HAWTHORN CHILDRENS PSYCHIATRIC HOSPITAL

5247 Fyler Ave, St Louis, MO 63139 (314) 644-8571 *Contact Person(s):* Donna Campbell PhD, Exec Dir
Setting and Background Information The facility was originally part of St Louis State Hospital and was separated in 1981 by state statute. Its 10-acre campus has a hospital, administration and education buildings.
Referral Information Contact the Intake Clinician. An appointment will be scheduled to determine eligibilty for admission.
Type of Facility
Funding Sources State.
Average Length of Stay Long term.
Types of Admissions Accepted Day treatment; Residential treatment; Wards of the state.
Sources of Referral State depts of education; Local depts of education; State depts of mental health; Psychiatrists; Private sources; Depts of correction; Social service depts; Parents.

Client Profile
Age Range of Clients Served Day programs: 12-18; Residential program: 12-18.
Characteristics Exhibited by Children Emotional handicaps; Learning disabilities; Speech/Language disorders; Neurological impairments; Mental disabilities.
IQ Range of Clients 60-130.
Tuition and Fees
Room and Board Long term: Sliding scale.
Placements Primarily Funded By State depts of mental health.
Social and Rehabilitative Services
Therapeutic Approach The facility has a psycho-educational approach to therapy.
Therapeutic Services Offered Individual therapy; Group therapy; Family therapy; Adjunctive therapy; Art therapy; Recreation activities; Substance abuse treatment; Aftercare program with follow up.
Professionals on Staff Psychiatrists; Psychologists; Social workers; Adjunctive therapists; Child care staff; Nurses.
Educational and Vocational Services
Type(s) of Educational Programs Offered On campus.
Profile of On Campus School Program Number of teachers 4; *Number of classrooms* 4; *Student to teacher ratio* 10:1; *Credentials of teachers* BA; *Grades taught* 1-12; Special curriculum electives offered; Remedial courses offered (Spec Ed).

MARIAN HALL RESIDENTIAL CARE

325 N Newstead, St Louis, MO 63108 (314) 531-0511 *Contact Person(s):* Patricia A Bednara, Dir
Setting and Background Information The facility was established in 1960 by the Sisters of Mercy under the auspices of the Roman Catholic Orphan Board. The facility accepts girls only.
Referral Information Contact the facility for referral information..
Type of Facility
Funding Sources Private; State; Grants.
Average Length of Stay Long term.
Types of Admissions Accepted Residential treatment.
Sources of Referral Local depts of education; Psychiatrists; Private sources; Social service depts; City & County courts; City & County Div of Family Services.
Client Profile
Age Range of Clients Served Residential program: 12-18.
Characteristics Exhibited by Children Emotional handicaps; Learning disabilities; Mental disabilities; Behavior disorders; Abused and neglected; Runaways.
Tuition and Fees
Room and Board Long term: $56.86/diem.
Placements Primarily Funded By Private sources; Social service depts.
Social and Rehabilitative Services
Therapeutic Approach The facility uses reality therapy, including behavior modification and a structured level system.
Therapeutic Services Offered Individual therapy; Group therapy; Family therapy; Adjunctive therapy; Independent living skills program; Recreation activities; Aftercare program with follow up.
Professionals on Staff Psychiatrists; Psychologists; Social workers; Adjunctive therapists; Child care staff; Nurses.
Educational and Vocational Services
Type(s) of Educational Programs Offered On campus (Resource center); Off campus (Public/parochial).
Profile of On Campus School Program Number of teachers 1; *Number of classrooms* 1; *Student to teacher ratio* 4:1; *Credentials of teachers* MA; Special curriculum electives offered (Reading, Math, Language, Computers); Remedial courses offered.

ST JOSEPH'S HOME FOR BOYS

4753 S Grand Blvd, St Louis, MO 63111 (314) 481-9121, 481-0121 *Contact Person(s):* Gladys Dorsey
Setting and Background Information The facility was originally established as an orphanage in 1846. It has since expanded it programs and services to become a treatment center. The campus is located in south St Louis and consists of a 3-story building housing large living units, classrooms, dining area, and a playroom. There are also 2 large recreational fields and a swimming pool on the grounds.
Referral Information Referrals can be made by parents, school districts, hospitals, and psychologists. To make a referral, contact the social workers at the facility to start the intake process.

ST JOSEPH'S HOME FOR BOYS *(continued)*

Type of Facility
Funding Sources Private.
Average Length of Stay Long term.
Types of Admissions Accepted Day treatment; Residential treatment; Group home placement.
Sources of Referral Local depts of education; Psychiatrists; Private sources; Social service depts.
Client Profile
Age Range of Clients Served Day programs: 7-14; Residential program: 7-14.
Characteristics Exhibited by Children Emotional handicaps; Learning disabilities.
Tuition and Fees
Room and Board Long term: Sliding scale.
Placements Primarily Funded By Insurance; Private sources; Social service depts.
Social and Rehabilitative Services
Therapeutic Approach The philosophy of the treatment program is based on reality therapy, goal-directed therapy, and parent effectiveness training.
Therapeutic Services Offered Individual therapy; Group therapy; Family therapy; Recreation activities; Aftercare program with follow up.
Professionals on Staff Psychiatrists; Psychologists; Social workers; Child care staff.
Educational and Vocational Services
Type(s) of Educational Programs Offered On campus; Off campus; Summer campus.
Profile of On Campus School Program Number of teachers 5; *Number of classrooms* 5; *Student to teacher ratio* 10:1; *Grades taught* 1-8; Remedial courses offered.
Degrees Offered 8th grade diploma.

ST VINCENT HOME

7401 Florissant Rd, St Louis, MO 63121 (314) 261-6011 *Contact Person(s):* Sr Virginia Kuhn, Admin
Setting and Background Information The facility was privately established in 1850 as an orphanage. The 20-acre campus has a main building and a gym.
Referral Information Referrals are made through Catholic Charities. The facility accepts youth up to 12 years of age.
Type of Facility
Funding Sources Private; State; Federal; United Way.
Average Length of Stay 2-3 yrs.
Types of Admissions Accepted Residential treatment; Wards of the state.
Sources of Referral Private sources; Social service depts; Catholic Charities; Families.
Client Profile
Age Range of Clients Served Residential program: 6-16.
Characteristics Exhibited by Children Emotional handicaps; Learning disabilities; Hearing impairments/deafness; Speech/Language disorders; Behavior disorders.
IQ Range of Clients 80+.
Tuition and Fees
Placements Primarily Funded By Social service depts; Title XX.
Social and Rehabilitative Services
Therapeutic Services Offered Individual therapy; Group therapy; Family therapy; Art therapy; Physical therapy; Recreation activities; Aftercare program with follow up.
Professionals on Staff Psychiatrists; Psychologists; Social workers; Adjunctive therapists; Child care staff; Nurses; Art therapists.
Educational and Vocational Services
Type(s) of Educational Programs Offered On campus (Spec Ed).
Profile of On Campus School Program Number of teachers 5; *Number of classrooms* 5; *Student to teacher ratio* 10:1; *Credentials of teachers* BA, Certified Spec Ed; *Grades taught* Ungraded; Special curriculum electives offered (Individualized program); Remedial courses offered.

THE SALVATION ARMY RESIDENCE FOR CHILDREN

3740 Marine Ave, St Louis, MO 63118 (314) 773-0980 *Contact Person(s):* Susan Stepleton, Prog Dir

Setting and Background Information The facility was originally established in 1929 as a maternity hospital and home for unwed mothers. There is one large building with a playground.
Referral Information Referrals to the facility are primarily made by state social service depts. Referrals may also be made by hospitals, day care centers, and private practitioners.
Type of Facility
Funding Sources Private; State; Federal.
Average Length of Stay Long term.
Types of Admissions Accepted Day treatment; Residential treatment; Wards of the state; Foster care; Day care.
Sources of Referral State depts of mental health; Social service depts.
Client Profile
Age Range of Clients Served Day programs: Birth-6; Residential program: Birth-6.
Characteristics Exhibited by Children Emotional handicaps; Learning disabilities; Speech/Language disorders.
Tuition and Fees
Room and Board Long term: $35/diem.
Placements Primarily Funded By Social service depts.
Social and Rehabilitative Services
Therapeutic Services Offered Individual therapy; Group therapy; Family therapy; Adjunctive therapy; Aftercare program with follow up.
Professionals on Staff Psychiatrists; Psychologists; Social workers; Adjunctive therapists; Child care staff; Nurses.
Educational and Vocational Services
Type(s) of Educational Programs Offered On campus.
Profile of On Campus School Program Number of teachers 1; *Number of classrooms* 4; *Student to teacher ratio* 4:1.

MONTANA

BILLINGS

YELLOWSTONE TREATMENT CENTER

1732 S 72nd St W, Billings, MT 59106-3599 (406) 656-3001 *Contact Person(s):* Loren L Soft, Exec Dir; Trisha Eik, Intake Coord
Setting and Background Information The ranch is a non-profit, private residential treatment center for adolescents and children. It was established in 1956 as a custodial care facility. Currently, the facility offers residential psychiatric treatment and day services on their 400-acre campus in the Yellowstone River Valley. The campus consists of 9 housing units, a school, a clinic, vocational facilities, recreation facilities, a dining hall, a chapel, family guest homes as well as support facilities. The center also has 4 group homes in the area, several day treatment options, and a psychiatric hospital unit.
Referral Information Contact the facility for referral procedures.

Type of Facility
Funding Sources Private; State.
Average Length of Stay Long term; 12-14 mos.
Types of Admissions Accepted Day treatment; Residential treatment; Group home placement; Wards of the state.
Sources of Referral State depts of education; Local depts of education; State depts of mental health; Psychiatrists; Private sources; Depts of correction; Social service depts.

Client Profile
Age Range of Clients Served Day programs: 6-17; Residential program: 6-17.
Characteristics Exhibited by Children Emotional handicaps; Learning disabilities.
IQ Range of Clients 70+.

Tuition and Fees
Placements Primarily Funded By Local depts of education; State depts of mental health; Insurance; Private sources; Social service depts.

Social and Rehabilitative Services
Therapeutic Approach The treatment program is a comprehensive relationship-based program designed to benefit the child emotionally, physically, socially, academically and spiritually.
Therapeutic Services Offered Individual therapy; Group therapy; Family therapy; Adjunctive therapy; Art therapy; Physical therapy; Independent living skills program; Recreation activities; Substance abuse treatment.
Professionals on Staff Psychiatrists; Psychologists; Social workers; Adjunctive therapists; Child care staff; Nurses; Art therapists; Physical therapists; Pediatricians.

Educational and Vocational Services
Type(s) of Educational Programs Offered On campus; Off campus.
Profile of On Campus School Program Number of teachers 8 and 16 aides; *Number of classrooms* 9; *Student to teacher ratio* 3:1; *Credentials of teachers* Certified Spec Ed; *Grades taught* 1-12; Special curriculum electives offered (Individualized).
Vocational Education Programs/Degrees Offered #Carpentry; Auto Mechanics; Food service; Landscaping; Maintenance; Farming; Ranching; Child care#.
Degrees Offered 8th grade diploma; 12th grade diploma; GED.

HELENA

INTER-MOUNTAIN DEACONESS HOME

500 S Lamborn, Helena, MT 59601 (406) 442-7920 *Contact Person(s):* John Wilkenson, Admin
Setting and Background Information The facility was initially established as an orphanage in 1909. Since then, it has expanded its programs to become a treatment center with 4 residential units and a school and is located on a 40-acre campus.
Referral Information Referrals can be made by parents, agencies, physicians, clergy, and concerned individuals. To make a referral, forward the necessary background information to the Director of Social Services. Upon receipt of the referral material, a pre-placement visit will be scheduled, followed by a staff meeting to make a decision regarding admission.

Type of Facility
Funding Sources Private.
Average Length of Stay 2 ½ yrs.
Types of Admissions Accepted Residential treatment; Wards of the state.
Sources of Referral Social service depts; Courts.

Client Profile
Age Range of Clients Served Residential program: 5-15.
Characteristics Exhibited by Children Emotional handicaps; Learning disabilities.

Tuition and Fees
Room and Board Long term: $70/diem.
Placements Primarily Funded By State depts of mental health; Private sources; County.

Social and Rehabilitative Services
Therapeutic Services Offered Individual therapy; Group therapy; Family therapy.
Professionals on Staff Psychiatrists; Psychologists; Social workers; Child care staff; Nurses.

Educational and Vocational Services
Type(s) of Educational Programs Offered On campus; Off campus; Summer campus.
Profile of On Campus School Program Number of teachers 2 and 1 aide; *Student to teacher ratio* 6:1; *Credentials of teachers* Spec Ed; Special curriculum electives offered.

NEBRASKA

HENDERSON

GRACE CHILDREN'S HOME

Box 519, Henderson, NE 68371 (402) 723-5725 *Contact Person(s):*
Herb Mills

Setting and Background Information The facility was established in
1936 as a Christian child care institution, operated by people
from several denominations. Its campus is located in a small rural
community and consists of 3 cottages, gymnasium, shop, and
office building.

Referral Information Referrals can be made by the Dept of Welfare,
courts, probation officers, and families. To make a referral,
contact the facility and forward a social history, statement of
presenting problems and goals for placement, and an assessment
of services needed. A pre-placement visit is necessary before an
admission decision is made.

Type of Facility

Funding Sources Private; State; Federal.

Average Length of Stay Long term.

Types of Admissions Accepted Residential treatment; Group home
placement; Wards of the state.

Sources of Referral Private sources; Depts of correction; Social service depts.

Client Profile

Age Range of Clients Served Residential program: 6-16.

Characteristics Exhibited by Children Emotional handicaps; Learning
disabilities.

Tuition and Fees

Room and Board Long term: $750/mo.

Social and Rehabilitative Services

Therapeutic Services Offered Individual therapy; Group therapy; Independent living skills program.

Professionals on Staff Social workers; Child care staff.

LINCOLN

NEBRASKA CENTER FOR CHILDREN AND YOUTH

2320 N 57th, Lincoln, NE 68504 (402) 471-3305 *Contact Person(s):*
Brad Pope

Setting and Background Information The facility was initially
established as an orphanage in 1876 by a group of concerned
church women. Since then, it has expanded its services to become
a treatment center. The main campus is located on 7 acres and
consists of a mansion housing offices, 7 residential cottages,
school/administration building, and a 10-bed locked facility.
There are also group homes located in Auburn, Columbus,
Seward, Bellevue, and Lincoln.

Referral Information Referrals can be made by contacting the
facility.

Type of Facility

Funding Sources State; Federal.

Average Length of Stay Long term.

Types of Admissions Accepted Residential treatment; Group home
placement; Wards of the state.

Sources of Referral Social service depts.

Client Profile

Age Range of Clients Served Residential program: 12-17.

Characteristics Exhibited by Children Emotional handicaps; Learning
disabilities.

Social and Rehabilitative Services

Therapeutic Approach The treatment program utilizes a family systems model and a variety of other therapeutic approaches.

Therapeutic Services Offered Individual therapy; Group therapy;
Family therapy; Independent living skills program; Recreation
activities; Aftercare program with follow up.

Professionals on Staff Psychiatrists; Psychologists; Social workers;
Child care staff; Nurses.

Educational and Vocational Services

Type(s) of Educational Programs Offered On campus; Summer campus.

Profile of On Campus School Program Number of teachers 10;
Number of classrooms 10; *Student to teacher ratio* 5:1; Special
curriculum electives offered; Remedial courses offered.

WICS RESIDENCE FOR GIRLS

1935 'D' St, Lincoln, NE 68502 (402) 477-5256 *Contact Person(s):*
Lucy Nevels, Dir

Setting and Background Information The facility was established in
1970 with federal funds, foundation and organization grants,
church and individual contributions. It is located in a residential
area.

Referral Information Contact the facility for referral information.

Type of Facility

Funding Sources Private.

Average Length of Stay Long term.

Types of Admissions Accepted Residential treatment; Group home
placement; Foster care.

Sources of Referral State depts of mental health; Psychiatrists; Private sources; Depts of correction; Social service depts; Parents.

Client Profile

Age Range of Clients Served Residential program: 12-19.

Characteristics Exhibited by Children Emotional handicaps; Learning
disabilities; Mental disabilities.

Tuition and Fees

Room and Board Long term: $1,125/mo.

Placements Primarily Funded By Private sources; Social service
depts.

Social and Rehabilitative Services

Therapeutic Approach The program has a family systems approach
to therapy and uses reality therapy with behavior modification.

Therapeutic Services Offered Individual therapy; Group therapy;
Family therapy; Independent living skills program; Aftercare program with follow up.

Professionals on Staff Social workers; Child care staff.

Educational and Vocational Services

Type(s) of Educational Programs Offered Off campus (Public School).

OMAHA

AMI ST JOSEPH CENTER FOR MENTAL HEALTH

819 Dorcas St, Omaha, NE 68108 (402) 449-4650

Referral Information Referrals can be made by contacting the
facility.

Type of Facility

Funding Sources Private.

Average Length of Stay Short term.

Types of Admissions Accepted Day treatment; Residential treatment.

AMI ST JOSEPH CENTER FOR MENTAL HEALTH
(continued)

Sources of Referral State depts of education; Local depts of education; State depts of mental health; Psychiatrists; Private sources; Social service depts.
Client Profile
Age Range of Clients Served Day programs: 18-21+; Residential program: Birth-55+.
Characteristics Exhibited by Children Emotional handicaps.
Tuition and Fees
Placements Primarily Funded By Insurance.
Social and Rehabilitative Services
Therapeutic Services Offered Individual therapy; Group therapy; Family therapy; Adjunctive therapy; Recreation activities; Substance abuse treatment; Occupational therapy, Music therapy.
Professionals on Staff Psychiatrists; Psychologists; Social workers; Adjunctive therapists; Nurses; Music therapist; Movement therapist; Occupational therapist; Recreational therapists.
Educational and Vocational Services
Type(s) of Educational Programs Offered On campus.
Profile of On Campus School Program Number of teachers 6; *Number of classrooms* 5; *Credentials of teachers* MA Certified; *Grades taught* Pre school-12; Remedial courses offered.

UTA HALEE GIRLS VILLAGE
10625 Calhoun Rd, Omaha, NE 68112 (402) 453-0805 *Contact Person(s):* Richard Hays, Exec Dir
Setting and Background Information The village was founded in 1950 by Church Women United. It is located on 30 acres and has dormitories, a school, administration and maintenance buildings.
Referral Information Contact the facility for referral information.
Type of Facility
Funding Sources Private; State.
Average Length of Stay Long term.
Types of Admissions Accepted Residential treatment; Group home placement.
Sources of Referral State depts of mental health; Psychiatrists; Private sources; Social service depts.
Client Profile
Age Range of Clients Served Residential program: 12-18.
Characteristics Exhibited by Children Emotional handicaps.
IQ Range of Clients 80-125.
Tuition and Fees
Room and Board Long term: $105/diem.
Placements Primarily Funded By State depts of education; Local depts of education; Insurance; Social service depts.
Social and Rehabilitative Services
Therapeutic Services Offered Individual therapy; Group therapy; Family therapy; Independent living skills program; Recreation activities; Aftercare program with follow up.
Professionals on Staff Psychiatrists; Psychologists; Social workers; Child care staff; Nurses.
Educational and Vocational Services
Type(s) of Educational Programs Offered On campus.
Profile of On Campus School Program Number of teachers 7; *Number of classrooms* 6; *Student to teacher ratio* 8:1; *Grades taught* 7-12.

RICHARD H YOUNG MEMORIAL HOSPITAL
PO Box 3434, 415 S 25th Ave, Omaha, NE 68103-0434 (402) 536-6599 *Contact Person(s):* Terese Holm, Asst Admin, Psychiatric Svcs
Setting and Background Information The facility was established in 1928 by 9 local Missouri Synod Lutheran Churches. Currently, there are two main buildings—the Lutheran Medical Center, and the Richard H Young Memorial Hospital. The hospital is a comprehensive psychiatric facility.
Referral Information The hospital accepts self referrals and referrals from healthcare professionals, ministers, educators, and psychiatirc admissions.
Type of Facility
Funding Sources Private.
Average Length of Stay Short term.
Types of Admissions Accepted Day treatment; In-patient psychiatric treatment.

Sources of Referral State depts of education; Local depts of education; State depts of mental health; Psychiatrists; Private sources; Depts of correction; Social service depts.
Client Profile
Age Range of Clients Served Day programs: 6-21+; Residential program: 6-55+.
Characteristics Exhibited by Children Emotional handicaps; Learning disabilities; Neurological impairments; Mental disabilities; Physical illness; Chemical dependency.
Tuition and Fees
Placements Primarily Funded By Insurance; Private sources; Social service depts.
Social and Rehabilitative Services
Therapeutic Approach The basic approach of the facility is a medical model utilizing a variety of treatment options directed by private psychiatrists on the staff of the Dept of Psychiatry.
Therapeutic Services Offered Individual therapy; Group therapy; Family therapy; Adjunctive therapy; Art therapy; Physical therapy; Independent living skills program; Recreation activities; Substance abuse treatment; Aftercare program with follow up; Activity therapy; Occupational therapy.
Professionals on Staff Psychiatrists; Psychologists; Social workers; Adjunctive therapists; Child care staff; Nurses; Art therapists; Physical therapists; Occupational therapist.
Educational and Vocational Services
Type(s) of Educational Programs Offered On campus.
Profile of On Campus School Program Number of teachers 7; *Number of classrooms* 7; *Student to teacher ratio* 10:1; *Credentials of teachers* State certified; *Grades taught* K-12; Special curriculum electives offered (Individualized); Remedial courses offered.
Degrees Offered 8th grade diploma; 12th grade diploma; GED.

YOUTH AND FAMILY SERVICES
2555 Leavenworth St, Omaha, NE 68105 (402) 444-6656 *Contact Person(s):* William E Reay, Dir of Youth & Family Srvs
Setting and Background Information The community based facility was established in 1973 through an inter-local agreement between counties.
Referral Information Referrals to the facility are through the Dept of Social Services, the Dept of Education or the court system.
Type of Facility
Funding Sources Political subdivision.
Average Length of Stay Long term.
Types of Admissions Accepted Day treatment; Residential treatment; Home-based foster-care.
Sources of Referral State depts of education; Local depts of education; State depts of mental health; Psychiatrists; Private sources; Social service depts; Self.
Client Profile
Age Range of Clients Served Day programs: 6-21+; Residential program: 6-18.
Characteristics Exhibited by Children Emotional handicaps; Learning disabilities; Conduct disorders.
Tuition and Fees
Room and Board Long term: $1,193-2,100/mo.
Tuition $60/diem.
Placements Primarily Funded By State depts of education; Local depts of education; State depts of mental health; Social service depts.
Social and Rehabilitative Services
Therapeutic Approach The facility has a systems approach to therapy with emphasis on behavior modification.
Therapeutic Services Offered Individual therapy; Family therapy; Independent living skills program; Recreation activities; Aftercare program with follow up.
Professionals on Staff Psychiatrists; Psychologists; Social workers; Child care staff.
Educational and Vocational Services
Type(s) of Educational Programs Offered On campus; Off campus.
Profile of On Campus School Program Number of teachers 18; *Number of classrooms* 1; *Student to teacher ratio* 4:1; Special curriculum electives offered; Remedial courses offered.

YORK

EPWORTH VILLAGE, INC

Box 503, 21st & Division, York, NE 68467 (402) 362-3353 *Contact Person(s):* Mrs Jessie K Forney, Dir of Comm Relations

Setting and Background Information The facility was founded as an orphanage in 1889 by church women who wanted to meet the social needs of children and families. Currently, the 11-acre campus has two residences and an administration building, plus 2 off-campus group homes.

Referral Information For referral, contact the facility for an application packet. Contact-Linda Hirschfeld, Dir of Residential Treatment, Box 503, York, NE, 68467

Type of Facility

Funding Sources Private; State; Charitable contributions.

Average Length of Stay Short and long term.

Types of Admissions Accepted Day treatment; Residential treatment; Group home placement; Wards of the state; Out-patient.

Sources of Referral State depts of education; Local depts of education; State depts of mental health; Psychiatrists; Private sources; Depts of correction; Social service depts; Private referrals.

Client Profile

Age Range of Clients Served Day programs: 6-18; Residential program: 6-18.

Characteristics Exhibited by Children Emotional handicaps; Learning disabilities; Neurological impairments; Physical handicaps; Mental disabilities; Behavior disorders.

IQ Range of Clients 75-120.

Tuition and Fees

Placements Primarily Funded By State depts of education; Local depts of education; Private sources; Social service depts.

Social and Rehabilitative Services

Therapeutic Approach The basic therapeutic approach is eclectic and includes behavior modification, individual and group counseling in a milieu setting.

Therapeutic Services Offered Individual therapy; Group therapy; Family therapy; Adjunctive therapy; Art therapy; Independent living skills program; Recreation activities; Aftercare program with follow up.

Professionals on Staff Psychiatrists; Psychologists; Social workers; Adjunctive therapists; Child care staff; Nurses; Art therapists.

Educational and Vocational Services

Type(s) of Educational Programs Offered On campus; Off campus (Public school); Summer campus (Full program).

Profile of On Campus School Program Number of teachers 8; *Number of classrooms* 8; *Student to teacher ratio* 4:1; *Credentials of teachers* MA or MS, Spec Ed; *Grades taught* K-12; Special curriculum electives offered (Art, Recreation, Crafts, Music, Social skills); Remedial courses offered (Complete academic curriculum).

Vocational Education Programs/Degrees Offered Currently developing a program.

Degrees Offered 12th grade diploma through public school; GED through York Community Ed.

NEVADA

RENO

NORTHERN NEVADA CHILD AND ADOLESCENCE SERVICES

2655 Enterprise Rd, Reno, NV 89512 (702) 789-0300 *Contact Person(s):* Dr Darrell Downs, Dir of Outpatient Svcs

Setting and Background Information The programs were established in 1977 and are in 3 different areas of the city. There is an adolescent program, a child program, and a community-based treatment home.

Referral Information Referrals can be made by anyone.

Type of Facility

Funding Sources State.

Average Length of Stay Long term.

Types of Admissions Accepted Day treatment; Residential treatment; Group home placement.

Sources of Referral State depts of mental health.

Client Profile

Age Range of Clients Served Day programs: Birth-18; Residential program: 5-18.

Characteristics Exhibited by Children Emotional handicaps; Learning disabilities; Speech/Language disorders; Neurological impairments.

Tuition and Fees

Room and Board Long term: $84-$120/diem.

Placements Primarily Funded By State depts of mental health.

Social and Rehabilitative Services

Therapeutic Approach The program has an eclectic treatment approach, in conjunction with behavior therapy.

Therapeutic Services Offered Individual therapy; Group therapy; Family therapy; Aftercare program with follow up.

Professionals on Staff Psychiatrists; Psychologists; Social workers; Child care staff.

Educational and Vocational Services

Type(s) of Educational Programs Offered On campus.

Profile of On Campus School Program Number of teachers 1; *Student to teacher ratio* 8:1.

NEW HAMPSHIRE

CONCORD

ANNA PHILBROOK CENTER FOR CHILDREN AND YOUTH

121 S Fruit St, Concord, NH 03301 (603) 224-6531 ext 2366
Contact Person(s): Joseph Perry
Setting and Background Information The facility is located on the grounds of New Hampshire Hospital.
Referral Information Referrals to the psychiatric program can be made by district court orders under RSA 169B, C, or D for 30-60 day evaluations, petitions for involuntary emergency hospitalization, probate court commitment, and voluntary application. The special education program accepts referrals under the authority of House Bill 27. To make a referral to the psychiatric program, contact Joseph Perry. Referrals to the special education program should be directed to Ted Prizio.

Type of Facility
Funding Sources State.
Average Length of Stay Long term.
Types of Admissions Accepted Residential treatment; Wards of the state.
Sources of Referral Local depts of education; State depts of mental health; Psychiatrists; Social service depts.

Client Profile
Age Range of Clients Served Residential program: 5-17.
Characteristics Exhibited by Children Emotional handicaps.

Tuition and Fees
Placements Primarily Funded By State depts of mental health.

Social and Rehabilitative Services
Therapeutic Services Offered Individual therapy; Group therapy; Family therapy.

Educational and Vocational Services
Type(s) of Educational Programs Offered On campus (Spec Ed); Summer campus.
Profile of On Campus School Program Student to teacher ratio 3:1; *Grades taught* K-12; Special curriculum electives offered; Remedial courses offered.

TILTON

SPAULDING YOUTH CENTER

PO Box 189, Tilton, NH 03276 (603) 286-8901 *Contact Person(s):* Vincent Francisco, Admis Spec
Setting and Background Information The facility was originally established as an orphanage after the Civil War, but evolved into a treatment center in 1958. Its campus is located on 500 acres in rural central New Hampshire and consists of 4 residences (3 for emotionally disturbed residents and one for autistic residents), dining hall, classroom building, administration building, maintenance shed, and assorted outbuildings.
Referral Information Referral can be made by school districts, courts, social workers, parents, and any concerned individual. To make a referral, forward the following background information: family history, intelligence testing report, educational history, individualized educational plan, history of agency contacts, reports from previous treatment programs the child has been involved in, medical history, court and probation records (if appropriate), and a statement of who will be funding the placement. Upon receipt of completed application forms and the above information, a pre-placement visit and interview will take place and an admission decision made the same day. The facility accepts boys only.

Type of Facility
Funding Sources Private; State; Federal.
Average Length of Stay Short and long term.
Types of Admissions Accepted Day treatment; Residential treatment; Group home placement; Wards of the state.
Sources of Referral State depts of education; Local depts of education; State depts of mental health; Psychiatrists; Private sources; Depts of correction; Social service depts.

Client Profile
Age Range of Clients Served Day programs: 6-16; Residential program: 6-16.
Characteristics Exhibited by Children Emotional handicaps; Learning disabilities; Hearing impairments/deafness; Speech/Language disorders; Neurological impairments; Physical handicaps; Mental disabilities; Autism.

Tuition and Fees
Placements Primarily Funded By State depts of education; Local depts of education; State depts of mental health; Private sources; Social service depts.

Social and Rehabilitative Services
Therapeutic Approach The philosophy of the treatment program is eclectic with emphasis on behavioral approaches.
Therapeutic Services Offered Individual therapy; Group therapy; Family therapy; Art therapy; Independent living skills program; Recreation activities; Aftercare program with follow up.
Professionals on Staff Psychologists; Social workers; Adjunctive therapists; Child care staff; Nurses; Art therapists.

Educational and Vocational Services
Type(s) of Educational Programs Offered On campus; Off campus; Summer campus.
Profile of On Campus School Program Number of teachers 20; *Number of classrooms* 9; *Student to teacher ratio* 6:1; *Length of school day* 7 ½ hrs; Remedial courses offered.

NEW JERSEY

CEDAR GROVE

CEDAR GROVE RESIDENTIAL CENTER

240 Grove Ave, Cedar Grove, NJ 07009 (201) 857-0200 *Contact Person(s):* Delores Cox

Setting and Background Information The facility was established in 1975 by the Division of Youth and Family Services and Bureau of Residential Facilities. Its campus is located on 8 ½ acres of land and consists of 3 cottages, school and recreation building, gymnasium, administrative building, and an outdoor field area.

Referral Information Referrals are only accepted directly from district offices of the Division of Youth and Family Services.

Type of Facility

Funding Sources State.

Average Length of Stay Long term.

Types of Admissions Accepted Residential treatment.

Sources of Referral Social service depts; Div of Youth and Family Services.

Client Profile

Age Range of Clients Served Residential program: 13-17.

Characteristics Exhibited by Children Emotional handicaps; Learning disabilities; Neurological impairments.

IQ Range of Clients 75+.

Tuition and Fees

Placements Primarily Funded By Social service depts; Div of Youth and Family Svcs.

Social and Rehabilitative Services

Therapeutic Approach The residential treatment program utilizes the Teaching Parent Model, in conjunction with behavior modification in the form of a point system.

Therapeutic Services Offered Family therapy; Independent living skills program; Recreation activities.

Professionals on Staff Psychiatrists; Social workers; Child care staff; Nurses.

Educational and Vocational Services

Type(s) of Educational Programs Offered Off campus.

Profile of On Campus School Program Remedial courses offered.

Degrees Offered GED.

CHESTER

THE DEVEREUX CENTER—DEERHAVEN

PO Box 654, Chester, NJ 07930 (201) 879-4500 *Contact Person(s):* Bernice Manshel, Dir

Setting and Background Information This facility was established by the Devereux Foundation in 1982. Its 33-acre campus has residential cottages, an administration building and a school.

Referral Information For information, contact the admissions office and forward the necessary records. A pre-placement visit will be scheduled.

Type of Facility

Funding Sources Private.

Average Length of Stay Long term.

Types of Admissions Accepted Residential treatment.

Sources of Referral Local depts of education; Psychiatrists; Private sources; Social service depts.

Client Profile

Age Range of Clients Served Residential program: 12-18.

Characteristics Exhibited by Children Emotional handicaps; Learning disabilities.

IQ Range of Clients 85+.

Tuition and Fees

Room and Board Long term: $108/diem.

Tuition $11,000/yr.

Placements Primarily Funded By Local depts of education; Private sources; Social service depts.

Social and Rehabilitative Services

Therapeutic Services Offered Individual therapy; Group therapy; Family therapy; Art therapy; Recreation activities; Aftercare program with follow up.

Professionals on Staff Psychiatrists; Psychologists; Social workers; Child care staff; Nurses; Art therapists.

Educational and Vocational Services

Type(s) of Educational Programs Offered On campus (Self-contained high school).

Profile of On Campus School Program Number of classrooms 4; Student to teacher ratio 8:1; Credentials of teachers BA, MA; Grades taught 7-12; Special curriculum electives offered (Art, Drama).

Degrees Offered 12th grade diploma; GED.

FARMINGDALE

ARTHUR BRISBANE CHILD TREATMENT CENTER

PO Box 625, Farmingdale, NJ 07727 (201) 938-5061 *Contact Person(s):* Donald A Bruckman

Setting and Background Information The facility was established in 1947 by state law. There are three residential buildings, a clinical/office building, and a school.

Referral Information Clients are referred and placed by consensus of treatment team. Placements are often made through the Division of Youth and Family Services.

Type of Facility

Funding Sources State.

Average Length of Stay Long term.

Types of Admissions Accepted Residential treatment; Psychiatric committment.

Sources of Referral Psychiatrists; Courts; Div of Youth and Family Services.

Client Profile

Age Range of Clients Served Residential program: 6-15.

Characteristics Exhibited by Children Emotional handicaps; Learning disabilities; Neurological impairments; Mental disabilities.

IQ Range of Clients 30-132.

Tuition and Fees

Placements Primarily Funded By Insurance; Medicaid.

Social and Rehabilitative Services

Therapeutic Approach The facility offers individual and family therapy within a behavior modification program.

Therapeutic Services Offered Individual therapy; Group therapy; Art therapy; Recreation activities.

Professionals on Staff Psychiatrists; Psychologists; Social workers; Child care staff; Nurses; Occupational therapists.

Educational and Vocational Services

Type(s) of Educational Programs Offered On campus; Summer campus.

Profile of On Campus School Program Number of teachers 13; Number of classrooms 11; Student to teacher ratio 8:1; Credentials of teachers Certified Spec Ed; Grades taught K-7; Special curriculum electives offered (Library, Speech, PE, Shop, Art, Music, Home Ec, Reading, Family life, Computer instruction).

HACKENSACK

HOLLEY CHILD CARE AND DEVELOPMENT CENTER

260 Union St, Hackensack, NJ 07601 (201) 343-8803 *Contact Person(s):* Cynthia Chaltowitz, ACSW

Setting and Background Information The facility was established in 1971 by the Youth Consultation Service and the Episcopal Diocese of Newark. It is located in Hackensack, New Jersey and the school program is located in nearby Edgewater.

Referral Information Referrals can be made by parents, school districts, physicians, and state agencies. Applicants should contact Cynthia Chaltowitz for information concerning admission procedures.

Type of Facility

Funding Sources Private; State; Federal.

Average Length of Stay Long term.

Types of Admissions Accepted Day treatment; Residential treatment; Wards of the state.

Sources of Referral Local depts of education; Social service depts.

Client Profile

Age Range of Clients Served Day programs: 4-18; Residential program: 4-12.

Characteristics Exhibited by Children Emotional handicaps; Learning disabilities; Vision impairments/blindness; Speech/Language disorders; Neurological impairments; Mental disabilities.

Tuition and Fees

Room and Board Long term: $112/diem.

Tuition $12,800/yr.

Placements Primarily Funded By Social service depts; Medicare.

Social and Rehabilitative Services

Therapeutic Approach The program's philosophy is based on behavior therapy, cognitive behavior therapy, play therapy, and chemotherapy.

Therapeutic Services Offered Individual therapy; Group therapy; Family therapy; Adjunctive therapy; Art therapy; Recreation activities; Aftercare program with follow up.

Professionals on Staff Psychiatrists; Psychologists; Social workers; Adjunctive therapists; Child care staff; Nurses; Art therapists.

Educational and Vocational Services

Type(s) of Educational Programs Offered On campus; Off campus.

Profile of On Campus School Program Number of teachers 10; *Number of classrooms* 10; *Student to teacher ratio* 4:1; *Grades taught* K-12; Special curriculum electives offered; Remedial courses offered.

Degrees Offered 12th grade diploma.

HADDONFIELD

THE BANCROFT SCHOOL

Hopkins Lane, Haddonfield, NJ 08033 (609) 429-0010 *Contact Person(s):* Yolanda S Katona, Admis Dir

Setting and Background Information The school was established in 1883 by Margaret Bancroft, a teacher in the Philadelphia school system, as an educational center for developmentally disabled and multiply handicapped children. Its main campus is located on 16 acres and consists of 2 dormitory buildings, school, garden apartments, and a group home. There is also a community program located near Mullica Hill, New Jersey, on 300 acres, which provides handicapped young adults with the independent learning skills necessary to return to their community. The Bancroft School's vocational and summer program, located on 30 acres along Penobscot Bay at Owl's Head, Maine, is their year round residential school.

Referral Information Referrals can be made by physicians, psychologists, school districts, social agencies, parents, and guardians. To make a referral, contact the facility and forward all necessary background information including clinical evaluations. Upon receipt of the referral material, an interview will take place and the funding source established. Staff clinicians will then review the case and make a placement decision.

Type of Facility

Funding Sources Private; State.

Average Length of Stay Long term.

Types of Admissions Accepted Day treatment; Residential treatment; Group home placement.

Sources of Referral State depts of education; Local depts of education; Private sources; Social service depts.

Client Profile

Age Range of Clients Served Day programs: 5-21+; Residential program: 5-21+.

Characteristics Exhibited by Children Emotional handicaps; Learning disabilities; Hearing impairments/deafness; Vision impairments/blindness; Speech/Language disorders; Neurological impairments; Physical handicaps; Mental disabilities; Autism.

IQ Range of Clients 40-90.

Tuition and Fees

Room and Board Long term: $50,760/yr (Residential); $14,429/yr(Day treatment); $59,916/yr (Autism).

Placements Primarily Funded By State depts of education; Local depts of education; Private sources; Social service depts.

Social and Rehabilitative Services

Therapeutic Approach The treatment programs use reality therapy and behavior management. Eclectic therapeutic approaches are developed and utilized according to resident's individual needs.

Therapeutic Services Offered Individual therapy; Group therapy; Family therapy; Art therapy; Independent living skills program; Aftercare program with follow up.

Professionals on Staff Psychiatrists; Psychologists; Social workers; Child care staff; Nurses; Art therapists.

Educational and Vocational Services

Type(s) of Educational Programs Offered On campus; Summer campus.

Profile of On Campus School Program Number of teachers 75; *Number of classrooms* 34; Special curriculum electives offered.

MILLVILLE

CUMBERLAND COUNTY GUIDANCE CENTER, INC

PO Box 808, Rt 1, Carmel Rd, Millville, NJ 08332 (609) 825-6810 *Contact Person(s):* Client Svcs Suprv

Setting and Background Information This facility was established in 1970 with federal monies. The 15-acre campus has two buildings.

Referral Information Contact the Client Services Dept for referral information.

Type of Facility

Funding Sources Private; State; Federal; County.

Average Length of Stay Short and long term.

Types of Admissions Accepted Day treatment; Group home placement.

Sources of Referral State depts of education; Local depts of education; State depts of mental health; Psychiatrists; Private sources; Depts of correction; Social service depts.

Client Profile

Age Range of Clients Served Day programs: 6-55+; Residential program: 18-55+.

Characteristics Exhibited by Children Emotional handicaps.

Tuition and Fees

Room and Board Short term: Sliding scale; Long term: Sliding scale.

Social and Rehabilitative Services

Therapeutic Services Offered Individual therapy; Group therapy; Family therapy; Independent living skills program; Recreation activities; Aftercare program with follow up.

Professionals on Staff Psychiatrists; Psychologists; Social workers; Child care staff.

MOUNT HOLLY

THE CHILDREN'S HOME OF BURLINGTON COUNTY

243 Pine St, Mount Holly, NJ 08060 (609) 267-1550 *Contact Person(s):* William F Town, Exec Dir

Setting and Background Information The facility was originally established in 1864 as an orphanage. Currently, it is located on 10 acres and has 9 buildings.

Referral Information Referrals are made through the Division of Youth and Family Services. There will be a pre-placement visit of 1 to 3 days.

Type of Facility

Funding Sources Private; State.

Average Length of Stay Long term.

Types of Admissions Accepted Residential treatment.

Sources of Referral Division of Youth and Family Service.

THE CHILDREN'S HOME OF BURLINGTON COUNTY *(continued)*

Client Profile
Age Range of Clients Served Residential program: 12-18.
Characteristics Exhibited by Children Emotional handicaps; Learning disabilities.
Tuition and Fees
Room and Board Long term: $53.40-$76.32/diem.
Tuition $10,900/yr.
Placements Primarily Funded By Local depts of education; Social service depts.
Social and Rehabilitative Services
Therapeutic Approach The facility offers a therapeutic milieu.
Therapeutic Services Offered Individual therapy; Group therapy; Family therapy; Adjunctive therapy; Art therapy; Independent living skills program; Recreation activities.
Professionals on Staff Psychiatrists; Psychologists; Social workers; Adjunctive therapists; Child care staff; Nurses; Art therapists.
Educational and Vocational Services
Type(s) of Educational Programs Offered On campus.
Profile of On Campus School Program Number of teachers 6; *Number of classrooms* 5; *Student to teacher ratio* 8:1; *Credentials of teachers* Spec Ed; *Length of school day* 9-3; Special curriculum electives offered; Remedial courses offered.
Vocational Education Programs/Degrees Offered Job readiness training.
Degrees Offered GED; Degree conferred by the referring school district.

OCEAN

SEARCH DAY PROGRAM, INC.
73 Wickapecko Dr, Ocean, NJ 07712 (201) 531-0454 *Contact Person(s):* Kenneth F Appenzeller, Exec Dir
Setting and Background Information The program was established in 1971 by parents of autistic children. It is designed to serve the comprehensive needs of an autisic person from pre-school throughout adult life. There are three components to this program—a school, a group home, and an adult activity center.
Referral Information Contact the facility for referral information.
Type of Facility
Funding Sources Private; State.
Average Length of Stay Short and long term.
Types of Admissions Accepted Day treatment; Group home placement.
Sources of Referral State depts of education; Local depts of education; State depts of mental health; Psychiatrists; Private sources; Social service depts.
Client Profile
Age Range of Clients Served Day programs: 3-21+; Residential program: 18-21+.
Characteristics Exhibited by Children Autism.
Tuition and Fees
Tuition Established by State Dept of Education.
Placements Primarily Funded By State depts of education; Local depts of education; State depts of mental health.
Social and Rehabilitative Services
Therapeutic Services Offered Individual therapy; Group therapy; Family therapy; Speech/language therapy; Occupational therapy.
Professionals on Staff Psychiatrists; Psychologists; Social workers; Nurses.
Educational and Vocational Services
Type(s) of Educational Programs Offered On campus.
Profile of On Campus School Program Number of teachers 10; *Number of classrooms* 10; *Student to teacher ratio* 2:1; *Credentials of teachers* State Certified Spec Ed.

PRINCETON

THE EDEN FAMILY OF PROGRAMS
One Logan Dr, Princeton, NJ 08540 (609) 987-0099 *Contact Person(s):* Dr David L Holmes, Exec Dir
Setting and Background Information The facility was established in 1975. There are 5 group homes, 2 adult training centers, and a day school with administrative offices.

Referral Information For referral, contact the facility and forward the required materials. A pre-placement interview will be scheduled.
Type of Facility
Funding Sources Private; State.
Average Length of Stay Long term.
Types of Admissions Accepted Day treatment; Group home placement.
Sources of Referral State depts of education; Local depts of education; State depts of mental health; Psychiatrists; Private sources; Social service depts.
Client Profile
Age Range of Clients Served Day programs: Birth-21; Residential program: 12-21+.
Characteristics Exhibited by Children Autism.
IQ Range of Clients 25-75.
Tuition and Fees
Room and Board Long term: $35,000/yr.
Tuition $13,000/yr.
Placements Primarily Funded By State depts of education; Social service depts.
Social and Rehabilitative Services
Therapeutic Approach The facility has a behavioral approach to therapy.
Therapeutic Services Offered Individual therapy; Family therapy; Physical therapy; Independent living skills program; Recreation activities; Speech therapy; Occupational therapy.
Professionals on Staff Psychologists; Adjunctive therapists; Child care staff; Occupational therapist.
Educational and Vocational Services
Type(s) of Educational Programs Offered On campus; Summer campus.
Profile of On Campus School Program Student to teacher ratio 2:1; *Credentials of teachers* State certified; *Length of school day* 9-2:30; Remedial courses offered (Speech, PE).
Vocational Education Programs/Degrees Offered Employment orientation; Pre-vocational.
Degrees Offered GED.

PRINCETON CHILD DEVELOPMENT INSTITUTE
300 Cold Soil Rd, Princeton, NJ 08540 (609) 924-6280 *Contact Person(s):* Dr Patricia Krantz, Dr Lynn McClannahan, Co-Dirs
Setting and Background Information The facility was founded in 1971 and is a private, non-profit program offering a broad spectrum of services to autistic children, youth and young adults and their families. It is also involved in the development of models for effective education and treatment of autistic children.
Referral Information Contact the facility for referral information.
Type of Facility
Funding Sources Private; State; Federal; County.
Average Length of Stay Long term.
Types of Admissions Accepted Residential treatment; Group home placement.
Sources of Referral State Division of Youth and Family Svcs.
Client Profile
Age Range of Clients Served Day programs: Birth-21+; Residential program: 6-21+.
Characteristics Exhibited by Children Emotional handicaps; Autism.
Tuition and Fees
Tuition $10,900/10 mo.
Placements Primarily Funded By State depts of education.
Social and Rehabilitative Services
Therapeutic Approach The program uses behavioral analysis as a therapeutic approach.
Therapeutic Services Offered Individual therapy; Parent training/home program.
Professionals on Staff Psychologists.
Educational and Vocational Services
Type(s) of Educational Programs Offered On campus (Community-based).
Profile of On Campus School Program Number of teachers 10; *Number of classrooms* 10; *Student to teacher ratio* 1.5:1.
Vocational Education Programs/Degrees Offered Individualized career development programs.

SUMMIT

FAIR OAKS HOSPITAL

19 Prospect St, Summit, NJ 07901 (201) 522-7000; 1-800-672-1807 (toll free in NJ); 1-800-526-4494 (out of state) *Contact Person(s):* Wendy Calvin, Dir of Admis

Setting and Background Information The facility was established by two physicians in 1902. The hospital is located on 10 acres.
Referral Information Contact the facility for referral procedures.

Type of Facility
Funding Sources Private.
Average Length of Stay Long term.
Types of Admissions Accepted Day treatment; Residential treatment; Out-patient.
Sources of Referral Anyone may make a referral.

Client Profile
Age Range of Clients Served Day programs: 18-21+; Residential program: 12-21+.
Characteristics Exhibited by Children Emotional handicaps; Learning disabilities; Mental disabilities.

Tuition and Fees
Placements Primarily Funded By Insurance; Private sources.

Social and Rehabilitative Services
Therapeutic Services Offered Individual therapy; Group therapy; Family therapy; Art therapy; Recreation activities; Substance abuse treatment; Aftercare program with follow up.
Professionals on Staff Psychiatrists; Psychologists; Social workers; Nurses; Art therapists.

Educational and Vocational Services
Type(s) of Educational Programs Offered On campus; Summer campus.
Profile of On Campus School Program Number of teachers 5; *Number of classrooms* 5; *Student to teacher ratio* 7 or 8:1; *Length of school day* 8:45-3:30; *Grades taught* 7-12; Special curriculum electives offered; Remedial courses offered (Math, Reading).

PROSPECT LEARNING CENTER

19 Prospect St, Summit, NJ 07901 (201) 522-7039 *Contact Person(s):* Patricia Tarashuk, Dir

Setting and Background Information Prospect Learning Center is a private program which serves residents in the Fair Oaks Hospital Adolescent Program. Psychiatric and educational placements are accepted. The school program was established in 1981 at Fair Oaks Hospital. The facility is located 25 miles from New York City.
Referral Information Referrals can be made by therapists, school districts, physicians, courts, and parents by contacting the Admissions Office.

Type of Facility
Funding Sources Private.
Average Length of Stay Long term.
Types of Admissions Accepted Day treatment; Residential treatment.
Sources of Referral Psychiatrists; Private sources.

Client Profile
Age Range of Clients Served Day programs: 12-18; Residential program: 12-18.
Characteristics Exhibited by Children Emotional handicaps; Learning disabilities; Neurological impairments.

Tuition and Fees
Tuition $11,900/yr.
Placements Primarily Funded By Insurance; Private sources.

Social and Rehabilitative Services
Therapeutic Services Offered Individual therapy; Group therapy; Family therapy; Adjunctive therapy; Art therapy; Physical therapy; Independent living skills program; Recreation activities; Substance abuse treatment; Aftercare program with follow up.
Professionals on Staff Psychiatrists; Psychologists; Social workers; Adjunctive therapists; Child care staff; Nurses; Art therapists.

Educational and Vocational Services
Type(s) of Educational Programs Offered On campus.
Profile of On Campus School Program Number of teachers 6; *Number of classrooms* 5; *Student to teacher ratio* 8:1; Remedial courses offered.

TOTOWA

MOUNT ST JOSEPH CHILDREN'S CENTER

124 Shepherd Lane, Totowa, NJ 07512 (201) 595-5720 *Contact Person(s):* Linda Poskanzer, Dir

Setting and Background Information The facility was originally established as an orphanage in 1854 and, in 1974, expanded its programs to become a treatment center. The program is located in a red brick building built in 1908.
Referral Information Referrals can be made by the New Jersey Division of Youth and Family Services. To make a referral contact the facility to provide background information concerning the child, and schedule a pre-placement visit. The facility accepts boys only.

Type of Facility
Funding Sources State.
Average Length of Stay Long term.
Types of Admissions Accepted Residential treatment.
Sources of Referral State depts of education; Local depts of education; Social service depts; Div of Youth and Family Svcs.

Client Profile
Age Range of Clients Served Residential program: 6-12.
Characteristics Exhibited by Children Emotional handicaps.

Tuition and Fees
Room and Board Long term: $18,900/yr.
Placements Primarily Funded By State depts of education; Local depts of education; Social service depts.

Social and Rehabilitative Services
Therapeutic Approach The facility has an eclectic approach to therapy, which includes psychotherapy.
Therapeutic Services Offered Individual therapy; Group therapy; Family therapy; Recreation activities.
Professionals on Staff Psychiatrists; Psychologists; Social workers; Child care staff; Nurses.

Educational and Vocational Services
Type(s) of Educational Programs Offered On campus; Summer campus.
Profile of On Campus School Program Number of teachers 4; *Number of classrooms* 4; *Student to teacher ratio* 4:1.

VINELAND

AMERICAN INSTITUTE FOR MENTAL STUDIES

1667 E Landis Ave, Vineland, NJ 08360 (609) 691-0021 *Contact Person(s):* Barbara Nyce, Registrar

Setting and Background Information The facility was founded by Rev S Olin Garrison in 1888 as a training school for children with mental handicaps. It is situated in a semi-rural community on 200 acres of land. The campus consists of 15 residential homes, school, vocational opportunity center, senior enrichment center, and greenhouse complex.
Referral Information Referrals can be made by parents, professionals, and agency staff. Applicants are requested to submit an application form and referral packet consisting of a social history, current individualized educational plan, current psychological report, medical examination report, and other pertinent evaluation materials. A pre-placement interview will be held before an interdisciplinary team reviews the referral packet and makes a placement decision.

Type of Facility
Funding Sources Private; State.
Average Length of Stay Long term.
Types of Admissions Accepted Day treatment; Residential treatment; Group home placement.
Sources of Referral State depts of education; Local depts of education; Private sources; Social service depts.

Client Profile
Age Range of Clients Served Residential program: 8-21+.
Characteristics Exhibited by Children Emotional handicaps; Speech/Language disorders; Neurological impairments; Mental disabilities.

Tuition and Fees
Room and Board Long term: $36,000-$41,000/yr.
Placements Primarily Funded By State depts of education; Local depts of education; Private sources.

AMERICAN INSTITUTE FOR MENTAL STUDIES
(continued)

Social and Rehabilitative Services
Therapeutic Approach The therapeutic approach used is based on a developmental model.
Therapeutic Services Offered Adjunctive therapy; Independent living skills program; Recreation activities.
Professionals on Staff Psychiatrists; Psychologists; Social workers; Adjunctive therapists; Child care staff; Nurses.
Educational and Vocational Services
Type(s) of Educational Programs Offered On campus; Summer campus.
Profile of On Campus School Program Number of teachers 17; Student to teacher ratio 4:1; Special curriculum electives offered.
Vocational Education Programs/Degrees Offered Work activities center; Custodial training; Horticulture.

WARREN

SOMERSET HILLS SCHOOL
PO Box 4305, 201 Mt Horeb Rd, Warren, NJ 07060 (201) 469-6900
Contact Person(s): Jerome Amedeo, Exec Dir
Setting and Background Information The facility was originally established in 1926 as a private boarding school. Currently, it is located on 22 acres with 7 dormitories, a school, a gym and administrative offices.
Referral Information For referrals, contact the facility and forward information including social history, psychiatric evaluations, psychological and educational reports. After assessment by facility, a pre-placement visit with child and parents is scheduled.
Type of Facility
Funding Sources State; Local school districts.
Average Length of Stay 2-2 ½ yrs.
Types of Admissions Accepted Residential treatment.
Sources of Referral Local depts of education; State depts of mental health; Depts of correction; Social service depts.
Client Profile
Age Range of Clients Served Residential program: 6-15.
Characteristics Exhibited by Children Emotional handicaps; Learning disabilities; Neurological impairments; Mental disabilities.
IQ Range of Clients 70+.
Tuition and Fees
Room and Board Long term: $30,660/yr.
Tuition $10,900/yr.
Placements Primarily Funded By Local depts of education; Social service depts.
Social and Rehabilitative Services
Therapeutic Approach The facility uses behavior modification and individual psychotherapy.
Therapeutic Services Offered Individual therapy; Family therapy; Recreation activities.
Professionals on Staff Psychiatrists; Psychologists; Social workers; Child care staff; Nurses.
Educational and Vocational Services
Type(s) of Educational Programs Offered On campus.
Profile of On Campus School Program Number of teachers 16; Number of classrooms 10; Student to teacher ratio 8:1; Grades taught K-9.
Degrees Offered 8th grade diploma.

WASHINGTON

MOUNT SCOTT INSTITUTE
PO Box 129, Washington, NJ 07882 (201) 453-2486 *Contact Person(s):* Rona Silver, Dir
Setting and Background Information The facility was established in 1971. The campus is located on 50 acres and has 7 buildings.
Referral Information Contact the facility for referral procedures.
Type of Facility
Funding Sources State.
Average Length of Stay 2 yrs.
Types of Admissions Accepted Residential treatment.
Sources of Referral State depts of education; Local depts of education; State depts of mental health; Psychiatrists; Private sources; Depts of correction; Social service depts.

Client Profile
Age Range of Clients Served Residential program: 12-18.
Characteristics Exhibited by Children Emotional handicaps; Learning disabilities; Speech/Language disorders.
IQ Range of Clients 75-110.
Tuition and Fees
Placements Primarily Funded By State depts of education; Local depts of education; State depts of mental health.
Social and Rehabilitative Services
Therapeutic Services Offered Individual therapy; Group therapy; Family therapy; Independent living skills program; Recreation activities; Aftercare program with follow up.
Professionals on Staff Psychiatrists; Psychologists; Social workers; Adjunctive therapists; Child care staff; Nurses.
Educational and Vocational Services
Type(s) of Educational Programs Offered On campus.
Profile of On Campus School Program Number of teachers 7; Number of classrooms 5; Student to teacher ratio 4:1; Credentials of teachers BA, BS or MS, Spec Ed; Grades taught K-12.
Degrees Offered Diploma conferred through local school district.

NEW MEXICO

ALBUQUERQUE

HOGARES, INC
PO Box 6342, Albuquerque, NM 87107 (505) 345-8471 *Contact Person(s):* Nancy Archer, Dir; Kathy Lawrence, Intake Coord
Setting and Background Information Hogares is a private, non-profit agency which offers diagnostic services, counseling, and residential treatment in group homes. The agency was established in 1981. There are 10 residential facilities located in various parts of Albuquerque. The agency's office and school program is located at 1218 Greigus NW.
Referral Information Anyone can make a referral by contacting the agency and scheduling an interview.
Type of Facility
Funding Sources Private.
Average Length of Stay Long term.
Types of Admissions Accepted Residential treatment; Group home placement.
Sources of Referral State depts of mental health; Depts of correction; Courts.
Client Profile
Age Range of Clients Served Residential program: 13-18.
Characteristics Exhibited by Children Emotional handicaps; Learning disabilities.
Tuition and Fees
Room and Board Long term: Sliding scale.
Placements Primarily Funded By State depts of mental health; Social service depts; United Way.
Social and Rehabilitative Services
Therapeutic Approach The treatment programs utilize an eclectic therapeutic approach with emphasis on behavioral, psychodynamic, psychosocial, developmental, and personality theory.
Therapeutic Services Offered Individual therapy; Group therapy; Family therapy; Independent living skills program; Recreation activities; Substance abuse treatment.
Professionals on Staff Social workers; Adjunctive therapists; Child care staff.
Educational and Vocational Services
Type(s) of Educational Programs Offered On campus.
Profile of On Campus School Program Number of teachers 7 and 7 aides; *Number of classrooms* 7; *Student to teacher ratio* 7:1.
Degrees Offered 12th grade diploma; GED.

MUCH MORE
305 Lagunitas SW, Albuquerque, NM 87105 (505) 877-7318 *Contact Person(s):* Josephine Olson, Dir
Setting and Background Information Much More is a state residential treatment facilty. The program initially opened as a group home but later converted to a treatment center to meet community needs.
Referral Information Anyone can make a referral by contacting the Mental Health Panel at PO Box 968, Sante Fe, NM 87504.
Type of Facility
Funding Sources State.
Types of Admissions Accepted Residential treatment.
Sources of Referral Court.
Client Profile
Age Range of Clients Served Residential program: 10-13.
Characteristics Exhibited by Children Emotional handicaps; Learning disabilities.

Tuition and Fees
Placements Primarily Funded By State depts of mental health; Private sources; Dept of Health and Education.
Social and Rehabilitative Services
Therapeutic Services Offered Individual therapy; Group therapy; Family therapy; Adjunctive therapy; Independent living skills program; Recreation activities; Aftercare program with follow up.
Professionals on Staff Psychologists; Social workers; Adjunctive therapists; Child care staff.
Educational and Vocational Services
Type(s) of Educational Programs Offered On campus; Off campus.
Profile of On Campus School Program Number of teachers 1; *Student to teacher ratio* 2:1; Special curriculum electives offered; Remedial courses offered.
Degrees Offered 12th grade diploma.

VISTA SANDIA HOSPITAL
501 Alameda NE, Albuquerque, NM 87113 (505) 823-2000 *Contact Person(s):* Marie Williams, PhD
Setting and Background Information Vista Sandia Hospital is a private psychiatric hospital with 92 beds, divided into 4 units. The adolescent unit was established in 1973 and has 18 beds. There is also a residential treatment center, called Vista House, which serves as a transitional facility for adolescents who have been discharged from the the hospital.
Referral Information Referrals can be made by anyone by contacting the hospital or a physician on staff.
Type of Facility
Funding Sources Private.
Average Length of Stay Long term.
Types of Admissions Accepted Residential treatment.
Sources of Referral Psychiatrists; Private sources; Social service depts.
Client Profile
Age Range of Clients Served Residential program: 13-55+.
Characteristics Exhibited by Children Emotional handicaps; Learning disabilities; Mental disabilities.
Tuition and Fees
Placements Primarily Funded By State depts of mental health; Insurance; Private sources.
Social and Rehabilitative Services
Therapeutic Services Offered Individual therapy; Group therapy; Family therapy; Adjunctive therapy; Independent living skills program; Recreation activities.
Professionals on Staff Psychiatrists; Psychologists; Social workers; Child care staff; Nurses.
Educational and Vocational Services
Type(s) of Educational Programs Offered On campus.
Profile of On Campus School Program Number of teachers 3; *Student to teacher ratio* 6:1.

LAS VEGAS

LAS VEGAS MEDICAL CENTER—ADOLESCENT UNIT
PO Box 1388, Hot Springs Blvd, Las Vegas, NM 87701
(505) 454-2100 *Contact Person(s):* Will Matthew, Dir of Adolescent Unit

LAS VEGAS MEDICAL CENTER—ADOLESCENT UNIT *(continued)*

Setting and Background Information The Las Vegas Medical Center is a psychiatric hospital, which was established in 1978 in response to the need for an institution based residential treatment program for adolescents. The purpose of this program was to provide back up services for community programs and centers for young children. It is located on the Las Vegas Medical Center campus, housed in a 2-story building containing a dorm, recreational facilities, and classrooms.

Referral Information Referrals can be made by state juvenile evaluation teams, school districts, and private practitioners. The admission procedure requires the preparation of an evaluation report documenting the adolescent's need for residential placement. This evaluation report will then be reviewed by the state panel to identify the least restrictive program available. Arrangements must be made for expert testimony at committment hearings (except in the case of 20% of the adolescents who enter on a voluntary basis), as required by the New Mexico Mental Health Code.

Type of Facility

Funding Sources Private; State; Federal.

Average Length of Stay Long term.

Types of Admissions Accepted Residential treatment; Wards of the state.

Sources of Referral State depts of education; Local depts of education; State depts of mental health; Private sources; Depts of correction; Social service depts.

Client Profile

Age Range of Clients Served Residential program: 13-18.

Characteristics Exhibited by Children Emotional handicaps; Learning disabilities; Hearing impairments/deafness; Speech/Language disorders; Neurological impairments; Physical handicaps; Mental disabilities.

Tuition and Fees

Room and Board Long term: $135/diem.

Placements Primarily Funded By State depts of mental health; Private sources; Social service depts.

Social and Rehabilitative Services

Therapeutic Approach Students participate in a highly structured motivational program which uses a behavior oriented therapeutic approach in conjunction with milieu therapy.

Therapeutic Services Offered Individual therapy; Group therapy; Family therapy; Adjunctive therapy; Art therapy; Physical therapy; Independent living skills program; Recreation activities; Wilderness program.

Professionals on Staff Psychiatrists; Psychologists; Social workers; Adjunctive therapists; Child care staff; Nurses; Art therapists; Physical therapists.

Educational and Vocational Services

Type(s) of Educational Programs Offered On campus; Summer campus.

Profile of On Campus School Program Number of teachers 3; *Number of classrooms* 2; *Student to teacher ratio* 8:1; *Length of school day* 5 hrs; *Grades taught* 1-12; Remedial courses offered.

Degrees Offered GED.

NEW YORK

ALBANY

EQUINOX YOUTH SHELTER

214 Lark St, Albany, NY 12210 (518) 465-9524 *Contact Person(s):* Donna McIntosh, Youth Srvs Dir

Setting and Background Information The facility was established in 1976. The shelter is a 4-story brick building in Albany.

Referral Information Referrals to the facility can be made by anyone or any agency, 24-hours a day, for immediate intake.

Type of Facility

Funding Sources Private; State; Federal.

Average Length of Stay Short term.

Types of Admissions Accepted Emergency shelter.

Sources of Referral Social service depts; Family court.

Client Profile

Age Range of Clients Served Residential program: 12-18.

Characteristics Exhibited by Children Abused and neglected; Runaways.

Tuition and Fees

Placements Primarily Funded By Grants.

Social and Rehabilitative Services

Therapeutic Approach The facility has a client-centered approach to therapy.

Therapeutic Services Offered Individual therapy; Group therapy; Family therapy; Independent living skills program; Aftercare program with follow up.

Professionals on Staff Social workers; Child care staff.

Educational and Vocational Services

Type(s) of Educational Programs Offered Off campus.

LA SALLE SCHOOL, INC

391 Western Ave, Albany, NY 12203 (518) 489-4731 *Contact Person(s):* Al Hyland, Intake Coord

Setting and Background Information The intitial facility was established by the Brothers of the Christian Schools in 1854. Its main campus is located in a residential community and consists of 6 group living units, arranged according to age and grade along with a school complex. There are also 2 off-campus group homes and several semi-autonomous living units or apartments in the community. The facility accepts boys only.

Referral Information Referrals can be made by public agencies. To make a referral, contact the facility and forward the following background information: social history, current psychiatric and psychological evaluations, school records, medical records, and other pertinent information. A pre-placement visit will be arranged before an admission decision is made.

Type of Facility

Funding Sources State.

Average Length of Stay Long term.

Types of Admissions Accepted Day treatment; Residential treatment; Group home placement.

Sources of Referral State depts of education; Local depts of education; Social service depts; Div for Youth; Family court; Probation dept.

Client Profile

Age Range of Clients Served Day programs: 12-16; Residential program: 13-17.

Characteristics Exhibited by Children Emotional handicaps; Learning disabilities.

Tuition and Fees

Room and Board Long term: $72.88/diem.

Social and Rehabilitative Services

Therapeutic Services Offered Individual therapy; Group therapy; Family therapy; Adjunctive therapy; Independent living skills program; Recreation activities; Substance abuse treatment; Aftercare program with follow up.

Professionals on Staff Psychiatrists; Psychologists; Social workers; Adjunctive therapists; Child care staff; Nurses.

Educational and Vocational Services

Type(s) of Educational Programs Offered On campus.

Profile of On Campus School Program Number of teachers 35; Number of classrooms 28; Student to teacher ratio 10:1; Remedial courses offered.

Vocational Education Programs/Degrees Offered Woodwork; Computers; Business.

Degrees Offered 12th grade diploma.

PARSONS CHILD & FAMILY CENTER

845 Central Ave, Albany, NY 12206 (518) 438-4571 *Contact Person(s):* Deborah Singer, Intake Dir

Setting and Background Information The facility was established in 1829 as an orphanage. Currently, it has a campus setting with a school, residential cottages, a gym, a medical clinic, clinical buildings and an administration building.

Referral Information Referrals are made by New York State agencies or localities that have a contract with the facility. Assessment by multi-disciplinary staff is required prior to acceptance.

Type of Facility

Funding Sources Private; State; Federal.

Average Length of Stay Long term.

Types of Admissions Accepted Day treatment; Residential treatment; Group home placement; Foster-care; Adoption.

Sources of Referral State depts of education; Local depts of education; State depts of mental health; Psychiatrists; Private sources; Social service depts.

Client Profile

Age Range of Clients Served Day programs: 6-18; Residential program: 6-18.

Characteristics Exhibited by Children Emotional handicaps; Learning disabilities; Speech/Language disorders; Neurological impairments; Mental disabilities; Developmentally disabled.

Tuition and Fees

Placements Primarily Funded By State depts of education; Local depts of education; Social service depts; Medicaid.

Social and Rehabilitative Services

Therapeutic Services Offered Individual therapy; Group therapy; Family therapy; Art therapy; Independent living skills program; Recreation activities; Aftercare program with follow up.

Professionals on Staff Psychiatrists; Psychologists; Social workers; Child care staff; Nurses; Art therapists.

Educational and Vocational Services

Type(s) of Educational Programs Offered On campus; Off campus; Summer campus.

Profile of On Campus School Program Number of teachers 38; Number of classrooms 19; Student to teacher ratio 12:1; Credentials of teachers MA, BA, Spec Ed; Grades taught K-12; Remedial courses offered (Math, Reading, Art).

Vocational Education Programs/Degrees Offered Auto shop; Maintenance; Typing; Cooking; Woodworking;.

Degrees Offered 12th grade diploma.

ST ANNE INSTITUTE

160 N Main Ave, Albany, NY 12206 (518) 489-7411 *Contact Person(s):* Ralph Fedullo, Exec Dir

Setting and Background Information The facility was established in 1887 by the Sisters of The Good Shepherd. The 5.5-acre campus has residential facilities, a school, and a medical/administrative building.

Referral Information Contact the facility for referral information.

Type of Facility

Funding Sources Private; State; Federal; County; School districts.

Average Length of Stay Long term.

Types of Admissions Accepted Day treatment; Residential treatment; Group home placement.

Sources of Referral Local depts of education; Social service depts.

Client Profile

Age Range of Clients Served Day programs: 12-18; Residential program: 12-18.

Characteristics Exhibited by Children Emotional handicaps; Learning disabilities.

IQ Range of Clients 75+.

Tuition and Fees

Room and Board Long term: $68.97-85.93/diem.

Tuition $62-74.90/diem.

Placements Primarily Funded By Local depts of education; Social service depts.

Social and Rehabilitative Services

Therapeutic Services Offered Individual therapy; Group therapy; Family therapy; Art therapy; Independent living skills program.

Professionals on Staff Psychiatrists; Psychologists; Social workers; Adjunctive therapists; Child care staff; Nurses; Art therapists.

Educational and Vocational Services

Type(s) of Educational Programs Offered On campus; Summer campus.

Degrees Offered GED.

ST CATHERINE'S CENTER FOR CHILDREN

30 N Main Ave, Albany, NY 12203 (518) 482-3331 *Contact Person(s):* Patricia Putnam, MSW

Setting and Background Information St Catherine's Center for Children is a private, multi-service agency which operates the following residential programs: foster family care, boarding home, group home, group residence, and emergency shelter for homeless families. There are also a variety of day treatment services available.

Referral Information Referrals can be made by the Dept of Social Services and Committees for Special Education. To make a referral, contact the facility, forward the necessary background information, and schedule a pre-placement interview.

Type of Facility

Funding Sources State.

Types of Admissions Accepted Day treatment; Residential treatment.

Sources of Referral State depts of education; Local depts of education; Social service depts.

Client Profile

Age Range of Clients Served Day programs: 2-12; Residential program: 8-12.

Characteristics Exhibited by Children Emotional handicaps; Abused and neglected.

Tuition and Fees

Placements Primarily Funded By State depts of education; State depts of mental health; Social service depts.

Social and Rehabilitative Services

Therapeutic Approach The treatment programs use a variety of family-centered therapeutic approaches.

Therapeutic Services Offered Individual therapy; Group therapy; Family therapy; Adjunctive therapy; Recreation activities; Aftercare program with follow up.

Professionals on Staff Psychiatrists; Psychologists; Social workers; Adjunctive therapists; Child care staff; Nurses; Speech therapists.

Educational and Vocational Services

Type(s) of Educational Programs Offered On campus; Off campus; Summer campus.

Profile of On Campus School Program Number of teachers 11; *Number of classrooms* 11; *Student to teacher ratio* 10:1; Special curriculum electives offered.

BALLSTON SPA

DONOVAN HOUSE

30 E High St, Ballston Spa, NY 12151 (518) 885-8220 *Contact Person(s):* Dan Godfrey, Dir

Setting and Background Information The facility was established in 1979 under the auspices of Catholic Family and Community Services of Saratoga County. It is a large group home.

Referral Information Most referrals are made through local depts of social services. Youths with an extensive history of violence or drug abuse are not accepted.

Type of Facility

Funding Sources State.

Average Length of Stay Long term.

Types of Admissions Accepted Group home placement.

Sources of Referral Social service depts.

Client Profile

Age Range of Clients Served Residential program: 12-18.

Characteristics Exhibited by Children Emotional handicaps; Learning disabilities.

Tuition and Fees

Room and Board Long term: $66/diem.

Placements Primarily Funded By Social service depts.

Social and Rehabilitative Services

Therapeutic Approach The facility has a highly structured behavioral approach.

Therapeutic Services Offered Individual therapy; Group therapy; Family therapy; Recreation activities; Aftercare program with follow up.

Professionals on Staff Psychiatrists; Social workers; Adjunctive therapists.

Educational and Vocational Services

Type(s) of Educational Programs Offered Off campus.

BATH

KENNEDY HOUSE, BOYS HOME

PO Box 369, 16 Pultney Sq, Bath, NY 14810 (607) 776-7853 *Contact Person(s):* David Andreine, Supv

Setting and Background Information This facility was established in 1968. A local parish donated the property, which is a large farm house.

Referral Information All referrals are made through DSS/DFY. An intake assessment and overnight pre-placement visit will be scheduled.

Type of Facility

Funding Sources Private; State; Federal.

Average Length of Stay 18 mos.

Types of Admissions Accepted Group home placement.

Sources of Referral Social service depts; NY Division for Youth.

Client Profile

Age Range of Clients Served Residential program: 12-18.

Characteristics Exhibited by Children Emotional handicaps.

Tuition and Fees

Room and Board Long term: $63.50/diem.

Placements Primarily Funded By Social service depts; DFY.

Social and Rehabilitative Services

Therapeutic Services Offered Individual therapy; Group therapy; Family therapy; Independent living skills program.

Professionals on Staff Psychiatrists; Psychologists; Social workers; Adjunctive therapists; Child care staff.

Educational and Vocational Services

Type(s) of Educational Programs Offered Off campus (Public schools).

Degrees Offered 12th grade diploma.

KINSHIP FAMILY AND YOUTH SERVICES

16 Pultney Sq, Bath, NY 14810 (607) 776-7853, 776-6621, 776-3051 *Contact Person(s):* Cheryl L Drummond, Dir of Srvs

Setting and Background Information The agency was established in 1968. It is a rural group home program, with administrative offices in Bath.

Referral Information Contact the Director of Services. An intake assessment will be scheduled.

KINSHIP FAMILY AND YOUTH SERVICES
(continued)

Type of Facility
Funding Sources Private; State; Federal.
Average Length of Stay Short and long term.
Types of Admissions Accepted Group home placement; Wards of the state.
Sources of Referral Private sources; Social service depts.
Client Profile
Age Range of Clients Served Residential program: 6-18.
Characteristics Exhibited by Children Emotional handicaps.
IQ Range of Clients 70-130.
Tuition and Fees
Room and Board Long term: $64.62.
Placements Primarily Funded By State depts of mental health; Social service depts.
Social and Rehabilitative Services
Therapeutic Services Offered Individual therapy; Group therapy; Family therapy; Independent living skills program; Recreation activities.
Professionals on Staff Psychiatrists; Psychologists; Social workers; Child care staff.
Educational and Vocational Services
Type(s) of Educational Programs Offered Off campus (All community based).

NEW LIFE HOMES—SNELL FARM
RD #2 Snell Hill Rd, Bath, NY 14810 (607) 776-7723 *Contact Person(s):* Harry T Ballos, Dir
Setting and Background Information The facility was established in 1972. The 180-acre farm has residential buildings, a school, a vocational/office building and barns.
Referral Information Referrals are made directly to the facility and must include a history of the client, a psychiatric evaluation, a school history, and court records.
Type of Facility
Funding Sources Private; State.
Average Length of Stay Long term.
Types of Admissions Accepted Residential treatment; Group home placement; Wards of the state.
Sources of Referral State depts of education; Local depts of education; State depts of mental health; Psychiatrists; Private sources; Depts of correction; Social service depts.
Client Profile
Age Range of Clients Served Residential program: 12-18.
Characteristics Exhibited by Children Emotional handicaps; Learning disabilities.
IQ Range of Clients 80-125.
Tuition and Fees
Placements Primarily Funded By State depts of education; Private sources; Social service depts.
Social and Rehabilitative Services
Therapeutic Approach The facility uses cognitive therapy.
Therapeutic Services Offered Individual therapy; Group therapy; Family therapy; Independent living skills program; Substance abuse treatment; Aftercare program with follow up.
Professionals on Staff Social workers; Child care staff.
Educational and Vocational Services
Type(s) of Educational Programs Offered On campus; Off campus.
Profile of On Campus School Program Number of teachers 2; *Number of classrooms* 2; *Student to teacher ratio* 6:1; Remedial courses offered.
Vocational Education Programs/Degrees Offered Vocational shops.
Degrees Offered 8th grade diploma; 12th grade diploma; GED.

BETHPAGE

HOPE FOR YOUTH, INC
Northedge Bldg, Stewart Ave, Bethpage, NY 11714 (516) 579-6880
Contact Person(s): John Provost CSW, Exec Dir
Setting and Background Information The agency was established in 1969. There are 4 separate group homes in different communities on Long Island.
Referral Information Contact the facility for referral information.

Type of Facility
Funding Sources State.
Average Length of Stay 1 yr or more.
Types of Admissions Accepted Group home placement.
Sources of Referral Social service depts; Probation depts.
Client Profile
Age Range of Clients Served Residential program: 12-18.
Characteristics Exhibited by Children Emotional handicaps; Mental disabilities; Behavior disorders.
IQ Range of Clients 80+.
Tuition and Fees
Room and Board Long term: $68/diem.
Placements Primarily Funded By Social service depts; Probation depts.
Social and Rehabilitative Services
Therapeutic Services Offered Individual therapy; Group therapy; Independent living skills program; Aftercare program with follow up.
Professionals on Staff Psychiatrists; Psychologists; Social workers; Child care staff.
Educational and Vocational Services
Type(s) of Educational Programs Offered Off campus (Local school districts).
Degrees Offered Conferred through local school districts.

BINGHAMTON

CATHOLIC CHARITIES GROUP HOME
57 Chestnut St, Binghamton, NY 13905 (607) 723-6355 *Contact Person(s):* Diana E Schaumberg MSW CSW, Prog Dir
Setting and Background Information The facility was established in 1983 and is licensed by the state Office of Mental Health. It is a group home in a residential community setting.
Referral Information Referrals are made through or in conjunction with the Dept of Social Services.
Type of Facility
Funding Sources Local dept of social services.
Average Length of Stay Long term.
Types of Admissions Accepted Group home placement; Wards of the state.
Sources of Referral State depts of mental health; Psychiatrists; Depts of correction; Social service depts; Local psychiatric facilities.
Client Profile
Age Range of Clients Served Residential program: 14-18.
Characteristics Exhibited by Children Emotional handicaps; Learning disabilities; Mental disabilities.
IQ Range of Clients 70+.
Tuition and Fees
Room and Board Long term: $90/diem.
Placements Primarily Funded By Social service depts.
Social and Rehabilitative Services
Therapeutic Approach The facility has an eclectic approach, which includes reality therapy.
Therapeutic Services Offered Adjunctive therapy; Independent living skills program; Recreation activities; Aftercare program with follow up.
Professionals on Staff Social workers; Child care staff.

NEW YORK STATE DIVISION FOR YOUTH, BINGHAMTON COMMUNITY URBAN HOMES
43 Park Ave, Binghamton, NY 13903 (607) 772-9610 *Contact Person(s):* Walter Roscello, Facility Dir
Setting and Background Information This program was established in 1967 by the state in response to local need. There are three group homes.
Referral Information Placements are made by the Family Courts.
Type of Facility
Funding Sources State; Federal.
Average Length of Stay Long term.
Types of Admissions Accepted Group home placement.
Sources of Referral Social service depts; Family courts.
Client Profile
Age Range of Clients Served Residential program: 12-18.
Characteristics Exhibited by Children Emotional handicaps; Mental disabilities.
Tuition and Fees
Room and Board Long term: $135/diem.
Placements Primarily Funded By State Div for Youth.

NEW YORK STATE DIVISION FOR YOUTH, BINGHAMTON COMMUNITY URBAN HOMES *(continued)*

Social and Rehabilitative Services
Therapeutic Approach The basic therapeutic approach is reality therapy.
Therapeutic Services Offered Individual therapy; Group therapy; Independent living skills program; Aftercare program with follow up.
Professionals on Staff Psychologists; Child care staff.
Educational and Vocational Services
Type(s) of Educational Programs Offered Off campus (Public school).

BREWSTER

GREEN CHIMNEYS CHILDREN'S SERVICES, INC
Putnam Lake Rd, Brewster, NY 10509 (914) 279-2996, (212) 892-6810 *Contact Person(s):* Myra M Ross, Clinical Coord
Setting and Background Information The facility was established in 1948 as a private boarding school. In 1974, it was licensed as a social service agency. The campus program is located on 150 acres. There are 3 group homes in Westchester County and a group residence in New York City.
Referral Information Contact the facility for referral information. Admission is limited to New York State residents.
Type of Facility
Funding Sources State; Federal.
Average Length of Stay Long term.
Types of Admissions Accepted Residential treatment; Group home placement.
Sources of Referral State depts of education; Local depts of education; State depts of mental health; Psychiatrists; Social service depts; Psychiatric hospitals.
Client Profile
Age Range of Clients Served Residential program: 6-21.
Characteristics Exhibited by Children Emotional handicaps; Learning disabilities; Neurological impairments; Mental disabilities.
Tuition and Fees
Placements Primarily Funded By Local depts of education; Social service depts.
Social and Rehabilitative Services
Therapeutic Approach The facility has a eclectic approach to therapy.
Therapeutic Services Offered Individual therapy; Group therapy; Family therapy; Art therapy; Independent living skills program; Recreation activities; Aftercare program with follow up.
Professionals on Staff Psychiatrists; Psychologists.
Educational and Vocational Services
Type(s) of Educational Programs Offered On campus (Spec Ed).
Profile of On Campus School Program Student to teacher ratio 12:1; *Credentials of teachers* Certified Spec Ed; Special curriculum electives offered (Computer).
Vocational Education Programs/Degrees Offered Pre-vocational.

BRONX

ARGUS COMMUNITY, INC
760 E 160th St, Bronx, NY 10456 (212) 993-5300 *Contact Person(s):* Mary Taylor, Asst Dir
Setting and Background Information The facility was established in 1969 with funds from a federal grant. There are two group homes for adolescent girls and a treatment facility for adult males.
Referral Information Contact the facility for referral information.
Type of Facility
Funding Sources Private; State.
Average Length of Stay Long term.
Types of Admissions Accepted Day treatment; Residential treatment; Group home placement.
Sources of Referral Local depts of education; State depts of mental health; Psychiatrists; Depts of correction; Social service depts.
Client Profile
Age Range of Clients Served Day programs: 12-18; Residential program: 12-21+.
Characteristics Exhibited by Children Emotional handicaps; Learning disabilities.
IQ Range of Clients 70+.

Tuition and Fees
Placements Primarily Funded By Local depts of education; Social service depts.
Social and Rehabilitative Services
Therapeutic Services Offered Individual therapy; Group therapy; Family therapy; Art therapy; Physical therapy; Independent living skills program; Independent living skills program; Substance abuse treatment.
Professionals on Staff Social workers; Adjunctive therapists; Child care staff; Art therapists.
Educational and Vocational Services
Type(s) of Educational Programs Offered On campus.
Profile of On Campus School Program Number of teachers 13; *Number of classrooms* 12; *Student to teacher ratio* 10:1; *Grades taught* 5-12.
Degrees Offered GED.

BROOKLYN

ANGEL GUARDIAN HOME—MCAULEY RESIDENCE
372 Clinton Ave, Brooklyn, NY 11238 (718) 638-7424 *Contact Person(s):* Linda Mendoza, Prog Dir
Setting and Background Information The facility was established in 1975 as a joint placement center for teen mothers, ages 16-18, with their children.
Referral Information For referral information contact the program director and forward the necessary information including a psycho-social summary, psychiatric and psychological evaluations.
Type of Facility
Funding Sources Private; State; City.
Average Length of Stay Long term.
Types of Admissions Accepted Group home placement.
Sources of Referral Social service depts; City.
Client Profile
Age Range of Clients Served Residential program: 16-18.
Characteristics Exhibited by Children Emotional handicaps; Learning disabilities.
Tuition and Fees
Placements Primarily Funded By State depts of mental health; Social service depts; City.
Social and Rehabilitative Services
Therapeutic Services Offered Individual therapy; Group therapy; Family therapy; Art therapy; Independent living skills program.
Professionals on Staff Psychiatrists; Psychologists; Social workers; Art therapists.
Educational and Vocational Services
Type(s) of Educational Programs Offered Off campus.
Vocational Education Programs/Degrees Offered Secretarial; Word processing; Data entry; Food services.

BLUEBERRY TREATMENT CENTER
16 Court St, Brooklyn, NY 11241 (718) 834-4880 *Contact Person(s):* Tev Goldsman, Exec Dir
Setting and Background Information The facility was established in 1958.
Referral Information Contact the facility for referral information.
Type of Facility
Funding Sources State; Federal; City.
Average Length of Stay Long term.
Types of Admissions Accepted Day treatment; Residential treatment.
Sources of Referral Local depts of education; Social service depts.
Client Profile
Age Range of Clients Served Day programs: Birth-15; Residential program: Birth-15.
Characteristics Exhibited by Children Emotional handicaps; Learning disabilities; Speech/Language disorders; Mental disabilities.
Tuition and Fees
Tuition $13,101/yr.
Placements Primarily Funded By State depts of education; Local depts of education; State depts of mental health; Social service depts.
Social and Rehabilitative Services
Therapeutic Approach The facility uses behavior management.
Therapeutic Services Offered Individual therapy; Group therapy; Family therapy; Art therapy; Independent living skills program; Recreation activities.
Professionals on Staff Psychiatrists; Psychologists; Social workers; Child care staff; Nurses; Art therapists.

BLUEBERRY TREATMENT CENTER *(continued)*

Educational and Vocational Services
Type(s) of Educational Programs Offered Off campus.

MACDOUGAL DIAGNOSTIC RECEPTION CENTER

330 MacDougal St, Brooklyn, NY 11233 (718) 452-8800 *Contact Person(s):* Gerard T Grote, Dir
Setting and Background Information The facility was established in 1975 by New York City Dept of Social Services.
Referral Information All referrals come through the NYC Special Service for Children Allocation Unit or Evening Energy Children Services.
Type of Facility
Average Length of Stay Short and long term.
Types of Admissions Accepted Residential treatment; Diagnostic evaluations.
Sources of Referral City Bureau of Child Welfare.
Client Profile
Age Range of Clients Served Residential program: 12-21+.
Characteristics Exhibited by Children Emotional handicaps; Learning disabilities; Physical handicaps; Mental disabilities.
Tuition and Fees
Placements Primarily Funded By City of New York.
Social and Rehabilitative Services
Therapeutic Services Offered Individual therapy; Group therapy; Family therapy; Independent living skills program.
Professionals on Staff Psychiatrists; Psychologists; Social workers; Child care staff; Nurses.
Educational and Vocational Services
Type(s) of Educational Programs Offered On campus.
Profile of On Campus School Program Number of teachers 3; *Number of classrooms* 3; *Student to teacher ratio* 8:1; *Credentials of teachers* MA; *Grades taught* Ungraded.

BUFFALO

BUFFALO YOUTH DEVELOPMENT CENTER

567 Richmond Ave, Buffalo, NY 14222 (716) 882-6931 *Contact Person(s):* Louis C Benton, Dir
Setting and Background Information The facility was established in 1975 by the New York State Division for Youth. There are five group homes located thoughout the city of Buffalo.
Referral Information Referrals to the facility are made through the State Division of Youth Services.
Type of Facility
Funding Sources State.
Average Length of Stay 9-12 mos.
Types of Admissions Accepted Group home placement.
Sources of Referral Social service depts; Family courts.
Client Profile
Age Range of Clients Served Residential program: 12-21+.
Characteristics Exhibited by Children Emotional handicaps; Learning disabilities; Speech/Language disorders; Mental disabilities.
Tuition and Fees
Placements Primarily Funded By Social service depts; State division for youth.
Social and Rehabilitative Services
Therapeutic Approach The facility uses reality therapy.
Therapeutic Services Offered Aftercare program with follow up.
Professionals on Staff Adjunctive therapists; Child care staff.
Educational and Vocational Services
Type(s) of Educational Programs Offered On campus.
Profile of On Campus School Program Number of teachers 3; *Number of classrooms* 3; *Student to teacher ratio* 10:1; *Credentials of teachers* Certified; *Grades taught* 8-10; Remedial courses offered (Reading, Math, Language, Arts).

LONGVIEW PROTESTANT HOME FOR CHILDREN

605 Niagara St, Buffalo, NY 14201 (716) 883-4531 *Contact Person(s):* J Robert Oliver, Asst Exec Dir
Setting and Background Information This facility was privately established in 1917. There are five group homes serving the needs of adolescents with emotional, behavioral and social problems.
Referral Information Contact the facility for referral information.

Type of Facility
Funding Sources State; County.
Average Length of Stay Long term Average length of stay is 12 mos.
Types of Admissions Accepted Group home placement.
Sources of Referral Social service depts; Family courts.
Client Profile
Age Range of Clients Served Residential program: 12-18.
Characteristics Exhibited by Children Emotional handicaps; Behavior disorders.
IQ Range of Clients 75-135.
Tuition and Fees
Placements Primarily Funded By Social service depts.
Social and Rehabilitative Services
Therapeutic Services Offered Individual therapy; Group therapy; Family therapy; Independent living skills program; Aftercare program with follow up.
Professionals on Staff Psychiatrists; Social workers; Child care staff; Nurses.
Educational and Vocational Services
Type(s) of Educational Programs Offered Off campus (Local schools).

CANAAN

BERKSHIRE FARM CENTER AND SERVICES FOR YOUTH

Yaphank Ave, Bldg 58, Canaan, NY 12029 (518) 781-4567 *Contact Person(s):* Harold Novick, Exec Dir
Setting and Background Information The facility was originally established in 1886 by legislative action. Currently, the 1400-acre campus has 45 residential buildings, a school, a recreation facility, and administrative and support buildings.
Referral Information Referrals are made by the local Dept of Social Services and by the Division for Youth assigned by Family Court or Probation.
Type of Facility
Funding Sources Private; State; County.
Average Length of Stay Long term.
Types of Admissions Accepted Residential treatment.
Sources of Referral Local depts of education; Social service depts; State Division for Youth.
Client Profile
Age Range of Clients Served Residential program: 12-18.
Characteristics Exhibited by Children Emotional handicaps.
IQ Range of Clients 80+.
Tuition and Fees
Room and Board Long term: $73.78/diem.
Tuition $47.19/diem.
Placements Primarily Funded By Social service depts.
Social and Rehabilitative Services
Therapeutic Approach The facility offers individual and group therapy.
Therapeutic Services Offered Individual therapy; Group therapy; Family therapy; Recreation activities; Substance abuse treatment; Aftercare program with follow up.
Professionals on Staff Psychiatrists; Psychologists; Social workers; Child care staff; Nurses; Physician.
Educational and Vocational Services
Type(s) of Educational Programs Offered On campus (Spec Ed); Summer campus (Spec Ed).
Profile of On Campus School Program Number of teachers 40; *Number of classrooms* 30; *Student to teacher ratio* 9:1; *Credentials of teachers* Spec Ed; *Grades taught* 7-11, Ungraded.
Vocational Education Programs/Degrees Offered Horticulture; Food service.
Degrees Offered GED.

CLINTON CORNERS

HIGH VALLEY

Sunset Trail, Clinton Corners, NY 12514 (914) 266-3621 *Contact Person(s):* Olga Smylk
Setting and Background Information The facility is located on 200 acres with a farmhouse and a classroom building.
Referral Information Contact the facility for referral information.

HIGH VALLEY *(continued)*

Type of Facility
Funding Sources Private.
Average Length of Stay Short term.
Types of Admissions Accepted Residential treatment.
Sources of Referral Psychiatrists; Private sources.
Client Profile
Age Range of Clients Served Residential program: 6-21+.
Characteristics Exhibited by Children Emotional handicaps; Learning disabilities.
Tuition and Fees
Room and Board Short term: $500/wk.
Tuition $2,500/yr.
Placements Primarily Funded By Private sources.
Social and Rehabilitative Services
Therapeutic Services Offered Individual therapy.
Professionals on Staff Child care staff.
Educational and Vocational Services
Type(s) of Educational Programs Offered On campus.
Profile of On Campus School Program Student to teacher ratio 2:1;
Credentials of teachers Spec Ed.

DOBBS FERRY

CHILDREN'S VILLAGE

Dobbs Ferry, NY 10522 (914) 693-0600 *Contact Person(s):* Mona Swanson, Assoc Exec Dir for Quality Assurance
Setting and Background Information The facility was originally established as an institution for homeless and orphaned children in 1851. Currently, it resides on 200 acres with 21 cottages, a school, offices, a gym with a pool, an infirmary, a nature center and other small buildings.
Referral Information Contact the facility and forward psychological, psychiatric, and medical information to the Admissions Director. If appropriate, an interview will be held.
Type of Facility
Funding Sources Private; State; Federal.
Average Length of Stay Long term.
Types of Admissions Accepted Residential treatment; Group home placement.
Sources of Referral State depts of education; Local depts of education; State depts of mental health; Psychiatrists; Depts of correction; Social service depts.
Client Profile
Age Range of Clients Served Residential program: 6-18.
Characteristics Exhibited by Children Emotional handicaps; Learning disabilities; Speech/Language disorders; Neurological impairments; Mental disabilities.
IQ Range of Clients 60+.
Tuition and Fees
Room and Board Long term: $78/diem.
Tuition $108/diem.
Placements Primarily Funded By State depts of education; Social service depts.
Social and Rehabilitative Services
Therapeutic Approach The facility uses behavioral and family therapy.
Therapeutic Services Offered Individual therapy; Group therapy; Family therapy; Independent living skills program; Recreation activities; Aftercare program with follow up.
Professionals on Staff Psychiatrists; Psychologists; Social workers; Child care staff; Nurses.
Educational and Vocational Services
Type(s) of Educational Programs Offered On campus.
Profile of On Campus School Program Number of teachers 58;
Number of classrooms 43; *Student to teacher ratio* 5:1; *Credentials of teachers* Certified; *Grades taught* K-10; Special curriculum electives offered (PE, Art, Music, Library, Computer labs, Industrial art); Remedial courses offered (Reading, Speech therapy, Counseling).

FREEVILLE

GEORGE JUNIOR REPUBLIC

Freeville, NY 13068 (607) 844-8613 *Contact Person(s):* Karen Smith, Admis Dir
Setting and Background Information The facility was established in 1895 by William R George with the aid of Theodore Roosevelt. The campus is located on 1,200 acres of land and consists of 45 buildings, along with a farm, orchard, and garden.
Referral Information Referrals can be made by community agencies, school districts, physicians, and parents or guardians. Applicants should submit a social history, psychological evaluation, and school records to the admission office. A pre-placement interview will be scheduled.
Type of Facility
Funding Sources State.
Average Length of Stay Long term.
Types of Admissions Accepted Residential treatment.
Sources of Referral State depts of education; Local depts of education; Social service depts; Family court.
Client Profile
Age Range of Clients Served Residential program: 12-16.
Characteristics Exhibited by Children Emotional handicaps; Learning disabilities.
IQ Range of Clients 80+.
Tuition and Fees
Room and Board Long term: $48,000/yr.
Placements Primarily Funded By Social service depts.
Social and Rehabilitative Services
Therapeutic Services Offered Individual therapy; Group therapy; Family therapy; Independent living skills program; Recreation activities; Aftercare program with follow up.
Professionals on Staff Psychiatrists; Psychologists; Social workers; Child care staff; Nurses.
Educational and Vocational Services
Type(s) of Educational Programs Offered On campus; Summer campus.
Profile of On Campus School Program Number of teachers 18;
Number of classrooms 20; *Student to teacher ratio* 6:1; Remedial courses offered.
Degrees Offered 12th grade diploma.

GOSHEN

ASTOR HOME FOR CHILDREN, MARIAN GROUP HOME

36 Parkway, Goshen, NY 10924 (914) 294-7402 *Contact Person(s):* Beth Hoeffner, Supv
Setting and Background Information The facility was established in 1985 by the Astor Agency in response to a request from Orange County. It is a group home.
Referral Information Contact the facility for referral information.
Type of Facility
Funding Sources Private; Archdiocese; United Way.
Average Length of Stay Approx 1 yr.
Types of Admissions Accepted Group home placement.
Sources of Referral Private sources; Social service depts.
Client Profile
Age Range of Clients Served Residential program: 6-12.
Characteristics Exhibited by Children Emotional handicaps.
IQ Range of Clients 60-100.
Tuition and Fees
Placements Primarily Funded By Social service depts; County.
Social and Rehabilitative Services
Therapeutic Approach The facility uses behavior modification.
Therapeutic Services Offered Individual therapy; Group therapy; Family therapy; Recreation activities.
Professionals on Staff Psychiatrists; Psychologists; Social workers; Child care staff.
Educational and Vocational Services
Type(s) of Educational Programs Offered Off campus.

HAMBURG

HOPEVALE, INC
PO Box 828, 3780 Howard Rd, Hamburg, NY 14075
(716) 648-1964 *Contact Person(s):* Donna LaPatra, Dir of Intake
Setting and Background Information The facility was established in
1976. There are 20 buildings, including 7 cottages, 2
administration buildings, a school, and a recreation center.
Referral Information Contact the facility and submit a letter which
describes the required level of care (regular or critical care), a
social summary, a probation report, psychiatric/psychological
evaluations, a birth certificate, school records, and previous
reports from former institutions.
Type of Facility
Funding Sources Private.
Average Length of Stay 12-18 mos.
Types of Admissions Accepted Residential treatment.
Sources of Referral State depts of education; Social service depts;
Dept of Family & Youth.
Client Profile
Age Range of Clients Served Residential program: 12-21+.
Characteristics Exhibited by Children Emotional handicaps.
IQ Range of Clients 65+.
Tuition and Fees
Room and Board Long term: $72.92/diem.
Tuition $11,316/yr.
Placements Primarily Funded By State depts of education; Local
depts of education; Social service depts; Dept of Family & Youth.
Social and Rehabilitative Services
Therapeutic Approach The basic therapeutic approach of the facility
is behavior modification.
Therapeutic Services Offered Individual therapy; Group therapy;
Family therapy; Art therapy; Independent living skills program;
Recreation activities; Substance abuse treatment; Aftercare pro-
gram with follow up.
Professionals on Staff Psychiatrists; Psychologists; Social workers;
Adjunctive therapists; Child care staff; Nurses.
Educational and Vocational Services
Type(s) of Educational Programs Offered On campus; Off campus
(BOCES); Summer campus.
Profile of On Campus School Program Number of teachers 20;
Number of classrooms 21; *Student to teacher ratio* 12:1; *Creden-
tials of teachers* Dual certification in Spec Ed & subject area;
Grades taught 7-12; Remedial courses offered (Math, Reading).
Vocational Education Programs/Degrees Offered Medical aide; Cos-
metology; Food service; Office work.
Degrees Offered 8th grade diploma; 12th grade diploma; GED.

HAWTHORNE

HAWTHORNE CEDAR KNOLLS SCHOOL
226 Linda Ave, Hawthorne, NY 10532 (914) 769-2790 *Contact
Person(s):* Norman E Friedman, Dir
Setting and Background Information The facility was established in
1906 by the Jewish Board of Guardians and the Jewish
Protectorate Society. There is a clinic, a school, an infirmary,
along with residential units on a 200-acre campus.
Referral Information The referral procedure is to contact the facility
and forward educational, psychosocial and psychiatric material.
Type of Facility
Funding Sources Private; State; Federal.
Average Length of Stay 18 mos.
Types of Admissions Accepted Day treatment; Residential treatment;
Group home placement.
Sources of Referral State depts of education; Local depts of educa-
tion; State depts of mental health; Psychiatrists; Private sources;
Social service depts.
Client Profile
Age Range of Clients Served Day programs: 6-18; Residential pro-
gram: 6-21+.
Characteristics Exhibited by Children Emotional handicaps; Learning
disabilities; Mental disabilities.
IQ Range of Clients 70+.
Tuition and Fees
Placements Primarily Funded By State depts of mental health; Social
service depts.

Social and Rehabilitative Services
Therapeutic Approach Psychotherapy in a mileau setting is the basic
therapeutic approach of this facility.
Therapeutic Services Offered Individual therapy; Group therapy;
Family therapy; Independent living skills program; Recreation
activities; Aftercare program with follow up.
Professionals on Staff Psychiatrists; Psychologists; Social workers;
Child care staff; Nurses; Art therapists.
Educational and Vocational Services
Type(s) of Educational Programs Offered On campus (Academic,
Vocational).
Profile of On Campus School Program Number of teachers 47;
Number of classrooms 47; *Student to teacher ratio* 6:1; *Credentials
of teachers* Certified Spec Ed; *Length of school day* 9-3; *Grades
taught* 3-12; Remedial courses offered.
Degrees Offered 8th grade diploma; 12th grade diploma; GED.

HUNTINGTON

MADONNA HEIGHTS SERVICES
Burrs Lane, Huntington, NY 11743 (516) 643-8800 *Contact
Person(s):* Sr Mary James, ACSW, Exec Dir
Setting and Background Information The facility was originally
established in 1868 in Brooklyn and later moved to Huntington,
NY, in 1963. Its campus consists of an administration building,
school, gym, 6 group living apartments, cottage and gatehouse on
55 acres.
Referral Information Contact the facility and foreward the necessary
information, including psychosocial history, psychiatric reports,
and psychological evaluations.
Type of Facility
Funding Sources Private; State; Federal; County.
Average Length of Stay Short and long term.
Types of Admissions Accepted Day treatment; Residential treatment;
Group home placement; Wards of the state.
Sources of Referral State depts of education; Local depts of educa-
tion; Private sources; Depts of correction; Social service depts.
Client Profile
Age Range of Clients Served Day programs: 12-21+; Residential
program: 12-21+.
Characteristics Exhibited by Children Emotional handicaps; Neuro-
logical impairments; Mental disabilities.
IQ Range of Clients 75+.
Tuition and Fees
Tuition $9,367/yr.
Placements Primarily Funded By Local depts of education; Depts of
corrections; Social service depts.
Social and Rehabilitative Services
Therapeutic Approach The facility has psychiatric, psychological and
case work services, including family therapy and a substance
abuse program.
Therapeutic Services Offered Individual therapy; Group therapy;
Family therapy; Independent living skills program; Recreation
activities; Substance abuse treatment; Aftercare program with
follow up.
Professionals on Staff Psychiatrists; Psychologists; Social workers;
Adjunctive therapists; Child care staff; Nurses.
Educational and Vocational Services
Type(s) of Educational Programs Offered On campus (Spec Ed); Off
campus (Community schools); Summer campus (Spec Ed).
Profile of On Campus School Program Number of teachers 16;
Number of classrooms 12; *Student to teacher ratio* 6:1; *Credentials
of teachers* Spec Ed; *Grades taught* 6-12; Remedial courses of-
fered.
Degrees Offered 8th grade diploma; 12th grade diploma.

JOHNSTOWN

FOOTHILLS YOUTH SERVICES, INC
101 S Perry St, Johnstown, NY 12095 (518) 762-3361 *Contact
Person(s):* Hope Fried, Exec Dir
Setting and Background Information The facility was privately
established in 1976. It is a group home.
Referral Information For referral, contact the facility and forward
the necessary information. An interview and week-end
observation will be scheduled.

FOOTHILLS YOUTH SERVICES, INC (continued)

Type of Facility
Funding Sources Private.
Average Length of Stay Long term.
Types of Admissions Accepted Group home placement; Wards of the state.
Sources of Referral Social service depts.
Client Profile
Age Range of Clients Served Residential program: 12-18.
Characteristics Exhibited by Children Emotional handicaps; Learning disabilities; Abused and neglected.
Tuition and Fees
Placements Primarily Funded By Social service depts.
Social and Rehabilitative Services
Therapeutic Approach The approach of the facility is reality therapy.
Therapeutic Services Offered Individual therapy; Group therapy; Family therapy; Independent living skills program; Recreation activities; Aftercare program with follow up.
Professionals on Staff Social workers; Adjunctive therapists; Child care staff.

KINGSTON

CHILDREN'S HOME OF KINGSTON
PO Box 68, 26 Grove St, Kingston, NY 12401 (914) 331-1448
Contact Person(s): Connie Whitehurst, Exec Dir
Setting and Background Information The facility was originally established in 1876. Currently, it is located on 5 acres and has 4 dorms, a school and an administration building. There are also 2 group homes.
Referral Information Contact the Director of Intake for referral information.
Type of Facility
Funding Sources Private; State.
Average Length of Stay Long term.
Types of Admissions Accepted Day treatment; Residential treatment; Group home placement; Wards of the state.
Sources of Referral Social service depts; School districts.
Client Profile
Age Range of Clients Served Day programs: 6-15; Residential program: 6-15.
Characteristics Exhibited by Children Emotional handicaps; Learning disabilities; Mental disabilities.
Tuition and Fees
Room and Board Long term: $65-77/diem.
Tuition $48/diem.
Placements Primarily Funded By Local depts of education; Social service depts.
Social and Rehabilitative Services
Therapeutic Services Offered Individual therapy; Group therapy; Family therapy; Independent living skills program.
Professionals on Staff Psychiatrists; Psychologists; Social workers; Nurses.
Educational and Vocational Services
Type(s) of Educational Programs Offered On campus (For residential clients); Off campus (For group home clients).
Profile of On Campus School Program Number of teachers 12; Student to teacher ratio 8:1; Credentials of teachers MA; Grades taught 3-10; Special curriculum electives offered (Music, Art, PE); Remedial courses offered.

LACKAWANNA

BAKER HALL
125 Martin Rd, Lackawanna, NY 14218 (716) 827-9777 *Contact Person(s):* Robert Beuler, Dir of Residential Srvs & Group Homes
Setting and Background Information The facility was established in 1956 as an orphanage and working boy's home. Currently, it is a residential program. There are 3 group homes, two 12-bed DSS cottages, two 18-bed special service cottages, and three 15-bed OMH cottages (one for adolescent females).
Referral Information For referral to the residential and group home programs, contact the facility and submit the necessary information. Referrals to the OMH programs are made through the regional OMH office.

Type of Facility
Funding Sources Private; State; Federal.
Average Length of Stay Long term.
Types of Admissions Accepted Day treatment; Residential treatment; Group home placement; Wards of the state.
Sources of Referral Local depts of education; State depts of mental health; Social service depts; State Division for Youth.
Client Profile
Age Range of Clients Served Day programs: 12-15; Residential program: 12-21+.
Characteristics Exhibited by Children Emotional handicaps; Learning disabilities; Mental disabilities.
Tuition and Fees
Placements Primarily Funded By State depts of education; Local depts of education; State depts of mental health; Social service depts.
Social and Rehabilitative Services
Therapeutic Approach The facility has an individualized approach to therapy.
Therapeutic Services Offered Individual therapy; Group therapy; Family therapy; Adjunctive therapy; Independent living skills program; Recreation activities; Aftercare program with follow up.
Professionals on Staff Psychiatrists; Psychologists; Social workers; Child care staff; Nurses.
Educational and Vocational Services
Type(s) of Educational Programs Offered On campus (Academic; GED); Off campus (BOCES).
Profile of On Campus School Program Number of teachers 19; Number of classrooms 13; Student to teacher ratio 12:1; Credentials of teachers Spec Ed; Length of school day 8:30-2:30; Grades taught Ungraded; Special curriculum electives offered (Photography, Computer); Remedial courses offered (Reading, Math).
Vocational Education Programs/Degrees Offered Work study.
Degrees Offered GED; 9th grade credits.

OUR LADY OF VICTORY INFANT HOME
790 Ridge Rd, Lackawanna, NY 14218 (716) 827-9611 *Contact Person(s):* Virginia Purcell, Admin
Setting and Background Information This facility was established in 1907 as a home to care for pregnant unmarried women, their babies and homeless children. Currently, it offers several services to the community, including 2 group homes for girls, a special education nursery school and maternity residence.
Referral Information For referral information, contact the facility.
Type of Facility
Funding Sources Private; State; County.
Average Length of Stay Long term.
Types of Admissions Accepted Residential treatment; Group home placement; Wards of the state.
Sources of Referral State depts of education; Local depts of education; State depts of mental health; Psychiatrists; Private sources; Depts of correction; Social service depts.
Client Profile
Age Range of Clients Served Day programs: Birth-5; Residential program: Birth-21+.
Characteristics Exhibited by Children Emotional handicaps; Learning disabilities; Hearing impairments/deafness; Vision impairments/blindness; Speech/Language disorders; Neurological impairments; Physical handicaps; Mental disabilities; Unmarried mothers.
Tuition and Fees
Placements Primarily Funded By State depts of mental health; Social service depts; Medicaid.
Social and Rehabilitative Services
Therapeutic Approach This Christian program has a multi-disciplinary approach to therapy.
Therapeutic Services Offered Individual therapy; Group therapy; Family therapy; Adjunctive therapy; Art therapy; Physical therapy; Independent living skills program; Recreation activities; Aftercare program with follow up; Speech therapy.
Professionals on Staff Psychiatrists; Psychologists; Social workers; Adjunctive therapists; Child care staff; Nurses; Art therapists; Physical therapists; Dietician; Pediatrician.
Educational and Vocational Services
Type(s) of Educational Programs Offered On campus (Nursery school & day program); Off campus; Summer campus.
Profile of On Campus School Program Special curriculum electives offered; Remedial courses offered.

OUR LADY OF VICTORY INFANT HOME *(continued)*

Degrees Offered 8th grade diploma.

LOCKPORT

WYNDHAM LAWN HOME FOR CHILDREN

6395 Old Niagara Rd, Lockport, NY 14094 (716) 433-4487 *Contact Person(s):* Richard J Pyc, Assoc Dir
Setting and Background Information The facility was established in 1871 by the Lockport Ladies Relief Society. The 80-acre campus has an administration building, 4 cottages, an apartment, a school and a recreation building.
Referral Information Contact the facility and submit a referral packet, including a social history, medical information, psychological reports and educational records.
Type of Facility
Funding Sources Private; State; Federal; County.
Average Length of Stay Long term.
Types of Admissions Accepted Day treatment; Residential treatment; Group home placement; Wards of the state.
Sources of Referral State depts of education; Local depts of education; Psychiatrists; Private sources; Depts of correction; Social service depts.
Client Profile
Age Range of Clients Served Day programs: 11-15; Residential program: 11-15.
Characteristics Exhibited by Children Emotional handicaps; Learning disabilities; Behavior disorders.
IQ Range of Clients 80+.
Tuition and Fees
Room and Board Long term: $77.06/diem.
Tuition $47.84/diem.
Placements Primarily Funded By State depts of education; Local depts of education; Depts of corrections; Social service depts.
Social and Rehabilitative Services
Therapeutic Services Offered Individual therapy; Group therapy; Family therapy; Adjunctive therapy; Independent living skills program; Recreation activities; Substance abuse treatment; Aftercare program with follow up.
Professionals on Staff Psychiatrists; Psychologists; Social workers; Adjunctive therapists; Child care staff; Nurses.
Educational and Vocational Services
Type(s) of Educational Programs Offered On campus; Off campus; Summer campus.
Profile of On Campus School Program Number of teachers 11; *Number of classrooms* 10; *Student to teacher ratio* 6:1; *Grades taught* 4-10; Special curriculum electives offered (Independent living skills, Adaptive PE); Remedial courses offered (Reading, Math).

MELVILLE

MELVILLE HOUSE, INC

20 Ruland Rd, Melville, NY 11747 (516) 293-0044 *Contact Person(s):* Rhoda Cohen, Exec Dir
Setting and Background Information The facility was established in 1972 and has a residential group home on 5 acres.
Referral Information Referrals to the facility are accepted from all upstate county Depts of Social Services and from probation depts.
Type of Facility
Funding Sources Private; State; County.
Average Length of Stay Long term.
Types of Admissions Accepted Residential treatment; Group home placement; Wards of the state.
Sources of Referral Depts of correction; Social service depts; Private.
Client Profile
Age Range of Clients Served Residential program: 12-18.
Characteristics Exhibited by Children Emotional handicaps; Learning disabilities.
Social and Rehabilitative Services
Therapeutic Services Offered Individual therapy; Group therapy; Family therapy; Independent living skills program; Substance abuse treatment.
Professionals on Staff Psychiatrists; Psychologists; Social workers; Child care staff.

Educational and Vocational Services
Type(s) of Educational Programs Offered On campus; Off campus.
Profile of On Campus School Program Number of teachers 2; *Number of classrooms* 1; *Student to teacher ratio* 3:1; *Credentials of teachers* Spec Ed.
Vocational Education Programs/Degrees Offered Vocational tech.
Degrees Offered 12th grade diploma.

MINEOLA

NASSAU CHILDREN'S HOUSE

PO Box 510, Mineola, NY 11501 (516) 746-0350 *Contact Person(s):* Richard P Dina, Exec Dir
Setting and Background Information The facility was privately established in 1884 to provide shelter to abused and abandoned children. Currently, there are 6 residental programs for adolescents who are unable to remain at home.
Referral Information Contact the facility for referral information.
Type of Facility
Funding Sources Private; State; County.
Average Length of Stay Short and long term.
Types of Admissions Accepted Group home placement; Wards of the state.
Sources of Referral Social service depts; Voluntary; Family; Court.
Client Profile
Age Range of Clients Served Residential program: 12-21+.
Characteristics Exhibited by Children Emotional handicaps; Learning disabilities; Delinquency; Abused and neglected; Runaways.
IQ Range of Clients 80+.
Tuition and Fees
Placements Primarily Funded By Social service depts; Family probation.
Social and Rehabilitative Services
Therapeutic Approach The facility uses behavior modification.
Therapeutic Services Offered Individual therapy; Group therapy; Family therapy; Independent living skills program; Aftercare program with follow up.
Professionals on Staff Psychologists; Social workers; Child care staff.
Educational and Vocational Services
Type(s) of Educational Programs Offered Off campus (Local school).

NEW YORK

LAURENT CLERC GROUP HOME

490 2nd Ave #8A, New York, NY 10016 (212) 685-5921, 685-6904, 472-2233 *Contact Person(s):* Jeanne Fernekees, Prog Supv
Setting and Background Information This facility was established in 1981. It is a community based group home for hearing impaired adolescents.
Referral Information Contact the facility for referral information.
Type of Facility
Funding Sources Private; City.
Average Length of Stay Long term; 1-3 yrs.
Types of Admissions Accepted Day treatment; Group home placement.
Sources of Referral State depts of education; Local depts of education; State depts of mental health; Psychiatrists; Social service depts.
Client Profile
Age Range of Clients Served Day programs: 12-18; Residential program: 12-18.
Characteristics Exhibited by Children Emotional handicaps; Hearing impairments/deafness.
Tuition and Fees
Placements Primarily Funded By Social service depts.
Social and Rehabilitative Services
Therapeutic Approach The facility uses a combination of individual, group and family therapy, and uses behavior modification.
Therapeutic Services Offered Individual therapy; Group therapy; Family therapy; Adjunctive therapy; Physical therapy; Independent living skills program.
Professionals on Staff Psychiatrists; Social workers; Adjunctive therapists; Child care staff; Physical therapists.
Educational and Vocational Services
Type(s) of Educational Programs Offered Off campus (Public schools).

HARLEM COMMUNITY RESIDENTIAL HOME

419 W 145th St, New York, NY 10031 (212) 862-6969 *Contact Person(s):* Joseph Dennison, Dir

Setting and Background Information The facility was established in 1980 as a state program. It is located in a large brownstone.

Referral Information Referrals to the facility are made through the courts.

Type of Facility

Funding Sources State; Federal.

Average Length of Stay Long term.

Types of Admissions Accepted Residential treatment; Group home placement; Wards of the state.

Sources of Referral Court.

Client Profile

Age Range of Clients Served Residential program: 15-18.

Characteristics Exhibited by Children Emotional handicaps; Learning disabilities.

IQ Range of Clients 65-110.

Tuition and Fees

Room and Board Long term: $22,000/yr.

Placements Primarily Funded By State agencies.

Social and Rehabilitative Services

Therapeutic Approach The basic therapeutic approach of the facility is reality therapy.

Therapeutic Services Offered Individual therapy; Group therapy; Family therapy; Recreation activities; Substance abuse treatment.

Professionals on Staff Psychiatrists; Psychologists; Social workers; Child care staff; Counselors.

Educational and Vocational Services

Type(s) of Educational Programs Offered On campus; Off campus (High school; Training programs).

HEARTSEASE HOME, INC

216 E 70th St, New York, NY 10021 (212) 249-3107 *Contact Person(s):* Richard Frey, Exec Dir

Setting and Background Information The facility was established in 1969 as a non-profit maternity shelter. There are 2 community-based congregate care facilities.

Referral Information Referrals are received from other NYC approved child care agencies. Intake committee determines appropriateness and arranges for an interview.

Type of Facility

Funding Sources Private; State; City.

Average Length of Stay Long term.

Types of Admissions Accepted Group home placement; Wards of the state.

Sources of Referral Social service depts.

Client Profile

Age Range of Clients Served Residential program: 16-21.

Characteristics Exhibited by Children Behavior disorders.

IQ Range of Clients 70+.

Tuition and Fees

Placements Primarily Funded By Social service depts.

Social and Rehabilitative Services

Therapeutic Approach The facility offers a therapeutic milieu.

Therapeutic Services Offered Individual therapy; Independent living skills program.

Professionals on Staff Psychologists; Social workers; Child care staff; Nurses.

Educational and Vocational Services

Type(s) of Educational Programs Offered On campus (Tutoring).

Vocational Education Programs/Degrees Offered Vocational counseling and testing.

OSWEGO

OSWEGO COUNTY OPPORTUNITIES— ADOLESCENT GIRLS GROUP HOME

55 Erie St, Oswego, NY 13126 (315) 342-3772 *Contact Person(s):* Diane Steffen, Dir of Social Svcs, Group Home Supv

Setting and Background Information The facility was established in 1984 with joint funding from the State Office of Mental Health and the Dept of Social Services. It is a community-based group home.

Referral Information Referral packet should include a social summary, educational and health material, and psychological information.

Type of Facility

Funding Sources State.

Average Length of Stay Long term.

Types of Admissions Accepted Group home placement.

Sources of Referral State depts of mental health; Depts of correction; Social service depts; Probation dept.

Client Profile

Age Range of Clients Served Residential program: 12-18.

Characteristics Exhibited by Children Emotional handicaps; Learning disabilities.

IQ Range of Clients 70-110.

Tuition and Fees

Room and Board Long term: $79.58/diem.

Placements Primarily Funded By Social service depts.

Social and Rehabilitative Services

Therapeutic Approach The basic therapeutic approach is reality therapy.

Therapeutic Services Offered Individual therapy; Group therapy; Independent living skills program; Substance abuse treatment.

Professionals on Staff Psychologists; Social workers; Adjunctive therapists; Child care staff; Nurses; Dietician.

Educational and Vocational Services

Type(s) of Educational Programs Offered Off campus (Public school).

RANDOLPH

RANDOLPH CHILDREN'S HOME

PO Box 218, Randolph, NY 14772 (716) 358-3636 *Contact Person(s):* Albert L Richter, MA

Setting and Background Information The facility was initially established as a home for neglected and dependent children in 1878. It has since expanded its program to become a treatment center for emotionally disturbed children. The campus is located 15 miles east of Jamestown and 60 miles south of Buffalo, on 200 acres of land. There are 4 modern residential units (3 for males and 1 for females) and a recreation center.

Referral Information Referrals can be made by the state Division for Youth, family court, Committee on Special Education, and Dept of Social Services. Private and public referrals are also accepted from other states. To make a referral, contact the facility and forward the necessary background information. A pre-placement visit is necessary before an admission decision is made.

Type of Facility

Funding Sources State; County.

Average Length of Stay Long term.

Types of Admissions Accepted Residential treatment.

Sources of Referral State depts of education; Local depts of education; Social service depts; Div for Youth.

Client Profile

Age Range of Clients Served Residential program: 8-18.

Characteristics Exhibited by Children Emotional handicaps; Learning disabilities; Speech/Language disorders; Neurological impairments; Mental disabilities.

IQ Range of Clients 60+.

Tuition and Fees

Room and Board Long term: $77/diem.

Tuition $60/diem.

Placements Primarily Funded By State depts of education; Local depts of education; Social service depts.

Social and Rehabilitative Services

Therapeutic Approach The basic therapeutic approaches used at the facility are reality therapy and milieu.

Therapeutic Services Offered Individual therapy; Group therapy; Family therapy; Adjunctive therapy; Independent living skills program; Recreation activities; Aftercare program with follow up.

Professionals on Staff Psychiatrists; Psychologists; Social workers; Adjunctive therapists; Child care staff; Nurses.

Educational and Vocational Services

Type(s) of Educational Programs Offered On campus; Summer campus (6 weeks).

Profile of On Campus School Program Number of teachers 20; Number of classrooms 12; Student to teacher ratio 6:1; Remedial courses offered.

Degrees Offered 12th grade diploma.

RHINEBECK

THE ASTOR HOME FOR CHILDREN

36 Mill St, Rhinebeck, NY 12572 (914) 876-4081 *Contact Person(s):* Martha Parker, Intake Soc Wkr

Setting and Background Information The facility was established in 1953 as a pilot project of the state Office of Mental Health and is sponsored by Catholic Charities of the Archdiocese of New York. It is a non-profit agency which provides a continuum of services to meet the needs of children and their families, including early childhood programs, special education, community mental health and residential programs.

Referral Information Referral material should include psychological, psychiatric, psychosocial, educational and medical history. Contact the facility for more information.

Type of Facility

Funding Sources State; Federal; Counties.

Average Length of Stay Long term.

Types of Admissions Accepted Day treatment; Residential treatment; Group home placement.

Sources of Referral Local depts of education; State depts of mental health; Social service depts.

Client Profile

Age Range of Clients Served Day programs: Birth-12; Residential program: 6-21+.

Characteristics Exhibited by Children Emotional handicaps; Learning disabilities; Mental disabilities.

IQ Range of Clients 70-125.

Tuition and Fees

Room and Board Long term: $94.83-$163/diem.

Tuition $12,520/yr.

Placements Primarily Funded By Local depts of education; Social service depts; Medicaid.

Social and Rehabilitative Services

Therapeutic Services Offered Individual therapy; Group therapy; Family therapy; Independent living skills program; Recreation activities.

Professionals on Staff Psychiatrists; Psychologists; Social workers; Child care staff; Nurses.

Educational and Vocational Services

Type(s) of Educational Programs Offered Off campus.

Profile of On Campus School Program Number of teachers 15; *Number of classrooms* 14; *Student to teacher ratio* 6:1; *Credentials of teachers* BA/MS, Spec Ed; Special curriculum electives offered (Home Ec, Art, Gym, Computer); Remedial courses offered (Reading, Math).

RIVERDALE

HENRY ITTLESON CENTER FOR CHILD RESEARCH

5050 Iselin Ave, Riverdale, NY 10471 (212) 549-6700 *Contact Person(s):* Marilyn Tamarin, Acting Dir

Setting and Background Information This facility was established in 1953. Its 5-acre campus has a residential pavilion, a school and an administration building.

Referral Information Referrals are made through the State Office of Mental Health and through the Application Service Center of the Jewish Board of Family & Children's Services, Inc.

Type of Facility

Funding Sources State; Philanthropic.

Average Length of Stay Long term.

Types of Admissions Accepted Day treatment; Residential treatment.

Sources of Referral Local depts of education; State depts of mental health; Psychiatrists; Social service depts.

Client Profile

Age Range of Clients Served Day programs: 6-12; Residential program: 6-12.

Characteristics Exhibited by Children Emotional handicaps; Learning disabilities; Speech/Language disorders; Neurological impairments.

IQ Range of Clients 75+.

Tuition and Fees

Placements Primarily Funded By State depts of mental health.

Social and Rehabilitative Services

Therapeutic Approach The facility offers psychiatric therapies in a milieu setting.

Therapeutic Services Offered Individual therapy; Group therapy; Family therapy; Art therapy; Recreation activities; Music therapy.

Professionals on Staff Psychiatrists; Psychologists; Social workers; Adjunctive therapists; Child care staff; Nurses; Art therapists; Music therapist; Remedial reading therapist.

Educational and Vocational Services

Type(s) of Educational Programs Offered On campus (Spec Ed).

Profile of On Campus School Program Number of teachers 12; *Number of classrooms* 7; *Credentials of teachers* Certified Spec Ed; *Grades taught* Pre school-6th; Remedial courses offered (Reading, Speech).

Vocational Education Programs/Degrees Offered Pre-vocational.

RIVERHEAD

TIMOTHY HILL CHILDREN'S RANCH

810 E Main St, Riverhead, NY 11901 (516) 369-1190 *Contact Person(s):* Jerrell D Hill, Exec Dir

Setting and Background Information The facility was established in 1980. There are two residential houses located on 106 acres.

Referral Information Contact the facility for referral information.

Type of Facility

Funding Sources Private; State.

Average Length of Stay Long term.

Types of Admissions Accepted Group home placement; Wards of the state.

Sources of Referral Private sources; Depts of correction; Social service depts.

Client Profile

Age Range of Clients Served Residential program: 6-18.

Characteristics Exhibited by Children Emotional handicaps; Learning disabilities; Behavior disorders.

Tuition and Fees

Room and Board Long term: $84.65/diem.

Placements Primarily Funded By Depts of corrections; Social service depts; Donations.

Social and Rehabilitative Services

Therapeutic Approach The facility uses behavior modification.

Therapeutic Services Offered Individual therapy; Group therapy; Family therapy; Adjunctive therapy; Independent living skills program; Recreation activities; Substance abuse treatment; Aftercare program with follow up.

Professionals on Staff Psychiatrists; Psychologists; Social workers; Adjunctive therapists; Child care staff.

Educational and Vocational Services

Type(s) of Educational Programs Offered On campus; Off campus (Public school).

Profile of On Campus School Program Number of teachers 1; *Number of classrooms* 1; *Student to teacher ratio* 3:1; *Grades taught* 7-12.

ROCHESTER

CONVALESCENT HOSPITAL FOR CHILDREN

2075 Scottsville Rd, Rochester, NY 14623 (716) 436-4442 *Contact Person(s):* Mary Lou Segal, VP

Setting and Background Information The facility was initially established in 1885 as a hospital for infant summer fever. In 1958 it converted to a residential treatment center and, in 1967, became a community mental health center. The 50-acre campus has an administrative building, an educational center, a preschool educational center, and a summer camp pavillion on 50 acres of land.

Referral Information For referral information, contact the Intake Secretary.

Type of Facility

Funding Sources Private; State.

Average Length of Stay Long term.

Types of Admissions Accepted Day treatment; Residential treatment; Group home placement.

Sources of Referral State depts of education; Local depts of education; State depts of mental health; Psychiatrists; Private sources; Social service depts; Anyone may make a referral.

Client Profile

Age Range of Clients Served Day programs: Birth-18; Residential program: 6-18.

Characteristics Exhibited by Children Emotional handicaps; Learning disabilities; Speech/Language disorders; Neurological impairments; Mental disabilities.

IQ Range of Clients 70+.

CONVALESCENT HOSPITAL FOR CHILDREN
(continued)

Tuition and Fees
Room and Board Long term: $172/diem.
Tuition $12,196/yr.
Placements Primarily Funded By State depts of education; State depts of mental health.
Social and Rehabilitative Services
Therapeutic Approach The facility has a psychoanalytic/ego psychological approach to therapy.
Therapeutic Services Offered Individual therapy; Group therapy; Family therapy; Adjunctive therapy; Art therapy; Physical therapy; Independent living skills program; Recreation activities; Aftercare program with follow up.
Professionals on Staff Psychiatrists; Psychologists; Social workers; Adjunctive therapists; Child care staff; Nurses; Art therapists; Recreation therapist.
Educational and Vocational Services
Type(s) of Educational Programs Offered On campus.
Profile of On Campus School Program Number of teachers 35; Remedial courses offered (Reading, Math).
Degrees Offered 12th grade diploma.

DEPAUL MENTAL HEALTH, WELLINGTON GROUP HOME
287 Wellington Ave, Rochester, NY 14611 (716) 436-9455 *Contact Person(s):* Jeff McConnell, Mgr
Setting and Background Information The facility was established in 1982 by the DePaul Mental Health Services' adolescent program. It is a 5-bedroom group home with a capacity of 11.
Referral Information For referral, contact the intake worker at DePaul Mental Health Services.
Type of Facility
Funding Sources Foster System; DSS.
Average Length of Stay 12-18 mos.
Types of Admissions Accepted Group home placement.
Sources of Referral State depts of mental health; Psychiatrists; Social service depts.
Client Profile
Age Range of Clients Served Residential program: 14-18.
Characteristics Exhibited by Children Emotional handicaps.
Social and Rehabilitative Services
Therapeutic Services Offered Individual therapy; Group therapy; Family therapy; Independent living skills program; Recreation activities; Aftercare program with follow up.
Professionals on Staff Psychiatrists; Psychologists; Social workers; Child care staff.

HILLSIDE CHILDREN'S CENTER
1183 Monroe Ave, Rochester, NY 14620 (716) 244-4455 *Contact Person(s):* Barbara Conradt, Intake Dir
Setting and Background Information The facility was established in 1837 as an orphanage. Currently, the 26-acre campus has residential cottages, a gym and school, and an administrative office. There are also 6 community based group homes.
Referral Information Referrals to the facility are accepted in writing from approved funding sources. Candidates are interviewed on campus to determine formal acceptance.
Type of Facility
Funding Sources State; Federal; United Way.
Average Length of Stay Short and long term.
Types of Admissions Accepted Day treatment; Residential treatment; Group home placement; Wards of the state; Therapeutic foster home.
Sources of Referral Local depts of education; State depts of mental health; Depts of correction; Social service depts.
Client Profile
Age Range of Clients Served Day programs: 6-18; Residential program: 6-18.
Characteristics Exhibited by Children Emotional handicaps; Learning disabilities; Hearing impairments/deafness; Neurological impairments.
IQ Range of Clients 65+.

Tuition and Fees
Room and Board Long term: $84.90/diem.
Tuition $817.70/mo.
Placements Primarily Funded By State depts of education; State depts of mental health; Social service depts.
Social and Rehabilitative Services
Therapeutic Approach The facility uses behavior management in a therapeutic milieu.
Therapeutic Services Offered Individual therapy; Group therapy; Family therapy; Adjunctive therapy; Art therapy; Independent living skills program; Recreation activities; Substance abuse treatment; Aftercare program with follow up; Dance therapy; Occupational therapy.
Professionals on Staff Psychiatrists; Psychologists; Social workers; Adjunctive therapists; Child care staff; Nurses; Art therapists; Occupational therapist.
Educational and Vocational Services
Type(s) of Educational Programs Offered On campus.
Profile of On Campus School Program Number of teachers 26; *Number of classrooms* 19; *Student to teacher ratio* 3:1; *Credentials of teachers* Certified; *Grades taught* 1-12; Special curriculum electives offered.

ST JOSEPH'S VILLA
3300 Dewey Ave, Rochester, NY 14616 (716) 865-1550 *Contact Person(s):* Roger C Battoglia, Asst Exec Dir
Setting and Background Information The facility was originally established as an orphanage in 1942. Currently, the 40-acre campus has five cottages, an education complex, administration and social service buildings.
Referral Information Contact the facility for referral information which will be reviewed by the intake dept. A pre-placement visit will be scheduled.
Type of Facility
Funding Sources Private.
Average Length of Stay 12-14 mos.
Types of Admissions Accepted Day treatment; Residential treatment; Group home placement.
Sources of Referral Local depts of education; State depts of mental health; Social service depts; Family court.
Client Profile
Age Range of Clients Served Day programs: 12-18; Residential program: 12-18.
Characteristics Exhibited by Children Emotional handicaps; Learning disabilities; Mental disabilities.
IQ Range of Clients 70-120.
Tuition and Fees
Placements Primarily Funded By Local depts of education; State depts of mental health; Social service depts.
Social and Rehabilitative Services
Therapeutic Approach The facility has a multi-disciplinary approach to therapy and offers a therapeutic milieu.
Therapeutic Services Offered Individual therapy; Group therapy; Family therapy; Independent living skills program; Recreation activities; Substance abuse treatment; Aftercare program with follow up.
Professionals on Staff Psychiatrists; Psychologists; Social workers; Adjunctive therapists; Child care staff; Nurses.
Educational and Vocational Services
Type(s) of Educational Programs Offered On campus (Spec Ed); Summer campus.
Profile of On Campus School Program Number of teachers 17; *Number of classrooms* 11; *Student to teacher ratio* 10:1; *Credentials of teachers* BS, MS; *Grades taught* 7-12; Remedial courses offered (Reading, Math).

SCHENECTADY

NORTHEAST PARENT AND CHILD SOCIETY
120-122 Park Ave, Schenectady, NY 12019 (518) 346-2387 *Contact Person(s):* Richard J Kelly, Comm Liaison Coord
Setting and Background Information This facility was originally established in 1888 as an orphanage with private ownership. Currently, this facility offers a variety of programs designed to meet specific client needs, including group homes, residential units, and several community educational and prevention services.

NORTHEAST PARENT AND CHILD SOCIETY
(continued)

Referral Information Referrals are accepted from public and private agencies. The referring agency is requested to submit a comprehensive social history, medical report and school records. A pre-placement visit may be required.

Type of Facility
Funding Sources Private; State.
Average Length of Stay Short and long term.
Types of Admissions Accepted Day treatment; Residential treatment; Group home placement; Emergency shelter.
Sources of Referral Local depts of education; Social service depts; Probation depts; Family courts.

Client Profile
Age Range of Clients Served Day programs: 12-18; Residential program: 12-18.
Characteristics Exhibited by Children Emotional handicaps; Learning disabilities.
IQ Range of Clients 70+.

Tuition and Fees
Room and Board Short term: $67.68/diem; Long term: $67.68/diem.
Tuition $67.52/diem.
Placements Primarily Funded By Social service depts.

Social and Rehabilitative Services
Therapeutic Approach The basic therapeutic approach used is structural family therapy.
Therapeutic Services Offered Individual therapy; Group therapy; Family therapy; Independent living skills program; Aftercare program with follow up.
Professionals on Staff Psychiatrists; Psychologists; Social workers; Child care staff; Nurses.

Educational and Vocational Services
Type(s) of Educational Programs Offered On campus (Spec Ed); Off campus (Mainstreaming into public schools).
Profile of On Campus School Program Number of teachers 14; Number of classrooms 14; Student to teacher ratio 6:1; Credentials of teachers MS, Spec Ed; Grades taught 6-10; Special curriculum electives offered (Computers, Job readiness); Remedial courses offered.
Vocational Education Programs/Degrees Offered Job readiness.
Degrees Offered Credits are transferrable to home school district.

WAITT HOUSES, INC
PO Box 3455, Schenectady, NY 12303 (518) 382-8438 *Contact Person(s):* John Karbowski, Exec Dir
Setting and Background Information The facility was established in 1977 in response to a community need for a group home. Currently, there are 5 agency boarding homes and an office.
Referral Information Referrals to the facility are made by the family court through the Dept of Social Services and the State Division for Youth.

Type of Facility
Funding Sources Private; State; Fund raising.
Average Length of Stay Long term.
Types of Admissions Accepted Group home placement; Wards of the state.
Sources of Referral Depts of correction; Social service depts.

Client Profile
Age Range of Clients Served Residential program: 15-21+.
Characteristics Exhibited by Children Emotional handicaps; Learning disabilities.
IQ Range of Clients 64-100.

Tuition and Fees
Room and Board Long term: $77.25/diem.
Placements Primarily Funded By Depts of corrections; Social service depts.

Social and Rehabilitative Services
Therapeutic Services Offered Individual therapy; Group therapy; Family therapy; Independent living skills program; Recreation activities; Aftercare program with follow up.
Professionals on Staff Psychologists; Social workers; Child care staff; Nurses.

Educational and Vocational Services
Type(s) of Educational Programs Offered On campus (Tutoring); Off campus.
Vocational Education Programs/Degrees Offered Woodworking shop.

SPRING VALLEY

LAKESIDE SCHOOL
S Main St, Spring Valley, NY 10977 (914) 578-6829 *Contact Person(s):* Lorraine Carlson, Dir of Social Svcs
Setting and Background Information The facility was established in 1923 through the Edwin Gould Foundation. The 150-acre campus has 16 residential units, a school, restaurant, auto shop, and a health center.
Referral Information The facility accepts emergency placements and placements made through DFY and the county.

Type of Facility
Funding Sources State.
Average Length of Stay Long term.
Types of Admissions Accepted Residential treatment.
Sources of Referral Social service depts; Dept of Family & Youth.

Client Profile
Age Range of Clients Served Residential program: 12-18.
Characteristics Exhibited by Children Emotional handicaps.
IQ Range of Clients 77+.

Tuition and Fees
Placements Primarily Funded By Social service depts; Dept of Family & Youth.

Social and Rehabilitative Services
Therapeutic Approach The basic therapeutic approach used at the facility is behavior modification.
Therapeutic Services Offered Individual therapy; Group therapy; Independent living skills program; Recreation activities; Aftercare program with follow up.
Professionals on Staff Psychiatrists; Psychologists; Social workers; Child care staff; Nurses.

Educational and Vocational Services
Type(s) of Educational Programs Offered On campus; Off campus.
Profile of On Campus School Program Number of teachers 30; Number of classrooms 30; Student to teacher ratio 10:1; Credentials of teachers Certified; Grades taught Ungraded; Remedial courses offered (Reading, Math).
Degrees Offered GED.

STAATSBURG

THE ANDERSON SCHOOL
Rte 9, Albany Post Rd, Staatsburg, NY 12580 (914) 889-4046, 889-4034 *Contact Person(s):* Kate Haas, Intake Coord
Setting and Background Information The facility was established in 1927 by Dr V V Anderson, a psychiatrist. He believed that children and adolescents with special needs could benefit from a therapeutic environment, integrated with an educational program. The campus is located on over 100 acres, north of Hyde Park, New York, bordering the Hudson River. There are various recreational facilities, residential units, school buildings, and medical facilities residing on the property. There are 2 specific programs offered by the school: The Special Secondary Education Program and the Autistic Program.
Referral Information Referrals can be made by school districts and social service agencies. Applicants are requested to complete a referral packet to be sent to the Intake Coordinator for review. The Intake Coordinator will then schedule a pre-placement interview with the child and family.

Type of Facility
Funding Sources Private.
Average Length of Stay Long term.
Types of Admissions Accepted Residential treatment.
Sources of Referral Social service depts; School districts.

Client Profile
Age Range of Clients Served Residential program: 4-21.
Characteristics Exhibited by Children Emotional handicaps; Learning disabilities; Speech/Language disorders; Neurological impairments; Mental disabilities; Autism.

Tuition and Fees
Room and Board Long term: $100-$140/diem.
Tuition $16,288-$18,338/year.
Placements Primarily Funded By Local depts of education; Social service depts.

THE ANDERSON SCHOOL *(continued)*

Social and Rehabilitative Services

Therapeutic Approach The core of the program's treatment philosophy is based on problem-solving therapy and client centered therapy in conjunction with a 24-hour behavior management program.

Therapeutic Services Offered Individual therapy; Group therapy; Family therapy; Independent living skills program; Recreation activities.

Professionals on Staff Psychiatrists; Psychologists; Social workers; Child care staff; Nurses.

Educational and Vocational Services

Type(s) of Educational Programs Offered On campus; Summer campus.

Profile of On Campus School Program Student to teacher ratio 6:1, 3:1 (Autistic program); *Credentials of teachers* Certified Spec Ed; *Grades taught* Ungraded; Special curriculum electives offered; Remedial courses offered.

STATEN ISLAND

BOYS HOPE

40 Ackerman St, Staten Island, NY 10308 (718) 984-8466 *Contact Person(s):* Brother Lawrence Hartung FSC CSW, Exec Dir

Setting and Background Information The facility was established in 1979. It is a part of a national child care program which was founded in 1975. There are 2 group homes in a residential area.

Referral Information For referrals, contact the executive director.

Type of Facility

Funding Sources Private.

Average Length of Stay Long term.

Types of Admissions Accepted Group home placement.

Sources of Referral Local depts of education; Psychiatrists; Depts of correction; Social service depts.

Client Profile

Age Range of Clients Served Residential program: 12-18.

Characteristics Exhibited by Children Emotional handicaps.

Tuition and Fees

Placements Primarily Funded By Private sources.

Social and Rehabilitative Services

Therapeutic Services Offered Individual therapy; Group therapy; Family therapy; Independent living skills program; Aftercare program with follow up.

Professionals on Staff Psychiatrists; Psychologists; Social workers; Child care staff.

Educational and Vocational Services

Type(s) of Educational Programs Offered Off campus (Public school).

MARKET STREET RESIDENTIAL TREATMENT CENTER

171 Market St, Staten Island, NY 10310 (718) 727-3031 *Contact Person(s):* Robert Moss, Admin Dir

Setting and Background Information The facility was established in 1974 by approval of the State Dept of Social Services as a group residence.

Referral Information Contact the facility and submit a full clinical work-up to the allocations unit.

Type of Facility

Funding Sources State; City.

Average Length of Stay 18 mos+.

Types of Admissions Accepted Residential treatment.

Sources of Referral Social service depts.

Client Profile

Age Range of Clients Served Residential program: 12-18.

Characteristics Exhibited by Children Emotional handicaps.

IQ Range of Clients 50+.

Tuition and Fees

Placements Primarily Funded By Social service depts.

Social and Rehabilitative Services

Therapeutic Approach The facility uses reality therapy in a milieu setting.

Therapeutic Services Offered Individual therapy; Group therapy; Family therapy; Art therapy; Recreation activities; Aftercare program with follow up.

Professionals on Staff Psychiatrists; Psychologists; Social workers; Adjunctive therapists; Child care staff; Nurses; Art therapists.

Educational and Vocational Services

Type(s) of Educational Programs Offered On campus; Summer campus.

Profile of On Campus School Program Number of teachers 2; *Number of classrooms* 2; *Student to teacher ratio* 8:1; *Grades taught* 5-12; Special curriculum electives offered (Computer, Typing, Driver's Ed); Remedial courses offered.

Degrees Offered GED.

MISSION OF THE IMMACULATE VIRGIN

6581 Hylan Blvd, Staten Island, NY 10309 (718) 317-2600 *Contact Person(s):* Thomas O'Donnell, Dir Soc Srvs

Setting and Background Information The facility was established in 1871. Currently, it is located on 250 acres and has 20 buildings, a church and a school.

Referral Information Most of the referrals are from the Dept of Special Services for Children. Voluntary placements and court placements go through the Office of Mental Health.

Type of Facility

Funding Sources Private; State; Federal.

Average Length of Stay Short and long term.

Types of Admissions Accepted Residential treatment; Group home placement; Wards of the state.

Sources of Referral State depts of mental health; Social service depts.

Client Profile

Age Range of Clients Served Residential program: 12-21+.

Characteristics Exhibited by Children Emotional handicaps; Learning disabilities; Speech/Language disorders; Neurological impairments; Physical handicaps; Mental disabilities; Dually diagnosed.

IQ Range of Clients 40-130.

Tuition and Fees

Placements Primarily Funded By State depts of mental health; Social service depts.

Social and Rehabilitative Services

Therapeutic Approach The basic therapeutic approach is behavior modification.

Therapeutic Services Offered Individual therapy; Group therapy; Family therapy; Independent living skills program; Recreation activities; Substance abuse treatment; Aftercare program with follow up.

Professionals on Staff Psychiatrists; Psychologists; Social workers; Child care staff; Nurses; Art therapists.

Educational and Vocational Services

Type(s) of Educational Programs Offered On campus (Spec Ed and a school for handicapped children); Off campus.

Profile of On Campus School Program Number of teachers 100; *Credentials of teachers* Spec Ed; Remedial courses offered.

Vocational Education Programs/Degrees Offered Automotive; Woodwork; Baking; Typing; Computers; Food preparation.

Degrees Offered GED.

SYOSSETT

ST MARY'S FAMILY AND CHILDREN SERVICES

Convent Rd, Syossett, NY 11791 (516) 921-0808 *Contact Person(s):* Sr Mary Sean Foley, Exec Dir

Setting and Background Information The facility was originally established in 1894 as an orphanage. Currently, the 60-acre campus has 3 cottages, a school, a gym, and an administration building.

Referral Information Referrals are made through the Dept of Social Services.

Type of Facility

Funding Sources Private; State.

Average Length of Stay Short and long term.

Types of Admissions Accepted Residential treatment; Group home placement.

Sources of Referral Social service depts.

Client Profile

Age Range of Clients Served Residential program: 6-18.

Characteristics Exhibited by Children Emotional handicaps; Learning disabilities; Mental disabilities.

IQ Range of Clients 70-120.

Tuition and Fees

Placements Primarily Funded By Social service depts.

ST MARY'S FAMILY AND CHILDREN SERVICES
(continued)

Social and Rehabilitative Services
Therapeutic Services Offered Individual therapy; Group therapy; Family therapy; Independent living skills program; Recreation activities.
Professionals on Staff Psychiatrists; Psychologists; Social workers; Child care staff; Art therapists.
Educational and Vocational Services
Type(s) of Educational Programs Offered On campus; Off campus.
Profile of On Campus School Program Number of teachers 11; *Number of classrooms* 11; *Student to teacher ratio* 10:1; *Grades taught* ungraded.
Degrees Offered 12th grade diploma.

SYRACUSE

ELMCREST CHILDREN'S CENTER
960 Salt Springs Rd, Syracuse, NY 13224 (315) 446-6250 *Contact Person(s):* Charles L Stevens, Dir of Admis
Setting and Background Information The center was established by a church in 1845 to provide educational opportunities to deprived children of Syracuse. The 142-acre campus has residential cottages, a school, and recreational facilities.
Referral Information Contact the Director of Admissions for referral information.
Type of Facility
Funding Sources Private.
Average Length of Stay Short and long term.
Types of Admissions Accepted Day treatment; Residential treatment; Group home placement.
Sources of Referral Local depts of education; Depts of correction; Social service depts.
Client Profile
Age Range of Clients Served Day programs: 2-5; Residential program: 12-18.
Characteristics Exhibited by Children Emotional handicaps; Learning disabilities; Mental disabilities.
Tuition and Fees
Placements Primarily Funded By Local depts of education; Social service depts.
Social and Rehabilitative Services
Therapeutic Approach The facility uses psychotherapy in a therapeutic milieu.
Therapeutic Services Offered Individual therapy; Group therapy; Family therapy; Recreation activities; Aftercare program with follow up.
Professionals on Staff Psychiatrists; Psychologists; Social workers; Child care staff; Nurses.
Educational and Vocational Services
Type(s) of Educational Programs Offered On campus; Off campus.
Profile of On Campus School Program Number of teachers 7; *Number of classrooms* 5; *Student to teacher ratio* 6:1; *Credentials of teachers* NY State certified; *Grades taught* K-10; *Special curriculum electives offered* (Spec Ed).

SYRACUSE YOUTH DEVELOPMENT CENTER
3737 E Genesee St, Syracuse, NY 13214 (315) 445-1454 *Contact Person(s):* Charles M Jones, Facility Dir
Setting and Background Information The facility has four separate units—one is for pregnant adolescents.
Referral Information Court adjudicated youth are placed at the facility through the State Division for Youth.
Type of Facility
Funding Sources State.
Average Length of Stay Short and long term.
Types of Admissions Accepted Group home placement.
Sources of Referral Social service depts; Courts.
Client Profile
Age Range of Clients Served Residential program: 12-21+.
Characteristics Exhibited by Children Emotional handicaps; Learning disabilities; Physical handicaps; Mental disabilities; Delinquency.
IQ Range of Clients 75+.
Tuition and Fees
Placements Primarily Funded By State of NY.

Social and Rehabilitative Services
Therapeutic Services Offered Individual therapy; Group therapy.
Professionals on Staff Psychologists; Child care staff.
Educational and Vocational Services
Type(s) of Educational Programs Offered On campus; Off campus (Community schools).
Profile of On Campus School Program Number of teachers 9; *Number of classrooms* 5; *Student to teacher ratio* 2:1; *Credentials of teachers* State certified; *Length of school day* 8-3; *Grades taught* 7-12; *Special curriculum electives offered* (Shop, Art); *Remedial courses offered* (Math, Reading).

UTICA

THE HOUSE OF THE GOOD SHEPHERD
Champlin Ave, Utica, NY 13502 (315) 733-0436 *Contact Person(s):* William Holicky, Exec Dir
Setting and Background Information The facility was initially established as a home for destitute children by a group of Episcopalians in 1972. The main campus is located on 7 acres of land and consists of 4 cottages, school, and offices. There are also 5 group homes located throughout the Utica community.
Referral Information Referrals can be made by social service agencies, school districts, and family courts. To make a referral, forward the necessary background information on the child to the Intake Committee, who will then schedule a pre-placement interview.
Type of Facility
Funding Sources State.
Average Length of Stay Long term.
Types of Admissions Accepted Residential treatment; Group home placement.
Sources of Referral State depts of education; Local depts of education; Social service depts.
Client Profile
Age Range of Clients Served Residential program: 8-17.
Characteristics Exhibited by Children Emotional handicaps; Learning disabilities; Autism.
IQ Range of Clients 80+.
Tuition and Fees
Room and Board Long term: $75.46/diem; $72.03/diem (group home).
Tuition $54.97/diem.
Placements Primarily Funded By State depts of education; Local depts of education; Social service depts.
Social and Rehabilitative Services
Therapeutic Approach The philosophy of the treatment program is reality based and goal oriented.
Therapeutic Services Offered Individual therapy; Group therapy; Family therapy; Aftercare program with follow up.
Professionals on Staff Psychiatrists; Psychologists; Social workers; Child care staff; Nurses.
Educational and Vocational Services
Type(s) of Educational Programs Offered On campus.
Profile of On Campus School Program Number of teachers 53; *Number of classrooms* 15; *Special curriculum electives offered.*

WARKICK

PIUS XII YOUTH AND FAMILY SERVICES
338 Bellvale Lakes Rd, Warkick, NY 10918 (914) 469-9121 *Contact Person(s):* Don Schmidt
Setting and Background Information Pius XII Youth and Family Services is a private non-profit agency, which was established in 1959 by the Brothers of the Holy Cross. There are two separate campuses; one is located in Chester on 100 acres of land and serves adolescent boys who could not be cared for in other institutions. There are 6 residential cottages each with a capacity for 17. The other campus is in Rhinecliff and was originally established as a drug treatment center, but expanded to meet other needs. The 100-acre campus has 2 dorms, a school, tennis and basketball courts and a lake. The agency also operates five group homes—four are for boys (12 in each) and one is for girls.
Referral Information Referrals to the facility are made from the family court, Div for Youth, Dept of Social Services. For referral information, write, telephone or visit the facility.

PIUS XII YOUTH AND FAMILY SERVICES
(continued)

Type of Facility
Funding Sources Private; State.
Average Length of Stay Long term.
Types of Admissions Accepted Residential treatment; Group home placement.
Sources of Referral State depts of education; Local depts of education; Social service depts; Div for Youth; Family courts.
Client Profile
Age Range of Clients Served Residential program: 12-18.
Characteristics Exhibited by Children Emotional handicaps; Learning disabilities.
IQ Range of Clients 70+.
Tuition and Fees
Room and Board Long term: $76/diem.
Tuition $76/diem.
Placements Primarily Funded By Social service depts; County of origin.
Social and Rehabilitative Services
Therapeutic Approach The primary therapeutic approach used is behavior modification.
Therapeutic Services Offered Individual therapy; Group therapy; Family therapy; Independent living skills program; Recreation activities; Substance abuse treatment; Aftercare program with follow up.
Professionals on Staff Psychiatrists; Psychologists; Social workers; Child care staff; Nurses.
Educational and Vocational Services
Type(s) of Educational Programs Offered On campus; Off campus.
Profile of On Campus School Program Number of teachers 20; *Grades taught* 7-12; Special curriculum electives offered; Remedial courses offered.
Degrees Offered 8th grade diploma; 12th grade diploma; GED.

WHITE PLAINS

DAVIS AVE YOUTH RESIDENCE
56 Davis Ave, White Plains, NY 10605 (914) 948-8004, 686-0324 *Contact Person(s):* William A Baker, Dir
Setting and Background Information The facility was established in 1971 with foundation and government grants. There are two community residences, one is at the above address. The other residence is called Oakwood Ave Youth Residence, 14 Oakwood Ave. The phone number of this residence is (914) 949-0815.
Referral Information For referral, contact the facility and forward psychological, psychiatric, and social summaries to the program director.
Type of Facility
Funding Sources Private; State.
Average Length of Stay Long term.
Types of Admissions Accepted Group home placement.
Sources of Referral State depts of mental health; Social service depts.
Client Profile
Age Range of Clients Served Residential program: 15-18.
Characteristics Exhibited by Children Emotional handicaps.
Tuition and Fees
Room and Board Long term: $66/diem.
Placements Primarily Funded By Social service depts.
Social and Rehabilitative Services
Therapeutic Approach The facilities use supportive psychotherapy in a milieu setting.
Therapeutic Services Offered Individual therapy; Group therapy; Family therapy; Independent living skills program; Recreation activities.
Professionals on Staff Psychiatrists; Social workers; Child care staff.
Educational and Vocational Services
Type(s) of Educational Programs Offered Off campus (Public schools).

WILLIAMSVILLE

GATEWAY UNITED METHODIST YOUTH CENTER
6350 Main St, Williamsville, NY 14221 (716) 633-7266 *Contact Person(s):* Jan McGhee, Admin Asst
Setting and Background Information The facility was established in 1890 by the Buffalo Episcopal Deaconnesses as an orphanage. The 65-acre campus has 4 cottages and a school/administration building.
Referral Information Referrals are accepted from local DSS, family courts, and committees on special education. A pre-admission interview will be scheduled.
Type of Facility
Funding Sources Private; State; Federal; County.
Average Length of Stay Long term.
Types of Admissions Accepted Day treatment; Residential treatment; Foster homes.
Sources of Referral Local depts of education; Depts of correction; Social service depts.
Client Profile
Age Range of Clients Served Day programs: 8-16; Residential program: 8-16.
Characteristics Exhibited by Children Emotional handicaps; Learning disabilities.
IQ Range of Clients 75+.
Tuition and Fees
Room and Board Long term: $79.12/diem.
Tuition $47.05/diem.
Placements Primarily Funded By State depts of education; Local depts of education; Social service depts.
Social and Rehabilitative Services
Therapeutic Approach The facility has a behavioral approach in a therapeutic milieu.
Therapeutic Services Offered Individual therapy; Group therapy; Family therapy; Art therapy; Recreation activities; Substance abuse treatment; Aftercare program with follow up.
Professionals on Staff Psychiatrists; Psychologists; Social workers; Child care staff; Nurses; Art therapists.
Educational and Vocational Services
Type(s) of Educational Programs Offered On campus (Spec Ed); Off campus (Public schools); Summer campus.
Profile of On Campus School Program Number of teachers 9; *Number of classrooms* 11; *Student to teacher ratio* 8:1; *Credentials of teachers* Spec Ed; *Length of school day* 9-3:15; *Grades taught* K-12; Special curriculum electives offered (Remedial reading, Computer assisted Ed, PE); Remedial courses offered.

WYNANTSKILL

VANDERHEYDEN HALL
Box 219, Wynantskill, NY 12198 (518) 283-6500 *Contact Person(s):* Leonard Yaffe, Exec Dir
Setting and Background Information The facility was initially established as Troy Orphanage in 1833, but has since evolved into a treatment center for court referred adolescents. The campus is located in a rural area and consists of 6 residential cottages, a diagnostic unit, school, gym, and outdoor facilities.
Referral Information To make a referral, contact the facility and forward the necessary reports, educational records, medical and family histories.
Type of Facility
Funding Sources State.
Average Length of Stay Long term.
Types of Admissions Accepted Day treatment; Residential treatment; Group home placement.
Sources of Referral State depts of education; Local depts of education; State depts of mental health; Social service depts; Dept for Youth.
Client Profile
Age Range of Clients Served Day programs: 12-16; Residential program: 12-16.
Characteristics Exhibited by Children Emotional handicaps; Learning disabilities; Speech/Language disorders; Neurological impairments; Mental disabilities.
IQ Range of Clients 70+.

VANDERHEYDEN HALL (continued)

Social and Rehabilitative Services
Therapeutic Services Offered Individual therapy; Group therapy; Family therapy; Adjunctive therapy; Physical therapy; Independent living skills program; Recreation activities; Aftercare program with follow up.
Professionals on Staff Psychiatrists; Psychologists; Social workers; Adjunctive therapists; Child care staff; Nurses.
Educational and Vocational Services
Type(s) of Educational Programs Offered On campus; Off campus; Summer campus.
Profile of On Campus School Program Number of teachers 13; *Number of classrooms* 13; *Student to teacher ratio* 10:1.
Degrees Offered 8th grade diploma; 12th grade diploma.

YONKERS

ANDRUS CHILDREN'S HOME
1156 N Broadway, Yonkers, NY 10701 (914) 965-3700 *Contact Person(s):* Barbara Z Smith, MA, Adm Dir
Setting and Background Information The facility was established as a children's home for the needy by John E Andrus in 1928. By the 1980s it expanded its programs and services to become a treatment center for emotionally handicapped children. The campus is located north of Yonkers and consists of 4 residential cottages, a school, administrative building, swimming pool and infirmary.
Referral Information Referrals can be made by parents, teachers, physicians, mental health professionals, ministers, and private or public agencies. To make a referral, forward the necessary background information, including psychiatric reports, psychological evaluations, psychosocial history, and school records to the Director of Admissions. A pre-placement interview will take place before an admission decision is made.
Type of Facility
Funding Sources Private.
Average Length of Stay Long term.
Types of Admissions Accepted Residential treatment; Group home placement.
Sources of Referral State depts of education; Local depts of education; Psychiatrists; Private sources; Social service depts.
Client Profile
Age Range of Clients Served Residential program: 7-15.
Characteristics Exhibited by Children Emotional handicaps; Learning disabilities; Neurological impairments.
IQ Range of Clients 85+.
Tuition and Fees
Placements Primarily Funded By Private sources.
Social and Rehabilitative Services
Therapeutic Approach The treatment program utilizes a family systems approach.
Therapeutic Services Offered Individual therapy; Group therapy; Family therapy; Recreation activities; Aftercare program with follow up.
Professionals on Staff Psychiatrists; Social workers; Child care staff; Nurses.
Educational and Vocational Services
Type(s) of Educational Programs Offered On campus; Off campus.
Profile of On Campus School Program Number of teachers 9; *Number of classrooms* 8; *Student to teacher ratio* 8:1.
Degrees Offered 8th grade diploma.

LEAKE & WATTS SCHOOL
463 Hawthorne Ave, Yonkers, NY 10705 (914) 963-5220 *Contact Person(s):* Selma K Levy, Ed Dir
Setting and Background Information The school was originally established in 1831 as a home for orphans. Currently, the 27-acre campus has an administration building, cottages, an infirmary, a school and a gym.
Referral Information Referrals for residential treatment are made by the Dept of Social Services. Referrals for day placement are made by local boards of education.
Type of Facility
Funding Sources State; New York City Dept of Special Services for Children.
Average Length of Stay Long term.
Types of Admissions Accepted Residential treatment.

Sources of Referral Social service depts.
Client Profile
Age Range of Clients Served Day programs: 6-18; Residential program: 12-18.
Characteristics Exhibited by Children Emotional handicaps; Learning disabilities.
IQ Range of Clients 75-125.
Tuition and Fees
Room and Board Long term: determined by Dept of Social Services.
Tuition Determined by State Education Dept.
Placements Primarily Funded By Social service depts.
Social and Rehabilitative Services
Therapeutic Approach The facility offers group and individual therapy in a milieu setting.
Therapeutic Services Offered Individual therapy; Group therapy; Family therapy; Art therapy; Independent living skills program; Recreation activities; Aftercare program with follow up.
Professionals on Staff Psychiatrists; Psychologists; Social workers; Child care staff; Nurses; Art therapists.
Educational and Vocational Services
Type(s) of Educational Programs Offered On campus (Work/study and vocational training).
Profile of On Campus School Program Number of teachers 15; *Number of classrooms* 10; *Student to teacher ratio* 12:1; *Credentials of teachers* Spec Ed; *Grades taught* Ungraded; Remedial courses offered.
Degrees Offered GED.

NORTH CAROLINA

ALBERMARLE

UWHARRIE HOMES, INC

PO Box 1026, Albermarle, NC 28002 (704) 983-1808 *Contact Person(s):* Keith Wolf, Exec Dir

Setting and Background Information The facility was established in 1976. It is a residential treatment center for boys.

Referral Information Contact the facility and forward the social history, psychological evaluation and school records to the executive director. A pre-admission visit is required.

Type of Facility

Funding Sources Private; State; United Way.

Average Length of Stay Long term; 6-12 mos.

Types of Admissions Accepted Residential treatment.

Sources of Referral Psychiatrists; Social service depts; Mental health therapists; Court counselors.

Client Profile

Age Range of Clients Served Residential program: 12-18.

Characteristics Exhibited by Children Emotional handicaps.

IQ Range of Clients 70-120.

Tuition and Fees

Room and Board Long term: Sliding scale.

Placements Primarily Funded By Private sources; Social service depts; Willie M.

Social and Rehabilitative Services

Therapeutic Approach The basic approach of the facility is reality therapy.

Therapeutic Services Offered Individual therapy; Group therapy.

Professionals on Staff Psychiatrists; Psychologists; Child care staff.

Educational and Vocational Services

Type(s) of Educational Programs Offered Off campus.

ASHEBORO

RANDOLPH COUNTY MENTAL HEALTH CENTER, NORTH HOUSE RESIDENTIAL GROUP HOME

1718 N Asheboro Jr High School Rd, Asheboro, NC 27203.

Contact Person(s): Kara Davis Beust, North House Dir

Setting and Background Information This facility is a residential group home established with funds from Willie M.

Referral Information Referrals are made through the Randolph County Mental Health Willie M Coordinator.

Type of Facility

Funding Sources State; Willie M.

Average Length of Stay Long term.

Types of Admissions Accepted Group home placement; Willie M.

Sources of Referral State depts of mental health; Social service depts; Willie M.

Client Profile

Age Range of Clients Served Residential program: 12-18.

Characteristics Exhibited by Children Emotional handicaps; Mental disabilities.

IQ Range of Clients 70+.

Tuition and Fees

Room and Board Long term: $3/diem.

Placements Primarily Funded By Private sources.

Social and Rehabilitative Services

Therapeutic Approach The basic therapeutic approach is behavior modification.

Therapeutic Services Offered Individual therapy; Group therapy; Aftercare program with follow up.

Professionals on Staff Psychiatrists; Psychologists; Social workers; Child care staff; Art therapists.

Educational and Vocational Services

Type(s) of Educational Programs Offered Off campus.

Profile of On Campus School Program Number of teachers 5 and 3 aides; *Number of classrooms* 5; *Student to teacher ratio* 5:1; *Credentials of teachers* MEd.

ASHEVILLE

HIGHLAND HOSPITAL

PO Box 1101, 49 Zillicoa St, Asheville, NC 28802 (704) 254-3201

Contact Person(s): Joyce Bracewell ACSW, Dir of Admis

Setting and Background Information This psychiatric hospital was established in 1904. There are 25 buildings on the 80-acre grounds, including residential treatment units, an activities building, a school, a greenhouse, a halfway house, an out-patient clinic, and a day treatment facility.

Referral Information Contact the Director of Admissions for referral information.

Type of Facility

Funding Sources Private; Federal.

Average Length of Stay Long term.

Types of Admissions Accepted Day treatment; Residential treatment; Group home placement; In-patient.

Sources of Referral Local depts of education; Psychiatrists; Private sources.

Client Profile

Age Range of Clients Served Day programs: 15-55+; Residential program: 12-55+.

Characteristics Exhibited by Children Emotional handicaps; Learning disabilities; Mental disabilities.

Tuition and Fees

Room and Board Long term: $660-1,000/mo.

Tuition $700/mo.

Placements Primarily Funded By Insurance; Private sources.

Social and Rehabilitative Services

Therapeutic Approach The facility has a psychodynamic approach to therapy and offers a therapeutic community.

Therapeutic Services Offered Individual therapy; Group therapy; Family therapy; Adjunctive therapy; Art therapy; Physical therapy; Independent living skills program; Recreation activities; Substance abuse treatment; Aftercare program with follow up.

Professionals on Staff Psychiatrists; Psychologists; Social workers; Adjunctive therapists; Nurses; Art therapists; Physical therapists.

Educational and Vocational Services

Type(s) of Educational Programs Offered On campus.

Profile of On Campus School Program Number of teachers 7; *Number of classrooms* 14; *Student to teacher ratio* 6:1; *Credentials of teachers* Certified Spec Ed; *Grades taught* 7-12; Special curriculum electives offered; Remedial courses offered.

Vocational Education Programs/Degrees Offered Pre-vocational training and placement.

Degrees Offered 12th grade diploma; GED.

BESSEMER CITY

HOPE RUN GROUP HOME

Rt 1 Box 161, Bess Town Rd, Bessemer City, NC 28016
(704) 922-4872 *Contact Person(s):* Kelly B Ottinger, Dir
Setting and Background Information In 1983, the Gaston County
Mental Health Agency received funding to establish a residential
facility. A contract was offered to Lutheran Family Services, who
operate the facility.
Referral Information Referrals are made through Gaston County
mental health. A treatment team will assess the case for
placement. The child must be certified E.H.
Type of Facility
Funding Sources Private; State; County.
Average Length of Stay Long term.
Types of Admissions Accepted Group home placement.
Sources of Referral County.
Client Profile
Age Range of Clients Served Residential program: Birth-18 (average
age 12-15).
Characteristics Exhibited by Children Emotional handicaps.
IQ Range of Clients 65+.
Tuition and Fees
Placements Primarily Funded By State depts of mental health; Coun-
ty.
Social and Rehabilitative Services
Therapeutic Approach The basic therapeutic approach is reality ther-
apy.
Therapeutic Services Offered Individual therapy; Group therapy;
Family therapy; Recreation activities.
Professionals on Staff Psychologists; Child care staff.

BURLINGTON

LUTHERAN FAMILY SERVICES, LIGHTHOUSE

PO Box 1307, 604 S Broad St, Burlington, NC 27215
(919) 227-8146 *Contact Person(s):* Dwayne Harden, Prog Dir
Setting and Background Information This facility was established in
1982. It is a private, non-profit program operated by Lutheran
Family Services. It contracts with Alamance/Caswell County
Mental Health and provides long-term residential treatment
services to five youths who are certified Willie M Class Members.
Referral Information All referrals come from Alamance/Caswell
Mental Health Children-Services.
Type of Facility
Funding Sources State.
Average Length of Stay Long term.
Types of Admissions Accepted Group home placement.
Sources of Referral State depts of mental health.
Client Profile
Age Range of Clients Served Residential program: 6-18.
Characteristics Exhibited by Children Emotional handicaps; Learning
disabilities.
IQ Range of Clients 80+.
Tuition and Fees
Placements Primarily Funded By State depts of mental health; Willie
M.
Social and Rehabilitative Services
Therapeutic Approach The facility offers individual and group coun-
seling, personal and social skills development, and behavior man-
agement in a structured program.
Therapeutic Services Offered Individual therapy; Group therapy; Art
therapy; Independent living skills program; Recreation activities.
Professionals on Staff Psychiatrists; Psychologists; Adjunctive thera-
pists; Child care staff.

BUTNER

C A DILLON SCHOOL

Old Hwy 75, Butner, NC 27509 (919) 575-7926 *Contact Person(s):*
Malcolm Mangum, Admin Officer
Setting and Background Information The State of NC established the
facility in 1968. The facility has 5 buildings located on 82 acres.
Referral Information Referrals are made through the courts.

Type of Facility
Funding Sources State.
Average Length of Stay Long term.
Types of Admissions Accepted Residential treatment.
Sources of Referral Depts of correction; Courts.
Client Profile
Age Range of Clients Served Residential program: 12-18.
Tuition and Fees
Placements Primarily Funded By Local depts of education; State
depts of mental health; Depts of corrections.
Social and Rehabilitative Services
Therapeutic Approach The therapeutic approach is reality therapy,
combined with behavior modification.
Professionals on Staff Psychiatrists; Psychologists; Social workers;
Child care staff; Nurses; Art therapists; Counselor.
Educational and Vocational Services
Type(s) of Educational Programs Offered On campus; Off campus.
Profile of On Campus School Program Number of teachers 21;
Number of classrooms 25; *Student to teacher ratio* 10:1; *Creden-
tials of teachers* Certified; *Length of school day* 6 hrs; *Grades
taught* 6-12.
Degrees Offered GED.

THE WHITAKER SCHOOL

K St, Butner, NC 27509 (919) 575-7360 *Contact Person(s):* Liz
Eierman, Asst Dir
Setting and Background Information The facility was established in
1980 by state law for Willie M clients as a re-educational facility
for adolescents. The 6-wing hospital facility consists of: 3
dormitories, a recreation room, an administration wing, and a
school wing.
Referral Information Clients are referred to the facility through the
Regional Placement Committees.
Type of Facility
Funding Sources State; Federal.
Average Length of Stay Long term.
Types of Admissions Accepted Residential treatment; Willie M.
Sources of Referral Regional placement committees.
Client Profile
Age Range of Clients Served Residential program: 12-18.
Characteristics Exhibited by Children Emotional handicaps; Learning
disabilities.
IQ Range of Clients 47-144.
Tuition and Fees
Placements Primarily Funded By State depts of mental health; Social
service depts.
Social and Rehabilitative Services
Therapeutic Services Offered Individual therapy; Group therapy;
Family therapy; Adjunctive therapy; Independent living skills
program; Recreation activities; Aftercare program with follow up.
Professionals on Staff Psychiatrists; Psychologists; Child care staff;
Nurses.
Educational and Vocational Services
Type(s) of Educational Programs Offered On campus.
Profile of On Campus School Program Number of teachers 10;
Number of classrooms 3; *Student to teacher ratio* 3:1; *Credentials
of teachers* M SpecEd; *Grades taught* All grades.
Degrees Offered GED.

CHAPEL HILL

CARAMORE COMMUNITY

PO Box 2123, Chapel Hill, NC 27515 (919) 967-3402 *Contact
Person(s):* Russell Thomas, Clin Dir
Setting and Background Information The facility was established in
1978 by a group of parents who had chronically mentally ill
children. Located on 6 acres, there are 2 office buildings, 2
greenhouses and a retail garden store.
Referral Information Contact the facility for referral information.
Type of Facility
Funding Sources Private; State.
Average Length of Stay Long term.
Types of Admissions Accepted Day treatment; Residential treatment;
Group home placement.
Sources of Referral State depts of education; Local depts of educa-
tion; State depts of mental health; Psychiatrists; Private sources;
Social service depts; Hospitals.

CARAMORE COMMUNITY *(continued)*

Client Profile

Age Range of Clients Served Day programs: 15-21+; Residential program: 15-21+.

Characteristics Exhibited by Children Emotional handicaps; Mental disabilities.

IQ Range of Clients 70-125.

Tuition and Fees

Room and Board Long term: $58/week.

Tuition $1,300/mo.

Placements Primarily Funded By State depts of mental health; Private sources; Vocational Rehab.

Social and Rehabilitative Services

Therapeutic Approach The facility uses a psychosocial model as a therapeutic intervention.

Therapeutic Services Offered Individual therapy; Group therapy; Family therapy; Independent living skills program; Recreation activities.

Professionals on Staff Psychologists; Social workers; Vocational.

Educational and Vocational Services

Type(s) of Educational Programs Offered On campus (Vocational training).

CHARLOTTE

ALEXANDER CHILDREN'S CENTER 36

PO Box 220632, Charlotte, NC 28222 (704) 366-8712 *Contact Person(s):* Glenn B Robinson, Exec Dir

Setting and Background Information The facility was originally established in 1888. The 60-acre campus has 6 cottages, 3 houses, a school, a gym, a cafeteria, a pool, and clinical and administrative buildings.

Referral Information Contact the facility to arrange a visit and forward background information, including a physical examination, and educational and psychological reports.

Type of Facility

Funding Sources Private.

Average Length of Stay 20 mos.

Types of Admissions Accepted Day treatment; Residential treatment.

Sources of Referral State depts of education; Local depts of education; State depts of mental health; Psychiatrists; Private sources; Social service depts.

Client Profile

Age Range of Clients Served Day programs: Birth-12; Residential program: 6-12.

Characteristics Exhibited by Children Emotional handicaps; Learning disabilities; Neurological impairments.

IQ Range of Clients 70-140.

Tuition and Fees

Placements Primarily Funded By State depts of education; Local depts of education; State depts of mental health; Insurance; Private sources; Social service depts.

Social and Rehabilitative Services

Therapeutic Approach The facility employs therapeutic processes in all areas of the program.

Therapeutic Services Offered Individual therapy; Group therapy; Family therapy; Adjunctive therapy; Art therapy; Recreation activities; Aftercare program with follow up.

Professionals on Staff Psychiatrists; Psychologists; Social workers; Child care staff; Nurses; Art therapists.

Educational and Vocational Services

Type(s) of Educational Programs Offered On campus (Non-graded).

Profile of On Campus School Program Number of teachers 4; *Number of classrooms* 4; *Student to teacher ratio* 8:1; *Credentials of teachers* MA.

BRIDLEWOOD GROUP HOME, INTENSIVE RESIDENTIAL PROGRAM

9100 Moss Cove Ct, Charlotte, NC 28212 (704) 364-2020, 535-2646 *Contact Person(s):* Bet Levine, Supv

Setting and Background Information The facility was established in 1986 with 'Willie M' funds to treat clients in an intensive setting. It is a residential group home.

Referral Information Contact the Placement Committee for referral information.

Type of Facility

Funding Sources State.

Average Length of Stay Short and long term.

Types of Admissions Accepted Residential treatment; Group home placement.

Sources of Referral State depts of education; Local depts of education; State depts of mental health; Psychiatrists; Private sources; Social service depts.

Client Profile

Age Range of Clients Served Residential program: 12-18.

Characteristics Exhibited by Children Emotional handicaps; Learning disabilities; Speech/Language disorders; Neurological impairments; Mental disabilities.

IQ Range of Clients 50-100.

Tuition and Fees

Placements Primarily Funded By State depts of mental health.

Social and Rehabilitative Services

Therapeutic Approach The facility uses reality therapy and behavior modification.

Therapeutic Services Offered Individual therapy; Group therapy; Family therapy; Adjunctive therapy; Art therapy; Recreation activities; Substance abuse treatment.

Professionals on Staff Psychiatrists; Psychologists; Social workers; Adjunctive therapists.

Educational and Vocational Services

Type(s) of Educational Programs Offered Off campus (Public school).

TOM RAY YOUTH RESIDENTIAL TREATMENT CENTER

3430 Wheatley Ave, Charlotte, NC 28211 (704) 336-4232 *Contact Person(s):* Peter Bishop MD, Dir

Setting and Background Information This center was established in 1983 with state funding for Willie M certified youth. Located on an acre, it has a secure residential building.

Referral Information For referral information, contact the social worker. The facility accepts only youth from Mecklenbury County who are Willie M certified.

Type of Facility

Funding Sources State; Federal; County.

Average Length of Stay Short and long term.

Types of Admissions Accepted Day treatment; Residential treatment.

Sources of Referral Local depts of education; Psychiatrists; Depts of correction; Social service depts; Agencies; Private practician.

Client Profile

Age Range of Clients Served Day programs: 12-18; Residential program 12-18.

Characteristics Exhibited by Children Emotional handicaps; Learning disabilities; Hearing impairments/deafness; Neurological impairments.

IQ Range of Clients 40-140.

Tuition and Fees

Room and Board Short term: $190/diem; Long term: $190/diem.

Placements Primarily Funded By State depts of mental health; County.

Social and Rehabilitative Services

Therapeutic Approach The basic therapeutic approach is applied behavior analysis.

Therapeutic Services Offered Individual therapy; Group therapy; Family therapy; Adjunctive therapy; Recreation activities; Substance abuse treatment.

Professionals on Staff Psychiatrists; Psychologists; Social workers; Adjunctive therapists; Child care staff; Nurses; Behavior modification technicians.

Educational and Vocational Services

Type(s) of Educational Programs Offered On campus (Full school program).

Profile of On Campus School Program Number of teachers 3; *Number of classrooms* 3; *Student to teacher ratio* 8:1; *Credentials of teachers* MA; *Grades taught* Individualized instruction.

Degrees Offered Degrees are offered through the Charlotte Mecklenbury school system.

SPECIALIZED YOUTH SERVICES

4401 Colwick Rd, Ste 706, Charlotte, NC 28211 (704) 364-2020 *Contact Person(s):* John Webb, Dir

Setting and Background Information The agency was established in 1983 by state mandate. There are ten programs throughout the county.

SPECIALIZED YOUTH SERVICES *(continued)*

Referral Information Contact the facility for referral information.
Type of Facility
Funding Sources State.
Average Length of Stay Short and long term.
Types of Admissions Accepted Day treatment; Residential treatment; Group home placement.
Sources of Referral State depts of education; Local depts of education; State depts of mental health; Psychiatrists; Social service depts; Courts; Guardians.
Client Profile
Age Range of Clients Served Day programs: 12-18; Residential program: 12-18.
Characteristics Exhibited by Children Emotional handicaps; Learning disabilities; Hearing impairments/deafness; Speech/Language disorders; Neurological impairments; Physical handicaps; Mental disabilities.
IQ Range of Clients 60-130.
Tuition and Fees
Placements Primarily Funded By State depts of mental health; Social service depts.
Social and Rehabilitative Services
Therapeutic Approach The facility uses behavior management.
Therapeutic Services Offered Individual therapy; Group therapy; Family therapy; Independent living skills program; Recreation activities; Substance abuse treatment; Sex offenders and arson program.
Professionals on Staff Psychiatrists; Psychologists; Social workers; Child care staff; Nurses.
Educational and Vocational Services
Type(s) of Educational Programs Offered On campus; Off campus.
Profile of On Campus School Program Number of teachers 4; *Number of classrooms* 3; *Student to teacher ratio* 5:1; Remedial courses offered.
Degrees Offered 8th grade diploma; 12th grade diploma; GED.

THOMPSON CHILDREN'S HOME
PO Box 25129, Charlotte, NC 28229 (704) 536-0375 *Contact Person(s):* Intake Soc Wkr
Setting and Background Information The home was established in 1886 by the Episcopal Church. The 40-acre campus has an administration building, a school, 4 cottages, a chapel, a gym, and a pool.
Referral Information Contact the facility for referral information.
Type of Facility
Funding Sources Private.
Average Length of Stay Long term.
Types of Admissions Accepted Residential treatment.
Sources of Referral State depts of education; Local depts of education; Psychiatrists; Private sources; Social service depts.
Client Profile
Age Range of Clients Served Residential program: 6-12.
Characteristics Exhibited by Children Emotional handicaps; Learning disabilities.
Tuition and Fees
Placements Primarily Funded By State depts of mental health; Private sources; Social service depts.
Social and Rehabilitative Services
Therapeutic Services Offered Individual therapy; Group therapy; Family therapy; Aftercare program with follow up.
Professionals on Staff Psychiatrists; Social workers; Child care staff; Nurses.
Educational and Vocational Services
Type(s) of Educational Programs Offered On campus (Spec Ed).
Profile of On Campus School Program Number of teachers 3 and 3 aides; *Student to teacher ratio* 4:1; *Credentials of teachers* Certified; Special curriculum electives offered.

CHERRYVILLE

MT RIDGE GROUP HOME
Rt #1 Box 271, Cherryville, NC 28021 (704) 435-2439 *Contact Person(s):* Susan R Taylor, Dir
Setting and Background Information The facility was established in 1983 through Gaston Mental Health and Western Carolina Center. The 300-acre farm has one residence and a barn.

Referral Information Referrals to the facility are made through the Gaston Mental Health Dept.
Type of Facility
Funding Sources State.
Average Length of Stay Long term.
Types of Admissions Accepted Group home placement.
Sources of Referral State depts of mental health.
Client Profile
Age Range of Clients Served Residential program: 12-18.
Characteristics Exhibited by Children Emotional handicaps; Learning disabilities; Speech/Language disorders; Neurological impairments; Mental disabilities; Autism.
Tuition and Fees
Placements Primarily Funded By County mental health.
Social and Rehabilitative Services
Therapeutic Approach The facility uses behavior modification.
Therapeutic Services Offered Independent living skills program.
Professionals on Staff Psychiatrists; Psychologists; Child care staff.
Educational and Vocational Services
Type(s) of Educational Programs Offered Off campus (Autistic classroom; Adult day care/workshop).

CONCORD

STONEWALL JACKSON SCHOOL
1484 Old Charlotte Rd, Concord, NC 28025 (704) 786-5304 *Contact Person(s):* Paul E Kennedy, Center Dir
Setting and Background Information The facility was established in 1909. The 750-acre campus has dormitories, a cafeteria, a school and support buildings.
Referral Information Contact the facility for referral information.
Type of Facility
Funding Sources State.
Average Length of Stay Long term.
Types of Admissions Accepted Residential treatment.
Sources of Referral Juvenile judges.
Client Profile
Age Range of Clients Served Residential program: 11-17.
Characteristics Exhibited by Children Emotional handicaps; Learning disabilities; Delinquency.
Tuition and Fees
Placements Primarily Funded By Dept of Human Resources.
Social and Rehabilitative Services
Therapeutic Approach The basic approach of the facility is reality therapy.
Therapeutic Services Offered Individual therapy; Group therapy; Physical therapy; Independent living skills program; Substance abuse treatment.
Professionals on Staff Psychiatrists; Psychologists; Social workers; Child care staff; Nurses.
Educational and Vocational Services
Type(s) of Educational Programs Offered On campus.
Profile of On Campus School Program Number of teachers 19; *Number of classrooms* 20; *Student to teacher ratio* 8:1; *Credentials of teachers* Certified; *Grades taught* Non-graded; Remedial courses offered.
Vocational Education Programs/Degrees Offered Woodwork; Auto mechanics; Home economics; Business education.

DURHAM

GREENHOUSE
601 N Driver St, Durham, NC 27703 (919) 688-5350, 682-9248
Contact Person(s): Vivian Roberti, Clin Dir
Setting and Background Information The facility was established in 1975 as a private, non-profit facility to serve emotionally disturbed adolescents. It is a contract agency with Durham County Mental Health and is located in residential areas.
Referral Information The facility gives placement priority to residents of the North Central Region of NC. Referring materials should include social and family history, a psychological evaluation and school records. A DSM-III diagnosis and a specific recommendation for group care, signed by a licensed psychologist or psychiatrist, must be included.
Type of Facility
Funding Sources Private.
Average Length of Stay Long term.
Types of Admissions Accepted Group home placement.

GREENHOUSE *(continued)*

Sources of Referral State depts of education; Local depts of education; State depts of mental health; Psychiatrists; Private sources; Depts of correction; Social service depts; Psychologists; Social workers.

Client Profile

Age Range of Clients Served Residential program: 6-18.

Characteristics Exhibited by Children Emotional handicaps; Neurological impairments; Mental disabilities.

Tuition and Fees

Room and Board Short term: Sliding scale; Long term: Sliding scale.

Placements Primarily Funded By Title XX; Willie M.

Social and Rehabilitative Services

Therapeutic Approach The facility offers individual, group, and family therapy in a milieu setting.

Therapeutic Services Offered Individual therapy; Group therapy; Family therapy; Aftercare program with follow up.

Professionals on Staff Psychologists; Social workers; Child care staff.

Educational and Vocational Services

Type(s) of Educational Programs Offered Off campus (Public schools, Day treatment programs).

WRIGHT SCHOOL

3132 Roxboro Rd, Durham, NC 27704 (919) 471-1536

Setting and Background Information The facilty was established in 1963 as part of the North Carolina Division of Mental Health, Dept of Human Resources. The campus consists of ranch-style buildings located on 30 acres of land in a suburban community.

Referral Information Referrals can be made through local mental health facilities.

Type of Facility

Funding Sources State; Federal.

Average Length of Stay Long term.

Types of Admissions Accepted Day treatment; Residential treatment; Wards of the state.

Sources of Referral State depts of mental health.

Client Profile

Age Range of Clients Served Day programs: 6-12; Residential program: 6-12.

Characteristics Exhibited by Children Emotional handicaps; Learning disabilities.

Tuition and Fees

Placements Primarily Funded By State depts of mental health.

Social and Rehabilitative Services

Therapeutic Services Offered Individual therapy; Group therapy; Family therapy; Independent living skills program; Recreation activities; Aftercare program with follow up.

Professionals on Staff Social workers; Child care staff.

Educational and Vocational Services

Type(s) of Educational Programs Offered On campus; Summer campus.

Profile of On Campus School Program Number of teachers 12; *Number of classrooms* 3; *Student to teacher ratio* 2:1; *Grades taught* 1-8; Special curriculum electives offered; Remedial courses offered.

FAYETTEVILLE

HSA CUMBERLAND HOSPITAL

3425 Melrose Rd, Fayetteville, NC 28304 (919) 485-7181, 1-800-682-6003 *Contact Person(s):* Al Howard, Asst Admin

Setting and Background Information The facility was established in 1983 on 3 acres of land and has 2 buildings.

Referral Information Contact the referral coordinator at the facility.

Type of Facility

Funding Sources Private.

Average Length of Stay Short term.

Types of Admissions Accepted In-patient.

Sources of Referral State depts of education; Local depts of education; State depts of mental health; Psychiatrists; Private sources; Depts of correction; Social service depts.

Client Profile

Age Range of Clients Served Residential program: Birth-55+.

Characteristics Exhibited by Children Emotional handicaps; Learning disabilities; Hearing impairments/deafness; Vision impairments/ blindness; Speech/Language disorders; Neurological impairments; Physical handicaps; Mental disabilities.

IQ Range of Clients 70+.

Tuition and Fees

Room and Board Short term: $328/diem.

Placements Primarily Funded By Insurance.

Social and Rehabilitative Services

Therapeutic Approach The basic therapeutic approach of the hospital is eclectic, including intense psychotherapy.

Therapeutic Services Offered Individual therapy; Group therapy; Family therapy; Adjunctive therapy; Art therapy; Physical therapy; Independent living skills program; Recreation activities; Substance abuse treatment; Aftercare program with follow up.

Professionals on Staff Psychiatrists; Psychologists; Social workers; Adjunctive therapists; Child care staff; Nurses; Art therapists; Physical therapists.

Educational and Vocational Services

Type(s) of Educational Programs Offered On campus (Certified school); Off campus (Public school).

Profile of On Campus School Program Number of teachers 5; *Number of classrooms* 6; *Student to teacher ratio* 6:1; *Credentials of teachers* MA; *Grades taught* K-12; Special curriculum electives offered; Remedial courses offered.

Vocational Education Programs/Degrees Offered Determined by population.

Degrees Offered 12th grade diploma.

GOLDSBORO

CHERRY HOSPITAL, CHILDREN AND YOUTH UNIT

Caller Box 8000, Goldsboro, NC 27530 (919) 731-3317 *Contact Person(s):* Dr C Gicana

Setting and Background Information The facility was established in 1965 to provide treatment for emotionally disturbed children who were housed together with an adult population. It is located on the grounds of Cherry Hospital.

Referral Information Referrals are made through local mental health centers.

Type of Facility

Funding Sources Private; State; Federal.

Average Length of Stay Short and long term.

Types of Admissions Accepted Residential treatment.

Sources of Referral State depts of mental health; Psychiatrists; Depts of correction; Social service depts.

Client Profile

Age Range of Clients Served Residential program: 6-18.

Characteristics Exhibited by Children Emotional handicaps; Neurological impairments; Mental disabilities.

Tuition and Fees

Room and Board Short term: Sliding scale; Long term: Sliding scale.

Placements Primarily Funded By State depts of mental health.

Social and Rehabilitative Services

Therapeutic Services Offered Individual therapy; Group therapy; Family therapy; Recreation activities; Psychopharmacotherapy.

Professionals on Staff Psychiatrists; Psychologists; Social workers; Nurses.

Educational and Vocational Services

Type(s) of Educational Programs Offered On campus; Off campus (Vocational education program).

Profile of On Campus School Program Number of teachers 13; *Number of classrooms* 8; *Student to teacher ratio* 4:1; *Grades taught* K-12; Special curriculum electives offered (Life skills, Arts and crafts); Remedial courses offered.

GREENSBORO

GUILDORD RESIDENTIAL TREATMENT

6015 High Point Rd, Greensboro, NC 27407 (919) 454-5446

Contact Person(s): Michael Wright

Setting and Background Information This residential treatment center was established in 1982. Its 5-acre campus has a residential building, an activity building, and a barn.

Referral Information Referrals are made through Lutheran Family Services.

Type of Facility

Funding Sources Private; State.

Average Length of Stay Long term.

Types of Admissions Accepted Residential treatment.

Sources of Referral State depts of mental health; Social service depts.

GUILDORD RESIDENTIAL TREATMENT *(continued)*

Client Profile
Age Range of Clients Served Residential program: 12-18.
Characteristics Exhibited by Children Emotional handicaps; Mental disabilities.
Tuition and Fees
Placements Primarily Funded By State depts of mental health; Social service depts.
Social and Rehabilitative Services
Therapeutic Services Offered Individual therapy; Group therapy; Independent living skills program.
Professionals on Staff Social workers; Child care staff.
Educational and Vocational Services
Type(s) of Educational Programs Offered Off campus.

HIGH POINT

TRIAD HOMES FOR AUTISTIC INDIVIDUALS, INC
5405 W Wendover Ave, High Point, NC 27260 (919) 454-6578
Contact Person(s): Alene P Kiricoples, Exec Dir
Setting and Background Information The facility was established in 1978 by parents needing residential treatment for their autistic children. There are two residential 5-bed group homes in Guilford County.
Referral Information Contact the facility for referral information.
Type of Facility
Funding Sources Private; State; Federal.
Average Length of Stay Long term.
Types of Admissions Accepted Residential treatment.
Sources of Referral State depts of mental health; Social service depts.
Client Profile
Age Range of Clients Served Residential program: 12-21+.
Characteristics Exhibited by Children Emotional handicaps; Learning disabilities; Speech/Language disorders; Neurological impairments; Mental disabilities; Autism.
IQ Range of Clients 40-75+.
Tuition and Fees
Placements Primarily Funded By State depts of mental health; Social service depts.
Social and Rehabilitative Services
Therapeutic Approach The basic therapeutic approach of the facility is behavior modification.
Therapeutic Services Offered Individual therapy; Family therapy; Physical therapy; Independent living skills program; Recreation activities; Speech therapy.
Professionals on Staff Psychiatrists; Psychologists; Social workers; Adjunctive therapists; Child care staff; Physical therapists.
Educational and Vocational Services
Type(s) of Educational Programs Offered Off campus; Summer campus.

JACKSONVILLE

CAROBELL CHILDREN'S HOME, INC
311 Warn St, Jacksonville, NC 28540 (919) 455-3080, 455-2310
Contact Person(s): Karla Henry, Soc Wkr
Setting and Background Information The facility was privately established in 1969 as a residential treatment center for handicapped and brain-damaged children. There are 2 residential homes, an office and a school.
Referral Information Referrals can be made by contacting the facility.
Type of Facility
Funding Sources Private; State; Federal.
Average Length of Stay Long term.
Types of Admissions Accepted Residential treatment.
Sources of Referral State depts of education; Local depts of education; State depts of mental health; Private sources; Social service depts; Family.
Client Profile
Age Range of Clients Served Residential program: Birth-21.
Characteristics Exhibited by Children Hearing impairments/deafness; Vision impairments/blindness; Speech/Language disorders; Neurological impairments; Physical handicaps; Mental disabilities.
Tuition and Fees
Room and Board Long term: $2,283/mo.
Placements Primarily Funded By State/federal funds.

Social and Rehabilitative Services
Therapeutic Services Offered Family therapy; Physical therapy; Independent living skills program; Recreation activities; Occupational therapy; Educational services.
Professionals on Staff Social workers; Child care staff; Nurses; Physical therapists; Occupational therapist.
Educational and Vocational Services
Type(s) of Educational Programs Offered On campus.
Profile of On Campus School Program Number of teachers 8; Number of classrooms 2; Student to teacher ratio 3:1; Grades taught Ungraded.

LUTHERAN FAMILY SERVICES, STEPPING STONE GROUP HOME
143 Chaney Ave, Jacksonville, NC 28540 (919) 347-2040 *Contact Person(s):* Tommy Puckett, Prog Dir
Setting and Background Information The facility was established in 1983 by Onslow County Mental Health and is owned by Lutheran Family Services. It is a group home.
Referral Information Applicants for admission must be Willie M certified.
Type of Facility
Funding Sources State.
Average Length of Stay Long term.
Types of Admissions Accepted Group home placement.
Sources of Referral State depts of mental health.
Client Profile
Age Range of Clients Served Residential program: 12-18.
Characteristics Exhibited by Children Emotional handicaps.
IQ Range of Clients 80-120.
Tuition and Fees
Placements Primarily Funded By State depts of mental health.
Social and Rehabilitative Services
Therapeutic Approach The basic approach of the facility is reality therapy.
Therapeutic Services Offered Individual therapy; Group therapy; Family therapy; Independent living skills program; Recreation activities; Substance abuse treatment; Aftercare program with follow up.
Professionals on Staff Psychiatrists; Psychologists; Social workers; Adjunctive therapists; Child care staff.

KENANSVILLE

SUNRISE GROUP HOME
Rt 1 Box 149-D, Kenansville, NC 28349 (919) 296-1531 *Contact Person(s):* Doreen Cherry, Group Home Dir
Setting and Background Information The facility was established in 1984 by the Duplin-Sampson Mental Health Center. It is a large group home.
Referral Information Contact the facility for referral information.
Type of Facility
Funding Sources Local government; Willie M.
Average Length of Stay Long term.
Types of Admissions Accepted Group home placement; Emergency shelter.
Sources of Referral Social service depts.
Client Profile
Age Range of Clients Served Day programs: 12-18; Residential program: 12-18.
Characteristics Exhibited by Children Emotional handicaps; Learning disabilities; Speech/Language disorders; Mental disabilities; Conduct disorder.
IQ Range of Clients 56+.
Tuition and Fees
Room and Board Long term: $245/mo.
Placements Primarily Funded By Willie M; SSI.
Social and Rehabilitative Services
Therapeutic Services Offered Individual therapy; Group therapy; Recreation activities; Music therapy.
Professionals on Staff Psychiatrists; Psychologists; Social workers; Child care staff; Rehabilitation therapist.
Educational and Vocational Services
Type(s) of Educational Programs Offered On campus; Off campus.
Profile of On Campus School Program Number of teachers 4; Number of classrooms 4; Student to teacher ratio 4:1; Grades taught 3-12; Special curriculum electives offered (Music, Home Ec).

SUNRISE GROUP HOME *(continued)*

Vocational Education Programs/Degrees Offered Sheltered workshop; Woodwork.
Degrees Offered 12th grade diploma.

KINSTON

NOVA, INC

Rt 5, Box 62, Kinston, NC 28501 (919) 522-4233 *Contact Person(s):* Cecil Brown, Admin; George Lapas, Exec Dir
Setting and Background Information The facility was privately established in 1985. It is located on approximately 50 acres and has 6 residential units, an administration building and a school.
Referral Information Referrals are primarily made through mental health, social service, or school agencies.
Type of Facility
Funding Sources State.
Average Length of Stay Long term.
Types of Admissions Accepted Day treatment; Residential treatment; Group home placement; Respite care.
Sources of Referral State depts of education; Local depts of education; State depts of mental health; Psychiatrists; Private sources; Social service depts.
Client Profile
Age Range of Clients Served Day programs: 6-18; Residential program: 6-18.
Characteristics Exhibited by Children Emotional handicaps; Mental disabilities.
IQ Range of Clients 70+.
Tuition and Fees
Room and Board Short term: $104-125/diem; Long term: $104-125/diem.
Tuition $10/hr.
Placements Primarily Funded By State depts of education; State depts of mental health.
Social and Rehabilitative Services
Therapeutic Approach The facility uses behavior modification and insight therapy.
Therapeutic Services Offered Individual therapy; Group therapy; Family therapy; Independent living skills program.
Professionals on Staff Psychiatrists; Psychologists; Social workers; Child care staff; Nurses; Pediatrician.
Educational and Vocational Services
Type(s) of Educational Programs Offered On campus.
Profile of On Campus School Program Number of teachers 6; *Number of classrooms* 6; *Student to teacher ratio* 5:1; *Credentials of teachers* MA, Spec Ed; *Grades taught* 4-11; Special curriculum electives offered; Remedial courses offered.
Vocational Education Programs/Degrees Offered Work activity and pre-vocational skills.

MORGANTON

WESTERN CORRECTIONAL CENTER

PO Drawer 1439, Morganton, NC 28655 (704) 437-8335 *Contact Person(s):* Bill Hartley, Psychologist
Setting and Background Information The facility was established in 1973 and has a 50 acre campus.
Referral Information Contact the facility for referral information.
Type of Facility
Funding Sources State.
Average Length of Stay Long term.
Types of Admissions Accepted Residential treatment; Prison.
Sources of Referral Depts of correction.
Client Profile
Age Range of Clients Served Residential program: 15-18.
Characteristics Exhibited by Children Emotional handicaps; Learning disabilities.
IQ Range of Clients 50-130.
Tuition and Fees
Placements Primarily Funded By Depts of corrections.
Social and Rehabilitative Services
Therapeutic Approach The primary therapeutic approach used is based on a multidisciplinary structure.
Therapeutic Services Offered Individual therapy; Group therapy; Recreation activities; Substance abuse treatment.
Professionals on Staff Psychiatrists; Psychologists.

Educational and Vocational Services
Type(s) of Educational Programs Offered On campus.
Profile of On Campus School Program Number of teachers 20; *Number of classrooms* 20; *Student to teacher ratio* 6:1; *Credentials of teachers* Spec Ed; Remedial courses offered.
Vocational Education Programs/Degrees Offered Basic vocational skills.
Degrees Offered GED.

NEW BERN

WINDJAMMER GROUP HOME

1210 Ol' Cherry Pt Rd, New Bern, NC 28560 (919) 638-5388
Contact Person(s): Millard Godwin, Dir
Setting and Background Information The facility was established in 1980 with state funding. It is a residential group home.
Referral Information Contact the facility and submit the required records.
Type of Facility
Funding Sources State.
Average Length of Stay Long term.
Types of Admissions Accepted Group home placement.
Sources of Referral State depts of mental health; Social service depts.
Client Profile
Age Range of Clients Served Residential program: 6-12.
Characteristics Exhibited by Children Emotional handicaps.
IQ Range of Clients 80-110.
Tuition and Fees
Placements Primarily Funded By State depts of mental health; Social service depts.
Social and Rehabilitative Services
Therapeutic Approach The facility uses behavior management.
Therapeutic Services Offered Individual therapy; Group therapy; Family therapy.
Professionals on Staff Psychiatrists; Psychologists; Social workers; Adjunctive therapists.
Educational and Vocational Services
Type(s) of Educational Programs Offered Off campus (Public school).

RALEIGH

HOLLY HILL HOSPITAL

3019 Falstaff Rd, Raleigh, NC 27610 (919) 755-1840 *Contact Person(s):* Deo Garlock, Asst Exec Dir
Setting and Background Information The facility was founded in 1978 by five psychiatrists. It is an inpatient psychiatric hospital on 3 acres.
Referral Information Referrals are made by contacting the hospital. A psychiatrist must approve the admission.
Type of Facility
Funding Sources Private.
Average Length of Stay Short term.
Types of Admissions Accepted Day treatment; In-patient psychiatric hospitalization.
Sources of Referral State depts of education; Local depts of education; State depts of mental health; Psychiatrists; Private sources; Depts of correction; Social service depts; Only psychiatrists can admit patients; the sources listed may refer patients.
Client Profile
Age Range of Clients Served Day programs: 18-55+; Residential program: 12-55+.
Characteristics Exhibited by Children Emotional handicaps; Mental disabilities; Behavior disorders.
Tuition and Fees
Room and Board Short term: $165/diem.
Placements Primarily Funded By Insurance.
Social and Rehabilitative Services
Therapeutic Approach The facility has a comprehensive psychiatric approach to therapy.
Therapeutic Services Offered Individual therapy; Group therapy; Family therapy; Adjunctive therapy; Art therapy; Physical therapy; Independent living skills program; Recreation activities; Substance abuse treatment; Aftercare program with follow up.
Professionals on Staff Psychiatrists; Psychologists; Social workers; Adjunctive therapists; Child care staff; Nurses; Art therapists; Physical therapists.

HOLLY HILL HOSPITAL (continued)

Educational and Vocational Services
Type(s) of Educational Programs Offered On campus.
Profile of On Campus School Program Number of teachers 2; *Number of classrooms* 2; *Student to teacher ratio* 8:1; *Grades taught* 7-12.

WAKE COUNTY JUVENILE TREATMENT SYSTEM
401 E Whitake Mill Rd, Raleigh, NC 27608 (919) 755-6508 *Contact Person(s):* Martha F Waters, Asst Dir for Juvenile Svcs
Setting and Background Information The facility was established in 1981. It offers a continuum of care for Willie M youth, ranging from a locked setting to out-patient services.
Referral Information Admissions are screened by the state Willie M office. Children must be emotionally disturbed, mentally retarded, or neurologically impaired and must have exhibited a history of violent behavior.
Type of Facility
Funding Sources State.
Average Length of Stay From certification until age 18 unless otherwise signed out.
Types of Admissions Accepted Day treatment; Residential treatment; Group home placement; Willie M.
Sources of Referral Wake County.
Client Profile
Age Range of Clients Served Day programs: 12-18; Residential program: 6-18.
Characteristics Exhibited by Children Emotional handicaps; Learning disabilities; Neurological impairments; Mental disabilities; Willie M certified.
IQ Range of Clients 49-120.
Tuition and Fees
Placements Primarily Funded By State depts of mental health.
Social and Rehabilitative Services
Therapeutic Approach The facility has an individualized approach to therapy.
Therapeutic Services Offered Individual therapy; Group therapy; Family therapy; Adjunctive therapy; Independent living skills program; Substance abuse treatment.
Professionals on Staff Psychiatrists; Psychologists; Social workers; Adjunctive therapists; Child care staff; Nurses; Vocational staff.
Educational and Vocational Services
Type(s) of Educational Programs Offered On campus; Off campus (Public schools).
Profile of On Campus School Program Student to teacher ratio 2:1; *Credentials of teachers* State certification; Remedial courses offered.
Vocational Education Programs/Degrees Offered Pre-employment training; Job placement.

RUTHERFORDTON

RUTHERFORD COUNTY YOUTH SERVICES, INC—NORTH HOUSE
617 N Main St, Rutherfordton, NC 28139 (704) 287-7555 *Contact Person(s):* Glenn & Laura Arizmendi, Teaching Parents
Setting and Background Information The facility is located in a residential home.
Referral Information Contact the facility for referral information.
Type of Facility
Funding Sources Private; State; Federal; County; United Way.
Average Length of Stay Long term.
Types of Admissions Accepted Residential treatment; Group home placement.
Sources of Referral State depts of education; Local depts of education; State depts of mental health; Psychiatrists; Depts of correction; Social service depts.
Client Profile
Age Range of Clients Served Day programs: 12-15; Residential program: 12-15.
Characteristics Exhibited by Children Emotional handicaps; Learning disabilities.
Tuition and Fees
Placements Primarily Funded By State depts of education; Local depts of education; State depts of mental health; Private sources.

SALISBURY

TURNING POINT
Rt 2 Box 573, Salisbury, NC 28144 (704) 637-8900 *Contact Person(s):* Deborah McKinnon, Res Dir
Setting and Background Information This facility was established in 1983 through a private contract.
Referral Information Residential clients must be Willie M class members as determined by NC State.
Type of Facility
Funding Sources State.
Average Length of Stay Short and long term.
Types of Admissions Accepted Day treatment; Residential treatment; Group home placement; Willie M.
Sources of Referral State depts of education; Local depts of education; State depts of mental health; Psychiatrists; Social service depts.
Client Profile
Age Range of Clients Served Day programs: 12-18; Residential program: 12-18.
Characteristics Exhibited by Children Emotional handicaps.
Tuition and Fees
Placements Primarily Funded By State depts of mental health.
Social and Rehabilitative Services
Therapeutic Services Offered Individual therapy; Group therapy; Family therapy.
Professionals on Staff Psychiatrists; Psychologists; Social workers; Child care staff; Nurses.
Educational and Vocational Services
Type(s) of Educational Programs Offered On campus; Off campus (Public school).
Profile of On Campus School Program Number of teachers 1; *Number of classrooms* 1; *Student to teacher ratio* 10:1; *Credentials of teachers* Certified; *Grades taught* 6-12; Remedial courses offered.
Vocational Education Programs/Degrees Offered Pre-vocational.
Degrees Offered 12th grade diploma.

SANFORD

COLON ROAD HOME
1109 Colon Rd, Sanford, NC 27330 (919) 774-6218 *Contact Person(s):* Larry Paul, Dir
Setting and Background Information The facility was established in 1982 as a 'Willie M' program. There is a house and a barn on the 10-acre site.
Referral Information All referrals are made through the local mental health center.
Type of Facility
Funding Sources State.
Average Length of Stay Avg 8 mos.
Types of Admissions Accepted Residential treatment; Willie M certified.
Sources of Referral State depts of mental health.
Client Profile
Age Range of Clients Served Residential program: 12-18.
Characteristics Exhibited by Children Emotional handicaps.
Tuition and Fees
Room and Board Long term: $35,000/yr.
Placements Primarily Funded By State depts of mental health.
Social and Rehabilitative Services
Therapeutic Approach The facility has a reality-based approach to therapy.
Therapeutic Services Offered Individual therapy; Group therapy; Family therapy; Physical therapy; Independent living skills program; Recreation activities; Substance abuse treatment.
Professionals on Staff Psychiatrists; Psychologists; Social workers; Child care staff; Nurses.

WHITEVILLE

JOYNER THERAPEUTIC HOME
Rte 6, Box L20, Whiteville, NC 28472 (919) 642-3081
Setting and Background Information The facility was established in 1981 with funds from the local dept of social services.
Referral Information For referrals, contact the facility.

JOYNER THERAPEUTIC HOME *(continued)*

Type of Facility
Funding Sources State.
Average Length of Stay Long term.
Types of Admissions Accepted Residential treatment; Group home placement.
Sources of Referral State depts of education; State depts of mental health; Social service depts.
Client Profile
Age Range of Clients Served Residential program: 15-18.
Characteristics Exhibited by Children Emotional handicaps; Learning disabilities; Vision impairments/blindness.
Tuition and Fees
Room and Board Long term: $850/mo.
Social and Rehabilitative Services
Therapeutic Services Offered Family therapy; Physical therapy; Independent living skills program; Aftercare program with follow up.
Professionals on Staff Psychiatrists; Psychologists; Social workers.
Educational and Vocational Services
Type(s) of Educational Programs Offered Off campus (Public school); Summer campus.

NORTH DAKOTA

JAMESTOWN

CHILDREN AND ADOLESCENT TREATMENT CENTER

State Hospital, Jamestown, ND 58401 (701) 252-7733 ext 2760
Contact Person(s): Social Work Staff
Setting and Background Information The facility was established in 1966 by the state legislature to provide a treatment program for youth, separate from adults. Located on State Hospital grounds, the Center has child and adolescent wards, special education classrooms, recreation hall, and clinical team offices.
Referral Information Referrals can be made by parents, juvenile court, tribal court, State Youth Authority, and private clinicians. To make a referral, contact the facility's social work staff or Director to discuss the child and his/her presenting problems.

Type of Facility
Funding Sources State; Federal.
Average Length of Stay Short and long term.
Types of Admissions Accepted Residential treatment.
Sources of Referral State depts of mental health; Psychiatrists; Private sources; Depts of correction; Social service depts.

Client Profile
Age Range of Clients Served Residential program: 8-17.
Characteristics Exhibited by Children Emotional handicaps; Learning disabilities; Hearing impairments/deafness; Vision impairments/blindness; Speech/Language disorders; Neurological impairments; Mental disabilities.

Tuition and Fees
Room and Board Long term: $207.59/diem.
Placements Primarily Funded By Social service depts; Medicare.

Social and Rehabilitative Services
Therapeutic Approach The primary therapeutic approaches used are psycho-dynamic and behavioral therapy, in conjunction with milieu therapy and chemotherapy.
Therapeutic Services Offered Individual therapy; Group therapy; Family therapy; Adjunctive therapy; Independent living skills program; Recreation activities; Substance abuse treatment; Aftercare program with follow up.
Professionals on Staff Psychiatrists; Psychologists; Social workers; Child care staff; Nurses.

Educational and Vocational Services
Type(s) of Educational Programs Offered On campus.
Profile of On Campus School Program Number of teachers 10; *Number of classrooms* 10; *Student to teacher ratio* 4:1; *Length of school day* 5 ½ hrs; *Grades taught* 1-12; Remedial courses offered.

MINOT

DAKOTA BOYS RANCH

Box 5007, Minot, ND 58702 (701) 852-3628 *Contact Person(s):* Charles Fontaine, MSW
Setting and Background Information The facility was established by congregations of the Lutheran Church-Missouri Synod in 1952. The 200-acre campus is located in the Souris River Valley, 4 miles west of Minot. There is a large complex of modern buildings, including 5 residential cottages, industrial arts and apiary complex, school, chapel, gymnasium, livestock barn, recreational fields, tennis court, riding areas, and auxiliary buildings.

Referral Information Referrals can be made by anyone including school districts, courts, social service agencies, and parents or guardians. To make a referral, contact the facility and forward the necessary background information. Upon receiving the referral packet, the intake committee will review the case and make a placement decision within one week.

Type of Facility
Funding Sources Private.
Average Length of Stay Long term.
Types of Admissions Accepted Residential treatment.
Sources of Referral State depts of education; Local depts of education; State depts of mental health; Psychiatrists; Private sources; Depts of correction; Social service depts.

Client Profile
Age Range of Clients Served Residential program: 10-16.
Characteristics Exhibited by Children Emotional handicaps; Learning disabilities; Mental disabilities.

Tuition and Fees
Placements Primarily Funded By State depts of education; Local depts of education; Private sources; Social service depts.

Social and Rehabilitative Services
Therapeutic Approach The philosophy of the treatment program is based on reality therapy.
Therapeutic Services Offered Individual therapy; Group therapy; Family therapy; Adjunctive therapy; Art therapy; Recreation activities; Substance abuse treatment; Aftercare program with follow up.
Professionals on Staff Psychiatrists; Psychologists; Social workers; Adjunctive therapists; Child care staff; Art therapists.

Educational and Vocational Services
Type(s) of Educational Programs Offered On campus; Off campus; Summer campus.
Profile of On Campus School Program Number of teachers 6; *Student to teacher ratio* 4:1; Remedial courses offered.
Degrees Offered 8th grade diploma; GED.

OHIO

ASHTABULA

ASHTABULA COUNTY RESIDENTIAL TREATMENT CENTER

3914 Donahoe Center Dr, Ashtabula, OH 44004 (216) 998-1811
Contact Person(s): Catherine Stenroos
Setting and Background Information The facility was established in 1977 to provide more accessible and specific residential treatment for the children of Ashtabula County.
Referral Information Contact the facility and forward the necessary information including social history and psychological evaluations. A staffing will be held by the admissions committee to discuss appropriateness of placement.

Type of Facility
Funding Sources Private; State; Federal; Tax levy.
Average Length of Stay Long term.
Types of Admissions Accepted Residential treatment; Group home placement.
Sources of Referral State depts of education; Local depts of education; State depts of mental health; Psychiatrists; Private sources; Depts of correction; Social service depts.

Client Profile
Age Range of Clients Served Residential programs: 6-18.
Characteristics Exhibited by Children Emotional handicaps; Learning disabilities.
IQ Range of Clients 75-120.

Tuition and Fees
Room and Board Long term: $75/diem.
Tuition $218.73/mo.
Placements Primarily Funded By Ashtabula County.

Social and Rehabilitative Services
Therapeutic Approach The basic therapeutic approach is behavior modification.
Therapeutic Services Offered Individual therapy; Group therapy; Family therapy; Recreation activities; Substance abuse treatment; Aftercare program with follow up.
Professionals on Staff Psychologists; Social workers; Child care staff.

Educational and Vocational Services
Type(s) of Educational Programs Offered Off campus (Public school; Vocational school).

ATHENS

GENESIS

22 Stonybrook Dr, Athens, OH 45701 (614) 592-3061 *Contact Person(s):* Patricia Jones, Dir
Setting and Background Information This residential facility was established in 1986 with funds from the Ohio Dept of Youth Services and the Athens County Childrens Services.
Referral Information Contact the facility for referral information.

Type of Facility
Funding Sources State.
Average Length of Stay Long term.
Types of Admissions Accepted Residential treatment; Group home placement; Wards of the state.
Sources of Referral State depts of education; State depts of mental health; Depts of correction; Social service depts.

Client Profile
Age Range of Clients Served Residential program 12-18.
Characteristics Exhibited by Children Emotional handicaps; Delinquency.

Tuition and Fees
Room and Board Short term: $35/diem; Long term: $35/diem.
Placements Primarily Funded By Depts of corrections; Social service depts.

Social and Rehabilitative Services
Therapeutic Approach The basic therapeutic approach is reality therapy.
Therapeutic Services Offered Individual therapy; Group therapy; Independent living skills program; Substance abuse treatment.
Professionals on Staff Social workers; Child care staff.

Educational and Vocational Services
Type(s) of Educational Programs Offered Off campus (Local schools).

BEREA

OHIO BOYS TOWN, INC

PO Box 329, Berea, OH 44017 (216) 243-8770 *Contact Person(s):* Thomas N Gill, Exec Dir
Setting and Background Information The facility was originally established in 1960. Additional facilities were added in 1976 and 1986.
Referral Information Contact the facility and forward the social history, medical history, psychological evaluations, and school records.

Type of Facility
Funding Sources Private.
Average Length of Stay Long term.
Types of Admissions Accepted Residential treatment; Group home placement; Wards of the state.
Sources of Referral Social service depts.

Client Profile
Age Range of Clients Served Residential program: 11-18.
Characteristics Exhibited by Children Emotional handicaps.

Tuition and Fees
Placements Primarily Funded By Social service depts.

Social and Rehabilitative Services
Therapeutic Services Offered Individual therapy; Group therapy; Independent living skills program.
Professionals on Staff Psychologists; Social workers; Child care staff.

Educational and Vocational Services
Type(s) of Educational Programs Offered Off campus (Public school).

CINCINNATI

BOYS HOPE

600 N Bend Rd, Cincinnati, OH 45224 (513) 761-3535 *Contact Person(s):* Joseph P Sweeney, Exec Dir
Setting and Background Information The facility was established in 1984. There are 2 group homes.
Referral Information Contact the facility.

Type of Facility
Funding Sources Private.
Average Length of Stay Long term.
Types of Admissions Accepted Group home placement.
Sources of Referral State depts of education; Local depts of education; Psychiatrists; Private sources; Social service depts.

BOYS HOPE *(continued)*

Client Profile
Age Range of Clients Served Residential program: 9-18.
Characteristics Exhibited by Children Emotional handicaps; Homeless.
Tuition and Fees
Room and Board Long term: $16,900/yr.
Placements Primarily Funded By Foundations; Corporations.
Social and Rehabilitative Services
Therapeutic Approach The facility has a family-oriented environment.
Therapeutic Services Offered Individual therapy; Family therapy; Independent living skills program; Aftercare program with follow up.
Professionals on Staff Psychiatrists; Psychologists; Social workers; Adjunctive therapists; Child care staff.
Educational and Vocational Services
Type(s) of Educational Programs Offered On campus (Tutoring); Off campus (College prep); Summer campus (Camp).

THE CHILDREN'S HOME

5051 Duck Creek Rd, Cincinnati, OH 45227 (513) 272-2800
Contact Person(s): Barbara Schmidlapp MS, Intake Social Worker
Setting and Background Information The facility was established in 1864 for children who could not be cared for by their families. The 40-acre suburban campus has 3 residential cottages, an administrative building, school building, a cottage for the day treatment program, gymnasium, and outdoor pool.
Referral Information For referral, contact the intake social worker and forward a social history, current psychological evaluation, school reports, psychiatric and medical reports. A personal interview with the youth on the campus is also required.
Type of Facility
Average Length of Stay Long term.
Types of Admissions Accepted Day treatment; Residential treatment; Group home placement; Wards of the state.
Sources of Referral State depts of education; Local depts of education; State depts of mental health; Psychiatrists; Private sources; Depts of corrections; Social service depts.
Client Profile
Age Range of Clients Served Day Programs: 11-17; Residential program: 11-17.
Characteristics Exhibited by Children Emotional handicaps.
Tuition and Fees
Room and Board Long term: $70.43/diem.
Placements Primarily Funded By State depts of education; Local depts of education; State depts of mental health; Insurance; Private sources; Depts of corrections; Social service depts.
Social and Rehabilitative Services
Therapeutic Approach The facility has an individualized approach to treatment.
Therapeutic Services Offered Individual therapy; Group therapy; Family therapy; Recreation activities; Aftercare program with follow up.
Professionals on Staff Psychiatrists; Psychologists; Social workers; Adjunctive therapists; Child care staff; Nurses; Art therapists.
Educational and Vocational Services
Type(s) of Educational Programs Offered On campus.

ST ALOYSIUS TREATMENT CENTER

4721 Reading Rd, Cincinnati, OH 45237 (513) 242-7600 *Contact Person(s):* Sr Mary Ann Christine, Admin
Setting and Background Information The facility was established in 1837 to care for homeless children. Currently, it is located on 10 acres with one main building.
Referral Information Contact the facility for referral information.
Type of Facility
Funding Sources Private; County.
Average Length of Stay Long term.
Types of Admissions Accepted Day treatment; Residential treatment; Wards of the state.
Sources of Referral State depts of mental health; Psychiatrists; Private sources; Social service depts.

Client Profile
Age Range of Clients Served Day programs: 6-12; Residential program: 6-12.
Characteristics Exhibited by Children Emotional handicaps; Learning disabilities.
Tuition and Fees
Room and Board Long term: $84.06/diem.
Placements Primarily Funded By Social service depts.
Social and Rehabilitative Services
Therapeutic Approach The basic approach used is milieu therapy.
Therapeutic Services Offered Individual therapy; Group therapy; Family therapy; Art therapy; Recreation activities; Aftercare program with follow up.
Professionals on Staff Psychiatrists; Psychologists; Social workers; Child care staff; Art therapists; Physical therapists.
Educational and Vocational Services
Type(s) of Educational Programs Offered On campus; Off campus; Summer campus (6 wks).
Profile of On Campus School Program Number of teachers 5; *Number of classrooms* 5.
Degrees Offered 8th grade diploma.

ST JOSEPH ORPHANAGE—ALTERCREST

274 Sutton Rd, Cincinnati, OH 45230 (513) 231-5010 *Contact Person(s):* Fr William C Wagner, Exec Dir
Setting and Background Information The orphanage was established in 1830 and is located on 42 acres. There are 2 residences, a gym, offices and a school.
Referral Information Contact the facility and forward a referral packet, including a social history, psychological reports, education records, court contacts and rationale for placement.
Type of Facility
Funding Sources Private; State; Federal; Donations; Endowment.
Average Length of Stay Long term.
Types of Admissions Accepted Residential treatment.
Sources of Referral State depts of mental health; Depts of correction; Social service depts.
Client Profile
Age Range of Clients Served Residential program: 12-21+.
Characteristics Exhibited by Children Emotional handicaps; Learning disabilities; Mental disabilities.
IQ Range of Clients 70-90.
Tuition and Fees
Room and Board Long term: $65.21/diem.
Placements Primarily Funded By Social service depts.
Social and Rehabilitative Services
Therapeutic Approach The facility offers behavior modification and milieu therapy.
Therapeutic Services Offered Individual therapy; Group therapy; Family therapy; Adjunctive therapy; Independent living skills program; Recreation activities.
Professionals on Staff Psychiatrists; Psychologists; Social workers; Adjunctive therapists; Child care staff; Nurses.
Educational and Vocational Services
Type(s) of Educational Programs Offered On campus (SBH); Off campus.
Profile of On Campus School Program Number of teachers 4; *Number of classrooms* 4; *Student to teacher ratio* 4:1; *Credentials of teachers* MA; *Grades taught* 7-12.

ST JOSEPH ORPHANAGE—ST JOSEPH VILLA

5400 Edalbert Dr, Cincinnati, OH 45239 (513) 741-3100 *Contact Person(s):* Fr William C Wagner, Exec Dir
Setting and Background Information The facility was established in 1830.
Referral Information For referral, contact the facility and forward a social history, medical history, psychological reports, rationale for placement and court contacts.
Type of Facility
Funding Sources Private; State; Federal.
Average Length of Stay Long term.
Types of Admissions Accepted Residential treatment.
Sources of Referral Depts of correction; Social service depts.
Client Profile
Age Range of Clients Served Residential program: 6-21+.
Characteristics Exhibited by Children Emotional handicaps; Learning disabilities; Mental disabilities.
IQ Range of Clients 65-85.

ST JOSEPH ORPHANAGE—ST JOSEPH VILLA
(continued)

Tuition and Fees
Room and Board Long term: $61.79/diem.
Placements Primarily Funded By Social service depts.
Social and Rehabilitative Services
Therapeutic Approach The facility uses behavior modification in a therapeutic milieu.
Therapeutic Services Offered Individual therapy; Group therapy; Family therapy; Adjunctive therapy; Independent living skills program; Recreation activities.
Professionals on Staff Psychiatrists; Psychologists; Social workers; Adjunctive therapists; Child care staff; Nurses.
Educational and Vocational Services
Type(s) of Educational Programs Offered Off campus.

CLEVELAND

BELLEFAIRE RESIDENTIAL TREATMENT FACILITY
22001 Fairmount Blvd, Cleveland, OH 44118 (216) 932-2800
Contact Person(s): Margaret Culp, Adm Dir LISW
Setting and Background Information Bellefaire is a private, non-profit residential treatment facility which was initially established in 1868 as an orphanage for homeless Jewish children during the Civil War. It has since evolved into a treatment center, located in a residential area in eastern Cleveland.
Referral Information Referrals can be made by parents, psychiatrists, mental health specialists, psychiatric hospitals, and school districts. To make a referral, contact the Director of Intake and provide information regarding the child's family history, mental functioning, psychological test results, and diagnosis (according to DSM-III).
Type of Facility
Funding Sources Private; State; Federal.
Average Length of Stay Long term.
Types of Admissions Accepted Day treatment; Residential treatment; Out-patient.
Sources of Referral Psychiatrists; Private sources; Social service depts.
Client Profile
Age Range of Clients Served Day programs: 10-18; Residential program: 10-18.
Characteristics Exhibited by Children Emotional handicaps; Learning disabilities.
Tuition and Fees
Room and Board Long term: $67,580/yr.
Placements Primarily Funded By Private sources; Social service depts; United Way.
Social and Rehabilitative Services
Therapeutic Services Offered Individual therapy; Group therapy; Family therapy; Adjunctive therapy; Art therapy; Independent living skills program; Recreation activities; Substance abuse treatment; Aftercare program with follow up; Sexual abuse therapy.
Professionals on Staff Psychiatrists; Psychologists; Social workers; Adjunctive therapists; Child care staff; Nurses; Art therapists.
Educational and Vocational Services
Type(s) of Educational Programs Offered On campus; Off campus.
Profile of On Campus School Program Remedial courses offered.
Vocational Education Programs/Degrees Offered Vocational education.
Degrees Offered 12th grade diploma.

JONES HOME OF CHILDREN'S SERVICES
3518 W 25th St, Cleveland, OH 44144 (216) 741-2241 *Contact Person(s):* Thomas Hanrahan, Dir of Prof Srvs
Setting and Background Information The facility was established in 1886 by the estate of Carlos Jones. It is a residential treatment center for emotionally disturbed youth who have experienced extreme neglect or rejection and frequently are the victims of abuse.
Referral Information Contact the facility.
Type of Facility
Funding Sources Private.
Average Length of Stay Short and long term.
Types of Admissions Accepted Residential treatment; Emergency shelter.

Sources of Referral Private sources; Social service depts; Juvenile court.
Client Profile
Age Range of Clients Served Residential program 6-18.
Characteristics Exhibited by Children Emotional handicaps; Learning disabilities; Behavior disorders; Delinquency.
Tuition and Fees
Room and Board Short term: $71/diem; Long term: $72/diem (includes school tuition).
Placements Primarily Funded By Depts of corrections; Social service depts.
Social and Rehabilitative Services
Therapeutic Services Offered Individual therapy; Group therapy; Family therapy; Recreation activities.
Professionals on Staff Psychologists; Social workers; Child care staff; Nurses.
Educational and Vocational Services
Type(s) of Educational Programs Offered On campus (LD/BD); Off campus (Public school).
Profile of On Campus School Program Number of teachers 4; Number of classrooms 4; Student to teacher ratio 5:1; Credentials of teachers Certified; Grades taught Ungraded.

COLUMBUS

HANNAH NEIL CENTER FOR CHILDREN, THE STARR COMMONWEALTH SCHOOLS
301 Obetz Rd, Columbus, OH 43207 (614) 491-5784 *Contact Person(s):* JoAnne F Milburn PhD, Dir
Setting and Background Information The facility was originally established in 1858 to provide shelter care for homeless women and their children. Currently, the 21-acre campus has residential buildings and a day treatment facility.
Referral Information For referral, contact the facility for an admission packet. A pre-placement interview will be scheduled.
Type of Facility
Funding Sources Private; Federal; County.
Average Length of Stay Avg 15 mos.
Types of Admissions Accepted Day treatment; Residential treatment; Specialized foster care.
Sources of Referral State depts of education; Local depts of education; State depts of mental health; Psychiatrists; Private sources; Depts of correction; Social service depts.
Client Profile
Age Range of Clients Served Day programs: 6-12; Residential program: 6-12.
Characteristics Exhibited by Children Emotional handicaps.
Tuition and Fees
Room and Board Long term: $88/diem.
Tuition $42/diem.
Placements Primarily Funded By Social service depts.
Social and Rehabilitative Services
Therapeutic Approach The facility offers a therapeutic milieu.
Therapeutic Services Offered Individual therapy; Group therapy; Family therapy; Adjunctive therapy; Recreation activities; Substance abuse treatment; Music therapy; Occupational therapy.
Professionals on Staff Psychiatrists; Psychologists; Social workers; Child care staff; Nurses; Music therapist; Occupational therapist.
Educational and Vocational Services
Type(s) of Educational Programs Offered On campus (Spec Ed); Summer campus.
Profile of On Campus School Program Number of teachers 7 and 7 aides; Number of classrooms 7; Student to teacher ratio 6:1; Credentials of teachers Certified Spec Ed; Grades taught Ungraded elementary; Remedial courses offered (Tutoring in basic subjects).

ROSEMONT CENTER
2440 Dawnlight Ave, Columbus, OH 43211 (614) 471-2626 *Contact Person(s):* Sr M Elise Kramer, Exec Dir; Terri Maloney Houston, Public Affairs Dir
Setting and Background Information The facility was originally established in 1865 as an orphanage and shelter for the rehabilitation of Civil War prostitutes by the Sisters of the Good Shephard. Currently, the center offers three programs— residential care for adolescent girls, day treatment for adolescent boys and girls, and emergency shelter care for Franklin County adolescent girls. The 35-acre campus has five cottages, two group

ROSEMONT CENTER *(continued)*

homes, a pool, and an administration building which includes a school and a gym.

Referral Information Contact the program director for referral information. Ohio County Social Service agencies make referrals by letter with an information packet including child's social history, psychological evaluation, and school records.

Type of Facility

Funding Sources Private; State; Federal; County.

Average Length of Stay Short and long term.

Types of Admissions Accepted Day treatment; Residential treatment; Group home placement; Wards of the state; Emergency shelter.

Sources of Referral Local depts of education; Social service depts; County mental health board.

Client Profile

Age Range of Clients Served Day programs: 12-18; Residential program: 12-18.

Characteristics Exhibited by Children Emotional handicaps; Learning disabilities; Substance Abuse.

IQ Range of Clients 65+.

Tuition and Fees

Room and Board Short term: $87.44/diem (includes school tuition); Long term: $87.44/diem (includes school tuition).

Tuition $36/diem.

Placements Primarily Funded By Local depts of education; State depts of mental health; Social service depts; United Way; County Mental Health Board.

Social and Rehabilitative Services

Therapeutic Approach The basic approach of the facility is reality therapy.

Therapeutic Services Offered Individual therapy; Group therapy; Family therapy; Independent living skills program; Recreation activities; Substance abuse treatment; Aftercare program with follow up.

Professionals on Staff Psychiatrists; Psychologists; Social workers; Child care staff; Nurses.

Educational and Vocational Services

Type(s) of Educational Programs Offered On campus; Off campus (Public schools); Summer campus.

Profile of On Campus School Program Number of teachers 18; *Number of classrooms* 16; *Student to teacher ratio* 10:1; *Grades taught* 7-12; Special curriculum electives offered (Art, Wood shop, Communications); Remedial courses offered (Math, English).

Vocational Education Programs/Degrees Offered Typing/keyboarding; Career education.

Degrees Offered 8th grade diploma; 12th grade diploma.

WHITTIER GROUP HOME

740 E Whittier St, Columbus, OH 43207 (614) 444-0272 *Contact Person(s):* Jane E Heins, Dir of Group Homes

Setting and Background Information The facility was established in 1983 by the county children's service agency. It is a group home.

Referral Information Contact the intake worker for referral information.

Type of Facility

Funding Sources County.

Average Length of Stay Long term.

Types of Admissions Accepted Group home placement; Wards of the state.

Sources of Referral Agency only.

Client Profile

Age Range of Clients Served Residential program: 12-15.

Characteristics Exhibited by Children Emotional handicaps; Learning disabilities; Dependent/unruly; Parent and child conflict.

IQ Range of Clients 75+.

Tuition and Fees

Placements Primarily Funded By Social service depts.

Social and Rehabilitative Services

Therapeutic Approach The facility uses behavior management.

Therapeutic Services Offered Individual therapy; Group therapy; Aftercare program with follow up.

Professionals on Staff Social workers; Child care staff.

Educational and Vocational Services

Type(s) of Educational Programs Offered Off campus (Public schools).

FAIRFIELD

ONE WAY FARM, INC

PO Box 197, 6111 River Rd, Fairfield, OH 45014 (513) 829-3276

Contact Person(s): Barbara Condo, Exec Dir

Setting and Background Information The facility was established in 1976. There are two campuses. One is located on 15 ½ acres and has 2 buildings. The other campus is located on 52 acres and has 12 buildings.

Referral Information The referral procedure is to contact the facility and forward the necessary background information.

Type of Facility

Funding Sources Private; Federal; County.

Average Length of Stay Short and long term.

Types of Admissions Accepted Residential treatment; Group home placement.

Sources of Referral Private sources; Depts of correction; Social service depts; Dept of Human Svcs.

Client Profile

Age Range of Clients Served Residential program: 6-18.

Characteristics Exhibited by Children Emotional handicaps; Learning disabilities; Abused and neglected.

IQ Range of Clients 70+.

Tuition and Fees

Room and Board Long term: $37.50/diem.

Placements Primarily Funded By Private sources; Depts of corrections; Social service depts.

Social and Rehabilitative Services

Therapeutic Approach The facility uses reality therapy.

Therapeutic Services Offered Individual therapy; Independent living skills program; Recreation activities; Substance abuse treatment.

Professionals on Staff Child care staff.

Educational and Vocational Services

Type(s) of Educational Programs Offered On campus; Off campus.

Profile of On Campus School Program Number of teachers 1; *Student to teacher ratio* 5:1; *Credentials of teachers* Certified.

GAHANNA

SYNTAXIS, INC

5435 Morse Rd, Gahanna, OH 43230 (614) 855-1224 *Contact Person(s):* Joseph V Friend, Asst Dir

Setting and Background Information This facility was established in 1973 with funding from a SSDP grant. There are 6 group homes scattered throughout northeast Franklin County.

Referral Information For referral, contact the associate director. A pre-placement interview will be scheduled.

Type of Facility

Funding Sources State; County.

Average Length of Stay Long term.

Types of Admissions Accepted Residential treatment; Group home placement; Wards of the state.

Sources of Referral Depts of correction; Social service depts.

Client Profile

Age Range of Clients Served Residential program: 15-18.

Characteristics Exhibited by Children Emotional handicaps; Learning disabilities; Neurological impairments; Mental disabilities; Behavior disorders; Delinquency.

IQ Range of Clients 65+.

Tuition and Fees

Room and Board Long term: $56.25/diem.

Placements Primarily Funded By Depts of corrections; Social service depts.

Social and Rehabilitative Services

Therapeutic Approach The basic approach of the facility is reality therapy.

Therapeutic Services Offered Individual therapy; Group therapy; Independent living skills program.

Professionals on Staff Psychiatrists; Psychologists; Social workers; Child care staff.

Educational and Vocational Services

Type(s) of Educational Programs Offered On campus (Tutors; Industrial arts); Off campus (High school; Vocational school).

GROVE CITY

BUCKEYE BOYS RANCH, INC

5665 Hoover Road, Grove City, OH 43123 (614) 875-2371 *Contact Person(s):* Leslie A Bostic PhD, Exec Dir

Setting and Background Information This non-profit facility was privately established in 1961. Located on 80 acres, there are 3 residential buildings, an athletic center, a vocational center and support buildings. There is a group home at a separate location.

Referral Information Contact the facility for referral information.

Type of Facility

Funding Sources Private; State; Federal.

Average Length of Stay Long term.

Types of Admissions Accepted Day treatment; Residential treatment; Group home placement; Wards of the state.

Sources of Referral State depts of education; Private sources; Depts of correction; Social service depts; Juvenile courts.

Client Profile

Age Range of Clients Served Day programs: 10-18; Residential program: 10-18.

Characteristics Exhibited by Children Emotional handicaps; Learning disabilities; Hearing impairments/deafness; Vision impairments/blindness; Mental disabilities.

IQ Range of Clients 80+.

Tuition and Fees

Room and Board Long term: $66-$129/mo.

Placements Primarily Funded By Depts of corrections; Social service depts; Juvenile courts.

Social and Rehabilitative Services

Therapeutic Approach The facility primarily uses behavior modification and reality therapy in a therapeutic milieu.

Therapeutic Services Offered Individual therapy; Group therapy; Family therapy; Independent living skills program; Recreation activities; Aftercare program with follow up.

Professionals on Staff Psychiatrists; Social workers; Child care staff; Nurses.

Educational and Vocational Services

Type(s) of Educational Programs Offered On campus; Off campus.

Profile of On Campus School Program Number of teachers 9; *Number of classrooms* 9; *Student to teacher ratio* 10:1; *Credentials of teachers* Spec Ed; *Grades taught* 4-12; *Special curriculum electives offered;* Remedial courses offered.

Vocational Education Programs/Degrees Offered Vocational program.

Degrees Offered 12th grade diploma.

FRANKLIN VILLAGE

1951 Gantz Rd, Grove City, OH 43123 (614) 275-2603 *Contact Person(s):* Michael Fliegel, Dir Classification and Assignment

Setting and Background Information The facility was established in 1951. It is owned and operated by Franklin County Children Services and is located on 85 acres. The campus has administration, residential and recreation buildings, a dining facility and a gym.

Referral Information For referral to the facility, youth must be wards of Franklin County Juvenile Court and committed to Franklin County Children Services.

Type of Facility

Funding Sources State; Property taxes.

Average Length of Stay Long term.

Types of Admissions Accepted Residential treatment; Wards of the state county.

Sources of Referral Franklin County Children Services.

Client Profile

Age Range of Clients Served Residential program: 12-18.

Characteristics Exhibited by Children Emotional handicaps; Learning disabilities; Speech/Language disorders; Delinquency; Abused and neglected.

Tuition and Fees

Room and Board Long term: $90/diem.

Tuition The cost of school tuition is provided by the local school district..

Social and Rehabilitative Services

Therapeutic Approach A behavior modification point system is the basic therapeutic approach.

Therapeutic Services Offered Individual therapy; Group therapy; Family therapy; Adjunctive therapy; Art therapy; Independent living skills program; Recreation activities; Aftercare program with follow up.

Professionals on Staff Social workers; Adjunctive therapists; Child care staff; Nurses; Art therapists.

Educational and Vocational Services

Type(s) of Educational Programs Offered On campus; Off campus.

LIMA

ALLEN ACRES

1920 Slabtown Rd, Lima, OH 45801 (419) 227-6620 *Contact Person(s):* David Bingham, Dir

Setting and Background Information This is a residential treatment facility, located on 11 acres, with 6 buildings.

Referral Information Contact the facility for referral information.

Type of Facility

Funding Sources County.

Average Length of Stay Short and long term.

Types of Admissions Accepted Residential treatment; County custody.

Sources of Referral County.

Client Profile

Age Range of Clients Served Residential program: 12-18.

Characteristics Exhibited by Children Emotional handicaps; Learning disabilities; Abused and neglected.

Tuition and Fees

Room and Board Long term: $40/diem.

Placements Primarily Funded By County.

Social and Rehabilitative Services

Therapeutic Approach The facility uses behavior modification.

Therapeutic Services Offered Group therapy; Independent living skills program; Recreation activities.

Professionals on Staff Social workers; Child care staff; Physical therapists.

Educational and Vocational Services

Type(s) of Educational Programs Offered Off campus (Vocational school).

NORWALK

ALTERNATIVE RESOURCES FOR KIDS, INC—GIRLS HOME

75 S Linwood Ave, Norwalk, OH 44857 (419) 668-5813 *Contact Person(s):* Trudy Robertson, Dir

Setting and Background Information This facility was established in 1985. It is a transitional residential program.

Referral Information For referral, contact the facility and forward social and medical histories, school information and any psychological reports.

Type of Facility

Funding Sources Private; County.

Average Length of Stay Approx 1 yr.

Types of Admissions Accepted Group home placement; Wards of the state.

Sources of Referral State depts of mental health; Private sources; Social service depts; Dept of Human Svcs.

Client Profile

Age Range of Clients Served Residential program: 12-18.

Tuition and Fees

Room and Board Long term: $45/diem.

Placements Primarily Funded By Depts of corrections; Social service depts.

Social and Rehabilitative Services

Therapeutic Approach The basic therapeutic approach used is reality therapy with behavior modification.

Therapeutic Services Offered Individual therapy; Group therapy; Independent living skills program; Recreation activities.

Professionals on Staff Psychologists; Child care staff.

Educational and Vocational Services

Type(s) of Educational Programs Offered Off campus (Local schools).

Degrees Offered 8th grade diploma; 12th grade diploma; GED.

PAINESVILLE

ST JOHN'S HOME
173 W High St, Painesville, OH 44077 (216) 357-7523 *Contact Person(s):* Alberta Chokshi LISW, Soc Wkr
Setting and Background Information This facility was established in 1909 as an orphanage by the Sisters of the Transfiguration of the Episcopal Diocese of Ohio. The 4-acre campus has 3 cottages, a chapel, an administration building and others.
Referral Information Contact the facility and forward the necessary material.
Type of Facility
Funding Sources County.
Average Length of Stay Long term.
Types of Admissions Accepted Residential treatment.
Sources of Referral Depts of correction; Social service depts.
Client Profile
Age Range of Clients Served Residential program: 12-21+.
Characteristics Exhibited by Children Emotional handicaps; Learning disabilities; Neurological impairments.
IQ Range of Clients 85+.
Tuition and Fees
Room and Board Long term: $50/diem.
Placements Primarily Funded By Depts of corrections; Social service depts.
Social and Rehabilitative Services
Therapeutic Approach The basic approach is reality therapy.
Therapeutic Services Offered Individual therapy; Group therapy; Independent living skills program; Substance abuse treatment.
Professionals on Staff Psychologists; Social workers; Adjunctive therapists; Child care staff.
Educational and Vocational Services
Type(s) of Educational Programs Offered Off campus.

PARMA

PARMADALE
6753 State Rd, Parma, OH 44134 (216) 845-7700 *Contact Person(s):* Anne Mengerink, Dir of Intake
Setting and Background Information The facility was established in 1925 by Catholic Charities Corp. Its 200-acre campus has 21 buildings.
Referral Information For referral, contact the Intake Dept and forward social history, psychological and psychiatric evaluations, school records and medical history.
Type of Facility
Funding Sources Private; State; Federal; Foundations; Fund raising.
Average Length of Stay 9-18 mos.
Types of Admissions Accepted Day treatment; Residential treatment; Group home placement.
Sources of Referral Social service depts; Juvenile courts.
Client Profile
Age Range of Clients Served Day programs: 12-18; Residential program: 6-18.
Characteristics Exhibited by Children Emotional handicaps; Learning disabilities; Behavior disorders; Chemically dependent.
IQ Range of Clients 50+.
Tuition and Fees
Room and Board Long term: $73/diem (includes school tuition).
Placements Primarily Funded By Social service depts.
Social and Rehabilitative Services
Therapeutic Approach The basic therapeutic approach of the facility is behavioral.
Therapeutic Services Offered Individual therapy; Group therapy; Family therapy; Substance abuse treatment; Aftercare program with follow up.
Professionals on Staff Psychiatrists; Psychologists; Social workers; Adjunctive therapists; Child care staff; Nurses; Speech therapist.
Educational and Vocational Services
Type(s) of Educational Programs Offered On campus; Off campus (Spec Ed); Summer campus.
Profile of On Campus School Program Number of teachers 23; *Number of classrooms* 12; *Student to teacher ratio* 9:1; *Credentials of teachers* State certified; *Grades taught* 7-12; Remedial courses offered.
Degrees Offered 8th grade diploma; 12th grade diploma.

PEDRO

OHIO CENTER FOR YOUTH AND FAMILY DEVELOPMENT
PO Box 128, Paddle Creek Rd, Pedro, OH 45659 (614) 532-5787
Contact Person(s): Robert Haas, Dir
Setting and Background Information The program was started in 1982 and is located in Wayne National Forest. It has 4 new cottages and 2 transitional living units, school, gymnasium, workshop building, maintenance building, and 2 office buidings.
Referral Information Referrals can be made by the Depts of Welfare, Social Services, Mental Health, Youth Services, and Education, along with juvenile authorities. Referring agencies are requested to forward personal, social, and educational records on the child. If the placement is reviewed as appropriate, then the referring agency must make a formal application.
Type of Facility
Funding Sources Private.
Average Length of Stay Long term.
Types of Admissions Accepted Residential treatment.
Sources of Referral State depts of education; Local depts of education; Private sources; Social service depts.
Client Profile
Age Range of Clients Served Residential program: 12-17.
Characteristics Exhibited by Children Emotional handicaps; Learning disabilities; Speech/Language disorders; Neurological impairments; Mental disabilities.
IQ Range of Clients 50+.
Tuition and Fees
Room and Board Long term: $106/diem.
Social and Rehabilitative Services
Therapeutic Approach The treatment program uses a psychoeducational approach with emphasis on behaviorism, humanism, and acceptance of responsibility. A token economy is used for behavior management.
Therapeutic Services Offered Individual therapy; Group therapy; Independent living skills program; Recreation activities.
Professionals on Staff Social workers; Child care staff; Nurses.
Educational and Vocational Services
Type(s) of Educational Programs Offered On campus; Off campus.
Profile of On Campus School Program Number of teachers 8; *Number of classrooms* 7; *Student to teacher ratio* 6:1; Remedial courses offered.
Degrees Offered 12th grade diploma.

PIQUA

UPPER VALLEY CHARITABLE CORP—CLEAR CREEK FARM
PO Box 1433, Piqua, OH 45356 (513) 498-9445 *Contact Person(s):* Jim Gover, Admin
Setting and Background Information This program was privately established in 1980. Located on 100 acres, there are 2 family-style residences, a barn, and an office building.
Referral Information Contact the facility for referral information.
Type of Facility
Funding Sources Private.
Average Length of Stay Long term.
Types of Admissions Accepted Group home placement.
Sources of Referral State depts of education; Local depts of education; State depts of mental health; Psychiatrists; Private sources; Social service depts.
Client Profile
Age Range of Clients Served Residential program: 5 ½ -18.
Characteristics Exhibited by Children Emotional handicaps; Hearing impairments/deafness; Speech/Language disorders.
IQ Range of Clients 80+.
Tuition and Fees
Placements Primarily Funded By Private sources.
Social and Rehabilitative Services
Therapeutic Approach The facility offers a home-like environment. It relies on community resources to provide therapeutic intervention.
Professionals on Staff Psychologists; Social workers; Child care staff.
Educational and Vocational Services
Type(s) of Educational Programs Offered Off campus (Public and vocational schools).

SMITHVILLE

BOYS' VILLAGE, INC

PO Box 518, Smithville, OH 44677 (216) 264-3232 *Contact Person(s):* James Miller ACSW, Clinical Dir
Setting and Background Information This agency was established in 1946. The 148-acre campus has 7 cottages, an administration building, a school, a gym, and a recreation facility.
Referral Information Contact the facility and forward the necessary information. A pre-placement interview and visit will be arranged.
Type of Facility
Funding Sources Private; State; County.
Average Length of Stay Long term.
Types of Admissions Accepted Residential treatment; Treatment foster care.
Sources of Referral State depts of education; Local depts of education; State depts of mental health; Psychiatrists; Private sources; Depts of correction; Social service depts; Juvenile courts.
Client Profile
Age Range of Clients Served Residential program: 6-18.
Characteristics Exhibited by Children Emotional handicaps; Learning disabilities; Physical handicaps; Mental disabilities; Behavior disorders.
IQ Range of Clients 75-130.
Tuition and Fees
Room and Board Long term: $63.75/diem.
Tuition $243.61/mo.
Placements Primarily Funded By Private sources; Depts of corrections; Social service depts; Juvenile courts.
Social and Rehabilitative Services
Therapeutic Approach The therapeutic approach of the facility is based on S.T.E.P (systematic training for effective parenting) and reality therapy.
Therapeutic Services Offered Individual therapy; Group therapy; Family therapy; Art therapy; Independent living skills program; Recreation activities; Substance abuse treatment; Aftercare program with follow up; Treatment foster home.
Professionals on Staff Psychiatrists; Psychologists; Social workers; Child care staff; Art therapists; Music therapist.
Educational and Vocational Services
Type(s) of Educational Programs Offered On campus; Off campus; Summer campus.
Profile of On Campus School Program Number of teachers 9; Number of classrooms 8; Student to teacher ratio 6:1; Credentials of teachers SBH; Grades taught Ungraded; Special curriculum electives offered (SBH/LD curriculum).
Vocational Education Programs/Degrees Offered Local vocational programs.

SPRINGFIELD

OESTERLEN SERVICES FOR YOUTH

1918 Mechanicsburg Rd, Springfield, OH 45503 (513) 399-6101
Contact Person(s): Walter Brooker ACSW, Exec Dir
Setting and Background Information The facility was established in 1903. The 90-acre campus has 5 cottages, a school, administration building and others.
Referral Information Referrals are made through local children's services/welfare dept or the juvenile court.
Type of Facility
Funding Sources Private; State.
Average Length of Stay Long term.
Types of Admissions Accepted Residential treatment.
Sources of Referral Social service depts; Juvenile courts.
Client Profile
Age Range of Clients Served Residential program: 12-18.
Characteristics Exhibited by Children Emotional handicaps; Learning disabilities; Hearing impairments/deafness; Vision impairments/blindness; Speech/Language disorders; Neurological impairments; Mental disabilities.
IQ Range of Clients 70+.
Tuition and Fees
Room and Board Long term: $88.23/diem.
Tuition $5.41/diem.
Placements Primarily Funded By Social service depts; Juvenile courts.

Social and Rehabilitative Services
Therapeutic Approach The facility uses behavior modification.
Therapeutic Services Offered Individual therapy; Group therapy; Family therapy; Art therapy; Recreation activities; Drama therapy.
Professionals on Staff Psychiatrists; Psychologists; Social workers; Adjunctive therapists; Child care staff; Nurses; Art therapists.
Educational and Vocational Services
Type(s) of Educational Programs Offered On campus; Off campus; Summer campus (Remedial).
Profile of On Campus School Program Number of teachers 7; Number of classrooms 5; Student to teacher ratio 8:1; Credentials of teachers MEd; Length of school day 6 hrs; Special curriculum electives offered (Typing, Business, Values); Remedial courses offered (Math, English).
Vocational Education Programs/Degrees Offered Pre-vocational.
Degrees Offered 12th grade diploma.

TOLEDO

ST ANTHONY VILLA

2740 W Central Ave, Toledo, OH 43606 (419) 473-1353 *Contact Person(s):* Sandra VanDenBrink, Regional Dir
Setting and Background Information The facility was initially established in 1855 as an orphanage and later evolved into a residential treatment center. It is located on 9 ½ acres.
Referral Information Referrals are accepted from physicians, social service agencies, juvenile courts and voluntary placements. After a 30 day assessment, if necessary, the child goes into long term treatment or is referred to another more appropriate setting.
Type of Facility
Funding Sources Private.
Average Length of Stay Short and long term.
Types of Admissions Accepted Residential treatment; Wards of the state.
Sources of Referral Psychiatrists; Private sources; Depts of correction; Social service depts; Courts.
Client Profile
Age Range of Clients Served Day programs: Birth-15; Residential program: 6-17.
Characteristics Exhibited by Children Emotional handicaps; Learning disabilities; Speech/Language disorders; Neurological impairments; Mental disabilities.
IQ Range of Clients 60-130.
Tuition and Fees
Room and Board Short term: $43/diem (includes school tuition); Long term: $43/diem (includes school tuition).
Placements Primarily Funded By Private sources; Depts of corrections; Social service depts.
Social and Rehabilitative Services
Therapeutic Approach The therapeutic approach of the facility is reality therapy, which includes a positive peer culture.
Therapeutic Services Offered Individual therapy; Group therapy; Family therapy; Art therapy; Independent living skills program; Recreation activities; Substance abuse treatment; Aftercare program with follow up.
Professionals on Staff Psychiatrists; Psychologists; Social workers; Child care staff; Nurses.
Educational and Vocational Services
Type(s) of Educational Programs Offered On campus; Off campus; Summer campus.
Degrees Offered 8th grade diploma; 12th grade diploma.

VAN WERT

THE MARSH FOUNDATION HOME AND SCHOOL

PO Box 150, Van Wert, OH 45891 (419) 238-1695 *Contact Person(s):* Ronald R Bagley, Dir
Setting and Background Information This facility was established in 1919 by the estate of George H Marsh. The purpose of the foundation is to help families and children who are experiencing mild to moderate adjustment problems. Its 200-acre campus has 4 cottages, a health clinic, an administration building, a recreation center and other buildings. It is licensed to serve 22 counties in northwest Ohio.
Referral Information The foundation accepts referrals from families, county human service depts and other social service agencies. A pre-admission visit will be scheduled.

THE MARSH FOUNDATION HOME AND SCHOOL
(continued)

Type of Facility
Funding Sources Private.
Average Length of Stay Long term.
Types of Admissions Accepted Residential treatment.
Sources of Referral Social service depts; Parents.
Client Profile
Age Range of Clients Served Residential program: 6-18.
Characteristics Exhibited by Children Emotional handicaps; Learning disabilities; Behavior disorders.
IQ Range of Clients 85-120.
Tuition and Fees
Tuition $180/mo.
Placements Primarily Funded By State depts of education; Private sources; Social Security; Title IV-E.
Social and Rehabilitative Services
Therapeutic Approach The basic therapeutic approach is reality therapy.
Therapeutic Services Offered Individual therapy; Group therapy; Family therapy.
Professionals on Staff Psychologists; Social workers; Child care staff; School guidance counselor.
Educational and Vocational Services
Type(s) of Educational Programs Offered On campus; Off campus (High school; Vocational school); Summer campus (Summer school for grades 1-6).
Profile of On Campus School Program Number of teachers 5; *Number of classrooms* 4; *Student to teacher ratio* 4:1; *Credentials of teachers* BS, MS; *Length of school day* 5 ½ hrs; *Grades taught* 4-8; Special curriculum electives offered (Piano lessons).
Degrees Offered 8th grade diploma.

WORTHINGTON

UNITED METHODIST CHILDRENS HOME
1033 N High St, Worthington, OH 43085 (614) 885-5020 *Contact Person(s):* Marvin D Bean, Dir of Intake
Setting and Background Information The facility was established in 1911 as a home for dependent and neglected children. The 44-acre campus has 7 major buildings.
Referral Information Contact the Director of Intake and forward a social history, school records, a WISC report and any psychiatric hospital reports.
Type of Facility
Funding Sources Private; State; County; Juvenile courts.
Average Length of Stay Long term.
Types of Admissions Accepted Residential treatment; Group home placement.
Sources of Referral State depts of education; Local depts of education; State depts of mental health; Psychiatrists; Private sources; Depts of correction; Social service depts.
Client Profile
Age Range of Clients Served Residential program: 13-18.
Characteristics Exhibited by Children Emotional handicaps; Mental disabilities.
IQ Range of Clients 75+.
Tuition and Fees
Room and Board Long term: $69-87/diem.
Placements Primarily Funded By Social service depts.
Social and Rehabilitative Services
Therapeutic Services Offered Group therapy.
Professionals on Staff Psychiatrists; Psychologists; Social workers; Adjunctive therapists; Child care staff; Nurses.
Educational and Vocational Services
Type(s) of Educational Programs Offered On campus (Severe behavior handicapped); Off campus (Mainstream placements).
Profile of On Campus School Program Number of teachers 8; *Number of classrooms* 6; *Student to teacher ratio* 10:1; *Credentials of teachers* MA; *Length of school day* 8-3:30; *Grades taught* 7-12; Remedial courses offered (Reading, Math, Science, Health).
Degrees Offered 12th grade diploma.

YELLOW SPRINGS

SECOND CIRCLE
PO Box 296, Yellow Springs, OH 45387 (513) 767-1885 *Contact Person(s):* Kenney Olson, Exec Dir
Setting and Background Information The facility was established in 1973.
Referral Information Contact the facility for referral information. A pre-placement visit will be arranged prior to placement decision.
Type of Facility
Funding Sources State.
Average Length of Stay Long term.
Types of Admissions Accepted Group home placement; Wards of the state.
Sources of Referral Depts of correction; Social service depts.
Client Profile
Age Range of Clients Served Residential program: 6-18.
Characteristics Exhibited by Children Emotional handicaps; Learning disabilities; Behavior disorders.
IQ Range of Clients 70+.
Tuition and Fees
Room and Board Long term: $56/diem.
Placements Primarily Funded By Social service depts.
Social and Rehabilitative Services
Therapeutic Approach The facility uses the principles of reality therapy and behavior modification in a therapeutic milieu.
Therapeutic Services Offered Individual therapy; Group therapy; Recreation activities.
Professionals on Staff Psychiatrists; Adjunctive therapists.
Educational and Vocational Services
Type(s) of Educational Programs Offered Off campus.

ZANESVILLE

AVONDALE YOUTH CENTER
4155 Roseville Rd, Zanesville, OH 43701 (614) 452-0257 *Contact Person(s):* Charles G Jones
Setting and Background Information The facility was established in 1911 by the county as a children's home. There are 40-acres with a main building, a gym, a laundry and an apartment.
Referral Information Contact the facility for referral information.
Type of Facility
Funding Sources County.
Average Length of Stay Long term.
Types of Admissions Accepted Residential treatment.
Sources of Referral Psychiatrists; Private sources; Depts of correction; Social service depts.
Client Profile
Age Range of Clients Served Residential program: 12-18.
Characteristics Exhibited by Children Emotional handicaps.
IQ Range of Clients 60+.
Tuition and Fees
Room and Board Long term: $40/diem.
Placements Primarily Funded By Social service depts; County.
Social and Rehabilitative Services
Therapeutic Approach The basic therapeutic approach used by the facility is behavior modification.
Therapeutic Services Offered Individual therapy; Group therapy; Family therapy; Recreation activities; Substance abuse treatment; Aftercare program with follow up.
Professionals on Staff Social workers; Child care staff.
Educational and Vocational Services
Type(s) of Educational Programs Offered Off campus.

OKLAHOMA

ADA

MENTAL HEALTH SERVICES OF SOUTHERN OKLAHOMA
111 E 12th St, Ada, OK 74820 (405) 436-2690
Referral Information Contact the facility for referral information.
Type of Facility
Funding Sources State.
Types of Admissions Accepted Day treatment; Residential treatment; Group home placement.
Client Profile
Age Range of Clients Served Day programs: 6-55+; Residential program: 6-55+.
Characteristics Exhibited by Children Emotional handicaps; Drug and alcohol dependency.
Social and Rehabilitative Services
Therapeutic Services Offered Individual therapy; Group therapy; Family therapy; Substance abuse treatment; Psychological/psychiatric evaluations.

ARDMORE

MENTAL HEALTH SERVICES OF SOUTHERN OKLAHOMA
2530 S Commerce, Ardmore, OK 73401 (405) 223-5636
Referral Information Contact the facility for referral information.
Type of Facility
Funding Sources State.
Types of Admissions Accepted Day treatment; Residential treatment; Group home placement.
Client Profile
Age Range of Clients Served Day programs: 6-55+; Residential program: 6-55+.
Characteristics Exhibited by Children Emotional handicaps; Drug and alcohol dependency.
Social and Rehabilitative Services
Therapeutic Services Offered Individual therapy; Group therapy; Family therapy; Substance abuse treatment; Psychiatric/psychological evaluations.

DURANT

MENTAL HEALTH SERVICES OF SOUTHERN OKLAHOMA
North Hall, SOSU, Durant, OK 74701 (405) 924-7330
Referral Information Contact the facility for referral information.
Type of Facility
Funding Sources State.
Types of Admissions Accepted Day treatment; Residential treatment; Group home placement.
Client Profile
Age Range of Clients Served Day programs: 6-55+; Residential program: 6-55+.
Characteristics Exhibited by Children Emotional handicaps; Alcohol and drug dependency.
Social and Rehabilitative Services
Therapeutic Services Offered Individual therapy; Group therapy; Family therapy; Substance abuse treatment; Psychological/psychiatric evaluations.

LAWTON

GREAT PLAINS HOSPITAL
1601 SW 82, Lawton, OK 73505 (405) 248-0508
Referral Information Contact the hospital for referral information.
Type of Facility
Types of Admissions Accepted Day treatment; Residential treatment.
Client Profile
Age Range of Clients Served Day programs: 6-55+; Residential programs: 6-55+.
Characteristics Exhibited by Children Emotional handicaps; Drug and alcohol dependency.
Social and Rehabilitative Services
Therapeutic Services Offered Individual therapy; Group therapy; Recreation activities; Substance abuse treatment; Aftercare program with follow up.
Professionals on Staff Adjunctive therapists; Physical therapists; Occupational therapist.

JIM TALIAFERRO COMMUNITY MENTAL HEALTH CENTER
602 SW 38th, Lawton, OK 73505 (405) 248-5780
Referral Information Contact the facility for referral information.
Type of Facility
Types of Admissions Accepted Day treatment; Residential treatment.
Client Profile
Age Range of Clients Served Day programs: 12-55+; Residential program: 12-55+.
Characteristics Exhibited by Children Emotional handicaps; Drug and alcohol dependency.
Social and Rehabilitative Services
Therapeutic Services Offered Individual therapy; Group therapy; Substance abuse treatment; Aftercare program with follow up.

LONE WOLF

SOUTHWEST OKLAHOMA ADOLESCENT ADDICTION REHABILITATION RANCH, INC
Rte 1, Box 64, Lone Wolf, OK 73655 (405) 846-9041 *Contact Person(s):* Sue Billups, Clinical Dir; J Frank Claiborne III, Admin
Setting and Background Information The facility was established in 1982 as a non-profit corporation and is located on 5 acres.
Referral Information For referral information contact the facility.
Type of Facility
Funding Sources Private; State.
Average Length of Stay Long term.
Types of Admissions Accepted Residential treatment.
Sources of Referral Local depts of education; State depts of mental health; Private sources; Social service depts.
Client Profile
Age Range of Clients Served Residential program: 12-21+.
Characteristics Exhibited by Children Mental disabilities; Chemical dependencies.
IQ Range of Clients 80+.
Tuition and Fees
Room and Board Long term: Sliding scale.
Placements Primarily Funded By State depts of mental health.

SOUTHWEST OKLAHOMA ADOLESCENT ADDICTION REHABILITATION RANCH, INC *(continued)*

Social and Rehabilitative Services
Therapeutic Approach The primary therapeutic approach is behavior modification.
Therapeutic Services Offered Individual therapy; Group therapy; Family therapy; Adjunctive therapy; Independent living skills program; Recreation activities; Substance abuse treatment; Aftercare program with follow up.
Professionals on Staff Psychologists; Adjunctive therapists; Drug and alcohol counselor.
Educational and Vocational Services
Type(s) of Educational Programs Offered On campus.
Profile of On Campus School Program Number of teachers 1; *Number of classrooms* 1; *Student to teacher ratio* 15:1; *Credentials of teachers* State Certified; *Length of school day* 3 hrs.
Degrees Offered GED.

MADILL

MENTAL HEALTH SERVICES OF SOUTHERN OKLAHOMA

106 N 5th, Madill, OK 73446 (405) 795-5564
Referral Information Contact the facility for referral information.
Type of Facility
Funding Sources State.
Types of Admissions Accepted Day treatment; Residential treatment.
Client Profile
Age Range of Clients Served Day programs: 6-55+; Residential program: 6-55+.
Characteristics Exhibited by Children Emotional handicaps; Alcohol and drug dependency.
Social and Rehabilitative Services
Therapeutic Services Offered Individual therapy; Group therapy; Family therapy; Substance abuse treatment; Aftercare program with follow up.

MARIETTA

MENTAL HEALTH SERVICES OF SOUTHERN OKLAHOMA

101 SW 4th, Marietta, OK 73448 (405) 276-3323
Referral Information Contact the facility for referral information.
Type of Facility
Funding Sources State.
Types of Admissions Accepted Day treatment; Residential treatment.
Client Profile
Age Range of Clients Served Day programs: 6-55+; Residential program: 6-55+.
Characteristics Exhibited by Children Emotional handicaps; Drug and alcohol dependency.
Social and Rehabilitative Services
Therapeutic Services Offered Individual therapy; Group therapy; Family therapy; Substance abuse treatment; Aftercare program with follow up.

MIDWEST CITY

HOPE COMMUNITY SERVICES

1114 S Air Depot Blvd, Midwest City, OK 73110 (405) 732-2102
Referral Information Contact the facility for referral information.
Type of Facility
Types of Admissions Accepted Day treatment; Residential treatment.
Client Profile
Age Range of Clients Served Day programs: 12-18; Residential program: 12-18.
Characteristics Exhibited by Children Emotional handicaps; Drug and alcohol dependency.
Social and Rehabilitative Services
Therapeutic Services Offered Individual therapy; Group therapy; Family therapy; Substance abuse treatment.
Educational and Vocational Services
Vocational Education Programs/Degrees Offered Pre-vocational; Job placement.

NORMAN

CENTRAL OKLAHOMA COMMUNITY MENTAL HEALTH CENTER

PO Box 400, 909 E Alameda, Norman, OK 73071 (405) 360-5100
Referral Information Contact the facility for referral information.
Type of Facility
Types of Admissions Accepted Day treatment; Residential treatment.
Client Profile
Age Range of Clients Served Day programs: 13-55+; Residential program: 13-55+.
Characteristics Exhibited by Children Emotional handicaps; Drug and alcohol dependency.
Social and Rehabilitative Services
Therapeutic Services Offered Individual therapy; Substance abuse treatment; Aftercare program with follow up.

OKLAHOMA YOUTH CENTER

PO Box 1008, 1120 E Main, Norman, OK 73070 (405) 364-9004
Contact Person(s): Mick Jepsen PhD, Dir
Setting and Background Information The facility was established in 1971 by a Hill Borton Construction grant. The 10-acre campus has 3 buildings.
Referral Information Referrals are made through court committment.
Type of Facility
Funding Sources State; Federal.
Average Length of Stay Long term.
Types of Admissions Accepted Residential treatment.
Sources of Referral State depts of education; Local depts of education; State depts of mental health; Psychiatrists; Private sources; Social service depts; Courts.
Client Profile
Age Range of Clients Served Residential program: 6-18.
Characteristics Exhibited by Children Emotional handicaps.
Tuition and Fees
Room and Board Long term: $330/diem.
Placements Primarily Funded By State depts of mental health.
Social and Rehabilitative Services
Therapeutic Approach The facility uses cognitive therapy.
Therapeutic Services Offered Individual therapy; Group therapy; Family therapy; Recreation activities.
Professionals on Staff Psychiatrists; Psychologists; Social workers; Adjunctive therapists; Child care staff; Nurses.
Educational and Vocational Services
Type(s) of Educational Programs Offered On campus; Off campus.
Profile of On Campus School Program Number of teachers 15; *Number of classrooms* 13; *Student to teacher ratio* 5:1; *Credentials of teachers* Spec Ed; *Grades taught* K-12; Special curriculum electives offered (Computers); Remedial courses offered (Reading).
Vocational Education Programs/Degrees Offered Work-study; Sheltered workshop.
Degrees Offered 12th grade diploma.

OKLAHOMA CITY

HIGH POINTE

6501 NE 50th, Oklahoma City, OK 73141 (405) 424-3383 *Contact Person(s):* Marilee Monnot, Admis Dir
Setting and Background Information High Pointe is a residential treatment facility which was established in 1982 as a division of Dillon Family and Youth Services of Shadow Mountain Institute. It is accredited by the Joint Commission on Accreditation of Hospitals and is licensed by the Oklahoma Dept of Human Services. The large ranch-style facility is located on 40 acres of land, 15 minutes northeast of Oklahoma City.
Referral Information Anyone can make a referral by contacting the facility and forwarding the necessary background information. A placement decision will be made by a staff psychiatrist.
Type of Facility
Funding Sources Private; Federal.
Average Length of Stay Long term.
Types of Admissions Accepted Residential treatment.
Sources of Referral Psychiatrists; Private sources; Social service depts.

HIGH POINTE *(continued)*

Client Profile
Age Range of Clients Served Residential program: 12-18.
Characteristics Exhibited by Children Emotional handicaps; Learning disabilities; Speech/Language disorders.
IQ Range of Clients 80+.
Tuition and Fees
Room and Board Long term: $340-$378/diem.
Placements Primarily Funded By Insurance; Private sources.
Social and Rehabilitative Services
Therapeutic Approach The program is based on structured milieu therapy involving the use of insight-oriented therapy and a behavioral level system.
Therapeutic Services Offered Individual therapy; Group therapy; Family therapy; Art therapy; Recreation activities; Aftercare program with follow up; Occupational therapy; Music therapy; Sexual abuse counseling.
Professionals on Staff Psychiatrists; Psychologists; Social workers; Adjunctive therapists; Child care staff; Nurses; Art therapists.
Educational and Vocational Services
Type(s) of Educational Programs Offered On campus.
Profile of On Campus School Program Number of teachers 5; *Number of classrooms* 5; *Student to teacher ratio* 10:1.
Degrees Offered 12th grade diploma.

SUNBEAM FAMILY SERVICES, INC

616 NW 21st, Oklahoma City, OK 73103 (405) 528-7721
Referral Information Contact the facility for the following types of care: residential, group, and foster care for adolescents (528-7721); pre-school therapeutic care (685-2404, 424-5297); respite care for elderly (525-3663).
Type of Facility
Types of Admissions Accepted Day treatment; Residential treatment; Group home placement; Foster care; Respite; Pre-school.
Client Profile
Age Range of Clients Served Day programs: Birth-5; Residential program: 6-55+.
Characteristics Exhibited by Children Emotional handicaps.
Social and Rehabilitative Services
Therapeutic Services Offered Individual therapy; Group therapy; Family therapy.

TISHOMINGO

MENTAL HEALTH SERVICES OF SOUTHERN OKLAHOMA

105 N Neshoba, Tishomingo, OK 73460 (405) 371-2311
Referral Information Contact the facility for referral information.
Type of Facility
Funding Sources State.
Types of Admissions Accepted Day treatment; Residential treatment.
Client Profile
Age Range of Clients Served Day programs: 6-55+; Residential program: 6-55+.
Characteristics Exhibited by Children Emotional handicaps; Drug and alcohol dependency.
Social and Rehabilitative Services
Therapeutic Services Offered Individual therapy; Group therapy; Family therapy; Substance abuse treatment; Aftercare program with follow up.

TULSA

SHADOW MOUNTAIN INSTITUTE

6262 S Sheridan Rd, Tulsa, OK 74133 (918) 492-8200 *Contact Person(s):* Philip L Cottrell, ACSW
Setting and Background Information The facility has been involved in psychiatric residential treatment for approximately 10 years but the current program has been in existence since 1980. It is located on a 20-acre campus in the southeast part of Tulsa. There are 30 acute care beds and 60 psychiatric residential treatment beds in 5 separate living units. There is also a partial hospitalization program which offers day treatment for youth.
Referral Information Anyone can make a referral by contacting the Director of Admissions.

Type of Facility
Funding Sources Private; Federal.
Average Length of Stay Long term.
Types of Admissions Accepted Day treatment; Residential treatment.
Sources of Referral State depts of mental health; Psychiatrists; Private sources; Social service depts.
Client Profile
Age Range of Clients Served Day programs: 5-18; Residential program: 5-18.
Characteristics Exhibited by Children Emotional handicaps; Learning disabilities; Speech/Language disorders; Neurological impairments; Physical handicaps; Mental disabilities.
IQ Range of Clients 80+.
Tuition and Fees
Room and Board Long term: $340-$400/diem; $170/diem (Day treatment).
Placements Primarily Funded By State depts of mental health; Insurance; Private sources; Social service depts.
Social and Rehabilitative Services
Therapeutic Approach The facility has an eclectic approach to therapy.
Therapeutic Services Offered Individual therapy; Group therapy; Family therapy; Adjunctive therapy; Art therapy; Physical therapy; Independent living skills program; Recreation activities; Substance abuse treatment; Aftercare program with follow up; Dance therapy.
Professionals on Staff Psychiatrists; Psychologists; Social workers; Adjunctive therapists; Child care staff; Nurses; Art therapists; Physical therapists.
Educational and Vocational Services
Type(s) of Educational Programs Offered On campus.
Profile of On Campus School Program Number of teachers 7; *Number of classrooms* 7; *Student to teacher ratio* 7:1.
Degrees Offered 12th grade diploma.

OREGON

ASHLAND

SOUTHERN OREGON CHILD STUDY AND TREATMENT CENTER

1836 Fremont St, Ashland, OR 97520 (503) 482-5792 *Contact Person(s):* Marilyn Dapses MS, Dir of Admin
Referral Information Referrals to the facility are made through the Children's Services Division. The children are enrolled on a provisional 60 days stay during which time a comprehensive assessment is made.
Type of Facility
Funding Sources State; Federal.
Average Length of Stay 12 months.
Types of Admissions Accepted Day treatment; Residential treatment.
Sources of Referral Private sources; Social service depts.
Client Profile
Age Range of Clients Served Day programs: 3-16; Residential program: 5-10.
Characteristics Exhibited by Children Emotional handicaps; Learning disabilities; Hearing impairments/deafness; Vision impairments/blindness; Mental disabilities.
IQ Range of Clients 50+.
Tuition and Fees
Placements Primarily Funded By Insurance; Private sources; Social service depts; Medicaid.
Social and Rehabilitative Services
Therapeutic Services Offered Individual therapy; Group therapy; Family therapy.
Professionals on Staff Psychologists; Social workers; Child care staff.
Educational and Vocational Services
Type(s) of Educational Programs Offered Off campus.

BEAVERTON

ST MARY'S HOME FOR BOYS

16535 SW Tualatin Valley Hwy, Beaverton, OR 97006 (503) 649-5651 *Contact Person(s):* Rev H William Hamilton, Exec Dir
Setting and Background Information St Mary's Home for Boys is a residential treatment center with 2 large cottage living units for 20-25 boys each and an off-campus apartment. The facility also provides transitional services with an independent living program supervised by a MSW Coordinator.
Referral Information Contact the facility for referral information.
Type of Facility
Funding Sources Private.
Average Length of Stay 14 months.
Types of Admissions Accepted Residential treatment.
Sources of Referral Social service depts.
Client Profile
Age Range of Clients Served Residential program: 9-16.
Characteristics Exhibited by Children Emotional handicaps; Behavior disorders; Delinquency.
IQ Range of Clients 70+.
Tuition and Fees
Placements Primarily Funded By Social service depts; United Way; Contributions.
Social and Rehabilitative Services
Therapeutic Services Offered Individual therapy; Group therapy; Family therapy.

Educational and Vocational Services
Type(s) of Educational Programs Offered On campus; Off campus.

CORVALLIS

CHILDREN'S FARM HOME

4455 NE Hwy 20, Corvallis, OR 97330 (503) 757-1852 *Contact Person(s):* Millard Ryker, Admin Dir
Setting and Background Information Children's Farm Home is a residential care facility located between Corvallis and Albany serving children from the entire state. The campus has 3 living units for boys (12-16 boys per unit), a unit for girls (maximum of 12),and an on-campus school consisting of 4 separate buildings. The agency also operates two group homes.
Referral Information Placements in the facility are made through the Dept of Social Services. Requirements for admission are a court order, medical and consent forms, medical/psychological records, and family social history. An on-campus interview will be scheduled with the child and family.
Type of Facility
Funding Sources Private; State.
Average Length of Stay Long term; 16 mos.
Types of Admissions Accepted Residential treatment; Group home placement; Emergency shelter.
Sources of Referral Local depts of education; Private sources; Depts of correction; Social service depts; Court.
Client Profile
Age Range of Clients Served Residential program: 12-18.
Characteristics Exhibited by Children Emotional handicaps; Learning disabilities; Behavior disorders; Delinquency.
IQ Range of Clients 75+.
Tuition and Fees
Room and Board Short term: $60/diem (shelter); Long term: $90/diem.
Placements Primarily Funded By Social service depts; United Way.
Social and Rehabilitative Services
Therapeutic Approach The program philosophy is eclectic with primary emphasis on an eco-systems/family approach.
Therapeutic Services Offered Individual therapy; Group therapy; Family therapy; Adjunctive therapy; Art therapy; Independent living skills program; Substance abuse treatment.
Professionals on Staff Psychiatrists; Psychologists; Social workers; Adjunctive therapists; Nurses.
Educational and Vocational Services
Type(s) of Educational Programs Offered On campus; Off campus.
Profile of On Campus School Program Number of teachers 8; *Number of classrooms* 8; *Grades taught* 7-12; Special curriculum electives offered; Remedial courses offered.
Vocational Education Programs/Degrees Offered Pre-vocational development.

GRANTS PASS

SOUTHERN OREGON ADOLESCENT STUDY AND TREATMENT CENTER

210 Tacoma St, Grants Pass, OR 97526 (503) 476-3302 *Contact Person(s):* Frank Kennedy MA, Sr Therapist
Setting and Background Information Southern Oregon Adolescent Study and Treatment Center is a private, non-profit residential treatment facility for psychiatric placements. The facility was

SOUTHERN OREGON ADOLESCENT STUDY AND TREATMENT CENTER *(continued)*

established in July 1977 through a petition presented to the state legislature by local citizens. The program is temporarily housed in a large 5-bedroom house, in a wooded rural area.

Referral Information Referrals can be made by parents, schools, public agencies, and juvenile depts. To make a referral, contact the senior therapist. If the placement seems appropriate, then background information on the child will be requested and personal interviews scheduled before a placement decision is made.

Type of Facility

Funding Sources State.

Types of Admissions Accepted Residential treatment.

Sources of Referral State depts of education; Local depts of education; Psychiatrists; Social service depts; Juvenile depts.

Client Profile

Age Range of Clients Served Residential program: 12-18.

Characteristics Exhibited by Children Emotional handicaps; Learning disabilities; Speech/Language disorders.

IQ Range of Clients 80+.

Tuition and Fees

Placements Primarily Funded By State depts of education; Local depts of education; Social service depts; Juvenile depts.

Social and Rehabilitative Services

Therapeutic Approach The treatment program utilizes milieu therapy and behavior modification programs.

Therapeutic Services Offered Individual therapy; Group therapy; Family therapy; Adjunctive therapy; Recreation activities; Aftercare program with follow up.

Professionals on Staff Psychiatrists; Psychologists; Social workers; Adjunctive therapists.

Educational and Vocational Services

Type(s) of Educational Programs Offered On campus.

Profile of On Campus School Program Number of teachers 1; *Number of classrooms* 1; *Student to teacher ratio* 12:1; Remedial courses offered.

Degrees Offered 12th grade diploma; GED.

LA GRANDE

GRANDE RONDE CHILD CENTER

902 D Ave, La Grande, OR 97850 (503) 963-8666 *Contact Person(s):* Cindy Stenard, Exec Dir

Setting and Background Information Grande Ronde Child Center was established in 1972 as a psychiatric day and residential treatment facility for emotionally disturbed children. It also operates an outpatient family counseling program. It is a member of the Oregon Association of Treatment Programs which contracts with Oregon's Childrens Service Division. Grande Ronde Child Center is located in a residential neighborhood and has living quarters and a school program.

Referral Information Referrals can be made by the Children's Services Division, school districts, and the Educational Service District for Juveniles Dept. All referrals are directed to the Admission Office to arrange for the required background information to be forwarded to the facility. A pre-placement interview will be arranged for staff to observe the child and parents at home.

Type of Facility

Funding Sources State.

Average Length of Stay Long term.

Types of Admissions Accepted Day treatment; Residential treatment; Outreach.

Sources of Referral State depts of education; Local depts of education; Social service depts.

Client Profile

Age Range of Clients Served Day programs: 3-12; Residential program: 3-12; Outreach program: 12-14.

Characteristics Exhibited by Children Emotional handicaps; Learning disabilities.

IQ Range of Clients 70+.

Tuition and Fees

Placements Primarily Funded By Social service depts.

Social and Rehabilitative Services

Therapeutic Approach A behavioral therapeutic approach is used in conjunction with structured family therapy and reality therapy.

Therapeutic Services Offered Individual therapy; Group therapy; Family therapy; Adjunctive therapy; Aftercare program with follow up.

Professionals on Staff Psychiatrists; Psychologists; Adjunctive therapists; Child care staff.

Educational and Vocational Services

Type(s) of Educational Programs Offered On campus; Summer campus.

Profile of On Campus School Program Number of teachers 1; *Number of classrooms* 1; *Student to teacher ratio* 10:1.

OREGON CITY

YOUTH ADVENTURES, INC

15544 S Clackamas River Rd, Oregon City, OR 97045 (503) 656-8005 *Contact Person(s):* Richard S Patton, Admin Dir

Referral Information Referrals to the facility are made through the Children's Services Division. A copy of a completed referral report, with relevant court documents, a signed medical consent, psychological, and school reports, social security number, insurance carrier, and medical coverage forms are required.

Type of Facility

Funding Sources State.

Types of Admissions Accepted Group home placement.

Sources of Referral Social service depts.

Client Profile

Age Range of Clients Served Residential program: 13-18.

Characteristics Exhibited by Children Emotional handicaps; Learning disabilities; Mental disabilities; Delinquency.

Tuition and Fees

Placements Primarily Funded By Social service depts.

Social and Rehabilitative Services

Therapeutic Services Offered Individual therapy; Group therapy; Family therapy; Independent living skills program.

Educational and Vocational Services

Type(s) of Educational Programs Offered Off campus.

PORTLAND

BOYS AND GIRLS AID SOCIETY OF OREGON

2301 NW Glisan, Portland, OR 97210 (503) 222-9661 *Contact Person(s):* Jewel Goddard, Admin Dir

Setting and Background Information The agency is licensed to provide residential care for children and maternity cases in supervised foster family homes and group homes. The agency is also licensed for maternity and adoption services.

Referral Information Contact the facility for referral information.

Type of Facility

Funding Sources Private.

Average Length of Stay 90-120 days.

Types of Admissions Accepted Residential treatment; Group home placement; Emergency shelter; Foster care.

Client Profile

Age Range of Clients Served Residential program: 12-18.

Characteristics Exhibited by Children Emotional handicaps; Delinquency; Foster care.

Tuition and Fees

Placements Primarily Funded By Social service depts; Donations; United Way.

Educational and Vocational Services

Type(s) of Educational Programs Offered On campus.

Profile of On Campus School Program Student to teacher ratio 7:1; Grades taught 8-12.

Degrees Offered Conferred through public school.

CEDAR HILLS HOSPITAL

10300 SW Eastridge, Portland, OR 97225 (503) 297-2252 *Contact Person(s):* Chris Krenk MSW, Prog Dir

Setting and Background Information Cedar Hills is a psychiatric facility for children in need of short-term psychiatric care. There is a special day treatment program for drug and alcohol abusers and fire setters.

Referral Information Contact the facility for referral information.

CEDAR HILLS HOSPITAL *(continued)*

Type of Facility
Funding Sources Private.
Average Length of Stay Short term.
Types of Admissions Accepted Residential treatment.
Client Profile
Age Range of Clients Served Day programs: 6-18; Residential program: 6-18.
Characteristics Exhibited by Children Emotional handicaps; Behavior disorders; Drug and alcohol abuse; Arson.
Social and Rehabilitative Services
Therapeutic Services Offered Individual therapy; Group therapy; Family therapy; Recreation activities; Occupational therapy.
Educational and Vocational Services
Type(s) of Educational Programs Offered On campus.

JANIS YOUTH PROGRAMS, INC

738 NE Davis, Portland, OR 97232 (503) 233-6090 *Contact Person(s):* Dennis Morrow, Admin Dir
Setting and Background Information The agency offers a variety of services, including day and residential treatment and community-based group homes.
Referral Information Contact the facility for referral information.
Type of Facility
Funding Sources State.
Average Length of Stay Short and long term.
Types of Admissions Accepted Residential treatment; Group home placement.
Sources of Referral Social service depts.
Client Profile
Age Range of Clients Served Residential program: 12-18.
Characteristics Exhibited by Children Emotional handicaps; Learning disabilities; Behavior disorders; Delinquency; Drug and alcohol abuse.
Tuition and Fees
Placements Primarily Funded By Social service depts.
Social and Rehabilitative Services
Therapeutic Approach The residential treatment program is based on an intensive milieu therapy program.
Therapeutic Services Offered Individual therapy; Group therapy; Family therapy; Physical therapy; Recreation activities; Substance abuse treatment; Aftercare program with follow up.
Educational and Vocational Services
Type(s) of Educational Programs Offered On campus; Off campus.
Vocational Education Programs/Degrees Offered Job preparation and placements.

OUT-FRONT HOUSE

928 SE 18th, Portland, OR 97214 (503) 232-7644 *Contact Person(s):* Michael M Ware, Admin Dir
Referral Information Referrals to the facility are made through Children's Services Division.
Type of Facility
Types of Admissions Accepted Group home placement.
Client Profile
Age Range of Clients Served Residential program: 14-18.
Characteristics Exhibited by Children Emotional handicaps; Behavior disorders; Sexual abuse.
Tuition and Fees
Placements Primarily Funded By Social service depts; Title I; CETA.
Social and Rehabilitative Services
Therapeutic Services Offered Individual therapy; Group therapy; Family therapy; Independent living skills program; Aftercare program with follow up.
Educational and Vocational Services
Type(s) of Educational Programs Offered Off campus.
Profile of On Campus School Program Special curriculum electives offered (Tutorial); Remedial courses offered.
Vocational Education Programs/Degrees Offered Summer job placement.

PARRY CENTER FOR CHILDREN

3415 SE Powell Blvd, Portland, OR 97202 (503) 234-9591 *Contact Person(s):* Ross Miller, Admin Dir
Setting and Background Information Parry Center provides residential treatment services and has a group home program.
Referral Information Contact the facility for referral information.

Type of Facility
Funding Sources Private.
Types of Admissions Accepted Residential treatment; Group home placement.
Sources of Referral Social service depts.
Client Profile
Age Range of Clients Served Residential program: Birth-10.
Characteristics Exhibited by Children Emotional handicaps; Learning disabilities; Neurological impairments; Behavior disorders; Autism; Schizophrenia.
Tuition and Fees
Placements Primarily Funded By Social service depts.
Social and Rehabilitative Services
Therapeutic Services Offered Individual therapy; Group therapy; Family therapy; Recreation activities; Play therapy.
Educational and Vocational Services
Type(s) of Educational Programs Offered On campus; Off campus.

RIVERSIDE PSYCHIATRIC HOSPITAL

1400 SE Umatilla St, Portland, OR 97202 (503) 234-5353
Setting and Background Information Riverside has a 20-bed unit providing short term psychiatric treatment and evaluation.
Referral Information Contact the facility for referral information.
Type of Facility
Funding Sources Private.
Average Length of Stay Short term.
Types of Admissions Accepted Residential treatment.
Sources of Referral Psychiatrists; Private sources.
Client Profile
Age Range of Clients Served Day programs: 12-17; Residential program: 12-17.
Characteristics Exhibited by Children Emotional handicaps; Neurological impairments; Behavior disorders; Drug and alcohol abuse; Psychotic.
Tuition and Fees
Placements Primarily Funded By Insurance; Private sources.
Social and Rehabilitative Services
Therapeutic Services Offered Individual therapy; Group therapy; Family therapy; Recreation activities; Substance abuse treatment.
Professionals on Staff Psychiatrists; Psychologists; Child care staff; Physical therapists.
Educational and Vocational Services
Vocational Education Programs/Degrees Offered Vocational counseling.

ROSEMONT SCHOOL, INC

597 N Dekum, Portland, OR 97217 (503) 283-2205 *Contact Person(s):* Ray Micciche, Prog Dir
Setting and Background Information Rosemont conducts a structured residential treatment program for girls. There are also two community-based group homes.
Referral Information Referrals to the facility are made through the Chidren's Services Division. Inappropriate referrals are girls who are pregnant, physically abusive, overtly psychotic or severely retarded.
Type of Facility
Funding Sources Private.
Types of Admissions Accepted Residential treatment; Group home placement.
Sources of Referral Social service depts.
Client Profile
Age Range of Clients Served Residential program: 13-18.
Characteristics Exhibited by Children Emotional handicaps; Behavior disorders; Delinquency; Drug and alcohol abuse.
Tuition and Fees
Placements Primarily Funded By Social service depts; United Way.
Social and Rehabilitative Services
Therapeutic Services Offered Individual therapy; Group therapy; Family therapy; Substance abuse treatment.
Educational and Vocational Services
Type(s) of Educational Programs Offered On campus; Off campus.
Degrees Offered 12th grade diploma.

SALVATION ARMY WHITE SHIELD CENTER

PO Box 10027, 2640 NW Alexandra Ave, Portland, OR 97210-0027 (503) 226-4053 *Contact Person(s):* Capt Sherry Ann Downs, Admin Dir

SALVATION ARMY WHITE SHIELD CENTER
(continued)

Setting and Background Information The Center provides residential treatment, prenatal care and/or infant maternal training for 13 young women. The agency also operates a shelter care program for girls (12-18).

Referral Information Referrals to the facility are made through the Children's Services Division. Copies of court orders, medical consent forms and reports are required.

Type of Facility
Funding Sources Private.
Types of Admissions Accepted Residential treatment; Emergency shelter.
Sources of Referral Social service depts.

Client Profile
Age Range of Clients Served Residential program: Birth-18.
Characteristics Exhibited by Children Emotional handicaps; Behavior disorders; Pregnancy.

Tuition and Fees
Placements Primarily Funded By Social service depts; Contributions; Title I.

Social and Rehabilitative Services
Therapeutic Services Offered Individual therapy; Group therapy; Family therapy; Independent living skills program.

Educational and Vocational Services
Type(s) of Educational Programs Offered Off campus.
Vocational Education Programs/Degrees Offered Vocational and prevocational courses.

WAVERLY CHILDREN'S HOME
3550 SE Woodward, Portland, OR 97202 (503) 234-7532 *Contact Person(s):* Cynthia A Thompson, Dir

Setting and Background Information Waverly has 4 separate programs for children. Three small group home settings provide services for boys between the ages of 8 and 12 who have severe behavioral/emotional problems. The day treatment services are for children (8 to 14) with behavioral problems. AAnother program is for educable mentally retarded children (7 to 12) with emotional/behavioral problems. The shelter care unit provides emergency care and services to children from Multnomah County.

Referral Information Referrals to the facility are made by Children's Services Division, court orders, and voluntary commitment. Medical forms and psychological records are required along with a family information sheet.

Type of Facility
Funding Sources Private.
Average Length of Stay Short and long term.
Types of Admissions Accepted Day treatment; Residential treatment; Emergency shelter.
Sources of Referral Social service depts.

Client Profile
Age Range of Clients Served Day programs: 8-14; Residential program: 8-12.
Characteristics Exhibited by Children Emotional handicaps; Learning disabilities; Mental disabilities; Behavior disorders.

Tuition and Fees
Placements Primarily Funded By Social service depts; Contributions; United Way; Guilds.

Social and Rehabilitative Services
Therapeutic Services Offered Individual therapy; Group therapy; Family therapy.

Educational and Vocational Services
Type(s) of Educational Programs Offered On campus.

REDMOND

CASCADE CHILD CARE CENTER
PO Box 549, 1379 S 15th, Redmond, OR 97756 (503) 548-6166 *Contact Person(s):* Marilyn Keenan

Setting and Background Information Cascade Child Care Center is a private, non-profit residential and day treatment facility which was established in 1977 by a state legislature mandate to establish a child treatment center to serve the central Oregon region.

Referral Information Anyone can make a referral by contacting the facility or the Children's Services Division office in their area. The referral process requires the child to visit the program and participate in a family interview.

Type of Facility
Funding Sources State.
Average Length of Stay Long term.
Types of Admissions Accepted Day treatment; Residential treatment.
Sources of Referral State depts of education; Local depts of education; State depts of mental health; Psychiatrists; Social service depts.

Client Profile
Age Range of Clients Served Day programs: 5-12; Residential program: 5-12.
Characteristics Exhibited by Children Emotional handicaps; Learning disabilities; Hearing impairments/deafness; Vision impairments/blindness; Speech/Language disorders; Physical handicaps.

Tuition and Fees
Placements Primarily Funded By Social service depts.

Social and Rehabilitative Services
Therapeutic Approach The basic therapeutic approach of the facility is behavioral.
Therapeutic Services Offered Individual therapy; Group therapy; Family therapy; Art therapy; Recreation activities; Aftercare program with follow up.
Professionals on Staff Psychiatrists; Psychologists; Social workers; Adjunctive therapists; Child care staff.

Educational and Vocational Services
Type(s) of Educational Programs Offered On campus; Summer campus.
Profile of On Campus School Program Number of teachers 2.5; *Number of classrooms* 1; *Student to teacher ratio* 4:1.

TROUTDALE

EDGEFIELD LODGE, INC
2408 SW Halsey, Troutdale, OR 97060 (503) 665-0157, 661-4300 (Group Home) *Contact Person(s):* Buell E Goocher PhD, Admin Dir

Setting and Background Information Edgefield Lodge has three programs: day treatment, 5-day residential, and group home care. The day treatment program serves 28 boys and girls (6-11). The group home serves boys only (11-14).

Referral Information Families may contact the Lodge directly or be referred by the Children's Services Division. Residential placements must be able to return to their families for weekends and vacations.

Type of Facility
Funding Sources Private; State.
Average Length of Stay Short and long term.
Types of Admissions Accepted Day treatment; Residential treatment; Group home placement.
Sources of Referral Social service depts; Families.

Client Profile
Age Range of Clients Served Day Programs: 6-11; Residential program: 6-14.
Characteristics Exhibited by Children Emotional handicaps; Learning disabilities; Behavior disorders; Delinquency.

Tuition and Fees
Placements Primarily Funded By Social service depts.

Social and Rehabilitative Services
Therapeutic Services Offered Individual therapy; Group therapy; Family therapy.
Professionals on Staff Child care staff.

Educational and Vocational Services
Type(s) of Educational Programs Offered On campus; Off campus.
Profile of On Campus School Program Credentials of teachers Certified Spec Ed.

PENNSYLVANIA

ALLENTOWN

ALLENTOWN STATE HOSPITAL—CHILDREN'S UNIT
Allentown, PA 18103 (215) 821-6211
Setting and Background Information The hospital is JCAH accredited and Medicare certified.
Referral Information Contact the facility for referral information.
Type of Facility
Funding Sources State.
Types of Admissions Accepted Residential treatment.
Sources of Referral State depts of mental health.
Client Profile
Age Range of Clients Served Residential program: 12-18.
Characteristics Exhibited by Children Emotional handicaps.
Tuition and Fees
Placements Primarily Funded By State depts of mental health.

AMBLER

HORSHAM CLINIC
Welsh Rd and Butler Pike, Ambler, PA 19002 (215) 643-7800
Referral Information Contact the facility for referral information.
Type of Facility
Types of Admissions Accepted Residential treatment.
Sources of Referral State depts of mental health.
Client Profile
Age Range of Clients Served Residential program: 12-18.
Tuition and Fees
Placements Primarily Funded By State depts of mental health.
Social and Rehabilitative Services
Therapeutic Services Offered Individual therapy; Group therapy; Family therapy; Art therapy; Recreation activities; Psychodrama; Music therapy; Movement therapy; Occupational therapy.
Professionals on Staff Psychiatrists; Psychologists; Art therapists.
Educational and Vocational Services
Type(s) of Educational Programs Offered On campus.

BLOSSBURG

NORTHERN TIER YOUTH SERVICES
PO Box 8, Blossburg, PA 16912 (717) 638-2141 *Contact Person(s):* Mimi Bixby, Prog Dir
Setting and Background Information This facility is a division of North PA Comprehensive Health Services and was established in 1977. There are several sites throughout PA: three community-based residential treatment programs, foster care programs, and diagnostic programs.
Referral Information For referrals, contact the facility for a pre-placement application packet.
Type of Facility
Funding Sources State.
Average Length of Stay Short and long term.
Types of Admissions Accepted Residential treatment; Wards of the state.
Sources of Referral Depts of correction; Social service depts.

Client Profile
Age Range of Clients Served Day programs: 12-18; Residential program: 12-18.
Characteristics Exhibited by Children Emotional handicaps; Learning disabilities; Neurological impairments; Mental disabilities.
IQ Range of Clients 80-120.
Tuition and Fees
Room and Board Short term: $92.40/diem; Long term: $92.40/diem; 30 day diagnostic $113.40/diem.
Placements Primarily Funded By Depts of corrections; Social service depts.
Social and Rehabilitative Services
Therapeutic Approach The facility uses reality therapy as its basic therapeutic approach.
Therapeutic Services Offered Individual therapy; Group therapy; Family therapy; Adjunctive therapy; Independent living skills program; Recreation activities; Substance abuse treatment.
Professionals on Staff Psychiatrists; Psychologists; Social workers; Adjunctive therapists; Child care staff; Nurses.
Educational and Vocational Services
Type(s) of Educational Programs Offered On campus; Off campus (Public school); Summer campus (Vocational).
Profile of On Campus School Program Number of teachers 8; *Number of classrooms* 2; *Student to teacher ratio* 5:1; *Credentials of teachers* Spec Ed; *Grades taught* Individualized instruction; Special curriculum electives offered (Vocational experiences); Remedial courses offered.
Vocational Education Programs/Degrees Offered Building maintenance; Trades; Woodworking; Food service.
Degrees Offered 12th grade diploma; GED.

BRIDGEVILLE

MAYVIEW STATE HOSPITAL
1601 Mayview Rd, Bridgeville, PA 15017-1599 (412) 343-2700
Setting and Background Information The facility has a comprehensive treatment program for severely emotionally disturbed children and adolescents. The facility has JCAH accreditation and Medicare certification.
Referral Information Contact the facility for referral information.
Type of Facility
Types of Admissions Accepted Residential treatment.
Client Profile
Age Range of Clients Served Residential program: 6-18.
Characteristics Exhibited by Children Emotional handicaps.
Tuition and Fees
Placements Primarily Funded By State depts of mental health.
Social and Rehabilitative Services
Therapeutic Services Offered Individual therapy; Group therapy; Family therapy; Adjunctive therapy; Independent living skills program; Recreation activities; Substance abuse treatment; Aftercare program with follow up.
Professionals on Staff Psychiatrists; Psychologists; Social workers; Adjunctive therapists; Child care staff; Nurses.
Educational and Vocational Services
Type(s) of Educational Programs Offered On campus.

CHAMBERSBURG

CHILDREN'S AID SOCIETY OF FRANKLIN COUNTY
PO Box 353, 255 Miller St, Chambersburg, PA 17201
(717) 263-4150
Referral Information Contact the facility for referral information.
Type of Facility
Types of Admissions Accepted Residential treatment.
Sources of Referral Social service depts.
Client Profile
Age Range of Clients Served Residential program: 12-18.
Tuition and Fees
Placements Primarily Funded By Social service depts.
Social and Rehabilitative Services
Therapeutic Services Offered Individual therapy; Group therapy;
    Family therapy.

CLARKS SUMMIT

LOURDSMONT—GOOD SHEPHERD ADOLESCENT SERVICES
537 Venard Rd, Clarks Summit, PA 18411 (717) 587-4741
Referral Information Contact the facility for referral information.
    The facility accepts girls only.
Type of Facility
Types of Admissions Accepted Residential treatment.
Sources of Referral Social service depts.
Client Profile
Age Range of Clients Served Residential program: 12-18.
Tuition and Fees
Placements Primarily Funded By Social service depts.
Social and Rehabilitative Services
Therapeutic Services Offered Individual therapy; Group therapy;
    Family therapy; Art therapy; Recreation activities; Substance
    abuse treatment; Play therapy; Music therapy.
Professionals on Staff Psychiatrists; Social workers; Child care staff;
    Art therapists.
Educational and Vocational Services
Type(s) of Educational Programs Offered On campus (Spec Ed).

CONCORDVILLE

THE GLEN MILLS SCHOOLS
Concordville, PA 19331 (215) 459-8100, 1-800-441-2064,4334
Contact Person(s): Bernard J Kreig, Dir of Admis
Setting and Background Information This school was established in
    1826 by Quaker philanthropists. It is currently located on 800
    acres and has 26 buildings.
Referral Information For referrals, contact the admissions dept and
    forward social history, arrest history, and psychological and
    educational reports. The facility will respond within 24 hours.
Type of Facility
Funding Sources State; Federal.
Average Length of Stay 1 yr.
Types of Admissions Accepted Residential treatment.
Sources of Referral Social service depts; Juvenile courts.
Client Profile
Age Range of Clients Served Residential program: 15-18.
Characteristics Exhibited by Children Delinquency.
IQ Range of Clients 70+.
Tuition and Fees
Room and Board Long term: $73.50/diem.
Placements Primarily Funded By Social service depts; Juvenile
    courts.
Social and Rehabilitative Services
Therapeutic Approach The facility uses a sociological model as its
    approach to therapy, including peer pressure and confrontation.
Therapeutic Services Offered Individual therapy; Group therapy; In-
    dependent living skills program; Recreation activities; Aftercare
    program with follow up.
Professionals on Staff Psychologists; Child care staff; Nurses.
Educational and Vocational Services
Type(s) of Educational Programs Offered On campus; Off campus;
    Summer campus.
Profile of On Campus School Program Number of teachers 50;
    Number of classrooms 25; *Student to teacher ratio* 10:1; *Grades
    taught* 1-12.

Vocational Education Programs/Degrees Offered 20 areas of study.
Degrees Offered GED.

CONNELLSVILLE

ANCHOR HOUSE YOUTH SERVICES
201 E Fairview Ave, Connellsville, PA 15425 (412) 628-4386,
626-1120
Referral Information Referrals to the facility are made through the
    Office of Children, Youth and Families. For information contact
    the facility.
Type of Facility
Types of Admissions Accepted Residential treatment.
Sources of Referral Office of Children, Youth and Families.
Client Profile
Age Range of Clients Served Residential program: 12-18.
Social and Rehabilitative Services
Therapeutic Services Offered Individual therapy; Group therapy;
    Family therapy; Independent living skills program; Recreation
    activities.
Professionals on Staff Psychiatrists; Psychologists.

NEW DIRECTIONS, INC
201 E Fairview Ave, Connellsville, PA 15425 (412) 628-3041
Referral Information Referrals to the facility are made through the
    Office of Children, Youth and Families. Contact the facility for
    information.
Type of Facility
Types of Admissions Accepted Group home placement.
Sources of Referral Office of Children; Youth and Families.
Client Profile
Age Range of Clients Served Residential program: 12-18.
Social and Rehabilitative Services
Therapeutic Services Offered Group therapy.
Professionals on Staff Psychologists.

DEVON

THE DEVEREUX FOUNDATION
PO Box 400, 19 S Waterloo Rd, Devon, PA 19333 (215) 964-3000
Contact Person(s): Ellwood M Smith, Admis Dir
Referral Information Contact the facility for referral information.
Type of Facility
Types of Admissions Accepted Residential treatment; Crisis interven-
    tion.
Client Profile
Age Range of Clients Served Residential program: 5-18.
Characteristics Exhibited by Children Emotional handicaps; Learning
    disabilities; Mental disabilities.
Social and Rehabilitative Services
Therapeutic Services Offered Individual therapy; Group therapy;
    Family therapy; Art therapy; Physical therapy; Recreation activi-
    ties.
Professionals on Staff Psychiatrists; Psychologists; Art therapists;
    Physical therapists.
Educational and Vocational Services
Type(s) of Educational Programs Offered On campus.
Profile of On Campus School Program Grades taught K-12.
Vocational Education Programs/Degrees Offered Vocational assess-
    ment.

ELWYN

ELWYN INSTITUTE
111 Elwyn Rd, Elwyn, PA 19063 (215) 358-6400 *Contact Person(s):*
Agnes Bauer, Dir Acad Affairs
Setting and Background Information The facility is accredited by the
    Commission on Accreditation of Rehabilitative Facilities.
Referral Information Contact the facility for referral information.
Type of Facility
Types of Admissions Accepted Residential treatment.
Sources of Referral Social service depts.
Client Profile
Age Range of Clients Served Residential program: Birth-18.
Characteristics Exhibited by Children Emotional handicaps; Learning
    disabilities; Mental disabilities.

ELWYN INSTITUTE *(continued)*

Tuition and Fees
Placements Primarily Funded By Social service depts.
Social and Rehabilitative Services
Therapeutic Services Offered Individual therapy; Group therapy; Recreation activities.
Professionals on Staff Psychiatrists.
Educational and Vocational Services
Type(s) of Educational Programs Offered On campus.
Vocational Education Programs/Degrees Offered Vocational program.

ERIE

SARAH A REED CHILDREN'S CENTER
2445 W 34th St, Erie, PA 16506 (814) 838-1954
Referral Information Contact the facility for information.
Type of Facility
Types of Admissions Accepted Residential treatment.
Sources of Referral Office of Children, Youth and Families.
Client Profile
Age Range of Clients Served Residential program: 6-18.
Social and Rehabilitative Services
Therapeutic Services Offered Individual therapy; Group therapy; Family therapy; Independent living skills program; Recreation activities.
Professionals on Staff Psychiatrists.
Educational and Vocational Services
Type(s) of Educational Programs Offered On campus (Spec Ed).

FORT WASHINGTON

WORDSWORTH ACADEMY
Pennsylvania Ave & Camphill RD, Fort Washington, PA 19034
(215) 643-5400 *Contact Person(s):* Dr Bernard Cooper, Dir; Michael Curcio, Educ Dir
Referral Information For referral information contact the facility.
Type of Facility
Types of Admissions Accepted Residential treatment.
Client Profile
Age Range of Clients Served Residential program: 5-21.
Characteristics Exhibited by Children Emotional handicaps; Learning disabilities.
Social and Rehabilitative Services
Therapeutic Services Offered Individual therapy; Group therapy; Family therapy; Adjunctive therapy; Art therapy; Physical therapy; Recreation activities.
Professionals on Staff Psychiatrists; Psychologists; Adjunctive therapists; Art therapists; Physical therapists; Speech therapist.
Educational and Vocational Services
Type(s) of Educational Programs Offered On campus.
Vocational Education Programs/Degrees Offered Vocational assessment and education.

GLENMORE

CAMPHILL SPECIAL SCHOOLS, INC
Glenmore, PA (215) 469-9236 *Contact Person(s):* Ursel Pietzner, Exec Dir
Referral Information Contact the facility for referral information.
Type of Facility
Types of Admissions Accepted Residential treatment.
Client Profile
Age Range of Clients Served Residential program: 6-20.
Characteristics Exhibited by Children Emotional handicaps; Neurological impairments; Mental disabilities.
Social and Rehabilitative Services
Therapeutic Services Offered Individual therapy; Family therapy; Art therapy; Independent living skills program; Recreation activities.
Professionals on Staff Psychiatrists; Psychologists; Adjunctive therapists; Art therapists; Physical therapists; Speech therapist.
Educational and Vocational Services
Type(s) of Educational Programs Offered On campus (Pre-vocational education).

HARBOR CREEK

HARBOR CREEK SCHOOL FOR BOYS
5712 Iroquois Ave, Harbor Creek, PA 16421 (814) 899-7664
Referral Information Contact the facility for referral information.
Type of Facility
Types of Admissions Accepted Residential treatment.
Client Profile
Age Range of Clients Served Residential program: 10-18.
Social and Rehabilitative Services
Therapeutic Services Offered Individual therapy; Group therapy; Family therapy; Recreation activities; Occupational therapy.
Professionals on Staff Psychologists.
Educational and Vocational Services
Type(s) of Educational Programs Offered On campus.

JEFFERSONVILLE

THE PATHWAY SCHOOL
162 Egypt Rd, Jeffersonville, PA 19403 (215) 277-0660 *Contact Person(s):* Charlotte Prettyman, Adm Dir
Setting and Background Information The Pathway School is a private residential and day treatment facility which was established in 1961 on 13 acres adjacent to Valley Forge National Park. Its campus consists of an administration building, 4 educational buildings, and 5 residential cottages (16 residents in each).
Referral Information Referrals can be made by school districts, consultants, agencies, families, and private individuals. All applicants must forward the necessary background information for the screening process. If the placement seems appropriate, then an on-campus diagnostic evaluation will be performed before a final placement decision is made.
Type of Facility
Funding Sources Private; State.
Average Length of Stay Long term.
Types of Admissions Accepted Day treatment; Residential treatment.
Sources of Referral State depts of education; Local depts of education; Psychiatrists; Private sources; Social service depts.
Client Profile
Age Range of Clients Served Day programs: 6-18; Residential program: 6-18.
Characteristics Exhibited by Children Emotional handicaps; Learning disabilities.
IQ Range of Clients 70+.
Tuition and Fees
Room and Board Long term: $34,000/yr; $10,500/yr (Day treatment).
Placements Primarily Funded By Private sources.
Social and Rehabilitative Services
Therapeutic Approach The basic therapeutic approach of the facility is milieu therapy.
Therapeutic Services Offered Individual therapy; Group therapy; Family therapy; Art therapy; Aftercare program with follow up; Music therapy.
Professionals on Staff Psychiatrists; Psychologists; Social workers; Child care staff; Nurses.
Educational and Vocational Services
Type(s) of Educational Programs Offered On campus; Summer campus.
Profile of On Campus School Program Number of teachers 20; *Number of classrooms* 15; *Student to teacher ratio* 12:1; Remedial courses offered.
Degrees Offered 12th grade diploma.

JOHNSTOWN

ALOYSIA HALL—MERCY HOSPITAL OF JOHNSTOWN
1020 Franklin St, Johnstown, PA 15905 (814) 536-4461
Referral Information Contact the facility for referral information.
Type of Facility
Types of Admissions Accepted Residential treatment.
Sources of Referral Dept of Health.
Client Profile
Age Range of Clients Served Residential program: 6-18.

ALOYSIA HALL—MERCY HOSPITAL OF JOHNSTOWN *(continued)*

Tuition and Fees
Placements Primarily Funded By Social service depts.
Social and Rehabilitative Services
Therapeutic Services Offered Individual therapy; Group therapy; Art therapy; Recreation activities; Play therapy; Music therapy.

LAFAYETTE HILL

EUGENIA HOSPITAL
660 Thomas Rd, Lafayette Hill, PA 19444 (215) 836-1380 ext 446, 447
Referral Information Contact the facility for referral information.
Type of Facility
Types of Admissions Accepted Residential treatment.
Sources of Referral State depts of mental health.
Client Profile
Age Range of Clients Served Residential program: 12-18.
Tuition and Fees
Placements Primarily Funded By State depts of mental health.
Social and Rehabilitative Services
Therapeutic Services Offered Individual therapy; Group therapy; Family therapy; Art therapy; Physical therapy; Recreation activities; Occupational therapy.
Professionals on Staff Psychiatrists; Psychologists; Art therapists.

LANGHORNE

THE WOODS SCHOOLS
1 Winch St, Langhorne, PA 19047 (215) 750-4000 *Contact Person(s):* Laurie A Lemott, Admis Dir
Setting and Background Information The facility was established in 1913, 20 miles north of Philadelphia, and is licensed by the Pennsylvania Dept of Education, Dept of Public Welfare, and US Dept of Labor. The campus consists of 300 wooded acres with 2 lakes, hiking and riding trails. There are more than 70 buildings on the grounds, including the Child Study Research and Treatment Center, Gardner Education Center, Holland Vocational Training Center, Shannon Medical Pavilion, auditorium, gymnasium, and 22 residences. There are 3 residences specially designated for multi-handicapped persons and a special residential program designed for head-injury persons.
Referral Information Anyone can make a referral by contacting the Registrar and forwarding all neurological, medical, psychiatric, and educational reports. If the Admission Committee agrees that the applicant could benefit from the placement, then he or she will be evaluated by staff. Following the evaluation, an admission decision will be made.
Type of Facility
Funding Sources Private; State.
Average Length of Stay Long term.
Types of Admissions Accepted Day treatment; Residential treatment.
Sources of Referral State depts of education; Local depts of education; Social service depts.
Client Profile
Age Range of Clients Served Day programs: 6-76; Residential program: 6-76.
Characteristics Exhibited by Children Emotional handicaps; Learning disabilities; Hearing impairments/deafness; Speech/Language disorders; Neurological impairments; Physical handicaps; Mental disabilities; Head injuries.
Tuition and Fees
Placements Primarily Funded By State depts of education; Local depts of education; Social service depts.
Social and Rehabilitative Services
Therapeutic Approach The philosophy of the treatment program is based on the therapeutic milieu concept.
Therapeutic Services Offered Individual therapy; Group therapy; Adjunctive therapy; Art therapy; Physical therapy; Independent living skills program; Recreation activities; Occupational therapy.
Professionals on Staff Psychiatrists; Psychologists; Social workers; Adjunctive therapists; Nurses; Art therapists; Physical therapists.
Educational and Vocational Services
Type(s) of Educational Programs Offered On campus; Summer campus.

LIMA

SLEIGHTON SCHOOL
Forge and Valley Rds, Lima, PA 19037 (215) 459-8000 *Contact Person(s):* Gloria Levister
Setting and Background Information Sleighton School is a residential treatment facility for court ordered placements. The facility was established in 1828 by the Quakers. Its campus is located 20 miles west of Philadelphia and consists of 6 residential cottages (20 residents in each), gymnasium, vocational center, school, greenhouse, and chapel.
Referral Information Referrals are only accepted from the courts.
Type of Facility
Funding Sources State.
Average Length of Stay Long term.
Types of Admissions Accepted Residential treatment.
Sources of Referral Depts of correction.
Client Profile
Age Range of Clients Served Residential program: 12-18.
Characteristics Exhibited by Children Emotional handicaps; Learning disabilities.
Tuition and Fees
Placements Primarily Funded By Depts of corrections.
Social and Rehabilitative Services
Therapeutic Services Offered Individual therapy; Group therapy; Family therapy; Art therapy; Substance abuse treatment.
Professionals on Staff Psychiatrists; Psychologists; Social workers; Child care staff; Nurses; Art therapists.
Educational and Vocational Services
Type(s) of Educational Programs Offered On campus; Summer campus.
Vocational Education Programs/Degrees Offered Carpentry; Home improvement; Auto repair; Restaurant work; Greenhouse; Landscaping; Tailoring; Silk screening; Job placement.
Degrees Offered 12th grade diploma; GED.

MALVERN

THE DEVEREUX CENTER—MAPLETON
Sugartown Rd, Malvern, PA 19355 (215) 964-3000
Referral Information Contact the facility for referral information.
Type of Facility
Types of Admissions Accepted Residential treatment.
Sources of Referral State depts of education; State depts of mental health.
Client Profile
Age Range of Clients Served Residential program: 13-20.
Tuition and Fees
Placements Primarily Funded By State depts of education; State depts of mental health.
Social and Rehabilitative Services
Therapeutic Services Offered Individual therapy; Group therapy; Recreation activities.
Educational and Vocational Services
Type(s) of Educational Programs Offered On campus (Spec Ed).

MEADVILLE

BETHESDA YOUTH SERVICES
RD 9 Box 84, Meadville, PA 16335 (814) 724-7510
Referral Information Contact the facility for information.
Type of Facility
Types of Admissions Accepted Residential treatment.
Sources of Referral Office of Children, Youth and Families.
Client Profile
Age Range of Clients Served Residential program: 12-18.
Social and Rehabilitative Services
Therapeutic Services Offered Individual therapy; Group therapy; Family therapy.
Professionals on Staff Psychiatrists; Psychologists; Child care staff.

PHILADELPHIA

HAHNEMAN MEDICAL COLLEGE AND HOSPITAL
16th Flr, South Tower, 230 N Broad St, Philadelphia, PA 19102 (215) 448-4800
Referral Information Contact the facility for referral information.

HAHNEMAN MEDICAL COLLEGE AND HOSPITAL
(continued)

Type of Facility
Types of Admissions Accepted Residential treatment.
Sources of Referral State depts of mental health.
Client Profile
Age Range of Clients Served Residential program: 6-18.
Tuition and Fees
Placements Primarily Funded By State depts of mental health.
Social and Rehabilitative Services
Therapeutic Services Offered Individual therapy; Group therapy; Family therapy; Recreation activities; Crisis intervention; Diagnostic evaluations; Play therapy.
Educational and Vocational Services
Type(s) of Educational Programs Offered On campus.

SOUTHERN HOME SERVICES
3200 S Broad St, Philadelphia, PA 19145 (215) 334-4319 *Contact Person(s):* Inez Bruce, Dir of Intake
Setting and Background Information Southern Home Services is a residential treatment facility. It was initially established as an orphanage in 1849, but expanded its programs to become a treatment center in 1954. The campus is located in a residential area and consists of 2 living units, cafeteria, gymnasium, pool, activity rooms, and offices.
Referral Information Any funding agency can make a referral by forwarding the necessary background information and scheduling a pre-placement interview with facility staff, child, and family.
Type of Facility
Funding Sources Private.
Average Length of Stay Long term.
Types of Admissions Accepted Day treatment; Residential treatment.
Sources of Referral Psychiatrists; Social service depts.
Client Profile
Age Range of Clients Served Day programs: 13-17; Residential program: 13-17.
Characteristics Exhibited by Children Emotional handicaps; Learning disabilities; Hearing impairments/deafness; Vision impairments/blindness; Speech/Language disorders; Neurological impairments; Mental disabilities.
Tuition and Fees
Placements Primarily Funded By Private sources; Social service depts.
Social and Rehabilitative Services
Therapeutic Approach The facility has an eclectic approach to therapy.
Therapeutic Services Offered Individual therapy; Group therapy; Family therapy; Art therapy; Physical therapy; Independent living skills program; Recreation activities; Substance abuse treatment; Aftercare program with follow up.
Professionals on Staff Psychiatrists; Psychologists; Social workers; Child care staff; Nurses; Art therapists; Physical therapists.
Educational and Vocational Services
Type(s) of Educational Programs Offered Off campus.

PLYMOUTH MEETING

THE LUTHERAN HOME IN GERMANTOWN
Township Line Rd, Plymouth Meeting, PA 19462 (215) 825-4440
Referral Information Contact the facility for referral information.
Type of Facility
Types of Admissions Accepted Residential treatment; Foster care.
Sources of Referral Office of Children, Youth and Families.
Client Profile
Age Range of Clients Served Residential program: 6-18.
Tuition and Fees
Placements Primarily Funded By State depts of mental health.
Social and Rehabilitative Services
Therapeutic Services Offered Individual therapy; Group therapy; Family therapy; Recreation activities.
Professionals on Staff Psychiatrists.
Educational and Vocational Services
Type(s) of Educational Programs Offered On campus (Spec Ed).

SILVER SPRINGS
Township Line Rd, Plymouth Meeting, PA 19462 (215) 825-4440
Contact Person(s): John McCall, Soc Srvc Dir
Setting and Background Information Silver Springs is a residential treatment facility. It also offers specialized foster family care and services to children in their own homes. The facility was established in 1859 by a group of concerned Lutheran Church women. Its campus consists of 4 residential units with 18 children each, a center core for offices, and a 2-story school building.
Referral Information Referrals can be made by county offices for the Dept of Children, Youth and Families and by parents. Applicants are requested to forward a recent psychiatric evaluation, psychologicals performed by a certified school psychologist, social history, medical history, educational reports, and neurological reports.
Type of Facility
Funding Sources State.
Average Length of Stay Long term.
Types of Admissions Accepted Residential treatment; Foster care.
Sources of Referral Social service depts; Dept of Children, Youth and Families.
Client Profile
Age Range of Clients Served Residential program: 6-14.
Characteristics Exhibited by Children Emotional handicaps; Learning disabilities.
Tuition and Fees
Placements Primarily Funded By Social service depts.
Social and Rehabilitative Services
Therapeutic Approach The primary therapeutic approach used is based on a structured behavior management system.
Therapeutic Services Offered Individual therapy; Group therapy; Family therapy; Recreation activities.
Professionals on Staff Psychiatrists; Psychologists; Social workers; Child care staff; Nurses.
Educational and Vocational Services
Type(s) of Educational Programs Offered On campus; Off campus; Summer campus.
Profile of On Campus School Program Number of teachers 9; *Number of classrooms* 9; *Student to teacher ratio* 12:1; Remedial courses offered.

SCRANTON

FRIENDSHIP HOUSE CHILDREN'S CENTER
1020 Derby Ave, Scranton, PA 18505 (717) 342-8305
Referral Information Contact the facility for referral information.
Type of Facility
Types of Admissions Accepted Residential treatment.
Sources of Referral Social service depts.
Client Profile
Age Range of Clients Served Residential program: 6-18.
Tuition and Fees
Placements Primarily Funded By Social service depts.
Social and Rehabilitative Services
Therapeutic Services Offered Individual therapy; Group therapy; Family therapy; Art therapy; Recreation activities; Diagnostic Evaluations; Music therapy.
Professionals on Staff Psychiatrists; Social workers; Child care staff.

TREVOSE

EASTERN STATE SCHOOL AND HOSPITAL
3740 Lincoln Hwy, Trevose, PA 19047 (215) 671-4000
Setting and Background Information The facility is JCAH accredited and Medicare certified.
Referral Information Contact the facility for referral information.
Type of Facility
Types of Admissions Accepted Residential treatment.
Sources of Referral State depts of mental health.
Client Profile
Age Range of Clients Served Residential program: 6-18.
Characteristics Exhibited by Children Emotional handicaps; Hearing impairments/deafness.
Tuition and Fees
Placements Primarily Funded By State depts of mental health.
Educational and Vocational Services
Type(s) of Educational Programs Offered On campus.

WAYNESBURG

TRY-AGAIN HOMES, INC
32 Church St, Waynesburg, PA 15370 (412) 852-2227, 852-2228
Referral Information Referrals to the facility are made through the Office of Children, Youth and Families. Contact the facility for information.
Type of Facility
Types of Admissions Accepted Residential treatment.
Sources of Referral Office of Children; Youth and Families.
Client Profile
Age Range of Clients Served Residential program: 12-18.
Social and Rehabilitative Services
Therapeutic Services Offered Individual therapy; Group therapy; Family therapy.
Professionals on Staff Psychologists.

RHODE ISLAND

CHEPACHET

HARMONY HILL SCHOOL, INC
Absalona Hill Rd, RR1 Box 90, Chepachet, RI 02814
(401) 949-0690 *Contact Person(s):* Kristen Dexter
Setting and Background Information Harmony Hill School is a non-profit residential and day treatment facility. The campus is located 12 miles west of Providence on 40 acres of land. It consists of 3 separate residential units, school building, administration building, and several buildings housing an arts and crafts shop, music room, and recreation room. There is a large lake on the grounds and 150 acres of fields and woodlands in the surrounding area.
Referral Information For referral information contact the facility.
Type of Facility
Funding Sources Private; State.
Average Length of Stay Long term.
Types of Admissions Accepted Day treatment; Residential treatment.
Sources of Referral State depts of education; Local depts of education.
Client Profile
Age Range of Clients Served Day programs: 8-16; Residential program: 8-16.
Characteristics Exhibited by Children Emotional handicaps; Learning disabilities.
Tuition and Fees
Room and Board Long term: $42,844/yr; $25,730/yr (Day treatment).
Placements Primarily Funded By State depts of education; Local depts of education; State depts of mental health.
Social and Rehabilitative Services
Therapeutic Approach The facility has an eclectic approach to therapy.
Therapeutic Services Offered Individual therapy; Group therapy; Family therapy; Recreation activities.
Professionals on Staff Psychiatrists; Psychologists; Social workers; Child care staff; Nurses.
Educational and Vocational Services
Type(s) of Educational Programs Offered On campus; Off campus.
Profile of On Campus School Program Number of teachers 6.

CRANSTON

SOPHIA LITTLE HOME
135 Norwood Ave, Cranston, RI 02905 (401) 467-2410 *Contact Person(s):* Kathi M Crowe
Referral Information Referrals to the facility are made through the Rhode Island Dept for Children and Their Families. The facility accepts girls only.
Type of Facility
Average Length of Stay Long term.
Types of Admissions Accepted Residential treatment.
Sources of Referral Depts of correction.
Client Profile
Age Range of Clients Served Residential program: 13-18.
Characteristics Exhibited by Children Emotional handicaps.
Tuition and Fees
Placements Primarily Funded By Social service depts.
Social and Rehabilitative Services
Therapeutic Services Offered Individual therapy.

Educational and Vocational Services
Type(s) of Educational Programs Offered On campus.
Profile of On Campus School Program Special curriculum electives offered; Remedial courses offered.

RCA EVALUATION AND TREATMENT CENTER
735 New London Ave, Cranston, RI 02920 (401) 946-2020 *Contact Person(s):* James E Patrick
Referral Information Contact the facility for referral information.
Type of Facility
Funding Sources Private.
Types of Admissions Accepted Residential treatment.
Client Profile
Age Range of Clients Served Residential program: 13-18.
Characteristics Exhibited by Children Emotional handicaps; Behavior disorders; Delinquency.
Social and Rehabilitative Services
Therapeutic Services Offered Art therapy; Recreation activities.
Professionals on Staff Social workers; Art therapists; Physical therapists.
Educational and Vocational Services
Type(s) of Educational Programs Offered On campus.
Profile of On Campus School Program Number of teachers 3; *Credentials of teachers* Certified Spec Ed; Remedial courses offered (Math, Science, Social studies, Reading, Writing).
Vocational Education Programs/Degrees Offered Vocational evaluation and training.

EAST PROVIDENCE

BRADLEY HOSPITAL
1011 Veterans Memorial Pkwy, East Providence, RI 02915
(401) 434-3400 *Contact Person(s):* Joyce Selley, Intake Coord, ext 182
Setting and Background Information The hospital was established in 1931 as one of the nation's first psychiatric treatment centers for emotionally disturbed children. The facility provides psychiatric hospitalization with outpatient and day treatment services. Its campus is located 6 miles from downtown Providence on 37 acres and consists of 5 major buildings, outdoor swimming pool, tennis court, ball fields, tree houses, and special playing areas.
Referral Information Referrals are received from any source. To make a referral, contact the Intake Coordinator and provide the necessary referral information. If the case is accepted by the Intake Screenings Committee, then it is assigned to an evaluator and consulting psychiatrists, who will begin the process of evaluation. Emergency referrals are also accepted.
Type of Facility
Funding Sources Private.
Average Length of Stay Short term.
Types of Admissions Accepted Day treatment; Residential treatment.
Sources of Referral State depts of education; Local depts of education; State depts of mental health; Psychiatrists.
Client Profile
Age Range of Clients Served Day programs: 4-18; Residential program: 4-18.
Characteristics Exhibited by Children Emotional handicaps; Learning disabilities; Hearing impairments/deafness; Vision impairments/blindness; Speech/Language disorders; Neurological impairments; Physical handicaps; Mental disabilities.

BRADLEY HOSPITAL *(continued)*

Tuition and Fees
Room and Board Short term: $603/diem.
Placements Primarily Funded By Insurance; Private sources.
Social and Rehabilitative Services
Therapeutic Approach The treatment program uses a broad range of therapeutic approaches.
Therapeutic Services Offered Individual therapy; Group therapy; Family therapy; Adjunctive therapy; Independent living skills program; Recreation activities; Aftercare program with follow up.
Professionals on Staff Psychiatrists; Psychologists; Social workers; Adjunctive therapists; Child care staff; Nurses.
Educational and Vocational Services
Type(s) of Educational Programs Offered On campus; Summer campus.

GREENVILLE

ST ALOYSIUS HOME

40 Austin Ave, Greenville, RI 02828 (401) 949-1300 *Contact Person(s):* Frederick V Whiteside
Setting and Background Information The facility was established in 1852. It is located in northwest Rhode Island on 120 acres of land, in a suburban setting. There is one main building with a separate school building on campus.
Referral Information Each child must be screened and referred by the Dept of Children and Their Families.
Type of Facility
Funding Sources State.
Average Length of Stay Short and long term.
Types of Admissions Accepted Residential treatment; Emergency shelter.
Sources of Referral State depts of mental health.
Client Profile
Age Range of Clients Served Residential program: 6-14.
Characteristics Exhibited by Children Emotional handicaps; Learning disabilities.
Tuition and Fees
Room and Board Long term: $22,000-24,000/yr.
Placements Primarily Funded By State depts of mental health.
Social and Rehabilitative Services
Therapeutic Services Offered Individual therapy; Group therapy; Family therapy; Recreation activities; Aftercare program with follow up.
Professionals on Staff Psychiatrists; Psychologists; Social workers; Child care staff; Nurses.
Educational and Vocational Services
Type(s) of Educational Programs Offered On campus; Summer campus.
Profile of On Campus School Program Number of teachers 17.

NORTH PROVIDENCE

ST MARY'S CAMPUS SCHOOL

420 Fruit Hill Ave, North Providence, RI 02911 (401) 353-3900
Contact Person(s): Paul F Adams
Referral Information Contact the facility for referral information. The facility accepts girls only.
Type of Facility
Funding Sources Private.
Types of Admissions Accepted Day treatment; Residential treatment.
Sources of Referral Local depts of education.
Client Profile
Age Range of Clients Served Day programs: 9-15; Residential program: 9-15.
Characteristics Exhibited by Children Emotional handicaps; Behavior disorders.
Tuition and Fees
Placements Primarily Funded By Local depts of education.
Social and Rehabilitative Services
Therapeutic Services Offered Individual therapy.
Educational and Vocational Services
Type(s) of Educational Programs Offered On campus.

SPURWINK SCHOOL II

PO Box 3813, 622 Wooasquatucket Ave, North Providence, RI 02911 (401) 231-0330 *Contact Person(s):* Raymond A Arsenault
Referral Information Referrals to the school are made through the Rhode Island Dept for Children and Their Families.
Type of Facility
Funding Sources Private.
Average Length of Stay 6-8 mos.
Types of Admissions Accepted Day treatment.
Sources of Referral Social service depts.
Client Profile
Age Range of Clients Served Day programs: 6-15; Residential program: 6-15.
Characteristics Exhibited by Children Emotional handicaps; Behavior disorders.
Tuition and Fees
Placements Primarily Funded By Local depts of education.
Social and Rehabilitative Services
Therapeutic Approach The treatment program of the facility uses psycho-dynamic and psycho-educational therapeutic approaches.
Educational and Vocational Services
Type(s) of Educational Programs Offered On campus.

PROVIDENCE

BEHAVIOR RESEARCH INSTITUTE, INC

240 Laban St, Providence, RI 02909 (401) 944-1186 *Contact Person(s):* Marilyn Dunscomb; Jim Hayes
Setting and Background Information The Behavior Research Institute is a private residential and day school treatment facility and is licensed by the Rhode Island Dept of Mental Health, Retardation, and Hospitals and the Dept of Education. Small groups of residents live in homes located in suburban and semi-rural areas of Seekonk, Attleboro, and Rehoboth, Massachusetts. Students are transported to and from the Behavior Research Institute School each day.
Referral Information Referrals can be made by school systems, Dept of Mental Health, Dept of Social Services, and parents. All referrals are directed to contact Marilyn Dunscomb.
Type of Facility
Funding Sources Private; State.
Average Length of Stay Short and long term.
Types of Admissions Accepted Day treatment; Residential treatment.
Sources of Referral State depts of education; Local depts of education; State depts of mental health.
Client Profile
Age Range of Clients Served Day programs; 3-55+; Residential program: 3-55+.
Characteristics Exhibited by Children Emotional handicaps; Learning disabilities; Hearing impairments/deafness; Speech/Language disorders; Neurological impairments; Mental disabilities.
IQ Range of Clients 0-89.
Tuition and Fees
Room and Board Long term: $143,153/yr.
Placements Primarily Funded By State depts of education; Local depts of education; State depts of mental health.
Social and Rehabilitative Services
Therapeutic Approach The basic therapeutic approach used at the facility is behavior modification.
Professionals on Staff Psychiatrists; Psychologists; Social workers; Nurses.
Educational and Vocational Services
Type(s) of Educational Programs Offered On campus.
Profile of On Campus School Program Number of teachers 19.

BEHAVIORAL DEVELOPMENT CENTER, INC

86 Mount Hope Ave, Providence, RI 02906 (401) 274-6310 *Contact Person(s):* June Groden, PhD; Gerald Groden, PhD
Setting and Background Information The Behavioral Development Center is a non-profit day and residential agency which provides therapeutic placements.
Referral Information Contact the facility for referral information.
Type of Facility
Funding Sources Private; .
Types of Admissions Accepted Day treatment; Residential treatment.

BEHAVIORAL DEVELOPMENT CENTER, INC
(continued)

Client Profile
Age Range of Clients Served Day programs: 6-18; Residential program: 6-18.
Characteristics Exhibited by Children Autism; Behavior disorders.
Social and Rehabilitative Services
Therapeutic Services Offered Individual therapy.

SOUTH CAROLINA

BEAUFORT

COMMUNITY-BASED CHILDREN'S SERVICES

PO Box 2171, Beaufort, SC 29901 (803) 525-1158 *Contact Person(s):* Larry D Perry, Exec Dir

Setting and Background Information The facility was established in 1984 with grant monies from the state Dept of Mental Health.

Referral Information Contact the facility for referral information.

Type of Facility

Funding Sources State.

Average Length of Stay Long term.

Types of Admissions Accepted Day treatment; Group home placement.

Sources of Referral Local depts of education; State depts of mental health; Depts of correction; Social service depts.

Client Profile

Age Range of Clients Served Day programs: 12-15; Residential program: 6-18.

Characteristics Exhibited by Children Emotional handicaps; Learning disabilities.

Tuition and Fees

Placements Primarily Funded By State depts of mental health.

Social and Rehabilitative Services

Therapeutic Services Offered Individual therapy; Group therapy; Family therapy.

Professionals on Staff Psychologists; Social workers; Child care staff.

CHARLESTON

SOUTHERN PINES

2777 Speissegger Dr, Charleston, SC 29405 (803) 747-5830 *Contact Person(s):* Flo Sanders

Setting and Background Information The facility was established in 1982, as an affiliate of the Brown Schools of Texas. It is owned by Healthcare International of Austin, Texas. The campus is located on the Ashley River and consists of 7 residential units, administrative building, cafeteria, gymnasium, and school facilities.

Referral Information Referrals can be made by hospitals, state agencies, school districts, physicians, clergy, patients, and their families. To make a referral, contact the facility at any time.

Type of Facility

Funding Sources Private.

Average Length of Stay Short term.

Types of Admissions Accepted Day treatment; Residential treatment.

Sources of Referral State depts of mental health; Psychiatrists; Private sources; Social service depts.

Client Profile

Age Range of Clients Served Day programs: 8-18; Residential program: 5-55.

Characteristics Exhibited by Children Emotional handicaps; Learning disabilities; Speech/Language disorders; Neurological impairments; Physical handicaps; Mental disabilities.

IQ Range of Clients 40-139.

Tuition and Fees

Room and Board Short term: $2,220/wk; $850/wk (Day treatment).

Placements Primarily Funded By Insurance; Private sources.

Social and Rehabilitative Services

Therapeutic Approach The treatment program involves residents in family therapy, using a systems and structural model.

Therapeutic Services Offered Individual therapy; Group therapy; Family therapy; Adjunctive therapy; Art therapy; Independent living skills program; Recreation activities.

Professionals on Staff Psychiatrists; Psychologists; Social workers; Adjunctive therapists; Child care staff; Nurses; Art therapists; Physical therapists.

Educational and Vocational Services

Type(s) of Educational Programs Offered On campus; Summer campus.

Profile of On Campus School Program Number of teachers 6; *Number of classrooms* 6; *Student to teacher ratio* 8:1.

Degrees Offered 8th grade diploma; 12th grade diploma; GED.

COLUMBIA

ALSTON WILKES YOUTH HOME, COLUMBIA SOUTH

1103 Olympia Ave, Columbia, SC 29201 (803) 799-2406 *Contact Person(s):* Barbara Boultinghouse, Supv

Setting and Background Information This program was established in 1977 with a grant for status offenders. It is a residential treatment facility for juvenile offenders.

Referral Information Contact the facility.

Type of Facility

Funding Sources Private.

Average Length of Stay Long term.

Types of Admissions Accepted Group home placement.

Sources of Referral Dept of Youth Services.

Client Profile

Age Range of Clients Served Residential program: 6-18.

Characteristics Exhibited by Children Emotional handicaps; Delinquency.

IQ Range of Clients 70+.

Tuition and Fees

Placements Primarily Funded By Dept Youth Services.

Social and Rehabilitative Services

Therapeutic Services Offered Individual therapy; Independent living skills program.

Professionals on Staff Child care staff.

Educational and Vocational Services

Type(s) of Educational Programs Offered Off campus.

WILLIAM S HALL PSYCHIATRIC INSTITUTE

PO Box 202, Columbia, SC 29202 (803) 734-7320 *Contact Person(s):* John Morris Adm Dir

Setting and Background Information The facility was established in 1967 by state law as the research and training facility for the South Carolina Dept of Mental Health. The facility is located in the central part of the city of Columbia. Its campus consists of a large administration building, library, and 4 single-story cottages, and 2 adjoining renovated buildings.

Referral Information Referrals are made by the State Dept of Mental Health through community mental health centers. Referrals to the Adolescent Unit can be made by parents, professionals, and schools.

WILLIAM S HALL PSYCHIATRIC INSTITUTE
(continued)

Type of Facility
Funding Sources State.
Average Length of Stay Long term.
Types of Admissions Accepted Residential treatment.
Sources of Referral State depts of mental health; Psychiatrists.
Client Profile
Age Range of Clients Served Residential program: 6-17.
Characteristics Exhibited by Children Emotional handicaps; Learning disabilities.
Tuition and Fees
Placements Primarily Funded By State depts of mental health.
Social and Rehabilitative Services
Therapeutic Approach The facility has an eclectic approach to therapy.
Therapeutic Services Offered Individual therapy; Group therapy; Family therapy; Adjunctive therapy; Art therapy; Recreation activities; Aftercare program with follow up; Occupational therapy.
Professionals on Staff Psychiatrists; Psychologists; Social workers; Adjunctive therapists; Child care staff; Nurses; Art therapists.
Educational and Vocational Services
Type(s) of Educational Programs Offered On campus.
Profile of On Campus School Program Number of teachers 12; *Number of classrooms* 10; *Student to teacher ratio* 9:1; Remedial courses offered.
Degrees Offered 8th grade diploma; 12th grade diploma.

CORINE MORRIS COMMUNITY CARE HOME
429 Rockhaven Dr, Columbia, SC 29223 (803) 788-6819 *Contact Person(s):* Mo Morris, Admin
Setting and Background Information This facility was privately established in 1979 and has the capacity to serve twenty clients.
Referral Information For referral information, contact the facility.
Type of Facility
Funding Sources Private; State; Federal.
Average Length of Stay Short and long term.
Types of Admissions Accepted Residential treatment; Group home placement; Wards of the state.
Sources of Referral State depts of education; Local depts of education; State depts of mental health; Psychiatrists; Private sources; Depts of correction; Social service depts.
Client Profile
Age Range of Clients Served Residential program: 15-55+.
Characteristics Exhibited by Children Emotional handicaps; Learning disabilities; Hearing impairments/deafness; Vision impairments/blindness; Speech/Language disorders; Neurological impairments; Physical handicaps; Mental disabilities.
IQ Range of Clients 70+.
Tuition and Fees
Room and Board Short term: $35/diem; Long term: $20/diem.
Placements Primarily Funded By State depts of education; Local depts of education; State depts of mental health; Insurance; Private sources; Depts of corrections; Social service depts.
Social and Rehabilitative Services
Therapeutic Services Offered Individual therapy; Group therapy; Family therapy; Adjunctive therapy; Art therapy; Physical therapy; Independent living skills program; Recreation activities; Substance abuse treatment; Aftercare program with follow up.
Professionals on Staff Psychiatrists; Psychologists; Social workers; Adjunctive therapists; Child care staff; Nurses; Art therapists.
Educational and Vocational Services
Type(s) of Educational Programs Offered Off campus.

ELGIN

PINE GROVE SCHOOL
PO Box 100, Elgin, SC 29045 (803) 438-3011 *Contact Person(s):* Anita Gotwals, Dir
Referral Information For referral information contact the facility.
Type of Facility
Types of Admissions Accepted Residential treatment.
Client Profile
Age Range of Clients Served Residential program: 5-21.
Characteristics Exhibited by Children Emotional handicaps; Learning disabilities; Autism.

Social and Rehabilitative Services
Therapeutic Services Offered Family therapy; Adjunctive therapy; Art therapy; Physical therapy; Recreation activities.
Professionals on Staff Psychiatrists; Adjunctive therapists; Art therapists; Physical therapists; Occupational therapist; Speech therapist.
Educational and Vocational Services
Type(s) of Educational Programs Offered On campus.

GEORGETOWN

TARA HALL HOME FOR BOYS
PO Box 955, Rte 3, Rose Hill, Georgetown, SC 29442 (803) 546-3000 *Contact Person(s):* Jim Dumm, Dir
Setting and Background Information The facility was established in 1970. It is a non-profit home, licensed to provide care for 30 boys. The 11-acre campus has 5 cottages, a school/gym and a dining hall.
Referral Information Contact the facility for referral information. A pre-placement visit will be arranged.
Type of Facility
Funding Sources Private.
Average Length of Stay Min 2 yrs.
Types of Admissions Accepted Residential treatment; Wards of the state.
Sources of Referral State depts of education; Local depts of education; State depts of mental health; Psychiatrists; Private sources; Depts of correction; Social service depts.
Client Profile
Age Range of Clients Served Residential program: 6-18.
Characteristics Exhibited by Children Emotional handicaps; Learning disabilities; Behavior disorders.
IQ Range of Clients 70-120.
Tuition and Fees
Room and Board Long term: $11,500/yr.
Placements Primarily Funded By Donations.
Social and Rehabilitative Services
Therapeutic Approach The facility uses behavior modification in a 'System for Self-Achievement' program.
Therapeutic Services Offered Individual therapy; Independent living skills program.
Professionals on Staff Child care staff.
Educational and Vocational Services
Type(s) of Educational Programs Offered On campus.
Profile of On Campus School Program Number of teachers 6; *Number of classrooms* 6; *Student to teacher ratio* 5:1; *Credentials of teachers* Certified; *Grades taught* 2-8; Remedial courses offered.

GREENVILLE

MARSHALL I PICKENS HOSPITAL—THE CHILDREN'S PROGRAM
701 Grove Rd, Greenville, SC 29605 (803) 242-7807 *Contact Person(s):* Dr Laura Mohr EdD
Setting and Background Information The program was established in 1969 as an outgrowth of Project Re-ED in Nashville, Tennessee. It has a residential building and classroom/therapy building on the grounds of Greenville Hospital. The facility accepts boys only.
Referral Information Anyone can make a referral by contacting the facility and arranging a pre-placement visit.
Type of Facility
Funding Sources Private.
Average Length of Stay Long term.
Types of Admissions Accepted Day treatment; Residential treatment.
Sources of Referral State depts of education; Local depts of education; State depts of mental health; Psychiatrists; Private sources; Social service depts.
Client Profile
Age Range of Clients Served Day programs: 6-12; Residential program: 6-12.
Characteristics Exhibited by Children Emotional handicaps; Learning disabilities; Speech/Language disorders.
IQ Range of Clients 75+.
Tuition and Fees
Room and Board Long term: $146/diem.
Placements Primarily Funded By Private sources.

MARSHALL I PICKENS HOSPITAL—THE CHILDREN'S PROGRAM *(continued)*

Social and Rehabilitative Services
Therapeutic Approach The treatment program utilizes behavioral and psychiatric interventions.
Therapeutic Services Offered Individual therapy; Group therapy; Family therapy; Adjunctive therapy; Art therapy; Physical therapy; Independent living skills program; Recreation activities; Aftercare program with follow up.
Professionals on Staff Psychiatrists; Psychologists; Social workers; Adjunctive therapists; Child care staff; Art therapists; Physical therapists.
Educational and Vocational Services
Type(s) of Educational Programs Offered On campus.
Profile of On Campus School Program Number of teachers 2; *Number of classrooms* 2; *Student to teacher ratio* 8:1.

GREER

NEW BEGINNINGS
132 Circle Dr, Greer, SC 29651 (803) 877-0767 *Contact Person(s):* Nancy Curtis, Dir
Setting and Background Information The facility was established in 1980. It is a residential group home.
Referral Information Contact the facility.
Type of Facility
Funding Sources Private.
Average Length of Stay Short and long term.
Types of Admissions Accepted Group home placement.
Sources of Referral Private sources; Social service depts.
Client Profile
Age Range of Clients Served Residential program: Birth-18.
Characteristics Exhibited by Children Emotional handicaps; Learning disabilities; Physical handicaps; Mental disabilities; Abused and neglected; Sexual abuse.
Tuition and Fees
Room and Board Short term: $10/diem; Long term: $10/diem.
Placements Primarily Funded By Insurance; Private sources; Social service depts.
Educational and Vocational Services
Type(s) of Educational Programs Offered Off campus.

MAULDIN

CHURCH OF GOD HOME FOR CHILDREN
PO Box 430, Hwy 417, Mauldin, SC 29662 (803) 963-4751 *Contact Person(s):* Thomas H Ashley, Supt
Setting and Background Information The facility was established in 1955 by the Church of God in South Carolina. The 25-acre campus has 10 buildings, including cottages, a storehouse, and a gym.
Referral Information Referrals are made to the facility by pastors of local and statewide churches, and by state agencies.
Type of Facility
Funding Sources Private; State; Federal.
Average Length of Stay Long term.
Types of Admissions Accepted Group home placement; Wards of the state.
Sources of Referral Social service depts; Churches.
Client Profile
Age Range of Clients Served Residential program: 2-21.
Characteristics Exhibited by Children Emotional handicaps.
Tuition and Fees
Placements Primarily Funded By Private sources; Social service depts; Church.
Social and Rehabilitative Services
Therapeutic Services Offered Independent living skills program; Recreation activities.
Professionals on Staff Child care staff.
Educational and Vocational Services
Type(s) of Educational Programs Offered Off campus (Public schools).
Degrees Offered Degrees conferred through public schools.

NORTH AUGUSTA

NEW HORIZONS
753 W Five Notch Rd, North Augusta, SC 29841 (803) 279-6028
Contact Person(s): Rob Cantu, Coord of Children's Treatment Homes
Setting and Background Information The facility was established in 1984 with funding from the state. The five-acre campus has a house and a barn.
Referral Information Contact the facility for referral information. All applications are reviewed by an admissions committee, which consists of 6 people from various local agencies.
Type of Facility
Funding Sources State.
Average Length of Stay 12-16 mos.
Types of Admissions Accepted Day treatment; Residential treatment; Group home placement.
Sources of Referral State depts of mental health.
Client Profile
Age Range of Clients Served Day programs: 6-12; Residential program: 12-18.
Characteristics Exhibited by Children Emotional handicaps; Learning disabilities; Mental disabilities.
IQ Range of Clients 70-120.
Tuition and Fees
Placements Primarily Funded By State depts of mental health.
Social and Rehabilitative Services
Therapeutic Approach The facility uses behavior modification.
Therapeutic Services Offered Individual therapy; Group therapy; Family therapy; Adjunctive therapy; Independent living skills program; Recreation activities; Aftercare program with follow up.
Professionals on Staff Psychiatrists; Psychologists; Social workers; Child care staff.
Educational and Vocational Services
Type(s) of Educational Programs Offered Off campus.

NORTH CHARLESTON

CAROLINA YOUTH DEVELOPMENT CENTER
5055 Lackawanna Blvd, North Charleston, SC 29406-4522
(803) 744-5358 *Contact Person(s):* James F Gross, Residential Prog Dir
Setting and Background Information The facility was established in 1790 as the Charleston Orphan House. Currently, it consists of residential cottages and an activity center.
Referral Information Contact the facility for referral information.
Type of Facility
Funding Sources Private; State; Federal.
Average Length of Stay Short and long term.
Types of Admissions Accepted Day treatment; Residential treatment; Wards of the state.
Sources of Referral State depts of education; Local depts of education; State depts of mental health; Psychiatrists; Private sources; Depts of correction; Social service depts.
Client Profile
Age Range of Clients Served Day programs: 6-18; Residential program: 6-18.
Characteristics Exhibited by Children Emotional handicaps.
IQ Range of Clients 70+.
Social and Rehabilitative Services
Therapeutic Services Offered Individual therapy; Group therapy; Family therapy; Adjunctive therapy; Recreation activities.
Professionals on Staff Psychiatrists; Psychologists; Social workers; Adjunctive therapists; Child care staff; Nurses.
Educational and Vocational Services
Type(s) of Educational Programs Offered On campus; Off campus.
Profile of On Campus School Program Number of teachers 1; *Number of classrooms* 1; *Student to teacher ratio* 3:1; *Length of school day* 6 hrs.

ORANGEBURG

BROOKLAND PLANTATION HOME FOR BOYS

Rt 2, Box 125, Orangeburg, SC 29115 (803) 536-2456 *Contact Person(s):* L Philip Ross, Exec Dir

Setting and Background Information The facility was established in 1958. The 145-acre campus has 3 single-story brick cottages, a dining/school facility, a chapel, and a gym/shop.

Referral Information Contact the facility for referral information.

Type of Facility

Funding Sources Private.

Average Length of Stay 12-18 mos.

Types of Admissions Accepted Residential treatment.

Sources of Referral Private sources; Family court directive.

Client Profile

Age Range of Clients Served Residential program: 12-18.

Characteristics Exhibited by Children Emotional handicaps; Learning disabilities.

IQ Range of Clients 70-115.

Tuition and Fees

Placements Primarily Funded By Private sources.

Social and Rehabilitative Services

Therapeutic Services Offered Individual therapy; Group therapy; Family therapy; Independent living skills program; Recreation activities; Aftercare program with follow up.

Professionals on Staff Psychologists; Social workers; Child care staff.

Educational and Vocational Services

Type(s) of Educational Programs Offered On campus.

Profile of On Campus School Program Number of teachers 2; *Number of classrooms* 4; *Student to teacher ratio* 12:1; *Credentials of teachers* Certified; *Grades taught* 4-10; Remedial courses offered (Reading enrichment, German).

PICKENS

MIRACLE HILL CHILDREN'S HOME

Rt 3 Miralce Hill, Pickens, SC 29671 (803) 878-9987 *Contact Person(s):* Jane Pulido, Family Coord

Setting and Background Information The facility was established in 1957 as a group home and school. Currently, there are 2 boys dorms, a girls dorm, a tot dorm, a school, a day care center, staff housing, and an office building.

Referral Information Contact the facility for referral information. A pre-placement visit and interview will be scheduled.

Type of Facility

Funding Sources Private; Churches.

Average Length of Stay Short and long term.

Types of Admissions Accepted Residential treatment; Group home placement.

Sources of Referral Private sources; Depts of correction.

Client Profile

Age Range of Clients Served Residential program: Birth-21+.

Characteristics Exhibited by Children Emotional handicaps; Behavior disorders; Family dysfunction.

IQ Range of Clients 70+.

Tuition and Fees

Room and Board Long term: Sliding scale.

Placements Primarily Funded By Private sources; Churches; Donations.

Social and Rehabilitative Services

Therapeutic Services Offered Aftercare program with follow up.

Professionals on Staff Social workers; Child care staff; Nurses.

Educational and Vocational Services

Type(s) of Educational Programs Offered On campus; Off campus (Vocational center).

Profile of On Campus School Program Number of teachers 10; *Number of classrooms* 10; *Student to teacher ratio* 10:1; *Credentials of teachers* BS, BA; *Grades taught* K-12; Special curriculum electives offered (Computer science, Spanish, Art, Speech, Music, Instrumental); Remedial courses offered (Reading, English, Math, Science, History).

Degrees Offered 8th grade diploma; 12th grade diploma.

SIMPSONVILLE

PIEDMONT TREATMENT HOME FOR ADOLESCENTS, INC

12 Village Plaza West, Simpsonville, SC 29681 (803) 963-3421

Setting and Background Information This program was established in 1981 with state funding. It is a private non-profit corporation and provides community based treatment facilities for emotionally disturbed youth.

Referral Information For referrals, contact the facility.

Type of Facility

Funding Sources Private.

Average Length of Stay Long term.

Types of Admissions Accepted Residential treatment.

Sources of Referral Anyone may make referrals.

Client Profile

Age Range of Clients Served Residential program: 6-18.

Characteristics Exhibited by Children Emotional handicaps.

Tuition and Fees

Placements Primarily Funded By State depts of mental health.

Social and Rehabilitative Services

Therapeutic Approach The facility utilizes the teaching family concept, where the teaching parent relationship with each resident is one of parent, teacher, counselor and friend. The residents participate in role playing and individual counseling.

Therapeutic Services Offered Individual therapy; Group therapy; Family therapy; Independent living skills program.

Professionals on Staff Psychiatrists; Psychologists; Social workers; Nurses.

SPARTANBURG

ELLEN HINES SMITH GIRLS' HOME

241 Cedar Springs Rd, Spartanburg, SC 29302 (803) 573-9223 *Contact Person(s):* T David Tribble, Exec Dir

Setting and Background Information The facility was established in 1974 by the family court and the local Junior League. It is located on 5 ½ acres and has a residential building, administrative and office buildings, and a classroom building.

Referral Information Contact the facility. After a formal application is made, an intake interview is scheduled. The Advisory and Admission Committee then meets to decide on the appropriateness of the referral and possible admission.

Type of Facility

Funding Sources Private; State; Federal; County.

Average Length of Stay Long term.

Types of Admissions Accepted Residential treatment; Group home placement; Wards of the state.

Sources of Referral State depts of mental health; Psychiatrists; Private sources; Depts of correction; Social service depts.

Client Profile

Age Range of Clients Served Residential program: 12-18.

Characteristics Exhibited by Children Emotional handicaps; Learning disabilities.

IQ Range of Clients 70+.

Tuition and Fees

Room and Board Long term: $37.50/diem.

Placements Primarily Funded By Private sources; Depts of corrections; Social service depts.

Social and Rehabilitative Services

Therapeutic Approach The facility offers individual and family therapy, and uses behavior modification.

Therapeutic Services Offered Individual therapy; Group therapy; Family therapy; Independent living skills program; Substance abuse treatment; Aftercare program with follow up.

Professionals on Staff Psychiatrists; Psychologists; Social workers; Child care staff; Family therapist.

Educational and Vocational Services

Type(s) of Educational Programs Offered Off campus (Public schools).

TAYLORS

SOUTHEASTERN CHILDREN'S HOME, INC

3506 Edwards Rd, Taylors, SC 29687 (803) 292-3309 *Contact Person(s):* Mellisa A Thigpen, Exec Dir

Setting and Background Information The facility was established by the Church of Christ in 1968 as a single group home. It is currently a foster home program. A 50-acre facility is under construction to begin a residential treatment program in 1988.

Referral Information Referrals to the facility are made through the Dept of Social Services or by private placements.

Type of Facility

Funding Sources Private.

Average Length of Stay Short and long term.

Types of Admissions Accepted Residential treatment; Foster care.

Client Profile

Age Range of Clients Served Residential program: Birth-15.

Characteristics Exhibited by Children Abused and neglected.

Tuition and Fees

Placements Primarily Funded By Church; Private individuals.

Educational and Vocational Services

Type(s) of Educational Programs Offered Off campus (Public school).

WEST COLUMBIA

WIL LOU GRAY OPPORTUNITY SCHOOL

West Campus Rd, West Columbia, SC 29169 (803) 739-5480 *Contact Person(s):* Dr Johnie Spaulding

Setting and Background Information The facility was established in 1921 by Dr Wil Lou Gray to educate farmwomen who hadn't finished school. Since then, it has expanded its programs to become an alternative school. The campus is located on 100 acres near the Columbia Metropolitan Aiport and consists of an education building, administration building, 3 male dorms, 2 female dorms, cafeteria, gymnasium, auditorium, tennis courts, and ballfield.

Referral Information Anyone can make a referral by requesting an application and forwarding the necessary background information.

Type of Facility

Funding Sources State.

Average Length of Stay Long term.

Types of Admissions Accepted Residential treatment.

Sources of Referral State depts of education; Local depts of education; Social service depts; Dept of Youth Svcs.

Client Profile

Age Range of Clients Served Residential Program 15-18.

Characteristics Exhibited by Children Emotional handicaps; Learning disabilities; Hearing impairments/deafness; Physical handicaps.

IQ Range of Clients 65+.

Tuition and Fees

Room and Board Long term: $1,310/yr.

Placements Primarily Funded By State depts of education; Local depts of education; Social service depts.

Social and Rehabilitative Services

Therapeutic Approach The program uses a variety of therapeutic approaches, including reality therapy, and transactional analysis. Classes in assertiveness training and values clarification are also offered.

Therapeutic Services Offered Individual therapy; Group therapy; Family therapy; Independent living skills program; Recreation activities; Substance abuse treatment.

Professionals on Staff Psychologists; Nurses.

Educational and Vocational Services

Type(s) of Educational Programs Offered On campus.

Profile of On Campus School Program Number of teachers 25; *Number of classrooms* 21; *Student to teacher ratio* 12:1; Remedial courses offered.

Vocational Education Programs/Degrees Offered Food services; Nursing technician; Building construction; Auto mechanics; Carpentry; Building maintenance.

Degrees Offered 12th grade diploma; GED.

WESTMINSTER

FAIR PLAY WILDERNESS CAMP SCHOOL

Rt 2 Box 213-A, Westminster, SC 29693 (803) 972-9311 *Contact Person(s):* Floyd Yoder, Exec Dir

Setting and Background Information The facility was privately established in 1981. Located on 105 acres, there are residential buildings, offices, a chapel, a school, and other buildings.

Referral Information Contact the facility and forward the necessary information. A pre-placement visit will be scheduled.

Type of Facility

Funding Sources Private; State.

Average Length of Stay Long term.

Types of Admissions Accepted Residential treatment.

Sources of Referral Local depts of education; Private sources; Social service depts.

Client Profile

Age Range of Clients Served Residential program: 10-17.

Characteristics Exhibited by Children Emotional handicaps; Learning disabilities; Speech/Language disorders.

IQ Range of Clients 75-140.

Tuition and Fees

Room and Board Long term: $661.55/mo.

Tuition $610.67/mo.

Placements Primarily Funded By Private sources; Social service depts.

Social and Rehabilitative Services

Therapeutic Services Offered Individual therapy; Group therapy; Family therapy; Adjunctive therapy; Independent living skills program; Aftercare program with follow up.

Professionals on Staff Psychologists; Social workers; Adjunctive therapists; Child care staff.

Educational and Vocational Services

Type(s) of Educational Programs Offered On campus.

Profile of On Campus School Program Number of teachers 1; *Number of classrooms* 2; *Student to teacher ratio* 4:1; *Credentials of teachers* Certified EH; *Grades taught* 5-10; Special curriculum electives offered; Remedial courses offered.

Degrees Offered GED.

YORK

YORK PLACE

234 Kings Mountain St, York, SC 29745 (803) 684-4011 *Contact Person(s):* Sally Hart, Brian Phelps

Setting and Background Information The agency was initially established as a children's home, but by 1969 it had expanded its programs to become a treatment center. The campus is located on over 100 acres and consists of 3 treatment centers (9 children per cottage), gymnasium, chapel, and horse riding facilities.

Referral Information Referrals are primarily made by parents and agencies.

Type of Facility

Funding Sources Private; State.

Average Length of Stay Long term.

Types of Admissions Accepted Day treatment; Residential treatment.

Sources of Referral State depts of education; Local depts of education; State depts of mental health; Psychiatrists; Private sources; Social service depts.

Client Profile

Age Range of Clients Served Day programs: 6-12; Residential program: 6-12.

Characteristics Exhibited by Children Emotional handicaps; Learning disabilities; Speech/Language disorders; Neurological impairments; Mental disabilities.

IQ Range of Clients 70+.

Tuition and Fees

Room and Board Long term: $2,765/mo (sliding scale).

Placements Primarily Funded By State depts of education; Local depts of education; State depts of mental health; Insurance; Private sources; Social service depts.

Social and Rehabilitative Services

Therapeutic Approach The program has an eclectic therapeutic approach with an emphasis on behavioral therapy.

Therapeutic Services Offered Individual therapy; Group therapy; Family therapy; Recreation activities; Aftercare program with follow up.

YORK PLACE *(continued)*

Professionals on Staff Psychiatrists; Psychologists; Social workers; Adjunctive therapists; Child care staff.

Educational and Vocational Services

Type(s) of Educational Programs Offered On campus; Summer campus.

Profile of On Campus School Program Number of teachers 4; *Number of classrooms* 4; *Student to teacher ratio* 9:1.

SOUTH DAKOTA

ABERDEEN

NEW BEGINNINGS CENTER

1206 N 3rd St, Aberdeen, SD 57401 (605) 229-1239 *Contact Person(s):* Michael J McCafferty, Exec Dir
Setting and Background Information The center was established in 1974 in response to a community need for a short term intervention center. It is located in a residential area.
Referral Information Clients are referred by court services, DSS, school districts, and BIA-Tribal courts.
Type of Facility
Funding Sources Private; State.
Average Length of Stay Short and long term.
Types of Admissions Accepted Group home placement; 30 day evaluations.
Sources of Referral State depts of education; Local depts of education; Private sources; Depts of correction; Social service depts; BIA; Tribal Courts.
Client Profile
Age Range of Clients Served Day programs: 10-18; Residential program: 10-18.
Characteristics Exhibited by Children Emotional handicaps; Behavior disorders; Delinquency; Family dysfunction.
IQ Range of Clients 70+.
Tuition and Fees
Room and Board Short term: $36/diem (in-state residents); $45/diem (out-of-state residents).
Tuition Paid to Aberdeen School System by the referring area school district.
Placements Primarily Funded By Local depts of education; Depts of corrections; Social service depts; BIA; Tribes.
Social and Rehabilitative Services
Therapeutic Approach The center uses reality therapy, including behavior modification.
Therapeutic Services Offered Individual therapy; Group therapy; Family therapy; Adjunctive therapy; Independent living skills program; Recreation activities; Substance abuse treatment.
Professionals on Staff Psychiatrists; Psychologists; Social workers; Adjunctive therapists.
Educational and Vocational Services
Type(s) of Educational Programs Offered On campus; Off campus (Public school).

MITCHELL

ABBOTT HOUSE

1109 W University, Mitchell, SD 57301 (605) 996-2486 *Contact Person(s):* Ernest O Peters, Exec Dir
Setting and Background Information The facility was established in 1939 as a community project.
Referral Information Referral information availiable upon request.
Type of Facility
Funding Sources Private; State.
Average Length of Stay Long term.
Types of Admissions Accepted Residential treatment.
Sources of Referral State depts of education; Local depts of education; State depts of mental health; Private sources; Depts of correction; Social service depts.

Client Profile
Age Range of Clients Served Day programs: 12-18; Residential program: 12-18.
Characteristics Exhibited by Children Emotional handicaps; Learning disabilities; Mental disabilities.
IQ Range of Clients 80-120.
Tuition and Fees
Room and Board Long term: $50/diem.
Tuition $26/diem.
Placements Primarily Funded By State depts of education; Local depts of education; Social service depts.
Social and Rehabilitative Services
Therapeutic Approach The facility has an individualized approach to therapy.
Therapeutic Services Offered Individual therapy; Group therapy; Family therapy; Independent living skills program; Recreation activities; Substance abuse treatment; Incest survivors treatment.
Professionals on Staff Psychologists; Social workers; Child care staff.
Educational and Vocational Services
Type(s) of Educational Programs Offered On campus (Spec Ed); Off campus (Public schools).
Profile of On Campus School Program Number of teachers 3; Number of classrooms 3; Student to teacher ratio 4:1; Credentials of teachers Spec Ed; Grades taught 6-12; Special curriculum electives offered (Independent living).
Degrees Offered 12th grade diploma; GED.

RAPID CITY

WEST RIVER CHILDREN'S CENTER

HC 33, Box 7801, Rapid City, SD 57701 (605) 343-5422 *Contact Person(s):* Kathryn Crow
Referral Information Referrals can be made by parents, school districts, social service agencies, courts, and Bureau of Indian Affairs. To make a referral, contact the facility and schedule a 1, 3, 5, or 30 day evaluation for the child. If the child is appropriate for the program, then a referral packet is sent to the referral source for completion and the child is admitted.
Type of Facility
Funding Sources State.
Average Length of Stay Long term.
Types of Admissions Accepted Day treatment; Residential treatment.
Sources of Referral State depts of education; Local depts of education; Psychiatrists; Social service depts; Bureau of Indian Affairs.
Client Profile
Age Range of Clients Served Day programs: 5-13; Residential program: 5-13.
Characteristics Exhibited by Children Emotional handicaps; Learning disabilities; Neurological impairments; Mental disabilities.
IQ Range of Clients 80+.
Tuition and Fees
Room and Board Long term: $73.13/diem (includes school tuition).
Placements Primarily Funded By Social service depts.
Social and Rehabilitative Services
Therapeutic Approach The facility has an eclectic approach to therapy.
Therapeutic Services Offered Individual therapy; Group therapy; Family therapy; Recreation activities; Substance abuse treatment; Aftercare program with follow up.
Professionals on Staff Psychiatrists; Psychologists; Social workers; Child care staff.

WEST RIVER CHILDREN'S CENTER *(continued)*

Educational and Vocational Services
Type(s) of Educational Programs Offered On campus.
Profile of On Campus School Program Number of teachers 7; *Number of classrooms* 7; *Student to teacher ratio* 4:1.

SIOUX FALLS

CHILDRENS HOME SOCIETY

801 N Sycamore, Sioux Falls, SD 57103 (605) 336-1313 *Contact Person(s):* Sue Titze, Prog Dir
Setting and Background Information The facility was established in 1893 as an orphanage. Currently, it is a residential treatment center located on 28 acres.
Referral Information Contact the facility for a referral packet. A preplacement visit will be arranged.
Type of Facility
Funding Sources State.
Average Length of Stay 12-24 mos.
Types of Admissions Accepted Residential treatment; Wards of the state.
Sources of Referral State depts of education; Local depts of education; Depts of correction; Social service depts.
Client Profile
Age Range of Clients Served Residential program: 6-15.
Characteristics Exhibited by Children Emotional handicaps; Learning disabilities; Mental disabilities.
Tuition and Fees
Room and Board Long term: $72/diem.
Tuition $44/diem.
Placements Primarily Funded By State depts of education; Local depts of education; Depts of corrections; Social service depts.
Social and Rehabilitative Services
Therapeutic Services Offered Individual therapy; Group therapy; Family therapy; Independent living skills program.
Professionals on Staff Child care staff; Nurses; Family therapists.
Educational and Vocational Services
Type(s) of Educational Programs Offered On campus; Off campus; Summer campus.
Profile of On Campus School Program Number of teachers 7; *Number of classrooms* 7; *Student to teacher ratio* 4:1; *Credentials of teachers* Spec Ed; *Grades taught* K-12.

SOUTHEASTERN MENTAL HEALTH CENTER

2000 S Summit, Sioux Falls, SD 57105 (605) 336-0510 *Contact Person(s):* Marlys Waller, Dir of Children's Svcs
Setting and Background Information The facility was established in 1969. The school is in the Mental Health Center and there are 2 group homes in the surrounding community.
Referral Information To make a referral, contact the facility.
Type of Facility
Funding Sources State; Federal.
Average Length of Stay Long term.
Types of Admissions Accepted Day treatment; Residential treatment; Group home placement.
Sources of Referral State depts of education; Local depts of education; Social service depts.
Client Profile
Age Range of Clients Served Day programs: Birth-18; Residential program: Birth-18.
Characteristics Exhibited by Children Emotional handicaps; Learning disabilities; Hearing impairments/deafness; Vision impairments/blindness; Speech/Language disorders; Mental disabilities; Autism.
Tuition and Fees
Room and Board Long term: $64/diem.
Tuition $38.51/diem.
Placements Primarily Funded By Local depts of education; State depts of mental health.
Social and Rehabilitative Services
Therapeutic Approach The basic philosophy of the facility is social learning theory.
Therapeutic Services Offered Individual therapy; Family therapy; Physical therapy; Independent living skills program.
Professionals on Staff Psychiatrists; Psychologists; Social workers; Child care staff; Nurses; Physical therapists.

Educational and Vocational Services
Type(s) of Educational Programs Offered On campus.
Profile of On Campus School Program Number of teachers 3 and 3 aides; *Student to teacher ratio* 2:1; *Length of school day* Spec Ed Certified; *Grades taught* Spec Ed.
Vocational Education Programs/Degrees Offered Pre-vocational training.

SKY RANCH

SKY RANCH FOR BOYS

Sky Ranch Lane, Sky Ranch, SD 57724 (605) 797-4422 *Contact Person(s):* Scott Louks
Setting and Background Information The facility was established in rural Harding County in 1960. The campus consists of 11 buildings, including a gymnasium, school, chapel, and residences. The facility accepts boys only.
Referral Information Referrals can be made by any concerned agency or individual. Applicants are requested to submit an intake packet which includes school records, psychological evaluations, court reports, and social history. An intake team will review the material and decide whether the placement is appropriate.
Type of Facility
Funding Sources State.
Average Length of Stay Long term.
Types of Admissions Accepted Day treatment; Residential treatment.
Sources of Referral Psychiatrists; Private sources; Social service depts.
Client Profile
Age Range of Clients Served Day programs: 10-18; Residential program: 10-18.
Characteristics Exhibited by Children Emotional handicaps; Learning disabilities.
Tuition and Fees
Room and Board Long term: $39.14/diem.
Tuition $24.73/diem.
Placements Primarily Funded By Private sources.
Social and Rehabilitative Services
Therapeutic Approach The treatment program is based on reality therapy, milieu therapy, and behavior modification techniques.
Therapeutic Services Offered Individual therapy; Group therapy; Family therapy; Substance abuse treatment; Aftercare program with follow up.
Professionals on Staff Psychiatrists; Psychologists; Social workers; Child care staff.
Educational and Vocational Services
Type(s) of Educational Programs Offered On campus.
Profile of On Campus School Program Number of teachers 6; *Number of classrooms* 7; *Student to teacher ratio* 7:1.
Degrees Offered 8th grade diploma; 12th grade diploma; GED.

SPEARFISH

BLACK HILLS SPECIAL SERVICES—NORTHERN HILLS YOUTH SERVICES

1246 St Joe, Spearfish, SD 57783 (605) 578-1914, 642-3720 *Contact Person(s):* Ernest Bantam, Asst Dir for Residential Srvs
Setting and Background Information The facility was established in 1974 by an independent non-profit board and is a group home.
Referral Information Referrals for long-term care are considered by an interdisciplinary team.
Type of Facility
Funding Sources Public schools.
Average Length of Stay Short and long term.
Types of Admissions Accepted Day treatment; Residential treatment; Group home placement; Wards of the state.
Sources of Referral State depts of education; Local depts of education; State depts of mental health; Psychiatrists; Depts of correction; Social service depts; Court svcs.
Client Profile
Age Range of Clients Served Day programs: 12-18; Residential program: 12-18.
Characteristics Exhibited by Children Emotional handicaps; Learning disabilities; Mental disabilities.
IQ Range of Clients 80+.

BLACK HILLS SPECIAL SERVICES—NORTHERN HILLS YOUTH SERVICES *(continued)*

Tuition and Fees
Room and Board Short term: $42/diem; Long term: $42/diem.
Tuition $41/diem.
Placements Primarily Funded By State depts of education; Local depts of education; Depts of corrections; Social service depts; Court services.
Social and Rehabilitative Services
Therapeutic Services Offered Individual therapy; Group therapy; Art therapy; Independent living skills program; Recreation activities; Substance abuse treatment.
Professionals on Staff Psychologists; Social workers; Child care staff; Nurses; Art therapists; Physical therapists.
Educational and Vocational Services
Type(s) of Educational Programs Offered Off campus (Alternative school); Summer campus (Summer jobs program).
Profile of On Campus School Program Number of teachers 5; *Number of classrooms* 5; *Student to teacher ratio* 7:1; *Grades taught* 7-12; Special curriculum electives offered (Strong vocational emphasis).
Degrees Offered 12th grade diploma; GED.

YANKTON

SOUTH DAKOTA HUMAN SERVICES CENTER

PO Box 76, Hwy 81 & 50, Yankton, SD 57078-0076 (605) 668-3100
Contact Person(s): Karel S Sysel MBA, Assoc Admin
Setting and Background Information The facility was originally established in 1879 by the State Legislature. Currently, the 200-acre grounds have 71 buildings, including activity buildings, farm buildings, and penetentiary related buildings.
Referral Information All referrals to the facility are appropriately screened. Involuntary commitments must be screened by community mental health centers to determine if less restrictive placement/treatment can be made in the community. Voluntary admissions may be self-referred or referred by professionals.
Type of Facility
Funding Sources Private; State; Federal.
Average Length of Stay Short and long term.
Types of Admissions Accepted Residential treatment.
Sources of Referral State depts of education; Psychiatrists; Private sources; Depts of correction; Social service depts; Self referrals; County Boards of Mental Health.
Client Profile
Age Range of Clients Served Residential program: 12-55+.
Characteristics Exhibited by Children Emotional handicaps; Learning disabilities; Neurological impairments; Mental disabilities.
IQ Range of Clients 60+.
Tuition and Fees
Room and Board Short term: $154/diem; Long term: $80/diem.
Placements Primarily Funded By County.
Social and Rehabilitative Services
Therapeutic Approach The basic therapeutic approach of the facility is psycho-social rehabilitation.
Therapeutic Services Offered Individual therapy; Group therapy; Family therapy; Adjunctive therapy; Art therapy; Physical therapy; Independent living skills program; Recreation activities; Substance abuse treatment; Occupational therapy; Speech therapy; Vocational rehabilitation.
Professionals on Staff Psychiatrists; Psychologists; Social workers; Nurses; Physical therapists; Occupational therapist; Speech therapists; Chemical dependency counselors.
Educational and Vocational Services
Type(s) of Educational Programs Offered On campus.
Profile of On Campus School Program Number of teachers 3; *Number of classrooms* 4; *Student to teacher ratio* 10:1; *Credentials of teachers* BS; *Length of school day* 4 hrs; *Grades taught* 6-12; Special curriculum electives offered (Auto mechanics, Carpentry/shop, Business course); Remedial courses offered (Math).
Vocational Education Programs/Degrees Offered Auto mechanics; Carpentry/shop; Business courses.
Degrees Offered GED.

TENNESSEE

CHATTANOOGA

SMALLWOOD CHILDREN'S CENTER

Moccasin Bend Mental Institute, Moccasin Bend Rd, Chattanooga, TN 37405 (615) 265-2271 *Contact Person(s):* Catherine Sumburg, Prog Dir

Setting and Background Information The program was opened in 1967 as the Children's Unit of the Moccasin Bend Mental Institute, located on 356 acres of woodland bounded on 3 sides by the Tennessee River.

Referral Information Referrals can be made by mental health centers, physicians, mental health practioners, and parents. To make a referral, contact the facility and arrange to meet a social worker who will collect the necessary background information. The child will then be evaluated by a psychiatrist before a placement decision is made.

Type of Facility
Funding Sources State.
Average Length of Stay Long term.
Types of Admissions Accepted Residential treatment.
Sources of Referral State depts of education; Local depts of education; State depts of mental health; Psychiatrists; Social service depts.

Client Profile
Age Range of Clients Served Residential program: 5-13.
Characteristics Exhibited by Children Emotional handicaps; Learning disabilities.

Tuition and Fees
Room and Board Long term: $235/diem.
Placements Primarily Funded By State depts of education; Local depts of education; State depts of mental health; Insurance.

Social and Rehabilitative Services
Therapeutic Approach The treatment program utilizes an eclectic approach with emphasis on family therapy and parent training. A token economy system with contingency management procedures is the basic structure of the program.
Therapeutic Services Offered Individual therapy; Group therapy; Family therapy; Adjunctive therapy; Art therapy; Independent living skills program; Recreation activities.
Professionals on Staff Psychiatrists; Psychologists; Social workers; Adjunctive therapists; Child care staff; Nurses; Art therapists.

Educational and Vocational Services
Type(s) of Educational Programs Offered On campus.
Profile of On Campus School Program Number of teachers 30; *Number of classrooms* 4; Remedial courses offered.

COLUMBIA

THE KING'S DAUGHTERS' SCHOOL, INC

412 W 9th St, Columbia, TN 38401 (615) 388-3810 *Contact Person(s):* Charlotte Battles, Exec Dir

Setting and Background Information The facility was originally established in 1912 as a hospital. In 1954 it became a residential school for mentally retarded youth. There are 6 buildings.

Referral Information Contact the facility and forward a referral packet, including psychological reports and social history. Admission to the facility is determined by the placement committee.

Type of Facility
Funding Sources Private.
Average Length of Stay Long term.
Types of Admissions Accepted Residential treatment; Group home placement.
Sources of Referral State depts of education; Local depts of education; State depts of mental health; Psychiatrists; Private sources; Social service depts.

Client Profile
Age Range of Clients Served Day programs: Birth-5; Residential program: 6-21+.
Characteristics Exhibited by Children Emotional handicaps; Mental disabilities.

Tuition and Fees
Placements Primarily Funded By State depts of education; Local depts of education; State depts of mental health; Private sources; Social service depts.

Social and Rehabilitative Services
Therapeutic Services Offered Individual therapy; Group therapy; Physical therapy; Independent living skills program.
Professionals on Staff Psychiatrists; Psychologists; Adjunctive therapists; Nurses; Physical therapists.

Educational and Vocational Services
Type(s) of Educational Programs Offered On campus; Off campus; Summer campus.
Profile of On Campus School Program Number of teachers 7; *Number of classrooms* 15; *Student to teacher ratio* 3:1; *Credentials of teachers* Spec Ed; *Grades taught* Ungraded.
Vocational Education Programs/Degrees Offered On the job training.

ELIZABETHTON

EMERGENCY CHILD SHELTER, INC

308 S Main St, Elizabethton, TN 37643 (615) 543-3986 *Contact Person(s):* David L Maurice, Dir

Setting and Background Information The shelter was established in 1979.

Referral Information All clients are referred by the Tennessee Dept of Human Services.

Type of Facility
Funding Sources Private; State.
Average Length of Stay Short term.
Types of Admissions Accepted Emergency shelter.
Sources of Referral Social service depts; Dept of human svcs.

Client Profile
Age Range of Clients Served Residential program: Birth-18.
Characteristics Exhibited by Children Emotional handicaps.

Tuition and Fees
Placements Primarily Funded By Social service depts; Dept of human services.

Social and Rehabilitative Services
Professionals on Staff Psychologists; Social workers; Child care staff.

GREENVILLE

HOLSTON UNITED METHODIST HOME, INC

PO Box 188, Greenville, TN 37744-0188 (615) 638-4171 *Contact Person(s):* Arthur S Masker, Prog Admin

Referral Information Referrals are made by social service agencies.

HOLSTON UNITED METHODIST HOME, INC
(continued)

Type of Facility
Funding Sources Private; State; Federal.
Average Length of Stay Long term.
Types of Admissions Accepted Residential treatment.
Sources of Referral State depts of mental health; Psychiatrists; Private sources; Depts of correction; Social service depts.
Client Profile
Age Range of Clients Served Residential program: 6-15.
Characteristics Exhibited by Children Emotional handicaps; Learning disabilities; Physical handicaps.
IQ Range of Clients 70-120.
Tuition and Fees
Placements Primarily Funded By Social service depts.
Social and Rehabilitative Services
Therapeutic Services Offered Individual therapy; Group therapy; Family therapy; Recreation activities; Aftercare program with follow up.
Professionals on Staff Psychiatrists; Social workers; Adjunctive therapists; Child care staff; Physical therapists.
Educational and Vocational Services
Type(s) of Educational Programs Offered On campus; Off campus (Public school); Summer campus.
Profile of On Campus School Program Number of teachers 1; *Number of classrooms* 1; *Student to teacher ratio* 8:1; *Length of school day* 6 hrs; *Grades taught* K-8; Remedial courses offered (Individual instruction).

HIXSON

BETHEL BIBLE VILLAGE
PO Box 500, 3001 Hamill Rd, Hixson, TN 37343 (615) 842-5757
Contact Person(s): Ike Keay, Exec Dir
Setting and Background Information The facility was established in 1954 as a home for dependent and neglected children of prisoners. The 67-acre campus has 7 cottages, staff housing, an administration building and barns.
Referral Information Referrals are made by individuals, courts, and human service depts. Psychological, social history, and school records are required. One or both parents must have a record of incarceration.
Type of Facility
Funding Sources Private; State; Clubs; Churches; Foundations.
Average Length of Stay Long term.
Types of Admissions Accepted Group home placement; Wards of the state; Foster homes.
Sources of Referral Depts of correction; Social service depts; Juvenile court.
Client Profile
Age Range of Clients Served Residential program: Birth-18.
Characteristics Exhibited by Children Emotional handicaps; Learning disabilities.
IQ Range of Clients 70+.
Tuition and Fees
Placements Primarily Funded By Private.
Social and Rehabilitative Services
Therapeutic Approach The facility has an eclectic approach to therapy.
Therapeutic Services Offered Individual therapy; Group therapy; Family therapy; Adjunctive therapy; Recreation activities.
Professionals on Staff Psychiatrists; Psychologists; Social workers; Child care staff.
Educational and Vocational Services
Type(s) of Educational Programs Offered On campus (Tutorial); Off campus (Local schools); Summer campus (Title XX program).

KINGSTON

CAMELOT CARE CENTER
Rt 3 Box 267C, Kingston, TN 37763 (615) 376-2296 *Contact Person(s):* Heather Dziewulski ACSW, Facility Admin
Setting and Background Information This residential treatment center is located on 16 acres and has residential buildings, a barn, a recreational pavilion and office buildings.

Referral Information A telephone call to the facility activates the referral. Written materials will be requested.
Type of Facility
Funding Sources Private; State.
Average Length of Stay Long term.
Types of Admissions Accepted Day treatment; Residential treatment; Wards of the state.
Sources of Referral State depts of education; Local depts of education; State depts of mental health; Psychiatrists; Private sources; Social service depts.
Client Profile
Age Range of Clients Served Day programs: 6-18; Residential program: Birth-18.
Characteristics Exhibited by Children Emotional handicaps.
Tuition and Fees
Placements Primarily Funded By State depts of mental health; Insurance; Private sources; Social service depts.
Social and Rehabilitative Services
Therapeutic Approach The center has a developmental approach to therapy.
Therapeutic Services Offered Individual therapy; Group therapy; Family therapy; Adjunctive therapy; Recreation activities; Aftercare program with follow up.
Professionals on Staff Psychiatrists; Psychologists; Social workers; Child care staff; Nurses; Recreational therapists.
Educational and Vocational Services
Type(s) of Educational Programs Offered On campus; Off campus; Summer campus.
Profile of On Campus School Program Number of teachers 4; *Number of classrooms* 3; *Credentials of teachers* Certified Spec Ed; *Grades taught* 1-12; Special curriculum electives offered (Spec Ed, ED/LD); Remedial courses offered.
Degrees Offered 8th grade diploma; 12th grade diploma through local district.

KNOXVILLE

CHILD AND FAMILY SERVICES, INC
114 Dameron Ave, Knoxville, TN 37917 (615) 524-7483 *Contact Person(s):* Charles E Gentry ACSW IPSW, Exec Dir
Setting and Background Information The facility was established in 1960 as a church sponsored home for unwed mothers.
Referral Information Contact the facility for referral information.
Type of Facility
Funding Sources Private.
Average Length of Stay Long term.
Types of Admissions Accepted Residential treatment; Group home placement.
Sources of Referral Local depts of education; Psychiatrists; Depts of correction; Social service depts.
Client Profile
Age Range of Clients Served Day programs: 12-15; Residential program: 12-15.
Characteristics Exhibited by Children Emotional handicaps; Family dysfunction.
Tuition and Fees
Room and Board Long term: $3,000/yr.
Placements Primarily Funded By Social service depts.
Social and Rehabilitative Services
Therapeutic Approach The facility has a family oriented approach to therapy.
Therapeutic Services Offered Individual therapy; Group therapy; Family therapy.
Professionals on Staff Psychiatrists; Social workers.

LOUISVILLE

PENINSULA HOSPITAL
Jones Bend Rd, Louisville, TN 37777 (615) 573-7913 *Contact Person(s):* Cathy Rogers
Setting and Background Information The hospital was built in 1972 by Carl Knella on 50 acres, 10 miles south of Knoxville. The campus consists of a modern building which has residential units, classrooms, recreational rooms, swimming pool, gymnasium, tennis courts, crafts room, and cafeteria. Three treatment programs serve adolescents: adolescent psychiatric, youth chemical dependency, and The Village, an experiential outdoor program where the youth construct and live in log cabins.

PENINSULA HOSPITAL *(continued)*

Referral Information Referrals can be made by mental health professionals and other concerned individuals. Contact the hospital to make an appointment for admission.

Type of Facility
Funding Sources Private.
Average Length of Stay Long term.
Types of Admissions Accepted Residential treatment.
Sources of Referral State depts of education; Local depts of education; State depts of mental health; Psychiatrists; Private sources; Depts of correction; Social service depts.

Client Profile
Age Range of Clients Served Residential program: 12-17; The Village: 14-18.
Characteristics Exhibited by Children Emotional handicaps; Learning disabilities.

Tuition and Fees
Room and Board Long term: $431/diem; $135/diem (The Village).
Placements Primarily Funded By Private sources.

Social and Rehabilitative Services
Therapeutic Approach The program is psychodynamically oriented with an emphasis on milieu therapy.
Therapeutic Services Offered Individual therapy; Group therapy; Family therapy; Adjunctive therapy; Art therapy; Physical therapy; Independent living skills program; Recreation activities; Substance abuse treatment; Aftercare program with follow up.
Professionals on Staff Psychiatrists; Psychologists; Social workers; Adjunctive therapists; Art therapists.

Educational and Vocational Services
Type(s) of Educational Programs Offered On campus; Summer campus.
Degrees Offered 12th grade diploma.

MARYVILLE

BLOUNT COUNTY CHILDREN'S HOME
903 Louisville Rd, Maryville, TN 37801 (615) 982-6361 *Contact Person(s):* Chuck Gildrie, Admin
Setting and Background Information The facility was originally established in 1894.
Referral Information Contact the facility and forward social history, psychological reports and other information. An intake interview will be scheduled.

Type of Facility
Funding Sources Private; State; Fund raising.
Average Length of Stay Long term.
Types of Admissions Accepted Group home placement; Wards of the state.
Sources of Referral Private sources; Depts of correction; Social service depts.

Client Profile
Age Range of Clients Served Residential program: 6-21+.
Characteristics Exhibited by Children Emotional handicaps; Learning disabilities.
IQ Range of Clients 70+.

Tuition and Fees
Room and Board Long term: $307-481/mo.
Placements Primarily Funded By Social service depts.

Social and Rehabilitative Services
Therapeutic Approach The basic approach of the facility is behavior management.
Therapeutic Services Offered Individual therapy; Group therapy.
Professionals on Staff Social workers; Child care staff.

Educational and Vocational Services
Type(s) of Educational Programs Offered Off campus (Public school).

MEMPHIS

DOGWOOD VILLAGE
PO Box 341154, Memphis, TN 38134 (901) 867-8832 *Contact Person(s):* Luke Lukens, Prog Dir
Setting and Background Information The village was established in 1979. The 41-acre campus has 6 cottages; an administration building, an activity center, and two more cottages are under construction.
Referral Information For referral, contact the facility and forward the required data. A pre-placement interview will be scheduled.

Type of Facility
Funding Sources State; Federal.
Average Length of Stay Long term.
Types of Admissions Accepted Residential treatment.
Sources of Referral State depts of mental health; Psychiatrists; Social service depts.

Client Profile
Age Range of Clients Served Residential program: 12-18.
Characteristics Exhibited by Children Emotional handicaps; Mental disabilities.
IQ Range of Clients 75+.

Tuition and Fees
Room and Board Long term: $120/diem (including tuition).
Placements Primarily Funded By State depts of mental health; Social service depts.

Social and Rehabilitative Services
Therapeutic Approach The facility uses behavior management and verbal therapy.
Therapeutic Services Offered Individual therapy; Group therapy; Family therapy; Art therapy; Independent living skills program; Recreation activities; Aftercare program with follow up.
Professionals on Staff Psychiatrists; Psychologists; Social workers; Adjunctive therapists; Child care staff; Nurses.

Educational and Vocational Services
Type(s) of Educational Programs Offered On campus (Spec Ed).
Profile of On Campus School Program Number of teachers 5; Number of classrooms 5; Student to teacher ratio 4:1; Credentials of teachers Certified; Grades taught 4-12; Remedial courses offered.
Degrees Offered 8th grade diploma; 12th grade diploma.

MID-SOUTH HOSPITAL
135 N Pauline, Memphis, TN 38105 (901) 527-5211 *Contact Person(s):* Pati Land, Admis Dir; Juanese Clement, Intake Coord
Setting and Background Information The Child and Adolescent Psychiatric Program of Mid-South Hospital was established in 1978.
Referral Information Referrals can be made by parents, guardians, physicians, mental health professionals, school districts, and juvenile courts.

Type of Facility
Funding Sources Private.
Average Length of Stay Long term.
Types of Admissions Accepted Residential treatment.
Sources of Referral State depts of education; Local depts of education; State depts of mental health; Psychiatrists; Private sources; Social service depts; Juvenile courts.

Client Profile
Age Range of Clients Served Residential program: 8-18.
Characteristics Exhibited by Children Emotional handicaps; Learning disabilities; Hearing impairments/deafness; Vision impairments/blindness; Speech/Language disorders; Neurological impairments; Physical handicaps; Mental disabilities.
IQ Range of Clients 70+.

Tuition and Fees
Room and Board Long term: $5,000-$10,000/10 days.
Placements Primarily Funded By Private sources.

Social and Rehabilitative Services
Therapeutic Approach Treatment units use behavior modification and psychoanalytic therapeutic approaches.
Therapeutic Services Offered Individual therapy; Group therapy; Family therapy; Substance abuse treatment; Aftercare program with follow up.
Professionals on Staff Psychiatrists; Psychologists; Social workers; Child care staff; Nurses.

Educational and Vocational Services
Type(s) of Educational Programs Offered On campus; Summer campus.
Profile of On Campus School Program Number of teachers 20; Number of classrooms 5; Student to teacher ratio 10:1; Special curriculum electives offered.
Degrees Offered 8th grade diploma; 12th grade diploma; GED.

MORRISTOWN

YOUTH EMERGENCY SHELTER, INC

407 W 5th North St, Morristown, TN 37814 (615) 586-7740
Contact Person(s): Eddie R Davis, Exec Dir
Setting and Background Information The facility was established by the community in 1975.
Referral Information Contact the facility for referral information.
Type of Facility
Funding Sources Private; State; Federal; County.
Average Length of Stay Short term.
Types of Admissions Accepted Wards of the state; Emergency shelter.
Sources of Referral State depts of education; State depts of mental health; Depts of correction; Social service depts; Juvenile court.
Client Profile
Age Range of Clients Served Residential program: Birth-17.
Characteristics Exhibited by Children Emotional handicaps; Learning disabilities; Hearing impairments/deafness; Vision impairments/ blindness; Speech/Language disorders; Neurological impairments; Mental disabilities.
Tuition and Fees
Room and Board Short term: $35/diem.
Placements Primarily Funded By Counties.
Social and Rehabilitative Services
Professionals on Staff Psychiatrists; Psychologists; Social workers; Adjunctive therapists; Child care staff; Nurses.
Educational and Vocational Services
Type(s) of Educational Programs Offered Off campus (Public schools).

NASHVILLE

CROCKETT ACADEMY

3409 Belmont Blvd, Nashville, TN 37215 (615) 741-3841 *Contact Person(s):* Carol Baringer, Admis Dir
Setting and Background Information Crocket Academy is a residential treatment facility which is operated by the Child and Youth Div of Middle Tenn Mental Health Institute. The facility was established in 1962 as an alternative to psychiatric hospitalization. The campus is located in a middle-class residential area and consists of houses for administrative offices and classrooms, and 5 dorm buildings (8 students per dorm).
Referral Information Referrals can be made by community mental health centers, courts, psychiatrists, psychologists, and social workers. To make a referral, a letter from one of the above referrants should be sent to the Admission Office describing the child's problems and history of outpatient interventions. Background information on the child must also be forwarded, including a parent questionnaire, school reports, social history, and psychological evaluations. An admission committee will review the referral material and make a placement decision.
Type of Facility
Funding Sources State.
Average Length of Stay Long term.
Types of Admissions Accepted Residential treatment.
Sources of Referral State depts of mental health; Psychiatrists; Juvenile court.
Client Profile
Age Range of Clients Served Residential program: 13-18.
Characteristics Exhibited by Children Emotional handicaps; Learning disabilities; Behavior disorders.
Tuition and Fees
Room and Board Long term: $162.90/diem.
Placements Primarily Funded By State depts of mental health; Social service depts.
Social and Rehabilitative Services
Therapeutic Approach The program's philosophy is based on a multi-disciplinary team approach, which allows for the development of an individualized treatment plan for each child.
Therapeutic Services Offered Individual therapy; Group therapy; Family therapy; Art therapy; Independent living skills program; Recreation activities; Substance abuse treatment; Aftercare program with follow up.
Professionals on Staff Psychiatrists; Psychologists; Social workers; Child care staff; Nurses; Art therapists.

Educational and Vocational Services
Type(s) of Educational Programs Offered On campus; Off campus.
Profile of On Campus School Program Number of teachers 12; *Number of classrooms* 8; *Student to teacher ratio* 8:1; Special curriculum electives offered PE; Art; Music; Remedial courses offered.
Degrees Offered 12th grade diploma; GED.

CUMBERLAND HOUSE SCHOOL

3409 Belmont Blvd, Nashville, TN 37215 (615) 741-3841 *Contact Person(s):* Carol Baringer, Admis Dir
Setting and Background Information Cumberland House School is a residential treatment facility which is operated by the Child and Youth Div of Middle Tenn Mental Health Institute. The facility was established in 1962 as an alternative to psychiatric hospitalization. The campus is located in a middle-class residential area and consists of houses for administrative offices and classrooms, and 5 dorm buildings (8 students per dorm).
Referral Information Referrals can be made by community mental health centers, courts, psychiatrists, psychologists, and social workers. To make a referral, a letter from one of the above referrants should be sent to the Admission Office describing the child's problems and history of outpatient interventions. Background information on the child must also be forwarded, including a parent questionnaire, school reports, social history, and psychological evaluation. An admission committee will review the referral material and make a placement decision.
Type of Facility
Funding Sources State.
Average Length of Stay Long term.
Types of Admissions Accepted Residential treatment.
Sources of Referral State depts of mental health; Juvenile court.
Client Profile
Age Range of Clients Served Residential program: 5-12.
Characteristics Exhibited by Children Emotional handicaps; Learning disabilities.
Tuition and Fees
Room and Board Long term: $162.90/diem.
Placements Primarily Funded By Social service depts.
Social and Rehabilitative Services
Therapeutic Approach The program's philosophy is based on a multi-disciplinary team approach, which allows for the development of an individualized treatment plan for each child.
Therapeutic Services Offered Individual therapy; Group therapy; Family therapy; Art therapy; Independent living skills program; Recreation activities; Substance abuse treatment; Aftercare program with follow up.
Professionals on Staff Psychiatrists; Psychologists; Social workers; Child care staff; Nurses.
Educational and Vocational Services
Type(s) of Educational Programs Offered On campus; Off campus.
Profile of On Campus School Program Number of teachers 20-25; *Number of classrooms* 5; *Student to teacher ratio* 8:1.
Degrees Offered 8th grade diploma.

YWCA TRY ANGLE HOUSE

3137 Long Blvd, Nashville, TN 37203 (615) 298-3345 *Contact Person(s):* Doris Farley, Coord
Setting and Background Information The facility was established in 1975 as a group home for adolescent girls who are status offenders. It is sponsored by the YWCA.
Referral Information Most referrals are made through DHS. Application packet should include social history, psychological, school and medical records.
Type of Facility
Funding Sources Private; United Way.
Average Length of Stay Long term.
Types of Admissions Accepted Residential treatment; Group home placement; Wards of the state.
Sources of Referral Dept of Human Svcs.
Client Profile
Age Range of Clients Served Day programs: 14-18; Residential program: 14-18.
Characteristics Exhibited by Children Emotional handicaps; Delinquency; Abused and neglected.
IQ Range of Clients 70+.

YWCA TRY ANGLE HOUSE *(continued)*

Tuition and Fees
Room and Board Long term: $400/mo.
Placements Primarily Funded By Dept of Human Services.
Social and Rehabilitative Services
Therapeutic Services Offered Individual therapy; Group therapy; Family therapy, Independent living skills program; Aftercare program with follow up.
Professionals on Staff Social workers; Adjunctive therapists; Child care staff.
Educational and Vocational Services
Type(s) of Educational Programs Offered Off campus.

SEVIERVILLE

CHURCH OF GOD HOME FOR CHILDREN

Park Rd, Sevierville, TN 37862 (615) 453-4644 *Contact Person(s):* B J Moffett, Dir
Setting and Background Information The facility was established in 1920 by the Church of God. The 61-acre campus has 10 cottage-type units, with a capacity for 12 each.
Referral Information Contact the Director of Social Services for referral information.
Type of Facility
Funding Sources Private.
Average Length of Stay Long term.
Types of Admissions Accepted Group home placement; Wards of the state.
Sources of Referral State depts of mental health; Psychiatrists; Private sources; Depts of correction; Social service depts.
Client Profile
Age Range of Clients Served Residential program: Birth-18.
Characteristics Exhibited by Children Emotional handicaps; Learning disabilities.
IQ Range of Clients 80+.
Tuition and Fees
Room and Board Long term: $900/mo.
Placements Primarily Funded By Social service depts; Church of God.
Social and Rehabilitative Services
Therapeutic Services Offered Individual therapy; Recreation activities.
Professionals on Staff Psychologists; Social workers; Child care staff; Nurses.
Educational and Vocational Services
Type(s) of Educational Programs Offered Off campus (Public schools).

TEXAS

AMARILLO

BUCKNER CHILDREN'S SERVICES

PO Box 3907, 808 S Crockett, Amarillo, TX 79116 (806) 372-2622
Contact Person(s): Danny Wright, Clin Dir
Setting and Background Information This facility was established in 1982 as a private non-profit program. There are three residential facilities at two locations.
Referral Information Contact the facility and forward the application packet with psychological and social summaries.
Type of Facility
Funding Sources Private; State; Federal.
Average Length of Stay Long term; 1-2 yrs.
Types of Admissions Accepted Residential treatment.
Sources of Referral State depts of mental health; Psychiatrists; Private sources; Depts of correction; Social service depts; Child Protective Svcs; Juvenile Probation.
Client Profile
Age Range of Clients Served Residential program: 6-18.
Characteristics Exhibited by Children Emotional handicaps; Learning disabilities.
IQ Range of Clients 70-120.
Tuition and Fees
Room and Board Long term: $77/diem; $61/diem (DHS).
Placements Primarily Funded By Texas Dept of Health Services.
Social and Rehabilitative Services
Therapeutic Approach The facility uses milieu therapy.
Therapeutic Services Offered Individual therapy; Group therapy; Family therapy; Independent living skills program; Recreation activities; Aftercare program with follow up; Juvenile sex offender program.
Professionals on Staff Psychiatrists; Psychologists; Social workers; Child care staff.
Educational and Vocational Services
Type(s) of Educational Programs Offered Off campus.

AUSTIN

THE BROWN SCHOOLS

PO Box 4008, Austin, TX 78765 (800) 531-5305 *Contact Person(s):* Robert L Bennett, Jr, Dir of Admis
Setting and Background Information The Brown Schools are a group of private residential treatment facilities. Established by Kenneth Brown in 1940, The Brown Schools operates 8 separate facilities. The Oaks Treatment Center is located in Austin, Texas on 32 acres. Its campus consists of 10 treatment units (12 patients each), intensive care unit, dental clinic, medical treatment rooms, administrative and clinical offices, education complex, gymnasium, swimming pool, social center, dining room, and recreation fields. The San Marcos Treatment Center, in San Marcos, Texas, has 13 treatment units on 62 acres. Other on-ground facilities include an intensive care unit, dental clinic, medical treatment rooms, administrative and clinical offices, 2 dining rooms, education and pre-vocational classrooms, 2 pools, social center, 2 gymnasiums, music and craft room, and recreation fields. The Ranch Treatment Center is located in Austin, Texas, on 110 acres. Its campus consists of 7 treatment units, central dining room, medical treatment rooms, rehabilitation complex, classrooms, gymnasium, administrative and clinical offices, dental clinic, swimming pool, and recreation fields. Also in Austin, Texas, is the Transition Treatment Center, a 2-story home. The Brown Schools also operate 3 long-term group homes licensed by the Texas Dept of Health. The newest facility for adults, Laurel Ridge, is located in San Antonio.
Referral Information Referrals can be made by mental health professionals, social service agencies, school districts, and families. To make a referral, contact the facility and forward the following information: statement of need for residential treatment, psychological evaluation, family and developmental history, educational records, medical history, neurological assessment (if available), and summaries of previous treatment services. Upon review of the referral material, the admissions committee will determine if the placement is appropriate. If deemed appropriate, then a pre-admission evaluation will be done by a staff psychiatrist before a final decision is made.
Type of Facility
Funding Sources Private.
Average Length of Stay Long term.
Types of Admissions Accepted Residential treatment; Group home placement.
Sources of Referral State depts of education; Local depts of education; State depts of mental health; Psychiatrists; Private sources; Social service depts; National referral service.
Client Profile
Age Range of Clients Served Residential program: 4-18.
Characteristics Exhibited by Children Emotional handicaps; Learning disabilities; Hearing impairments/deafness; Vision impairments/blindness; Speech/Language disorders; Neurological impairments; Physical handicaps; Mental disabilities.
Tuition and Fees
Room and Board Long term: $200-$365/diem.
Placements Primarily Funded By Insurance; Private sources.
Social and Rehabilitative Services
Therapeutic Approach The treatment programs are generally behavioral and/or insight therapy oriented.
Therapeutic Services Offered Individual therapy; Group therapy; Family therapy; Adjunctive therapy; Art therapy; Physical therapy; Independent living skills program; Recreation activities; Substance abuse treatment; Aftercare program with follow up.
Professionals on Staff Psychiatrists; Psychologists; Social workers; Adjunctive therapists; Child care staff; Nurses; Art therapists; Physical therapists.
Educational and Vocational Services
Type(s) of Educational Programs Offered On campus; Off campus.

JUNIOR HELPING HAND HOME FOR CHILDREN

3804 Ave B, Austin, TX 78751 (512) 459-3353 *Contact Person(s):* Leslie M Clark, Exec Dir
Setting and Background Information The facility was established in 1893 as an orphanage.
Referral Information Contact the facility and forward the required information, including a social history and a psychological evaluation.
Type of Facility
Funding Sources Private; State.
Average Length of Stay Long term.
Types of Admissions Accepted Residential treatment; Wards of the state.
Sources of Referral State depts of education; Local depts of education; State depts of mental health; Psychiatrists; Private sources; Depts of correction; Social service depts.

JUNIOR HELPING HAND HOME FOR CHILDREN
(continued)

Client Profile
Age Range of Clients Served Residential program: Birth-12.
Characteristics Exhibited by Children Emotional handicaps; Learning disabilities; Neurological impairments; Mental disabilities.
IQ Range of Clients 80+.
Tuition and Fees
Room and Board Long term: $69/diem.
Placements Primarily Funded By Private sources; Social service depts.
Social and Rehabilitative Services
Therapeutic Approach The facility has a structured milieu.
Therapeutic Services Offered Individual therapy; Group therapy; Family therapy; Recreation activities.
Professionals on Staff Psychiatrists; Social workers; Child care staff; Nurses.
Educational and Vocational Services
Type(s) of Educational Programs Offered Off campus.

MERIDELL ACHIEVEMENT CENTER, INC— WINDRIDGE

PO Box 9383, Austin, TX 78766 (512) 258-1691 *Contact Person(s):* Eileen Krampitz, Dir of Admis
Setting and Background Information Meridell Achievement Center operates 2 private residential treatment facilities, one for boys and one coed. The first facility, Windridge, was founded by Wayne and Janet Lippold in 1961, as a day treatment program for autistic and emotionally disturbed children. In 1963, it expanded its programs to become a residential facility. A second facility was established in Liberty Hill called Westwood. The Windridge campus is located on 5 acres in a suburban setting in Austin. It includes residential units, office building, and a school. The Windridge facility accepts girls and younger boys.
Referral Information Referrals can be made by psychiatrists, psychologists, physicians, public and private agencies, and mental health professionals. To make a referral, contact the facility and forward the following background information: recent psychological or psychiatric evaluation, social history, medical history and examination, recent dental exam, immunization record, birth certificate, school records, court order, and completed application. A pre-placement visit is preferred before an admission decision is made.
Type of Facility
Funding Sources Private.
Average Length of Stay Long term.
Types of Admissions Accepted Residential treatment.
Sources of Referral Psychiatrists; Private sources; Depts of correction; Social service depts.
Client Profile
Age Range of Clients Served Residential program: 6-17.
Characteristics Exhibited by Children Emotional handicaps; Learning disabilities.
Tuition and Fees
Room and Board Long term: $275/diem.
Placements Primarily Funded By Insurance; Private sources.
Social and Rehabilitative Services
Therapeutic Approach The treatment programs use an existentialist approach, in conjunction with reality therapy and behaviorism.
Therapeutic Services Offered Individual therapy; Group therapy; Family therapy; Art therapy; Independent living skills program; Recreation activities; Aftercare program with follow up.
Professionals on Staff Psychiatrists; Social workers; Child care staff; Nurses.
Educational and Vocational Services
Type(s) of Educational Programs Offered On campus; Summer campus.
Profile of On Campus School Program Number of teachers 5; *Number of classrooms* 6; *Student to teacher ratio* 8:1.
Degrees Offered 8th grade diploma; 12th grade diploma.

BEAUMONT

DAYBREAK CHILD AND ADOLESCENT UNIT OF MHMR OF SOUTHEAST TEXAS

2750 S 8th St, Beaumont, TX 77701 (409) 838-3003 *Contact Person(s):* Nora Sollay, Soc Wkr
Setting and Background Information The program was initially established in 1978 as a 16-bed residential unit. It was expanded in 1985 and is now located on a 5-acre campus.
Referral Information Contact the facility. If appropriate, a screening will be performed by a treatment team.
Type of Facility
Funding Sources Private; State; Local.
Average Length of Stay Short and long term.
Types of Admissions Accepted Residential treatment; Wards of the state.
Sources of Referral Local depts of education; State depts of mental health; Psychiatrists; Private sources; Depts of correction; Social service depts.
Client Profile
Age Range of Clients Served Residential program: 6-18.
Characteristics Exhibited by Children Emotional handicaps; Mental disabilities.
IQ Range of Clients 70+.
Tuition and Fees
Room and Board Short term: $100/diem; Long term: $100/diem.
Placements Primarily Funded By State depts of mental health; Insurance; Private sources; Depts of corrections; Social service depts.
Social and Rehabilitative Services
Therapeutic Approach The facility has a holistic approach to therapy with a heavy emphasis on behavior modification.
Therapeutic Services Offered Individual therapy; Group therapy; Family therapy; Adjunctive therapy; Recreation activities; Substance abuse treatment; Aftercare program with follow up.
Professionals on Staff Psychiatrists; Psychologists; Social workers; Recreational therapist.
Educational and Vocational Services
Type(s) of Educational Programs Offered On campus.
Profile of On Campus School Program Number of teachers 4; *Number of classrooms* 3; *Student to teacher ratio* 10:1; *Credentials of teachers* Certified; *Grades taught* 2-12; Remedial courses offered.
Degrees Offered 8th grade diploma; 12th grade diploma.

CORPUS CHRISTI

YOUTH RESIDENTIAL TREATMENT CENTER

1546 S Brownlee, Corpus Christi, TX 78404 (512) 886-6960 *Contact Person(s):* Thomas D Winstead, Prog Dir
Referral Information Contact the facility for referral information. A personal interview will be arranged.
Type of Facility
Funding Sources Private; State.
Average Length of Stay Long term.
Types of Admissions Accepted Residential treatment.
Sources of Referral State depts of education; Local depts of education; State depts of mental health; Psychiatrists; Private sources; Depts of correction; Social service depts; Families.
Client Profile
Age Range of Clients Served Residential program: 12-18.
Characteristics Exhibited by Children Emotional handicaps; Learning disabilities; Abused and neglected.
Tuition and Fees
Room and Board Long term: $82/diem.
Social and Rehabilitative Services
Therapeutic Approach The basic approach of the center is milieu therapy.
Therapeutic Services Offered Individual therapy; Group therapy; Family therapy; Substance abuse treatment; Aftercare program with follow up.
Professionals on Staff Psychiatrists; Psychologists; Social workers; Child care staff; Nurses.
Educational and Vocational Services
Type(s) of Educational Programs Offered Off campus (Public school); Summer campus (Public school).

DALLAS

JULIETTE FOWLER HOMES
PO Box 140129, 100 S Fulton, Dallas, TX 75214 (214) 827-0813
Contact Person(s): Joe Fogle, Admin
Setting and Background Information The facility was established in 1906 as an orphanage and aged care facility. The 15.5-acre campus has cottages, an activity building with a gym, an outdoor swimming pool and a therapy building.
Referral Information Contact the facility for referral information.
Type of Facility
Funding Sources Private; State.
Average Length of Stay Long term.
Types of Admissions Accepted Residential treatment.
Sources of Referral State depts of education; Local depts of education; State depts of mental health; Psychiatrists; Private sources; Depts of correction; Social service depts.
Client Profile
Age Range of Clients Served Residential program: 12-18.
Characteristics Exhibited by Children Emotional handicaps; Learning disabilities.
IQ Range of Clients 79+.
Tuition and Fees
Room and Board Long term: $115/diem.
Placements Primarily Funded By Insurance; Private sources; Depts of corrections; Social service depts.
Social and Rehabilitative Services
Therapeutic Approach The facility has a cognitive behavioral approach to therapy.
Therapeutic Services Offered Individual therapy; Group therapy; Family therapy; Independent living skills program; Recreation activities; Aftercare program with follow up.
Professionals on Staff Psychiatrists; Psychologists; Social workers; Adjunctive therapists; Child care staff; Nurses.
Educational and Vocational Services
Type(s) of Educational Programs Offered On campus; Off campus; Summer campus.
Profile of On Campus School Program Number of teachers 2; *Number of classrooms* 2; *Student to teacher ratio* 8:1; *Credentials of teachers* MA; *Grades taught* 7-12.
Degrees Offered 12th grade diploma.

ST JOSEPH YOUTH CENTER/JOHN A MATZNER SCHOOL
901 S Madison Ave, Dallas, TX 75208 (214) 941-3900 *Contact Person(s):* Debbie Brown
Setting and Background Information St Joseph Youth Center is a non-profit residential treatment facility which was originally established as an orphanage by Catholic Charities in 1903. It evolved into a treatment center by 1979 and became licensed by the Texas Dept of Human Resources. The campus is located on 13 acres and consists of an administration building, recreation center, gymnasium, and 6 residences (3 for boys and 3 for girls) with 8 youths in each.
Referral Information Anyone can make a referral by contacting the facility and making an appointment for the applicant to be evaluated at the Center. This evaluation consists of an interview involving the child, parents, referring agency worker, and the Center's staff, who will assess whether the placement is appropriate.
Type of Facility
Funding Sources Private.
Average Length of Stay Long term.
Types of Admissions Accepted Residential treatment.
Sources of Referral State depts of education; Local depts of education; State depts of mental health; Psychiatrists; Private sources; Social service depts.
Client Profile
Age Range of Clients Served Residential program: 13-17.
Characteristics Exhibited by Children Emotional handicaps; Learning disabilities.
Tuition and Fees
Room and Board Long term: Sliding scale.
Placements Primarily Funded By Private sources.
Social and Rehabilitative Services
Therapeutic Approach The treatment program utilizes a multidisciplinary approach, with ego oriented psychotherapy and milieu therapy.

Therapeutic Services Offered Individual therapy; Group therapy; Family therapy; Adjunctive therapy; Art therapy; Independent living skills program; Recreation activities; Substance abuse treatment; Aftercare program with follow up.
Professionals on Staff Psychiatrists; Psychologists; Social workers; Adjunctive therapists; Child care staff.
Educational and Vocational Services
Type(s) of Educational Programs Offered On campus; Summer campus.
Profile of On Campus School Program Number of teachers 7.
Degrees Offered 8th grade diploma; 12th grade diploma.

DRIFTWOOD

DARDEN HILL RANCH SCHOOL
PO Box 40, Driftwood, TX 78619.
Contact Person(s): Charles Campise, Exec Dir
Setting and Background Information The facility was established in 1973.
Referral Information For referral information contact the facility.
Type of Facility
Funding Sources Private; State.
Average Length of Stay Long term.
Types of Admissions Accepted Residential treatment.
Sources of Referral State depts of mental health; Depts of correction; Social service depts.
Client Profile
Age Range of Clients Served Residential program: 6-18.
Characteristics Exhibited by Children Emotional handicaps; Learning disabilities; Neurological impairments; Mental disabilities.
IQ Range of Clients 68-118.
Tuition and Fees
Room and Board Long term: $61/diem.
Tuition $61/diem.
Placements Primarily Funded By State depts of mental health.
Social and Rehabilitative Services
Therapeutic Approach The facility uses behavior modification in a therapeutic milieu.
Therapeutic Services Offered Individual therapy; Group therapy; Family therapy; Physical therapy; Independent living skills program.
Professionals on Staff Psychiatrists; Psychologists; Social workers; Child care staff.
Educational and Vocational Services
Type(s) of Educational Programs Offered On campus.
Profile of On Campus School Program Number of teachers 2; *Number of classrooms* 2; *Student to teacher ratio* 5:1; *Grades taught* K-11; Remedial courses offered.

EL PASO

EL PASO CENTER FOR CHILDREN
3700 Altura, El Paso, TX 79930 (915) 565-8361 *Contact Person(s):* Neva Black, Intake Coord
Setting and Background Information The facility was founded in 1919 as an orphanage and later evolved into a home for dependent and neglected children. In 1971 the programs changed to become a residential treatment center and in 1982 expanded to include adolescents. The campus is located in west Texas and consists of an adolescent cottage, children's cottage, administration building, cafeteria, and service building.
Referral Information Referrals can be made by parents, physicians, and state agencies throughout the year. The Intake Coordinator should be contacted to obtain information on admission procedures. Information regarding the applicant will be given to the Clinical Director of the program. An intake worker will contact the client for additional information and to arrange an interview.
Type of Facility
Funding Sources Private; State.
Average Length of Stay Long term.
Types of Admissions Accepted Residential treatment.
Sources of Referral Private sources; Social service depts.
Client Profile
Age Range of Clients Served Residential program: 5-17.
Characteristics Exhibited by Children Emotional handicaps.

EL PASO CENTER FOR CHILDREN *(continued)*

Tuition and Fees
Room and Board Long term: $100/diem.
Placements Primarily Funded By Private sources; Social service depts; United Way.
Social and Rehabilitative Services
Therapeutic Approach The Center emphasizes the use of family therapy within the context of General Systems theory.
Therapeutic Services Offered Individual therapy; Group therapy; Family therapy; Recreation activities; Aftercare program with follow up.
Professionals on Staff Psychiatrists; Psychologists; Social workers; Child care staff; Nurses.
Educational and Vocational Services
Type(s) of Educational Programs Offered Off campus.

EL PASO STATE CENTER

6700 Delta, El Paso, TX 79922 (915) 779-0800 *Contact Person(s):* Michael Smith, Admin Res Svcs
Setting and Background Information The facility was established in 1974 by a state mandate. There are 6 MR living facilities and 3 MH living facilities.
Referral Information Contact the facility for referral information.
Type of Facility
Funding Sources State.
Average Length of Stay Short and long term.
Types of Admissions Accepted Residential treatment; Acute psychiatric care.
Sources of Referral Any citizen or agency may make a referral.
Client Profile
Age Range of Clients Served Day programs: 22-55+; Residential program: 6-55+.
Characteristics Exhibited by Children Emotional handicaps; Physical handicaps; Mental disabilities.
IQ Range of Clients 2-69.
Tuition and Fees
Room and Board Short term: $159/diem; Long term: $159/diem.
Placements Primarily Funded By State depts of mental health.
Social and Rehabilitative Services
Therapeutic Services Offered Individual therapy; Group therapy; Family therapy; Adjunctive therapy; Physical therapy; Independent living skills program; Recreation activities; Substance abuse treatment.
Professionals on Staff Psychiatrists; Psychologists; Social workers; Adjunctive therapists; Child care staff; Nurses.
Educational and Vocational Services
Type(s) of Educational Programs Offered On campus.

FORT DAVIS

THE HIGH FRONTIER, INC

PO Box 1325, Fort Davis, TX 79734 (915) 364-2241 *Contact Person(s):* Lee Lowry
Setting and Background Information The ranch-like facility was established in 1976 in a rural area of the Davis Mountains, 20 miles north of Alpine, Texas.
Referral Information Referrals are primarily made by the Dept of Human Resources, Texas Youth Commission, other institutions, and private individuals. All applicants must complete a referral packet which includes a psychological/psychiatric examination and an updated social history; both should have been completed within the past 6 months.
Type of Facility
Funding Sources Private; State; Federal.
Average Length of Stay Long term.
Types of Admissions Accepted Residential treatment.
Sources of Referral State depts of mental health; Psychiatrists; Private sources; Social service depts.
Client Profile
Age Range of Clients Served Residential program: 12-17.
Characteristics Exhibited by Children Emotional handicaps; Learning disabilities.
IQ Range of Clients 80+.
Tuition and Fees
Room and Board Long term: $61/diem.

Social and Rehabilitative Services
Therapeutic Approach The basic therapeutic approach used at the facility is positive peer culture.
Therapeutic Services Offered Individual therapy; Group therapy; Family therapy; Art therapy; Substance abuse treatment.
Professionals on Staff Psychiatrists; Social workers; Child care staff; Nurses.
Educational and Vocational Services
Type(s) of Educational Programs Offered On campus; Summer campus.
Profile of On Campus School Program Number of teachers 8; *Number of classrooms* 6.
Degrees Offered 8th grade diploma; 12th grade diploma; GED.

FORT WORTH

LENA POPE HOME

4701 W Rosedale, Fort Worth, TX 76107 (817) 731-8681 *Contact Person(s):* Pattye Mochek
Setting and Background Information The facility was intitially established as an orphanage in 1930, but has since evolved into a treatment center.
Referral Information Referrals can be made by community and state government agencies, as well as by parents. To make a referral, contact the facility and complete the necessary application materials. A psychiatric evaluation and pre-placement interview are required before an admission decision is made.
Type of Facility
Funding Sources State.
Average Length of Stay Long term.
Types of Admissions Accepted Residential treatment.
Sources of Referral State depts of mental health; Social service depts; Juvenile courts.
Client Profile
Age Range of Clients Served Residential program: 10-17.
Characteristics Exhibited by Children Emotional handicaps; Learning disabilities.
Tuition and Fees
Room and Board Long term: $61/diem.
Social and Rehabilitative Services
Therapeutic Approach The treatment program utilizes behavior modification and psychotherapy.
Therapeutic Services Offered Individual therapy; Group therapy; Aftercare program with follow up.
Professionals on Staff Psychiatrists; Psychologists; Child care staff; Nurses.
Educational and Vocational Services
Type(s) of Educational Programs Offered On campus; Off campus; Summer campus.
Profile of On Campus School Program Number of teachers 3; *Number of classrooms* 3; *Student to teacher ratio* 8:1.
Degrees Offered 8th grade diploma; 12th grade diploma.

GALVESTON

GULF COAST REGIONAL MENTAL HEALTH MENTAL RETARDATION CENTER

PO Box 2490, 123 Rosenburg, Ste 600, Galveston, TX 77553 (409) 763-2373 *Contact Person(s):* Norma Flory, Continuity of Care Dir
Setting and Background Information The facility was established in 1969. The objective of the center is to provide quality non-institutional community based services to mentally handicapped citizens of Galveston and Brazorra Counties.
Referral Information Contact any of the four Out-patient Clinics for referral information.
Type of Facility
Funding Sources State; Local.
Average Length of Stay Long term.
Types of Admissions Accepted Day treatment; Residential treatment; Group home placement; Wards of the state; Out-patient.
Sources of Referral State depts of mental health; Psychiatrists; Private sources; Social service depts.

GULF COAST REGIONAL MENTAL HEALTH MENTAL RETARDATION CENTER (continued)

Client Profile
Age Range of Clients Served Day programs: Birth-55+; Residential program: 12-55+.
Characteristics Exhibited by Children Emotional handicaps; Learning disabilities; Neurological impairments; Mental disabilities.
Tuition and Fees
Placements Primarily Funded By State depts of mental health; Insurance.
Social and Rehabilitative Services
Therapeutic Services Offered Individual therapy; Group therapy; Family therapy; Adjunctive therapy; Independent living skills program; Recreation activities; Substance abuse treatment; Aftercare program with follow up.
Professionals on Staff Psychiatrists; Psychologists; Social workers; Adjunctive therapists; Nurses.

GOLDTHWAITE

NEW HORIZONS RANCH AND CENTER

PO Box 549, Goldthwaite, TX 76844 (915) 938-5518 *Contact Person(s):* Mike Snider, Shirlene Gothrie
Setting and Background Information The facility was established in 1970 as an outgrowth of the Meridell Achievement Center in Austin, Texas. Its campus is located in central Texas in a semi-rustic setting.
Referral Information Anyone can make a referral by contacting the facility and forwarding the necessary background information, including psychological testing and social history.
Type of Facility
Funding Sources State.
Average Length of Stay Long term.
Types of Admissions Accepted Group home placement.
Sources of Referral State depts of education; Local depts of education; Private sources; Social service depts; Probation.
Client Profile
Age Range of Clients Served Residential program: 8-18.
Characteristics Exhibited by Children Emotional handicaps.
IQ Range of Clients 80+.
Tuition and Fees
Room and Board Long term: $61-$79/diem.
Placements Primarily Funded By Social service depts.
Social and Rehabilitative Services
Therapeutic Approach The treatment program is primarily based on milieu therapy.
Therapeutic Services Offered Individual therapy; Group therapy; Family therapy; Independent living skills program; Recreation activities.
Professionals on Staff Psychiatrists; Psychologists; Social workers; Child care staff.
Educational and Vocational Services
Type(s) of Educational Programs Offered On campus; Summer campus.
Profile of On Campus School Program Number of teachers 9; *Number of classrooms* 8; *Student to teacher ratio* 6:1.
Degrees Offered 8th grade diploma; 12th grade diploma; GED.

GROVETON

HOPE CENTER FOR YOUTH, GIRLS WILDERNESS PROGRAM

PO Box 760, Groveton, TX 75845 (409) 642-2384 *Contact Person(s):* Jeff Jamar
Setting and Background Information The agency was established in 1976 to provide day and residential treatment services to emotionally disturbed youth. There are 2 Wilderness Camp programs for boys and girls located in the wooded areas of east Texas. There is also a supervised apartment living program, which operates 2 small apartment complexes to prepare residents for independent living. An alternative school program offers special education instruction to students unable to attend public school.
Referral Information Referrals can be made by parents or guardians, and public or private agencies, Child Protection Services, Juvenile Probation, Dept of Human Services, and Texas Youth

Commission. Applicants must be residing in the state of Texas. Contact the facility for referral information.
Type of Facility
Funding Sources Private; State.
Average Length of Stay Long term.
Types of Admissions Accepted Residential treatment.
Sources of Referral Social service depts.
Client Profile
Age Range of Clients Served Residential program: 13-17.
Characteristics Exhibited by Children Emotional handicaps; Learning disabilities.
Tuition and Fees
Placements Primarily Funded By Social service depts.
Social and Rehabilitative Services
Therapeutic Services Offered Individual therapy; Group therapy; Family therapy; Independent living skills program; Recreation activities; Substance abuse treatment; Aftercare program with follow up.
Professionals on Staff Psychiatrists; Psychologists; Social workers; Child care staff; Nurses.
Educational and Vocational Services
Type(s) of Educational Programs Offered On campus.
Profile of On Campus School Program Number of teachers 5; *Number of classrooms* 4; *Student to teacher ratio* 10:1; Remedial courses offered.

KEENE

ODYSSEY HARBOR, INC

Box 409, Keene, TX 76059 (817) 641-4093 *Contact Person(s):* Amine Varga MSW, Exec Dir
Setting and Background Information This non-profit organization was established in 1983 in response to a need for residential services for multi-problem children. It is located on 30 acres and has 4 residential buildings, a barn, administration and activities buildings.
Referral Information For referral, contact facility and follow up with psychiatric, psychological, social history and educational reports.
Type of Facility
Funding Sources Private.
Average Length of Stay Long term.
Types of Admissions Accepted Residential treatment; Wards of the state.
Sources of Referral State depts of education; Local depts of education; State depts of mental health; Psychiatrists; Depts of correction; Social service depts.
Client Profile
Age Range of Clients Served Residential program: 5-18.
Characteristics Exhibited by Children Emotional handicaps; Learning disabilities; Hearing impairments/deafness; Vision impairments/blindness; Speech/Language disorders; Neurological impairments; Physical handicaps; Mental disabilities.
IQ Range of Clients 30-150.
Tuition and Fees
Room and Board Long term: $105/diem (includes school tuition).
Placements Primarily Funded By State depts of education; Local depts of education; State depts of mental health; Depts of corrections; Social service depts.
Social and Rehabilitative Services
Therapeutic Approach The facility has a multi-disciplinary approach to therapy which includes play therapy. The program is designed for the multi-problem emotionally disturbed child who has had multiple failed placements.
Therapeutic Services Offered Individual therapy; Group therapy; Family therapy; Art therapy; Physical therapy; Independent living skills program; Recreation activities; Aftercare program with follow up.
Professionals on Staff Psychiatrists; Psychologists; Social workers; Adjunctive therapists; Child care staff; Nurses; Art therapists; Recreational therapist.
Educational and Vocational Services
Type(s) of Educational Programs Offered On campus (Spec Ed); Off campus (Local school); Summer campus.
Profile of On Campus School Program Number of teachers 3; *Number of classrooms* 3; *Student to teacher ratio* 3:1; *Credentials of teachers* Certified Spec Ed; *Grades taught* K-12; Special curriculum electives offered (Computers); Remedial courses offered (Basic subjects).

ODYSSEY HARBOR, INC *(continued)*

Vocational Education Programs/Degrees Offered Beauty school.
Degrees Offered 8th grade diploma; 12th grade diploma; GED.

LAREDO

LAREDO STATE CENTER
413 Cherry Hill Dr, Laredo, TX 78044-1835 (512) 723-2926
Contact Person(s): Delores V Rodriguez, Dir
Setting and Background Information The center was established in
1969 with a federal grant from NIMH. The 15-acre campus has a
building with out-patient services, day treatment programs and
administrative offices and has two 15 bed cottages.
Referral Information Contact the facility for referral information.
Type of Facility
Funding Sources State; Federal.
Average Length of Stay Short term.
Types of Admissions Accepted Day treatment; Residential treatment;
Group home placement.
Sources of Referral State depts of education; Local depts of educa-
tion; State depts of mental health; Psychiatrists; Private sources;
Depts of correction; Social service depts.
Client Profile
Age Range of Clients Served Day programs: 6-55+; Residential pro-
gram: 15-55+.
Characteristics Exhibited by Children Emotional handicaps; Mental
disabilities.
Tuition and Fees
Room and Board Short term: $131/diem.
Placements Primarily Funded By State depts of mental health.
Social and Rehabilitative Services
Therapeutic Approach The facility has a multidisciplinary approach
to therapy.
Therapeutic Services Offered Individual therapy; Group therapy;
Family therapy; Adjunctive therapy; Physical therapy; Indepen-
dent living skills program; Recreation activities; Substance abuse
treatment; Aftercare program with follow up.
Professionals on Staff Psychiatrists; Psychologists; Social workers;
Adjunctive therapists; Nurses.

LIBERTY HILL

MERIDELL ACHIEVEMENT CENTER, INC—
WESTWOOD
PO Box 87, Liberty Hill, TX 78642 (512) 259-0774 *Contact
Person(s):* Eileen Krampitz, Dir of Admis
Setting and Background Information Meridell Achievement Center
operates 2 private residential treatment facilities, one for boys
and one coed. The first facility, Windridge, was founded by
Wayne and Janet Lippold in 1961, The Westwood facility was
established in 1964 and accepts older boys. The Westwood
campus is located in Liberty Hill on 225 acres of rural
countryside. It consists of 6 cabins, an administrative office,
therapy buildings, school, vocational/shop building, community
center, and several buildings.
Referral Information Referrals can be made by psychiatrists,
psychologists, physicians, public and private agencies, and mental
health professionals. To make a referral, contact the facility and
forward the following background information: recent
psychological or psychiatric evaluation, social history, medical
history and examination, recent dental exam, immunization
record, birth certificate, school records, court order, and
completed application. A pre-placement visit is preferred before
an admission decision is made.
Type of Facility
Funding Sources Private.
Average Length of Stay Long term.
Types of Admissions Accepted Residential treatment.
Sources of Referral State depts of education; Local depts of education; State depts of mental health; Private sources; Social service
depts.
Client Profile
Age Range of Clients Served Residential program: 11-17.
Characteristics Exhibited by Children Emotional handicaps; Learning
disabilities; Speech/Language disorders.

Tuition and Fees
Room and Board Long term: $275/diem.
Placements Primarily Funded By Insurance; Private sources.
Social and Rehabilitative Services
Therapeutic Approach The treatment programs use an existentialist
approach, in conjunction with reality therapy and behaviorism.
Therapeutic Services Offered Individual therapy; Group therapy;
Family therapy; Art therapy; Physical therapy; Independent living
skills program; Recreation activities; Aftercare program with fol-
low up; Sexual abuse therapy.
Professionals on Staff Psychiatrists; Psychologists; Social workers;
Child care staff; Nurses.
Educational and Vocational Services
Type(s) of Educational Programs Offered On campus.
Profile of On Campus School Program Number of teachers 7; Num-
ber of classrooms 6.
Degrees Offered 8th grade diploma; 12th grade diploma.

RICHARDSON

AUTISTIC TREATMENT CENTER
PO Box 529, Richardson, TX 75080 (214) 644-2076 *Contact
Person(s):* Mary York, Soc Wkr
Setting and Background Information The facility was established in
1976 and has 5 group homes, a day school and a vocational
workshop.
Referral Information Contact the facility and forward psychological
information, a social history and medical reports. Client must
have a diagnosis of autism and pervasive developmental delay.
Type of Facility
Funding Sources Private.
Average Length of Stay Long term.
Types of Admissions Accepted Day treatment; Residential treatment.
Sources of Referral State depts of education; Local depts of educa-
tion; State depts of mental health; Private sources; Social service
depts.
Client Profile
Age Range of Clients Served Day programs: Birth-15; Residential
program: Birth-55+.
Characteristics Exhibited by Children Autism.
Tuition and Fees
Placements Primarily Funded By State depts of education; Local
depts of education; State depts of mental health; Insurance; Pri-
vate sources.
Social and Rehabilitative Services
Therapeutic Approach The facility uses behavior management.
Therapeutic Services Offered Individual therapy; Family therapy;
Independent living skills program; Recreation activities.
Professionals on Staff Psychiatrists; Psychologists; Social workers;
Adjunctive therapists; Child care staff; Nurses; Physical therapists.
Educational and Vocational Services
Type(s) of Educational Programs Offered Off campus.
Vocational Education Programs/Degrees Offered Vocational work-
shop.

SAN ANTONIO

BAPTIST CHILDREN'S HOME AT SAN ANTONIO
7404 Hwy 90 W, San Antonio, TX 78227 (512) 674-3010 *Contact
Person(s):* Ben Spicer
Setting and Background Information The facility was initially
established in 1944 by the Mexican Baptist General Convention
of Texas to provide services to Mexican-American children. Since
then, its programs have expanded to accept children of all races.
The campus is located on 120 acres of land with 12 cottages (6
for boys and 6 for girls), commissary, barn, swimming pool,
chalet for parties, and an administration building.
Referral Information Anyone can make a referral, but admission
papers must be signed by the child's parent or guardian. To make
a referral, contact the Director of Social Services to provide
background information on the child. If the referral is
appropriate, then an intake packet must be completed by the
applicant and returned to the social worker. Several interviews,
accompanied by a pre-placement visit, will be scheduled before
an admission decision is made.

BAPTIST CHILDREN'S HOME AT SAN ANTONIO
(continued)

Type of Facility
Funding Sources Private.
Average Length of Stay Long term.
Types of Admissions Accepted Residential treatment.
Sources of Referral Local depts of education; State depts of mental health; Social service depts.
Client Profile
Age Range of Clients Served Residential program: 2-18.
Characteristics Exhibited by Children Emotional handicaps; Learning disabilities; Speech/Language disorders.
IQ Range of Clients 80+.
Tuition and Fees
Room and Board Long term: Sliding scale.
Placements Primarily Funded By Private sources.
Social and Rehabilitative Services
Therapeutic Services Offered Individual therapy; Family therapy; Aftercare program with follow up.
Professionals on Staff Social workers; Child care staff.
Educational and Vocational Services
Type(s) of Educational Programs Offered Off campus.

BEXAR COUNTY MHMR CENTER—RESIDENTIAL PROGRAM
227 Old Guilbeau, San Antonio, TX 78204 (512) 225-3864 *Contact Person(s):* Al Flores, Prog Dir
Setting and Background Information This facility is a group home social services agency, with 7 group homes in the San Antonio area. In addition, there are semi-independent apartments.
Referral Information Contact the facility for referral information.
Type of Facility
Funding Sources Private; State; County.
Average Length of Stay Short and long term.
Types of Admissions Accepted Residential treatment; Group home placement.
Sources of Referral State depts of mental health; Psychiatrists; Depts of correction; Social service depts.
Client Profile
Age Range of Clients Served Residential program: 12-55+.
Characteristics Exhibited by Children Emotional handicaps; Learning disabilities; Mental disabilities.
Tuition and Fees
Room and Board Short term: Sliding scale; Long term: Sliding scale.
Placements Primarily Funded By State depts of mental health; Depts of corrections.
Social and Rehabilitative Services
Therapeutic Services Offered Individual therapy; Group therapy; Family therapy; Independent living skills program; Recreation activities; Substance abuse treatment.
Professionals on Staff Psychiatrists; Psychologists; Social workers; Nurses; Community service workers.
Educational and Vocational Services
Type(s) of Educational Programs Offered Off campus (Public school).

COLONIAL HILLS HOSPITAL
4330 Vance Jackson Rd, San Antonio, TX 78230 (512) 341-5131
Contact Person(s): Admissions Office
Referral Information For referral information, contact the admissions office.
Type of Facility
Funding Sources Private.
Average Length of Stay Long term.
Types of Admissions Accepted Residential treatment.
Sources of Referral State depts of education; Local depts of education; State depts of mental health; Psychiatrists; Private sources; Depts of correction; Social service depts.
Client Profile
Age Range of Clients Served Residential program: 6-18.
Characteristics Exhibited by Children Emotional handicaps; Drug/alcohol use and abuse.
Tuition and Fees
Placements Primarily Funded By Insurance; Private sources.

Social and Rehabilitative Services
Therapeutic Approach The facility has a multi-disciplinary approach to therapy.
Therapeutic Services Offered Individual therapy; Group therapy; Family therapy; Adjunctive therapy; Art therapy; Recreation activities; Substance abuse treatment; Aftercare program with follow up.
Professionals on Staff Psychiatrists; Psychologists; Social workers; Adjunctive therapists; Child care staff; Nurses; Art therapists; Physical therapists.
Educational and Vocational Services
Type(s) of Educational Programs Offered On campus.
Profile of On Campus School Program Credentials of teachers State Certified.

SAN ANTONIO CHILDREN'S CENTER
2939 W Woodlawn Ave, San Antonio, TX 78228 (512) 736-4273
Contact Person(s): Cathi Hanna, Admis Coord
Setting and Background Information The facility was initially established as an orphanage in 1886 and later evolved into a home for emotionally disturbed youth. It became licensed as a psychiatric hopsital in 1975. The campus is located on 10 acres of land in northwest San Antonio. There are 11 buildings, including 6 separate treatment units, gymnasium, outdoor pool, and recreational fields.
Referral Information Referrals can be made by physicians, mental health professionals, education personnel, parents, and agencies. To make a referral, the child must be interviewed by a staff psychiatrist and the necessary background information must be forwarded to the Admissions Coordinator for review.
Type of Facility
Funding Sources Private.
Average Length of Stay Short and long term.
Types of Admissions Accepted Residential treatment.
Sources of Referral State depts of education; Local depts of education; Parents; Mental health professionals.
Client Profile
Age Range of Clients Served Residential program: 3-18.
Characteristics Exhibited by Children Emotional handicaps; Learning disabilities; Speech/Language disorders; Neurological impairments; Primary psychiatric diagnosis.
Tuition and Fees
Room and Board Long term: $240/diem (residential); $280/diem (intensive care).
Tuition $240/diem Residential.
Placements Primarily Funded By Insurance.
Social and Rehabilitative Services
Therapeutic Approach The facility has a structured therapeutic milieu.
Therapeutic Services Offered Individual therapy; Group therapy; Family therapy; Adjunctive therapy; Recreation activities; Aftercare program with follow up.
Professionals on Staff Psychiatrists; Psychologists; Social workers; Adjunctive therapists; Child care staff; Nurses.
Educational and Vocational Services
Type(s) of Educational Programs Offered On campus; Summer campus.
Profile of On Campus School Program Number of teachers 8; *Number of classrooms* 7; *Student to teacher ratio* 7:1; Remedial courses offered.
Degrees Offered 8th grade diploma; 12th grade diploma; GED.

YOUTH ALTERNATIVES, INC
3103 West Ave, San Antonio, TX 78213 (512) 340-8077 *Contact Person(s):* Bart Kelly
Setting and Background Information Youth Alternatives operates an emergency shelter, long-term residential faciliates for boys and girls (separately) and a long-term group home for boys. The first facility, Bridge Emergency Shelter, was established in 1976 by a group of concerned citizens who had received grant money from the Runaway Act. Over the years, additional programs for long-term residential care have opened.
Referral Information Referrals can be made by juvenile probation, Texas Youth Commission, Child Welfare, school districts, and parents. Upon acceptance, an agreement with the child's parent or guardian will be made regarding length of stay.

YOUTH ALTERNATIVES, INC (continued)

Type of Facility
Funding Sources State.
Average Length of Stay Short and long term.
Types of Admissions Accepted Residential treatment; Emergency shelter.
Sources of Referral Social service depts; Juvenile probation.
Client Profile
Age Range of Clients Served Residential program: 8-17.
Characteristics Exhibited by Children Emotional handicaps; Learning disabilities.
IQ Range of Clients 70+.
Tuition and Fees
Room and Board Long term: $61/diem.
Placements Primarily Funded By Social service depts; United Way; Civic groups.
Social and Rehabilitative Services
Therapeutic Approach The treatment program uses an eclectic approach with an emphasis on developing skills for social interaction.
Therapeutic Services Offered Individual therapy; Group therapy; Family therapy; Recreation activities; Substance abuse treatment; Aftercare program with follow up.
Professionals on Staff Psychiatrists; Psychologists; Social workers; Child care staff.
Educational and Vocational Services
Type(s) of Educational Programs Offered On campus; Off campus; Summer campus.
Profile of On Campus School Program Number of teachers 1; *Number of classrooms* 2; *Student to teacher ratio* 3:1.

TERRELL

TERRELL STATE HOSPITAL, CHILD/ADOLESCENT UNIT

PO Box 70, Terrell, TX 75160 (214) 563-6452 ext 2587 *Contact Person(s):* John Wyckoff, Admin
Setting and Background Information This unit was established in 1973 by separating adolescents from the adult unit of the Terrell State Hospital.
Referral Information For referral, contact the facility and forward pertinent information. A pre-placement evaluation will be held.
Type of Facility
Funding Sources State.
Average Length of Stay Long term.
Types of Admissions Accepted Residential treatment.
Sources of Referral State depts of education; Local depts of education; State depts of mental health; Psychiatrists; Social service depts.
Client Profile
Age Range of Clients Served Residential program: Birth-18.
Characteristics Exhibited by Children Emotional handicaps; Mental disabilities; Drug/alcohol abuse.
IQ Range of Clients 70+.
Tuition and Fees
Placements Primarily Funded By State depts of mental health.
Social and Rehabilitative Services
Therapeutic Approach The facility offers individual, group and family therapy.
Therapeutic Services Offered Individual therapy; Group therapy; Family therapy; Adjunctive therapy; Art therapy; Independent living skills program; Recreation activities; Substance abuse treatment; Aftercare program with follow up; Music therapy; Dance therapy.
Professionals on Staff Psychiatrists; Psychologists; Social workers; Child care staff; Nurses; Art therapists.
Educational and Vocational Services
Type(s) of Educational Programs Offered On campus.
Profile of On Campus School Program Number of teachers 10; *Number of classrooms* 7; *Student to teacher ratio* 5:1; *Credentials of teachers* BS; *Grades taught* 1-12; Special curriculum electives offered (Vocational programs).
Degrees Offered GED.

TYLER

EAST TEXAS GUIDANCE CENTER

PO Box 6648, Tyler, TX 75711 (214) 839-4374 *Contact Person(s):* Robert Main
Setting and Background Information East Texas Guidance Center is a residential treatment facility for boys which was established in 1968 on 18 acres of land in a rural area.
Referral Information Anyone can make a referral by contacting the facility and forwarding the necessary background information on the child. A pre-placement interview will take place before a placement decision is made.
Type of Facility
Funding Sources State.
Average Length of Stay Long term.
Types of Admissions Accepted Residential treatment.
Sources of Referral Social service depts.
Client Profile
Age Range of Clients Served Residential program: 6-18.
Characteristics Exhibited by Children Emotional handicaps; Learning disabilities; Speech/Language disorders.
IQ Range of Clients 40-139.
Tuition and Fees
Room and Board Long term: $61/diem.
Placements Primarily Funded By Social service depts.
Social and Rehabilitative Services
Therapeutic Approach The treatment program utilizes a therapeutic approach based on behavior modification, in conjunction with milieu therapy.
Therapeutic Services Offered Individual therapy; Group therapy; Family therapy; Art therapy; Independent living skills program; Recreation activities; Aftercare program with follow up.
Professionals on Staff Psychiatrists; Psychologists; Social workers; Child care staff.
Educational and Vocational Services
Type(s) of Educational Programs Offered Off campus.

WACO

WACO CENTER FOR YOUTH

PO Box 5117, 3501 N 19th, Waco, TX 76708 (817) 756-2171
Contact Person(s): Charles Locklin, Dir
Setting and Background Information The facility was established in 1979 by the Texas State Legislature. The 94.5-acre campus has 7 patient units, school buildings, gymnasium, recreational areas, and an intensive care unit.
Referral Information Referrals to the facility are accepted directly through community MHMR centers; state operated mental health facilities; Texas Dept of Human Services; and the Texas Education Agency.
Type of Facility
Funding Sources State.
Average Length of Stay Long term.
Types of Admissions Accepted Residential treatment.
Sources of Referral State depts of education; State depts of mental health; Social service depts; Texas Dept of Human Svcs.
Client Profile
Age Range of Clients Served Residential program: 10-18.
Characteristics Exhibited by Children Emotional handicaps; Learning disabilities.
Tuition and Fees
Placements Primarily Funded By State depts of mental health; Insurance.
Social and Rehabilitative Services
Therapeutic Approach The facility uses the psychiatric therapies which are associated with residential treatment.
Therapeutic Services Offered Individual therapy; Group therapy; Family therapy; Art therapy; Independent living skills program; Recreation activities; Aftercare program with follow up.
Professionals on Staff Psychiatrists; Psychologists; Social workers; Child care staff; Nurses; Art therapists.

Educational and Vocational Services

Type(s) of Educational Programs Offered On campus.

Profile of On Campus School Program Number of teachers 15;
Number of classrooms 8; *Student to teacher ratio* 6:1; *Credentials
of teachers* Spec Ed; *Grades taught* Spec Ed; Special curriculum
electives offered; Remedial courses offered.

Vocational Education Programs/Degrees Offered Pre-vocational education.

Degrees Offered Credits transfer to public school.

UTAH

PROVO

PROVO CANYON SCHOOL

PO Box 1441, Provo, UT 84603 (801) 227-2000 *Contact Person(s):*
Jannett Benson, Admis Supv
Setting and Background Information The facility was privately
established in 1971. Its 10-acre campus has one building. There is
also a recreation center.
Referral Information Contact the facility for referral information.
Type of Facility
Funding Sources Private.
Average Length of Stay 15 mos.
Types of Admissions Accepted Residential treatment.
Sources of Referral State depts of education; Local depts of educa-
tion; State depts of mental health; Psychiatrists; Private sources;
Depts of correction; Social service depts.
Client Profile
Age Range of Clients Served Residential program: 12-18.
Characteristics Exhibited by Children Emotional handicaps; Learning
disabilities.
IQ Range of Clients 80-140.
Tuition and Fees
Tuition $29,800/yr.
Placements Primarily Funded By Private sources.
Social and Rehabilitative Services
Therapeutic Approach The facility uses reality therapy.
Therapeutic Services Offered Individual therapy; Group therapy;
Family therapy; Substance abuse treatment.
Professionals on Staff Psychiatrists; Psychologists; Social workers;
Nurses.
Educational and Vocational Services
Type(s) of Educational Programs Offered On campus; Off campus
(Work experience).
Profile of On Campus School Program Number of teachers 20;
Number of classrooms 12; *Student to teacher ratio* 12:1; *Creden-
tials of teachers* BA/BS or MA, MS, MEd; *Grades taught* 7-12.
Vocational Education Programs/Degrees Offered Woodshop; Draft-
ing; Auto mechanics (theory); Photography; Painting; Drawing;
Ceramics; Sculpture.
Degrees Offered 12th grade diploma; Special education diploma.

UTAH STATE HOSPITAL, YOUTH CENTER

PO Box 270, 1300 E Center, Provo, UT 84604 (801) 373-4400 ext
515 *Contact Person(s):* Spence Wood, Admin Dir; Ron Kelley,
Admis Dir
Setting and Background Information The program was established in
1964 as part of the Utah State Hospital to provide services to
emotionally disturbed youth. The Youth Center is divided into
two separate dorm unit programs; the Children's Program (6-12)
and the Adolescent Unit (13-18).
Referral Information Referrals can be made by parents, mental
health centers, social service agencies, juvenile courts, and district
courts. Applicants are screened by mental health centers in their
geographical area and then referred by them.
Type of Facility
Funding Sources Private; State.
Average Length of Stay Short and long term.
Types of Admissions Accepted Residential treatment.
Sources of Referral State depts of mental health; Psychiatrists; Pri-
vate sources; Depts of correction.

Client Profile
Age Range of Clients Served Residential program: 6-18.
Characteristics Exhibited by Children Emotional handicaps; Learning
disabilities; Neurological impairments.
Tuition and Fees
Room and Board Long term: Sliding scale.
Placements Primarily Funded By State depts of education; State
depts of mental health; Insurance; Private sources.
Social and Rehabilitative Services
Therapeutic Approach The program's treatment philosophy involves
the use of a therapeutic community.
Therapeutic Services Offered Individual therapy; Group therapy;
Family therapy; Adjunctive therapy; Independent living skills
program; Recreation activities.
Professionals on Staff Psychiatrists; Psychologists; Social workers;
Adjunctive therapists; Child care staff; Nurses.
Educational and Vocational Services
Type(s) of Educational Programs Offered On campus.
Profile of On Campus School Program Number of teachers 8; *Num-
ber of classrooms* 8; *Student to teacher ratio* 8:1; *Credentials of
teachers* Certified; *Grades taught* Ungraded; Special curriculum
electives offered; Remedial courses offered.
Vocational Education Programs/Degrees Offered Food service; Build-
ing maintenance; Construction; Nursing care; Mechanic; Custodial.
Degrees Offered GED.

SALT LAKE CITY

AUTISM TEACHING HOME

1319 S 1000 E, Salt Lake City, UT 84105 (801) 328-4284, 359-8876
Contact Person(s): Don Robinson, Dir Childrens' Srvs
Setting and Background Information This facility was established in
1980 with funding from a federal grant.
Referral Information Contact the facility.
Type of Facility
Funding Sources State; Federal.
Average Length of Stay Long term.
Types of Admissions Accepted Residential treatment; Group home
placement; Respite care.
Sources of Referral State depts of education; Local depts of educa-
tion; State depts of mental health; Social service depts.
Client Profile
Age Range of Clients Served Residential program: 6-15.
Characteristics Exhibited by Children Neurological impairments; Au-
tism.
Tuition and Fees
Room and Board Long term: $280/diem.
Placements Primarily Funded By Social service depts.
Social and Rehabilitative Services
Therapeutic Approach The facility offers behavioral analysis.
Therapeutic Services Offered Independent living skills program; Re-
creation activities; Aftercare program with follow up; Home based
support service for autism.
Professionals on Staff Adjunctive therapists; Speech pathologists.

Educational and Vocational Services

Type(s) of Educational Programs Offered On campus; Off campus.

Profile of On Campus School Program Number of teachers 2; *Number of classrooms* 3; *Student to teacher ratio* 2:1; *Credentials of teachers* MA, BS.

Vocational Education Programs/Degrees Offered Pre-vocational home based training.

VERMONT

BENNINGTON

BENNINGTON SCHOOL, INC
19 Fairview St, Bennington, VT 05201 (802) 447-1557 *Contact Person(s):* Judith Fun, Dir
Setting and Background Information The school and residences were established in 1980 in the Green Mountains of Vermont for children who function academically at an elementary grade level.
Referral Information Anyone can make a referral by contacting the facility, forwarding the necessary background information, and scheduling a pre-placement visit.
Type of Facility
Funding Sources Private; State.
Average Length of Stay Long term.
Types of Admissions Accepted Residential treatment.
Sources of Referral Local depts of education; Private sources; Depts of correction; Social service depts; Courts; Schools.
Client Profile
Age Range of Clients Served Residential program: 10-18.
Characteristics Exhibited by Children Emotional handicaps; Learning disabilities; Mental disabilities.
IQ Range of Clients 75-110.
Tuition and Fees
Room and Board Long term: $32,448-37,648/yr (includes school tuition).
Placements Primarily Funded By State depts of education; State depts of mental health; Private sources.
Social and Rehabilitative Services
Therapeutic Approach The treatment program utilizes reality therapy, in conjunction with a behavioral level system whereby students earn points to exchange for privileges.
Therapeutic Services Offered Individual therapy; Group therapy; Family therapy; Independent living skills program.
Professionals on Staff Psychiatrists; Psychologists; Social workers; Adjunctive therapists; Child care staff; Clinicians.
Educational and Vocational Services
Type(s) of Educational Programs Offered On campus.
Profile of On Campus School Program Number of teachers 5; Number of classrooms 5; Student to teacher ratio 6:1; Credentials of teachers Certified; Grades taught Individualized.
Degrees Offered 12th grade diploma; GED.

BENSON

ECKERD WILDERNESS EDUCATIONAL CAMPING PROGRAM
Camp E-Wen-Akee, Benson, VT 05731 (802) 537-4101 *Contact Person(s):* James Holland
Setting and Background Information The program was founded in 1945 by Campbell Loughmiller with the support of the Jack and Ruth Eckerd Foundation and the Salesmanship Club of Dallas. The program was established as an alternative to institutionalization. In March, 1968, the first camp was opened for 50 emotionally disturbed boys in Brooksville, Florida. later, in June 1969, a second camp for girls was opened in Floral City, Florida. Since then, the camp program has expanded to include locations in Rhode Island, Vermont, and North Carolina. All camps operate a year round program. The camp locations vary in size from 150 to over 800 acres. Children build their own shelter to accommodate 10 children per living unit, plus 2 counselor-

teachers. They are also expected to cut their own wood, maintain their residence, repair their equipment, and initiate their own recreational activities.
Referral Information Referrals can be made by state agencies, school systems, psychologists, psychiatrists, and family counselors.
Type of Facility
Funding Sources Private; State.
Average Length of Stay 12-15 mos.
Types of Admissions Accepted Residential treatment.
Sources of Referral State depts of mental health; Private sources; Social service depts.
Client Profile
Age Range of Clients Served Residential program: 11-16.
Characteristics Exhibited by Children Emotional handicaps; Learning disabilities; Mental disabilities.
IQ Range of Clients 70-140.
Tuition and Fees
Placements Primarily Funded By State contracts.
Social and Rehabilitative Services
Therapeutic Approach The primary therapeutic approach used is reality therapy, in conjunction with a peer group pressure to process conflict situations. The counselor-teachers are present to help campers intitiate and carry out group plans, developing proper attitudes, learning problem-solving skills, acquiring a value system, and developing academic skills.
Therapeutic Services Offered Individual therapy; Group therapy; Independent living skills program; Recreation activities; Substance abuse treatment; Family intervention.
Professionals on Staff Social workers; Child care staff.
Educational and Vocational Services
Type(s) of Educational Programs Offered On campus.
Profile of On Campus School Program Number of teachers 13; Student to teacher ratio 5:1; Credentials of teachers Certified; Grades taught Individualized; Special curriculum electives offered; Remedial courses offered.
Degrees Offered GED.

BRATTLEBORO

BRATTLEBORO RETREAT
75 Linden St, Brattleboro, VT 05301 (802) 257-7785 *Contact Person(s):* Glenna Annis, Dir of Admis
Setting and Background Information Brattleboro Retreat is a private non-profit psychiatric residential and day treatment facility. The facility was established in 1834 on 1,600 acres of land in the southeastern corner of Vermont. Its campus consists of a large complex of buildings housing a variety of programs and services. Recreational facilities include hiking, cross country skiing, tennis courts, softball field, arts and crafts rooms, billiards, bowling alleys, gymnasium, etc. Brattleboro Retreat also operates the Wheeler Vocational and Rehabilitation Center and a working Holstein dairy farm.
Referral Information Referrals can be made by families, physicians, mental health professionals, school districts, religious leaders, and other professionals. To make a referral, contact the facility to arrange for a pre-admission evaluation.
Type of Facility
Funding Sources Private.
Average Length of Stay Avg 10 wks.
Types of Admissions Accepted Day treatment; Residential treatment.
Sources of Referral Psychiatrists; Hospitals.

BRATTLEBORO RETREAT *(continued)*

Client Profile
Age Range of Clients Served Day programs: 13-18; Residential program: 13-18.
Characteristics Exhibited by Children Emotional handicaps; Learning disabilities; Substance abuse.
IQ Range of Clients 75+.
Tuition and Fees
Room and Board Long term: $187/diem.
Placements Primarily Funded By State depts of mental health; Insurance; Private sources.
Social and Rehabilitative Services
Therapeutic Approach A wide range of treatment modalities are used through an interdisciplinary team format.
Therapeutic Services Offered Individual therapy; Group therapy; Family therapy; Adjunctive therapy; Art therapy; Recreation activities.
Professionals on Staff Psychiatrists; Psychologists; Social workers; Adjunctive therapists; Child care staff; Nurses; Art therapists.
Educational and Vocational Services
Type(s) of Educational Programs Offered On campus.
Profile of On Campus School Program Student to teacher ratio 8:1; *Length of school day* 8:15-11:30.
Vocational Education Programs/Degrees Offered Work assessment and job training.

BURLINGTON

BAIRD CHILDREN'S CENTER
1110 Pine St, Burlington, VT 05401 (802) 863-1326 *Contact Person(s):* Cynthia Fagan, Exec Dir
Setting and Background Information This facility was established initially as an orphanage in 1865. Its programs expanded to become a residential treatment center in 1960. The campus is located on the outskirts of Burlington, Vermont.
Referral Information Referrals can be made by anyone throughout the year. Applicants should contact the Admission Office and request a referral packet to be completed before screening by a mental health agency can take place. There will also be a home visit by a social worker, who will then present the necessary information to the Baird Screening Team for review.
Type of Facility
Funding Sources Private; State.
Average Length of Stay Long term.
Types of Admissions Accepted Residential treatment.
Client Profile
Age Range of Clients Served Residential program: 6-14.
Characteristics Exhibited by Children Emotional handicaps; Learning disabilities; Speech/Language disorders.
IQ Range of Clients 70+.
Tuition and Fees
Placements Primarily Funded By State depts of education; State depts of mental health.
Social and Rehabilitative Services
Therapeutic Approach The facility has a behavioral systems approach to therapy.
Therapeutic Services Offered Individual therapy; Group therapy; Family therapy; Recreation activities; Aftercare program with follow up; In-home intervention.
Professionals on Staff Psychiatrists; Social workers; Adjunctive therapists; Child care staff; Nurses.
Educational and Vocational Services
Type(s) of Educational Programs Offered On campus.
Profile of On Campus School Program Number of teachers 3 and 2 aides; *Number of classrooms* 2; *Student to teacher ratio* 5:1; *Credentials of teachers* Certified; Special curriculum electives offered; Remedial courses offered.

FERRISBURG

KINGSLAND BAY SCHOOL
Hawkins Rd, Ferrisburg, VT 05456 (802) 877-2006 *Contact Person(s):* Peter M Quinn MSW, Exec Dir
Setting and Background Information The facility was established in 1974 as an alternative school. The 19-acre campus has 3 residential buildings, a school, a barn, and other buildings.

Referral Information Contact the facility and forward an information packet. An interview and 2 day pre-placement visit will be arranged. The admission decision will be made following a one-month trial period.
Type of Facility
Funding Sources Private; State.
Average Length of Stay Short and long term.
Types of Admissions Accepted Group home placement; Crisis intervention.
Sources of Referral Social service depts.
Client Profile
Age Range of Clients Served Residential program: 12-18.
Characteristics Exhibited by Children Emotional handicaps; Learning disabilities.
IQ Range of Clients 75-120.
Tuition and Fees
Room and Board Short term: $212/diem; Long term: $24,000/yr.
Placements Primarily Funded By Social service depts.
Social and Rehabilitative Services
Therapeutic Approach The facility offers a therapeutic milieu.
Therapeutic Services Offered Individual therapy; Group therapy; Family therapy; Independent living skills program.
Professionals on Staff Social workers; Child care staff.
Educational and Vocational Services
Type(s) of Educational Programs Offered Off campus (Local school).

PLAINFIELD

MAPLEHILL COMMUNITY
PO Box 248, Plainfield, VT 05667 (802) 454-7368 *Contact Person(s):* Fredric C Woogmaster
Setting and Background Information The facility was established in 1966 on 220 acres and has 4 buildings.
Referral Information For referral, contact the facility.
Type of Facility
Average Length of Stay Long term.
Types of Admissions Accepted Residential treatment.
Sources of Referral State depts of education; Local depts of education; State depts of mental health; Psychiatrists; Private sources; Depts of correction; Social service depts.
Client Profile
Age Range of Clients Served Residential program: 6-18.
Characteristics Exhibited by Children Emotional handicaps; Learning disabilities; Delinquency.
Tuition and Fees
Room and Board Long term: $24,000/yr.
Placements Primarily Funded By Social service depts.
Social and Rehabilitative Services
Therapeutic Approach The basic therapeutic approach used is milieu therapy.
Educational and Vocational Services
Type(s) of Educational Programs Offered Off campus.
Vocational Education Programs/Degrees Offered Farming program.

VIRGINIA

ALEXANDRIA

FAIRFAX COUNTY DRUG ABUSE CONTROL
5801 N King Hwy, Alexandria, VA 22303 (703) 960-3276 *Contact Person(s):* Joan Volpe, Dir
Referral Information Contact the facility for referral information.
Client Profile
Age Range of Clients Served Residential program: 15-17.
Characteristics Exhibited by Children Emotional handicaps.

RESIDENTIAL YOUTH SERVICES, INC
2701 Cameron Mills Rd, Alexandria, VA 22302 (703) 548-8334
Contact Person(s): Nancy H Richardson, Exec Dir
Setting and Background Information The facility was privately established in 1969. There are 4 long-term group homes and 2 short-term emergency/diagnostic shelters.
Referral Information Contact the facility for referral information.
Type of Facility
Funding Sources Private; State; Federal.
Average Length of Stay Short and long term.
Types of Admissions Accepted Group home placement; Emergency shelter.
Sources of Referral Depts of correction; Social service depts.
Client Profile
Age Range of Clients Served Residential program: 12-17.
Characteristics Exhibited by Children Emotional handicaps; Learning disabilities.
Tuition and Fees
Room and Board Short term: $121.12/diem; Long term: $89.95/diem.
Placements Primarily Funded By Private sources.
Social and Rehabilitative Services
Therapeutic Approach The facility has a reality-based therapeutic milieu and uses behavior management.
Therapeutic Services Offered Individual therapy; Group therapy; Independent living skills program; Case management.
Professionals on Staff Social workers; Child care staff.
Educational and Vocational Services
Type(s) of Educational Programs Offered On campus (Shelters); Off campus (Group homes).
Profile of On Campus School Program Number of teachers 1; *Number of classrooms* 2; *Student to teacher ratio* 8:1; *Length of school day* 3 hrs; *Grades taught* 9-12; Remedial courses offered.

ANNANDALE

HARBOR HOUSE
6435 Columbia Pike, Annandale, VA 22003 (703) 549-5950 *Contact Person(s):* Lynne Kozma, Dir
Setting and Background Information This facility was established in 1980. It is a short-term (90 days) diagnostic program for DSS clients.
Referral Information Referrals are made through the Dept of Social Service.
Type of Facility
Funding Sources State; Federal.
Average Length of Stay Short term.
Types of Admissions Accepted Residential treatment; Wards of the state.
Sources of Referral Social service depts.

Client Profile
Age Range of Clients Served Residential program: 12-18.
Characteristics Exhibited by Children Emotional handicaps; Learning disabilities; Mental disabilities.
Tuition and Fees
Placements Primarily Funded By Title XX.
Social and Rehabilitative Services
Therapeutic Services Offered Individual therapy; Group therapy; Family therapy; Recreation activities; Substance abuse treatment.
Professionals on Staff Psychologists; Social workers; Adjunctive therapists; Child care staff.
Educational and Vocational Services
Type(s) of Educational Programs Offered On campus; Summer campus.
Profile of On Campus School Program Number of teachers 1; *Number of classrooms* 1; *Student to teacher ratio* 8:1; *Credentials of teachers* Spec Ed; *Grades taught* 7-12; Remedial courses offered.
Degrees Offered GED.

BERRYVILLE

GRAFTON SCHOOL
PO Box 112, Berryville, VA 22611 (703) 955-2400 *Contact Person(s):* Tammy Miller Tucker, Admin Supv
Setting and Background Information This program was established in 1958 by a parent whose learning-disabled child was not receiving services. The school is located on 15 acres. There are 3 off-campus sites. Residential and academic facilities are on all sites.
Referral Information Contact the facility for a referral packet. If appropriate, a pre-placement interview will be held.
Type of Facility
Funding Sources Private.
Average Length of Stay Long term.
Types of Admissions Accepted Day treatment; Residential treatment; Group home placement.
Sources of Referral State depts of education; Local depts of education; State depts of mental health; Private sources; Depts of correction; Social service depts.
Client Profile
Age Range of Clients Served Day programs: Birth-21+; Residential program: Birth-21+.
Characteristics Exhibited by Children Emotional handicaps; Learning disabilities; Hearing impairments/deafness; Speech/Language disorders; Neurological impairments; Mental disabilities; Autism.
IQ Range of Clients 40+.
Tuition and Fees
Room and Board Long term: Rates set yearly by state of Virginia.
Placements Primarily Funded By State depts of education; Local depts of education; State depts of mental health; Depts of corrections; Social service depts.
Social and Rehabilitative Services
Therapeutic Approach The therapeutic approach of the facility is behavior modification.
Therapeutic Services Offered Individual therapy; Group therapy; Independent living skills program; Recreation activities.
Professionals on Staff Psychologists; Social workers; Adjunctive therapists; Child care staff; Nurses.

GRAFTON SCHOOL *(continued)*

Educational and Vocational Services
Type(s) of Educational Programs Offered On campus (Spec Ed); Off campus.
Vocational Education Programs/Degrees Offered Small vocational program initiated recently.

BOYD TAVERN

OAKLAND SCHOOL
Oakland Farm, Boyd Tavern, VA 22947 (804) 293-9059 *Contact Person(s):* Joanne Dondero, Dir
Referral Information Contact the facility for referral information.
Client Profile
Age Range of Clients Served Residential program: 7-17.
Characteristics Exhibited by Children Emotional handicaps.

BRISTOL

JANIE HAMMIT CHILDREN'S HOME
1225 Janie Hammit Drive, Bristol, VA 24201 (703) 669-9221
Contact Person(s): Fay Buchanan, Exec Dir
Setting and Background Information The facility was originally established as an orphanage in 1938. Currently, it is a group home for abused and neglected children.
Referral Information Referrals are made through DSS or the juvenile courts.
Type of Facility
Funding Sources Private; State; Federal; United Way.
Average Length of Stay Short and long term.
Types of Admissions Accepted Group home placement; Wards of the state.
Sources of Referral Depts of correction; Social service depts.
Client Profile
Age Range of Clients Served Day programs: Birth-18; Residential program: Birth-15.
Characteristics Exhibited by Children Emotional handicaps; Learning disabilities; Mental disabilities.
IQ Range of Clients 70+.
Tuition and Fees
Room and Board Short term: $14.47/diem; Long term: $14.47/diem.
Placements Primarily Funded By Depts of corrections; Social service depts.
Social and Rehabilitative Services
Therapeutic Approach The facility uses behavior modification.
Therapeutic Services Offered Individual therapy; Group therapy; Family therapy; Independent living skills program; Recreation activities.
Professionals on Staff Psychiatrists; Psychologists; Social workers; Adjunctive therapists; Child care staff.
Educational and Vocational Services
Type(s) of Educational Programs Offered Off campus (Public schools).

CHARLOTTESVILLE

BOYS ATTENTION HOME
907 E Jefferson St, Charlottesville, VA 22901 (804) 971-3333
Contact Person(s): Jack Gallagher, Prog Coord
Setting and Background Information The facility was established in 1973 with a federal grant. It is a residential group home.
Referral Information Contact the facility for referral information.
Type of Facility
Funding Sources State; City.
Average Length of Stay Short and long term.
Types of Admissions Accepted Group home placement.
Sources of Referral Local depts of education; Psychiatrists; Depts of correction; Social service depts; Court.
Client Profile
Age Range of Clients Served Residential program: 14-18.
Characteristics Exhibited by Children Emotional handicaps; Learning disabilities.
IQ Range of Clients 70-110.

Tuition and Fees
Room and Board Short term: $39.30/diem; Long term: $39.30/diem.
Placements Primarily Funded By Private sources; Depts of corrections; Social service depts.
Social and Rehabilitative Services
Therapeutic Services Offered Individual therapy; Group therapy; Family therapy; Recreation activities; Aftercare program with follow up.
Professionals on Staff Child care staff.
Educational and Vocational Services
Type(s) of Educational Programs Offered Off campus (Public school).

COMMUNITY ATTENTION RESIDENTIAL CARE SYSTEM
PO Box 155, Charlottesville, VA 22902 (804) 971-3353 *Contact Person(s):* Paul D McWhinney, Admin; Orlean W Carter, Public Affairs Off
Setting and Background Information The facility was established in 1971 by a group of local citizens in response to a community need. There are boys' and girls' attention homes, 6 family group homes, and administrative offices on the grounds.
Referral Information For referral, contact the program coordinator, complete the admissions packet, and set up a personal interview.
Type of Facility
Funding Sources Private; State; Federal; City.
Average Length of Stay Short and long term.
Types of Admissions Accepted Residential treatment; Group home placement.
Sources of Referral Psychiatrists; Private sources; Depts of correction; Social service depts.
Client Profile
Age Range of Clients Served Residential program: 10-18.
Characteristics Exhibited by Children Emotional handicaps; Learning disabilities.
Tuition and Fees
Room and Board Short term: $19.92-$39.30/diem; Long term: $19.92-$39.30/diem.
Placements Primarily Funded By Private sources; Depts of corrections; Social service depts; City.
Social and Rehabilitative Services
Therapeutic Approach The basic therapeutic approach is cognitive behavior modification.
Therapeutic Services Offered Individual therapy; Group therapy; Family therapy; Independent living skills program; Aftercare program with follow up.
Professionals on Staff Psychologists; Social workers; Child care staff.

CHARLOTTSVILLE

ADVENTURE BOUND SCHOOL—BOONESVILLE RESIDENTIAL CENTER
PO Box 574, Charlottesville, VA 22902 (804) 973-3381 *Contact Person(s):* Gary Duncan, Exec Dir
Setting and Background Information The facility has a capacity for 30 youth and accepts males only.
Referral Information Contact the facility for referral information.
Client Profile
Age Range of Clients Served Residential program: 8-17.
Characteristics Exhibited by Children Emotional handicaps.

CHESAPEAKE

CENTERVILLE GROUP HOME
916 Centerville Tnpke S, Chesapeake, VA 23322 (804) 482-4744
Contact Person(s): Becky China, Dir
Setting and Background Information The facility was established in 1979 with funds from the Dept of Corrections. It is a large home in a semi-rural setting.
Referral Information Contact the facility and forward the necessary information, including a social history and psychological evaluation. A pre-placement interview will be scheduled. The child must be in foster care with the Dept of Social Services and not have any felony charges.
Type of Facility
Funding Sources State.
Average Length of Stay 6-12 mos.
Types of Admissions Accepted Group home placement.

CENTERVILLE GROUP HOME *(continued)*

Sources of Referral Social service depts.
Client Profile
Age Range of Clients Served Residential program: 12-18.
Characteristics Exhibited by Children Emotional handicaps; Learning disabilities.
IQ Range of Clients 75-120.
Tuition and Fees
Room and Board Long term: $17.04/diem.
Placements Primarily Funded By Depts of corrections.
Social and Rehabilitative Services
Therapeutic Approach The facility has a family systems approach to therapy.
Therapeutic Services Offered Individual therapy; Group therapy; Family therapy; Independent living skills program; Aftercare program with follow up.
Professionals on Staff Social workers; Child care staff.
Educational and Vocational Services
Type(s) of Educational Programs Offered Off campus (Public school).

COVINGTON

BOY'S HOME, INC

Rt 3, Covington, VA 24426 (703) 962-2867 *Contact Person(s):* Sarwat Chaudhry, Admis Coord
Setting and Background Information The facility was established in 1906 and is located in the Allegheny mountains on more than 1200 acres. There are 7 cottages, a dining hall, administrative offices, a complete gymnasium and a chapel.
Referral Information Contact the facility and forward referral information, including a social history, a psychological evaluation, court reports and school transcripts.
Type of Facility
Funding Sources Private; State; Donations.
Average Length of Stay Long term.
Types of Admissions Accepted Group home placement; Wards of the state.
Sources of Referral Local depts of education; Psychiatrists; Private sources; Depts of correction; Social service depts.
Client Profile
Age Range of Clients Served Residential program: 6-18.
Characteristics Exhibited by Children Learning disabilities; Behavior disorders.
IQ Range of Clients 80+.
Tuition and Fees
Room and Board Long term: Sliding scale (private); $13.35/diem (Title XX; court placement).
Placements Primarily Funded By Private sources; Depts of corrections; Social service depts.
Social and Rehabilitative Services
Therapeutic Services Offered Independent living skills program; Aftercare program with follow up.
Professionals on Staff Psychiatrists; Psychologists; Social workers; Child care staff; Nurses.
Educational and Vocational Services
Type(s) of Educational Programs Offered Off campus (Public school).

DANVILLE

ADOLESCENT GROUP HOME

504 Middle St, Danville, VA 24540 (804) 799-3178 *Contact Person(s):* Raymond A Ruocco, Res Coord
Setting and Background Information The facility was established in 1984 with funding from both private and state organizations. There are three buildings; an adult group home, an adolescent group home, and supervised apartments.
Referral Information Referrals are initiated by phone. Forward current available professional materials.
Type of Facility
Funding Sources State.
Average Length of Stay Short and long term.
Types of Admissions Accepted Residential treatment; Group home placement; Wards of the state.
Sources of Referral State depts of mental health; Depts of correction; Social service depts; Families/Legal guardians.

Client Profile
Age Range of Clients Served Residential program: 12-18.
Characteristics Exhibited by Children Emotional handicaps; Mental disabilities.
IQ Range of Clients 50+.
Tuition and Fees
Room and Board Short term: $49/diem; Long term: $306/mo.
Placements Primarily Funded By State depts of mental health; Private sources; Depts of corrections; Social service depts.
Social and Rehabilitative Services
Therapeutic Approach The facility uses behavior management.
Therapeutic Services Offered Individual therapy; Group therapy; Independent living skills program; Aftercare program with follow up.
Professionals on Staff Psychologists; Social workers; Child care staff; Nurses.
Educational and Vocational Services
Type(s) of Educational Programs Offered On campus; Off campus.

HUGHES MEMORIAL HOME FOR CHILDREN

1501 Franklin Turnpike, Danville, VA 24540 (804) 836-7050
Contact Person(s): Rux Cannady, Dir of Support Srvs
Setting and Background Information The facility was originally established in 1927 as an orphanage with funds from an endowment. The 365-acre campus has 5 residential cottages, 2 administrative buildings, a dining hall, a gym, and 3 agricultural barns.
Referral Information For referral, contact the facility and forward background information, including a social history, psychological and academic records, and a history of previous placement. A pre-placement visit and interview will be arranged.
Type of Facility
Funding Sources Private; State.
Average Length of Stay Long term.
Types of Admissions Accepted Residential treatment.
Sources of Referral Local depts of education; Depts of correction; Social service depts; Juvenile courts.
Client Profile
Age Range of Clients Served Residential program: 11-18.
Characteristics Exhibited by Children Emotional handicaps; Learning disabilities.
IQ Range of Clients 70+.
Tuition and Fees
Room and Board Long term: $92.03/diem.
Tuition $41.61/diem.
Placements Primarily Funded By Local depts of education; Depts of corrections; Social service depts; Juvenile courts.
Social and Rehabilitative Services
Therapeutic Approach The basic therapeutic approach of the facility is behavior management.
Therapeutic Services Offered Individual therapy; Group therapy; Family therapy; Adjunctive therapy; Independent living skills program; Independent living skills program; Recreation activities; Substance abuse treatment; Aftercare program with follow up.
Professionals on Staff Psychiatrists; Psychologists; Social workers; Adjunctive therapists; Child care staff; Recreation therapist.
Educational and Vocational Services
Type(s) of Educational Programs Offered On campus (ED/LD); Off campus (Public school).
Profile of On Campus School Program Number of teachers 6; *Number of classrooms* 3; *Student to teacher ratio* 5:1; *Credentials of teachers* Certified; Special curriculum electives offered (Individualized); Remedial courses offered (Individualized).
Degrees Offered GED.

DILLWYN

NEW DOMINION SCHOOL

PO Box 540, Dillwyn, VA 23936 (804) 983-2051 *Contact Person(s):* James M O'Connor, Admin
Setting and Background Information The school was established in 1977. The 350-acre campus has 6 separate group residences and an administrative area.
Referral Information Referrals are made by agencies, parents and professionals. The school also accepts court placements.
Type of Facility
Types of Admissions Accepted Residential treatment.

NEW DOMINION SCHOOL (continued)

Client Profile
Age Range of Clients Served Residential program: 13-18.
Characteristics Exhibited by Children Emotional handicaps; Learning disabilities.
Tuition and Fees
Placements Primarily Funded By State depts of education; State depts of mental health; Private sources; Depts of corrections.
Social and Rehabilitative Services
Therapeutic Approach The basic therapeutic approach of the facility is behavior modification.
Therapeutic Services Offered Individual therapy; Group therapy; Family therapy; Independent living skills program; Recreation activities; Substance abuse treatment.
Professionals on Staff Psychologists; Social workers; Adjunctive therapists; Child care staff; Nurses.
Educational and Vocational Services
Type(s) of Educational Programs Offered On campus.
Profile of On Campus School Program Number of teachers 6; *Number of classrooms* 8; *Student to teacher ratio* 3:1; *Credentials of teachers* Certified; Remedial courses offered.
Degrees Offered 12th grade diploma; GED.

GOOCHLAND

ELK HILL FARM, INC

PO Box 99, Goochland, VA 23063 (804) 457-4866, 784-4392
Contact Person(s): Richard Munchel, Exec Dir; Michael Farley, Prog Coord
Setting and Background Information In 1970 Buford Scott and James Ball donated 200 acres, along with a mansion (circa 1840) and 2 out buildings for the purpose of establishing a child care facility. The campus is located in a rural community and consists of a mansion housing administrative offices, 2 resident cottages, school building, and a vocational arts building. Elk Hill farm is a private, non-profit residential treatment facility.
Referral Information Referrals can be made by Court Service Unit Probation Officers, social workers, mental health professionals, school districts, and concerned individuals. To make a referral, forward the necessary background information, including social history, psychological reports, educational records, and medical records. If the adolescent appears to be appropriate for the program, then a 5 day pre-placement visit will be arranged.
Type of Facility
Funding Sources Private.
Average Length of Stay Long term.
Types of Admissions Accepted Residential treatment.
Sources of Referral Depts of correction; Social service depts; Courts; Parents.
Client Profile
Age Range of Clients Served Residential program: 13-17.
Characteristics Exhibited by Children Emotional handicaps; Learning disabilities.
IQ Range of Clients 80+.
Tuition and Fees
Placements Primarily Funded By State depts of education; State depts of mental health; Depts of corrections; Social service depts.
Social and Rehabilitative Services
Therapeutic Approach The philosophy of the treatment program is based on the positive peer culture therapeutic approach.
Therapeutic Services Offered Individual therapy; Group therapy; Family therapy; Independent living skills program; Recreation activities; Wilderness program.
Professionals on Staff Child care staff; Program director.
Educational and Vocational Services
Type(s) of Educational Programs Offered On campus (State accredited); Summer campus.
Profile of On Campus School Program Number of teachers 4; *Student to teacher ratio* 5:1; *Grades taught* 7-12; Special curriculum electives offered (Health, PE, Substance abuse); Remedial courses offered.
Vocational Education Programs/Degrees Offered Auto mechanics; Carpentry; Welding.
Degrees Offered GED.

HAMPTON

THE CHILDREN'S RESIDENCE

1520 Aberdeen Rd, Ste 202, Hampton, VA 23666 (804) 872-9482
Contact Person(s): Marilyn P Lovett, Children's Svcs Coord
Setting and Background Information The facility was established by local agencies in 1983. It is a large group home in a residential neighborhood.
Referral Information Contact the Children's Services Coordinator for referral information. Information on the child's living situation and behaviors must be provided by the referring agency.
Type of Facility
Funding Sources State; Local.
Average Length of Stay Long term.
Types of Admissions Accepted Group home placement.
Sources of Referral Local depts of education; Psychiatrists; Depts of correction; Social service depts; Parents; Psychologists.
Client Profile
Age Range of Clients Served Residential program: 6-18.
Characteristics Exhibited by Children Emotional handicaps.
IQ Range of Clients 74+.
Tuition and Fees
Room and Board Long term: $72/diem.
Placements Primarily Funded By Depts of corrections; Social service depts; Scholarships.
Social and Rehabilitative Services
Therapeutic Approach The facility uses reality therapy.
Therapeutic Services Offered Individual therapy; Group therapy; Family therapy; Independent living skills program; Recreation activities.
Professionals on Staff Psychiatrists; Social workers; Child care staff.

KESWICK

LITTLE KESWICK SCHOOL, INC

PO Box 24, Keswick, VA 22947 (804) 295-0457 *Contact Person(s):* Terry Columbus
Setting and Background Information The facility was initially established as a summer camp for learning disabled children in 1943. It has since evolved into a residential school for emotionally disturbed, learning disabled, and mentally retarded boys. The grounds include a main house, gymnasium, school, several tutorial cottages, recreational facilities, stables, workshop, athletic fields, and pool.
Referral Information Anyone can make a referral by contacting the facility and forwarding the necessary background information, including application, medical form, medical reports, psychological evaluation, educational reports, social history, and behavioral reports. If the applicant appears appropriate following the review of the referral packet, then a 2-day placement visit will take place before an admission decision is made.
Type of Facility
Funding Sources Private.
Average Length of Stay 24 mos.
Types of Admissions Accepted Residential treatment.
Sources of Referral Local depts of education; Private sources; Social service depts.
Client Profile
Age Range of Clients Served Residential program: 7-17.
Characteristics Exhibited by Children Emotional handicaps; Learning disabilities; Speech/Language disorders; Neurological impairments; Mental disabilities.
IQ Range of Clients 65-139.
Tuition and Fees
Room and Board Long term: $27,000/9 mos; $2,600/summer.
Placements Primarily Funded By State depts of mental health; Private sources.
Social and Rehabilitative Services
Therapeutic Approach The treatment program uses a psycho-educational approach, in conjunction with an individualized behavioral program.
Therapeutic Services Offered Individual therapy; Group therapy; Family therapy; Independent living skills program; Recreation activities; Substance abuse treatment; Aftercare program with follow up.
Professionals on Staff Psychiatrists; Psychologists; Nurses.

LITTLE KESWICK SCHOOL, INC *(continued)*

Educational and Vocational Services
Type(s) of Educational Programs Offered On campus; Summer campus.
Profile of On Campus School Program Number of teachers 7; *Student to teacher ratio* 5:1; *Grades taught* Individualized.

LEESBURG

GLAYDIN SCHOOL
Rte 3, Box 334, Leesburg, VA 22075 (703) 777-3505 *Contact Person(s):* Curtis Harstad, Dir
Referral Information Contact the facility for referral information.
Client Profile
Age Range of Clients Served Residential program: 13-17.
Characteristics Exhibited by Children Emotional handicaps.

SPRINGWOOD PSYCHIATRIC INSTITUTE
Rt 4, Box 50, Leesburg, VA 22075 (703) 777-0800 *Contact Person(s):*
Penny Thompson, Admin Sec
Setting and Background Information The facility was established in 1977. The 45-acre grounds have a hospital, a school, and administrative and physician offices.
Referral Information Contact the Intake Coordinator and forward referral information, including medical information, psychological history, prior hospitalization records, and health insurance carrier.
Type of Facility
Funding Sources Private.
Average Length of Stay Short and long term.
Types of Admissions Accepted Day treatment; Residential treatment.
Sources of Referral State depts of education; Local depts of education; State depts of mental health; Psychiatrists; Private sources; Depts of correction; Social service depts.
Client Profile
Age Range of Clients Served Day programs: 12-55+; Residential program: 12-55+.
Characteristics Exhibited by Children Emotional handicaps; Learning disabilities; Mental disabilities.
IQ Range of Clients 80+.
Tuition and Fees
Room and Board Short term: $17,200/mo; Long term: $17,200/mo.
Tuition $60/diem.
Placements Primarily Funded By Private sources.
Social and Rehabilitative Services
Therapeutic Approach The facility uses ego psychology and offers psychosocial orientation.
Therapeutic Services Offered Individual therapy; Group therapy; Family therapy; Adjunctive therapy; Art therapy; Independent living skills program; Recreation activities; Substance abuse treatment; Aftercare program with follow up.
Professionals on Staff Psychiatrists; Psychologists; Adjunctive therapists; Nurses; Art therapists.
Educational and Vocational Services
Type(s) of Educational Programs Offered On campus.
Profile of On Campus School Program Number of teachers 6; *Number of classrooms* 5; *Student to teacher ratio* 6:1; *Credentials of teachers* BA, BS, MA, Certified; *Length of school day* 9-3; *Grades taught* 7-12; Special curriculum electives offered (Art, Drama, Typing, Computer, Marketing); Remedial courses offered (Math, Reading).
Vocational Education Programs/Degrees Offered Vocational assessments; Vocational career development course.
Degrees Offered 8th grade diploma; 12th grade diploma; GED.

LYNCHBURG

OPPORTUNITY HOUSE
805 15th St, Lynchburg, VA 24504 (804) 847-1665 *Contact Person(s):* Linda L Blass, Asst Supt
Setting and Background Information The facility was established in 1974 by a local women's group. It is a group home affiliated with the State Dept of Corrections.
Referral Information Contact the facility and submit a referral form, social history, school records, and psychological data.

Type of Facility
Funding Sources State; City.
Average Length of Stay Long term.
Types of Admissions Accepted Group home placement; Outreach detention.
Sources of Referral Depts of correction; Social service depts; Juvenile courts.
Client Profile
Age Range of Clients Served Residential program: 13-17 ½ .
Characteristics Exhibited by Children Delinquency.
Tuition and Fees
Placements Primarily Funded By Depts of corrections; Social service depts; Local government; Title XX.
Social and Rehabilitative Services
Therapeutic Approach The facility has a behavioral approach to therapy.
Therapeutic Services Offered Individual therapy; Group therapy; Family therapy; Recreation activities.
Professionals on Staff Social workers; Child care staff.
Educational and Vocational Services
Type(s) of Educational Programs Offered Off campus (Public school).

SPARC HOUSE
1517 Jackson St, Lynchburg, VA 24504 (804) 847-1713 *Contact Person(s):* Mary Clayton Blackwell, Supt
Setting and Background Information The facility was established in 1980 by the city. It is a group home for girls.
Referral Information Contact the facility for referral information and forward the required information, including a social history, school records, a psychological report and medical information.
Type of Facility
Funding Sources State; Federal; City.
Average Length of Stay Long term.
Types of Admissions Accepted Group home placement.
Sources of Referral Depts of correction; Social service depts; Courts; Parents.
Client Profile
Age Range of Clients Served Residential program: 12-18.
Characteristics Exhibited by Children Emotional handicaps; Family dysfunction.
IQ Range of Clients 70+.
Tuition and Fees
Room and Board Long term: $16.75/diem.
Placements Primarily Funded By Depts of corrections; Social service depts; City.
Social and Rehabilitative Services
Therapeutic Approach The facility uses reality therapy.
Therapeutic Services Offered Individual therapy; Group therapy; Family therapy; Independent living skills program; Aftercare program with follow up.
Professionals on Staff Social workers; Adjunctive therapists; Child care staff.
Educational and Vocational Services
Type(s) of Educational Programs Offered Off campus (Public schools).

MARION

SOUTHWESTERN STATE HOSPITAL
502 E Main St, Marion, VA 24354 (703) 783-6921 *Contact Person(s):* David A Rosenquist MHA, Dir
Setting and Background Information The facility was established in 1887 by the general assembly. Currently, it is located on 100 acres and has residential and support services.
Referral Information Referrals are made by state depts of mental health and psychiatrists. Prior to admission, patients are screened by community services board staff.
Type of Facility
Funding Sources State.
Average Length of Stay Short and long term.
Types of Admissions Accepted Residential treatment.
Sources of Referral State depts of mental health; Psychiatrists.
Client Profile
Age Range of Clients Served Residential program: 12-55+.
Characteristics Exhibited by Children Emotional handicaps; Mental disabilities.
IQ Range of Clients 70+.

SOUTHWESTERN STATE HOSPITAL (continued)

Tuition and Fees
Room and Board Long term: $250/diem (includes school tuition; cost is dependent on treatment).
Placements Primarily Funded By Commonwealth of VA; The school program is funded by the Smyth County School Board..
Social and Rehabilitative Services
Therapeutic Approach The facility offers a therapeutic milieu.
Therapeutic Services Offered Individual therapy; Group therapy; Adjunctive therapy; Physical therapy; Independent living skills program; Recreation activities; Aftercare program with follow up; Occupational therapy.
Professionals on Staff Psychiatrists; Psychologists; Social workers; Adjunctive therapists; Child care staff; Nurses; Art therapists; Physical therapists.
Educational and Vocational Services
Type(s) of Educational Programs Offered On campus.
Profile of On Campus School Program Number of teachers 7; Number of classrooms 6; Student to teacher ratio 1:1; Credentials of teachers Certified; Grades taught K-12; Special curriculum electives offered; Remedial courses offered.
Degrees Offered GED.

MARTINSVILLE

ANCHOR I

100 Cleveland Ave, Martinsville, VA 24115 (703) 638-6530 *Contact Person(s):* Dale Hamann, Dir
Setting and Background Information The facility was established in 1971 by the Dept of Corrections. It is a community-based group home.
Referral Information Contact the facility for an admissions application.
Type of Facility
Funding Sources State; Local.
Average Length of Stay 5-6 mos.
Types of Admissions Accepted Group home placement.
Sources of Referral Depts of correction; Social service depts.
Client Profile
Age Range of Clients Served Residential program: 12-18.
Characteristics Exhibited by Children Emotional handicaps; Learning disabilities.
IQ Range of Clients 95+.
Tuition and Fees
Room and Board Long term: $11/diem.
Placements Primarily Funded By Social service depts.
Social and Rehabilitative Services
Therapeutic Approach The basic approach of the facility is reality therapy.
Therapeutic Services Offered Individual therapy; Group therapy; Family therapy; Independent living skills program; Recreation activities.
Professionals on Staff Social workers; Child care staff.
Educational and Vocational Services
Type(s) of Educational Programs Offered Off campus.

MISSION HOME

FAITH MISSION HOME

Box 114, Mission Home, VA 22940 (804) 985-2294 *Contact Person(s):* Ruben Yoder, Admin
Referral Information Contact the facility for referral information.
Client Profile
Age Range of Clients Served Residential program: 3-17.
Characteristics Exhibited by Children Emotional handicaps.

NEWPORT NEWS

CHARTER COLONIAL INSTITUTE

17579 Warwick Blvd, Newport News, VA 23603 (804) 887-2611
Contact Person(s): Helen Cullen, Admis Coord
Setting and Background Information The facility was privately established in 1980. The 30-acre campus has 5 buildings.
Referral Information Contact the facility for referral information.

Type of Facility
Funding Sources Private; State; Federal.
Average Length of Stay Short and long term.
Types of Admissions Accepted Day treatment; Residential treatment; Acute care.
Sources of Referral State depts of education; Local depts of education; State depts of mental health; Psychiatrists; Private sources; Depts of correction; Social service depts.
Client Profile
Age Range of Clients Served Day programs: Birth-18; Residential program: Birth-18.
Characteristics Exhibited by Children Emotional handicaps.
IQ Range of Clients 80-140.
Tuition and Fees
Placements Primarily Funded By Insurance.
Social and Rehabilitative Services
Therapeutic Services Offered Individual therapy; Group therapy; Family therapy; Adjunctive therapy; Art therapy; Recreation activities; Substance abuse treatment; Aftercare program with follow up.
Professionals on Staff Psychiatrists; Psychologists; Social workers; Adjunctive therapists; Child care staff; Nurses; Art therapists.
Educational and Vocational Services
Type(s) of Educational Programs Offered On campus; Summer campus.
Profile of On Campus School Program Number of teachers 8; Number of classrooms 8; Student to teacher ratio 6:1; Credentials of teachers MEd; Grades taught K-12; Special curriculum electives offered; Remedial courses offered.
Degrees Offered 12th grade diploma; GED.

NORFOLD

ST MARY'S INFANT HOME

317 Chapel St, Norfold, VA 23504 (804) 622-2208 *Contact Person(s):* William Jolly, Admin
Referral Information Contact the facility for referral information.
Client Profile
Age Range of Clients Served Residential program: Birth-11.
Characteristics Exhibited by Children Emotional handicaps.

NORFOLK

EASTERN VIRGINIA CENTER FOR CHILDREN AND YOUTH

721 Fairfax Ave, Norfolk, VA 23501 (804) 446-5000, 446-5046, 446-5039 *Contact Person(s):* Fred Weston LCSW, Unit Dir
Setting and Background Information The facility was established in 1984 as part of a CMHC facility. It is a 36-bed residential treatment unit located within a children's psychiatric hospital.
Referral Information Contact the facility and forward clinical information . An intake interview will be scheduled.
Type of Facility
Funding Sources Private.
Average Length of Stay Short and long term.
Types of Admissions Accepted Residential treatment.
Sources of Referral Psychiatrists; Private sources.
Client Profile
Age Range of Clients Served Residential Program: Birth-18.
Characteristics Exhibited by Children Emotional handicaps; Learning disabilities.
IQ Range of Clients 80-120.
Tuition and Fees
Room and Board Short term: $298/diem; Long term: $298/diem.
Placements Primarily Funded By Insurance.
Social and Rehabilitative Services
Therapeutic Services Offered Individual therapy; Group therapy; Family therapy; Adjunctive therapy; Art therapy; Recreation activities; Substance abuse treatment.
Professionals on Staff Psychiatrists; Psychologists; Social workers; Adjunctive therapists; Child care staff; Nurses; Art therapists.
Educational and Vocational Services
Type(s) of Educational Programs Offered On campus; Summer campus.
Profile of On Campus School Program Student to teacher ratio 8:1; Credentials of teachers MA; Grades taught 1-12; Remedial courses offered (Tutoring).

EASTERN VIRGINIA CENTER FOR CHILDREN AND YOUTH *(continued)*

Vocational Education Programs/Degrees Offered Vocational-tech studies through public school system.
Degrees Offered 12th grade diploma; GED.

JAMES BARRY-ROBINSON INSTITUTE

443 Kempsville Rd, Norfolk, VA 23502 (804) 461-1107 *Contact Person(s):* Morton E Hecht III, Exec Dir
Setting and Background Information The facility has a capacity for 35 youth and accepts males only.
Referral Information Contact the facility for referral information.
Client Profile
Age Range of Clients Served Residential program: 12-17.
Characteristics Exhibited by Children Emotional handicaps.

PETERSBURG

CENTRAL STATE HOSPITAL

PO Box 4030, Petersburg, VA 23803 (804) 861-7162 *Contact Person(s):* Olivia Garland, Dir
Referral Information Contact the facility for referral information.
Client Profile
Age Range of Clients Served Residential program: 14-17.
Characteristics Exhibited by Children Emotional handicaps.

PORTSMOUTH

THE PINES TREATMENT CENTER

1801 Portsmouth Blvd, Portsmouth, VA 23704 (804) 398-0777
Contact Person(s): Edward C Irby, Admin
Setting and Background Information The facility was established in 1986 as a residential treatment center for ED, LD and/or EMR children and adolescents. Its 28-acre campus has townhouses, a cottage, a dorm, an administration building, a classroom building and others.
Referral Information For referral, submit physical, medical and social development summaries and educational reports to admissions.
Type of Facility
Funding Sources Private; State; Federal; Champus.
Average Length of Stay Long term; 9-14 mos.
Types of Admissions Accepted Residential treatment.
Sources of Referral State depts of education; Local depts of education; State depts of mental health; Psychiatrists; Private sources; Depts of correction; Social service depts.
Client Profile
Age Range of Clients Served Residential program: Birth-18.
Characteristics Exhibited by Children Emotional handicaps; Learning disabilities; Speech/Language disorders; Mental disabilities; Sexual perpetrators; Firesetters.
IQ Range of Clients 60+.
Tuition and Fees
Room and Board Long term: $220-$280.
Placements Primarily Funded By State depts of education; Local depts of education; State depts of mental health; Insurance; Private sources; Depts of corrections; Social service depts; Champus.
Social and Rehabilitative Services
Therapeutic Approach The facility uses positive peer culture techniques and behavior modification.
Therapeutic Services Offered Individual therapy; Group therapy; Family therapy; Adjunctive therapy; Art therapy; Physical therapy; Independent living skills program; Recreation activities; Substance abuse treatment; Aftercare program with follow up.
Professionals on Staff Psychiatrists; Psychologists; Social workers; Adjunctive therapists; Child care staff; Nurses; Art therapists; Physical therapists.
Educational and Vocational Services
Type(s) of Educational Programs Offered On campus (Reg & Spec Ed; Vocational training); Off campus (Voc training; Wilderness experience); Summer campus.
Profile of On Campus School Program Number of classrooms 16; *Student to teacher ratio* 5:1; *Grades taught* K-12; Special curriculum electives offered (Wildrness exp).
Vocational Education Programs/Degrees Offered On campus-mechanical repairs; Carpentry.

Degrees Offered 8th grade diploma; 12th grade diploma; GED.

RICHMOND

PSYCHIATRIC INSTITUTE OF RICHMOND

3001 5th Ave, Richmond, VA 23222 (804) 329-4392, 329-3400
Contact Person(s): Rose Mary Jones, Prog Dir
Setting and Background Information The facility was founded in 1980. It is an 84-bed private mental health care facility designed for children and adolescents. It is owned by Psychiatric Institutes of America.
Referral Information For referral information, contact the facility.
Type of Facility
Funding Sources Private.
Average Length of Stay Long term.
Types of Admissions Accepted Residential treatment.
Sources of Referral State depts of mental health; Psychiatrists; Private sources; Depts of correction; Social service depts; Psychiatric in-patient hospitals.
Client Profile
Age Range of Clients Served Residential program: 12-18.
Characteristics Exhibited by Children Emotional handicaps; Chemical dependency.
IQ Range of Clients 70+.
Tuition and Fees
Room and Board Long term: $11,500/mo.
Tuition $1,400/mo.
Placements Primarily Funded By Insurance.
Social and Rehabilitative Services
Therapeutic Approach The basic therapeutic approach of the facility is psychosocial, using behavior modification.
Therapeutic Services Offered Individual therapy; Group therapy; Family therapy; Recreation activities; Substance abuse treatment; Aftercare program with follow up.
Professionals on Staff Psychiatrists; Psychologists; Social workers; Adjunctive therapists; Child care staff; Nurses; Art therapists; Physical therapists; Chemical dependency counselors.
Educational and Vocational Services
Type(s) of Educational Programs Offered On campus.
Profile of On Campus School Program Student to teacher ratio 5:1; *Grades taught* 1-12; Special curriculum electives offered; Remedial courses offered.
Vocational Education Programs/Degrees Offered Vocational counseling through the Educational Development Center.
Degrees Offered 12th grade diploma; GED.

ST JOSEPH'S VILLA

8000 Brook Rd, Richmond, VA 23227 (804) 266-2447 *Contact Person(s):* Pamela Alterescu, Dir, Res School Div
Setting and Background Information The facility was originally established to provide residential and educational services to children. It has since expanded its program to become a multiservice agency offering special services to children, adults, and families. Saint Joseph's Villa is licensed and certified by the state of Virginia, Depts of Welfare, Education, and Mental Retardation. The campus is located on spacious grounds north of Richmond and consists of cottage-type living units housing 6 to 12 children in each.
Referral Information Referrals can be made by social services, school districts, juvenile courts, mental health agencies, and the Dept of Corrections. To make a referral, an intake packet must be completed to be reviewed by the Admissions Committee. If the referral is appropriate, then an intake interview will be scheduled. Following the interview, the facility's staff will make a decision as to the appropriateness of the placement.
Type of Facility
Funding Sources Private.
Average Length of Stay Long term.
Types of Admissions Accepted Day treatment; Residential treatment; Group home placement.
Sources of Referral Local depts of education; Private sources; Social service depts; Courts; Hospitals.
Client Profile
Age Range of Clients Served Day programs: 11-18; Residential program: 11-18.
Characteristics Exhibited by Children Emotional handicaps; Learning disabilities; Mental disabilities; Behavior disorders.
IQ Range of Clients 80+.

ST JOSEPH'S VILLA (continued)

Tuition and Fees
Room and Board Long term: $49.76/diem.
Tuition $51.33/diem.
Placements Primarily Funded By State depts of mental health; Private sources; Social service depts.
Social and Rehabilitative Services
Therapeutic Approach The facility has an individualized approach to therapy.
Therapeutic Services Offered Individual therapy; Group therapy; Family therapy; Recreation activities.
Professionals on Staff Psychiatrists; Social workers; Child care staff.
Educational and Vocational Services
Type(s) of Educational Programs Offered On campus; Off campus (Public school).
Profile of On Campus School Program Number of teachers 4 and 4 aides; *Number of classrooms* 4; *Student to teacher ratio* 2:1; *Grades taught* (Individualized); Special curriculum electives offered (Driver's Ed).
Degrees Offered GED.

UNITED METHODIST FAMILY SERVICES OF VIRGINIA
3900 W Broad St, Richmond, VA 23230 (804) 353-4461 *Contact Person(s):* Paul Reaves, Admis Dir
Setting and Background Information This service agency was founded in 1962 by the Virginia Methodist Church. The campus is located in the city of Richmond and consists of individual cottages, administrative building, school, and gymnasium.
Referral Information Referrals can be made by court systems, dept of corrections, welfare agencies, school districts, churches, parents, and guardians. Applicants will be requested to submit a social history, psychological report, medical history with examination, and school records. A pre-placement interview will be scheduled before a placement decision is made.
Type of Facility
Funding Sources Private.
Average Length of Stay Long term.
Types of Admissions Accepted Residential treatment.
Sources of Referral Local depts of education; State depts of mental health; Psychiatrists; Social service depts.
Client Profile
Age Range of Clients Served Residential program: 11-17.
Characteristics Exhibited by Children Emotional handicaps; Learning disabilities.
Tuition and Fees
Placements Primarily Funded By State depts of mental health; Insurance; Private sources.
Social and Rehabilitative Services
Therapeutic Approach The use of a positive peer culture along with milieu therapy is the program's basic therapeutic approach.
Therapeutic Services Offered Individual therapy; Group therapy; Family therapy; Independent living skills program; Recreation activities; Aftercare program with follow up.
Professionals on Staff Social workers; Child care staff; Nurses.
Educational and Vocational Services
Type(s) of Educational Programs Offered On campus; Summer campus.
Profile of On Campus School Program Number of teachers 5; *Student to teacher ratio* 8:1; *Grades taught* Individualized.

VIRGINIA HOME FOR BOYS
8716 W Broad St, Richmond, VA 23229 (804) 270-6566 *Contact Person(s):* Cindy Smith, Intake Coord
Setting and Background Information Virginia Home for Boys is a residential treatment facility which was established in 1846 by concerned civic and church groups. It is located on a 27-acre campus in a residential neighborhood of Henrico County. The campus includes 6 cottages, vocational school, dining room, gymnasium, and athletic field.
Referral Information Referrals can be made by any private or public agency in Virginia. Upon receiving the necessary referral material, a pre-placement visit lasting 2 to 3 days will be scheduled. A final placement decision will be made within 5 days following the visit. The facility does not accept boys who are suicidal, psychotic, assaultive, or mentally retarded.

Type of Facility
Funding Sources Private.
Average Length of Stay Long term.
Types of Admissions Accepted Residential treatment; Group home placement.
Sources of Referral State depts of mental health; Private sources; Depts of correction; Social service depts.
Client Profile
Age Range of Clients Served Residential program: 10-17.
Characteristics Exhibited by Children Emotional handicaps; Learning disabilities.
IQ Range of Clients 75+.
Tuition and Fees
Room and Board Long term: $909/mo.
Tuition $7,616/9 mos.
Placements Primarily Funded By Local depts of education; State depts of mental health; Private sources; Depts of corrections; Social service depts; Donations.
Social and Rehabilitative Services
Therapeutic Approach The primary therapeutic approach used is reality therapy.
Therapeutic Services Offered Individual therapy; Group therapy; Recreation activities; Aftercare program with follow up.
Professionals on Staff Psychologists; Social workers; Adjunctive therapists; Child care staff; Nurses.
Educational and Vocational Services
Type(s) of Educational Programs Offered On campus (Vocational center); Off campus (Public school).
Profile of On Campus School Program Number of teachers 4; *Student to teacher ratio* 8:1.
Vocational Education Programs/Degrees Offered Printing and building maintenance.
Degrees Offered GED.

VIRGINIA TREATMENT CENTER
515 N 10th St, Richmond, VA 23201 (804) 786-3129, 786-3105 *Contact Person(s):* Clara Tarham, LCSW
Setting and Background Information The facility was established in 1956 by an act of the General Assembly and opened in 1962. It is located in the Medical College of Virginia complex and consists of living units, gymnasium, auditorium, classrooms, therapy offices, and an art-music studio.
Referral Information Referrals can be made by anyone through the Community Service Board for Admission. The program only serves residents of Virginia.
Type of Facility
Funding Sources State.
Average Length of Stay 3-6 mos.
Types of Admissions Accepted Day treatment; Residential treatment.
Sources of Referral State depts of education; Local depts of education; Psychiatrists.
Client Profile
Age Range of Clients Served Day programs: 4-16; Residential program: 4-16.
Characteristics Exhibited by Children Emotional handicaps; Learning disabilities; Hearing impairments/deafness; Vision impairments/blindness; Speech/Language disorders; Physical handicaps.
Tuition and Fees
Room and Board Long term: $505/diem (children's ward); $345/diem (adolescent ward); $140/diem (partial hospitalization).
Placements Primarily Funded By State depts of mental health; Insurance; Private sources; Donations.
Social and Rehabilitative Services
Therapeutic Approach The treatment program is psychoanalytically oriented with an emphasis on milieu therapy.
Therapeutic Services Offered Individual therapy; Group therapy; Family therapy; Recreation activities; Aftercare program with follow up.
Professionals on Staff Psychiatrists; Psychologists; Social workers; Nurses.
Educational and Vocational Services
Type(s) of Educational Programs Offered On campus; Summer campus.
Profile of On Campus School Program Number of teachers 6; *Number of classrooms* 6; *Student to teacher ratio* 3:1; *Grades taught* K-12, Individualized; Remedial courses offered.

ROANOKE

KIWANIS INDEPENDENCE PROGRAM

1336 Maple Ave SW, Roanoke, VA 24016 (703) 345-0039 *Contact Person(s):* Lynn McDowell, Coord

Setting and Background Information DSS and the Kiwanis Club established the facility in 1974. It is currently operated by the Mental Health Services at Roanoke Valley. The facility is located on 18 acres, adjacent to a school.

Referral Information Referrals are made by contacting the coordinator and applying to the admissions committee.

Type of Facility

Funding Sources Private; State; Federal; Title XX.

Average Length of Stay Long term.

Types of Admissions Accepted Residential treatment; Group home placement.

Sources of Referral Private sources; Depts of correction; Social service depts.

Client Profile

Age Range of Clients Served Residential program: 15-21+.

Characteristics Exhibited by Children Emotional handicaps; Learning disabilities; Mental disabilities.

IQ Range of Clients 70+.

Tuition and Fees

Room and Board Long term: $19.95/diem.

Placements Primarily Funded By Private sources; Depts of corrections; Social service depts.

Social and Rehabilitative Services

Therapeutic Approach Behavior management, individual and family counseling are the therapeutic approaches used.

Therapeutic Services Offered Individual therapy; Group therapy; Family therapy; Adjunctive therapy; Independent living skills program; Recreation activities; Substance abuse treatment; After-care program with follow up.

Professionals on Staff Psychologists; Adjunctive therapists.

Educational and Vocational Services

Type(s) of Educational Programs Offered On campus; Off campus.

Profile of On Campus School Program Number of teachers 1; *Number of classrooms* 1; *Student to teacher ratio* 8:1; *Length of school day* 3 hrs; *Grades taught* 8-12.

Degrees Offered 12th grade diploma.

MENTAL HEALTH SERVICES OF THE ROANOKE VALLEY—CHILDREN'S CENTER

2417 Salem Turnpike, Roanoke, VA 24017 (703) 981-0122 *Contact Person(s):* Gina Wilburn, Coord

Setting and Background Information The facility was jointly established in 1977 by CSB and local DSS. It is a residential house.

Referral Information Contact the facility for referral information.

Type of Facility

Funding Sources Private; State; Federal; Title XX.

Average Length of Stay Long term.

Types of Admissions Accepted Day treatment; Residential treatment.

Sources of Referral Local depts of education; Psychiatrists; Private sources; Depts of correction; Social service depts.

Client Profile

Age Range of Clients Served Day programs: 6-12; Residential program: 5-12.

Characteristics Exhibited by Children Emotional handicaps; Learning disabilities; Speech/Language disorders; Neurological impairments; Mental disabilities.

IQ Range of Clients 50+.

Tuition and Fees

Room and Board Long term: $33.20/diem.

Placements Primarily Funded By Social service depts.

Social and Rehabilitative Services

Therapeutic Approach The facility uses milieu therapy and behavior modification.

Therapeutic Services Offered Individual therapy; Group therapy; Family therapy; Adjunctive therapy; Recreation activities; After-care program with follow up.

Professionals on Staff Psychiatrists; Adjunctive therapists; Nurses.

Educational and Vocational Services

Type(s) of Educational Programs Offered On campus (Group homebound); Off campus (Mainstream into public schools); Summer campus (Group homebound).

Profile of On Campus School Program Number of teachers 1; *Number of classrooms* 1; *Student to teacher ratio* 3:1; *Credentials of teachers* BA, ED/LD; *Length of school day* 3 ½ hrs; *Grades taught* K-7; Remedial courses offered.

STANLEY

RIVER'S BEND FARM SCHOOL

Rt 1, Box 405, Stanley, VA 22851 (703) 652-6137 *Contact Person(s):* Jeff Lambert, Exec Dir

Referral Information Contact the facility and forward a letter of referral, a psychological evaluation, an educational evaluation, a social history, and medical information.

Type of Facility

Funding Sources State.

Average Length of Stay 1 yr or more.

Types of Admissions Accepted Residential treatment.

Sources of Referral State depts of education; Local depts of education; Private sources; Depts of correction; Social service depts.

Client Profile

Age Range of Clients Served Residential program: 12-18.

Characteristics Exhibited by Children Emotional handicaps; Learning disabilities; Speech/Language disorders; Neurological impairments; Mental disabilities.

IQ Range of Clients 60-120.

Tuition and Fees

Room and Board Long term: $76.17/diem.

Tuition $45.53/diem.

Placements Primarily Funded By State depts of education; Depts of corrections; Social service depts.

Social and Rehabilitative Services

Therapeutic Approach The basic therapeutic approach used at the facility is behavior modification.

Therapeutic Services Offered Individual therapy; Group therapy; Family therapy; Independent living skills program; Recreation activities.

Professionals on Staff Psychologists; Child care staff.

Educational and Vocational Services

Type(s) of Educational Programs Offered On campus (Spec Ed).

Profile of On Campus School Program Number of teachers 3; *Number of classrooms* 3; *Student to teacher ratio* 8:1; *Credentials of teachers* BA; *Grades taught* 6-12; Special curriculum electives offered; Remedial courses offered (Individualized).

Vocational Education Programs/Degrees Offered Building trades; Food services; Landscape.

Degrees Offered 12th grade diploma.

STAUNTON

DEJARNETTE CENTER FOR HUMAN DEVELOPMENT

PO Box 2309, Staunton, VA 24401 (703) 885-9085 *Contact Person(s):* Andrea Newsome, Dir

Referral Information Contact the facility for referral information.

Client Profile

Age Range of Clients Served Residential program: 2-17.

Characteristics Exhibited by Children Emotional handicaps.

STERLING

LOUDOUN YOUTH SHELTER

Rt 2 Box 319, Sterling, VA 22170 (703) 450-4858 *Contact Person(s):* Jerry Tracy, Admin

Setting and Background Information The facility was established in 1981 by the local government and community effort with a DOC block grant. It is a residential treatment program located on 3 acres.

Referral Information Referrals to the facility are made through social services, courts, depts of mental health, or by private therapists.

Type of Facility

Funding Sources State; Local.

Average Length of Stay Short and long term.

Types of Admissions Accepted Residential treatment; Emergency shelter.

Sources of Referral Psychiatrists; Depts of correction; Social service depts; Local mental health center.

LOUDOUN YOUTH SHELTER *(continued)*

Client Profile
Age Range of Clients Served Residential program: 12-18.
Characteristics Exhibited by Children Emotional handicaps.
Tuition and Fees
Room and Board Short term: $38/diem; (Free to Loudoun residents); Long term: $38/diem; (Free to Loudoun residents).
Placements Primarily Funded By Depts of corrections; Local.
Social and Rehabilitative Services
Therapeutic Approach The therapeutic approaches of the facility combine structured behavioral control with development of relationships and responsibility for behavior.
Therapeutic Services Offered Individual therapy; Group therapy; Family therapy; Aftercare program with follow up.
Professionals on Staff Psychologists; Social workers; Adjunctive therapists; Child care staff.
Educational and Vocational Services
Type(s) of Educational Programs Offered Off campus (Public school).

VIENNA

ALTERNATIVE HOUSE

2009 Gallows Rd, Vienna, VA 22180 (703) 356-8385 *Contact Person(s):* Judy Abrahams, Exec Dir
Setting and Background Information The facility was established in 1972 by a community group as a place for troubled adolescents. It is a residential home with the capacity for eight clients.
Referral Information Contact the facility for referral procedures.
Type of Facility
Funding Sources State; Federal; Community contribution.
Average Length of Stay Short term.
Types of Admissions Accepted Day treatment; Residential treatment.
Sources of Referral Private sources; Social service depts.
Client Profile
Age Range of Clients Served Residential program: 13-17.
Characteristics Exhibited by Children Emotional handicaps; Learning disabilities.
Tuition and Fees
Placements Primarily Funded By State depts of mental health; Social service depts.
Social and Rehabilitative Services
Therapeutic Approach The basic therapeutic approach is milieu therapy.
Therapeutic Services Offered Individual therapy; Group therapy; Family therapy; Art therapy; Recreation activities; Aftercare program with follow up.
Professionals on Staff Psychologists; Social workers.
Educational and Vocational Services
Type(s) of Educational Programs Offered Off campus.

WILLIAMSBURG

EASTERN STATE HOSPITAL—CHILDREN/ ADOLESCENT UNIT

PO Drawer N, Williamsburg, VA 23187 (804) 253-5259 *Contact Person(s):* David Pribble, Dir
Referral Information Contact the facility for referral information.
Client Profile
Age Range of Clients Served Residential program: 7-17.
Characteristics Exhibited by Children Emotional handicaps.

WINCHESTER

TIMBER RIDGE

PO Box 3160, Winchester, VA 22601 (703) 888-3456, 667-6303 (business office) *Contact Person(s):* Phillip Arlotta MSW
Setting and Background Information The facility was established by a group of concerned citizens, 19 miles northwest of Winchester, in the Blue Ridge Mountains. The campus is located on 126 acres and consists of individual residential units with their own classrooms, educational resource room, recreation hall, arts and crafts room. The facility accepts males only.
Referral Information For referral information contact the facility. The program does not accept applicants who are mentally retarded, physically handicapped, or psychotic.

Type of Facility
Funding Sources Private.
Average Length of Stay Long term.
Types of Admissions Accepted Residential treatment.
Sources of Referral State depts of education; Local depts of education; Private sources; Depts of correction; Social service depts.
Client Profile
Age Range of Clients Served Residential program: 11-21.
Characteristics Exhibited by Children Emotional handicaps; Learning disabilities; Delinquency.
Tuition and Fees
Room and Board Long term: $36,900-$37,500/yr (includes school tuition).
Placements Primarily Funded By State depts of education; Local depts of education; Private sources; Depts of corrections; Social service depts.
Social and Rehabilitative Services
Therapeutic Approach A psychoeducational model is used, stressing sequential development, behavior managements, and reality-based therapy.
Therapeutic Services Offered Individual therapy; Group therapy; Adjunctive therapy; Independent living skills program; Recreation activities; Aftercare program with follow up.
Professionals on Staff Psychiatrists; Psychologists; Social workers; Adjunctive therapists; Child care staff; Nurses.
Educational and Vocational Services
Type(s) of Educational Programs Offered On campus.
Profile of On Campus School Program Number of teachers 9; *Number of classrooms* 10; *Student to teacher ratio* 6:1; *Credentials of teachers* Certified Spec Ed; *Grades taught* Individualized; Remedial courses offered.
Vocational Education Programs/Degrees Offered Vocational educational.

WASHINGTON

ANACORTES

SECRET HARBOR SCHOOL
PO Box 440, 1809 Commercial Ave, Anacortes, WA 98221
(206) 293-5151 *Contact Person(s):* Cleo Schroeder, Susan Street, Admissions

Setting and Background Information Secret Harbor School is a private residential treatment facility for boys. There is also a transitional group home for boys who are discharged. The facility was established in 1949 by Lillian J Johnson and Thomas Gallagher, both former directors of Ryther Child Center in Seattle. It is owned and operated by the non-profit Johnson-Gallagher Foundation. The purpose of this facility was to fulfill the need for a treatment center with an open setting separated from urban influences. Located on 343 acres on Cypress Island, the campus is isolated from the mainland and can only be reached by private boat or sea plane. The waterfront setting offers opportunities for sailing, fishing, and skin diving. A central building houses a kitchen, dining room, living room, professional office, music, craft, and study rooms. Dormitories are adjacent to this building and a school building with a gymnasium is nearby. The center operates its own farm for therapeutic and vocational pruposes.

Referral Information Referrals can be made by parents, clinicians, psychiatrists, psychologists, physicians, social agencies, school districts, and other interested individuals. To make a referral, contact the facility and forward the necessary background information including psychiatric/psychological reports and social history. The referral material will be reviewed by the Admission Committee to determine if the placement is appropriate.

Type of Facility
Funding Sources Private; State.
Average Length of Stay 18 mos.
Types of Admissions Accepted Residential treatment; Group home placement.
Sources of Referral State depts of mental health; Private sources; Social service depts.

Client Profile
Age Range of Clients Served Residential program: 11-17.
Characteristics Exhibited by Children Emotional handicaps; Learning disabilities; Mental disabilities.

Tuition and Fees
Room and Board Long term: $3,350/mo (includes school tuition).
Placements Primarily Funded By State depts of mental health; Private sources.

Social and Rehabilitative Services
Therapeutic Approach An eclectic therapeutic approach is used involving reality therapy, accountability, and the work ethic.
Therapeutic Services Offered Individual therapy; Group therapy; Family therapy; Adjunctive therapy; Independent living skills program; Recreation activities; Aftercare program with follow up.
Professionals on Staff Psychiatrists; Psychologists; Social workers; Child care staff; Nurses.

Educational and Vocational Services
Type(s) of Educational Programs Offered On campus; Summer campus.
Profile of On Campus School Program Number of teachers 4; *Student to teacher ratio* 7:1; Remedial courses offered.
Degrees Offered GED; Credits are transferred to home school district.

BELLINGHAM

CATHOLIC COMMUNITY SERVICES NORTHWEST
2806 Douglas Ave, Bellingham, WA 98225 (206) 733-5800 *Contact Person(s):* Janice Condrin (Psychiatric Program); Cathy McAughton (Day Treatment)

Setting and Background Information Catholic Community Services Northwest is a private organization which operates a psychiatric residential treatment facility and a group home program. The agency also offers outpatient/day treatment programs at 1780 Iowa St. The group home program was established in 1971. An 18-bed psychiatric facility opened in 1982.

Referral Information Anyone can make a referral by contacting the facility.

Type of Facility
Funding Sources Private; State.
Average Length of Stay Short and long term.
Types of Admissions Accepted Day treatment; Residential treatment; Group home placement; Wards of the state.
Sources of Referral State depts of mental health; Social service depts; Courts.

Client Profile
Age Range of Clients Served Day programs: 4-17; Residential program: 4-17.
Characteristics Exhibited by Children Emotional handicaps; Learning disabilities; Neurological impairments; Mental disabilities.

Tuition and Fees
Placements Primarily Funded By State depts of mental health; United Way.

Social and Rehabilitative Services
Therapeutic Services Offered Individual therapy; Group therapy; Family therapy; Adjunctive therapy; Independent living skills program; Recreation activities; Aftercare program with follow up.
Professionals on Staff Psychiatrists; Psychologists; Social workers; Adjunctive therapists; Child care staff; Nurses.

Educational and Vocational Services
Type(s) of Educational Programs Offered On campus; Off campus (Public school).

BREMERTON

FRANCES HADDON MORGAN CENTER
3423 6th St, Bremerton, WA 98312-3555 (206) 478-4824 *Contact Person(s):* Marvin Bruno PhD

Setting and Background Information The Center was established in 1972 by an appropriation of the Washington State Legislature and the assistance of the Division of Developmental Disabilities, Department of Social and Health Services.

Referral Information Contact the facility for referral information.

Type of Facility
Funding Sources State; Federal.
Average Length of Stay Long term.
Types of Admissions Accepted Residential treatment; Respite care.
Sources of Referral State depts of mental health; Social service depts.

Client Profile
Age Range of Clients Served Residential program: 3-22.
Characteristics Exhibited by Children Emotional handicaps; Mental disabilities; Autism; Developmental Disabilities.

FRANCES HADDON MORGAN CENTER *(continued)*

Tuition and Fees
Placements Primarily Funded By State depts of mental health; Title XIX.
Social and Rehabilitative Services
Therapeutic Services Offered Individual therapy; Group therapy; Family therapy; Adjunctive therapy; Physical therapy; Independent living skills program; Recreation activities.
Professionals on Staff Psychologists; Social workers; Adjunctive therapists; Child care staff; Nurses; Occupational therapist.
Educational and Vocational Services
Type(s) of Educational Programs Offered On campus; Off campus.
Profile of On Campus School Program Special curriculum electives offered; Remedial courses offered.

RENTON

FRIENDS OF YOUTH

2500 Lake Washington Blvd N, Renton, WA 98056 (206) 228-5775 *Contact Person(s):* Claude Carlson, Dir of Prof Srvs
Setting and Background Information The facility was established in 1950 by volunteer efforts. There are five separate locations.
Referral Information Contact the facility for referral information. There is a 24-hour crisis line for short term care and counseling.
Type of Facility
Funding Sources Private; State; Federal.
Average Length of Stay Short and long term.
Types of Admissions Accepted Day treatment; Residential treatment; Group home placement; Wards of the state; Emergency shelter.
Sources of Referral State depts of education; Local depts of education; State depts of mental health; Psychiatrists; Private sources; Depts of correction; Social service depts.
Client Profile
Age Range of Clients Served Day programs: 12-18; Residential program: 12-18.
Characteristics Exhibited by Children Emotional handicaps; Learning disabilities.
Tuition and Fees
Room and Board Short term: $12/diem; Long term: $1,300-2,100/mo.
Placements Primarily Funded By State depts of education; Local depts of education; Private sources; Depts of corrections; Social service depts.
Social and Rehabilitative Services
Therapeutic Approach The facility has a behavioral approach to therapy.
Therapeutic Services Offered Individual therapy; Group therapy; Family therapy; Adjunctive therapy; Independent living skills program; Recreation activities; Substance abuse treatment; Aftercare program with follow up.
Professionals on Staff Psychiatrists; Psychologists; Social workers; Child care staff.
Educational and Vocational Services
Type(s) of Educational Programs Offered On campus; Off campus; Summer campus.
Profile of On Campus School Program Number of teachers 4; *Number of classrooms* 2; *Student to teacher ratio* 5:1; *Credentials of teachers* Certified; *Length of school day* 8:30-2:30; *Grades taught* 1-12; Special curriculum electives offered (Life skills); Remedial courses offered.
Degrees Offered 12th grade diploma.

SEATTLE

KEYSTONE RESOURCES

3515 Woodland Pk Ave N, Seattle, WA 98103 (206) 632-3872
Contact Person(s): Jana J Brumbaugh, Prog Mgr
Setting and Background Information This facility was established in 1982 as a private, non-private corporation by the Community Psychiatric Clinic. It is a 46-bed residential facility.
Referral Information Referrals are made by contacting the facility. A pre-placement interview will be scheduled. All placements, unless privately funded, must be approved by the state Dept of Social and Health Services.

Type of Facility
Funding Sources Private; State; Federal.
Average Length of Stay Long term; Minimum 6 mos.
Types of Admissions Accepted Group home placement.
Sources of Referral State depts of mental health; Psychiatrists; Private sources; Depts of correction; Social service depts.
Client Profile
Age Range of Clients Served Residential program: 18-21+.
Characteristics Exhibited by Children Emotional handicaps.
Tuition and Fees
Room and Board Long term: $20.19/diem.
Placements Primarily Funded By State depts of mental health.
Social and Rehabilitative Services
Therapeutic Approach The facility has a psychosocial approach to therapy.
Therapeutic Services Offered Recreation activities; Case management.

PARKVIEW HOMES I, II, & III

1918 33rd Ave S, Seattle, WA 98144 (206) 324-4113 *Contact Person(s):* Elizabeth Detels MSW, Exec Dir
Setting and Background Information This facility was established in 1969 by the parents of a developmentally disabled child. They wanted to provide an alternative to institutional placement. In 1973, two additional facilites were opened with funds from government and private sources. This is a group home and has two buildings in separate parts of town.
Referral Information For referral information contact the facility.
Type of Facility
Funding Sources Private; State.
Average Length of Stay Long term.
Types of Admissions Accepted Residential treatment; Group home placement.
Sources of Referral Social service depts.
Client Profile
Age Range of Clients Served Residential program: 9-21.
Characteristics Exhibited by Children Emotional handicaps; Learning disabilities; Speech/Language disorders; Neurological impairments; Mental disabilities; Autism.
Tuition and Fees
Room and Board Long term: The cost of room and board is provided by a state contract.
Placements Primarily Funded By Social service depts.
Social and Rehabilitative Services
Therapeutic Approach The facility uses behavior modification and offers training in independent living skills.
Therapeutic Services Offered Independent living skills program.
Professionals on Staff Social workers.
Educational and Vocational Services
Type(s) of Educational Programs Offered Off campus (Public schools).

RYTHER CHILD CENTER

2400 N E 95th, Seattle, WA 98115 (206) 525-5050 *Contact Person(s):* Robert L Roy, Exec Dir
Setting and Background Information The facility was established in 1935 by the community funds welfare council. It is a residential treatment facility and also offers day treatment programs. There are 6 cottages, a school, an administration building, and a day-treatment facility.
Referral Information Contact the intake worker for referral information. A pre-placement visit will be arranged. A psychiatric evaluation may be required.
Type of Facility
Funding Sources Private; State; Federal.
Average Length of Stay Long term.
Types of Admissions Accepted Day treatment; Residential treatment.
Sources of Referral Local depts of education; Psychiatrists; Private sources; Social service depts.
Client Profile
Age Range of Clients Served Day programs: Birth-12; Residential program: 6-18.
Characteristics Exhibited by Children Emotional handicaps; Learning disabilities; Mental disabilities.
IQ Range of Clients 80+.
Tuition and Fees
Room and Board Long term: $120/diem.
Placements Primarily Funded By Insurance; Private sources; Social service depts.

RYTHER CHILD CENTER *(continued)*

Social and Rehabilitative Services
Therapeutic Services Offered Individual therapy; Group therapy; Family therapy; Art therapy; Recreation activities; Substance abuse treatment; Aftercare program with follow up.
Professionals on Staff Psychiatrists; Psychologists; Social workers; Child care staff; Art therapists.
Educational and Vocational Services
Type(s) of Educational Programs Offered On campus.
Profile of On Campus School Program Number of teachers 5; *Number of classrooms* 6; *Student to teacher ratio* 6:1; *Credentials of teachers* Spec Ed; *Length of school day* 9-3; *Grades taught* 4-12; Remedial courses offered.

SEATTLE CHILDRENS HOME

2142 10th Ave W, Seattle, WA 98119 (206) 283-3300 *Contact Person(s):* Robert L DeLong, Exec Dir
Setting and Background Information The facility was privately established in 1884. The 3-acre campus has a day treatment center, a residential unit, an administrative building, an office and other buildings.
Referral Information Contact the facility for referral information.
Type of Facility
Funding Sources Private; State.
Average Length of Stay Long term.
Types of Admissions Accepted Day treatment; Residential treatment.
Sources of Referral State depts of education; Local depts of education; State depts of mental health; Private sources; Social service depts.
Client Profile
Age Range of Clients Served Day programs: 6-18; Residential program: 12-18.
Characteristics Exhibited by Children Emotional handicaps; Learning disabilities; Neurological impairments; Mental disabilities.
Tuition and Fees
Room and Board Long term: $245/diem.
Placements Primarily Funded By State depts of mental health.
Social and Rehabilitative Services
Therapeutic Services Offered Individual therapy; Group therapy; Family therapy; Adjunctive therapy; Art therapy; Independent living skills program; Recreation activities; Aftercare program with follow up.
Professionals on Staff Psychiatrists; Psychologists.
Educational and Vocational Services
Type(s) of Educational Programs Offered On campus; Off campus; Summer campus.
Vocational Education Programs/Degrees Offered Food services; Horticulture.
Degrees Offered 12th grade diploma; GED.

SPOKANE

BERNARD ST CCF

S 605 Bernard, Spokane, WA 99204 (509) 624-0419 *Contact Person(s):* Carol Robertson LPN, Facility Mgr
Referral Information Referrals are made by Eastern State Hospital, Sacred Heart Medical Center, and social service agencies.
Type of Facility
Funding Sources Private; State.
Average Length of Stay Long term.
Types of Admissions Accepted Group home placement.
Sources of Referral State depts of mental health; Psychiatrists; Private sources; Social service depts.
Client Profile
Age Range of Clients Served Residential program: 18-21+.
Characteristics Exhibited by Children Mental disabilities.
IQ Range of Clients 70+.
Tuition and Fees
Room and Board Long term: $20.19/diem.
Placements Primarily Funded By Social service depts.
Social and Rehabilitative Services
Therapeutic Services Offered Independent living skills program.
Professionals on Staff Psychiatrists; Psychologists; Social workers.

TACOMA

CHILD STUDY AND TREATMENT CENTER

PO Box 97036, 8919 Steilacoom Blvd, Tacoma, WA 98498 (206) 756-2504 *Contact Person(s):* Donna Douglass, MSW
Setting and Background Information The Child Study and Treatment Center is a state residential and day treatment facility, which evolved from a children's ward in a state hospital to become a JCAH-accredited child/adolescent psychiatric hospital in 1962. The campus consists of a 3-building complex located on the grounds of Western State Hospital. One building provides offices, conference rooms, occupational therapy rooms, school facilities, and a gymnasium. There are 2 residential cottages which house 16 residents each, along with treatment rooms, recreation rooms, day room, dining room, kitchen, and bedrooms. In 1979, a unit for 8 adolescents was opened on the main campus of Western State Hospital and has similar accomodations to that of the cottages.
Referral Information Voluntary admissions can be referred by parent or guardian; however, if the child is 13 years or older, their written consent must also be obtained. If a parent, guardian, or the court wants to commit a child over 13 years involuntarily, then a petition must be filed. This petition must explain why committment is necessary and why other alternative treatments have not or will not benefit the child. The court will then conduct a hearing to decide whether committment would be the best alternative for the child. If the placement is deemed appropriate, then admission can take place. The program does not accept children who are primarily delinquent, mentally retarded, autistic, multiply handicapped or sensory impaired.
Type of Facility
Funding Sources Private; State.
Average Length of Stay 3-5 mos (adolescent), 1 yr (pre-adolescent).
Types of Admissions Accepted Day treatment; Residential treatment.
Sources of Referral State depts of mental health; Psychiatrists; Private sources; Depts of correction; Social service depts.
Client Profile
Age Range of Clients Served Day programs: 6-11; Residential program: 7-18.
Characteristics Exhibited by Children Emotional handicaps; Mental disabilities; Psychotic; Depression; Self-destructive; Agressiveness; Hyperactivity.
Tuition and Fees
Room and Board Long term: $220/diem (Sliding scale).
Placements Primarily Funded By State depts of mental health; Insurance; Private sources; Champus; Title 19.
Social and Rehabilitative Services
Therapeutic Approach The basic therapeutic approach used at the facility is psychodynamic.
Therapeutic Services Offered Individual therapy; Group therapy; Family therapy; Adjunctive therapy.
Professionals on Staff Psychiatrists; Psychologists; Social workers; Adjunctive therapists; Child care staff; Nurses.
Educational and Vocational Services
Type(s) of Educational Programs Offered On campus (Operated by local school system).
Profile of On Campus School Program Number of teachers 10; *Student to teacher ratio* 8:1; *Grades taught* K-12.
Degrees Offered GED; Credits are transferable to home school district.

COMPREHENSIVE MENTAL HEALTH, PEARL ST CENTER

815 S Pearl St, Tacoma, WA 98465 (206) 756-5290 *Contact Person(s):* Michael K Laederich Phd, Prog Dir
Setting and Background Information The program was established by the state legislature in 1984.
Referral Information Contact the facility for referral information.
Type of Facility
Funding Sources State.
Average Length of Stay 18-24 mos.
Types of Admissions Accepted Psychiatric in-patient.
Sources of Referral State Admission Committee.
Client Profile
Age Range of Clients Served Residential program: 13-17.
Characteristics Exhibited by Children Emotional handicaps; Mental disabilities.

COMPREHENSIVE MENTAL HEALTH, PEARL ST CENTER *(continued)*

Tuition and Fees
Placements Primarily Funded By State depts of mental health.
Social and Rehabilitative Services
Therapeutic Approach The facility has a therapeutic milieu and offers supportive therapies.
Therapeutic Services Offered Individual therapy; Group therapy; Family therapy; Art therapy; Independent living skills program; Recreation activities; Aftercare program with follow up.
Professionals on Staff Psychiatrists; Psychologists; Social workers; Child care staff; Nurses.
Educational and Vocational Services
Type(s) of Educational Programs Offered On campus.
Profile of On Campus School Program Number of teachers 2; *Number of classrooms* 1.
Vocational Education Programs/Degrees Offered Pre-vocational; Vocational evaluation.

WEST VIRGINIA

BARBOURSVILLE

BARBOURSVILLE SCHOOL
1535 Martha Rd, Barboursville, WV 25705 (304) 736-0915 *Contact Person(s):* Lester Cohen, Dir
Setting and Background Information This residential school was established by a court decree in 1983. Its 10-acre campus has 3 cottages and an administration/school building.
Referral Information Contact the facility for referral information..
Type of Facility
Funding Sources State.
Average Length of Stay Long term.
Types of Admissions Accepted Residential treatment.
Sources of Referral State depts of education; Local depts of education; State depts of mental health; Psychiatrists; Private sources; Depts of correction; Social service depts.
Client Profile
Age Range of Clients Served Residential program: 12-18.
Characteristics Exhibited by Children Emotional handicaps; Learning disabilities; Mental disabilities.
IQ Range of Clients 65+.
Tuition and Fees
Placements Primarily Funded By State depts of mental health.
Social and Rehabilitative Services
Therapeutic Services Offered Individual therapy; Group therapy; Family therapy; Adjunctive therapy; Independent living skills program; Recreation activities; Aftercare program with follow up.
Professionals on Staff Psychiatrists; Psychologists; Social workers; Child care staff; Nurses.
Educational and Vocational Services
Type(s) of Educational Programs Offered On campus.
Profile of On Campus School Program Number of teachers 12; *Number of classrooms* 5; *Student to teacher ratio* 3:1; *Credentials of teachers* BA; *Grades taught* Individualized instruction; Special curriculum electives offered (Vocational education).
Degrees Offered GED.

BECKLEY

BECKLEY CHILD CARE CENTER
PO Box 250, Beckley, WV 25801 (304) 252-8508 *Contact Person(s):* Melvin D Coy
Referral Information To make a referral, contact the facility by phone or mail in order to determine if space is available and to determine if the referral is appropriate. Forward the necessary information. The facility does not accept severely emotionally disturbed, handicapped, or violent youth.
Type of Facility
Average Length of Stay 9 mos-2 yrs.
Types of Admissions Accepted Residential treatment.
Sources of Referral Dept of Human Svcs; Juvenile courts; Mental health facilities; Private individuals.
Client Profile
Age Range of Clients Served Residential program: 6-17.
Characteristics Exhibited by Children Emotional handicaps.
Tuition and Fees
Room and Board Long term: Sliding scale.
Placements Primarily Funded By Private sources; Depts of corrections; Dept of Human Svcs.

Social and Rehabilitative Services
Therapeutic Services Offered Individual therapy; Group therapy; Family therapy; Adjunctive therapy; Independent living skills program; Aftercare program with follow up.
Educational and Vocational Services
Type(s) of Educational Programs Offered Off campus (Public school; Vocational school).

BUCKHANNON

NEW DAWN YOUTH CENTER, INC
PO Box 163, Buckhannon, WV 26201 (304) 472-9354 *Contact Person(s):* James K Pritchard
Referral Information Referrals are made through the Dept of Human Services, juvenile court, or call the Director for information.
Type of Facility
Average Length of Stay 12-18 mos.
Types of Admissions Accepted Residential treatment; Group home placement.
Sources of Referral Social service depts; Juvenile court.
Client Profile
Age Range of Clients Served Residential program: 8-18.
Characteristics Exhibited by Children Emotional handicaps; Displaced youth.
Social and Rehabilitative Services
Therapeutic Services Offered Individual therapy; Group therapy; Recreation activities.
Professionals on Staff Child care staff.
Educational and Vocational Services
Type(s) of Educational Programs Offered Off campus.

BURLINGTON

BURLINGTON UNITED METHODIST HOME FOR CHILDREN AND YOUTH, INC
PO Box 96, Burlington, WV 26710 (304) 289-3511, 289-3512, 289-3903 *Contact Person(s):* Gary Wilson, Admin
Setting and Background Information Burlington United Methodist Home is a private residential treatment facility. The facility was initially a child care institution founded in 1913. In 1950, it became the property of the West Virginia Conference of the Methodist Church and when they merged with the Evangelical United Bretheren Church in 1968, the facility became known as the Burlington United Methodist Home. The campus is located in a rural setting on 16 acres of land and consists of 3 residential cottages, a group home, school, administration building, and a maintenance facility.
Referral Information Referrals can be made by the West Virginia Dept of Human Services, courts, mental health centers, private individuals, families, and other agencies. To make a referral, complete an application and send it to the facility's Welfare Area-4 Liaison Worker. The necessary background information on the child should also be forwarded, including psychological reports, physical exam, immunization records, social security number, birth certificate, and medical insurance numbers. Upon receipt of the referral material, a pre-placement interview will take place with the Intake Committee before an admission decision is made.

BURLINGTON UNITED METHODIST HOME FOR CHILDREN AND YOUTH, INC *(continued)*

Type of Facility
Funding Sources Private.
Average Length of Stay 3 mos-3 yrs.
Types of Admissions Accepted Residential treatment; Group home placement; Foster care.
Sources of Referral State depts of mental health.
Client Profile
Age Range of Clients Served Residential program: 8-18.
Characteristics Exhibited by Children Emotional handicaps; Learning disabilities.
Tuition and Fees
Placements Primarily Funded By United Methodist Church.
Social and Rehabilitative Services
Therapeutic Approach The treatment program utilizes reality therapy as its primary therapeutic modality, although behavior modification programs are used.
Therapeutic Services Offered Individual therapy; Group therapy; Family therapy; Independent living skills program; Recreation activities; Aftercare program with follow up.
Professionals on Staff Social workers; Child care staff.
Educational and Vocational Services
Type(s) of Educational Programs Offered Off campus (Public school).

CHARLES TOWN

BETH-SUR BOY'S HOME

Rte 1 Box 1930, Charles Town, WV 25414 (304) 725-2717 *Contact Person(s):* David Zimmerman, Dir
Referral Information Contact the facility directly for a referral. Any youth serving agency or parent can make a referral. The facility accepts boys only.
Type of Facility
Average Length of Stay Avg 2 yrs.
Types of Admissions Accepted Residential treatment.
Sources of Referral Family; Individuals; Any agency.
Client Profile
Age Range of Clients Served Residential program: 9-17.
Tuition and Fees
Room and Board Long term: $33.211/diem.
Placements Primarily Funded By Private sources.
Social and Rehabilitative Services
Therapeutic Services Offered Family therapy.
Educational and Vocational Services
Type(s) of Educational Programs Offered On campus.

CHARLESTON

CHILDREN'S HOME SOCIETY OF WEST VIRGINIA

PO Box 2942, 1118 Kanawha Blvd E, Charleston, WV 25330 (304) 346-0795
Referral Information Anyone may make a referral to the facility.
Type of Facility
Average Length of Stay Long term.
Types of Admissions Accepted Residential treatment; Emergency shelter; Foster care; Adoption services.
Client Profile
Age Range of Clients Served Residential program: Birth-21+.
Characteristics Exhibited by Children Homeless children; Pregnant women.
Social and Rehabilitative Services
Therapeutic Services Offered Individual therapy; Independent living skills program; Aftercare program with follow up.

DAYMARK, INC—TURNING POINT

1021 Lawndale Lane, Charleston, WV 25314 (304) 343-7256
Referral Information Referrals to the facility are made by any public or private agency with coordination through the Charleston Area 17 office, Dept of Human Services.
Type of Facility
Average Length of Stay Avg 12 mos.
Types of Admissions Accepted Residential treatment.
Sources of Referral Social service depts.

Client Profile
Age Range of Clients Served Residential program: 12-17.
Characteristics Exhibited by Children Emotional handicaps; Delinquency.
Tuition and Fees
Placements Primarily Funded By Social service depts.
Social and Rehabilitative Services
Therapeutic Services Offered Individual therapy; Group therapy; Family therapy; Adjunctive therapy; Independent living skills program; Aftercare program with follow up.
Educational and Vocational Services
Type(s) of Educational Programs Offered Off campus.

CLARKSBURG

GENESIS YOUTH CENTER

PO Box 546, Clarksburg, WV 26303 (304) 622-1907, 623-9346
Contact Person(s): Dave Majic, Dir
Referral Information Referrals to the facility are made by juvenile court or juvenile referees, Dept of Human Servcies, and parent or guardians of the youth. A signed contract by the parent or court order is needed for admission along with a social security number, birth certificate, and medical card number. Walk-ins or referrals by law enforcement agencies are acceptable.
Type of Facility
Average Length of Stay Short term.
Types of Admissions Accepted Emergency shelter.
Sources of Referral Juvenile court; Dept of Human Svcs; Parent; Guardian.
Client Profile
Age Range of Clients Served Residential Program: 10-18.
Characteristics Exhibited by Children Delinquency.
Tuition and Fees
Placements Primarily Funded By Depts of corrections; Social service depts.

ELKINS

WEST VIRGINIA CHILDREN'S HOME—DEPT OF HUMAN SERVICES

230 Heavner Ave, Elkins, WV 26241 (304) 636-0728, 348-3482
Contact Person(s): Carson W Markley, Dir
Referral Information Referrals to the facility are made by parents, schools, courts, and community agencies through the local Human Services office.
Type of Facility
Funding Sources State.
Average Length of Stay 90-120 days.
Types of Admissions Accepted Residential treatment; Diagnostic/evaluation.
Sources of Referral Social service depts.
Client Profile
Age Range of Clients Served Residential program: 11-16.
Characteristics Exhibited by Children Emotional handicaps.
Tuition and Fees
Placements Primarily Funded By Social service depts.
Social and Rehabilitative Services
Therapeutic Services Offered Individual therapy; Group therapy; Family therapy; Adjunctive therapy; Physical therapy; Recreation activities; Psychological/psychiatric evaluation.

FAIRMONT

STEPPING STONE, INC

PO Box 386, 900 State St, Fairmont, WV 26554 (304) 366-8571
Contact Person(s): John Trickett, Dir
Referral Information Referrals to the facility are made by the Dept of Human Services. The facility accepts boys only.
Type of Facility
Average Length of Stay 12-18 mos.
Types of Admissions Accepted Residential treatment.
Sources of Referral Social service depts.
Client Profile
Age Range of Clients Served Residential program: 12-18.
Characteristics Exhibited by Children Emotional handicaps; Displaced.

STEPPING STONE, INC *(continued)*

Tuition and Fees
Placements Primarily Funded By Social service depts; Title XX.
Social and Rehabilitative Services
Therapeutic Services Offered Individual therapy; Group therapy.

HUNTINGTON

CAMMACK CHILDREN'S CENTER, INC
PO Box 846, 64 W 6th Ave, Huntington, WV 25712 (304) 523-3497
Contact Person(s): George H Tinsman, Jr; Janet Knight
Referral Information Contact the facility for referral information.
Type of Facility
Average Length of Stay 6-18 mos.
Types of Admissions Accepted Residential treatment.
Sources of Referral Dept of Human Svcs; Courts; Community mental health facilities.
Client Profile
Age Range of Clients Served Residential program: 12-18.
Tuition and Fees
Placements Primarily Funded By Private sources; Dept of Human Svcs.
Social and Rehabilitative Services
Therapeutic Services Offered Individual therapy; Adjunctive therapy.

LAKIN

LAKIN HOSPITAL—ADOLESCENT SERVICES
PO Box 570, Lakin, WV 25250 (304) 675-3230 *Contact Person(s):*
Robert L Howes, Admin
Referral Information Referrals to the facility are made by courts, schools, Dept of Human Services, health care providers, families, and private agencies.
Type of Facility
Funding Sources State.
Types of Admissions Accepted Residential treatment.
Sources of Referral Local depts of education; State depts of mental health; Depts of correction; Health care providers; Family; Courts.
Client Profile
Age Range of Clients Served Residential program: 12-17.
Characteristics Exhibited by Children Emotional handicaps; Mental disabilities; Behavior disorders.
Social and Rehabilitative Services
Therapeutic Services Offered Individual therapy; Art therapy; Recreation activities; Foster grandparent program.
Educational and Vocational Services
Type(s) of Educational Programs Offered On campus.

LEWISBURG

DAVIS-STUART, INC
Davis-Stuart Rd, Lewisburg, WV 24901 (304) 647-5577 *Contact Person(s):* Terry Lusher, Prog Dir
Setting and Background Information Davis-Stuart, Inc is a private residential treatment facility. The facility was established by Synod of Virginia's Presbyterian Church, in 1919. Its 350-acre campus has 5 cottages, a pool, horseback riding, canoes, tennis, fully equipped gym, and video facilities on a cattle farm, located in a rural area 5 miles from Lewisburg. There are also 3 community based group homes.
Referral Information Referrals can be made by the Dept of Human Services, courts, and family. To make a referral, contact the facility and forward the necessary bacground information on the child. A placement decision will be made within a week.
Type of Facility
Funding Sources Private.
Average Length of Stay Avg 1 yr.
Types of Admissions Accepted Residential treatment; Group home placement.
Sources of Referral State depts of mental health; Private sources; Depts of correction; Social service depts; Courts.
Client Profile
Age Range of Clients Served Residential program: 12-18.
Characteristics Exhibited by Children Emotional handicaps; Learning disabilities.

Tuition and Fees
Room and Board Long term: $1,600/mo.
Placements Primarily Funded By State depts of mental health; Private sources; Foundations.
Social and Rehabilitative Services
Therapeutic Approach The treatment program is based on a positive peer group modality with reality therapy.
Therapeutic Services Offered Individual therapy; Group therapy; Family therapy; Recreation activities; Aftercare program with follow up.
Professionals on Staff Social workers; Adjunctive therapists; Child care staff; Recreation therapist.
Educational and Vocational Services
Type(s) of Educational Programs Offered On campus (Spec Ed); Off campus (Public school).
Profile of On Campus School Program Number of teachers 4; *Student to teacher ratio* 4:1; *Grades taught* 6-12; Special curriculum electives offered; Remedial courses offered.
Vocational Education Programs/Degrees Offered Vocational training.
Degrees Offered GED.

MARTINSBURG

GATEWAY YOUTH HOME
Rte 1 Box 146-A, Martinsburg, WV 25401 (304) 263-7932 *Contact Person(s):* Jim Schmidt
Referral Information Referrals are accepted from any public or private agency, friend or family member. The facility accepts boys only.
Type of Facility
Average Length of Stay 6 mos.
Types of Admissions Accepted Residential treatment; Wards of the state.
Client Profile
Age Range of Clients Served Residential program: 14-17.
Characteristics Exhibited by Children Emotional handicaps; Abused and neglected.
Tuition and Fees
Placements Primarily Funded By Dept of Human Services.
Social and Rehabilitative Services
Therapeutic Services Offered Individual therapy; Group therapy; Family therapy; Adjunctive therapy; Independent living skills program; Substance abuse treatment; Aftercare program with follow up.
Professionals on Staff Social workers; Adjunctive therapists; Child care staff; Physical therapists.

MARTINSBURG CHILDREN'S SHELTER
Rte 5, Box 282, Martinsburg, WV 25401 (304) 263-5014 *Contact Person(s):* Gail Brown, Dir
Referral Information Referrals to the shelter are made by the Dept of Human Services.
Type of Facility
Average Length of Stay Short and long term.
Types of Admissions Accepted Residential treatment; Emergency shelter.
Sources of Referral Dept of Human Svcs.
Client Profile
Age Range of Clients Served Residential program: 7-17.
Characteristics Exhibited by Children Abused and neglected; Runaways.
Tuition and Fees
Placements Primarily Funded By Social service depts.
Social and Rehabilitative Services
Therapeutic Services Offered Individual therapy.

MORGANTOWN

ODYSSEY—FAMILY SERVICE ASSOCIATION GROUP HOME
364 High St, Morgantown, WV 26505 (304) 296-8271 *Contact Person(s):* Lisa M Shepard, Exec Dir
Referral Information For referral information contact the facility.

ODYSSEY—FAMILY SERVICE ASSOCIATION GROUP HOME (continued)

Type of Facility
Funding Sources State.
Average Length of Stay Long term.
Types of Admissions Accepted Residential treatment; Group home placement.
Sources of Referral Social service depts.
Client Profile
Age Range of Clients Served Residential program: 12-17.
Characteristics Exhibited by Children Emotional handicaps.
Tuition and Fees
Room and Board Long term: Sliding scale.
Placements Primarily Funded By Insurance; Private sources; Social service depts; Title XX.
Social and Rehabilitative Services
Therapeutic Services Offered Individual therapy; Group therapy; Family therapy.

MOUNDSVILLE

HELINSKI SHELTER

RD 4 Box 17, Moundsville, WV 26041 (304) 843-1577 *Contact Person(s):* Kenny Fisher; Larry Creech
Referral Information Referrals to the facility are made by parents or guardians, juvenile court, police or the Dept of Human Services.
Type of Facility
Average Length of Stay Short term.
Types of Admissions Accepted Emergency shelter.
Sources of Referral Depts of correction; Social service depts; Juvenile courts; Walk-ins.
Client Profile
Age Range of Clients Served Residential program: 12-17.
Characteristics Exhibited by Children Crisis situation.
Social and Rehabilitative Services
Therapeutic Services Offered Individual therapy; Independent living skills program; Recreation activities; Peer group sessions.
Educational and Vocational Services
Type(s) of Educational Programs Offered On campus (Spec Ed).

NEWELL

BROOKE-HANCOCK GROUP HOME, INC

610 Washington St, Newell, WV 26050 (304) 387-0651 *Contact Person(s):* Perry G Stanley, Exec Dir; Joanne Dobrzanski, Prog Dir
Referral Information Referrals to the facility are made through the Dept of Human Services and probation depts. The facility accepts boys only.
Type of Facility
Average Length of Stay Avg 12 mos.
Types of Admissions Accepted Residential treatment; Group home placement.
Sources of Referral Dept of Human Svcs; Probation depts.
Client Profile
Age Range of Clients Served Residential program: 14-18.
Characteristics Exhibited by Children Emotional handicaps; Learning disabilities.
Tuition and Fees
Placements Primarily Funded By Depts of corrections; Dept of Human Svcs.
Social and Rehabilitative Services
Therapeutic Services Offered Individual therapy; Group therapy; Family therapy; Recreation activities.
Educational and Vocational Services
Type(s) of Educational Programs Offered Off campus (Public school).

PARKERSBURG

WOOD COUNTY CHILD CARE CENTER

PO Box 837, 1011 Mission Dr, Parkersburg, WV 26102 (304) 424-5145 *Contact Person(s):* Susan Latimer, Exec Dir; Phil Stephens, Prog Dir
Setting and Background Information Wood County Child Care Center is a private residential treatment facility. The establishment of this facility was the result of individuals in the community lobbying the state legislature and community officials for the funding of a residential center. The campus consists of 2 separate cottages on 3 acres of land located on the Ohio River in Parkersburg.
Referral Information Referrals can be made by anyone but the child must be in custody of the West Virginia Dept of Human Services. Applicants must submit the completed referral forms provided by the Dept of Human Services.
Type of Facility
Funding Sources Private; State.
Average Length of Stay 9 mos.
Types of Admissions Accepted Residential treatment; Group home placement.
Sources of Referral State depts of mental health; Courts.
Client Profile
Age Range of Clients Served Residential program: 12-18.
Characteristics Exhibited by Children Emotional handicaps; Delinquency; Abused and neglected.
IQ Range of Clients 70+.
Tuition and Fees
Room and Board Long term: $50/diem.
Placements Primarily Funded By State depts of mental health.
Social and Rehabilitative Services
Therapeutic Approach The basic therapeutic approach underlining the treatment program is that of reality therapy.
Therapeutic Services Offered Individual therapy; Group therapy; Family therapy; Adjunctive therapy; Independent living skills program; Recreation activities; Aftercare program with follow up.
Professionals on Staff Social workers; Adjunctive therapists; Child care staff.
Educational and Vocational Services
Type(s) of Educational Programs Offered Off campus.
Degrees Offered GED.

PHILIPPI

SUGAR CREEK CHILDREN'S CENTER

Rte 2, Box 127-A, Philippi, WV 26416 (304) 457-3098 *Contact Person(s):* Emily Strum; Dawn Norman
Referral Information Referrals to the facility are made through the Dept of Human Services, mental health centers, and the courts.
Type of Facility
Average Length of Stay Short and long term.
Types of Admissions Accepted Residential treatment.
Sources of Referral Social service depts.
Client Profile
Age Range of Clients Served Residential program: 10-17.
Characteristics Exhibited by Children Delinquency; Abused and neglected.
Tuition and Fees
Placements Primarily Funded By Social service depts.
Social and Rehabilitative Services
Therapeutic Services Offered Individual therapy; Group therapy.
Educational and Vocational Services
Type(s) of Educational Programs Offered On campus; Off campus.

ROMNEY

POTOMAC COMPREHENSIVE DIAGNOSTIC AND GUIDANCE CENTER

1 Blue St, Romney, WV 26757 (304) 822-3861 *Contact Person(s):* Joe S Pancake
Referral Information Referrals can be made through the Depts of Human Services or Mental Health, and through school boards.
Type of Facility
Funding Sources County.
Average Length of Stay 6 mos.
Types of Admissions Accepted Residential treatment; Emergency shelter; Respite care.
Sources of Referral State depts of mental health; Private sources; Depts of correction; School boards.
Client Profile
Age Range of Clients Served Residential program: 8-21+.
Characteristics Exhibited by Children Autism; Developmentally disabled.

POTOMAC COMPREHENSIVE DIAGNOSTIC AND GUIDANCE CENTER *(continued)*

Tuition and Fees
Room and Board Long term: Sliding scale.
Placements Primarily Funded By Insurance; Private sources; Social service depts.
Educational and Vocational Services
Type(s) of Educational Programs Offered On campus; Summer campus.

WHEELING

CHILDREN'S HOME OF WHEELING
14 Orchard Rd, Wheeling, WV 26003 (304) 233-2585 *Contact Person(s):* David Olds
Referral Information Contact the facility for referral information.
Type of Facility
Types of Admissions Accepted Residential treatment; Group home placement; Wards of the state; Foster care.
Sources of Referral Dept of Human Svcs; Court.
Client Profile
Age Range of Clients Served Residential program: 6-16.
Characteristics Exhibited by Children Abused and neglected.
Social and Rehabilitative Services
Therapeutic Services Offered Individual therapy; Group therapy; Family therapy; Adjunctive therapy; Independent living skills program; Aftercare program with follow up.

FLORENCE CRITTENTON HOME OF WHEELING
2606 National Rd, Wheeling, WV 26003 (304) 242-7060 *Contact Person(s):* Jamie Warton, Case Worker
Referral Information Referrals to the agency are primarily made through the Dept of Human Services, but are also accepted from private individuals or agencies.
Type of Facility
Average Length of Stay Short and long term.
Types of Admissions Accepted Residential treatment; Emergency shelter; Maternity services.
Sources of Referral Dept of Human Svcs; Schools; Hospitals; United Methodist Agency; Children's Home Society.
Client Profile
Age Range of Clients Served Residential program: 12-18.
Characteristics Exhibited by Children Pregnancy; Sheltered care.
Social and Rehabilitative Services
Therapeutic Services Offered Individual therapy; Group therapy; Independent living skills program; Aftercare program with follow up.
Professionals on Staff Social workers; Child care staff.

ST JOHN'S HOME FOR CHILDREN
141 Key Ave, Wheeling, WV 26003 (304) 242-5633 *Contact Person(s):* Kenny Fisher, Dir
Setting and Background Information St John's Home for Children is a private residential treatment facility. Its campus consists of 3 cottages, administration building, pool, basketball courts, and playground.
Referral Information Anyone can make a referral by contacting the facility and forwarding the necessary background information. A pre-placement interview is necessary before an admission decision is made.
Type of Facility
Funding Sources Private.
Average Length of Stay 6-18 mos.
Types of Admissions Accepted Residential treatment.
Sources of Referral State depts of mental health.
Client Profile
Age Range of Clients Served Day programs: 8-12; Residential program: 8-12.
Characteristics Exhibited by Children Emotional handicaps; Learning disabilities; Vision impairments/blindness; Speech/Language disorders.
Tuition and Fees
Room and Board Long term: $75/diem.
Placements Primarily Funded By State depts of mental health; Catholic Diocese.

Social and Rehabilitative Services
Therapeutic Approach The facility has an eclectic approach to therapy, which emphasizes family-based treatment.
Therapeutic Services Offered Individual therapy; Group therapy; Family therapy; Recreation activities; Aftercare program with follow up.
Professionals on Staff Social workers; Adjunctive therapists; Child care staff.
Educational and Vocational Services
Type(s) of Educational Programs Offered Off campus (Public school).

WISCONSIN

BELOIT

FIRST LIGHT GROUP HOME, INC
444 Wisconsin Ave, Beloit, WI 53511 (608) 365-2442 *Contact Person(s):* Jaimie Dyer, Dir
Setting and Background Information The facility was established in 1976 with donations from local civic organizations. It is a residential group home for girls.
Referral Information Referrals are made through probation officers or county social workers. A pre-placement visit will be scheduled.
Type of Facility
Funding Sources County.
Average Length of Stay 9-18 mos.
Types of Admissions Accepted Group home placement.
Sources of Referral Depts of correction; Social service depts.
Client Profile
Age Range of Clients Served Residential program: 13-17.
Characteristics Exhibited by Children Emotional handicaps; Learning disabilities; Mental disabilities; Alcohol and drug dependencies.
IQ Range of Clients 70+.
Tuition and Fees
Room and Board Long term: $1,552.27/mo.
Placements Primarily Funded By Depts of corrections; Social service depts.
Social and Rehabilitative Services
Therapeutic Approach The facility uses rational behavior therapy.
Therapeutic Services Offered Individual therapy; Group therapy; Family therapy; Independent living skills program; Recreation activities; Substance abuse treatment.
Professionals on Staff Social workers; Adjunctive therapists; Child care staff; Probation officers.
Educational and Vocational Services
Type(s) of Educational Programs Offered Off campus (Public schools).
Vocational Education Programs/Degrees Offered Vocational testing and training; Work experience.

DOUSMAN

LAD LAKE, INC
PO Box 158, W 350 S 1401 Waterville Dr, Dousman, WI 53118 (414) 965-2131 *Contact Person(s):* Gary Erdmann, Exec Dir
Setting and Background Information Lad Lake is a private non-sectarian treatment facility for boys which is located on 300 acres. There is an independent living skills program which was established to help boys transition back into the community. There are also 2 foster homes located in Milwaukee.
Referral Information Referrals can be made by social agencies, school districts, courts, guidance clinics, and private individuals. Applicants are requested to forward a family history, summary of problems, psychological and psychiatric evaluations, educational testing reports, and court reports to the Director of Treatment Services. A pre-placement visit and interview will then be scheduled involving staff, child, family, and the referring source before a placement decision is made.
Type of Facility
Funding Sources Private.
Average Length of Stay 90 days.
Types of Admissions Accepted Residential treatment; Foster care.

Sources of Referral Local depts of education; State depts of mental health; County; Courts.
Client Profile
Age Range of Clients Served Residential program: 8-17.
Characteristics Exhibited by Children Emotional handicaps.
Tuition and Fees
Placements Primarily Funded By State depts of mental health; County.
Social and Rehabilitative Services
Therapeutic Approach The treatment program is based on an eclectic therapeutic approach involving the use of multi-disciplinary teams.
Therapeutic Services Offered Individual therapy; Group therapy; Family therapy; Recreation activities.
Professionals on Staff Psychiatrists; Psychologists; Social workers.
Educational and Vocational Services
Type(s) of Educational Programs Offered On campus; Off campus (Public school).
Profile of On Campus School Program Number of teachers 10; Student to teacher ratio 8:1; Student to teacher ratio Certified Spec Ed; Special curriculum electives offered (Art, PE); Remedial courses offered (Reading, Math).
Vocational Education Programs/Degrees Offered Auto mechanics.

EAU CLAIRE

LUTHERAN SOCIAL SERVICES, EPIC GROUP HOME
1223 Menomonie St, Eau Claire, WI 54703 (715) 834-2046 *Contact Person(s):* Ted Hakala, Prog Serv Dir
Setting and Background Information The facility was established in 1976 with funds from the county and the state. There are two group homes, licensed for eight residents each.
Referral Information Referrals are made by contacting Lutheran Social Services and forwarding a social history. A pre-placement interview and visit will be scheduled.
Type of Facility
Funding Sources State; County.
Average Length of Stay Long term.
Types of Admissions Accepted Group home placement.
Sources of Referral State depts of mental health; Depts of correction; Social service depts.
Client Profile
Age Range of Clients Served Residential program: 12-18.
Characteristics Exhibited by Children Emotional handicaps; Learning disabilities; Behavior disorders.
Tuition and Fees
Room and Board Long term: $58.55/diem.
Placements Primarily Funded By Depts of corrections; Social service depts.
Social and Rehabilitative Services
Therapeutic Approach The facility uses reality therapy and behavior modification. It also offers an AA program.
Therapeutic Services Offered Individual therapy; Group therapy; Family therapy; Adjunctive therapy; Independent living skills program; Recreation activities; Substance abuse treatment; After-care program with follow up.
Professionals on Staff Psychiatrists; Psychologists; Social workers; Adjunctive therapists; Child care staff.
Educational and Vocational Services
Type(s) of Educational Programs Offered Off campus (Public school).

FORT ATKINSON

TEIPNER TREATMENT HOMES, INC

323 E Sherman Ave, Fort Atkinson, WI 53538 (414) 563-4449
Contact Person(s): Jackie Schoening, Agency Exec; John Teipner, Owner
Setting and Background Information This private corporation was established in 1984. There are 15 family-operated group homes in Wisconsin.
Referral Information Contact the facility and forward intake material, which should include psychological evaluations, a medical history, and court reports.

Type of Facility
Funding Sources County.
Average Length of Stay 6-9 mos.
Types of Admissions Accepted Group home placement.
Sources of Referral State depts of education; Local depts of education; State depts of mental health; Psychiatrists; Private sources; Depts of correction; Social service depts.

Client Profile
Age Range of Clients Served Day programs: 10-17; Residential program: 10-17.
Characteristics Exhibited by Children Emotional handicaps; Learning disabilities.
IQ Range of Clients 70+.

Tuition and Fees
Room and Board Long term: $1,429/mo.
Placements Primarily Funded By Social service depts.

Social and Rehabilitative Services
Therapeutic Services Offered Individual therapy; Group therapy; Family therapy; Adjunctive therapy; Independent living skills program; Recreation activities; Substance abuse treatment; Aftercare program with follow up.
Professionals on Staff Social workers; Adjunctive therapists; Child care staff.

Educational and Vocational Services
Type(s) of Educational Programs Offered Off campus.

GREEN BAY

ETHAN HOUSE I

1470 Emilie St, Green Bay, WI 54301 (414) 437-1942 *Contact Person(s):* Mike Washechek, Dir
Setting and Background Information This facility was established in 1972 as a private non-profit corporation contracting with the state. It is a residential home.
Referral Information All referrals are made through Brown County Social Service Dept and placed by the same.

Type of Facility
Funding Sources State; County.
Average Length of Stay Long term.
Types of Admissions Accepted Group home placement.
Sources of Referral Social service depts.

Client Profile
Age Range of Clients Served Residential program: 12-18.
Characteristics Exhibited by Children Emotional handicaps; Learning disabilities; Neurological impairments; Mental disabilities; Delinquency.
IQ Range of Clients 80+.

Tuition and Fees
Room and Board Long term: $223/mo.
Placements Primarily Funded By Social service depts.

Social and Rehabilitative Services
Therapeutic Approach The basic therapeutic approach used is behavior modification.
Therapeutic Services Offered Individual therapy; Group therapy; Recreation activities.
Professionals on Staff Social workers; Child care staff.

ETHAN HOUSE II

644 S Quincy St, Green Bay, WI 54301 (414) 437-5079 *Contact Person(s):* Pat Tweedale, Dir
Setting and Background Information This facility was established in 1972 as a private non-profit corporation, contracting with the county. It is a residential home.
Referral Information All referrals are made through Brown County Social Service Dept and placed by the same.

Type of Facility
Funding Sources County.
Average Length of Stay Long term.
Types of Admissions Accepted Group home placement.
Sources of Referral Social service depts.

Client Profile
Age Range of Clients Served Residential program: 6-18.
Characteristics Exhibited by Children Emotional handicaps; Learning disabilities; Neurological impairments; Mental disabilities; Delinquency.
IQ Range of Clients 80+.

Tuition and Fees
Room and Board Long term: $223/mo.
Placements Primarily Funded By Social service depts.

Social and Rehabilitative Services
Therapeutic Approach The basic therapeutic approach used is behavior modification.
Therapeutic Services Offered Individual therapy; Group therapy; Recreation activities.
Professionals on Staff Psychologists; Social workers; Child care staff.

Educational and Vocational Services
Type(s) of Educational Programs Offered Summer campus.
Profile of On Campus School Program Number of teachers 1; *Number of classrooms* 1; *Student to teacher ratio* 5:1.

EUDES FAMILY PROGRAMS—GROUP HOME, TRIUMPH II

1019 Neufeld, Green Bay, WI 54304 (414) 494-8708, 499-3201
Contact Person(s): Sr Sheila Rooney, Admin Dir
Setting and Background Information The facility was established in 1958 as an extension of a residential institutional program. It is a group home for adolescent girls.
Referral Information Referrals are made by social service agencies. A pre-admission interview will be scheduled.

Type of Facility
Funding Sources Private; County.
Average Length of Stay Long term.
Types of Admissions Accepted Group home placement.
Sources of Referral Private sources; Depts of correction; Social service depts.

Client Profile
Age Range of Clients Served Residential program: 12-18.
Characteristics Exhibited by Children Emotional handicaps; Character disorders.

Tuition and Fees
Room and Board Long term: $1,900/mo.
Placements Primarily Funded By Depts of corrections; Social service depts.

Social and Rehabilitative Services
Therapeutic Approach The facility uses the systemic family approach to therapy.
Therapeutic Services Offered Individual therapy; Group therapy; Family therapy; Independent living skills program; Recreation activities; Substance abuse treatment; Aftercare program with follow up.
Professionals on Staff Psychiatrists; Social workers; Child care staff; Family therapist.

Educational and Vocational Services
Type(s) of Educational Programs Offered Off campus (Public schools/ vocational schools).

EUDES FAMILY PROGRAMS—RESIDENTIAL CENTER

2640 W Point Rd, Green Bay, WI 54303 (414) 494-8708 *Contact Person(s):* Sr Sheila Rooney, Admin Dir; Kenneth Utech, Treatment Dir
Setting and Background Information The facility was established in 1883 by the Sisters of Our Lady of Charity. Currently, the 60-acre campus has 4 cottages, a school, a gym with a pool, and an administration building.
Referral Information Referrals are made to the facility by social service agencies. A pre-admission interview will be scheduled.

Type of Facility
Funding Sources Private; State; Federal.
Average Length of Stay Long term.
Types of Admissions Accepted Residential treatment.
Sources of Referral Private sources; Depts of correction; Social service depts.

EUDES FAMILY PROGRAMS—RESIDENTIAL CENTER *(continued)*

Client Profile
Age Range of Clients Served Residential program: 10-17.
Characteristics Exhibited by Children Emotional handicaps; Sexual abuse.
Tuition and Fees
Room and Board Long term: $3,134/mo.
Placements Primarily Funded By Depts of corrections; Social service depts.
Social and Rehabilitative Services
Therapeutic Approach The facility uses the systemic family approach to therapy.
Therapeutic Services Offered Individual therapy; Group therapy; Family therapy; Independent living skills program; Recreation activities; Substance abuse treatment; Aftercare program with follow up; Sexual abuse therapy.
Professionals on Staff Psychiatrists; Psychologists; Social workers; Child care staff; Family therapists.
Educational and Vocational Services
Type(s) of Educational Programs Offered On campus; Summer campus.
Profile of On Campus School Program Number of teachers 4; *Number of classrooms* 6; *Student to teacher ratio* 5:1; *Credentials of teachers* MEd; *Grades taught* 2-12; Special curriculum electives offered.

KENOSHA

PHOENIX HOUSE
2210 56th St, Kenosha, WI 53140 (414) 652-5827, 657-7188 *Contact Person(s):* Kathy Belshaw, Consultant
Setting and Background Information The facility was established in 1976 as a private, non-profit organization. It is a community based group home.
Referral Information Referrals should be made to Kenosha Youth Development Services, 5407 8th Ave, Kenosha, WI.
Type of Facility
Funding Sources State.
Average Length of Stay Long term.
Types of Admissions Accepted Group home placement.
Sources of Referral Depts of correction; Social service depts.
Client Profile
Age Range of Clients Served Residential program: 12-18.
Characteristics Exhibited by Children Emotional handicaps; Learning disabilities.
Tuition and Fees
Room and Board Long term: $56/diem.
Social and Rehabilitative Services
Therapeutic Services Offered Individual therapy; Group therapy; Family therapy; Independent living skills program; Recreation activities.
Professionals on Staff Social workers.
Educational and Vocational Services
Type(s) of Educational Programs Offered Off campus.

LA CROSSE

FAMILY AND CHILDREN'S CENTER
2507 Weston St, La Crosse, WI 54601 (608) 788-6762, 788-6333
Contact Person(s): Mr Burgess, MSSW, Prog Dir
Setting and Background Information Family and Children's Center is a mulit-service mental health center including residential treatment, foster care, an intensive home based treatment program, respite care, parent aid, and out-patient services. The agency has a history of providing services to children and familes for over 100 years. The Center is housed in a modern building, located in a residential area.
Referral Information Referrals can be made by anyone by forwarding the child's school records, psychiatric and psychological evaluations, social history, and previous treatment records. The facility does not accept children with severe psychiatric problems.

Type of Facility
Funding Sources Private.
Average Length of Stay 6-8 mos.
Types of Admissions Accepted Day treatment; Residential treatment.
Sources of Referral County; Self.
Client Profile
Age Range of Clients Served Day program: 4-55+; Residential program: 6-16.
Characteristics Exhibited by Children Emotional handicaps; Learning disabilities; Mental disabilities; Conduct disorders.
Tuition and Fees
Room and Board Long term: $2,978/mo (Residential); Sliding scale (Out-patient).
Placements Primarily Funded By Insurance; United Way; County.
Social and Rehabilitative Services
Therapeutic Approach The primary therapeutic approach used is eclectic in conjunction with behavior management programs and milieu therapy.
Therapeutic Services Offered Individual therapy; Group therapy; Family therapy; Adjunctive therapy; Aftercare program with follow up.
Professionals on Staff Psychiatrists; Psychologists; Social workers; Adjunctive therapists; Child care staff; Nurses.
Educational and Vocational Services
Type(s) of Educational Programs Offered On campus (In conjunction with public school); Off campus (Public school).
Profile of On Campus School Program Number of teachers 2; *Student to teacher ratio* 5:1; *Credentials of teachers* MA; *Grades taught* K-12; Individualized; Special curriculum electives offered; Remedial courses offered.
Degrees Offered 12th grade diploma; GED.

LACROSSE

COULEE YOUTH CENTERS, INC
231 Copeland Ave, LaCrosse, WI 54603 (608) 782-7152 *Contact Person(s):* Steven T Eide, Exec Dir
Setting and Background Information The facility was established in 1971 by the state Dept of Community Services. There are 4 group homes at different sites in the city.
Referral Information Referrals are made primarily by county or state social workers. Contact the facility for more information.
Type of Facility
Funding Sources Private.
Average Length of Stay Long term.
Types of Admissions Accepted Group home placement.
Sources of Referral State depts of mental health; Depts of correction; Social service depts.
Client Profile
Age Range of Clients Served Residential program: 12-18.
Characteristics Exhibited by Children Emotional handicaps; Learning disabilities; Behavior disorders.
Tuition and Fees
Room and Board Long term: $1,716.78/mo.
Placements Primarily Funded By State depts of mental health; Depts of corrections; Social service depts.
Social and Rehabilitative Services
Therapeutic Approach The facility uses reality therapy and behavior modification.
Therapeutic Services Offered Individual therapy; Group therapy; Independent living skills program.
Professionals on Staff Psychologists; Social workers; Child care staff.
Educational and Vocational Services
Type(s) of Educational Programs Offered On campus (Homebound); Off campus.
Profile of On Campus School Program Number of teachers 1; *Number of classrooms* 2; *Student to teacher ratio* 8:1.

LADYSMITH

CORNELL GROUP HOMES, INC
N 5520, Ladysmith, WI 54848 (715) 532-3098 *Contact Person(s):* Jerry Phelps, Admin
Setting and Background Information The facility was privately established in 1981. There are three facilities—Riverside, Log House, and Earthbound. Each is located on approximately 2 acres and has 2 buildings.
Referral Information For referral, contact the facility.

CORNELL GROUP HOMES, INC *(continued)*

Type of Facility
Funding Sources State; Federal.
Average Length of Stay Long term.
Types of Admissions Accepted Group home placement.
Sources of Referral Depts of correction; Social service depts.
Client Profile
Age Range of Clients Served Residential program: 12-18.
Characteristics Exhibited by Children Learning disabilities.
Tuition and Fees
Room and Board Long term: $46/diem.
Placements Primarily Funded By Depts of corrections; Social service depts.
Social and Rehabilitative Services
Therapeutic Services Offered Individual therapy; Group therapy; Recreation activities; Substance abuse treatment.
Professionals on Staff Social workers; Child care staff.
Educational and Vocational Services
Type(s) of Educational Programs Offered On campus; Off campus.
Profile of On Campus School Program Number of teachers 1; *Number of classrooms* 1; *Student to teacher ratio* 3:1.
Degrees Offered GED.

MADISON

DANE CO GROUP HMS, INC

3240 E Wash Ave, Madison, WI 53704 (608) 249-8411 *Contact Person(s):* Sandy Schult, Dir
Setting and Background Information This facility was established in 1974 by contracting with Dane County as a non-profit agency. It is a residential group home. There is another home, Coventry House, located at 1838 Sphon Ave.
Referral Information Referrals are made through Dane County Social Services.
Type of Facility
Funding Sources Private.
Average Length of Stay Long term.
Types of Admissions Accepted Group home placement; Wards of the state.
Sources of Referral Private sources; Social service depts.
Client Profile
Age Range of Clients Served Residential program: 12-18.
Characteristics Exhibited by Children Emotional handicaps.
Tuition and Fees
Placements Primarily Funded By Social service depts.
Social and Rehabilitative Services
Therapeutic Approach The facility utilizes a structured living program.
Therapeutic Services Offered Individual therapy; Group therapy; Family therapy; Independent living skills program; Substance abuse treatment; Aftercare program with follow up.
Professionals on Staff Social workers; Child care staff.
Educational and Vocational Services
Type(s) of Educational Programs Offered Off campus.

THOREAU HOUSE

1102 Spaight St, Madison, WI 53703 (608) 255-2493 *Contact Person(s):* George Nestler, Prog Dir
Setting and Background Information The facility was established in 1971 with state funding. It is a group home.
Referral Information Referrals are made through Dane County Dept of Social Services.
Type of Facility
Funding Sources State; County.
Average Length of Stay 6 mos.
Types of Admissions Accepted Group home placement.
Sources of Referral Social service depts.
Client Profile
Age Range of Clients Served Residential program: 13-17.
Characteristics Exhibited by Children Emotional handicaps; Learning disabilities; Mental disabilities.
IQ Range of Clients 70+.
Tuition and Fees
Room and Board Long term: $1,900/mo.
Placements Primarily Funded By Social service depts.

Social and Rehabilitative Services
Therapeutic Approach The facility offers a therapeutic milieu.
Therapeutic Services Offered Individual therapy; Group therapy; Family therapy; Recreation activities; Substance abuse treatment.
Professionals on Staff Social workers; Adjunctive therapists; Child care staff; Counselors.
Educational and Vocational Services
Type(s) of Educational Programs Offered Off campus (High school).

MENOMONEE FALLS

HEYDINGER HOUSE GROUP HOME

W 161 N 9013 Hayes Ave, Menomonee Falls, WI 53051 (414) 6558
Contact Person(s): Cindy Locke, Group Home Mgr
Setting and Background Information This group home was established in 1983 and is located in a residential area.
Referral Information Referrals are made through DSS.
Type of Facility
Funding Sources Private.
Average Length of Stay 6 mos-1 yr.
Types of Admissions Accepted Group home placement.
Sources of Referral Social service depts.
Client Profile
Age Range of Clients Served Residential program: 12-18.
Characteristics Exhibited by Children Emotional handicaps.
Social and Rehabilitative Services
Therapeutic Services Offered Individual therapy; Group therapy; Family therapy; Independent living skills program; Recreation activities; Substance abuse treatment.
Professionals on Staff Psychiatrists; Social workers; Child care staff.
Educational and Vocational Services
Type(s) of Educational Programs Offered Off campus (High school).
Degrees Offered GED.

MENOMONIE

ALPHA HOUSE YOUTH CARE, INC

121 12th Ave W, Menomonie, WI 54751 (715) 235-9552 *Contact Person(s):* Tisha Bolger, Dir
Setting and Background Information The facility was established in 1975 by a federal grant. It is a large residential house.
Referral Information To make a referral, contact the director or the educational coordinator.
Type of Facility
Funding Sources Private.
Average Length of Stay Short and long term.
Types of Admissions Accepted Group home placement.
Sources of Referral State depts of mental health; Depts of correction; Social service depts.
Client Profile
Age Range of Clients Served Residential program: 13-17.
Characteristics Exhibited by Children Emotional handicaps; Learning disabilities; Mental disabilities; Delinquency.
Tuition and Fees
Room and Board Short term: $49/diem; Long term: $56/diem.
Placements Primarily Funded By Depts of corrections; Social service depts.
Social and Rehabilitative Services
Therapeutic Approach The facility uses behavior modification.
Therapeutic Services Offered Individual therapy; Group therapy; Family therapy; Adjunctive therapy; Independent living skills program; Recreation activities.
Professionals on Staff Psychiatrists; Psychologists; Social workers; Adjunctive therapists; Child care staff.
Educational and Vocational Services
Type(s) of Educational Programs Offered On campus; Off campus (Public school).
Profile of On Campus School Program Number of teachers 1-3; *Number of classrooms* 2; *Student to teacher ratio* 2:1; *Credentials of teachers* BA; *Grades taught* 7-12; Remedial courses offered.

MERRILL

PARK HOUSE GROUP HOME

1508 E Main St, Merrill, WI 54452 (715) 536-4685 *Contact Person(s):* Scot Stark, Prog Dir

Setting and Background Information The facility was established in 1978 by Catholic Charities. It is a large group home.

Referral Information Referrals should be made to the program director.

Type of Facility

Funding Sources Private.

Average Length of Stay Long term.

Types of Admissions Accepted Group home placement.

Sources of Referral State depts of education; State depts of mental health; Depts of correction; Social service depts.

Client Profile

Age Range of Clients Served Residential program: 12-18.

Characteristics Exhibited by Children Emotional handicaps; Learning disabilities; Mental disabilities.

Tuition and Fees

Room and Board Long term: $68/diem.

Placements Primarily Funded By Social service depts.

Social and Rehabilitative Services

Therapeutic Approach The facility has a behavioral approach to therapy.

Therapeutic Services Offered Individual therapy; Group therapy; Family therapy; Independent living skills program.

Professionals on Staff Psychologists; Social workers; Adjunctive therapists.

Educational and Vocational Services

Type(s) of Educational Programs Offered Off campus (Public school).

MILWAUKEE

ATTUCKS CENTER, INC

2701 N 56th St, Milwaukee, WI 53210 (414) 447-7411 *Contact Person(s):* Jeanette Malone, Pres

Setting and Background Information The facility was established in 1985. There are 2 group homes.

Referral Information Referrals are made through Milwaukee County Dept of Social Services.

Type of Facility

Funding Sources State; Federal.

Average Length of Stay Long term; Avg 2 yrs.

Types of Admissions Accepted Group home placement.

Sources of Referral Social service depts.

Client Profile

Age Range of Clients Served Residential program: 12-18.

Characteristics Exhibited by Children Delinquency.

Tuition and Fees

Placements Primarily Funded By Social service depts.

Social and Rehabilitative Services

Therapeutic Services Offered Individual therapy; Group therapy; Family therapy; Independent living skills program; Aftercare program with follow up.

Professionals on Staff Psychologists; Social workers; Child care staff.

Educational and Vocational Services

Type(s) of Educational Programs Offered Off campus (Public schools).

LAKESIDE CHILD & FAMILY CENTER, INC

2220 E North Ave, Milwaukee, WI 53202 (414) 271-9494 *Contact Person(s):* David J Johnson, Exec Dir

Setting and Background Information The facility was established in 1850 as a non-denominational orphanage. There are 5 buildings on the 7 acres.

Referral Information Contact the facility for referral. The child and parents will be scheduled for a pre-placement interview and visit.

Type of Facility

Funding Sources State; Federal.

Average Length of Stay Short and long term.

Types of Admissions Accepted Residential treatment.

Sources of Referral State depts of education; Local depts of education; State depts of mental health; Psychiatrists; Private sources; Social service depts.

Client Profile

Age Range of Clients Served Residential program: 6-18.

Characteristics Exhibited by Children Emotional handicaps; Learning disabilities; Hearing impairments/deafness; Speech/Language disorders; Neurological impairments; Mental disabilities.

IQ Range of Clients 60+.

Tuition and Fees

Room and Board Long term: $3,220/mo.

Tuition $73.98/diem.

Placements Primarily Funded By State depts of education; Local depts of education; State depts of mental health; Social service depts.

Social and Rehabilitative Services

Therapeutic Approach The basic therapeutic approach of the facility is psycho-dynamic.

Therapeutic Services Offered Individual therapy; Group therapy; Family therapy; Adjunctive therapy; Art therapy; Independent living skills program.

Professionals on Staff Psychiatrists; Psychologists; Social workers; Adjunctive therapists; Child care staff; Nurses; Art therapists.

Educational and Vocational Services

Type(s) of Educational Programs Offered On campus; Off campus (Public schools).

Profile of On Campus School Program Number of teachers 7; *Number of classrooms* 7; *Student to teacher ratio* 6:1; *Credentials of teachers* ED; *Grades taught* 1-12; *Special curriculum electives offered.*

Vocational Education Programs/Degrees Offered Career education.

LUTHERAN SOCIAL SERVICES, HAMPTON HOUSE GROUP HOME

4507 N 47th St, Milwaukee, WI 53218 (414) 464-8113 *Contact Person(s):* Jan Nielsen, Dir, Soc Wkr

Setting and Background Information The facility was established through a contract with Milwaukee County in 1984. It is a large group home.

Referral Information Residents are adjudicated delinquent adolescent males. Referrals to the facility are made through the Dept of Social Services or by probation officers and are court ordered by a judge.

Type of Facility

Funding Sources County.

Average Length of Stay Long term.

Types of Admissions Accepted Group home placement.

Sources of Referral Depts of correction; Social service depts.

Client Profile

Age Range of Clients Served Residential program: 12-18.

Characteristics Exhibited by Children Delinquency.

Tuition and Fees

Room and Board Long term: $58.63/diem.

Placements Primarily Funded By Depts of corrections; Social service depts.

Social and Rehabilitative Services

Therapeutic Services Offered Individual therapy; Group therapy; Family therapy; Independent living skills program; Recreation activities; Aftercare program with follow up.

Professionals on Staff Social workers; Child care staff.

Educational and Vocational Services

Type(s) of Educational Programs Offered Off campus.

MARTIN CENTER, INC

2548 N 29th St, Milwaukee, WI 53210 (414) 264-4900 *Contact Person(s):* Lateefah Muhammad, Exec Dir

Setting and Background Information Martin Center is a private residential treatment facility which was established in 1970 for the purpose of working with emotionally disturbed/delinquent inner-city adolescent males. Its campus is located in Milwaukee's central city and consists of a building which has classrooms, 2 residential floors, a cafeteria, administrative offices, and recreation areas.

Referral Information Most referrals come through the Milwaukee County Dept of Health and Social Services and the Wisconsin Division of Corrections. Referrals can also come from surrounding counties. To make a referral, forward the necessary background information. A pre-placement visit and interview will take place before an admission decision is made.

MARTIN CENTER, INC (continued)

Type of Facility
Funding Sources Private.
Average Length of Stay Avg 1 yr.
Types of Admissions Accepted Residential treatment; Group home placement.
Sources of Referral Depts of correction; Social service depts; Courts.
Client Profile
Age Range of Clients Served Residential program: 12-18.
Characteristics Exhibited by Children Emotional handicaps; Learning disabilities; Speech/Language disorders.
Tuition and Fees
Placements Primarily Funded By Social service depts.
Social and Rehabilitative Services
Therapeutic Approach The treatment program utilizes a variety of treatment approaches, which are time-limited, reality-oriented, and supportive.
Therapeutic Services Offered Individual therapy; Group therapy; Family therapy; Independent living skills program; Recreation activities; Aftercare program with follow up; Family outreach.
Professionals on Staff Psychiatrists; Psychologists; Social workers; Adjunctive therapists; Child care staff.
Educational and Vocational Services
Type(s) of Educational Programs Offered On campus.
Profile of On Campus School Program Number of teachers 2; *Student to teacher ratio* 9:1; *Grades taught* 7-12; *Special curriculum electives offered; Remedial courses offered.*
Vocational Education Programs/Degrees Offered Vocational counseling.
Degrees Offered GED.

PATHFINDERS FOR RUNAWAYS

1614 E Kane Pl, Milwaukee, WI 53211 (414) 271-1560 *Contact Person(s):* Robin Ahrens
Setting and Background Information This program was established in 1971 in response to a need for a runaway shelter. It was funded with United Way and county grants. It is a group home and, also, has non-residential programs for families.
Referral Information Contact the facility for referral information.
Type of Facility
Funding Sources Private; State; Federal.
Average Length of Stay Short term.
Types of Admissions Accepted Group home placement; Wards of the state; Emergency shelter.
Sources of Referral State depts of education; Local depts of education; State depts of mental health; Psychiatrists; Private sources; Depts of correction; Social service depts; Parents; Youth (self referral); Friends.
Client Profile
Age Range of Clients Served Residential program: 12-18.
Characteristics Exhibited by Children Runaways.
IQ Range of Clients 70+.
Tuition and Fees
Placements Primarily Funded By Federal and state grants; United Way; Foundation; Community donations.
Social and Rehabilitative Services
Therapeutic Approach The facility uses crisis/short-term counseling models.
Therapeutic Services Offered Individual therapy; Group therapy; Family therapy; Recreation activities; Aftercare program with follow up.
Professionals on Staff Social workers; Child care staff.
Educational and Vocational Services
Type(s) of Educational Programs Offered Off campus.

ST AEMILIAN, INC

8901 W Capitol Dr, Milwaukee, WI 53222 (414) 463-1880 *Contact Person(s):* Alfred L Kasprowicz, Pres
Setting and Background Information The facility was established in 1854 by the Archdiocese of Milwaukee. The 14-acre campus has a large building which houses the residential program and the day treatment program.
Referral Information Referrals to the facility are usually made through social service depts.

Type of Facility
Funding Sources Private; State.
Average Length of Stay Short and long term.
Types of Admissions Accepted Day treatment; Residential treatment; Group home placement; Wards of the state.
Sources of Referral State depts of education; Local depts of education; State depts of mental health; Psychiatrists; Private sources; Social service depts.
Client Profile
Age Range of Clients Served Day programs: 6-15; Residential program: 6-15.
Characteristics Exhibited by Children Emotional handicaps; Learning disabilities; Speech/Language disorders; Mental disabilities.
IQ Range of Clients 70+.
Tuition and Fees
Room and Board Long term: $3,280/mo (includes school tuition).
Placements Primarily Funded By Insurance; Social service depts.
Social and Rehabilitative Services
Therapeutic Approach The facility has an eclectic approach to therapy.
Therapeutic Services Offered Individual therapy; Group therapy; Family therapy; Adjunctive therapy; Art therapy; Recreation activities; Aftercare program with follow up.
Professionals on Staff Psychiatrists; Psychologists; Social workers; Adjunctive therapists; Child care staff; Nurses; Art therapists.
Educational and Vocational Services
Type(s) of Educational Programs Offered On campus; Off campus; Summer campus.
Profile of On Campus School Program Number of teachers 16; *Number of classrooms* 8; *Student to teacher ratio* 5:1; *Credentials of teachers* BA, MA, Certified; Remedial courses offered.
Vocational Education Programs/Degrees Offered Pre-vocational.
Degrees Offered 8th grade diploma.

ST CHARLES, INC

PO Box 14005, 151 S 84th St, Milwaukee, WI 53214
(414) 476-3710 *Contact Person(s):* James Sampson, Exec Dir
Setting and Background Information The facility was established in 1923 as an alternative to a correctional facility for adolescent boys. Currently, the facility is located on 37 acres and has 11 brick buildings.
Referral Information Referrals can be made by the county and state Dept of Social Services. Applicants are requested to forward background information, including a social history, psychiatric evaluations, and psychological reports. A pre-placement visit will be scheduled before a placement decision is made.
Type of Facility
Funding Sources Private.
Average Length of Stay 6-12 mos.
Types of Admissions Accepted Day treatment; Residential treatment.
Sources of Referral Courts.
Client Profile
Age Range of Clients Served Day programs: 13-17; Residential program: 13-17.
Characteristics Exhibited by Children Emotional handicaps; Learning disabilities; Behavior disorders; Delinquency.
IQ Range of Clients 65+.
Tuition and Fees
Placements Primarily Funded By State depts of mental health; Social service depts; Referring county.
Social and Rehabilitative Services
Therapeutic Approach The primary therapeutic approach used is based on the priciples of reality therapy.
Therapeutic Services Offered Individual therapy; Group therapy; Family therapy; Independent living skills program; Recreation activities; Aftercare program with follow up.
Professionals on Staff Psychiatrists; Psychologists; Social workers; Child care staff.
Educational and Vocational Services
Type(s) of Educational Programs Offered On campus; Summer campus.
Profile of On Campus School Program Number of teachers 10; *Student to teacher ratio* 6:1; Special curriculum electives offered; Remedial courses offered.

ST ROSE RESIDENCE

3801 N 88th St, Milwaukee, WI 53222 (414) 466-9450 *Contact Person(s):* Kenneth Czaplewski, Dir
Setting and Background Information St Rose is a residential treatment facility for girls. The campus consists of a 2-story building built in 1973 containing 4 separate living units.
Referral Information Referrals can be made by social agencies, public schools, and private individuals. Applicants are requested to forward a social history, along with other pertinent information, before a pre-placement interview can take place.
Type of Facility
Funding Sources Private.
Average Length of Stay 14-16 mos.
Types of Admissions Accepted Day treatment; Residential treatment.
Sources of Referral State depts of mental health; Private sources; Social service depts; Court.
Client Profile
Age Range of Clients Served Day programs: 8-17; Residential program: 8-17.
Characteristics Exhibited by Children Emotional handicaps; Learning disabilities; Speech/Language disorders; Neurological impairments.
Tuition and Fees
Placements Primarily Funded By State depts of mental health; Social service depts.
Social and Rehabilitative Services
Therapeutic Approach The core of the treatment program is based on relationship therapy with strong behavioral expectations.
Therapeutic Services Offered Individual therapy; Group therapy; Family therapy; Art therapy; Recreation activities; Aftercare program with follow up.
Professionals on Staff Psychiatrists; Social workers; Child care staff; Nurses.
Educational and Vocational Services
Type(s) of Educational Programs Offered On campus; Off campus; Summer campus.
Profile of On Campus School Program Number of teachers 7; *Student to teacher ratio* 5:1; *Credentials of teachers* Certified; *Grades taught* 7-12; Special curriculum electives offered; Remedial courses offered.
Degrees Offered GED.

TRANSCENTER FOR YOUTH, GROUP FOSTER HOME

2506 W Uliet, Milwaukee, WI 53205 (414) 933-8002 *Contact Person(s):* Michael Harper, Prog Dir
Setting and Background Information The facility was established in 1969. It is a transitional living facility for delinquent boys.
Referral Information Referrals are made through Dept of Juvenile Services.
Type of Facility
Funding Sources State.
Average Length of Stay Long term.
Types of Admissions Accepted Group home placement.
Sources of Referral Depts of correction.
Client Profile
Age Range of Clients Served Residential program: 12-18.
Characteristics Exhibited by Children Delinquency.
IQ Range of Clients 70-110.
Tuition and Fees
Room and Board Short term: $79.96/diem; Long term: $79.96/diem.
Placements Primarily Funded By Depts of corrections.
Social and Rehabilitative Services
Therapeutic Services Offered Individual therapy; Group therapy; Family therapy; Independent living skills program.
Professionals on Staff Social workers; Child care staff; Parole officer.
Educational and Vocational Services
Type(s) of Educational Programs Offered Off campus (Community programs).

WILLOWGLEN

1235 N Milwaukee St, Milwaukee, WI 53202 (414) 272-2750
Contact Person(s): Gail Braun, Prog Dir
Setting and Background Information The facility was established in 1969 by Dr Balistrieri as a residential treatment center for dually-diagnosed adolescents. Its campus is located one mile from downtown Milwaukee and consists of a residential unit, school, and recreational facilities.

Referral Information Referrals can be made by the Dept of Social Services, Dept of Mental Health, school districts, correctional personnel, and other interested individuals. To make a referral, contact the facility and forward the following background information: social history, psychological reports, psychiatric evaluations, educational records, medical records, and any other relevant information. Upon reviewing the referral packet, an admission decision will be made.
Type of Facility
Funding Sources Private.
Average Length of Stay Avg 2 yrs.
Types of Admissions Accepted Residential treatment.
Sources of Referral Local depts of education; State depts of mental health; Social service depts; Courts.
Client Profile
Age Range of Clients Served Residential program: 12-18.
Characteristics Exhibited by Children Emotional handicaps; Learning disabilities; Speech/Language disorders; Neurological impairments; Mental disabilities; Developmentally disabled.
Tuition and Fees
Placements Primarily Funded By State depts of mental health; Private sources; Social service depts.
Social and Rehabilitative Services
Therapeutic Approach A variety of therapeutic approaches are used, including reality therapy, relationship therapy, and problem-solving techniques.
Therapeutic Services Offered Individual therapy; Group therapy; Family therapy; Independent living skills program; Recreation activities.
Professionals on Staff Psychiatrists; Social workers; Child care staff.
Educational and Vocational Services
Type(s) of Educational Programs Offered On campus; Off campus (Public schools; Technical college).
Profile of On Campus School Program Number of teachers 4; *Student to teacher ratio* 9:1; *Credentials of teachers* MA; *Grades taught* 7-12; Remedial courses offered.
Degrees Offered 8th grade diploma; 12th grade diploma; GED.

MONTFORT

MELODY RANCH, INC

Box 100C, Montfort, WI 53569 (608) 943-8448 *Contact Person(s):* Merlin Gorsline, Dir
Setting and Background Information The facility was established in 1973. It is a private non-profit corporation group home for adolescent boys.
Referral Information Contact the facility for referral information.
Type of Facility
Funding Sources County.
Average Length of Stay Long term.
Types of Admissions Accepted Group home placement.
Sources of Referral Social service depts.
Client Profile
Age Range of Clients Served Residential program: 12-18.
Characteristics Exhibited by Children Emotional handicaps; Delinquency.
Tuition and Fees
Room and Board Long term: $950/mo.
Placements Primarily Funded By Social service depts.
Social and Rehabilitative Services
Therapeutic Services Offered Individual therapy; Group therapy; Family therapy; Recreation activities.
Professionals on Staff Psychologists; Social workers.
Educational and Vocational Services
Type(s) of Educational Programs Offered Off campus (Public high school).

NEILLSVILLE

SUNBURST YOUTH HOMES

1210 W 5th St, Neillsville, WI 54456 (715) 743-3154 *Contact Person(s):* Rev Gale Wolf, Admin
Referral Information Contact the facility for referral information.
Type of Facility
Funding Sources Private; State.
Average Length of Stay Long term.
Types of Admissions Accepted Day treatment; Residential treatment.

SUNBURST YOUTH HOMES *(continued)*

Sources of Referral Private sources; Depts of correction; Social service depts.

Client Profile

Age Range of Clients Served Day Programs: 6-18; Residential program: 6-18.

Characteristics Exhibited by Children Emotional handicaps; Learning disabilities; Neurological impairments; Mental disabilities.

IQ Range of Clients 75+.

Tuition and Fees

Room and Board Short term: $111.29/diem; Long term: $111.29/diem.

Placements Primarily Funded By Social service depts.

Social and Rehabilitative Services

Therapeutic Services Offered Individual therapy; Group therapy; Recreation activities.

Professionals on Staff Psychiatrists; Psychologists; Child care staff.

Educational and Vocational Services

Type(s) of Educational Programs Offered On campus; Off campus; Summer campus.

Profile of On Campus School Program Number of teachers 12; *Number of classrooms* 12; *Student to teacher ratio* 10:1; *Credentials of teachers* BA; *Grades taught* K-12; Special curriculum electives offered (Art, Music, Home Ec, Industrial Arts); Remedial courses offered (Reading).

Vocational Education Programs/Degrees Offered Employment planning.

Degrees Offered 12th grade diploma.

NEW LONDON

RAWHIDE, INC

Route 1, New London, WI 54961 (414) 982-6100 *Contact Person(s):* Terry Egan, Soc Srvs Dir

Setting and Background Information This ranch was established in 1965 and is located on 500 acres. There are two main living facilities and a vocational shop.

Referral Information Contact the facility and forward referral materials. A pre-placement interview will be scheduled. The facility accepts boys only.

Type of Facility

Funding Sources Private; State; County.

Average Length of Stay Long term.

Types of Admissions Accepted Residential treatment; Wards of the state.

Sources of Referral State depts of mental health; Private sources; Depts of correction; Social service depts.

Client Profile

Age Range of Clients Served Residential program: 15-18.

Characteristics Exhibited by Children Emotional handicaps; Learning disabilities.

IQ Range of Clients 80+.

Tuition and Fees

Room and Board Long term: $2,950/mo (all inclusive).

Placements Primarily Funded By Social service depts.

Social and Rehabilitative Services

Therapeutic Approach The program uses behavior modification and reality therapy.

Therapeutic Services Offered Individual therapy; Group therapy; Family therapy; Independent living skills program; Recreation activities; Substance abuse treatment; Aftercare program with follow up.

Professionals on Staff Psychiatrists; Psychologists; Social workers; Child care staff.

Educational and Vocational Services

Type(s) of Educational Programs Offered On campus; Summer campus.

Profile of On Campus School Program Number of teachers 1; *Number of classrooms* 1; *Student to teacher ratio* 4:1; *Grades taught* 9-12; Remedial courses offered.

Vocational Education Programs/Degrees Offered Variety of vocational courses.

Degrees Offered GED.

OCONOMOWOC

OCONOMOWOC DEVELOPMENTAL TRAINING CENTER, INC

36100 Genesee Lake Rd, Oconomowoc, WI 53066-9202

(414) 567-5515 *Contact Person(s):* Debbie Frisk, Dir

Setting and Background Information Oconomowoc Developmental Training Center is a private residential treatment center for emotionally disturbed and mentally retarded children and young adults. The facility was established in 1975 and is located in southeastern Wisconsin. The campus consists of a school, gymnasium, dormitories for 60 children, play areas, administrative offices, 2 group homes and a sheltered workshop.

Referral Information Referrals can be made by anyone. The admission procedure requests that background information on the child be sent to the facility and then a pre-placement interview will be scheduled. Representatives from the facility are able to travel out of state to screen program candidates.

Type of Facility

Funding Sources Private.

Average Length of Stay Avg 2 yrs.

Types of Admissions Accepted Day treatment; Residential treatment; Group home placement.

Sources of Referral State depts of education; Local depts of education; State depts of mental health; Psychiatrists.

Client Profile

Age Range of Clients Served Day programs: 4-35; Residential program: 4-35.

Characteristics Exhibited by Children Emotional handicaps; Learning disabilities; Speech/Language disorders; Neurological impairments; Mental disabilities; Dually diagnosed.

IQ Range of Clients 0-89.

Tuition and Fees

Room and Board Long term: $3,197/mo; $1,825/mo (group home).

Placements Primarily Funded By Social service depts; County.

Social and Rehabilitative Services

Therapeutic Approach The facility has a behavioral approach to therapy.

Therapeutic Services Offered Individual therapy; Group therapy; Family therapy; Adjunctive therapy; Independent living skills program; Recreation activities; Aftercare program with follow up.

Professionals on Staff Psychiatrists; Psychologists; Social workers; Adjunctive therapists; Child care staff; Nurses.

Educational and Vocational Services

Type(s) of Educational Programs Offered On campus (State accredited); Off campus (Vocational; Sheltered workshops; Public schools).

Profile of On Campus School Program Special curriculum electives offered; Remedial courses offered.

Degrees Offered GED.

PRESCOTT

RIVERWOOD CENTER

445 Court St N, Prescott, WI 54021 (715) 262-3286 (WI), (612) 437-2133 (MN) *Contact Person(s):* Chris Cobb, Admis Coord

Setting and Background Information The facility was originally established in 1928. Currently, it is a residential center for children and adolescents, and an acute care psychiatric hospital.

Referral Information For referrals, contact the admissions coordinator. A psychiatrist will screen all applicants.

Type of Facility

Funding Sources Private.

Average Length of Stay Long term.

Types of Admissions Accepted Day treatment; Residential treatment.

Sources of Referral Local depts of education; State depts of mental health; Psychiatrists; Private sources; Social service depts; Parents.

Client Profile

Age Range of Clients Served Day programs: 6-18; Residential program: 12-18.

Characteristics Exhibited by Children Emotional handicaps; Learning disabilities; Speech/Language disorders; Mental disabilities.

IQ Range of Clients 80+.

Tuition and Fees

Room and Board Long term: $250/diem (all inclusive).

Placements Primarily Funded By Insurance; Private sources.

RIVERWOOD CENTER *(continued)*

Social and Rehabilitative Services
Therapeutic Approach The facility has a psychodynamic approach to therapy.
Therapeutic Services Offered Individual therapy; Group therapy; Family therapy; Adjunctive therapy; Recreation activities; Substance abuse treatment; Aftercare program with follow up.
Professionals on Staff Psychiatrists; Psychologists; Social workers; Adjunctive therapists; Child care staff; Nurses.
Educational and Vocational Services
Type(s) of Educational Programs Offered On campus (Tutoring); Summer campus (Enrichment).
Profile of On Campus School Program Number of teachers 3; *Number of classrooms* 4; *Student to teacher ratio* 6:1; *Credentials of teachers* State licensed; *Grades taught* 1-12; *Remedial courses offered* (LD tutoring).

RACINE

TAYLOR HOME
3131 Taylor Ave, Racine, WI 53405 (414) 554-8511 *Contact Person(s):* Dr M Sathya Babu, Exec Dir
Setting and Background Information The facility was privately established in 1897. Currently, there are four residential units, a dining hall, a gym and other buildings.
Referral Information Referrals are made through social services depts.
Type of Facility
Funding Sources Private; State.
Average Length of Stay Long term.
Types of Admissions Accepted Day treatment; Residential treatment; Group home placement.
Sources of Referral Local depts of education; Private sources; Depts of correction; Social service depts.
Client Profile
Age Range of Clients Served Day programs: 6-18; Residential program: 10-17.
Characteristics Exhibited by Children Emotional handicaps; Learning disabilities; Speech/Language disorders; Neurological impairments; Mental disabilities.
IQ Range of Clients 75+.
Tuition and Fees
Room and Board Short term: $79.92/diem; Long term: $79.92/diem.
Placements Primarily Funded By Local depts of education; Depts of corrections; Social service depts; Donations.
Social and Rehabilitative Services
Therapeutic Services Offered Individual therapy; Group therapy; Family therapy; Independent living skills program; Recreation activities; Aftercare program with follow up.
Professionals on Staff Psychiatrists; Psychologists; Social workers; Adjunctive therapists; Child care staff.
Educational and Vocational Services
Type(s) of Educational Programs Offered On campus; Summer campus.
Profile of On Campus School Program Number of teachers 4; *Number of classrooms* 3; *Student to teacher ratio* 10:1; *Credentials of teachers* Certified; *Grades taught* 6-12; *Remedial courses offered.*

SHEBOYGAN

FRIENDSHIP HOUSE
721 Ontario Ave, Sheboygan, WI 53081 (414) 452-9011 *Contact Person(s):* Robert J DePagter, Pres
Setting and Background Information The facility was originally established as an orphanage in 1910. In 1965, it became a group home for boys. There is one facility with a capacity for 8.
Referral Information Referrals are made through the Dept of Social Services and the juvenile courts.
Type of Facility
Funding Sources Private; State; Federal.
Average Length of Stay Long term.
Types of Admissions Accepted Group home placement.
Sources of Referral Social service depts.
Client Profile
Age Range of Clients Served Residential program: 12-15.
Characteristics Exhibited by Children Emotional handicaps; Drug and alcohol dependent.

IQ Range of Clients 80-120.
Tuition and Fees
Room and Board Long term: $1,333/mo.
Placements Primarily Funded By Social service depts.
Social and Rehabilitative Services
Therapeutic Approach The facility uses behavior modification.
Therapeutic Services Offered Individual therapy; Group therapy; Family therapy; Independent living skills program; Recreation activities; Substance abuse treatment; Aftercare program with follow up.
Professionals on Staff Psychiatrists; Social workers.
Educational and Vocational Services
Type(s) of Educational Programs Offered Off campus (High school; Tech school).

SPARTA

MONROE COUNTY SHELTER CARE, INC
PO Box 374, Sparta, WI 54656 (608) 269-6308 *Contact Person(s):* Ruth Schroeder MS, Dir
Setting and Background Information The non-profit agency was privately established in 1973. There are two group homes in Sparta.
Referral Information Contact the facility for referral information.
Type of Facility
Funding Sources County.
Average Length of Stay Short and long term.
Types of Admissions Accepted Group home placement.
Sources of Referral Social service depts.
Client Profile
Age Range of Clients Served Residential program: Birth-18.
Characteristics Exhibited by Children Emotional handicaps.
Tuition and Fees
Room and Board Short term: $54.82/diem; Long term: $54.82/diem.
Placements Primarily Funded By Social service depts.
Social and Rehabilitative Services
Therapeutic Approach The facility uses reality therapy and behavior modification.
Therapeutic Services Offered Individual therapy; Group therapy; Family therapy; Recreation activities.
Professionals on Staff Psychologists; Social workers; Child care staff.
Educational and Vocational Services
Type(s) of Educational Programs Offered Off campus (Public school).

STEVENS POINT

SOMA HOUSE
2201 Julia St, Stevens Point, WI 54481 (715) 341-6765 *Contact Person(s):* Mrs. William Konopacky
Setting and Background Information The facility was established in 1985 by Lutheran Social Services. It is a residential group home.
Referral Information Contact the facility for referral information.
Type of Facility
Funding Sources State.
Average Length of Stay Long term.
Types of Admissions Accepted Group home placement; Wards of the state.
Sources of Referral Social service depts.
Client Profile
Age Range of Clients Served Residential program: 12-18.
Characteristics Exhibited by Children Emotional handicaps; Learning disabilities; Mental disabilities; Delinquency.
IQ Range of Clients 70+.
Tuition and Fees
Room and Board Long term: $1,750/mo.
Placements Primarily Funded By Social service depts.
Social and Rehabilitative Services
Therapeutic Services Offered Individual therapy; Group therapy; Family therapy; Independent living skills program; Substance abuse treatment; Aftercare program with follow up.
Professionals on Staff Psychologists; Social workers; Child care staff.
Educational and Vocational Services
Type(s) of Educational Programs Offered Off campus.

TWO RIVERS

TRY GROUP HOME, INC
2317 Jefferson St, Two Rivers, WI 59241 (414) 794-7010 *Contact Person(s):* Pat Bannen
Setting and Background Information The facility was converted from a foster home to a group home in 1984.
Referral Information For referral information, contact the Bureau of Juvenile Services at the State Dept of Corrections.
Type of Facility
Funding Sources Private; State.
Average Length of Stay Long term.
Types of Admissions Accepted Group home placement.
Sources of Referral Depts of correction; Social service depts.
Client Profile
Age Range of Clients Served Residential program: 12-21+.
Characteristics Exhibited by Children Emotional handicaps; Drug and alcohol abuse.
Tuition and Fees
Room and Board Long term: $61.32/diem.
Placements Primarily Funded By Depts of corrections.
Social and Rehabilitative Services
Therapeutic Approach The basic approach of the facility is reality therapy.
Therapeutic Services Offered Individual therapy; Group therapy; Independent living skills program; Recreation activities; Substance abuse treatment; Aftercare program with follow up.
Professionals on Staff Psychiatrists; Psychologists; Social workers; Probation officer.
Educational and Vocational Services
Type(s) of Educational Programs Offered Off campus.

WAUTOMA

NOVA HOUSE
PO Box 110, 608 Cummings Rd, Wautoma, WI 54982
(414) 787-3522 *Contact Person(s):* John L Parrish, Admin
Setting and Background Information The facility was established in 1978 through a federal grant. It is a group home.
Referral Information Contact the facility and submit a social history, school records, psychological evaluation, and court records.
Type of Facility
Funding Sources State; Federal.
Average Length of Stay Long term.
Types of Admissions Accepted Group home placement.
Sources of Referral State depts of mental health; Private sources; Depts of correction; Social service depts.
Client Profile
Age Range of Clients Served Residential program: 12-18.
Characteristics Exhibited by Children Emotional handicaps; Learning disabilities.
IQ Range of Clients 85+.
Tuition and Fees
Room and Board Long term: $71.50/diem.
Placements Primarily Funded By Social service depts.
Social and Rehabilitative Services
Therapeutic Approach The facility has an eclectic approach to therapy.
Therapeutic Services Offered Individual therapy; Group therapy; Family therapy; Physical therapy; Independent living skills program; Recreation activities; Substance abuse treatment; Aftercare program with follow up; Foster care.
Professionals on Staff Psychologists; Social workers; Child care staff; Physical therapists; Chemical abuse therapist.
Educational and Vocational Services
Type(s) of Educational Programs Offered Off campus (Public school; Technical school).

WAUWATOSA

CARMELITE HOME, INC
1214 Kavanaugh Pl, Wauwatosa, WI 53213 (414) 258-4791 *Contact Person(s):* Jim Lewis, Dir
Setting and Background Information Carmelite Home is a private residential treatment facility which was initially established as an orphanage in 1923 by the Carmelite sisters. In 1967, its programs expanded to become a treatment center. The program is located in a 3-story brick building with a gymnasium located in a residential neighborhood outside Milwaukee.
Referral Information Referrals can be made by courts, county liaison workers, corrections officials, and parents. To make a referral, forward the following background information on the child: social history, school records, psychiatric evaluation, medical history, and court history. Upon receipt of the referral materials, a pre-placement visit will take place before a placement decision is made.
Type of Facility
Funding Sources Private.
Average Length of Stay 6-8 mos.
Types of Admissions Accepted Residential treatment; Wards of the state.
Sources of Referral Local depts of education; Private sources; Social service depts; Courts.
Client Profile
Age Range of Clients Served Residential program: 11-17.
Characteristics Exhibited by Children Emotional handicaps; Learning disabilities; Speech/Language disorders; Mental disabilities.
IQ Range of Clients 65+.
Tuition and Fees
Room and Board Long term: $2,540/mo.
Placements Primarily Funded By State depts of mental health; Social service depts.
Social and Rehabilitative Services
Therapeutic Approach The treatment program utilizes individualized treatment plans, in conjunction with milieu therapy and behavior modification.
Therapeutic Services Offered Individual therapy; Group therapy; Family therapy; Adjunctive therapy; Recreation activities.
Professionals on Staff Psychiatrists; Psychologists; Social workers; Adjunctive therapists; Child care staff; Reading specialist.
Educational and Vocational Services
Type(s) of Educational Programs Offered On campus; Off campus (Public school).
Profile of On Campus School Program Number of teachers 4; *Student to teacher ratio* 6:1.
Degrees Offered GED.

PASSAGES GROUP HOME
2555 N 75th St, Wauwatosa, WI 53213 (414) 475-5250 *Contact Person(s):* James Andreoni ACSW, Supv
Setting and Background Information The facility was established in 1985 with county funding. It is a residential group home.
Referral Information All referrals are made through the Milwaukee County Dept of Social Services. Clients must be residents of Milwaukee County.
Type of Facility
Funding Sources State; County.
Average Length of Stay Long term.
Types of Admissions Accepted Group home placement.
Sources of Referral Social service depts.
Client Profile
Age Range of Clients Served Residential program: 12-18.
Characteristics Exhibited by Children Emotional handicaps.
IQ Range of Clients 85+.
Tuition and Fees
Room and Board Long term: $63/diem.
Placements Primarily Funded By Social service depts; County.
Social and Rehabilitative Services
Therapeutic Services Offered Individual therapy; Group therapy; Family therapy; Independent living skills program; Recreation activities; Aftercare program with follow up.
Professionals on Staff Psychologists; Social workers; Adjunctive therapists; Child care staff.
Educational and Vocational Services
Type(s) of Educational Programs Offered Off campus (Public schools).

WEST BEND

NOVA SERVICES, INC

236 5th Ave, West Bend, WI 53095 (414) 338-8842 *Contact Person(s):* Paul VanDemark, Dir

Setting and Background Information The facility was established in 1976 in response to a community need for alternative care placements. There are 3 group homes with a capacity for 8 in each.

Referral Information All referrals are made through the Dept of Social Services.

Type of Facility

Funding Sources County.

Average Length of Stay Short term (14 days); Long term (10 mos).

Types of Admissions Accepted Group home placement.

Sources of Referral Depts of correction; Social service depts; Juvenile courts.

Client Profile

Age Range of Clients Served Residential program: 12-18.

Characteristics Exhibited by Children Emotional handicaps; Learning disabilities; Delinquency.

IQ Range of Clients 85-120.

Tuition and Fees

Room and Board Short term: $1,780/mo; Long term: $1,800/mo.

Placements Primarily Funded By Depts of corrections; Social service depts.

Social and Rehabilitative Services

Therapeutic Approach The facility uses reality therapy, including behavior modification.

Therapeutic Services Offered Individual therapy; Group therapy; Family therapy; Independent living skills program; Recreation activities; Aftercare program with follow up.

Professionals on Staff Social workers; Child care staff.

Educational and Vocational Services

Type(s) of Educational Programs Offered Off campus; Summer campus (Work program).

WHITE LAKE

WOLF RIVER GROUP HOME

Star Route, White Lake, WI 54491 (715) 882-4821 *Contact Person(s):* Carol Rewey, Soc Worker; Lee and Leslie Stewart, Admin

Setting and Background Information The facility was established in 1983 by a county juvenile court worker and is sponsored by Lutheran Social Services. The 23-acre campus has a large brick farmhouse and 3 outbuildings.

Referral Information Referrals to the facility are made through the Lutheran Social Services of Wisconsin and Upper Michigan, North Central Area.

Type of Facility

Funding Sources State; County.

Average Length of Stay 6-12 mos.

Types of Admissions Accepted Group home placement.

Sources of Referral Depts of correction; Social service depts.

Client Profile

Age Range of Clients Served Residential program: 12-18.

Characteristics Exhibited by Children Emotional handicaps; Learning disabilities.

Tuition and Fees

Room and Board Long term: $1,470/mo.

Placements Primarily Funded By Social service depts.

Social and Rehabilitative Services

Therapeutic Approach The facility uses behavior modification.

Therapeutic Services Offered Individual therapy; Group therapy; Independent living skills program; Recreation activities.

Professionals on Staff Psychiatrists; Psychologists; Social workers; Child care staff.

Educational and Vocational Services

Type(s) of Educational Programs Offered Off campus (Public school).

Degrees Offered Diploma conferred through public schools.

WYOMING

CASPER

CREST VIEW HOSPITAL
2521 E 15th St, Casper, WY 82609 (307) 237-7444 *Contact Person(s):* Jerry Wetherbee, Admin
Setting and Background Information The facility was privately established in 1985. It is a 54 bed hospital.
Referral Information Contact the facility for referral information.
Type of Facility
Funding Sources Private.
Average Length of Stay Short and long term.
Types of Admissions Accepted Day treatment; Residential treatment.
Sources of Referral State depts of education; Local depts of education; Psychiatrists; Private sources; Depts of correction; Social service depts.
Client Profile
Age Range of Clients Served Day programs: 12-55+; Residential program: 12-55+.
Characteristics Exhibited by Children Emotional handicaps; Mental disabilities; Chemical dependency.
Tuition and Fees
Room and Board Short term: $205/diem; Long term: $205/diem.
Placements Primarily Funded By Insurance; Private sources; Social service depts.
Social and Rehabilitative Services
Therapeutic Approach The facility uses a multi-disciplinary team approach.
Therapeutic Services Offered Individual therapy; Group therapy; Family therapy; Art therapy; Independent living skills program; Recreation activities; Substance abuse treatment; Aftercare program with follow up.
Professionals on Staff Psychiatrists; Psychologists; Social workers; Nurses; Art therapists.

WYOMING YOUTH TREATMENT CENTER
1514 E 12th St, Casper, WY 82601 (307) 261-2200 *Contact Person(s):* George Brown, Supt
Setting and Background Information The facility was established in 1936 as a home for dependent and neglected children. Located on 24 acres, there are 4 treatment cottages, a school, a gym and an administration building.
Referral Information Referrals are made by arrangement with the admissions coordinator and are court ordered.
Type of Facility
Funding Sources State.
Average Length of Stay Long term.
Types of Admissions Accepted Residential treatment.
Sources of Referral Juvenile courts.
Client Profile
Age Range of Clients Served Residential program: 12-18.
Characteristics Exhibited by Children Emotional handicaps.
Tuition and Fees
Placements Primarily Funded By Dept of Institutions.
Social and Rehabilitative Services
Therapeutic Approach The facility uses cognitive therapy and behavior modification.
Therapeutic Services Offered Recreation activities.
Professionals on Staff Psychiatrists; Psychologists; Adjunctive therapists; Child care staff; Nurses.

Educational and Vocational Services
Type(s) of Educational Programs Offered On campus.
Profile of On Campus School Program Number of teachers 7; Student to teacher ratio 6:1; Credentials of teachers Certified.

TORRINGTON

ST JOSEPH'S CHILDREN'S HOME
PO Box 1117, Torrington, WY 82240 (307) 532-4197 *Contact Person(s):* Steve Bogus, Prog Dir
Setting and Background Information The facility was initially established as an orphanage in 1930 by the Roman Catholic Diocese of Cheyene. In 1970, programs were altered and expanded to become a treatment center for emotionally disturbed children. The campus is located in eastern Wyoming in a rural community of 5,500 people and consists of self-contained living units, school, gymnasium, swimming pool, recreational areas, and a church.
Referral Information Referrals can be made by public assistance social workers, school districts, mental health professionals, and parents. To make a referral, forward the necessary background information, including medical records, school records, social summaries, and psychological reports. A pre-placement interview will be scheduled before a placement decision is made.
Type of Facility
Funding Sources Private.
Average Length of Stay Long term.
Types of Admissions Accepted Residential treatment; Group home placement.
Sources of Referral Local depts of education; State depts of mental health; Social service depts; Courts.
Client Profile
Age Range of Clients Served Residential program: 6-18.
Characteristics Exhibited by Children Emotional handicaps; Learning disabilities.
Tuition and Fees
Room and Board Long term: $79/diem.
Tuition $73/diem.
Placements Primarily Funded By State depts of mental health; Private sources; Social service depts; School districts.
Social and Rehabilitative Services
Therapeutic Approach The primary therapeutic approach used is Adlerian psychology.
Therapeutic Services Offered Individual therapy; Group therapy; Family therapy; Adjunctive therapy; Recreation activities; Aftercare program with follow up.
Professionals on Staff Psychiatrists; Social workers; Adjunctive therapists; Child care staff.
Educational and Vocational Services
Type(s) of Educational Programs Offered On campus; Off campus (Public school); Summer campus.
Profile of On Campus School Program Number of teachers 5; Student to teacher ratio 5:1; Credentials of teachers Certified; Special curriculum electives offered (College Prep).

WORLAND

WYOMING BOYS SCHOOL

R#2, 1550 Hwy 20 S, Worland, WY 82401 (307) 347-6144 *Contact Person(s):* David Renaud, Supt

Setting and Background Information The facility was established in 1921 by a state statute. The 40-acre campus has dormitories, a school, an administration building, vocational buildings and other support buildings.

Referral Information All referrals to the facility are made by the courts.

Type of Facility

Funding Sources State.

Average Length of Stay Long term.

Types of Admissions Accepted Residential treatment; Wards of the state.

Sources of Referral Courts.

Client Profile

Age Range of Clients Served Residential program: 12-18.

Characteristics Exhibited by Children Emotional handicaps; Learning disabilities; Behavior disorders; Delinquency.

IQ Range of Clients 69-120.

Tuition and Fees

Room and Board Long term: $61/diem.

Placements Primarily Funded By State depts of mental health.

Social and Rehabilitative Services

Therapeutic Approach The basic therapeutic approach of the facility is behavior modification.

Therapeutic Services Offered Individual therapy; Group therapy; Independent living skills program.

Professionals on Staff Social workers; Child care staff.

Educational and Vocational Services

Type(s) of Educational Programs Offered On campus (Educational; Vocational).

Profile of On Campus School Program Number of teachers 10; *Number of classrooms* 6; *Student to teacher ratio* 10:1; *Credentials of teachers* BA; *Grades taught* 7-12; Special curriculum electives offered; Remedial courses offered (Reading, English, Math).

Vocational Education Programs/Degrees Offered Auto mechanics; Welding; Carpentry.

Degrees Offered 12th grade diploma; GED.

GUAM

GUAM MAIN FACILITY

SANCTUARY, INC
PO Box 21030, Guam Main Facility, GU 96921
(671) 734-2661,734-2537, 646-5014 *Contact Person(s):* Tony C
Champaco, Exec Dir

Setting and Background Information This facility was established in
1987 with federal funding through LEAA. It cosists of a co-ed
shelter and an office.

Referral Information Referrals are made directly through the hotline
or office. Assessment and intake are provided by a caseworker.

Type of Facility

Funding Sources Private; State; Federal.

Average Length of Stay Short term.

Types of Admissions Accepted Day treatment; Residential treatment;
Group home placement; Wards of the state.

Sources of Referral State depts of education; Local depts of education; State depts of mental health; Psychiatrists; Private sources;
Social service depts; Court; Parents; Self.

Client Profile

Age Range of Clients Served Day programs: 12-18; Residential program: 12-18.

Characteristics Exhibited by Children Emotional handicaps; Learning
disabilities.

IQ Range of Clients 75-115.

Tuition and Fees

Placements Primarily Funded By Private sources; Social service
depts; Federal grants.

Social and Rehabilitative Services

Therapeutic Approach The facility offers crisis, supportive and in-
depth counseling.

Therapeutic Services Offered Individual therapy; Group therapy;
Family therapy; Independent living skills program; Recreation
activities; Aftercare program with follow up.

Professionals on Staff Psychologists; Social workers.

Educational and Vocational Services

Type(s) of Educational Programs Offered Off campus.

PUERTO RICO

CAGUAS

CAGUAS EMERGENCY CARE SHELTER
Calle 7 B-16, Urb Mariolga, Caguas, PR.
Setting and Background Information The facility is an temporary, emergency shelter for 8 children and youth.
Referral Information Contact the facility for referral information.
Type of Facility
Funding Sources State.
Types of Admissions Accepted Emergency shelter.
Client Profile
Age Range of Clients Served Residential program: 6-15.
Tuition and Fees
Placements Primarily Funded By State depts of mental health.

GUAYNABO

TORRIMAR GROUP HOME FOR GIRLS
Ave Lomas Verdes #55, Urb Torrimar, Guaynabo, PR 00657.
Setting and Background Information The facility is a group home for 8 girls.
Referral Information Contact the facility for referral information.
Type of Facility
Funding Sources State.
Types of Admissions Accepted Group home placement.
Client Profile
Age Range of Clients Served Residential program: 15-20.
Tuition and Fees
Placements Primarily Funded By State depts of mental health.

NAGUABO

RIO BLANCO GROUP HOME FOR DEPENDENT AND NEGLECTED
Bo Rio Blanco, Naguabo, PR.
Setting and Background Information The facility is a group home for 8 dependent and neglected girls.
Referral Information Contact the facility for referral information.
Type of Facility
Funding Sources State.
Types of Admissions Accepted Group home placement.
Client Profile
Age Range of Clients Served Residential program: 12-20.
Characteristics Exhibited by Children Dependent and neglected.
Tuition and Fees
Placements Primarily Funded By State depts of mental health.

PONCE

ARCOIRIS GROUP HOME FOR GIRLS
Calle F-5 Urb. Santa Maria, Ponce, PR 00731.
Setting and Background Information The facility is a group home for 8 girls.
Type of Facility
Funding Sources State.
Types of Admissions Accepted Group home placement.
Client Profile
Age Range of Clients Served Residential program: 14-20.
Tuition and Fees
Placements Primarily Funded By State depts of mental health.

PONCE GROUP HOME FOR GIRLS
Calle Sol #92, Esq Torres, Ponce, PR 00731.
Setting and Background Information The facility is a group home for 8 girls.
Referral Information Contact the facility for referral information.
Type of Facility
Funding Sources State.
Types of Admissions Accepted Group home placement.
Client Profile
Age Range of Clients Served Residential program: 13-18.
Tuition and Fees
Placements Primarily Funded By State depts of mental health.

RIO PIEDRAS

EL CARIBE GROUP HOME FOR BOYS
Calle Alda #1605, Urb Caribe, Rio Piedras, PR 00927.
Setting and Background Information The facility is a group home for 8 boys.
Referral Information Contact the facility for referral information.
Type of Facility
Funding Sources State.
Types of Admissions Accepted Group home placement.
Client Profile
Age Range of Clients Served Residential program: 15-20.
Tuition and Fees
Placements Primarily Funded By Local depts of education.

SAN GERMAN

LA SULTANA GROUP HOME FOR BOYS
Carr. #34 Km 1.8, Bo Cotto, San German, PR 00753.
Setting and Background Information The facility is a group home for 8 boys.
Referral Information Contact the facility for referral information.
Type of Facility
Funding Sources State.
Types of Admissions Accepted Group home placement.
Client Profile
Age Range of Clients Served Residential program: 14-20.
Tuition and Fees
Placements Primarily Funded By State depts of mental health.

Characteristics Exhibited by Children Index

ABUSED AND NEGLECTED

Allen Acres, Lima, OH
Arizona Youth Association, Inc, Phoenix, AZ
Children's Home of Wheeling, Wheeling, WV
Rhonda Crane Memorial Youth Shelter, Pascagoula, MS
Equinox Youth Shelter, Albany, NY
Foothills Youth Services, Inc, Johnstown, NY
Franklin Village, Grove City, OH
Gateway Youth Home, Martinsburg, WV
Hays House, Boise, ID
Johnson County Youth Service Bureau, Inc, Franklin, IN
MacDonell United Methodist Children's Services, Inc, Houma, LA
Marian Hall Residential Care, St Louis, MO
Martinsburg Children's Shelter, Martinsburg, WV
The Methodist Home of New Orleans, New Orleans, LA
Nassau Children's House, Mineola, NY
New Beginnings, Greer, SC
Olive Crest Treatment Centers, Santa Ana, CA
One Way Farm, Inc, Fairfield, OH
The Open Gate, Marietta, GA
Riverview Residential Treatment Facilities, Lowell, MI
St Catherine's Center for Children, Albany, NY
Shelter Services of Carlton County, Inc, Cloquet, MN
Southeastern Children's Home, Inc, Taylors, SC
Sugar Creek Children's Center, Philippi, WV
Transitional Living, Chicago, IL
Ulrey Homes, Inc, San Lorenzo, CA
Wood County Child Care Center, Parkersburg, WV
Youth Residential Treatment Center, Corpus Christi, TX
YWCA Try Angle House, Nashville, TN

AUTISM

The Anderson School, Staatsburg, NY
Archway, Inc, Leicester, MA
Au Clair School, Bear, DE
Autism Teaching Home, Salt Lake City, UT
Autistic Treatment Center, Richardson, TX
The Bancroft School, Haddonfield, NJ
Bar-None Residential Treatment Services, Anoka, MN
Behavioral Development Center, Inc, Providence, RI
Benhaven, East Haven, CT
Burt Children's Center, San Francisco, CA
The Devereux Center, Scottsdale, AZ
The Eden Family of Programs, Princeton, NJ
Glenwood Mental Health Services, Children's Residential, Birmingham, AL
Grafton School, Berryville, VA
The House of the Good Shepherd, Utica, NY
Kaplan Foundation, Inc, Orangevale, CA
May Institute, Chatham, MA
Frances Haddon Morgan Center, Bremerton, WA
Mt Ridge Group Home, Cherryville, NC
Parkview Homes I, II, & III, Seattle, WA
Parry Center for Children, Portland, OR
Pine Grove School, Elgin, WA
Potomac Comprehensive Diagnostic and Guidance Center, Romney, WV
Princeton Child Development Institute, Princeton, NJ
St John's Child Development Center, Washington, DC
Search Day Program, Inc., Ocean, NJ

Southeastern Mental Health Center, Sioux Falls, SD
Spaulding Youth Center, Tilton, NH
Triad Homes for Autistic Individuals, Inc, High Point, NC
Wheeler Clinic, Plainville, CT

BEHAVIOR DISORDERS

American School for the Deaf, Paces Program, West Hartford, CT
Appleton Family Ministries, Juliette, GA
Baby Fold Residential Treatment Center, Normal, IL
Behavioral Development Center, Inc, Providence, RI
Boy's Home, Inc, Covington, VA
Boys Republic, Chino, CA
Boys' Village, Inc, Smithville, OH
Bremwood Lutheran Children's Home Society, Waverly, IA
Maude Carpenter's Childrens Home, Wichita, KS
Cedar Hills Hospital, Portland, OR
Cedar House, Lewiston, ID
Center for Therapeutic Learning Annex, Loveland, CO
Challenge Group Home, Eagle, ID
Children's Farm Home, Corvallis, OR
Children's Home of Cedar Rapids, Cedar Rapids, IA
Coulee Youth Centers, Inc, LaCrosse, WI
Florence Crittenton of Arizona, Inc, Phoenix, AZ
Crockett Academy, Nashville, TN
Cunningham Children's Home, Urbana, IL
Diocesan Human Relations Service, Christopher Home of Aroostook, Caribou, ME
Edgefield Lodge, Inc, Troutdale, OR
Jennie Edmundson Memorial Hospital, Council Bluffs, IA
Epworth Village, Inc, York, NE
Fairway, Mobile, AL
Forest Ridge Community Youth Center, Wallingford, IA
Girl's Ranch, Inc, Scottsdale, AZ
Mary Greeley Medical Center, Ames, IA
Heartsease Home, Inc, New York, NY
Timothy Hill Children's Ranch, Riverhead, NY
Holly Hill Hospital, Raleigh, NC
Hope for Youth, Inc, Bethpage, NY
Huckleberry House II, San Francisco, CA
Iowa Children's and Family Services, Des Moines, IA
Janis Youth Programs, Inc, Portland, OR
Jewish Family and Children's Services, Phoenix, AZ
Jones Home of Children's Services, Cleveland, OH
K-Bar-B Youth Ranch, Lacombe, LA
Klein Bottle Social Advocates for Youth, Santa Barbara, CA
Lakin Hospital—Adolescent Services, Lakin, WV
Jane Lamb Health Center, Clinton, IA
Linnhaven, Inc, Marion, IA
Longview Protestant Home for Children, Buffalo, NY
Lutheran Social Services, Epic Group Home, Eau Claire, WI
MacDonell United Methodist Children's Services, Inc, Houma, LA
Mainstream Living, Inc, Ames, IA
Marian Hall Residential Care, St Louis, MO
The Marsh Foundation Home and School, Van Wert, OH
McCauley Girl's Home, Buhl, ID

Mercy Health Center, Dubuque, IA
The Methodist Home of Kentucky, Inc, Versailles, KY
Midwest Christian Children's Home, Peterson, IA
Miracle Hill Children's Home, Pickens, SC
Nampa Boys Group Home, Nampa, ID
New Beginnings Center, Aberdeen, SD
North Idaho Children's Home, Lewiston, ID
Ottumwa Regional Health Center, Ottumwa, IA
Out-Front House, Portland, OR
Parmadale, Parma, OH
Parry Center for Children, Portland, OR
Penikese Island School, Woods Hole, MA
RCA Evaluation and Treatment Center, Cranston, RI
Riverside Psychiatric Hospital, Portland, OR
Rosemont School, Inc, Portland, OR
St Charles, Inc, Milwaukee, WI
St Francis Hospital, Waterloo, IA
St Joseph Mercy Hospital, Mason City, IA
St Joseph's Villa, Richmond, VA
St Mary's Campus School, North Providence, RI
St Mary's Home for Boys, Beaverton, OR
St Vincent Home, St Louis, MO
Salvation Army White Shield Center, Portland, OR
San Pablo Residential Treatment School, Phoenix, AZ
Second Circle, Yellow Springs, OH
Norman C Sleezer Juvenile Homes, Inc, Freeport, IL
Spurwink School II, North Providence, RI
Sunny Ridge Family Center, Wheaton, IL
Syntaxis, Inc, Gahanna, OH
Tara Hall Home for Boys, Georgetown, SC
Touchstone Community, Inc—Arizona Boys Community, Phoenix, AZ
Trinity Regional Hospital, Fort Dodge, IA
Washington Street Homes, Fresno, CA
Waverly Children's Home, Portland, OR
The Constance Bultman Wilson Center, Faribault, MN
Wyndham Lawn Home for Children, Lockport, NY
Wyoming Boys School, Worland, WY
Youth Service Bureau, Muncie, IN

DELINQUENCY

Alaska Children's Services, Inc, Anchorage, AK
Alpha House Youth Care, Inc, Menomonie, WI
Alston Wilkes Youth Home, Columbia South, Columbia, SC
Aquarius House, Colrain, MA
Attucks Center, Inc, Milwaukee, WI
The Boyd School, Green Pond, AL
Boys and Girls Aid Society of Oregon, Portland, OR
Cary Home for Children, Lafayette, IN
Casa Victoria I, Whittier, CA
Children's Farm Home, Corvallis, OR
Children's Home of Stockton, Stockton, CA
Colbert-Lauderdale Attention Home, Inc, Florence, AL
Cortez House, Phoenix, AZ
Day Group Home, Inc, Buellton, CA
Daymark, Inc—Turning Point, Charleston, WV
Edgefield Lodge, Inc, Troutdale, OR
Ethan House I, Green Bay, WI
Ethan House II, Green Bay, WI
Franklin Village, Grove City, OH
Gateway Group Home, Excelsior, MN
Genesis, Athens, OH

Genesis Youth Center, Clarksburg, WV
Girl's Ranch, Inc, Scottsdale, AZ
The Glen Mills Schools, Concordville, PA
Good Samaritan Homes, Sacramento, CA
Hillcrest Family Services, Dubuque, IA
Stonewall Jackson School, Concord, NC
Janis Youth Programs, Inc, Portland, OR
Jefferson County Family Court Detention Center, Birmingham, AL
Jewish Family and Children's Services, Phoenix, AZ
Jones Home of Children's Services, Cleveland, OH
Littleton Girls House, Secure Treatment Facility, Littleton, MA
Lutheran Social Services, Hampton House Group Home, Milwaukee, WI
Maplehill Community, Plainfield, VT
Melody Ranch, Inc, Montfort, WI
Nassau Children's House, Mineola, NY
New Beginnings Center, Aberdeen, SD
The New Foundation, Phoenix, AZ
Northern Kentucky Treatment Center, Crittenden, KY
Nova Services, Inc, West Bend, WI
Opportunity House, Lynchburg, VA
Our House, Inc, Greenfield, MA
Pathway, Inc, New Brockton, AL
Penikese Island School, Woods Hole, MA
Prehab of Arizona, Mesa, AZ
Jerry Rabiner Memorial Boys Ranch, Inc, Fort Dodge, IA
RCA Evaluation and Treatment Center, Cranston, RI
Rosemont School, Inc, Portland, OR
St Charles, Inc, Milwaukee, WI
St Mary's Home for Boys, Beaverton, OR
Shelter for Women, Inc—Gray Lodge, Hartford, CT
Soma House, Stevens Point, WI
Maurice Spear Campus, Adrian, MI
Sugar Creek Children's Center, Philippi, WV
Sunshine Acres Children's Home, Mesa, AZ
Syntaxis, Inc, Gahanna, OH
Syracuse Youth Development Center, Syracuse, NY
Timber Ridge, Winchester, VA
Touchstone Community, Inc—Arizona Boys Community, Phoenix, AZ
Transcenter for Youth, Group Foster Home, Milwaukee, WI
Trinity School for Children, Ukiah, CA
Tumbleweed, Phoenix, AZ
Visionquest National Ltd, Tucson, AZ
Washington Street Homes, Fresno, CA
Wood County Child Care Center, Parkersburg, WV
Wyoming Boys School, Worland, WY
Youth Adventures, Inc, Oregon City, OR
Youth Care Center, Evansville, IN
Youth Rehabilitation Camps—Nokomis, Prudenville, MI
Youth Service Bureau, Muncie, IN
YWCA Try Angle House, Nashville, TN

EMOTIONAL HANDICAPS

Abbott House, Mitchell, SD
ABCS Little Canyon School, Phoenix, AZ
Adolescent Group Home, Danville, VA
Adventure Bound School—Boonesville Residential Center, Charlottsville, VA
Advocate Group Homes, Riverside, CA
Alaska Children's Services, Inc, Anchorage, AK
Aldea, Inc, Napa, CA
Alexander Children's Center 36, Charlotte, NC
Allen Acres, Lima, OH
Allendale, Lake Villa, IL
Allentown State Hospital—Children's Unit, Allentown, PA
Alpha House Youth Care, Inc, Menomonie, WI
Alpha Omega, Littleton, MA
Alston Wilkes Youth Home, Columbia South, Columbia, SC
Alternative Homes, Inc, St Paul, MN
Alternative House, Vienna, VA
American Institute for Mental Studies, Vineland, NJ
American School for the Deaf, Paces Program, West Hartford, CT
AMI St Joseph Center for Mental Health, Omaha, NE
Anchor I, Martinsville, VA
Paul Anderson Youth Home, Inc, Vidalia, GA
The Anderson School, Staatsburg, NY
Andrus Children's Home, Yonkers, NY

Angel Guardian Home—McAuley Residence, Brooklyn, NY
Apostolic Christian Childrens Home, Leo, IN
Appleton Family Ministries, Juliette, GA
Aquarius House, Colrain, MA
Arbor Heights Center, Ann Arbor, MI
Arden Shore, Highland Park, IL
Argus Community, Inc, Bronx, NY
Arizona Children's Home Association, Tucson, AZ
Arizona State Hospital—Child and Adolescent Treatment Unit, Phoenix, AZ
Arizona Youth Association, Inc, Phoenix, AZ
The ARK, Jackson, MS
Arrowhead Ranch, Coal Valley, IL
Ashtabula County Residential Treatment Center, Ashtabula, OH
The Astor Home for Children, Rhinebeck, NY
Astor Home for Children, Marian Group Home, Goshen, NY
Attleboro Youth Shelter, Attleboro, MA
Augusta Mental Health Institute, Augusta, ME
Aviva Center, Los Angeles, CA
Avondale Youth Center, Zanesville, OH
Baby Fold Residential Treatment Center, Normal, IL
The Baird Center, Plymouth, MA
Baird Children's Center, Burlington, VT
Baker Hall, Lackawanna, NY
The Bancroft School, Haddonfield, NJ
Baptist Children's Home and Family Ministries, Valparaiso, IN
Baptist Children's Home at San Antonio, San Antonio, TX
Baptist Children's Home, Inc, Carmi, IL
Baptist Home for Children, Bethesda, MD
Barboursville School, Barboursville, WV
Bar-None Residential Treatment Services, Anoka, MN
Bashor Home of the United Methodist Church, Inc, Goshen, IN
Beckley Child Care Center, Beckley, WV
Behavior Research Institute, Inc, Providence, RI
Bella Vida Group Home, Fresno, CA
Bellefaire Residential Treatment Facility, Cleveland, OH
Benhaven, East Haven, CT
Bennington School, Inc, Bennington, VT
Berkeley Academy, Berkeley, CA
Berkshire Farm Center and Services for Youth, Canaan, NY
Berkshire Learning Center, Pittsfield, MA
Bethany Home, Inc, Moline, IL
Bethel Bible Village, Hixson, TN
The Bethel Group Home, Bethel, AK
Bethesda PsycHealth System, Denver, CO
Bethlehem Children's Center, New Orleans, LA
Bexar County MHMR Center—Residential Program, San Antonio, TX
Black Hills Special Services—Northern Hills Youth Services, Spearfish, SD
Blount County Children's Home, Maryville, TN
Blueberry Treatment Center, Brooklyn, NY
The Boise Girls Home, Boise, ID
Boselli Residential Services, Inc, Lemon Grove, CA
The Boyd School, Green Pond, AL
Boys and Girls Aid Society of Oregon, Portland, OR
Boys and Girls Aid Society of San Diego—Cottonwood Center, El Cajon, CA
Boys Attention Home, Charlottesville, VA
Boys Hope, Staten Island, NY
Boys Hope, Cincinnati, OH
Boys Hope, St Louis, MO
Boys Republic, Chino, CA
Boys' Village, Inc, Smithville, OH
Boy's Village Youth and Family Services, Inc, Milford, CT
Bradley Hospital, East Providence, RI
Brandon School, Natick, MA
Brattleboro Retreat, Brattleboro, VT
Braun Programs, Inc., Braun Place, San Rafael, CA
Brehm Preparatory School, Carbondale, IL
Bremwood Lutheran Children's Home Society, Waverly, IA
Brewer-Porch Childrens Center, University, AL
The Bridge, San Diego, CA
Bridgeport Academy, Bridgeport, CT
Bridlewood Group Home, Intensive Residential Program, Charlotte, NC
Arthur Brisbane Child Treatment Center, Farmingdale, NJ
Broad Horizons of Ramona, Inc, Ramona, CA
Brooke-Hancock Group Home, Inc, Newell, WV

Brookland Plantation Home for Boys, Orangeburg, SC
The Brown Schools, Austin, TX
Buckeye Boys Ranch, Inc, Grove City, OH
Buckner Children's Services, Amarillo, TX
Buffalo Youth Development Center, Buffalo, NY
Burlington United Methodist Home for Children and Youth, Inc, Burlington, WV
Burt Children's Center, San Francisco, CA
The Calabasas Academy, Calabasas, CA
California Crest Diagnostic and Treatment Center, El Cajon, CA
Cambridge House, Inc, Muncie, IN
Camelot Care Center, Kingston, TN
Camelot Care Center, Inc, Palatine, IL
Camphill Special Schools, Inc, Glenmore, PA
CaraMore Community, Chapel Hill, NC
Caravan House, Palo Alto, CA
Cardinal Treatment Center, Louisville, KY
Carmelite Home for Boys, Hammond, IN
Carmelite Home, Inc, Wauwatosa, WI
Carolina Youth Development Center, North Charleston, SC
Maude Carpenter's Childrens Home, Wichita, KS
Walter P Carter Community Mental Health Center, Baltimore, MD
Cary Home for Children, Lafayette, IN
Casa de Luz, Santa Rosa, CA
Casa Victoria I, Whittier, CA
Cascade Child Care Center, Redmond, OR
Castle School, Inc, Cambridge, MA
Catholic Charities Group Home, Binghamton, NY
Catholic Children's Home, Alton, IL
Catholic Community Services Northwest, Bellingham, WA
Cedar Grove Residential Center, Cedar Grove, NJ
Cedar Hills Hospital, Portland, OR
Cedar House, Lewiston, ID
Cedar Ridge Children's Home and School, Williamsport, MD
Cedu School, Running Springs, CA
Center for Therapeutic Learning Annex, Loveland, CO
Center of Progressive Education, Newtown, CT
Centerville Group Home, Chesapeake, VA
Central Kentucky Re-Ed Center, Lexington, KY
Central Louisiana State Hospital, Adolescent Service, Pineville, LA
Central Oklahoma Community Mental Health Center, Norman, OK
Central State Hospital, Petersburg, VA
Chaddock, Quincy, IL
Challenge Group Home, Eagle, ID
Chamberlain's Children's Center, Inc, Hollister, CA
Charlee Family Care, Inc, Tucson, AZ
Charter Colonial Institute, Newport News, VA
Cherry Hospital, Children and Youth Unit, Goldsboro, NC
Chestnut Lodge Hospital, Rockville, MD
Chicago-Read Mental Health Center, Chicago, IL
Child and Family Services, Inc, Knoxville, TN
Child Center of Our Lady, St Louis, MO
Child Study and Treatment Center, Tacoma, WA
Children and Adolescent Treatment Center, Jamestown, ND
The Children's Campus, Mishawaka, IN
Children's Emergency Shelter, Cartersville, GA
Children's Farm Home, Corvallis, OR
Children's Garden, San Rafael, CA
The Children's Home, Cincinnati, OH
The Children's Home of Burlington County, Mount Holly, NJ
Children's Home of Cedar Rapids, Cedar Rapids, IA
Children's Home of Kingston, Kingston, NY
Children's Home of Stockton, Stockton, CA
Childrens Home Society, Sioux Falls, SD
The Children's Residence, Hampton, VA
Children's Study Home, Springfield, MA
Children's Treatment Service, Louisville, KY
Children's Village, Dobbs Ferry, NY
Christian Haven Homes, Inc, Wheatfield, IN
Church of God Home for Children, Sevierville, TN
Church of God Home for Children, Mauldin, SC
The City, Inc—Group Home, Minneapolis, MN
Laurent Clerc Group Home, New York, NY
Colon Road Home, Sanford, NC
Colonial Hills Hospital, San Antonio, TX
Colorado Boys Ranch Foundation, La Junta, CO
Colorado Christian Home, Denver, CO
Community Attention Residential Care System, Charlottesville, VA
Community Treatment Complex, Worcester, MA

Rawhide, Inc, New London, WI
Tom Ray Youth Residential Treatment Center, Charlotte, NC
RCA Evaluation and Treatment Center, Cranston, RI
Reed Academy, Framingham, MA
Re-Ed Treatment Program, Louisville, KY
Regional Institute for Children & Adolescents—Rockville, Rockville, MD
Regional Institute for Children and Adolescents—Cheltenham, Cheltenham, MD
Residential Center for Youth, Inc, Pittsburg, KS
Residential Youth Services, Inc, Alexandria, VA
Ridgeview Institute, Smyrna, GA
River's Bend Farm School, Stanley, VA
Riverside Psychiatric Hospital, Portland, OR
Riverview Residential Treatment Facilities, Lowell, MI
Riverwood Center, Prescott, WI
FD Roosevelt Wilderness Camp—Outdoor Therapeutic Program, Warm Springs, GA
Rosemont Center, Columbus, OH
Rosemont School, Inc, Portland, OR
Rumford Group Home, Inc, Rumford, ME
Rutherford County Youth Services, Inc—North House, Rutherfordton, NC
Ryther Child Center, Seattle, WA
St Aemilian, Inc, Milwaukee, WI
St Aloysius Home, Greenville, RI
St Aloysius Treatment Center, Cincinnati, OH
St Andre Group Home, Lewiston, ME
St Ann's Home, Inc, Methuen, MA
St Anne Institute, Albany, NY
St Anthony Villa, Toledo, OH
St Bernard Group Homes, Meraux, LA
St Catherine's Center for Children, Albany, NY
St Charles, Inc, Milwaukee, WI
St Cloud Children's Home, St Cloud, MN
St Elizabeth's Hospital—Division of Children and Adolescent Services, Washington, DC
The St Francis Boys' Homes, Salina, KS
St Francis Hospital, Waterloo, IA
St Joseph's Children's Home, Torrington, WY
St John's Home, Painesville, OH
St John's Home for Children, Wheeling, WV
St Joseph Mercy Hospital, Mason City, IA
St Joseph Orphanage—Altercrest, Cincinnati, OH
St Joseph Orphanage—St Joseph Villa, Cincinnati, OH
St Joseph Youth Center/John A Matzner School, Dallas, TX
St Joseph's Cardendelet Child Center, Chicago, IL
St Joseph's Villa, Rochester, NY
St Joseph's Home for Boys, St Louis, MO
St Joseph's Villa, Richmond, VA
St Mary's Family and Children Services, Syossett, NY
St Mary's Infant Home, Norfold, VA
St Mary's Campus School, North Providence, RI
St Mary's Home for Boys, Beaverton, OR
St Rose Residence, Milwaukee, WI
St Vincent Home, St Louis, MO
St Vincent—Sarah Fisher Center, Farmington Hills, MI
St Vincent's Center—Child and Family Care, Timonium, MD
St Vincent's Home, Fall River, MA
Salem Children's Home, Flanagan, IL
The Salvation Army Booth Brown House Services, St Paul, MN
The Salvation Army Residence for Children, St Louis, MO
The Salvation Army Residential Treatment Facilities For Children And Youth, Honolulu, HI
Salvation Army White Shield Center, Portland, OR
San Antonio Children's Center, San Antonio, TX
San Diego Center for Children, San Diego, CA
San Diego Youth Involvement Program, San Diego, CA
San Pablo Residential Treatment School, Phoenix, AZ
Sanctuary, Inc, Guam Main Facility, GU
Sanford Society, Inc, Oakland, CA
Savio House, Denver, CO
Jeanine Schultz Memorial School, Park Ridge, IL
Scott Center, Bloomington, IL
Seattle Childrens Home, Seattle, WA
Second Circle, Yellow Springs, OH
Secret Harbor School, Anacortes, WA
Seneca Center, Oakland, CA
Shadow Mountain Institute, Tulsa, OK
Sonia Shankman Orthogenic School, Chicago, IL
Shelter for Women, Inc—Gray Lodge, Hartford, CT

Shelter Services of Carlton County, Inc, Cloquet, MN
Anne Elizabeth Shepherd Home, Columbus, GA
Sheridan House, Ft Lauderdale, FL
Sheriffs Youth Programs, Austin, MN
Silver Springs, Plymouth Meeting, PA
Anne Sippi Clinic, Los Angeles, CA
Sky Ranch for Boys, Sky Ranch, SD
Sleighton School, Lima, PA
Smallwood Children's Center, Chattanooga, TN
Ellen Hines Smith Girls' Home, Spartanburg, SC
Sojourn, Mobile, AL
Solstice Adolescent Program, Rowley, MA
Soma House, Stevens Point, WI
Somerset Hills School, Warren, NJ
South Coast Children's Society, Costa Mesa, CA
South Dakota Human Services Center, Yankton, SD
South Forty Ranch, Summit City, CA
Southeast Louisiana Hospital, Mandeville, LA
Southeastern Mental Health Center, Sioux Falls, SD
Southern Home Services, Philadelphia, PA
Southern Oregon Adolescent Study and Treatment Center, Grants Pass, OR
Southern Oregon Child Study and Treatment Center, Ashland, OR
Southern Pines, Charleston, SC
Southwestern State Hospital, Marion, VA
Southwestern State Hospital—Child and Adolescent Unit, Thomasville, GA
Southwood Psychiatric Residential Treatment Center, South Bay, Chula Vista, CA
SPARC House, Lynchburg, VA
Spaulding Youth Center, Tilton, NH
Maurice Spear Campus, Adrian, MI
Specialized Youth Services, Charlotte, NC
The Spofford Home, Kansas City, MO
Springwood Psychiatric Hospital, Leesburg, VA
The Spurwink School, Portland, ME
Spurwink School II, North Providence, RI
Stepping Stone, Inc, Fairmont, WV
Ann Storck Center, Inc., Ft Lauderdale, FL
Summit School, Manchester, CT
Sun Porch Group Home, Palo Alto, CA
Sunbeam Family Services, Inc, Oklahoma City, OK
Sunburst Youth Homes, Neillsville, WI
Sunny Hills Children's Services, San Anselmo, CA
Sunny Ridge Family Center, Wheaton, IL
Sunrise Group Home, Kenansville, NC
Sweetser Childrens Home, Saco, ME
The Sycamores, Altadena, CA
Syntaxis, Inc, Gahanna, OH
Syracuse Youth Development Center, Syracuse, NY
Jim Taliaferro Community Mental Health Center, Lawton, OK
Tara Hall Home for Boys, Georgetown, SC
Taylor Home, Racine, WI
Teen Acres, Inc, Sterling, CO
Teens World Group Home, Inc, Los Angeles, CA
Teipner Treatment Homes, Fort Atkinson, WI
Terrell State Hospital, Child/Adolescent Unit, Terrell, TX
Terry Children's Psychiatric Center, New Castle, DE
Therapeutic Services Agency, Pine City, MN
Thompson Children's Home, Charlotte, NC
Thoreau House, Madison, WI
Thresholds, Chicago, IL
Timber Ridge, Winchester, VA
Topeka State Hospital—Capital City Schools, Topeka, KS
Touchstone Community, Inc—Arizona Boys Community, Phoenix, AZ
Towering Pines Center, Slidell, LA
Toyon Mesa School, Inc #1, Paradise, CA
Transitional Living Community for Girls, St Joseph, MO
The Treasure Cove, Atwater, CA
Triad Homes for Autistic Individuals, Inc, High Point, NC
Trinity Regional Hospital, Fort Dodge, IA
Trinity School for Children, Ukiah, CA
Tri-Wil, Inc—Porta Cras School, Greenpond, AL
True to Life Counseling and Company, Sebastopol, CA
TRY Group Home, Inc, Two Rivers, WI
Try House Center, Marshall, MN
Tumbleweed, Phoenix, AZ
Turning Point, Salisbury, NC
Ulrey Homes, Inc, San Lorenzo, CA
United Methodist Childrens Home, Worthington, OH

United Methodist Family Services of Virginia, Richmond, VA
United Methodist Youth Home, Evansville, IN
The University School, Bridgeport, CT
Upper Valley Charitable Corp—Clear Creek Farm, Piqua, OH
Utah State Hospital, Youth Center, Provo, UT
Uwharrie Homes, Inc, Albermarle, NC
Valley View School, North Brookfield, MA
Valleyhead, Lenox, MA
Valley-Lake Boys Home, Inc, Breckenridge, MN
Vanderheyden Hall, Wynantskill, NY
Veterans of Foreign Wars National Home, Eaton Rapids, MI
Victor Residential Center, Inc—dba Regional Adolescent Treatment Program, Stockton, CA
Victor Residential Center—Willow Creek Residential Center, Santa Rosa, CA
Village of St. Joseph, Atlanta, GA
The Villages of Indiana, Inc, Bloomington, IN
Virginia Home for Boys, Richmond, VA
Virginia Treatment Center, Richmond, VA
Vista Del Mar Child Care Service, Los Angeles, CA
Vista Maria, Dearborn Heights, MI
Vista Sandia Hospital, Albuquerque, NM
Vitam Center, Inc, Norwalk, CT
Waco Center for Youth, Waco, TX
WAITT Houses, Inc, Schenectady, NY
Wake County Juvenile Treatment System, Raleigh, NC
Walden Environment, Lancaster, CA
The Walker Home and School, Needham, MA
Cleo Wallace Center, Broomfield, CO
Wareham Key, Family Reunification Program, Wareham, MA
Warren G Murray Developmental Center, Centralia, IL
Waterford County School, Inc, Quaker Hill, CT
Wateroak Specialty Hospital Treatment Program, Tallahassee, FL
Waverly Children's Home, Portland, OR
Jane Wayland Center, Phoenix, AZ
We Care, San Jose, CA
Webster-Cantrell Hall, Decatur, IL
West GA Youth Council, Inc, LaGrange, GA
West River Children's Center, Rapid City, SD
West Virgina Children's Home—Dept of Human Services, Elkins, WV
Westbridge, Phoenix, AZ
Western Correctional Center, Morganton, NC
Westlake Academy, Westboro, MA
Wheeler Clinic, Plainville, CT
The Whitaker School, Butner, NC
White's, Wabash, IN
Whittier Group Home, Columbus, OH
Wichita Children's Home, Inc, Wichita, KS
WICS Residence for Girls, Lincoln, NE
Wide Horizons Ranch, Inc, Oak Run, CA
Willmar Regional Treatment Center, Willmar, MN
Willowglen, Milwaukee, WI
The Constance Bultman Wilson Center, Faribault, MN
Windjammer Group Home, New Bern, NC
Wolf River Group Home, White Lake, WI
Wood County Child Care Center, Parkersburg, WV
Woodland Hills, Duluth, MN
The Woods Schools, Langhorne, PA
Woodstock School, Hartford, CT
Wordsworth Academy, Fort Washington, PA
Wreath House, Middleton, MA
Wright Direction Home, Waverly, MN
Wright School, Durham, NC
Wyandotte House, Corydon, IN
Wyndham Lawn Home for Children, Lockport, NY
Wyoming Boys School, Worland, WY
Wyoming Youth Treatment Center, Casper, WY
Yellowstone Treatment Center, Billings, MT
YMCA Oz North Coast, Carlsbad, CA
YMCA Youth & Family Counseling Center, Redding, CA
York Place, York, SC
Young Acres, Peoria, AZ
Richard H Young Memorial Hospital, Omaha, NE
Youth Adventures, Inc, Oregon City, OR
Youth Alternatives, Inc, San Antonio, TX
Youth and Family Services, Omaha, NE
Youth Care Center, Evansville, IN
Youth Emergency Shelter, Inc, Morristown, TN
Youth Evaluation and Treatment Centers, Phoenix, AZ
Youth Home, Little Rock, AR
Youth Homes, Walnut Creek, CA

Youth House of Ouachita, Inc, West Monroe, LA
Youth in Need, St Charles, MO
Youth Rehabilitation Camps—Nokomis, Pruden-
ville, MI
Youth Residential Treatment Center, Corpus
Christi, TX
Youth Resources, Inc, Pilgrim Center, Braintree,
MA
Youth Service Bureau, Muncie, IN
YWCA Try Angle House, Nashville, TN

HEARING IMPAIRMENT/ DEAFNESS

American School for the Deaf, Paces Program,
West Hartford, CT
The Bancroft School, Haddonfield, NJ
Behavior Research Institute, Inc, Providence, RI
Benhaven, East Haven, CT
Bradley Hospital, East Providence, RI
Brehm Preparatory School, Carbondale, IL
The Brown Schools, Austin, TX
Buckeye Boys Ranch, Inc, Grove City, OH
Carobell Children's Home, Inc, Jacksonville, NC
Cascade Child Care Center, Redmond, OR
Catholic Children's Home, Alton, IL
Central Louisiana State Hospital, Adolescent Ser-
vice, Pineville, LA
Children and Adolescent Treatment Center,
Jamestown, ND
The Children's Campus, Mishawaka, IN
Children's Home of Cedar Rapids, Cedar Rapids,
IA
Laurent Clerc Group Home, New York, NY
Delta Treatment Centers of Indiana, Inc, Bloom-
ington, IN
Eastern State School and Hospital, Trevose, PA
Jennie Edmundson Memorial Hospital, Council
Bluffs, IA
Florence Crittenton Home, Sioux City, IA
Gerard of Minnesota, Austin, MN
Grafton School, Berryville, VA
Wil Lou Gray Opportunity School, West Colum-
bia, SC
Mary Greeley Medical Center, Ames, IA
Group Foster Homes, Inc, Redding, CA
The Charles Hayden Goodwill School, Dorches-
ter, MA
Hillcrest Educational Centers, Inc, Lenox, MA
Hillside Children's Center, Rochester, NY
Hope Haven, Inc, Rock Valley, IA
Houston County Group Home, LaCrescent,
LaCrescent, MN
HSA Cumberland Hospital, Fayetteville, NC
Indiana United Methodist Children's Home, Inc.,
Lebanon, IN
Jamestown, Stillwater, MN
Kaleidoscope, Bloomington, IL
Lakeside Child & Family Center, Inc, Milwaukee,
WI
Jane Lamb Health Center, Clinton, IA
Las Vegas Medical Center—Adolescent Unit, Las
Vegas, NM
Linnhaven, Inc, Marion, IA
Mainstream Living, Inc, Ames, IA
Manor Foundation, Jonesville, MI
Maxey Training School, Whitmore Lake, MI
McDowell Youth Homes, Inc, Soquel, CA
The Methodist Home of Kentucky, Inc, Ver-
sailles, KY
The Methodist Home of New Orleans, New Or-
leans, LA
Mid-South Hospital, Memphis, TN
Corine Morris Community Care Home, Colum-
bia, SC
Mount St Vincent's Home, Denver, CO
Odyssey Harbor, Inc, Keene, TX
Oesterlen Services for Youth, Springfield, OH
Our Lady of Victory Infant Home, Lackawanna,
NY
Tom Ray Youth Residential Treatment Center,
Charlotte, NC
St Francis Hospital, Waterloo, IA
St Joseph Mercy Hospital, Mason City, IA
St Vincent Home, St Louis, MO
Shelter Services of Carlton County, Inc, Cloquet,
MN
South Coast Children's Society, Costa Mesa, CA
Southeastern Mental Health Center, Sioux Falls,
SD
Southern Home Services, Philadelphia, PA
Southern Oregon Child Study and Treatment
Center, Ashland, OR
Spaulding Youth Center, Tilton, NH
Specialized Youth Services, Charlotte, NC
Ann Storck Center, Inc, Ft Lauderdale, FL
Trinity Regional Hospital, Fort Dodge, IA

United Methodist Youth Home, Evansville, IN
Upper Valley Charitable Corp—Clear Creek
Farm, Piqua, OH
Virginia Treatment Center, Richmond, VA
Cleo Wallace Center, Broomfield, CO
We Care, San Jose, CA
The Constance Bultman Wilson Center, Fari-
bault, MN
The Woods Schools, Langhorne, PA
Youth Emergency Shelter, Inc, Morristown, TN

LEARNING DISABILITIES

Abbott House, Mitchell, SD
ABCS Little Canyon School, Phoenix, AZ
Advocate Group Homes, Riverside, CA
Alaska Children's Services, Inc, Anchorage, AK
Alexander Children's Center 36, Charlotte, NC
Allen Acres, Lima, OH
Allendale, Lake Villa, IL
Alpha House Youth Care, Inc, Menomonie, WI
Alpha Omega, Littleton, MA
Alternative Homes, Inc, St Paul, MN
Alternative House, Vienna, VA
Anchor I, Martinsville, VA
Paul Anderson Youth Home, Inc, Vidalia, GA
The Anderson School, Staatsburg, NY
Andrus Children's Home, Yonkers, NY
Angel Guardian Home—McAuley Residence,
Brooklyn, NY
Apostolic Christian Childrens Home, Leo, IN
Arbor Heights Center, Ann Arbor, MI
Arden Shore, Highland Park, IL
Argus Community, Inc, Bronx, NY
Arizona State Hospital—Child and Adolescent
Treatment Unit, Phoenix, AZ
The ARK, Jackson, MS
Arrowhead Ranch, Coal Valley, IL
Ashtabula County Residential Treatment Center,
Ashtabula, OH
The Astor Home for Children, Rhinebeck, NY
Attleboro Youth Shelter, Attleboro, MA
Baby Fold Residential Treatment Center, Nor-
mal, IL
The Baird Center, Plymouth, MA
Baird Children's Center, Burlington, VT
Baker Hall, Lackawanna, NY
The Bancroft School, Haddonfield, NJ
Baptist Children's Home and Family Ministries,
Valparaiso, IN
Baptist Children's Home at San Antonio, San
Antonio, TX
Baptist Children's Home, Inc, Carmi, IL
Baptist Home for Children, Bethesda, MD
Barboursville School, Barboursville, WV
Bar-None Residential Treatment Services, Anoka,
MN
Bashor Home of the United Methodist Church,
Inc, Goshen, IN
Behavior Research Institute, Inc, Providence, RI
Bella Vida Group Home, Fresno, CA
Bellefaire Residential Treatment Facility, Cleve-
land, OH
Benhaven, East Haven, CT
Bennington School, Inc, Bennington, VT
Berkeley Academy, Berkeley, CA
Berkshire Learning Center, Pittsfield, MA
Bethany Home, Inc, Moline, IL
Bethel Bible Village, Hixson, TN
Bethesda PsycHealth System, Denver, CO
Bethlehem Children's Center, New Orleans, LA
Bexar County MHMR Center—Residential Pro-
gram, San Antonio, TX
Black Hills Special Services—Northern Hills
Youth Services, Spearfish, SD
Blount County Children's Home, Maryville, TN
Blueberry Treatment Center, Brooklyn, NY
Boselli Residential Services, Inc, Lemon Grove,
CA
The Boyd School, Green Pond, AL
Boys and Girls Aid Society of San Diego—Cot-
tonwood Center, El Cajon, CA
Boys Attention Home, Charlottesville, VA
Boy's Home, Inc, Covington, VA
Boys Republic, Chino, CA
Boys' Village, Inc, Smithville, OH
Boy's Village Youth and Family Services, Inc,
Milford, CT
Bradley Hospital, East Providence, RI
Brandon School, Natick, MA
Brattleboro Retreat, Brattleboro, VT
Braun Programs, Inc., Braun Place, San Rafael,
CA
Brehm Preparatory School, Carbondale, IL
Brewer-Porch Childrens Center, University, AL
The Bridge, San Diego, CA
Bridgeport Academy, Bridgeport, CT

Bridlewood Group Home, Intensive Residential
Program, Charlotte, NC
Arthur Brisbane Child Treatment Center, Far-
mingdale, NJ
Brooke-Hancock Group Home, Inc, Newell, WV
Brookland Plantation Home for Boys, Oran-
geburg, SC
The Brown Schools, Austin, TX
Buckeye Boys Ranch, Inc, Grove City, OH
Buckner Children's Services, Amarillo, TX
Buffalo Youth Development Center, Buffalo, NY
Burlington United Methodist Home for Children
and Youth, Inc, Burlington, WV
The Calabasas Academy, Calabasas, CA
California Crest Diagnostic and Treatment Cen-
ter, El Cajon, CA
Cambridge House, Inc, Muncie, IN
Caravan House, Palo Alto, CA
Carmelite Home for Boys, Hammond, IN
Carmelite Home, Inc, Wauwatosa, WI
Casa de Luz, Santa Rosa, CA
Casa Victoria I, Whittier, CA
Cascade Child Care Center, Redmond, OR
Castle School, Inc, Cambridge, MA
Catholic Charities Group Home, Binghamton,
NY
Catholic Children's Home, Alton, IL
Catholic Community Services Northwest, Belling-
ham, WA
Cedar Grove Residential Center, Cedar Grove,
NJ
Cedar Ridge Children's Home and School, Wil-
liamsport, MD
Center for Therapeutic Learning Annex, Love-
land, CO
Center of Progressive Education, Newtown, CT
Centerville Group Home, Chesapeake, VA
Central Kentucky Re-Ed Center, Lexington, KY
Central Louisiana State Hospital, Adolescent Ser-
vice, Pineville, LA
Chaddock, Quincy, IL
Chamberlain's Children's Center, Inc, Hollister,
CA
Charlee Family Care, Inc, Tucson, AZ
Chestnut Lodge Hospital, Rockville, MD
Children and Adolescent Treatment Center,
Jamestown, ND
The Children's Campus, Mishawaka, IN
Children's Emergency Shelter, Cartersville, GA
Children's Farm Home, Corvallis, OR
Children's Garden, San Rafael, CA
The Children's Home of Burlington County,
Mount Holly, NJ
Children's Home of Kingston, Kingston, NY
Children's Home of Stockton, Stockton, CA
Childrens Home Society, Sioux Falls, SD
Children's Study Home, Springfield, MA
Children's Village, Dobbs Ferry, NY
Christian Haven Homes, Inc, Wheatfield, IN
Church of God Home for Children, Sevierville,
TN
Colorado Boys Ranch Foundation, La Junta, CO
Colorado Christian Home, Denver, CO
Community Attention Residential Care System,
Charlottesville, VA
Community-Based Children's Services, Beaufort,
SC
Connecticut Junior Republic, Litchfield, CT
Convalescent Hospital for Children, Rochester,
NY
Convenant Children's Home, Princeton, IL
Cool Springs of Logansport, Logansport, LA
Cornell Group Homes, Inc, Ladysmith, WI
Cornerstone, St Charles, MO
Coulee Youth Centers, Inc, LaCrosse, WI
Cranwood, East Freetown, MA
Crittenton Center, Kansas City, MO
Crockett Academy, Nashville, TN
Crossroad, Fort Wayne, IN
Cumberland House School, Nashville, TN
Cunningham Children's Home, Urbana, IL
Curtis School, Meriden, CT
Dade County Dept of Youth and Family Devel-
opment—Group Home Program, Miami, FL
Dakota Boys Ranch, Minot, ND
Daniel Memorial, Inc, Jacksonville, FL
Darden Hill Ranch School, Driftwood, TX
Davis-Stuart, Inc, Lewisburg, WV
Day Group Home, Inc, Buellton, CA
Delta Treatment Centers of Indiana, Inc, Bloom-
ington, IN
The Denver Children's Home, Denver, CO
The Devereaux Foundation, Rutland, MA
The Devereux Center, Scottsdale, AZ
The Devereux Center—Deerhaven, Chester, NJ
The Devereux Center in Georgia, Kennesaw, GA
The Devereux Foundation, Devon, PA

The Devereux Foundation, Santa Barbara, CA
The Devereux Foundation—Glenholm, Washington, CT
Diagnostic and Educational Services, Palm Desert, CA
Donovan House, Ballston Spa, NY
Eagleton School, Great Barrington, MA
East Texas Guidance Center, Tyler, TX
Eastern Virginia Center for Children and Youth, Norfolk, VA
Eastfield Ming Quong, Campbell, CA
Eckerd Wilderness Educational Camping Program, Benson, VT
Edgefield Lodge, Inc, Troutdale, OR
Edgewood Children's Center, St Louis, MO
Edgewood Children's Center, San Francisco, CA
Edison Park Home, Park Ridge, IL
Elk Hill Farm, Inc, Goochland, VA
Elmcrest Children's Center, Syracuse, NY
Elwyn Institute, Elwyn, PA
Epworth Village, Inc, York, NE
Equinox Adolescent Treatment Center, Auburn, CA
Ethan House I, Green Bay, WI
Ethan House II, Green Bay, WI
Eufaula Adolescent Adjustment Center, Eufaula, AL
Evangelical Children's Home, Kansas City, MO
Evangelical Children's Home, St Louis, MO
Fair Oaks Hospital, Summit, NJ
Fair Play Wilderness Camp School, Westminster, SC
Fairmont Group Home, Fresno, CA
Fairway, Mobile, AL
Family and Children's Center, La Crosse, WI
Family Life Center, Petaluma, CA
Family Solutions, El Toro, CA
First Light Group Home, Inc, Beloit, WI
Five Acres, Altadena, CA
Florence Crittenton Services, San Francisco, CA
Foothills Youth Services, Inc, Johnstown, NY
Forest Heights Lodge, Evergreen, CO
Juliette Fowler Homes, Dallas, TX
Franklin Village, Grove City, OH
Freeport West Treatment Group Home, Minneapolis, MN
Fresno Treatment Center, Fresno, CA
Friends of Youth, Renton, WA
Friendship House, Minneapolis, MN
Full Circle Sonoma, Sebastopol, CA
Galloway Boys Ranch, Wahkon, MN
Gaston Family Home, Oakland, CA
Gateway Group Home, Excelsior, MN
Gateway Ranch, Auburn, CA
Gateway United Methodist Youth Center, Williamsville, NY
General Protestant Children's Home, St Louis, MO
George Junior Republic, Freeville, NY
Gerard of Iowa, Mason City, IA
Gerard of Minnesota, Austin, MN
The Germaine Lawrence School, Arlington, MA
Gibault School for Boys, Terre Haute, IN
Good News School, Inc, Boonville, CA
Good Samaritan Boys Ranch, Brighton, MO
Good Samaritan Homes, Sacramento, CA
Grace Children's Home, Henderson, NE
Grafton School, Berryville, VA
Grande Ronde Child Center, La Grande, OR
Grandview Children's Ranch, Inc, Angwin, CA
Grant County Residential Treatment Center, Marion, IN
Wil Lou Gray Opportunity School, West Columbia, SC
Green Chimneys Children's Services, Inc, Brewster, NY
The Griffith Center, Golden, CO
Group Foster Homes, Inc, Redding, CA
Grove School, Inc, Madison, CT
Gulf Coast Regional Mental Health Mental Retardation Center, Galveston, TX
Edward Hall of Guardian Angel Home, Peoria, IL
William S Hall Psychiatric Institute, Columbia, SC
Hall-Brooke Foundation, Westport, CT
Hamilton Centers YSB, Arcadia Home, Arcadia, IN
Hamilton Centers YSB—Cherry St Home, Noblesville, IN
Hamilton Centers YSB—Regional Shelter Home, Noblesville, IN
Janie Hammit Children's Home, Bristol, VA
Harambee House, San Diego, CA
Harbor House, Annandale, VA
The Harbor Schools, Inc, Newburyport, MA

Harbor Shelter & Counseling Center, Inc, Stillwater, MN
Harlem Community Residential Home, New York, NY
Harmony Hill School, Inc, Chepachet, RI
Hawthorn Childrens Psychiatric Hospital, St Louis, MO
Hawthorne Cedar Knolls School, Hawthorne, NY
The Charles Hayden Goodwill School, Dorchester, MA
HCA Grant Center Hospital, Miami, FL
Hickory House, Mobile, AL
The High Frontier, Inc, Fort Davis, TX
High Pointe, Oklahoma City, OK
High Valley, Clinton Corners, NY
Highland Heights, New Haven, CT
Highland Hospital, Asheville, NC
Timothy Hill Children's Ranch, Riverhead, NY
Hillcrest Educational Centers, Inc, Lenox, MA
Hillcrest Family Services, Dubuque, IA
Hillhaven Center, Middletown, DE
Hillside Children's Center, Rochester, NY
Hillside, Inc, Atlanta, GA
Hogares, Inc, Albuquerque, NM
Holley Child Care and Development Center, Hackensack, NJ
Holston United Methodist Home, Inc, Greenville, TN
Home Away Centers, Inc., Minneapolis, MN
Hoosier Boys Town, Inc, Schererville, IN
Hope Center for Youth, Girls Wilderness Program, Groveton, TX
Hope Haven-Madonna Manor Residential Treatment Center, Marrero, LA
The House of the Good Shepherd, Utica, NY
Houston County Group Home, LaCrescent, MN
HSA Cumberland Hospital, Fayetteville, NC
Huckleberry House II, San Francisco, CA
Hughes Memorial Home for Children, Danville, VA
Indiana Children's Christian Home, Ladoga, IN
Indiana United Methodist Children's Home, Inc., Lebanon, IN
Institute for Family and Life Learning, Danvers, MA
Inter-Mountain Deaconess Home, Helena, MT
Interventions, SMA Residential School, Matteson, IL
Henry Ittleson Center for Child Research, Riverdale, NY
Stonewall Jackson School, Concord, NC
Jamestown, Stillwater, MN
Janis Youth Programs, Inc, Portland, OR
Jefferson House, Stockton, CA
John/Mar Group Home for Children, Inc, Compton, CA
Johnson County Youth Service Bureau, Inc, Franklin, IN
Jones Home of Children's Services, Cleveland, OH
Joy Home for Boys II, Greenwood, LA
Joyner Therapeutic Home, Whiteville, NC
Juneau Youth Services, Inc, Juneau, AK
Junior Helping Hand Home for Children, Austin, TX
Justice Resource Institute, The Butler Center, Westboro, MA
K-Bar-B Youth Ranch, Lacombe, LA
Kaleidoscope, Bloomington, IL
KAM, Inc—Reality Ranch, Palms, CA
Kaplan Foundation, Inc, Orangevale, CA
Robert F Kennedy Action Corps, Lancaster, MA
Robert F Kennedy Action Corps Adolescent Treatment Unit, Lancaster, MA
Robert F Kennedy Action Corps Children's Center, Lancaster, MA
Keystone Adolescent Program, Northeastern Family Institute, Newton, MA
The King's Ranch—Oneonta, Oneonta, AL
Kingsland Bay School, Ferrisburg, VT
Kiwanis Independence Program, Roanoke, VA
Klingberg Family Centers, New Britain, CT
The Kolburne School, Inc, New Marlborough, MA
Kona Association for Retarded Citizens dba Kona Krafts, Kealakekua, HI
Kuubba Extended Family, Modesto, CA
La Salle School, Inc, Albany, NY
La Selva, Palo Alto, CA
Lakeside Child & Family Center, Inc, Milwaukee, WI
Lakeside School, Peabody, MA
Larkin Home For Children, Elgin, IL
Las Vegas Medical Center—Adolescent Unit, Las Vegas, NM
The Latham School, Brewster, MA

Lawrence Hall School for Boys, Chicago, IL
Leake & Watts School, Yonkers, NY
Little Keswick School, Inc, Keswick, VA
Littleton Girls House, Secure Treatment Facility, Littleton, MA
Lutheran Family Services, Lighthouse, Burlington, NC
Lutheran Social Services, Epic Group Home, Eau Claire, WI
Lutheran Social Services of Illinois, Nachusa Lutheran Home, Nachusa, IL
Lutherbrook Children's Center, Addison, IL
Lutherwood Residential Treatment Center, Indianapolis, IN
MacDonell United Methodist Children's Services, Inc, Houma, LA
MacDougal Diagnostic Reception Center, Brooklyn, NY
Madison County Boys Residential Unit, Anderson, IN
Maison Marie Group Home, Metairie, LA
Manatee Palms, Residential Treatment Center, Bradenton, FL
Manor Foundation, Jonesville, MI
Maple Valley School, Wendell, MA
Maplehill Community, Plainfield, VT
Maria Group Home, St Paul, MN
Marian Hall Residential Care, St Louis, MO
Marillac Center for Children, Kansas City, MO
The Marsh Foundation Home and School, Van Wert, OH
Marshall I Pickens Hospital—The Children's Program, Greenville, SC
Martin Center, Inc, Milwaukee, WI
Maui Youth & Family Services Boys' Group Home, Makawao, HI
Maxey Training School, Whitmore Lake, MI
McCormick House, Chicago, IL
McDowell Youth Homes, Inc, Soquel, CA
Melville House, Inc, Melville, NY
The Menninger Foundation—Childrens Division, Topeka, KS
Mental Health Services of the Roanoke Valley—Children's Center, Roanoke, VA
Mercy Boys Home, Chicago, IL
Meridell Achievement Center, Inc—Westwood, Liberty Hill, TX
Meridell Achievement Center, Inc—Windridge, Austin, TX
The Methodist Home of Kentucky, Inc, Versailles, KY
The Methodist Home of New Orleans, New Orleans, LA
Miami Children's Hospital—Division of Psychiatry, Miami, FL
Mid-South Hospital, Memphis, TN
Mingus Mountain Estate—Residential & Educational Center for Girls, Prescott, AZ
Minnesota Learning Center, Brainerd, MN
Mission of the Immaculate Virgin, Staten Island, NY
Mississippi Children's Home Society and Family Service Association, Jackson, MS
Elizabeth Mitchell Children's Center, Little Rock, AR
Mobile Group Home, Mobile, AL
Corine Morris Community Care Home, Columbia, SC
Mount Saint John, Deep River, CT
Mount St Vincent's Home, Denver, CO
Mount Scott Institute, Washington, NJ
Mt Ridge Group Home, Cherryville, NC
Much More, Albuquerque, NM
Murphy-Harpst United Methodist Children and Family Services, Cedartown, GA
Nassau Children's House, Mineola, NY
Natividad Ranch, Salinas, CA
Nebraska Center for Children and Youth, Lincoln, NE
New Beginnings, Greer, SC
New Chance, Inc, Ben Lomond, CA
New Dominion School, Dillwyn, VA
The New Foundation, Phoenix, AZ
New Hope Treatment Centers, San Bernardino, CA
New Horizons, North Augusta, SC
New Life Homes—Snell Farm, Bath, NY
New Orleans Adolescent Hospital, New Orleans, LA
Niles Home for Children, Kansas City, MO
North Star, Minneapolis, MN
Northeast Parent and Child Society, Schenectady, NY
Northeastern Family Institute—North Crossing Adolescent and Family Treatment Program, Bedford, MA

Youth Rehabilitation Camps—Nokomis, Prudenville, MI
Youth Residential Treatment Center, Corpus Christi, TX
Youth Resources, Inc, Pilgrim Center, Braintree, MA
Youth Service Bureau, Muncie, IN

MENTAL DISABILITIES

Abbott House, Mitchell, SD
ABCS Little Canyon School, Phoenix, AZ
Adolescent Group Home, Danville, VA
Allendale, Lake Villa, IL
Alpha House Youth Care, Inc, Menomonie, WI
Alternative Homes, Inc, St Paul, MN
American Institute for Mental Studies, Vineland, NJ
The Anderson School, Staatsburg, NY
Apostolic Christian Childrens Home, Leo, IN
Archway, Inc, Leicester, MA
Arizona State Hospital—Child and Adolescent Treatment Unit, Phoenix, AZ
Arizona Youth Association, Inc, Phoenix, AZ
The ARK, Jackson, MS
The Astor Home for Children, Rhinebeck, NY
Augusta Mental Health Institute, Augusta, ME
Baby Fold Residential Treatment Center, Normal, IL
The Baird Center, Plymouth, MA
Baker Hall, Lackawanna, NY
The Bancroft School, Haddonfield, NJ
Baptist Children's Home, Inc, Carmi, IL
Baptist Home for Children, Bethesda, MD
Barboursville School, Barboursville, WV
Bar-None Residential Treatment Services, Anoka, MN
Behavior Research Institute, Inc, Providence, RI
Benhaven, East Haven, CT
Bennington School, Inc, Bennington, VT
Berkeley Academy, Berkeley, CA
Bernard St CCF, Spokane, WA
Bethany Home, Inc, Moline, IL
Bexar County MHMR Center—Residential Program, San Antonio, TX
Black Hills Special Services—Northern Hills Youth Services, Spearfish, SD
Blueberry Treatment Center, Brooklyn, NY
Boselli Residential Services, Inc, Lemon Grove, CA
Boys and Girls Aid Society of San Diego—Cottonwood Center, El Cajon, CA
Boys Republic, Chino, CA
Boys' Village, Inc, Smithville, OH
Bradley Hospital, East Providence, RI
Braun Programs, Inc., Braun Place, San Rafael, CA
Brehm Preparatory School, Carbondale, IL
Bremwood Lutheran Children's Home Society, Waverly, IA
Brewer-Porch Childrens Center, University, AL
Bridlewood Group Home, Intensive Residential Program, Charlotte, NC
Arthur Brisbane Child Treatment Center, Farmingdale, NJ
Broad Horizons of Ramona, Inc, Ramona, CA
The Brown Schools, Austin, TX
Buckeye Boys Ranch, Inc, Grove City, OH
Buffalo Youth Development Center, Buffalo, NY
The Calabasas Academy, Calabasas, CA
California Crest Diagnostic and Treatment Center, El Cajon, CA
Cambridge House, Inc, Muncie, IN
Camphill Special Schools, Inc, Glenmore, PA
CaraMore Community, Chapel Hill, NC
Caravan House, Palo Alto, CA
Carmelite Home for Boys, Hammond, IN
Carmelite Home, Inc, Wauwatosa, WI
Carobell Children's Home, Inc, Jacksonville, NC
Walter P Carter Community Mental Health Center, Baltimore, MD
Casa de Luz, Santa Rosa, CA
Catholic Charities Group Home, Binghamton, NY
Catholic Children's Home, Alton, IL
Catholic Community Services Northwest, Bellingham, WA
Central Kentucky Re-Ed Center, Lexington, KY
Central Louisiana State Hospital, Adolescent Service, Pineville, LA
Challenge Group Home, Eagle, ID
Chamberlain's Children's Center, Inc, Hollister, CA
Charlee Family Care, Inc, Tucson, AZ
Cherry Hospital, Children and Youth Unit, Goldsboro, NC
Child Study and Treatment Center, Tacoma, WA

Children and Adolescent Treatment Center, Jamestown, ND
The Children's Campus, Mishawaka, IN
Children's Home of Cedar Rapids, Cedar Rapids, IA
Children's Home of Kingston, Kingston, NY
Children's Home of Stockton, Stockton, CA
Childrens Home Society, Sioux Falls, SD
Children's Treatment Service, Louisville, KY
Children's Village, Dobbs Ferry, NY
Colorado Christian Home, Denver, CO
Comprehensive Mental Health, Pearl St Center, Tacoma, WA
Convalescent Hospital for Children, Rochester, NY
Crest View Hospital, Casper, WY
Crittenton Center, Kansas City, MO
Cunningham Children's Home, Urbana, IL
Dade County Dept of Youth and Family Development—Group Home Program, Miami, FL
Dakota Boys Ranch, Minot, ND
Darden Hill Ranch School, Driftwood, TX
Day Group Home, Inc, Buellton, CA
Daybreak Child and Adolescent Unit of MHMR of Southeast Texas, Beaumont, TX
Delta Treatment Centers of Indiana, Inc, Bloomington, IN
The Devereaux Foundation, Rutland, MA
The Devereux Center, Scottsdale, AZ
The Devereux Center in Georgia, Kennesaw, GA
The Devereux Foundation, Devon, PA
The Devereux Foundation, Santa Barbara, CA
Diagnostic and Educational Services, Palm Desert, CA
Dogwood Village, Memphis, TN
Drake House Group Home, Pleasant Hill, CA
Eagleton School, Great Barrington, MA
Eckerd Wilderness Educational Camping Program, Benson, VT
Edgewood Children's Center, St Louis, MO
Edgewood Children's Center, San Francisco, CA
Jennie Edmundson Memorial Hospital, Council Bluffs, IA
Educational Therapy Center, Edwardsville, IL
El Paso State Center, El Paso, TX
Elmcrest Children's Center, Syracuse, NY
Elwyn Institute, Elwyn, PA
Epworth Village, Inc, York, NE
Equinox Adolescent Treatment Center, Auburn, CA
Ethan House I, Green Bay, WI
Ethan House II, Green Bay, WI
Eufaula Adolescent Adjustment Center, Eufaula, AL
Evangelical Children's Home, Kansas City, MO
Fair Oaks Hospital, Summit, NJ
Family and Children's Center, La Crosse, WI
Family Life Center, Petaluma, CA
Family Solutions, El Toro, CA
First Light Group Home, Inc, Beloit, WI
Florence Crittenton Home, Sioux City, IA
Forest Heights Lodge, Evergreen, CO
Forest Ridge Community Youth Center, Wallingford, IA
Fresno Treatment Center, Fresno, CA
Full Circle Sonoma, Sebastopol, CA
Galloway Boys Ranch, Wahkon, MN
Gaston Family Home, Oakland, CA
Gateway Ranch, Auburn, CA
Gerard of Iowa, Mason City, IA
Gerard of Minnesota, Austin, MN
Good Samaritan Boys Ranch, Brighton, MO
Grafton School, Berryville, VA
Grandview Children's Ranch, Inc, Angwin, CA
Mary Greeley Medical Center, Ames, IA
Green Chimneys Children's Services, Inc, Brewster, NY
Greenhouse, Durham, NC
Greentree Girls Program, Brockton, MA
Group Foster Homes, Inc, Redding, CA
Guildord Residential Treatment, Greensboro, NC
Gulf Coast Regional Mental Health Mental Retardation Center, Galveston, TX
Edward Hall of Guardian Angel Home, Peoria, IL
Hamilton Centers YSB, Arcadia Home, Arcadia, IN
Hamilton Centers YSB—Cherry St Home, Noblesville, IN
Hamilton Centers YSB—Regional Shelter Home, Noblesville, IN
Janie Hammit Children's Home, Bristol, VA
Harbor House, Annandale, VA
Hawthorn Childrens Psychiatric Hospital, St Louis, MO
Hawthorne Cedar Knolls School, Hawthorne, NY
HCA Grant Center Hospital, Miami, FL

Hickory House, Mobile, AL
Highland Hospital, Asheville, NC
Hillcrest Educational Centers, Inc, Lenox, MA
Hillcrest Family Services, Dubuque, IA
Hillhaven Center, Middletown, DE
Hillside, Inc, Atlanta, GA
Holley Child Care and Development Center, Hackensack, NJ
Holly Hill Hospital, Raleigh, NC
Hope for Youth, Inc, Bethpage, NY
Hope Haven, Inc, Rock Valley, IA
Hope Haven-Madonna Manor Residential Treatment Center, Marrero, LA
Houston County Group Home, LaCrescent, LaCrescent, MN
HSA Cumberland Hospital, Fayetteville, NC
Indiana United Methodist Children's Home, Inc., Lebanon, IN
Iowa Children's and Family Services, Des Moines, IA
Jamestown, Stillwater, MN
Junior Helping Hand Home for Children, Austin, TX
K-Bar-B Youth Ranch, Lacombe, LA
Kaleidoscope, Bloomington, IL
Kaplan Foundation, Inc, Orangevale, CA
Robert F Kennedy Action Corps, Lancaster, MA
Keystone Adolescent Program, Northeastern Family Institute, Newton, MA
The King's Daughters' School, Inc, Columbia, TN
Kiwanis Independence Program, Roanoke, VA
The Kolburne School, Inc, New Marlborough, MA
Kona Association for Retarded Citizens dba Kona Krafts, Kealakekua, HI
Kuubba Extended Family, Modesto, CA
La Selva, Palo Alto, CA
Lake Grove at Durham, Durham, CT
Lakeside Child & Family Center, Inc, Milwaukee, WI
Lakin Hospital—Adolescent Services, Lakin, WV
Jane Lamb Health Center, Clinton, IA
Laredo State Center, Laredo, TX
Larkin Home For Children, Elgin, IL
Larned State Hospital, Larned, KS
Las Vegas Medical Center—Adolescent Unit, Las Vegas, NM
The Latham School, Brewster, MA
Lawrence Hall School for Boys, Chicago, IL
Linnhaven, Inc, Marion, IA
Little Keswick School, Inc, Keswick, VA
Lutheran Social Services of Illinois, Nachusa Lutheran Home, Nachusa, IL
Lutherwood Residential Treatment Center, Indianapolis, IN
MacDougal Diagnostic Reception Center, Brooklyn, NY
Madonna Heights Services, Huntington, NY
Mainstream Living, Inc, Ames, IA
Manatee Palms, Residential Treatment Center, Bradenton, FL
Manor Foundation, Jonesville, MI
Marian Hall Residential Care, St Louis, MO
Maxey Training School, Whitmore Lake, MI
McCormick House, Chicago, IL
McDowell Youth Homes, Inc, Soquel, CA
McLean Hospital—Community Residential and Treatment Services, Belmont, MA
Mental Health Services of the Roanoke Valley—Children's Center, Roanoke, VA
The Methodist Home of Kentucky, Inc, Versailles, KY
The Methodist Home of New Orleans, New Orleans, LA
Miami Children's Hospital—Division of Psychiatry, Miami, FL
Mid-South Hospital, Memphis, TN
Minnesota Learning Center, Brainerd, MN
Mission of the Immaculate Virgin, Staten Island, NY
Frances Haddon Morgan Center, Bremerton, WA
Corine Morris Community Care Home, Columbia, SC
Mt Ridge Group Home, Cherryville, NC
New Beginnings, Greer, SC
The New Foundation, Phoenix, AZ
New Hope Treatment Centers, San Bernardino, CA
New Horizons, North Augusta, SC
New York State Division for Youth, Binghamton Community Urban Homes, Binghamton, NY
Niles Home for Children, Kansas City, MO
Northeastern Family Institute—North Crossing Adolescent and Family Treatment Program, Bedford, MA
Northern Tier Youth Services, Blossburg, PA

Northwood Children's Home, Duluth, MN
Nova, Inc, Kinston, NC
Oconomowoc Developmental Training Center, Inc, Oconomowoc, WI
Odd Fellow Rebekah Children's Home, Gilroy, CA
Odyssey Harbor, Inc, Keene, TX
Oesterlen Services for Youth, Springfield, OH
Ohio Center for Youth and Family Development, Pedro, OH
Orchard Place, Des Moines Children's Home, Des Moines, IA
Ottumwa Regional Health Center, Ottumwa, IA
Our Lady of Victory Infant Home, Lackawanna, NY
Outreach Broward—Solomon Center for Boys, Ft Lauderdale, FL
Outreach Broward—Solomon Center for Girls, Ft Lauderdale, FL
Ozanam Home for Boys, Inc, Kansas City, MO
Ozark Center Youth Residential Services, Joplin, MO
Park House Group Home, Merrill, WI
Parkview Homes I, II, & III, Seattle, WA
Parsons Child & Family Center, Albany, NY
The Pines Treatment Center, Portsmouth, VA
Pineview Homes, Inc, Evart, MI
Po'Ailani, Inc, Honolulu, HI
PORT of Crow Wing County, Inc, Brainerd, MN
Project Six, Van Nuys, CA
Rainbow Mental Health Facility, Kansas City, KS
Randolph Children's Home, Randolph, NY
Randolph County Mental Health Center, North House Residential Group Home, Asheboro, NC
Regional Institute for Children and Adolescents—Cheltenham, Cheltenham, MD
Ridgeview Institute, Smyrna, GA
River's Bend Farm School, Stanley, VA
Riverview Residential Treatment Facilities, Lowell, MI
Riverwood Center, Prescott, WI
FD Roosevelt Wilderness Camp—Outdoor Therapeutic Program, Warm Springs, GA
Ryther Child Center, Seattle, WA
St Aemilian, Inc, Milwaukee, WI
St Anthony Villa, Toledo, OH
St Francis Hospital, Waterloo, IA
St John's Child Development Center, Washington, DC
St Joseph Mercy Hospital, Mason City, IA
St Joseph Orphanage—Altercrest, Cincinnati, OH
St Joseph Orphanage—St Joseph Villa, Cincinnati, OH
St Joseph's Villa, Rochester, NY
St Joseph's Villa, Richmond, VA
St Mary's Family and Children Services, Syosett, NY
St Vincent—Sarah Fisher Center, Farmington Hills, MI
St Vincent's Center—Child and Family Care, Timonium, MD
Salem Children's Home, Flanagan, IL
Sanford Society, Inc, Oakland, CA
Jeanine Schultz Memorial School, Park Ridge, IL
Seattle Childrens Home, Seattle, WA
Secret Harbor School, Anacortes, WA
Seneca Center, Oakland, CA
Shadow Mountain Institute, Tulsa, OK
Shelter Services of Carlton County, Inc, Cloquet, MN
Sheriffs Youth Programs, Austin, MN
Anne Sippi Clinic, Los Angeles, CA
Sojourn, Mobile, AL
Soma House, Stevens Point, WI
Somerset Hills School, Warren, NJ
South Coast Children's Society, Costa Mesa, CA
South Dakota Human Services Center, Yankton, SD
Southeastern Mental Health Center, Sioux Falls, SD
Southern Home Services, Philadelphia, PA
Southern Oregon Child Study and Treatment Center, Ashland, OR
Southern Pines, Charleston, SC
Southwest Oklahoma Adolescent Addiction Rehabilitation Ranch, Inc, Lone Wolf, OK
Southwestern State Hospital, Marion, VA
Spaulding Youth Center, Tilton, NH
Specialized Youth Services, Charlotte, NC
The Spofford Home, Kansas City, MO
Springwood Psychiatric Institute, Leesburg, VA
The Spurwink School, Portland, ME
Ann Storck Center, Inc., Ft Lauderdale, FL
Sun Porch Group Home, Palo Alto, CA
Sunburst Youth Homes, Neillsville, WI

Sunny Hills Children's Services, San Anselmo, CA
Sunrise Group Home, Kenansville, NC
Sweetser Childrens Home, Saco, ME
The Sycamores, Altadena, CA
Syntaxis, Inc, Gahanna, OH
Syracuse Youth Development Center, Syracuse, NY
Taylor Home, Racine, WI
Terrell State Hospital, Child/Adolescent Unit, Terrell, TX
Terry Children's Psychiatric Center, New Castle, DE
Thoreau House, Madison, WI
Thresholds, Chicago, IL
Topeka State Hospital—Capital City Schools, Topeka, KS
Towering Pines Center, Slidell, LA
Toyon Mesa School, Inc #1, Paradise, CA
Transitional Living Community for Girls, St Joseph, MO
The Treasure Cove, Atwater, CA
Triad Homes for Autistic Individuals, Inc, High Point, NC
Trinity Regional Hospital, Fort Dodge, IA
Trinity School for Children, Ukiah, CA
Ulrey Homes, Inc, San Lorenzo, CA
United Methodist Childrens Home, Worthington, OH
United Methodist Youth Home, Evansville, IN
Valleyhead, Lenox, MA
Vanderheyden Hall, Wynantskill, NY
Victor Residential Center, Inc—dba Regional Adolescent Treatment Program, Stockton, CA
The Villages of Indiana, Inc, Bloomington, IN
Vista Sandia Hospital, Albuquerque, NM
Wake County Juvenile Treatment System, Raleigh, NC
Walden Environment, Lancaster, CA
Cleo Wallace Center, Broomfield, CO
Warren G Murray Developmental Center, Centralia, IL
Waterford County School, Inc, Quaker Hill, CT
Waverly Children's Home, Portland, OR
Jane Wayland Center, Phoenix, AZ
We Care, San Jose, CA
West River Children's Center, Rapid City, SD
Westlake Academy, Westboro, MA
WICS Residence for Girls, Lincoln, NE
Wide Horizons Ranch, Inc, Oak Run, CA
Willmar Regional Treatment Center, Willmar, MN
Willowglen, Milwaukee, WI
The Constance Bultman Wilson Center, Faribault, MN
The Woods Schools, Langhorne, PA
Wright Direction Home, Waverly, MN
York Place, York, SC
Richard H Young Memorial Hospital, Omaha, NE
Youth Adventures, Inc, Oregon City, OR
Youth Care Center, Evansville, IN
Youth Emergency Shelter, Morristown, TN
Youth Evaluation and Treatment Centers, Phoenix, AZ
Youth House of Ouachita, Inc, West Monroe, LA
Youth Rehabilitation Camps—Nokomis, Prudenville, MI
Youth Resources, Inc, Pilgrim Center, Braintree, MA
Youth Service Bureau, Muncie, IN

NEUROLOGICAL IMPAIRMENTS

ABCS Little Canyon School, Phoenix, AZ
Alexander Children's Center 36, Charlotte, NC
Alternative Homes, Inc, St Paul, MN
American Institute for Mental Studies, Vineland, NJ
The Anderson School, Staatsburg, NY
Andrus Children's Home, Yonkers, NY
Archway, Inc, Leicester, MA
Autism Teaching Home, Salt Lake City, UT
The Bancroft School, Haddonfield, NJ
Baptist Home for Children, Bethesda, MD
Bar-None Residential Treatment Services, Anoka, MN
Behavior Research Institute, Inc, Providence, RI
Bella Vida Group Home, Fresno, CA
Benhaven, East Haven, CT
Berkeley Academy, Berkeley, CA
Berkshire Learning Center, Pittsfield, MA
Boys Republic, Chino, CA
Bradley Hospital, East Providence, RI
Brehm Preparatory School, Carbondale, IL
Bridlewood Group Home, Intensive Residential Program, Charlotte, NC

Arthur Brisbane Child Treatment Center, Farmingdale, NJ
The Brown Schools, Austin, TX
Camphill Special Schools, Inc, Glenmore, PA
Carmelite Home for Boys, Hammond, IN
Carobell Children's Home, Inc, Jacksonville, NC
Catholic Children's Home, Alton, IL
Catholic Community Services Northwest, Bellingham, WA
Cedar Grove Residential Center, Cedar Grove, NJ
Central Kentucky Re-Ed Center, Lexington, KY
Central Louisiana State Hospital, Adolescent Service, Pineville, LA
Charlee Family Care, Inc, Tucson, AZ
Cherry Hospital, Children and Youth Unit, Goldsboro, NC
Children and Adolescent Treatment Center, Jamestown, ND
The Children's Campus, Mishawaka, IN
Children's Home of Stockton, Stockton, CA
Children's Village, Dobbs Ferry, NY
Colorado Christian Home, Denver, CO
Convalescent Hospital for Children, Rochester, NY
Darden Hill Ranch School, Driftwood, TX
The Denver Children's Home, Denver, CO
The Devereaux Foundation, Rutland, MA
The Devereux Foundation, Santa Barbara, CA
Diagnostic and Educational Services, Palm Desert, CA
Eastfield Ming Quong, Campbell, CA
Edgewood Children's Center, St Louis, MO
Epworth Village, Inc, York, NE
Ethan House I, Green Bay, WI
Ethan House II, Green Bay, WI
Floberg Center for Children, Rockton, IL
Fresno Treatment Center, Fresno, CA
Galloway Boys Ranch, Wahkon, MN
Gateway Ranch, Auburn, CA
Gerard of Iowa, Mason City, IA
Gerard of Minnesota, Austin, MN
Grafton School, Berryville, VA
Green Chimneys Children's Services, Inc, Brewster, NY
Greenhouse, Durham, NC
Group Foster Homes, Inc, Redding, CA
Gulf Coast Regional Mental Health Mental Retardation Center, Galveston, TX
Edward Hall of Guardian Angel Home, Peoria, IL
Hawthorn Childrens Psychiatric Hospital, St Louis, MO
HCA Grant Center Hospital, Miami, FL
Hillcrest Educational Centers, Inc, Lenox, MA
Hillside Children's Center, Rochester, NY
Holley Child Care and Development Center, Hackensack, NJ
Houston County Group Home, LaCrescent, LaCrescent, MN
HSA Cumberland Hospital, Fayetteville, NC
Indiana United Methodist Children's Home, Inc., Lebanon, IN
Interventions, SMA Residential School, Matteson, IL
Henry Ittleson Center for Child Research, Riverdale, NY
Jamestown, Stillwater, MN
Junior Helping Hand Home for Children, Austin, TX
Kaleidoscope, Bloomington, IL
Robert F Kennedy Action Corps, Lancaster, MA
The Kolburne School, Inc, New Marlborough, MA
Lakeside Child & Family Center, Inc, Milwaukee, WI
Larkin Home For Children, Elgin, IL
Larned State Hospital, Larned, KS
Las Vegas Medical Center—Adolescent Unit, Las Vegas, NM
The Latham School, Brewster, MA
Linnhaven, Inc, Marion, IA
Little Keswick School, Inc, Keswick, VA
Lutheran Social Services of Illinois, Nachusa Lutheran Home, Nachusa, IL
Lutherbrook Children's Center, Addison, IL
Lutherwood Residential Treatment Center, Indianapolis, IN
Madonna Heights Services, Huntington, NY
Manatee Palms, Residential Treatment Center, Bradenton, FL
Marillac Center for Children, Kansas City, MO
Maxey Training School, Whitmore Lake, MI
McDowell Youth Homes, Inc, Soquel, CA
McLean Hospital—Community Residential and Treatment Services, Belmont, MA

Mental Health Services of the Roanoke Valley—Children's Center, Roanoke, VA
The Methodist Home of Kentucky, Inc, Versailles, KY
Miami Children's Hospital—Division of Psychiatry, Miami, FL
Mid-South Hospital, Memphis, TN
Mission of the Immaculate Virgin, Staten Island, NY
Corine Morris Community Care Home, Columbia, SC
Mount St Vincent's Home, Denver, CO
Mt Ridge Group Home, Cherryville, NC
New Hope Treatment Centers, San Bernardino, CA
Northern Nevada Child and Adolescence Services, Reno, NV
Northern Tier Youth Services, Blossburg, PA
Northside Community Mental Health Center, Inc, Tampa, FL
Northwood Children's Home, Duluth, MN
Oconomowoc Developmental Training Center, Inc, Oconomowoc, WI
Odd Fellow Rebekah Children's Home, Gilroy, CA
Odyssey Harbor, Inc, Keene, TX
Oesterlen Services for Youth, Springfield, OH
Ohio Center for Youth and Family Development, Pedro, OH
Orchard Place, Des Moines Children's Home, Des Moines, IA
Our Lady of Victory Infant Home, Lackawanna, NY
Ozanam Home for Boys, Inc, Kansas City, MO
Parkview Homes I, II, & III, Seattle, WA
Parry Center for Children, Portland, OR
Parsons Child & Family Center, Albany, NY
Pinellas Emergency Mental Health Services, Pinellas Park, FL
Pineview Homes, Inc, Evart, MI
Project Six, Van Nuys, CA
Prospect Learning Center, Summit, NJ
Randolph Children's Home, Randolph, NY
Tom Ray Youth Residential Treatment Center, Charlotte, NC
Reed Academy, Framingham, MA
Regional Institute for Children and Adolescents—Cheltenham, Cheltenham, MD
River's Bend Farm School, Stanley, VA
Riverside Psychiatric Hospital, Portland, OR
Riverview Residential Treatment Facilities, Lowell, MI
FD Roosevelt Wilderness Camp—Outdoor Therapeutic Program, Warm Springs, GA
St Anthony Villa, Toledo, OH
St John's Home, Painesville, OH
St Joseph's Cardendelet Child Center, Chicago, IL
St Rose Residence, Milwaukee, WI
St Vincent—Sarah Fisher Center, Farmington Hills, MI
St Vincent's Center—Child and Family Care, Timonium, MD
San Antonio Children's Center, San Antonio, TX
Seattle Childrens Home, Seattle, WA
Seneca Center, Oakland, CA
Shadow Mountain Institute, Tulsa, OK
Shelter Services of Carlton County, Inc, Cloquet, MN
Anne Sippi Clinic, Los Angeles, CA
Somerset Hills School, Warren, NJ
South Coast Children's Society, Costa Mesa, CA
South Dakota Human Services Center, Yankton, SD
Southern Home Services, Philadelphia, PA
Southern Pines, Charleston, SC
Spaulding Youth Center, Tilton, NH
Specialized Youth Services, Charlotte, NC
The Spurwink School, Portland, ME
Ann Storck Center, Inc., Ft Lauderdale, FL
Sunburst Youth Homes, Neillsville, WI
Sweetser Childrens Home, Saco, ME
The Sycamores, Altadena, CA
Syntaxis, Inc, Gahanna, OH
Taylor Home, Racine, WI
Terry Children's Psychiatric Center, New Castle, DE
The Treasure Cove, Atwater, CA
Triad Homes for Autistic Individuals, Inc, High Point, NC
Trinity School for Children, Ukiah, CA
Utah State Hospital, Youth Center, Provo, UT
Vanderheyden Hall, Wynantskill, NY
Wake County Juvenile Treatment System, Raleigh, NC
Cleo Wallace Center, Broomfield, CO
Jane Wayland Center, Phoenix, AZ

Webster-Cantrell Hall, Decatur, IL
West River Children's Center, Rapid City, SD
Westlake Academy, Westboro, MA
Wide Horizons Ranch, Inc, Oak Run, CA
Willowglen, Milwaukee, WI
The Constance Bultman Wilson Center, Faribault, MN
The Woods Schools, Langhorne, PA
York Place, York, SC
Richard H Young Memorial Hospital, Omaha, NE
Youth Emergency Shelter, Inc, Morristown, TN
Youth Evaluation and Treatment Centers, Phoenix, AZ
Youth House of Ouachita, Inc, West Monroe, LA
Youth Rehabilitation Camps—Nokomis, Prudenville, MI

PHYSICAL HANDICAPS

The Bancroft School, Haddonfield, NJ
Baptist Children's Home, Inc, Carmi, IL
Boys' Village, Inc, Smithville, OH
Bradley Hospital, East Providence, RI
Brehm Preparatory School, Carbondale, IL
The Brown Schools, Austin, TX
Carobell Children's Home, Inc, Jacksonville, NC
Cascade Child Care Center, Redmond, OR
Charlee Family Care, Inc, Tucson, AZ
The Children's Campus, Mishawaka, IN
Children's Home of Cedar Rapids, Cedar Rapids, IA
Convenant Children's Home, Princeton, IL
Jennie Edmundson Memorial Hospital, Council Bluffs, IA
El Paso State Center, El Paso, TX
Epworth Village, Inc, York, NE
Floberg Center for Children, Rockton, IL
Florence Crittenton Home, Sioux City, IA
Gerard of Iowa, Mason City, IA
Gerard of Minnesota, Austin, MN
Wil Lou Gray Opportunity School, West Columbia, SC
Mary Greeley Medical Center, Ames, IA
Group Foster Homes, Inc, Redding, CA
Hamilton Centers YSB, Arcadia Home, Arcadia, IN
Hamilton Centers YSB—Cherry St Home, Noblesville, IN
Holston United Methodist Home, Inc, Greenville, TN
Hope Haven, Inc, Rock Valley, IA
Houston County Group Home, LaCrescent, LaCrescent, MN
HSA Cumberland Hospital, Fayetteville, NC
Indiana United Methodist Children's Home, Inc., Lebanon, IN
Iowa Children's and Family Services, Des Moines, IA
Kaleidoscope, Bloomington, IL
Jane Lamb Health Center, Clinton, IA
Las Vegas Medical Center—Adolescent Unit, Las Vegas, NM
Linnhaven, Inc, Marion, IA
Lutherbrook Children's Center, Addison, IL
MacDougal Diagnostic Reception Center, Brooklyn, NY
Mainstream Living, Inc, Ames, IA
Manatee Palms, Residential Treatment Center, Bradenton, FL
Maxey Training School, Whitmore Lake, MI
McCormick House, Chicago, IL
McDowell Youth Homes, Inc, Soquel, CA
Mercy Health Center, Dubuque, IA
The Methodist Home of Kentucky, Inc, Versailles, KY
Miami Children's Hospital—Division of Psychiatry, Miami, FL
Mid-South Hospital, Memphis, TN
Mission of the Immaculate Virgin, Staten Island, NY
Corine Morris Community Care Home, Columbia, SC
New Beginnings, Greer, SC
Odyssey Harbor, Inc, Keene, TX
Orchard Place, Des Moines Children's Home, Des Moines, IA
Ottumwa Regional Health Center, Ottumwa, IA
Our Lady of Victory Infant Home, Lackawanna, NY
Pineview Homes, Inc, Evart, MI
St Francis Hospital, Waterloo, IA
St Joseph Mercy Hospital, Mason City, IA
St Vincent—Sarah Fisher Center, Farmington Hills, MI
The Salvation Army Booth Brown House Services, St Paul, MN

Shadow Mountain Institute, Tulsa, OK
Shelter Services of Carlton County, Inc, Cloquet, MN
South Coast Children's Society, Costa Mesa, CA
Southern Pines, Charleston, SC
Spaulding Youth Center, Tilton, NH
Specialized Youth Services, Charlotte, NC
Ann Storck Center, Inc., Ft Lauderdale, FL
Sweetser Childrens Home, Saco, ME
Syracuse Youth Development Center, Syracuse, NY
Trinity Regional Hospital, Fort Dodge, IA
Virginia Treatment Center, Richmond, VA
We Care, San Jose, CA
Webster-Cantrell Hall, Decatur, IL
The Constance Bultman Wilson Center, Faribault, MN
The Woods Schools, Langhorne, PA
Youth Evaluation and Treatment Centers, Phoenix, AZ

SPEECH/LANGUAGE DISORDERS

ABCS Little Canyon School, Phoenix, AZ
American Institute for Mental Studies, Vineland, NJ
The Anderson School, Staatsburg, NY
Arbor Heights Center, Ann Arbor, MI
Archway, Inc, Leicester, MA
Arizona State Hospital—Child and Adolescent Treatment Unit, Phoenix, AZ
Baird Children's Center, Burlington, VT
The Bancroft School, Haddonfield, NJ
Baptist Children's Home at San Antonio, San Antonio, TX
Baptist Home for Children, Bethesda, MD
Bar-None Residential Treatment Services, Anoka, MN
Behavior Research Institute, Inc, Providence, RI
Bethlehem Children's Center, New Orleans, LA
Blueberry Treatment Center, Brooklyn, NY
Bradley Hospital, East Providence, RI
Brehm Preparatory School, Carbondale, IL
Bridlewood Group Home, Intensive Residential Program, Charlotte, NC
The Brown Schools, Austin, TX
Buffalo Youth Development Center, Buffalo, NY
The Calabasas Academy, Calabasas, CA
Carmelite Home for Boys, Hammond, IN
Carmelite Home, Inc, Wauwatosa, WI
Carobell Children's Home, Inc, Jacksonville, NC
Cascade Child Care Center, Redmond, OR
Catholic Children's Home, Alton, IL
Chamberlain's Children's Center, Inc, Hollister, CA
Children and Adolescent Treatment Center, Jamestown, ND
The Children's Campus, Mishawaka, IN
Children's Home of Stockton, Stockton, CA
Children's Village, Dobbs Ferry, NY
Colorado Christian Home, Denver, CO
Colorado Christian Home, Denver, CO
Connecticut Junior Republic, Litchfield, CT
Convalescent Hospital for Children, Rochester, NY
Delta Treatment Centers of Indiana, Inc, Bloomington, IN
The Devereaux Foundation, Rutland, MA
The Devereux Center, Scottsdale, AZ
The Devereux Center in Georgia, Kennesaw, GA
The Devereux Foundation, Santa Barbara, CA
Diagnostic and Educational Services, Palm Desert, CA
East Texas Guidance Center, Tyler, TX
Eastfield Ming Quong, Campbell, CA
Edgewood Children's Center, St Louis, MO
Edgewood Children's Center, San Francisco, CA
Fair Play Wilderness Camp School, Westminster, SC
Forest Heights Lodge, Evergreen, CO
Franklin Village, Grove City, OH
Gerard of Minnesota, Austin, MN
Grafton School, Berryville, VA
Grandview Children's Ranch, Inc, Angwin, CA
The Griffith Center, Golden, CO
Group Foster Homes, Inc, Redding, CA
Grove School, Inc, Madison, CT
Hawthorn Childrens Psychiatric Hospital, St Louis, MO
High Pointe, Oklahoma City, OK
Hillcrest Educational Centers, Inc, Lenox, MA
Holley Child Care and Development Center, Hackensack, NJ
Houston County Group Home, LaCrescent, LaCrescent, MN
HSA Cumberland Hospital, Fayetteville, NC

Indiana United Methodist Children's Home, Inc., Lebanon, IN
Henry Ittleson Center for Child Research, Riverdale, NY
Jamestown, Stillwater, MN
K-Bar-B Youth Ranch, Lacombe, LA
Kaleidoscope, Bloomington, IL
Kaplan Foundation, Inc, Orangevale, CA
Robert F Kennedy Action Corps, Lancaster, MA
The Kolburne School, Inc, New Marlborough, MA
Lakeside Child & Family Center, Inc, Milwaukee, WI
Lakeside School, Peabody, MA
Las Vegas Medical Center—Adolescent Unit, Las Vegas, NM
The Latham School, Brewster, MA
Little Keswick School, Inc, Keswick, VA
Manatee Palms, Residential Treatment Center, Bradenton, FL
Manor Foundation, Jonesville, MI
Marillac Center for Children, Kansas City, MO
Marshall I Pickens Hospital—The Children's Program, Greenville, SC
Martin Center, Inc, Milwaukee, WI
Maxey Training School, Whitmore Lake, MI
McDowell Youth Homes, Inc, Soquel, CA
Mental Health Services of the Roanoke Valley—Children's Center, Roanoke, VA
Meridell Achievement Center, Inc—Westwood, Liberty Hill, TX
The Methodist Home of Kentucky, Inc, Versailles, KY
The Methodist Home of New Orleans, New Orleans, LA
Mid-South Hospital, Memphis, TN
Mission of the Immaculate Virgin, Staten Island, NY
Corine Morris Community Care Home, Columbia, SC
Mount St Vincent's Home, Denver, CO
Mount Scott Institute, Washington, NJ
Mt Ridge Group Home, Cherryville, NC
Northern Nevada Child and Adolescence Services, Reno, NV
Northwood Children's Home, Duluth, MN
Oconomowoc Developmental Training Center, Inc, Oconomowoc, WI
Odyssey Harbor, Inc, Keene, TX
Oesterlen Services for Youth, Springfield, OH
Ohio Center for Youth and Family Development, Pedro, OH
Our Lady of Providence Children's Center, West Springfield, MA
Our Lady of Victory Infant Home, Lackawanna, NY
Ozanam Home for Boys, Inc, Kansas City, MO
Parkview Homes I, II, & III, Seattle, WA
Parsons Child & Family Center, Albany, NY
The Pines Treatment Center, Portsmouth, VA
Pineview Homes, Inc, Evart, MI
Project Six, Van Nuys, CA
Randolph Children's Home, Randolph, NY
Reed Academy, Framingham, MA
River's Bend Farm School, Stanley, VA
Riverwood Center, Prescott, WI
St Aemilian, Inc, Milwaukee, WI
St Ann's Home, Inc, Methuen, MA
St Anthony Villa, Toledo, OH
St John's Home for Children, Wheeling, WV
St Joseph's Cardendelet Child Center, Chicago, IL
St Rose Residence, Milwaukee, WI
St Vincent Home, St Louis, MO
St Vincent—Sarah Fisher Center, Farmington Hills, MI
St Vincent's Center—Child and Family Care, Timonium, MD
St Vincent's Home, Fall River, MA
The Salvation Army Booth Brown House Services, St Paul, MN
The Salvation Army Residence for Children, St Louis, MO
San Antonio Children's Center, San Antonio, TX
Shadow Mountain Institute, Tulsa, OK
Shelter Services of Carlton County, Inc, Cloquet, MN
South Coast Children's Society, Costa Mesa, CA
Southeastern Mental Health Center, Sioux Falls, SD
Southern Home Services, Philadelphia, PA
Southern Oregon Adolescent Study and Treatment Center, Grants Pass, OR
Southern Pines, Charleston, SC
Spaulding Youth Center, Tilton, NH
Maurice Spear Campus, Adrian, MI
Specialized Youth Services, Charlotte, NC

The Spofford Home, Kansas City, MO
Ann Storck Center, Inc., Ft Lauderdale, FL
Sunrise Group Home, Kenansville, NC
Sweetser Childrens Home, Saco, ME
The Sycamores, Altadena, CA
Taylor Home, Racine, WI
Terry Children's Psychiatric Center, New Castle, DE
The Treasure Cove, Atwater, CA
Triad Homes for Autistic Individuals, Inc, High Point, NC
Trinity School for Children, Ukiah, CA
United Methodist Youth Home, Evansville, IN
Upper Valley Charitable Corp—Clear Creek Farm, Piqua, OH
Vanderheyden Hall, Wynantskill, NY
Virginia Treatment Center, Richmond, VA
Cleo Wallace Center, Broomfield, CO
Waterford County School, Inc, Quaker Hill, CT
We Care, San Jose, CA
Wide Horizons Ranch, Inc, Oak Run, CA
Willowglen, Milwaukee, WI
The Constance Bultman Wilson Center, Faribault, MN
The Woods Schools, Langhorne, PA
York Place, York, SC
Young Acres, Peoria, AZ
Youth Emergency Shelter, Inc, Morristown, TN
Youth Resources, Inc, Pilgrim Center, Braintree, MA

VISION IMPAIRMENT/ BLINDNESS

The Bancroft School, Haddonfield, NJ
Benhaven, East Haven, CT
Bradley Hospital, East Providence, RI
Brehm Preparatory School, Carbondale, IL
The Brown Schools, Austin, TX
Buckeye Boys Ranch, Inc, Grove City, OH
Carobell Children's Home, Inc, Jacksonville, NC
Cascade Child Care Center, Redmond, OR
Children and Adolescent Treatment Center, Jamestown, ND
The Children's Campus, Mishawaka, IN
Children's Home of Cedar Rapids, Cedar Rapids, IA
Jennie Edmundson Memorial Hospital, Council Bluffs, IA
Floberg Center for Children, Rockton, IL
Florence Crittenton Home, Sioux City, IA
Gerard of Minnesota, Austin, MN
Mary Greeley Medical Center, Ames, IA
Hillcrest Educational Centers, Inc, Lenox, MA
Holley Child Care and Development Center, Hackensack, NJ
Hope Haven, Inc, Rock Valley, IA
Houston County Group Home, LaCrescent, LaCrescent, MN
HSA Cumberland Hospital, Fayetteville, NC
Indiana United Methodist Children's Home, Inc., Lebanon, IN
Iowa Children's and Family Services, Des Moines, IA
Joyner Therapeutic Home, Whiteville, NC
Kaleidoscope, Bloomington, IL
Jane Lamb Health Center, Clinton, IA
Linnhaven, Inc, Marion, IA
Maxey Training School, Whitmore Lake, MI
McDowell Youth Homes, Inc, Soquel, CA
The Methodist Home of Kentucky, Inc, Versailles, KY
Mid-South Hospital, Memphis, TN
Corine Morris Community Care Home, Columbia, SC
Mount St Vincent's Home, Denver, CO
Odyssey Harbor, Inc, Keene, TX
Oesterlen Services for Youth, Springfield, OH
Ottumwa Regional Health Center, Ottumwa, IA
Our Lady of Victory Infant Home, Lackawanna, NY
St Francis Hospital, Waterloo, IA
St John's Home for Children, Wheeling, WV
St Joseph Mercy Hospital, Mason City, IA
Shelter Services of Carlton County, Inc, Cloquet, MN
South Coast Children's Society, Costa Mesa, CA
Southeastern Mental Health Center, Sioux Falls, SD
Southern Home Services, Philadelphia, PA
Southern Oregon Child Study and Treatment Center, Ashland, OR
Ann Storck Center, Inc., Ft Lauderdale, FL
Trinity Regional Hospital, Fort Dodge, IA
United Methodist Youth Home, Evansville, IN
Virginia Treatment Center, Richmond, VA
We Care, San Jose, CA

The Constance Bultman Wilson Center, Faribault, MN
Youth Emergency Shelter, Inc, Morristown, TN

Funding Sources Index

DEPARTMENTS OF CORRECTION

Adolescent Group Home, Danville, VA
Advocate Group Homes, Riverside, CA
Alaska Children's Services, Inc, Anchorage, AK
Allendale, Lake Villa, IL
Alpha House Youth Care, Inc, Menomonie, WI
Alternative Homes, Inc, St Paul, MN
Alternative Resources for Kids, Inc—Girls Home, Norwalk, OH
Arizona Children's Home Association, Tucson, AZ
Bashor Home of the United Methodist Church, Inc, Goshen, IN
Beckley Child Care Center, Beckley, WV
The Bethel Group Home, Bethel, AK
Bexar County MHMR Center—Residential Program, San Antonio, TX
Black Hills Special Services—Northern Hills Youth Services, Spearfish, SD
Boys Attention Home, Charlottesville, VA
Boy's Home, Inc, Covington, VA
Boys Republic, Chino, CA
Boys' Village, Inc, Smithville, OH
The Bridge, San Diego, CA
Brooke-Hancock Group Home, Inc, Newell, WV
Buckeye Boys Ranch, Inc, Grove City, OH
California Crest Diagnostic and Treatment Center, El Cajon, CA
Caravan House, Palo Alto, CA
Casa de Luz, Santa Rosa, CA
Centerville Group Home, Chesapeake, VA
The Children's Home, Cincinnati, OH
Children's Home of Stockton, Stockton, CA
Childrens Home Society, Sioux Falls, SD
The Children's Residence, Hampton, VA
Christian Haven Homes, Inc, Wheatfield, IN
Colbert-Lauderdale Attention Home, Inc, Florence, AL
Community Attention Residential Care System, Charlottesville, VA
Convenant Children's Home, Princeton, IL
Cool Springs of Logansport, Logansport, LA
Cornell Group Homes, Inc, Ladysmith, WI
Coulee Youth Centers, Inc, LaCrosse, WI
Crossroad, Fort Wayne, IN
Cunningham Children's Home, Urbana, IL
Day Group Home, Inc, Buellton, CA
Daybreak Child and Adolescent Unit of MHMR of Southeast Texas, Beaumont, TX
The Devereaux Foundation, Rutland, MA
The Devereux Center in Georgia, Kennesaw, GA
C A Dillon School, Butner, NC
Drake House Group Home, Pleasant Hill, CA
Edison Park Home, Park Ridge, IL
Elan School, Poland Spring, ME
Elk Hill Farm, Inc, Goochland, VA
Equinox Adolescent Treatment Center, Auburn, CA
Eudes Family Programs—Group Home, Triumph II, Green Bay, WI
Eudes Family Programs—Residential Center, Green Bay, WI
Fairmont Group Home, Fresno, CA
Family Life Center, Petaluma, CA
First Light Group Home, Inc, Beloit, WI
Juliette Fowler Homes, Dallas, TX
Freeport West Treatment Group Home, Minneapolis, MN
Friends of Youth, Renton, WA
Galloway Boys Ranch, Wahkon, MN
Gateway Group Home, Excelsior, MN

Gateways Hospital and Mental Health Center, Los Angeles, CA
Genesis, Athens, OH
Genesis Youth Center, Clarksburg, WV
Gerard of Minnesota, Austin, MN
Gibault School for Boys, Terre Haute, IN
Good News School, Inc, Boonville, CA
Good Samaritan Homes, Sacramento, CA
Grafton School, Berryville, VA
Group Foster Homes, Inc, Redding, CA
Guardian Angel Home of Joliet, Joliet, IL
Gundry Hospital, Baltimore, MD
Janie Hammit Children's Home, Bristol, VA
Harambee House, San Diego, CA
The Harbor Schools, Inc, Newburyport, MA
Timothy Hill Children's Ranch, Riverhead, NY
Hillside, Inc, Atlanta, GA
Leo A Hoffmann Center, St Peter, MN
Home Away Centers, Inc., Minneapolis, MN
Hoosier Boys Town, Inc, Schererville, IN
Huckleberry House II, San Francisco, CA
Hughes Memorial Home for Children, Danville, VA
Indiana United Methodist Children's Home, Inc., Lebanon, IN
Jamestown, Stillwater, MN
John/Mar Group Home for Children, Inc, Compton, CA
Jones Home of Children's Services, Cleveland, OH
The King's Ranch—Oneonta, Oneonta, AL
Kiwanis Independence Program, Roanoke, VA
Klein Bottle Social Advocates for Youth, Santa Barbara, CA
Kuubba Extended Family, Modesto, CA
La Selva, Palo Alto, CA
Francis Lauer Youth Services, Mason City, IA
Loudoun Youth Shelter, Sterling, VA
Lutheran Social Services, Epic Group Home, Eau Claire, WI
Lutheran Social Services, Hampton House Group Home, Milwaukee, WI
Madonna Heights Services, Huntington, NY
Manor Foundation, Jonesville, MI
Maria Group Home, St Paul, MN
Maui Youth & Family Services Boys' Group Home, Makawao, HI
McCormick Foundation, Calistoga, CA
Mingus Mountain Estate—Residential & Educational Center for Girls, Prescott, AZ
Corine Morris Community Care Home, Columbia, SC
Natividad Ranch, Salinas, CA
New Beginnings Center, Aberdeen, SD
New Chance, Inc, Ben Lomond, CA
New Connection Programs, Inc., St Paul, MN
New Dominion School, Dillwyn, VA
New Family Vision, Los Olivos, CA
The New Foundation, Phoenix, AZ
New Hope Treatment Centers, San Bernardino, CA
Northern Tier Youth Services, Blossburg, PA
Northwestern Minnesota Juvenile Training Center, Bemidji, MN
Nova Services, Inc, West Bend, WI
Odd Fellow Rebekah Children's Home, Gilroy, CA
Odyssey Harbor, Inc, Keene, TX
Olive Crest Treatment Centers, Santa Ana, CA
One Way Farm, Inc, Fairfield, OH
Opportunity House, Lynchburg, VA
Orchard Place, Des Moines Children's Home, Des Moines, IA
Perrin House, Roxbury, MA

Phoenix House, Whiting, IN
The Pines Treatment Center, Portsmouth, VA
PORT of Crow Wing County, Inc, Brainerd, MN
Prehab of Arizona, Mesa, AZ
Quakerdale Home, New Providence, IA
River's Bend Farm School, Stanley, VA
St Anthony Villa, Toledo, OH
St Bernard Group Homes, Meraux, LA
St Cloud Children's Home, St Cloud, MN
St John's Home, Painesville, OH
The Salvation Army Booth Brown House Services, St Paul, MN
San Pablo Residential Treatment School, Phoenix, AZ
Sanford Society, Inc, Oakland, CA
Sheriffs Youth Programs, Austin, MN
Norman C Sleezer Juvenile Homes, Inc, Freeport, IL
Sleighton School, Lima, PA
Ellen Hines Smith Girls' Home, Spartanburg, SC
SPARC House, Lynchburg, VA
Maurice Spear Campus, Adrian, MI
Sun Porch Group Home, Palo Alto, CA
Sunny Hills Children's Services, San Anselmo, CA
Sunny Ridge Family Center, Wheaton, IL
The Sycamores, Altadena, CA
Syntaxis, Inc, Gahanna, OH
Taylor Home, Racine, WI
Timber Ridge, Winchester, VA
Toyon Mesa School, Inc #1, Paradise, CA
Transcenter for Youth, Group Foster Home, Milwaukee, WI
TRY Group Home, Inc, Two Rivers, WI
Try House Center, Marshall, MN
Ulrey Homes, Inc, San Lorenzo, CA
United Citizen Community Organization, Chicago, IL
The Villages of Indiana, Inc, Bloomington, IN
Virginia Home for Boys, Richmond, VA
Vista Maria, Dearborn Heights, MI
WAITT Houses, Inc, Schenectady, NY
Western Correctional Center, Morganton, NC
Wyndham Lawn Home for Children, Lockport, NY
Young Acres, Peoria, AZ
Youth Evaluation and Treatment Centers, Phoenix, AZ
Youth House of Ouachita, Inc, West Monroe, LA
Youth in Need, St Charles, MO
Youth Resources, Inc, Pilgrim Center, Braintree, MA
Youth Service Bureau, Muncie, IN

DEPARTMENTS OF EDUCATION

Abbott House, Mitchell, SD
ABCS Little Canyon School, Phoenix, AZ
Alexander Children's Center 36, Charlotte, NC
Allendale, Lake Villa, IL
Alpha Omega, Littleton, MA
American Institute for Mental Studies, Vineland, NJ
American School for the Deaf, Paces Program, West Hartford, CT
The Anderson School, Staatsburg, NY
Archway, Inc, Leicester, MA
Argus Community, Inc, Bronx, NY
Arizona Children's Home Association, Tucson, AZ
The Astor Home for Children, Rhinebeck, NY
Autistic Treatment Center, Richardson, TX
Baby Fold Residential Treatment Center, Normal, IL

The Baird Center, Plymouth, MA
Baird Children's Center, Burlington, VT
Baker Hall, Lackawanna, NY
The Bancroft School, Haddonfield, NJ
Bar-None Residential Treatment Services, Anoka, MN
Behavior Research Institute, Inc, Providence, RI
Bennington School, Inc, Bennington, VT
Berkeley Academy, Berkeley, CA
Berkshire Learning Center, Pittsfield, MA
Black Hills Special Services—Northern Hills Youth Services, Spearfish, SD
Blueberry Treatment Center, Brooklyn, NY
Boy's Village Youth and Family Services, Inc, Milford, CT
Brandon School, Natick, MA
Burt Children's Center, San Francisco, CA
The Calabasas Academy, Calabasas, CA
California Crest Diagnostic and Treatment Center, El Cajon, CA
Castle School, Inc, Cambridge, MA
Catholic Children's Home, Alton, IL
Center for Therapeutic Learning Annex, Loveland, CO
Chaddock, Quincy, IL
Child Center of Our Lady, St Louis, MO
The Children's Home, Cincinnati, OH
The Children's Home of Burlington County, Mount Holly, NJ
Children's Home of Kingston, Kingston, NY
Children's Home of Stockton, Stockton, CA
Childrens Home Society, Sioux Falls, SD
Children's Study Home, Springfield, MA
Children's Village, Dobbs Ferry, NY
Community Treatment Complex, Worcester, MA
Concord Assabet Adolescent Services, Concord, MA
Connecticut Junior Republic, Litchfield, CT
Convalescent Hospital for Children, Rochester, NY
Convenant Children's Home, Princeton, IL
Cunningham Children's Home, Urbana, IL
Dakota Boys Ranch, Minot, ND
The Devereaux Foundation, Rutland, MA
The Devereux Center, Scottsdale, AZ
The Devereux Center—Deerhaven, Chester, NJ
The Devereux Center in Georgia, Kennesaw, GA
The Devereux Center—Mapleton, Malvern, PA
The Devereux Foundation, Santa Barbara, CA
C A Dillon School, Butner, NC
Eckerd Wilderness Educational System Camping Progams, Clearwater, FL
The Eden Family of Programs, Princeton, NJ
Edgewood Children's Center, St Louis, MO
Edgewood Children's Center, San Francisco, CA
Edison Park Home, Park Ridge, IL
Educational Therapy Center, Edwardsville, IL
El Caribe Group Home for Boys, Rio Piedras, PR
Elan School, Poland Spring, ME
Elk Hill Farm, Inc, Goochland, VA
Elmcrest Children's Center, Syracuse, NY
Epworth Village, Inc, York, NE
Evangelical Children's Home, St Louis, MO
Evanston Children's Center, Evanston, IL
Five Acres, Altadena, CA
Fresno Treatment Center, Fresno, CA
Friends of Youth, Renton, WA
Full Circle Sonoma, Sebastopol, CA
Galloway Boys Ranch, Wahkon, MN
Gaston Family Home, Oakland, CA
Gateway United Methodist Youth Center, Williamsville, NY
Gateways Hospital and Mental Health Center, Los Angeles, CA
Gerard of Minnesota, Austin, MN
The Germaine Lawrence School, Arlington, MA
Glenwood Mental Health Services, Children's Residential, Birmingham, AL
Grafton School, Berryville, VA
Wil Lou Gray Opportunity School, West Columbia, SC
Green Chimneys Children's Services, Inc, Brewster, NY
The Griffith Center, Golden, CO
Guardian Angel Home of Joliet, Joliet, IL
Uta Halee Girls Village, Omaha, NE
Edward Hall of Guardian Angel Home, Peoria, IL
Hall-Brooke Foundation, Westport, CT
Harambee House, San Diego, CA
The Harbor Schools, Inc, Newburyport, MA
Harbor Shelter & Counseling Center, Inc, Stillwater, MN
Harmony Hill School, Inc, Chepachet, RI
The Charles Hayden Goodwill School, Dorchester, MA

HCA Grant Center Hospital, Miami, FL
Highland Heights, New Haven, CT
Hillcrest Educational Centers, Inc, Lenox, MA
Hillside Children's Center, Rochester, NY
Hillside, Inc, Atlanta, GA
Homestead Residential Center, Ellsworth, ME
Hopevale, Inc, Hamburg, NY
The House of the Good Shepherd, Utica, NY
Hughes Memorial Home for Children, Danville, VA
Institute for Family and Life Learning, Danvers, MA
Interventions, SMA Residential School, Matteson, IL
Jamestown, Stillwater, MN
Justice Resource Institute, The Butler Center, Westboro, MA
Kaplan Foundation, Inc, Orangevale, CA
Robert F Kennedy Action Corps Adolescent Treatment Unit, Lancaster, MA
Robert F Kennedy Action Corps Children's Center, Lancaster, MA
Keystone Adolescent Program, Northeastern Family Institute, Newton, MA
The King's Daughters' School, Inc, Columbia, TN
Klingberg Family Centers, New Britain, CT
The Kolburne School, Inc, New Marlborough, MA
Lakeside Child & Family Center, Inc, Milwaukee, WI
Lakeside School, Peabody, MA
Larkin Home For Children, Elgin, IL
The Latham School, Brewster, MA
Lawrence Hall School for Boys, Chicago, IL
Lutheran Social Services of Illinois, Nachusa Lutheran Home, Nachusa, IL
Lutherwood Residential Treatment Center, Indianapolis, IN
Madonna Heights Services, Huntington, NY
Marillac Center for Children, Kansas City, MO
The Marsh Foundation Home and School, Van Wert, OH
Marygrove, Florissant, MO
Corine Morris Community Care Home, Columbia, SC
Mount St Joseph Children's Center, Totowa, NJ
Mount Scott Institute, Washington, NJ
Murphy-Harpst United Methodist Children and Family Services, Cedartown, GA
New Beginnings Center, Aberdeen, SD
New Dominion School, Dillwyn, VA
The New Foundation, Phoenix, AZ
New Life Homes—Snell Farm, Bath, NY
Nova, Inc, Kinston, NC
Odyssey Harbor, Inc, Keene, TX
Orchard Home, Watertown, MA
Orchard Place, Des Moines Children's Home, Des Moines, IA
Our Lady of Providence Children's Center, West Springfield, MA
Pace Center, West Springfield, MA
Park Ridge Youth Campus, Park Ridge, IL
Parsons Child & Family Center, Albany, NY
Pathway, Inc, New Brockton, AL
Penikese Island School, Woods Hole, MA
The Pines Treatment Center, Portsmouth, VA
Presbyterian Hospitality House, Fairbanks, AK
Princeton Child Development Institute, Princeton, NJ
Randolph Children's Home, Randolph, NY
Reed Academy, Framingham, MA
River's Bend Farm School, Stanley, VA
Rosemont Center, Columbus, OH
Rutherford County Youth Services, Inc—North House, Rutherfordton, NC
St Anne Institute, Albany, NY
St Catherine's Center for Children, Albany, NY
St Joseph's Villa, Rochester, NY
St Mary's Campus School, North Providence, RI
The Salvation Army Residential Treatment Facilities For Children And Youth, Honolulu, HI
Jeanine Schultz Memorial School, Park Ridge, IL
Scott Center, Bloomington, IL
Search Day Program, Inc., Ocean, NJ
Seneca Center, Oakland, CA
Shelter for Women, Inc—Gray Lodge, Hartford, CT
Norman C Sleezer Juvenile Homes, Inc, Freeport, IL
Smallwood Children's Center, Chattanooga, TN
Solstice Adolescent Program, Rowley, MA
Somerset Hills School, Warren, NJ
Southeastern Mental Health Center, Sioux Falls, SD
Southern Oregon Adolescent Study and Treatment Center, Grants Pass, OR

Spaulding Youth Center, Tilton, NH
The Spurwink School, Portland, ME
Spurwink School II, North Providence, RI
Summit School, Manchester, CT
Sweetser Childrens Home, Saco, ME
The Sycamores, Altadena, CA
Taylor Home, Racine, WI
Thresholds, Chicago, IL
Timber Ridge, Winchester, VA
Topeka State Hospital—Capital City Schools, Topeka, KS
Transitional Living, Chicago, IL
Tri-Wil, Inc—Porta Cras School, Greenpond, AL
Utah State Hospital, Youth Center, Provo, UT
Virginia Home for Boys, Richmond, VA
Vitam Center, Inc, Norwalk, CT
The Walker Home and School, Needham, MA
Cleo Wallace Center, Broomfield, CO
Westbridge, Phoenix, AZ
Wide Horizons Ranch, Inc, Oak Run, CA
The Constance Bultman Wilson Center, Faribault, MN
The Woods Schools, Langhorne, PA
Wreath House, Middleton, MA
Wyndham Lawn Home for Children, Lockport, NY
Yellowstone Treatment Center, Billings, MT
York Place, York, SC
Youth and Family Services, Omaha, NE
Youth in Need, St Charles, MO
Youth Resources, Inc, Pilgrim Center, Braintree, MA

DEPARTMENTS OF MENTAL HEALTH

Adolescent Group Home, Danville, VA
Alexander Children's Center 36, Charlotte, NC
Allendale, Lake Villa, IL
Allentown State Hospital—Children's Unit, Allentown, PA
Alternative House, Vienna, VA
American School for the Deaf, Paces Program, West Hartford, CT
Angel Guardian Home—McAuley Residence, Brooklyn, NY
Archway, Inc, Leicester, MA
Arcoiris Group Home for Girls, Ponce, PR
Arizona Children's Home Association, Tucson, AZ
The ARK, Jackson, MS
Augusta Mental Health Institute, Augusta, ME
Autistic Treatment Center, Richardson, TX
The Baird Center, Plymouth, MA
Baird Children's Center, Burlington, VT
Barboursville School, Barboursville, WV
Bar-None Residential Treatment Services, Anoka, MN
Bashor Home of the United Methodist Church, Inc, Goshen, IN
Behavior Research Institute, Inc, Providence, RI
Bella Vida Group Home, Fresno, CA
Bennington School, Inc, Bennington, VT
Berkshire Learning Center, Pittsfield, MA
Bethlehem Children's Center, New Orleans, LA
Bexar County MHMR Center—Residential Program, San Antonio, TX
Blueberry Treatment Center, Brooklyn, NY
Brattleboro Retreat, Brattleboro, VT
Bridlewood Group Home, Intensive Residential Program, Charlotte, NC
Caguas Emergency Care Shelter, Caguas, PR
California Crest Diagnostic and Treatment Center, El Cajon, CA
Camelot Care Center, Kingston, TN
Camelot Care Center, Inc, Palatine, IL
CaraMore Community, Chapel Hill, NC
Cardinal Treatment Center, Louisville, KY
Carmelite Home, Inc, Wauwatosa, WI
Walter P Carter Community Mental Health Center, Baltimore, MD
Catholic Community Services Northwest, Bellingham, WA
Central Kentucky Re-Ed Center, Lexington, KY
Central Louisiana State Hospital, Adolescent Service, Pineville, LA
Chaddock, Quincy, IL
Cherry Hospital, Children and Youth Unit, Goldsboro, NC
Child Center of Our Lady, St Louis, MO
Child Study and Treatment Center, Tacoma, WA
The Children's Home, Cincinnati, OH
Children's Home of Stockton, Stockton, CA
Colbert-Lauderdale Attention Home, Inc, Florence, AL
Colon Road Home, Sanford, NC

INSURANCE

Autistic Treatment Center, Richardson, TX
Bar-None Residential Treatment Services, Anoka, MN
Bethesda PsycHealth System, Denver, CO
Boys and Girls Aid Society of San Diego—Cottonwood Center, El Cajon, CA
Bradley Hospital, East Providence, RI
Brattleboro Retreat, Brattleboro, VT
Arthur Brisbane Child Treatment Center, Farmingdale, NJ
Broad Horizons of Ramona, Inc, Ramona, CA
The Brown Schools, Austin, TX
Camelot Care Center, Kingston, TN
Camelot Care Center, Inc, Palatine, IL
Cedu School, Running Springs, CA
Central Louisiana State Hospital, Adolescent Service, Pineville, LA
Charter Colonial Institute, Newport News, VA
Chestnut Lodge Hospital, Rockville, MD
Child Study and Treatment Center, Tacoma, WA
The Children's Home, Cincinnati, OH
Colonial Hills Hospital, San Antonio, TX
Colorado Boys Ranch Foundation, La Junta, CO
Colorado Christian Home, Denver, CO
Convenant Children's Home, Princeton, IL
Crest View Hospital, Casper, WY
Crittenton Center, Kansas City, MO
Cunningham Children's Home, Urbana, IL
Daniel Memorial, Inc, Jacksonville, FL
Daybreak Child and Adolescent Unit of MHMR of Southeast Texas, Beaumont, TX
De Paul Hospital, New Orleans, LA
Delta Treatment Centers of Indiana, Inc, Bloomington, IN
The Denver Children's Home, Denver, CO
Desert Hills, Tucson, AZ
The Devereux Center, Scottsdale, AZ
The Devereux Center in Georgia, Kennesaw, GA
The Devereux Foundation, Santa Barbara, CA
Eastern Virginia Center for Children and Youth, Norfolk, VA
Elan School, Poland Spring, ME
Fair Oaks Hospital, Summit, NJ
Fairway, Mobile, AL
Family and Children's Center, La Crosse, WI
Family Solutions, El Toro, CA
Florence Crittenton Services, San Francisco, CA
Forest Heights Lodge, Evergreen, CO
Juliette Fowler Homes, Dallas, TX
Friendship House, Minneapolis, MN
Galloway Boys Ranch, Wahkon, MN
Gateways Hospital and Mental Health Center, Los Angeles, CA
Gerard of Iowa, Mason City, IA
Gerard of Minnesota, Austin, MN
The Griffith Center, Golden, CO
Grove School, Inc, Madison, CT
Gulf Coast Regional Mental Health Mental Retardation Center, Galveston, TX
Uta Halee Girls Village, Omaha, NE
Hall-Brooke Foundation, Westport, CT
HCA Grant Center Hospital, Miami, FL
Hickory House, Mobile, AL
High Pointe, Oklahoma City, OK
Highland Hospital, Asheville, NC
Hillside, Inc, Atlanta, GA
Holly Hill Hospital, Raleigh, NC
HSA Cumberland Hospital, Fayetteville, NC
HSA Heartland Hospital, Nevada, MO
Iowa Lutheran Hospital, Children's Services, Des Moines, IA
Jamestown, Stillwater, MN
Kaplan Foundation, Inc, Orangevale, CA
Klingberg Family Centers, New Britain, CT
La Selva, Palo Alto, CA
Lutherwood Residential Treatment Center, Indianapolis, IN
Manatee Palms, Residential Treatment Center, Bradenton, FL
Marillac Center for Children, Kansas City, MO
The Menninger Foundation—Childrens Division, Topeka, KS
Meridell Achievement Center, Inc—Westwood, Liberty Hill, TX
Meridell Achievement Center, Inc—Windridge, Austin, TX
Miami Children's Hospital—Division of Psychiatry, Miami, FL
Mississippi Children's Home Society and Family Service Association, Jackson, MS
Elizabeth Mitchell Children's Center, Little Rock, AR
Corine Morris Community Care Home, Columbia, SC
Murphy-Harpst United Methodist Children and Family Services, Cedartown, GA
New Beginnings, Greer, SC

New Connection Programs, Inc., St Paul, MN
Northside Community Mental Health Center, Inc, Tampa, FL
Odyssey—Family Service Association Group Home, Morgantown, WV
Ozanam Home for Boys, Inc, Kansas City, MO
Ozark Center Youth Residential Services, Joplin, MO
The Pines Treatment Center, Portsmouth, VA
Potomac Comprehensive Diagnostic and Guidance Center, Romney, WV
Prospect Learning Center, Summit, NJ
Psychiatric Institute of Richmond, Richmond, VA
Ridgeview Institute, Smyrna, GA
Riverside Psychiatric Hospital, Portland, OR
Riverwood Center, Prescott, WI
Ryther Child Center, Seattle, WA
St Aemilian, Inc, Milwaukee, WI
St Cloud Children's Home, St Cloud, MN
The St Francis Boys' Homes, Salina, KS
St Joseph's Home for Boys, St Louis, MO
The Salvation Army Booth Brown House Services, St Paul, MN
San Antonio Children's Center, San Antonio, TX
San Diego Center for Children, San Diego, CA
Shadow Mountain Institute, Tulsa, OK
Smallwood Children's Center, Chattanooga, TN
Sojourn, Mobile, AL
Southern Oregon Child Study and Treatment Center, Ashland, OR
Southern Pines, Charleston, SC
Southwestern State Hospital—Child and Adolescent Unit, Thomasville, GA
Southwood Psychiatric Residential Treatment Center, South Bay, Chula Vista, CA
The Spofford Home, Kansas City, MO
Summit School, Manchester, CT
United Methodist Family Services of Virginia, Richmond, VA
Utah State Hospital, Youth Center, Provo, UT
Virginia Treatment Center, Richmond, VA
Vista Sandia Hospital, Albuquerque, NM
Vitam Center, Inc, Norwalk, CT
Waco Center for Youth, Waco, TX
Cleo Wallace Center, Broomfield, CO
Wateroak Specialty Hospital Treatment Program, Tallahassee, FL
Wide Horizons Ranch, Inc, Oak Run, CA
The Constance Bultman Wilson Center, Faribault, MN
Woodland Hills, Duluth, MN
Yellowstone Treatment Center, Billings, MT
York Place, York, SC
Richard H Young Memorial Hospital, Omaha, NE
Youth Home, Little Rock, AR

SOCIAL SERVICE DEPARTMENTS

Abbott House, Mitchell, SD
ABCS Little Canyon School, Phoenix, AZ
Adolescent Group Home, Danville, VA
Advocate Group Homes, Riverside, CA
Alaska Children's Services, Inc, Anchorage, AK
Aldea, Inc, Napa, CA
Alexander Children's Center 36, Charlotte, NC
Allendale, Lake Villa, IL
Aloysia Hall—Mercy Hospital of Johnstown, Johnstown, PA
Alpha House Youth Care, Inc, Menomonie, WI
Alpha Omega, Littleton, MA
Alternative House, Vienna, VA
Alternative Resources for Kids, Inc—Girls Home, Norwalk, OH
American School for the Deaf, Paces Program, West Hartford, CT
Anchor I, Martinsville, VA
The Anderson School, Staatsburg, NY
Angel Guardian Home—McAuley Residence, Brooklyn, NY
Apostolic Christian Childrens Home, Leo, IN
Appleton Family Ministries, Juliette, GA
Arbor Heights Center, Ann Arbor, MI
Archway, Inc, Leicester, MA
Argus Community, Inc, Bronx, NY
Arizona Children's Home Association, Tucson, AZ
The Astor Home for Children, Rhinebeck, NY
Astor Home for Children, Marian Group Home, Goshen, NY
Attleboro Youth Shelter, Attleboro, MA
Attucks Center, Inc, Milwaukee, WI
Autism Teaching Home, Salt Lake City, UT
Aviva Center, Los Angeles, CA
Avondale Youth Center, Zanesville, OH

Baby Fold Residential Treatment Center, Normal, IL
The Baird Center, Plymouth, MA
Baker Hall, Lackawanna, NY
The Bancroft School, Haddonfield, NJ
Baptist Home for Children, Bethesda, MD
Bar-None Residential Treatment Services, Anoka, MN
Bashor Home of the United Methodist Church, Inc, Goshen, IN
Bellefaire Residential Treatment Facility, Cleveland, OH
Berkeley Academy, Berkeley, CA
Berkshire Farm Center and Services for Youth, Canaan, NY
Berkshire Learning Center, Pittsfield, MA
Bernard St CCF, Spokane, WA
Bethany Home, Inc, Moline, IL
The Bethel Group Home, Bethel, AK
Black Hills Special Services—Northern Hills Youth Services, Spearfish, SD
Blount County Children's Home, Maryville, TN
Blueberry Treatment Center, Brooklyn, NY
Boselli Residential Services, Inc, Lemon Grove, CA
Boys and Girls Aid Society of Oregon, Portland, OR
Boys and Girls Aid Society of San Diego—Cottonwood Center, El Cajon, CA
Boys Attention Home, Charlottesville, VA
Boy's Home, Inc, Covington, VA
Boys Republic, Chino, CA
Boys' Village, Inc, Smithville, OH
Brandon School, Natick, MA
The Bridge, San Diego, CA
Broad Horizons of Ramona, Inc, Ramona, CA
Buckeye Boys Ranch, Inc, Grove City, OH
Buffalo Youth Development Center, Buffalo, NY
Burt Children's Center, San Francisco, CA
The Calabasas Academy, Calabasas, CA
California Crest Diagnostic and Treatment Center, El Cajon, CA
Camelot Care Center, Kingston, TN
Caravan House, Palo Alto, CA
Carmelite Home for Boys, Hammond, IN
Carmelite Home, Inc, Wauwatosa, WI
Cary Home for Children, Lafayette, IN
Casa de Luz, Santa Rosa, CA
Casa Victoria I, Whittier, CA
Cascade Child Care Center, Redmond, OR
Castle School, Inc, Cambridge, MA
Catholic Charities Group Home, Binghamton, NY
Catholic Children's Home, Alton, IL
Cedar Grove Residential Center, Cedar Grove, NJ
Cedar Ridge Children's Home and School, Williamsport, MD
Chaddock, Quincy, IL
Chamberlain's Children's Center, Inc, Hollister, CA
Charlee Family Care, Inc, Tucson, AZ
Child and Family Services, Inc, Knoxville, TN
Child Center of Our Lady, St Louis, MO
Children and Adolescent Treatment Center, Jamestown, ND
Children's Aid Society of Franklin County, Chambersburg, PA
Children's Emergency Shelter, Cartersville, GA
Children's Farm Home, Corvallis, OR
Children's Garden, San Rafael, CA
The Children's Home, Cincinnati, OH
The Children's Home of Burlington County, Mount Holly, NJ
Children's Home of Kingston, Kingston, NY
Children's Home of Stockton, Stockton, CA
Childrens Home Society, Sioux Falls, SD
The Children's Residence, Hampton, VA
Children's Study Home, Springfield, MA
Children's Village, Dobbs Ferry, NY
Christian Haven Homes, Inc, Wheatfield, IN
Church of God Home for Children, Sevierville, TN
Church of God Home for Children, Mauldin, SC
The City, Inc—Group Home, Minneapolis, MN
Laurent Clerc Group Home, New York, NY
Colbert-Lauderdale Attention Home, Inc, Florence, AL
Colorado Boys Ranch Foundation, La Junta, CO
Colorado Christian Home, Denver, CO
Community Attention Residential Care System, Charlottesville, VA
Community Treatment Complex, Worcester, MA
Concord Assabet Adolescent Services, Concord, MA
Connecticut Junior Republic, Litchfield, CT
Convenant Children's Home, Princeton, IL

Specialized Programs Index

EARLY CHILDHOOD PROGRAMS

Alexander Children's Center 36, Charlotte, NC
AMI St Joseph Center for Mental Health, Omaha, NE
The Anderson School, Staatsburg, NY
The Astor Home for Children, Rhinebeck, NY
Autistic Treatment Center, Richardson, TX
Baby Fold Residential Treatment Center, Normal, IL
The Bancroft School, Haddonfield, NJ
Baptist Children's Home at San Antonio, San Antonio, TX
Behavior Research Institute, Inc, Providence, RI
Bethel Bible Village, Hixson, TN
Blueberry Treatment Center, Brooklyn, NY
Bradley Hospital, East Providence, RI
The Brown Schools, Austin, TX
Burt Children's Center, San Francisco, CA
Camelot Care Center, Kingston, TN
Camelot Care Center, Inc, Palatine, IL
Carobell Children's Home, Inc, Jacksonville, NC
Catholic Community Services Northwest, Bellingham, WA
Center for Therapeutic Learning Annex, Loveland, CO
Charter Colonial Institute, Newport News, VA
Children's Emergency Shelter, Cartersville, GA
Children's Garden, San Rafael, CA
Church of God Home for Children, Sevierville, TN
Church of God Home for Children, Mauldin, SC
Convalescent Hospital for Children, Rochester, NY
Rhonda Crane Memorial Youth Shelter, Pascagoula, MS
Daniel Memorial, Inc, Jacksonville, FL
Day Group Home, Inc, Buellton, CA
Diagnostic and Educational Services, Palm Desert, CA
Eastern Virginia Center for Children and Youth, Norfolk, VA
Eastfield Ming Quong, Campbell, CA
The Eden Family of Programs, Princeton, NJ
Elmcrest Children's Center, Syracuse, NY
Elwyn Institute, Elwyn, PA
Emergency Child Shelter, Inc, Elizabethton, TN
Evangelical Children's Home, St Louis, MO
Family and Children's Center, La Crosse, WI
Five Acres, Altadena, CA
Florence Crittenton Services, San Francisco, CA
Georgia Baptist Children's Homes and Family Ministries, Inc, Palmetto, GA
Glenwood Mental Health Services, Children's Residential, Birmingham, AL
Grafton School, Berryville, VA
Grande Ronde Child Center, La Grande, OR
Grandview Children's Ranch, Inc, Angwin, CA
Gulf Coast Regional Mental Health Mental Retardation Center, Galveston, TX
Janie Hammit Children's Home, Bristol, VA
HCA Grant Center Hospital, Miami, FL
Holley Child Care and Development Center, Hackensack, NJ
Hope Run Group Home, Bessemer City, NC
HSA Cumberland Hospital, Fayetteville, NC
Inter-Mountain Deaconess Home, Helena, MT
Junior Helping Hand Home for Children, Austin, TX
Kaplan Foundation, Inc, Orangevale, CA
The King's Daughters' School, Inc, Columbia, TN
Larkin Home For Children, Elgin, IL

MacDonell United Methodist Children's Services, Inc, Houma, LA
Manatee Palms, Residential Treatment Center, Bradenton, FL
Marillac Center for Children, Kansas City, MO
The Menninger Foundation—Childrens Division, Topeka, KS
The Methodist Home of Kentucky, Inc, Versailles, KY
The Methodist Home of New Orleans, New Orleans, LA
Miracle Hill Children's Home, Pickens, SC
Mississippi Children's Home Society and Family Service Association, Jackson, MS
Monroe County Shelter Care, Inc, Sparta, WI
Frances Haddon Morgan Center, Bremerton, WA
Mount St Vincent's Home, Denver, CO
New Beginnings, Greer, SC
New Orleans Adolescent Hospital, New Orleans, LA
Northeast Mississippi Emergency Shelter for Children, Corinth, MS
Northern Nevada Child and Adolescence Services, Reno, NV
Oconomowoc Developmental Training Center, Inc, Oconomowoc, WI
Olive Crest Treatment Centers, Santa Ana, CA
The Open Gate, Marietta, GA
Orchard Place, Des Moines Children's Home, Des Moines, IA
Our Lady of Victory Infant Home, Lackawanna, NY
Parry Center for Children, Portland, OR
Anna Philbrook Center for Children and Youth, Concord, NH
Pinellas Emergency Mental Health Services, Pinellas Park, FL
The Pines Treatment Center, Portsmouth, VA
Presbyterian Home for Children, Talladega, AL
Princeton Child Development Institute, Princeton, NJ
Rainbow Mental Health Facility, Kansas City, KS
Re-Ed Treatment Program, Louisville, KY
Ryther Child Center, Seattle, WA
St Anthony Villa, Toledo, OH
St Catherine's Center for Children, Albany, NY
St Vincent—Sarah Fisher Center, Farmington Hills, MI
St Vincent's Center—Child and Family Care, Timonium, MD
The Salvation Army Residence for Children, St Louis, MO
Salvation Army White Shield Center, Portland, OR
San Antonio Children's Center, San Antonio, TX
Jeanine Schultz Memorial School, Park Ridge, IL
Search Day Program, Inc, Ocean, NJ
Shelter Services of Carlton County, Inc, Cloquet, MN
Smallwood Children's Center, Chattanooga, TN
Southeastern Children's Home, Inc, Taylors, SC
Southeastern Mental Health Center, Sioux Falls, SD
Southern Oregon Child Study and Treatment Center, Ashland, OR
Southern Pines, Charleston, SC
Southwestern State Hospital—Child and Adolescent Unit, Thomasville, GA
The Spofford Home, Kansas City, MO
The Spurwink School, Portland, ME
Ann Storck Center, Inc., Ft Lauderdale, FL
Terrell State Hospital, Child/Adolescent Unit, Terrell, TX

Terry Children's Psychiatric Center, New Castle, DE
Topeka State Hospital—Capital City Schools, Topeka, KS
The Treasure Cove, Atwater, CA
Veterans of Foreign Wars National Home, Eaton Rapids, MI
Virginia Treatment Center, Richmond, VA
Walden Environment, Lancaster, CA
Warren G Murray Developmental Center, Centralia, IL
Jane Wayland Center, Phoenix, AZ
We Care, San Jose, CA
Wichita Children's Home, Inc, Wichita, KS
Wyandotte House, Corydon, IN
Youth Emergency Shelter, Inc, Morristown, TN
Youth Service Bureau, Muncie, IN

EMERGENCY SHELTERS

Attleboro Youth Shelter, Attleboro, MA
Augusta Mental Health Institute, Augusta, ME
Boys and Girls Aid Society of Oregon, Portland, OR
The Bridge, San Diego, CA
Caguas Emergency Care Shelter, Caguas, PR
Cary Home for Children, Lafayette, IN
Charlee Family Care, Inc, Tucson, AZ
Children's Emergency Shelter, Cartersville, GA
Children's Farm Home, Corvallis, OR
Concord Assabet Adolescent Services, Concord, MA
Coosa Valley Youth Services, Attention Home, Anniston, AL
Rhonda Crane Memorial Youth Shelter, Pascagoula, MS
Emergency Child Shelter, Inc, Elizabethton, TN
Equinox Youth Shelter, Albany, NY
Five Acres, Altadena, CA
Friends of Youth, Renton, WA
Genesis Youth Center, Clarksburg, WV
Harbor Shelter & Counseling Center, Inc, Stillwater, MN
Jones Home of Children's Services, Cleveland, OH
Klein Bottle Social Advocates for Youth, Santa Barbara, CA
Kodiak Baptist Mission, Inc, Kodiak, AK
Loudoun Youth Shelter, Sterling, VA
MacDonell United Methodist Children's Services, Inc, Houma, LA
Madison County Boys Residential Unit, Anderson, IN
Martinsburg Children's Shelter, Martinsburg, WV
Northeast Mississippi Emergency Shelter for Children, Corinth, MS
Northeast Parent and Child Society, Schenectady, NY
The Open Gate, Marietta, GA
Pathfinders for Runaways, Milwaukee, WI
Pinellas Emergency Mental Health Services, Pinellas Park, FL
Po'Ailani, Inc, Honolulu, HI
Potomac Comprehensive Diagnostic and Guidance Center, Romney, WV
Prehab of Arizona, Mesa, AZ
Presbyterian Home for Children, Talladega, AL
Residential Youth Services, Inc, Alexandria, VA
Rosemont Center, Columbus, OH
St Aloysius Home, Greenville, RI
The Salvation Army Booth Brown House Services, St Paul, MN
Salvation Army White Shield Center, Portland, OR

Shelter Services of Carlton County, Inc, Cloquet, MN
Sojourn, Mobile, AL
Sunrise Group Home, Kenansville, NC
Transitional Living, Chicago, IL
Try House Center, Marshall, MN
Vista Maria, Dearborn Heights, MI
Waverly Children's Home, Portland, OR
Wichita Children's Home, Inc, Wichita, KS
YMCA Youth & Family Counseling Center, Redding, CA
Youth Alternatives, Inc, San Antonio, TX
Youth Care Center, Evansville, IN
Youth Emergency Shelter, Inc, Morristown, TN
Youth Homes, Walnut Creek, CA
Youth in Need, St Charles, MO

GROUP HOME PROGRAMS

Adolescent Group Home, Danville, VA
Advocate Group Homes, Riverside, CA
Aldea, Inc, Napa, CA
Alpha House Youth Care, Inc, Menomonie, WI
Alpha Omega, Littleton, MA
Alston Wilkes Youth Home, Columbia South, Columbia, SC
Alternative Resources for Kids, Inc—Girls Home, Norwalk, OH
American Institute for Mental Studies, Vineland, NJ
Anchor I, Martinsville, VA
Andrus Children's Home, Yonkers, NY
Angel Guardian Home—McAuley Residence, Brooklyn, NY
Apostolic Christian Childrens Home, Leo, IN
Arcoiris Group Home for Girls, Ponce, PR
Argus Community, Inc, Bronx, NY
Arizona Children's Home Association, Tucson, AZ
The ARK, Jackson, MS
Ashtabula County Residential Treatment Center, Ashtabula, OH
The Astor Home for Children, Rhinebeck, NY
Astor Home for Children, Marian Group Home, Goshen, NY
Attucks Center, Inc, Milwaukee, WI
Autism Teaching Home, Salt Lake City, UT
Baker Hall, Lackawanna, NY
The Bancroft School, Haddonfield, NJ
Baptist Children's Home and Family Ministries, Valparaiso, IN
Bella Vida Group Home, Fresno, CA
Bernard St CCF, Spokane, WA
Bethel Bible Village, Hixson, TN
The Bethel Group Home, Bethel, AK
Bethlehem Children's Center, New Orleans, LA
Bexar County MHMR Center—Residential Program, San Antonio, TX
Black Hills Special Services—Northern Hills Youth Services, Spearfish, SD
Blount County Children's Home, Maryville, TN
Boselli Residential Services, Inc, Lemon Grove, CA
The Boyd School, Green Pond, AL
Boys and Girls Aid Society of Oregon, Portland, OR
Boys and Girls Aid Society of San Diego—Cottonwood Center, El Cajon, CA
Boys Attention Home, Charlottesville, VA
Boy's Home, Inc, Covington, VA
Boys Hope, Staten Island, NY
Boys Hope, Cincinnati, OH
Boys Hope, St Louis, MO
Boys Republic, Chino, CA
Brandon School, Natick, MA
Bridlewood Group Home, Intensive Residential Program, Charlotte, NC
Brooke-Hancock Group Home, Inc, Newell, WV
The Brown Schools, Austin, TX
Buckeye Boys Ranch, Inc, Grove City, OH
Buffalo Youth Development Center, Buffalo, NY
Burlington United Methodist Home for Children and Youth, Inc, Burlington, WV
Burt Children's Center, San Francisco, CA
The Calabasas Academy, Calabasas, CA
California Crest Diagnostic and Treatment Center, El Cajon, CA
CaraMore Community, Chapel Hill, NC
Caravan House, Palo Alto, CA
Carmelite Home for Boys, Hammond, IN
Casa de Luz, Santa Rosa, CA
Casa Victoria I, Whittier, CA
Castle School, Inc, Cambridge, MA
Catholic Charities Group Home, Binghamton, NY
Catholic Children's Home, Alton, IL

Catholic Community Services Northwest, Bellingham, WA
Cedu School, Running Springs, CA
Centerville Group Home, Chesapeake, VA
Chamberlain's Children's Center, Inc, Hollister, CA
Charlee Family Care, Inc, Tucson, AZ
Child and Family Services, Inc, Knoxville, TN
Children's Farm Home, Corvallis, OR
Children's Garden, San Rafael, CA
The Children's Home, Cincinnati, OH
Children's Home of Kingston, Kingston, NY
Children's Home of Stockton, Stockton, CA
The Children's Residence, Hampton, VA
Children's Village, Dobbs Ferry, NY
Church of God Home for Children, Sevierville, TN
Church of God Home for Children, Mauldin, SC
The City, Inc—Group Home, Minneapolis, MN
Laurent Clerc Group Home, New York, NY
Community Attention Residential Care System, Charlottesville, VA
Community Treatment Complex, Worcester, MA
Community-Based Children's Services, Beaufort, SC
Connecticut Junior Republic, Litchfield, CT
Convalescent Hospital for Children, Rochester, NY
Cornell Group Homes, Inc, Ladysmith, WI
Cornerstone, St Charles, MO
Coulee Youth Centers, Inc, LaCrosse, WI
Cranwood, East Freetown, MA
Crittenton Center, Kansas City, MO
Cunningham Children's Home, Urbana, IL
Dade County Dept of Youth and Family Development—Group Home Program, Miami, FL
Dane Co Group Hms, Inc, Madison, WI
Davis Ave Youth Residence, White Plains, NY
Davis-Stuart, Inc, Lewisburg, WV
Day Group Home, Inc, Buellton, CA
The Devereux Center, Scottsdale, AZ
The Devereux Foundation, Santa Barbara, CA
Donovan House, Ballston Spa, NY
Drake House Group Home, Pleasant Hill, CA
The Eden Family of Programs, Princeton, NJ
Edgefield Lodge, Inc, Troutdale, OR
Edison Park Home, Park Ridge, IL
Educational Therapy Center, Edwardsville, IL
El Caribe Group Home for Boys, Rio Piedras, PR
Elmcrest Children's Center, Syracuse, NY
Epworth Village, Inc, York, NE
Ethan House I, Green Bay, WI
Ethan House II, Green Bay, WI
Eudes Family Programs—Group Home, Triumph II, Green Bay, WI
Evangelical Children's Home, St Louis, MO
Fairmont Group Home, Fresno, CA
Family Life Center, Petaluma, CA
Family Solutions, El Toro, CA
First Light Group Home, Inc, Beloit, WI
Five Acres, Altadena, CA
Florence Crittenton Services, San Francisco, CA
Foothills Youth Services, Inc, Johnstown, NY
Freeport West Treatment Group Home, Minneapolis, MN
Fresno Treatment Center, Fresno, CA
Friends of Youth, Renton, WA
Friendship House, Minneapolis, MN
Friendship House, Sheboygan, WI
Full Circle Sonoma, Sebastopol, CA
Gaston Family Home, Oakland, CA
Gateway Group Home, Excelsior, MN
Gateway Ranch, Auburn, CA
Gateways Hospital and Mental Health Center, Los Angeles, CA
General Protestant Children's Home, St Louis, MO
Genesis, Athens, OH
Georgia Baptist Children's Homes and Family Ministries, Inc, Palmetto, GA
Good News School, Inc, Boonville, CA
Grafton School, Berryville, VA
Grandview Children's Ranch, Inc, Angwin, CA
Green Chimneys Children's Services, Inc, Brewster, NY
Greenhouse, Durham, NC
Greentree Girls Program, Brockton, MA
Group Foster Homes, Inc, Redding, CA
Gulf Coast Regional Mental Health Mental Retardation Center, Galveston, TX
Uta Halee Girls Village, Omaha, NE
Hamilton Centers YSB, Arcadia Home, Arcadia, IN
Hamilton Centers YSB—Cherry St Home, Noblesville, IN

Hamilton Centers YSB—Regional Shelter Home, Noblesville, IN
Janie Hammit Children's Home, Bristol, VA
Harlem Community Residential Home, New York, NY
Hawthorne Cedar Knolls School, Hawthorne, NY
The Charles Hayden Goodwill School, Dorchester, MA
Heartsease Home, Inc, New York, NY
Highland Hospital, Asheville, NC
Timothy Hill Children's Ranch, Riverhead, NY
Hillside Children's Center, Rochester, NY
Hogares, Inc, Albuquerque, NM
Home Away Centers, Inc., Minneapolis, MN
Hope for Youth, Inc, Bethpage, NY
Hope Run Group Home, Bessemer City, NC
The House of the Good Shepherd, Utica, NY
Houston County Group Home, LaCrescent, LaCrescent, MN
Huckleberry House II, San Francisco, CA
Indiana United Methodist Children's Home, Inc., Lebanon, IN
Jamestown, Stillwater, MN
Janis Youth Programs, Inc, Portland, OR
Jefferson House, Stockton, CA
John/Mar Group Home for Children, Inc, Compton, CA
Joy Home for Boys II, Greenwood, LA
Kaleidoscope, Bloomington, IL
KAM, Inc—Reality Ranch, Palms, CA
Kennedy House, Boys Home, Bath, NY
Keystone Resources, Seattle, WA
The King's Daughters' School, Inc, Columbia, TN
Kingsland Bay School, Ferrisburg, VT
Kinship Family and Youth Services, Bath, NY
Kiwanis Independence Program, Roanoke, VA
Kodiak Baptist Mission, Inc, Kodiak, AK
The Kolburne School, Inc, New Marlborough, MA
Kuubba Extended Family, Modesto, CA
La Sultana Group Home for Boys, San German, PR
Laredo State Center, Laredo, TX
Larkin Home For Children, Elgin, IL
Lawrence Hall School for Boys, Chicago, IL
Longview Protestant Home for Children, Buffalo, NY
Lutheran Family Services, Lighthouse, Burlington, NC
Lutheran Family Services, Stepping Stone Group Home, Jacksonville, NC
Lutheran Social Services, Epic Group Home, Eau Claire, WI
Lutheran Social Services, Hampton House Group Home, Milwaukee, WI
Madison County Boys Residential Unit, Anderson, IN
Madonna Heights Services, Huntington, NY
Maison Marie Group Home, Metairie, LA
Maria Group Home, St Paul, MN
Martin Center, Inc, Milwaukee, WI
Maui Youth & Family Services Boys' Group Home, Makawao, HI
McCormick Foundation, Calistoga, CA
McCormick House, Chicago, IL
McDowell Youth Homes, Inc, Soquel, CA
Melody Ranch, Inc, Montfort, WI
The Methodist Home of Kentucky, Inc, Versailles, KY
Mingus Mountain Estate—Residential & Educational Center for Girls, Prescott, AZ
Miracle Hill Children's Home, Pickens, SC
Mission of the Immaculate Virgin, Staten Island, NY
Mississippi Children's Home Society and Family Service Association, Jackson, MS
Monroe County Shelter Care, Inc, Sparta, WI
Corine Morris Community Care Home, Columbia, SC
Mt Ridge Group Home, Cherryville, NC
Mystic Valley Adolescent Residence, Lexington, MA
Nassau Children's House, Mineola, NY
Natividad Ranch, Salinas, CA
New Beginnings, Greer, SC
New Beginnings Center, Aberdeen, SD
New Chance, Inc, Ben Lomond, CA
New Family Vision, Los Olivos, CA
New Hope Treatment Centers, San Bernardino, CA
New Horizons, North Augusta, SC
New Horizons Ranch and Center, Goldthwaite, TX
New Life Homes—Snell Farm, Bath, NY
New York State Division for Youth, Binghamton Community Urban Homes, Binghamton, NY

North Idaho Children's Home, Lewiston, ID
Northeast Parent and Child Society, Schenectady, NY
Northern Nevada Child and Adolescence Services, Reno, NV
Northside Community Mental Health Center, Inc, Tampa, FL
Northwood Children's Home, Duluth, MN
Nova House, Wautoma, WI
Nova, Inc, Kinston, NC
Nova Services, Inc, West Bend, WI
Oconomowoc Developmental Training Center, Inc, Oconomowoc, WI
Odyssey—Family Service Association Group Home, Morgantown, WV
Ohio Boys Town, Inc, Berea, OH
Olive Crest Treatment Centers, Santa Ana, CA
One Way Farm, Inc, Fairfield, OH
Opportunity House, Lynchburg, VA
Orchard Home, Watertown, MA
Oswego County Opportunities—Adolescent Girls Group Home, Oswego, NY
Our Lady of Providence Children's Center, West Springfield, MA
Our Lady of Victory Infant Home, Lackawanna, NY
Out-Front House, Portland, OR
Outreach Broward—The Chord, Pompano Beach, FL
Oz, San Diego, San Diego, CA
Ozanam Home for Boys, Inc, Kansas City, MO
Palomares Group Home, San Jose, CA
Park House Group Home, Merrill, WI
Park Ridge Youth Campus, Park Ridge, IL
Parkview Homes I, II, & III, Seattle, WA
Parmadale, Parma, OH
Parry Center for Children, Portland, OR
Parsons Child & Family Center, Albany, NY
Passages Group Home, Wauwatosa, WI
Pathfinders for Runaways, Milwaukee, WI
Perrin House, Roxbury, MA
Pinellas Emergency Mental Health Services, Pinellas Park, FL
Pius XII Youth and Family Services, Warkick, NY
Ponce Group Home for Girls, Ponce, PR
PORT of Crow Wing County, Inc, Brainerd, MN
Powers Therapeutic Group Home for Adolescent Girls, Jackson, MS
Presbyterian Home for Children, Talladega, AL
Presbyterian Home for Children, Farmington, MO
Princeton Child Development Institute, Princeton, NJ
Randolph County Mental Health Center, North House Residential Group Home, Asheboro, NC
Residential Youth Services, Inc, Alexandria, VA
Rio Blanco Group Home for Dependent and Neglected, Naguabo, PR
Rosemont Center, Columbus, OH
Rosemont School, Inc, Portland, OR
Rumford Group Home, Inc, Rumford, ME
Rutherford County Youth Services, Inc—North House, Rutherfordton, NC
St Aemilian, Inc, Milwaukee, WI
St Andre Group Home, Lewiston, ME
St Ann's Home, Inc, Methuen, MA
St Anne Institute, Albany, NY
St Bernard Group Homes, Meraux, LA
St Joseph's Children's Home, Torrington, WY
St Joseph's Villa, Rochester, NY
St Joseph's Home for Boys, St Louis, MO
St Joseph's Villa, Richmond, VA
St Mary's Family and Children Services, Syossett, NY
Salem Children's Home, Flanagan, IL
The Salvation Army Booth Brown House Services, St Paul, MN
San Diego Center for Children, San Diego, CA
San Pablo Residential Treatment School, Phoenix, AZ
Sanctuary, Inc, Guam Main Facility, GU
Sanford Society, Inc, Oakland, CA
Scott Center, Bloomington, IL
Search Day Program, Inc., Ocean, NJ
Second Circle, Yellow Springs, OH
Secret Harbor School, Anacortes, WA
Seneca Center, Oakland, CA
Anne Elizabeth Shepherd Home, Columbus, GA
Sheriffs Youth Programs, Austin, MN
Ellen Hines Smith Girls' Home, Spartanburg, SC
Soma House, Stevens Point, WI
South Forty Ranch, Summit City, CA
Southeastern Mental Health Center, Sioux Falls, SD
SPARC House, Lynchburg, VA
Spaulding Youth Center, Tilton, NH

Specialized Youth Services, Charlotte, NC
The Spurwink School, Portland, ME
Ann Storck Center, Inc., Ft Lauderdale, FL
Summit School, Manchester, CT
Sun Porch Group Home, Palo Alto, CA
Sunrise Group Home, Kenansville, NC
Sweetser Childrens Home, Saco, ME
The Sycamores, Altadena, CA
Syntaxis, Inc, Gahanna, OH
Syracuse Youth Development Center, Syracuse, NY
Taylor Home, Racine, WI
Teen Acres, Inc, Sterling, CO
Teens World Group Home, Inc, Los Angeles, CA
Teipner Treatment Homes, Inc, Fort Atkinson, WI
Terra Residential Center, San Jose, CA
Thoreau House, Madison, WI
Thresholds, Chicago, IL
Torrimar Group Home for Girls, Guaynabo, PR
Toyon Mesa School, Inc #1, Paradise, CA
Transcenter for Youth, Group Foster Home, Milwaukee, WI
Transitional Living Community for Girls, St Joseph, MO
The Treasure Cove, Atwater, CA
Trinity School for Children, Ukiah, CA
True to Life Counseling and Company, Sebastopol, CA
TRY Group Home, Inc, Two Rivers, WI
Turning Point, Salisbury, NC
Ulrey Homes, Inc, San Lorenzo, CA
United Citizen Community Organization, Chicago, IL
United Methodist Childrens Home, Worthington, OH
United Methodist Youth Home, Evansville, IN
Upper Valley Charitable Corp—Clear Creek Farm, Piqua, OH
Valley-Lake Boys Home, Inc, Breckenridge, MN
Veterans of Foreign Wars National Home, Eaton Rapids, MI
Victor Residential Center—Willow Creek Residential Center, Santa Rosa, CA
The Villages of Indiana, Inc, Bloomington, IN
Virginia Home for Boys, Richmond, VA
Vista Del Mar Child Care Service, Los Angeles, CA
Vista Maria, Dearborn Heights, MI
WAITT Houses, Inc, Schenectady, NY
Wake County Juvenile Treatment System, Raleigh, NC
Walden Environment, Lancaster, CA
Washington Street Homes, Fresno, CA
Waterford County School, Inc, Quaker Hill, CT
Jane Wayland Center, Phoenix, AZ
Whittier Group Home, Columbus, OH
WICS Residence for Girls, Lincoln, NE
Wide Horizons Ranch, Inc, Oak Run, CA
The Constance Bultman Wilson Center, Faribault, MN
Windjammer Group Home, New Bern, NC
Wolf River Group Home, White Lake, WI
Wood County Child Care Center, Parkersburg, WV
Wright Direction Home, Waverly, MN
Wyandotte House, Corydon, IN
Wyndham Lawn Home for Children, Lockport, NY
Yellowstone Treatment Center, Billings, MT
Young Acres, Peoria, AZ
Youth Adventures, Inc, Oregon City, OR
Youth Homes, Walnut Creek, CA
Youth House of Ouachita, Inc, West Monroe, LA
Youth in Need, St Charles, MO
Youth Resources, Inc, Pilgrim Center, Braintree, MA
Youth Service Bureau, Muncie, IN
YWCA Try Angle House, Nashville, TN

SUBSTANCE ABUSE PROGRAMS

Abbott House, Mitchell, SD
Advocate Group Homes, Riverside, CA
Alpha Omega, Littleton, MA
Alternative Homes, Inc, St Paul, MN
AMI St Joseph Center for Mental Health, Omaha, NE
Paul Anderson Youth Home, Inc, Vidalia, GA
Argus Community, Inc, Bronx, NY
The ARK, Jackson, MS
Ashtabula County Residential Treatment Center, Ashtabula, OH
Augusta Mental Health Institute, Augusta, ME
Aviva Center, Los Angeles, CA
Avondale Youth Center, Zanesville, OH
The Baird Center, Plymouth, MA

Bar-None Residential Treatment Services, Anoka, MN
Bellefaire Residential Treatment Facility, Cleveland, OH
Berkshire Farm Center and Services for Youth, Canaan, NY
The Bethel Group Home, Bethel, AK
Bexar County MHMR Center—Residential Program, San Antonio, TX
Black Hills Special Services—Northern Hills Youth Services, Spearfish, SD
Boselli Residential Services, Inc, Lemon Grove, CA
Boys and Girls Aid Society of San Diego—Cottonwood Center, El Cajon, CA
Boys Republic, Chino, CA
Boys' Village, Inc, Smithville, OH
Bridlewood Group Home, Intensive Residential Program, Charlotte, NC
Broad Horizons of Ramona, Inc, Ramona, CA
The Brown Schools, Austin, TX
The Calabasas Academy, Calabasas, CA
California Crest Diagnostic and Treatment Center, El Cajon, CA
Camelot Care Center, Inc, Palatine, IL
Caravan House, Palo Alto, CA
Carmelite Home for Boys, Hammond, IN
Cary Home for Children, Lafayette, IN
Casa de Luz, Santa Rosa, CA
Casa Victoria I, Whittier, CA
Castle School, Inc, Cambridge, MA
Charter Colonial Institute, Newport News, VA
Chestnut Lodge Hospital, Rockville, MD
Children and Adolescent Treatment Center, Jamestown, ND
Children's Farm Home, Corvallis, OR
Christian Haven Homes, Inc, Wheatfield, IN
Colon Road Home, Sanford, NC
Colonial Hills Hospital, San Antonio, TX
Colorado Boys Ranch Foundation, La Junta, CO
Coosa Valley Youth Services, Attention Home, Anniston, AL
Cornell Group Homes, Inc, Ladysmith, WI
Crest View Hospital, Casper, WY
Crittenton Center, Kansas City, MO
Crockett Academy, Nashville, TN
Cumberland House School, Nashville, TN
Cunningham Children's Home, Urbana, IL
Dakota Boys Ranch, Minot, ND
Dane Co Group Hms, Inc, Madison, WI
Daybreak Child and Adolescent Unit of MHMR of Southeast Texas, Beaumont, TX
De Paul Hospital, New Orleans, LA
Delta Treatment Centers of Indiana, Inc, Bloomington, IN
The Denver Children's Home, Denver, CO
The Devereux Center in Georgia, Kennesaw, GA
Diagnostic and Educational Services, Palm Desert, CA
Drake House Group Home, Pleasant Hill, CA
Eastern Virginia Center for Children and Youth, Norfolk, VA
Eckerd Wilderness Educational Camping Program, Benson, VT
Edgewood Children's Center, St Louis, MO
El Paso State Center, El Paso, TX
Eudes Family Programs—Group Home, Triumph II, Green Bay, WI
Eudes Family Programs—Residential Center, Green Bay, WI
Fair Oaks Hospital, Summit, NJ
Fairmont Group Home, Fresno, CA
Family Life Center, Petaluma, CA
First Light Group Home, Inc, Beloit, WI
Fresno Treatment Center, Fresno, CA
Friends of Youth, Renton, WA
Friendship House, Sheboygan, WI
Full Circle Sonoma, Sebastopol, CA
Galloway Boys Ranch, Wahkon, MN
Gateway United Methodist Youth Center, Williamsville, NY
Gateway Youth Home, Martinsburg, WV
Genesis, Athens, OH
The Germaine Lawrence School, Arlington, MA
Gibault School for Boys, Terre Haute, IN
Good Samaritan Boys Ranch, Brighton, MO
Good Samaritan Homes, Sacramento, CA
Grant County Residential Treatment Center, Marion, IN
Wil Lou Gray Opportunity School, West Columbia, SC
Gulf Coast Regional Mental Health Mental Retardation Center, Galveston, TX
Hall-Brooke Foundation, Westport, CT
Harbor House, Annandale, VA
Harlem Community Residential Home, New York, NY

Barbara Smiley Sherman has a MA in Education, with an emphasis on special education working with emotionally handicapped children. Her teaching and clinical experience includes working in private day school programs and in psychiatric residential care programs. She was the Director of the Old Orchard Psychiatric Hospital School Program and, since then, has been an educational consultant to that program. Barbara Smiley Sherman was the editor for *Directory of Residential Treatment Facilities for Emotionally Disturbed Children,* also published by Oryx Press.